QUANTITY SURVEY

[Principles and Applications]
includes
Computerised Estimation, Costing, Specification, Valuation and Construction Management

P.K. Guha

B.A. (Cal.) M.I.S., F.I.E. (India)
Chartered Engineer and valuer, Retired Executive Engineer,
Public Works Department, Govt. of West Bengal,
Formerly Director, Planning and Development, Kolkata Muncipal Corporation

KHANNA PUBLISHERS
Operational Office
4575/15, Onkar House, Ground Floor,
Darya Ganj, New Delhi 110 002
Phones : 011-23243042, 011-23243043 & Mob. 09811541460
email : contactus@khannapublishers.in

Published by :

Romesh Chander Khanna & Vineet Khanna
for **KHANNA PUBLISHERS**
2-B, Nath Market, Nai Sarak
Delhi- 110 006 (India)

Website : www.khannapublishers.in

Hologram & Description

To all readers of our books, from yourself if being defrauded by pirates to prevent, please make sure that there is a Hologram on the cover of our books with the below specifications. If you find any book without Hologram and Description, please mail us at **contactus@khannapublishers.in**

Thanking you

ISBN No. 978-81-7409-242-7

First Edition : 2009
Second Reprint : 2013

Price : **₹ 299.00**

Dedicated to my

Grand-daughters

Abheree Roy
and
Prajna Paramita Guha

Dedicated to my

Grand-daughters

Abheree Roy

and

Prajna Pāramita Guha

Foreword

In these days of super-technology, when physical distances have melted away to conceptual nearness, among the international communities, with heterogeneous level of development; It is the scientists and technologists of the developing countries, who have to bear the burnt of the tremendous techno-economic upsurgence, to meet the aspirations of their nations. Timely completion of ecofriendly, environmentally-compatible projects and structures, achieving maximum cost-benefit, by employing optimum latest technology in man, machine and material is the motto of the day. This is the crux of the national strategy of developing nations. And the study, teaching and employment of all the branches of technologies, including 'Quantity Survey' are to follow that.

The subject 'Quantity Survey' of Civil Engineering structures, has long transcended its basic boundaries of estimation of probable quantities of work prior to construction, in commensurate with the drawings, details, sketches, specifications of works etc., as laid down by the Architect and Civil Engineer. It now includes measurement of quantities of works completed or partly completed in stages, including additional and supplementary works required to be done to complete the work; Assessment of progressing physical and financial status, project management, payment, Arbitration and allied works, etc.

Shri P.K. Guha, in his book 'Quantity Survey', has very nicely incorporated the entire spectrum of it, in its broadest concept. While dealing the subject mostly with modern technique and concept, the rudimentary elements even were not lost sight of by him; which has made the book versatile and useful for all. Chapter 17 needs a special emphasis. In this chapter, he has included computerised estimation of quantities of work and drawn its comparison with that of the manually calculated method. This is befitting with time. And will go a long way towards encouraging the students, teachers and professionals in the field alike. Wide employment of computerised systems in estimation and other fields of project management are inescapable need of the day.

The author, by virtue of his vast experience in the academic and practical fields, has dealt with the subject exhaustively from appropriate angles, which has made the subject more penetrating, pragmatic and interesting, I am sure, this book will be acceptable with eagerness by students, teachers and professionals alike.

Block GD, Plot No. 371
Salt Lake City,
Kolkata-700106

Sd/- A. K. Dan, B,E. (Cal.) C.E.
Diploma in Housing,
(School of Planning and Architecture, New Delhi)
Retired Engineer in Chief,
Public Works Department,
Govt. of West Bengal.
Formerly, Housing Commissioner,
West Bengal Housing Board.

Preface

Quantity survey is generally considered as one subject, *i.e.* Estimation of the probable quantities of work prior to construction. But actually it is not so. Quantity Survey comprises of a group of subjects of which Estimation is one. Estimation of the quantities of items of work prior to commencement of work involved is a part of the Quantity Survey. It also involves measurement of the completed work and preparation of bills for interim and final payment. It also includes costing and preparation of specification and Analysis of Rates.

Apart from the above, Quantity Survey involves other various subjects Building Economics, Tendering procedure, Arbitration, Valuation and Construction Management. All these are now parts of Quantity Survey Subject. Quantity Survey is now included in the all Syllabus in many Universities in India and in foreign countries.

While teaching the subject in the Institution of Urban Management of K.M.C., difficulties of the students in reading the drawings and taking out the quantities was observed. Attempts have been made to remedy those and make the subject easy and acceptable.

Construction Management has become essential for implementation of the project small or large. Quantity Surveyor does the most important functions in this respect. He is the man behind Construction Management. Appreciating the contribution of Quantity Surveyor in Construction Management a chapter on the subject has been incorporated.

Now a days in the era of computer, incorporation of computer in estimation has become essential to eliminate human error and expediting the process. A chapter has been devoted on this which has been possible due to the kind help extended by Dr. P.N. Basu of CMC.

A Quantity Surveyor is often asked to solve Valuation problems. He has to deal the Arbitration cases and often he has to scrutinize the arbitration papers and prepare the cases for presentation before the Arbitrator. A chapter each for Valuation and Arbitration has been incorporated for the persons dealing in the subjects.

Efforts have been made to make the book useful for the students of the subject and for practising Engineers both of Degree and Diploma streams.

In spite of all attempts, there is possibility of lapses leaving scope for improvement. There may be shortcomings in conception or mistakes may have crept in. Any reference, correction and/or suggestion for improvement of any matter will be gratefully acknowledged.

—P.K. Guha
Anand Lok- A/8,
A/1/1, C.I.T. Scheme VIIM
Kolkata-700054.

N.B. All calculations have been based on Schedule of rates of Public Works Department, Government of West Bengal, Presidency Circle - 2002—03.

Acknowledgment

Extensive help has been received in all aspects in writing the book from Shree Shyambenode Banerjee, an Engineer and my friend, for which I shall remain ever grateful.

Help has been taken from the book "Estimating, costing, specification, Valuation in Civil Engineering by Shree M. Chakravorty and the books as mentioned under Reference. I am deeply indebted to them all and take the opportunity to extend my gratefulness to them and also thank them.

—Author

Contents

1

QUANTITY SURVEY

1.1.0 QUANTITY SURVEY

The term Quantity Survey covers a wide range of functions related to any Civil Engineering work. Quantity Survey is misunderstood as 'estimating' the probable quantities of items of works to be done; Estimating is a part of Quantity Survey but not the whole.

Quantity Survey is not limited to working out quantities of work only, but in actual fact is a separate specialised subject embracing Civil Engineering, Construction Economics, Tendering procedures and Contractual arrangements, Taking measurement of work done, Preparation of bill for payment, etc. In view of the above, the subject covers the following :

(*i*) Estimation : Taking out quantities, preparation of abstract of cost and bill of quantities of works,

(*ii*) Building economics,

(*iii*) Tendering and contractual procedures and drafting of Contract document,

(*iv*) Specifications of items of works,

(*v*) Procedure for taking measurements of work done and preparation of bills,

(*vi*) Analysis of prices of items of works,

(*vii*) Arbitration, and

(*viii*) Valuation of land and immovable properties.

In addition to the above activities, it also includes construction management, Law relevant to construction and Accountancy, Construction technology, Financial administration of contracts, Contract law and other allied subjects of Civil Engineering such as Building materials and Construction drawing, Engineering mathematics, Structural design, Land survey, etc. These are separate independent subjects and to be studied separately in details.

1.2.0 STUDY OF QUANTITY SURVEY AND APPLICATION

A comprehensive study of Quantity Survey and its application need detailed study of the following :

1.2.1 Estimation

Estimation is computation of the quantities required and cost likely to be incurred in the construction work. It is prepared by calculating the quantities from the dimensions furnished in the drawings of various items of work to complete the project/work and computing the cost of the work on the basis of unit cost of the items.

Purpose of estimation

Preparation of estimate for a work or project is necessary mainly for the following :

(*i*) To ascertain the probable cost of the work for knowing the probable fund required for the work. In the Public Works Department system, estimate is required for obtaining Administrative Approval and Technical Sanction of the work or project.

(*ii*) To ascertain the quantities of different materials that would be required and programming for procurement of the same.

(*iii*) To ascertain the mandays required of different categories of labour that would be required for completion of the work in the desired period of time.

(*iv*) To ascertain the requirement of tools, plants, equipments and appliances which would be required during execution of the work.

(*v*) To fix up a probable date of completion on the basis of quantities of works to be done.

(*vi*) It helps in drawing up a comprehensive work programme for management of the construction by Bar-Chart or PERT or CPM. It also helps in financial planning and programming of the work.

(*vii*) To evaluate the cost benefit ratio and economic viability of the work/project.

(*viii*) It is required for inviting tenders and for preparation of bill of quantities.

(*ix*) Estimate for existing property is required for assessing the valuation of it.

Estimates are of different kinds

(*i*) **Preliminary estimate** is an estimate prepared on the basis of any of the approximate methods e.g., Plinth area of the structure, Cubic content of the structure, Number of units, Kilometer length, etc., for a quick assessment of the cost.

(*ii*) **Detailed estimate** is a comprehensive estimate in which the quantities of various items of work are worked out and the estimated cost of each item is arrived at on the basis of the prevalent schedule of Rates or at Market Rates in an abstract form with the Bill of Quantities.

(*iii*) **Revised estimate** is the estimate required to be framed when substantial deviation is observed from the original detailed estimate either in cost or quantity or due to any other reason inviting revised administrative approval of the work.

(*iv*) **Supplementary estimate** is required to be prepared for execution of additional item or items of work not included in the original detailed estimate.

(*v*) **Supplementary and Revised estimate** is initiated when there is deviation from the original detailed estimate due to both the causes necessitating initiation of supplementary and Revised estimates.

(*vi*) **Maintenance estimate** need be prepared for 'Maintenance and Repair works'. These are prepared for undertaking any repair work to an already damaged structure or as protective measure against any anticipated damage. Maintenance estimates are also prepared for routine maintenance works to be done annually.

(*vii*) **Annual maintenance estimate** is prepared for routine maintenance works that are to be undertaken during the year for keeping the structure serviceable and useful. It is prepared on percentage basis of the capital cost of the structure excluding the cost of land. While preparing the estimate, Capital cost need be updated and then the amount of the estimate shall be found out. The percentage varies from 2% to 9% according to the nature of construction and life of the structure.

However, now a days the method of preparation of the estimate on percentage basis has been discontinued. The quantities of work to be done are assessed after surveying the structure and then the estimate is prepared on the basis of actual requirement.

(*viii*) **Special Repairs estimate** Annual Repair estimates are meant for meeting the cost of routine maintenance works. When the amount required is large and cannot be met from the Annual Repairs fund, Special Repairs estimate is prepared to meet the cost of actual requirement. The estimate is prepared after actually surveying the structure and assessing the quantities. The work is treated as a separate work. Sometimes, addition and alteration works are also included in the Special Repairs estimates.

(*ix*) **Estimates for Emergent Repair works** The estimate is required to be framed to meet the cost of emergent works necessitated for restoration of a structure damaged due to natural calamities, like flood, storm, earthquake, etc. The estimate is prepared after proper survey of the structure, ascertaining the actual requirement of works to be done. The work is treated as a separate work.

1.3.0 DEFINITION OF TERMS

Some of the terms used in connection with estimating :

1.3.1 Abstract Cost

Abstract cost is the summary of the cost of various items of work shown in the detailed estimate.

1.3.2 Administrative Approval

The concerned department or the client on receipt of the estimate will go through the same and study it along with the report, examine the physical and financial viability and specially the availability of the fund in the department. When the estimate is found to be acceptable, the concerned department shall accord Administrative Approval of the estimate and communicate the approval to the department entrusted for the execution in writing.

Administrative approval of the estimate is normally accorded on the detailed estimate. Preparation of detailed estimate require considerable time. For saving time and expediting the work, Administrative approval is often accorded on the basis of preliminary estimate with report.

1.3.3 Technical Sanction

Technical sanction is the sanction accorded by the competent authority in the technical department of the executive agency on the detailed estimate prepared complying with the requirements of the requisitioning department and for which administrative approval has been accorded. If the detailed estimate on which technical sanction is sought for varies exceeding the permissible limit of 5%, revised administrative approval is to be obtained prior to technical sanction.

1.3.4 Capital Cost

Capital cost of a project is the cost including building structure, external and internal services and contingent expenditure, including cost of land. Capital cost required in connection with the repair estimate shall be excluding the cost of land.

1.3.5 Schedule of Rates

Various items of works are involved in construction of Civil Engineering Projects *e.g.* Buildings, Roads, Water Supply, Sewerage, Drainage, etc.

Government Departments and large organisations who often undertake such works, standardise the major items of works and compile in a schedule, called Schedule of Items. The rates of cost of the schedule items are analysed and incorporated in the schedule and a book is compiled. The book is called 'Schedule of Rates'.

1.3.6 Contingency

Provision for contingency in the detailed estimate is made varying from 1/2 to 5% to meet the cost of unforeseen items of works. Contingency is not meant for meeting the excess cost arising due to extra item of works or due to quantitative excess of any item for which supplementary or revised estimate shall be prepared.

1.3.7 Plinth Area

Plinth area is the area covered by the structure at the plinth level. The area is also called covered area.

1.3.8 Carpet Area

Carpet area is the net area of a building comprising of the living rooms *i.e.* area of living excluding the space where carpet is not generally spread *e.g.* kitchen, pantry, store, boxroom, verandah, toilet bath, etc.

1.3.9 Bill of Quantities

Bill of quantities is the abstract of quantities with rates and amount.

1.3.10 Service Charges

Charges levied on percentage basis on the actual cost of work, when work of a department or a statutory body or a municipal body is proposed to be executed by another department of the Government to meet the administrative charges of the department that would be required for the work.

2

ESTIMATION OF BUILDING

2.1.0 ESTIMATION

Before undertaking any construction work, it is necessary to know the probable cost of the concerned work. Estimate provides for the probable cost of the work. It is calculated from the plans and drawings and the cost is worked out on the basis of current 'Schedule of Rates', if there be any or on the basis of current market rates of materials and labour.

2.1.1 Requirement for Preparation of Estimate

(*i*) Complete and fully dimensioned plans and sections of the structure with all possible details, so that all information regarding the structure is available,

(*ii*) Detailed specification of the items of works provided in the plan, and

(*iii*) Rates of various items of works.

2.2.0 UNITS OF MEASUREMENTS

(*i*) Mass or voluminous and thick works shall be taken in cubic unit or volume—Earthwork, Brickwork, concrete, etc.

(*ii*) Thin, shallow and surface works shall be taken in square unit or in area—Plaster, Door and window shutters, painting, white washing, etc.

(*iii*) Long and thin works shall be taken in linear or running unit and linear measurement shall be taken—Coping, Water supply pipe lines, Sewer lines, etc.

(*iv*) Piece work, job work, etc. shall be taken in number.

2.3.0 LIMITS OF MEASUREMENT AND DEGREE OF ACCURACY

(*a*) Dimensions shall be measured to the nearest 0.01 m, except for

(*i*) Thickness of slab or R.C.C. slab which shall be measured to the nearest of 0.005 m,

(*ii*) Wood work to the nearest of 0.002 m,

(*iii*) Steel work to the nearest of 0.001 m, and Reinforcement to the nearest of 0.002 m.

(*b*) Areas shall be worked out to the nearest of 0.001 sqm. For steel work areas excluding cross-sectional measurements shall be worked out to the nearest of 0.001 sqm.

(*c*) Cubic contents shall be worked out to the nearest of 0.01 cum except for woodwork which shall be worked out to the nearest of 0.001 cum.

(*d*) Weights shall be worked out to the nearest of 1 kg.

2.4.0 MODE OF MEASUREMENT

While taking out the measurements of the items of works, attempts shall be made for accuracy. However, for speedy work and for avoiding unnecessary complication having very little financial implication, some mode of measurements have been adopted as per convention and as recommended by the I.S. Code.

(*a*) **Concrete work.** Item shall be measured in cubic meter and no deduction shall be made for :

(*i*) Openings up to 0.10 sqm.,

(*ii*) Volume occupied by reinforcements,

(*iii*) Volume occupied by pipes up to 100 sq cm. each in cross-section, and

(*iv*) Small voids not exceeding 40 sq cm. each in cross-section.

(*b*) **Brickwork.** Item shall be measured in cubic metre in general. However, walls less than one brick thick shall be measured in sqm.

Brick edging shall be measured in running meter.

Deductions shall be made for openings or voids or both when such features shall refer within the space measured.

Honeycomb brickwork shall be measured separately in sqm.

(*c*) **Formwork.** Formwork shall be measured in sqm. Actual surface in contact with the concrete or any other material requiring formwork shall be taken into consideration.

(*d*) **Plastering.** No addition in measurement shall be made for reveals, jambs, soffits, sills, etc. and no deduction shall be made for the ends of the joints and beams below 0.5 sqm in area. When such opening exceed 0.5 sqm but not exceeding 3 sqm deduction shall be made as below :

(*i*) When both faces of wall are plastered, deduction shall be made for one face only.

(*ii*) When only one face is plastered, full deduction shall be made from the plaster, if width of the reveals on the plastered side is less than that on the unplastered side.

(*iii*) If the two faces of the wall have different plaster, deductions shall be made from the side on which width of the reveals are less.

(*iv*) Full deduction for wall opening shall be made for each plastered surface of the wall, when the width of door frame is equal to the thickness of the wall.

(*v*) When the areas of openings exceed 3 sqm each deduction shall be made for the openings on each face, but jambs, soffits and sills shall be measured.

(*e*) **Painting and varnishing.** Measurement for painting work in doors and windows, grills, gratings, collapsible gates, corrugated roofing, etc. shall be made in area. The area measured shall be multiplied by the factor given below for arriving at the actually covered by painting.

Nature of surface painted	*Multiplication factor for painting one side only*	*Multiplication factor for painting both sides*
(*a*) Timber doors and windows		
(*i*) Fully glazed	0.67	1.33
(*ii*) Fully panelled or flush or battened	1.00	2.00
(*iii*) Fully venetian or fixed louverd	1.50	3.00
(*iv*) 2/3rd panelled, 1/3rd glazed	0.875	1.75
(*v*) 1/3rd panelled, 2/3rd glazed	0.75	1.50
(*vi*) 1/3rd panelled, 2/3rd venetian or fixed louverd	1.33	2.67
(*vii*) 1/3rd glazed, 2/3rd venetian or fixed louverd	1.25	2.50

Nature of surface painted	Multiplication factor for painting one side only	Multiplication factor for painting both sides
(viii) Netted without painting to the net	0.25	0.50
(ix) Netted with painting to the net	0.63	1.25
(x) Corrugated *i.e.* with leaves of C. I. sheet	1.25	2.50
(b) Corrugated iron sheet roof or wall	1.17	2.33
(c) Corrugated asbestos sheet roof or wall	1.20	2.40
(d) Trafford asbestos sheet roof or wall	1.10	2.20
(e) Cast iron or wooden railing	–	1.50
(f) Grills, gratings (welded mesh)	–	1.00
(g) Heavy type grating or grated doors as in Jails etc.	–	1.50
(h) Collapsible gate	–	1.50
(i) Steel roll-top shutters (including top casting)	1.25	2.50
(j) Steel windows	0.33	0.67

(*f*) **Woodwork and joinery.** Measurement shall be made in linear metre, sqm or cum as the case may be.

Door and window frames — Sections shall be measured as full without any deduction for rebates and the length of each piece shall be measured in full including the mortice or tenon.

(*g*) **Shrinkage.** Freshly stacked materials like sand, stone chips, gravel, clay, murrum, rock, etc. show increase in volume in the loose state due to increase in void than that in normal state. The material after a few days reduces in volume in normal condition. This reduction in volume from freshly stacked state is termed shrinkage and is reflected in calculation of volume of the materials received in stacks either by reducing the height of the stacks of the materials or by introducing a shrinkage allowance on the volume of the freshly stacked materials.

Shrinkage allowance generally adopted are:

Materials	Minimum height of stack	Factor
Stone metal, ballast, chips, shingles or gravel	325 mm	1/7
Stone boulders below 150 mm size	450 mm	1/9
Jhama bats or brick bats	530 mm	1/7
Jhama metal khoa or chips	340 mm	1/9
Sand	610 mm	1/8
Surki	610 mm	1/4
Lime	610 mm	1/4
Moorum	335 mm	1/13
Carried earth	340 mm	1/9
Rubbish (building or kiln)	340 mm	1/9
Steam coal or slack coal	610 mm	1/8
Cinder	430 mm	1/9

2.5.0 ESTIMATION OF BUILDING

There are three methods of measuring the length of wall of a building for computing the quantity of different items of work.

2.5.1 Long and Short Wall Method

In this method, the longer walls in a building are taken as long walls and measured from out to out, and shorter or partition walls, in a perpendicular direction of long walls are considered as short walls and are measured from out in to out in for a particular layer of work. The long and short walls are multiplied separately by the breadth and height of the corresponding layer and are added to get the quantity.

2.5.2 Centre Line Method

In this method, computation is made of the total centre line length of walls of a building and the same is multiplied by the breadth and depth of the respective layer to get the total quantity at a time.

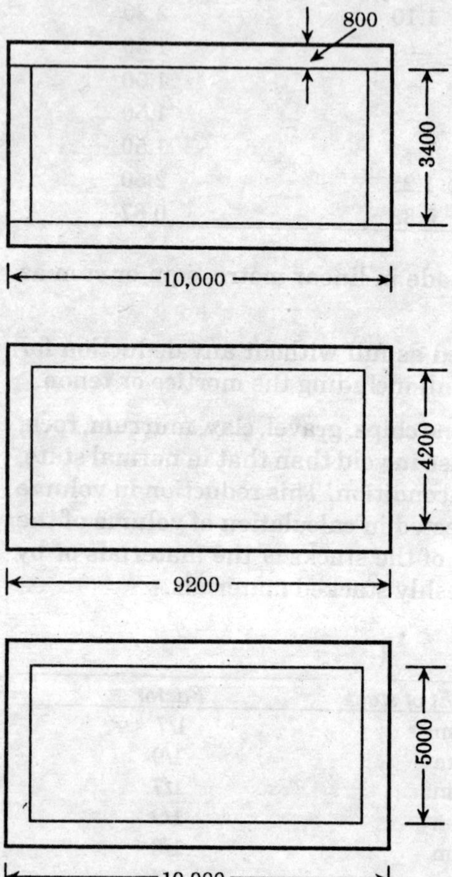

Figure 2.1 Shape of wall.

2.5.3 Crossing Method

In this method computation is made of the overall perimeter of the building. Four times the thickness of the wall is then subtracted to obtain the centre line length. Quantity is computed as usual like centre line method.

Example 2.1

Long wall short wall method

Length of wall

Long walls 2 × 10.00 = 20.00

Short walls 2 × (5.00 – 2 × 0.80) = 6.80

26.80 m

Centre line method

Centre line = 9.20 + 4.20 + 9.20 + 4.20 = 26.80 m

Cross wall method

Perimeter = 10.00 + 5.00 + 10.00 + 5.00 = 30.00 m

Deduct (–)4 × 0.80 = 30.00 – 3.20 m

= 26.80 m

Example 2.2 *Calculate the quantity of Brickwork of a wall as shown in Figure 2.2.*

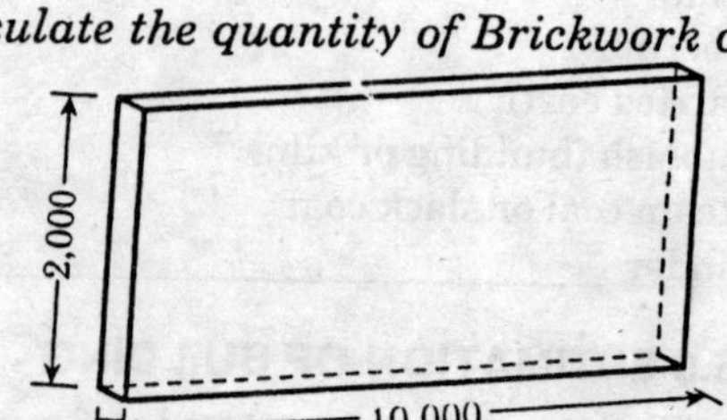

Figure 2.2 Shape of wall.

Volume of Brickwork

= 1 × 10.00 × 0.20 × 2.00

= 4.00 cum

Example 2.3 *Calculate the quantity of items of works of the wall 20.00 m long of section as shown in Figure 2.3.*

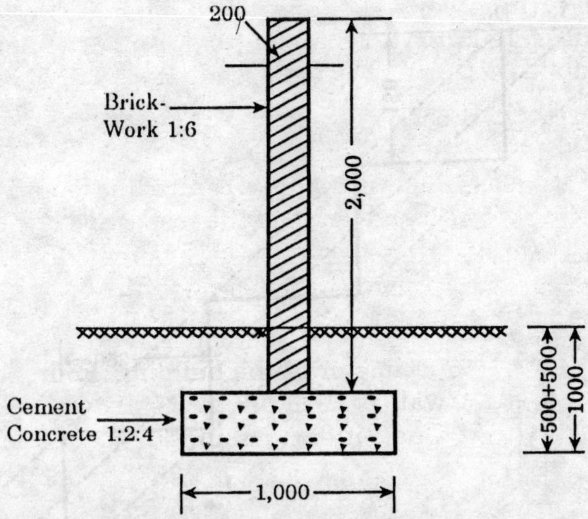

Figure 2.3 Section of wall.

1. Earthwork in excavation.
   $1 \times 20.00 \times 1.00 \times 1.00$ = 20.00 cum
2. Cement concrete 1 : 2 : 4.
   $1 \times 20.00 \times 1.00 \times 0.50$ = 10.00 cum
3. Brickwork 1 : 6 in foundation.
   $1 \times 20.00 \times 0.20 \times 0.50$ = 2.00 cum
4. Brickwork in cement mortar 1 : 6 in superstructure.
   $1 \times 20.00 \times 0.20 \times 2.00$ = 8.00 cum
5. Earthwork in back filling of foundation trench.
   as per item no. 1

Volume of Earthwork in excavation =20.00 cum

Less volume of cement concrete as per item no. 2 = 10.00

Less volume of Brickwork as per item no. 3 = 2.00

(–) 12.00 cum

8.00 cum

2.6.0 COMPUTATION OF DIFFERENT TYPICAL SECTIONS

Steps.

Volume of masonry steps can be calculated in four different methods. Whichever seems to easier may be adopted.

Calculate the sectional area then multiply it by the length.

Calculation of the sectional area

(*i*) Calculate the sectional area of each step,

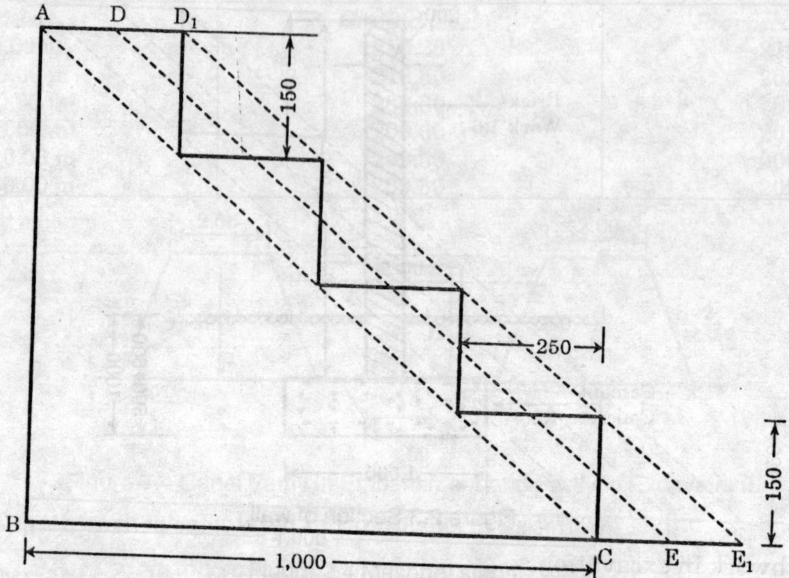

Figure 2.4 Masonry steps.

(*ii*) Calculate the sectional area A B C and then add the four triangles left,

(*iii*) Calculate the sectional area A B E D,

(*iv*) Calculate the sectional area AB E′ D′ and then subtract the four triangles.

Example 2.4 *Calculate the volume of the step shown in Figure 2.4.*

(*i*) As per method *i*.

$$1 \times 1.00 \times 0.15 = 0.15$$
$$1 \times 0.75 \times 0.15 = 0.1125$$
$$1 \times 0.50 \times 0.15 = 0.075$$
$$1 \times 0.25 \times 0.15 = 0.0375$$

0.375 sqm

Volume = 0.375L cum

(*ii*) As per method *ii*.

Area of section A B C $= 1/2 \times 1.00 \times 0.60 = 0.30$

Add for triangles $= 4 \times 1/2 \times 0.25 \times 0.15 = 0.075$

0.375 sqm

Volume = 0.375L cum

(*iii*) As per method *iii*.

$$\text{Area of section A, B, E, D} = \frac{0.125 + 1.125}{2} \times 0.60 = 0.375 \text{ sqm.}$$

Volume = 0.375L cum

(*iv*) As per method *iv*.

$$\text{Area of section ABE'D'} = \frac{0.25 + 1.25}{2} \times 0.60 = 0.45$$

Deduct area of 4 triangles $= 4 \times 1/2 \times 0.25 \times 0.15 = \dfrac{0.075}{0.375 \text{ sqm.}}$

Volume = 0.375L cum

2.7.0 CALCULATION OF QUANTITIES OF PRISM SHAPED OBJECTS

The quantities are calculated by applying prismoidal formula.

Volume, $V = L/6\,(A_1 + A_2 + 4A_m)$

Where L = Length

A_1, A_2 are the cross-sectional areas at the ends and A_m is the mid cross-sectional area between the two ends.

Example 2.5 *Calculate the volume of an isolated footing as shown in the Figure 2.5.*

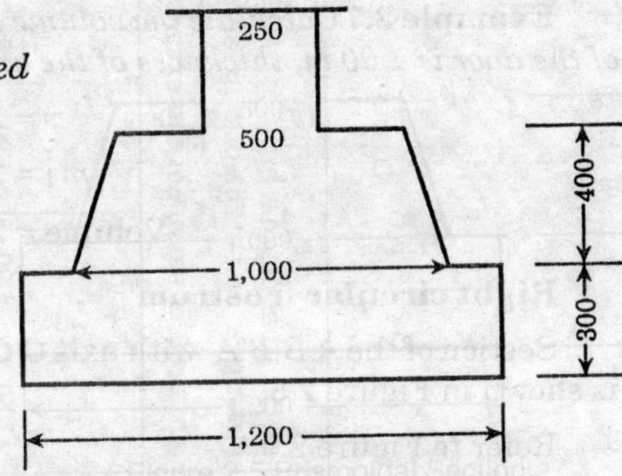

Figure 2.5 Prismoidal Section.

Prismoidal section

$V = L/6\,(A_1 + A_2 + 4A_m),\ L = 0.40$

$A_1 = 0.50 \times 0.50 = 0.25$ sqm

$A_2 = 1.00 \times 1.00 = 1.00$ sqm

$A_m = 0.75 \times 0.75 = 0.563$ sqm

$V = 0.40/6\,(0.25 + 1.00 + 4 \times 0.563) = 0.233$ cu

Rectangular section

$V = 1 \times 1.2 \times 1.2 \times 0.30 = 0.432$ cum

Total volume $= 0.233 + 0.432 = 0.665$ cum

2.7.1 Computation of Volume of Arch

Semi-circular arch

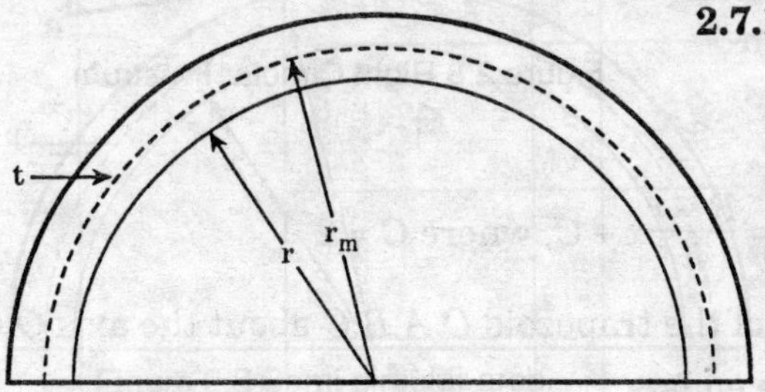

Figure 2.6 Semi-circular arch.

Radius = r

Mean radius = $r_m = r + t/2$

Mean length = $2\pi\, r_m/2 = \pi\, r_m$

$= \pi\,(r + t/2)$

Example 2.6 *Calculate the volume of a semi-circular arch of span 2 m, thickne·s of the arch 300 mm and width 500 mm.*

Span = 2.00 m, r = 1.00 mm.

$$\text{Mean length } = \pi\,(r + t/2) = \frac{22}{7}\left(1.00 + \frac{0.30}{2}\right) = \frac{22}{7} \times 1.15$$

$$\text{Volume } = \frac{22}{7} \times 1.15 \times 0.50 \times 0.30 = 0.542 \text{ cum.}$$

Segmental arch subtending an angle of 60° at the centre

a = Span, r = Radius, t = Thickness of arch, m_r = Mean radius and w = Width of arch

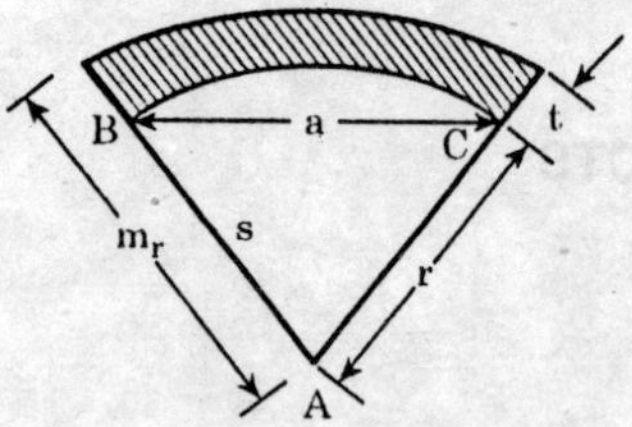

Figure 2.7 Segmental arch.

$A\,B\,C$ is an equilateral triangle,

$$A\,B = s = r$$

$$m_1 = 2\pi\, m_r \times \theta/360,$$

where θ = Angle subtended at the centre = 60°

Volume $= m_1 \times t \times w$.

Example 2.7 *Calculate the volume of an arch subtending an angle of 60° at the centre, width of the door is 1.00 m, thickness of the arch = 200 mm and width of the wall = 300 mm.*

$$r = 1.00 \text{ m}, \theta = 60°, t = 0.20 \text{ m and } w = 0.30 \text{ m},$$

$$m_1 = 2\pi\ mr \times \theta/360 = 2\pi \times \theta/360 \times (1.00 + 0.10)$$

$$\text{Volume} = 2\pi \times 1.10 \times 60/360 \times 0.20 \times 0.30 = 0.069 \text{ cum.}$$

Right circular frustrum

Section of the $A\,B\,B'A'$ with axis $O\,C$ horizontal is shown in Figure 2.8.

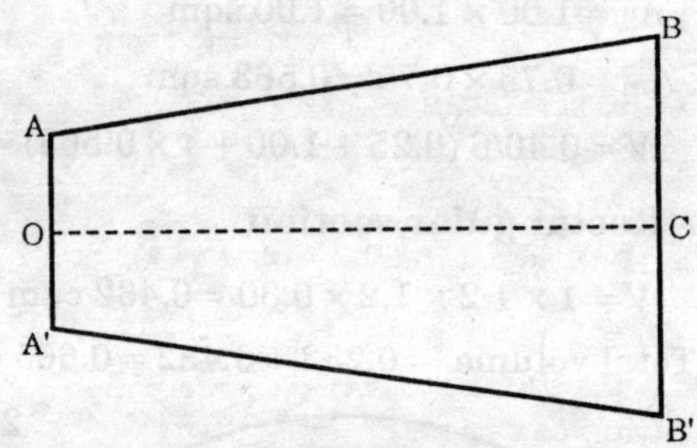

Figure 2.8 Right Circular Frustrum.

Refer to Figure 2.9,

With mid point O of the diameter $A\,A'$ as origin and with OX and OY as co-ordinate axis

Let P be any point (x, y) on the line $A\,B$.

$$OQ = x,\ Qp = y,$$

From A and B in a length of h, gradient increases by $\dfrac{(R-r)}{h}$,

Gradient of $AB = \dfrac{R-r}{h}$. Equation of AB is $Y = \dfrac{R-r}{h}x + C$, where $C = 2$

The frustrum is generated by the revolution of the trapezoid $O\,A\,B\,C$ about the axis $O\,C$.

Consider strip $P\,Q$ of width dx parallel to the ends.

Volume of frustrum generated by revolution of strip $P\,Q$ about the axis $O\,C = \pi\, Y^2 dx$

Required volume of the frustrum is the sum of volume of revolution of all the strips like PQ between the end faces. At end O, $x = 0$, at end C, $x = h$.

$$\text{Required volume} = \int_0^h \pi y^2\, dx = \pi \int_0^h \left[\left(\frac{R-r}{h}x\right) + 2\right]^2 dx$$

$$= \pi \int_0^h \left[\left(\frac{R-r}{h}x\right)^2 + 2.2x\left(\frac{R-r}{h}\right) + 4\right]_0 dx$$

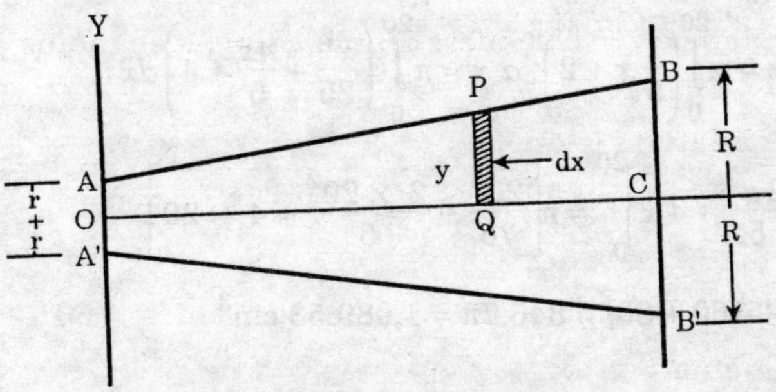

Figure 2.9 Right Circular Frustrum.

$$= \pi \left[\left(\frac{R-r}{h}\right)^2 \frac{x^3}{3} + \frac{4x^2}{2}\left(\frac{R-r}{h}\right) + 4x \right]_0^h$$

$$= \pi \left[\left(\frac{R-r}{h}\right) \times \frac{h^3}{3} + \frac{4h^2}{2}\,\frac{R-r}{h} + 4h \right]$$

$$= \pi \left[(R-r)^2 \times \frac{h}{3} + 2h\,(R-r) + 4h \right]$$

$$= \pi \left[\frac{h}{3}(R-r)^2 + 2\,h\,(R-r) + 4h \right]$$

Example 2.8 *Find out the volume of a frustrum of a right circular cone having radii 2 cm and 6 cm at the two ends and a total length 20 cm.*

Here, $R = 6$ cm, $r = 2$ cm and $h = 20$ cm.

Volume of a regular frustrum $= \pi \left[\frac{h}{3}(R-r)^2 + 2h\,(R-r) + 4h \right]$

Putting the values of h, R, and r,

Required volume $= \pi \left[\frac{20}{3} \times (6-2)^2 + 2 \times 20\,(6-2) + 4 \times 20 \right]$

$$= \pi \left[\frac{20}{3} \times 4^2 + 40 \times 4 + 4 \times 20 \right] = \pi \left[\frac{320}{3} + 160 + 80 \right]$$

$$= \pi\,(106.7 + 160 + 80) = \pi\,346.67 = 1{,}089.53 \text{ cm}^3$$

The problem can be solved directly without application of the formula.

Section of the frustrum $A\,B\,B'A'$ with its axis OC horizontal is shown in the figure. With mid point O of end diameter A' as origin and with OX and OY as co-ordinate axes, let p be any point (x, y) on the line $A\,B$.

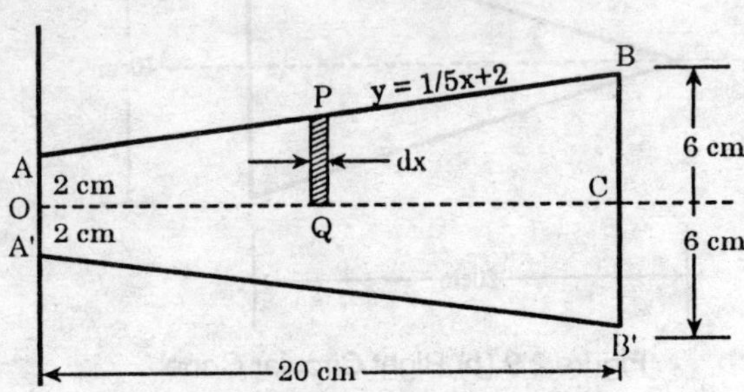

Fig. 2.9 (*a*) Right Circular Frustrum

Right circular frustrum

Then $OQ = x$, and $OP = y$;

From A to B in a length of 20 cm, radius increases by 4 cm.

$\therefore$ Gradient of $A\,B = 1/5$

$\therefore$ Equation of $A\,B$ is $Y = \frac{1}{5}x + 2$

The frustrum is generated by the revolution of trapezoid $O\,A\,B\,C$ about axis $O\,C$.

Consider strip PQ of the width dx parallel to the ends.

Volume of frustrum generated by revolution of strip $P\,Q$ about axis $O\,C = \pi\,y^2\,dx$.

Required volume of the frustrum is the sum of volume of revolution of all strips like $P\,Q$

between the end faces. At end O, $x = O$; at end C, $x = 20$

$$\therefore \quad \text{Required volume} = \int_0^{20} \pi y^2\, dx = \pi \int_0^{20} \left(\frac{1}{5}x + 2\right)^2 dx = \pi \int_0^{20} \left(\frac{x^2}{25} + \frac{4x}{5} + 4\right) dx$$

$$= \pi \left[\frac{x^3}{75} + \frac{2x^2}{5} + 4x\right]_0^{20} = \pi \left[\frac{20^3}{75} + \frac{2 \times 20^2}{5} + 4 \times 20\right]$$

$$= \pi\,[106.7 + 160 + 80] = 346.7\pi = 1{,}089.53 \text{ cm}^3$$

Right circular cone

In case of right circular cone A and A' meet at 0

Gradient of AB $= \dfrac{R}{h}$

Equation of AB is $y = \dfrac{R}{h}x + C$, here $C = 0$

Required volume $= \displaystyle\int_0^h \pi y^2\, dx = \int_0^h \pi \left(\frac{R}{h}x\right)^2 dx$

$$= \pi \left[\frac{R^2}{h^2}\frac{x^3}{3}\right]_3^h = \pi \frac{R^2}{h^2} \times \frac{h^3}{3} = \pi \frac{R^2 h}{3}$$

Example 2.9 *Find the volume of a right circular cone having base diameter 10 cm and height 20 cm.*

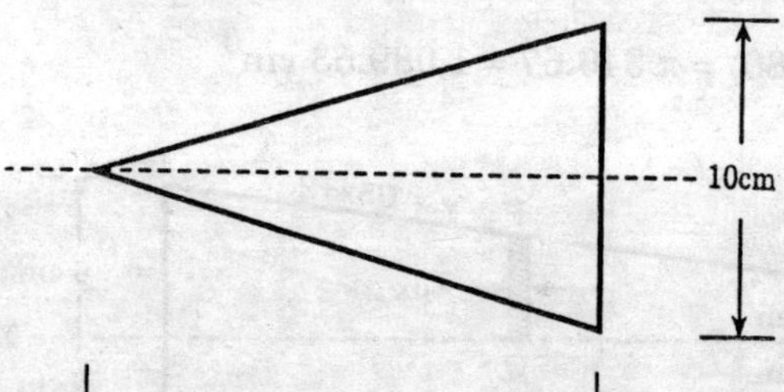

Figure 2.9 (*b*) Right Circular Cone.

Volume of right circular cone $= \pi R^2 \dfrac{h}{3}$

Putting the values of R and h,

$$= \pi\, 5^2 \times \frac{20}{3}$$

$$= \pi \frac{25 \times 20}{3} = \frac{\pi}{3} \times 500 = 525.33 \text{ cm}^3$$

Volume of regular solids can be calculated by using Prismoidal formula, Simpson's Rule or by using formula for frustrum of right square pyramid.

Formula for frustrum of right square pyramid is —

Volume $= \dfrac{1}{3} h\,(A + B + AB)$

Where, A and B are the areas of the two ends, and h = height.

Simpson's rule which is commonly known as Simpson's one-third rule is mostly used in calculation of quantities of Road Embankment.

This has been discussed in details under Chapter — Road Works.

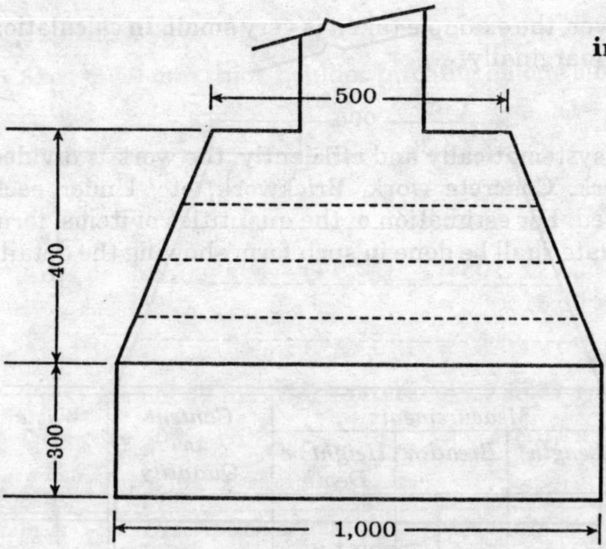

Figure 2.10 Trapezoidal section.

Comparison of quantities calculated in three methods

Reference example 2.5

(*i*) Calculation of volume of the trapezoidal section by Prismoidal formula.

Volume of the trapezoidal section

$$V = \frac{L}{6}(A_1 + A_n + 4A_m)$$

$$= \frac{0.40}{6}(0.25 + 1.00 + 4 \times 0.563) = 0.233 \text{ m}^3$$

Here, L = length = 0.40

A_1 and A_n = Cross sectional areas at the ends

$A_1 = 0.25, A_n = 1.00$ m

A_m = Area of mid section = 0.563

(*ii*) Calculation of volume as per Simpson's Rule

Dividing the length 400 mm in 4 sections of equal 100 mm length,

$$A_1 = 0.25 \text{ m}^2, A_2 = 0.625 \times 0.625 = 0.39 \text{ m}^2$$

$$A_3 = 0.75 \times 0.75 = 0.563 \text{ m}^2, A_4 = 0.875 \times 0.875 = 0.766 \text{ m}^2$$

and $$A_n = 1.0 \times 1.0 = 1.0 \text{ m}^2$$

Volume, $$V = \frac{L}{3}[0.25 + 1.0 + 2 \times 0.563 + 4 \times (0.39 + 0.766)]$$

$$= \frac{0.1}{3}[0.25 + 1.0 + 2 \times 0.563 + 4 \times (0.39 + 0.766)]$$

$$= \frac{0.1}{3}(1.25 + 1.126 + 4 \times 1.156)$$

$$= \frac{0.1}{3}(2.376 + 4.624) = 0.233 \text{ m}^3$$

(*iii*) Calculation as per formula for right square frustrum.

Volume, $V = \frac{h}{3}(A + B + \sqrt{AB})$, where, A and B are the areas of the two ends, and h = height.

$$A = 0.50 \times 0.50 = 0.25 \text{ m}^2$$
$$B = 1.00 \times 1.00 = 1.00 \text{ m}^2$$
$$h = 0.40 \text{ m}$$

Volume, $$V = \frac{0.40}{3}(0.25 + 1.00 + \sqrt{0.25 \times 1.00})$$

$$= \frac{0.40}{3}(0.25 + 1.00 + 0.50) = \frac{0.40}{3} \times 1.75 = 0.233 \text{ m}^3$$

All the three results are the same. However, the example taken is very small. In calculation of large quantities, the quantities may vary marginally.

2.8.0 ESTIMATE FORM

For the sake of preparation of estimate systematically and efficiently, the work is divided into different sub-heads such as Earthwork, Concrete work, Brickwork, etc. Under each sub-head several items of works are computed. For estimation of the quantities of items, form has been developed and standardised. Estimate shall be done in such form showing the details measurements of the items of work.

Specimen Estimate Form

Item no.	*Description of item or Particulars*	*No.*	*Measurements*			*Content or Quantity*	*Waste*
			Length	*Breadth*	*Height or Depth*		

Note: The column 'waste' is meant for noting the rough calculations.

2.9.0 ABSTRACT FORM

The cost of each item of work sub-headwise is computed from the quantities taken from the detailed estimate form, multiplied by the rate (current market or schedule) in the form developed for the purpose and standardised. The form is termed 'Abstract estimate form'.

Specimen Abstract Estimate Form

Item no.	*Description of item or Particulars of items*	*Quantity*	*Unit*	*Rate*	*Amount*	*Remarks*

Example 2.10 *Estimate the quantities of items of works up to plinth of the building plan given below.*

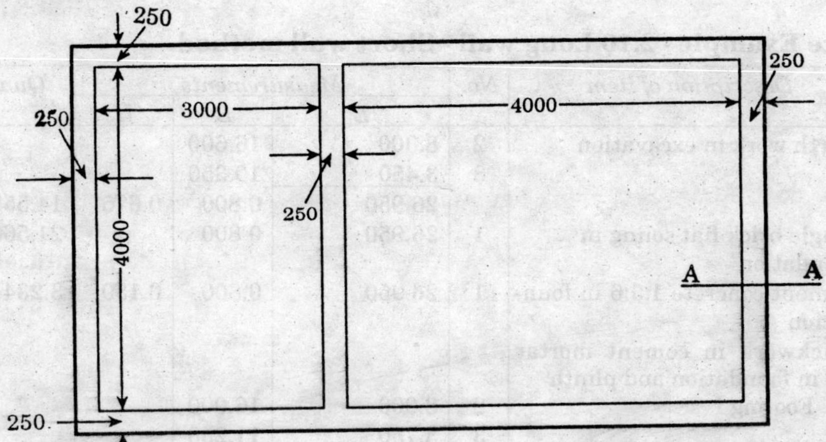

PLANAT PLINTH

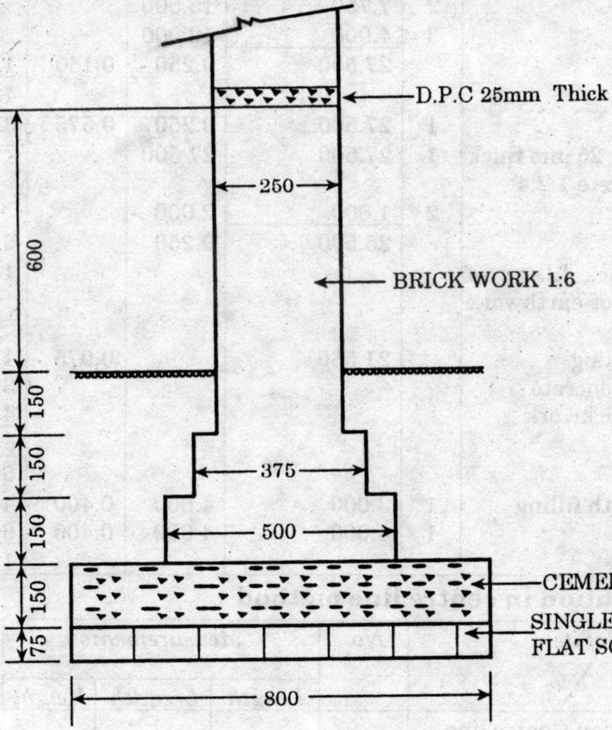

Section a-a

Figure 2.11 Plan and Section.

Estimate Example - 2.10 Long wall - Short wall method

Item no.	*Description of item*	*No.*	*Measurements*			*Quantity*	*Waste*
			L	*B*	*H*		
1	Earth work in excavation	2	8.300	16.600			
		3	3.450	10.350			
			26.950	0.800	0.675	14.553 cum	
2	Single brick flat soling in foundation	1	26.950	0.800		21.560 sqm	
3	Cement concrete 1:3:6 in foundation	1	26.950	0.800	0.150	3.234 cum	
4	Brickwork in cement mortar 1:6 in foundation and plinth						
	Footing I	2	8.000	16.000			
		3	3.750	11.250			
			27.250	0.500	0.150	2.044	
	Footing II	2	7.875	15.750			
		3	3.875	11.625			
			27.375	0.375	0.150	1.540	
	Footing III	2	7.750	15.500			
		3	4.000	12.000			
			27.500	0.250	0.150	1.031	
						4.615 cum	
	Plinth	1	27.500	0.250	0.575	3.953 cum	
5	Damp proof course 25 mm thick with cement concrete 1:2:4	1	27.500	27.500			
	Less for door	2	1.000	2.000			
			25.500	0.250		6.375 sqm	
6	Earthwork in back filling of trenches Volume of earthwork in excavation					14.553 cum	
	Less Volume of soling		21.560		0.075	1.617	
	Less Volume of concrete					3.234	
	Less Volume of brickwork					4.615	
						(–) 9.466	
						5.087 cum	
7	Earthwork in plinth filling	1	3.000	4.000	0.400	4.800	
		1	4.000	4.000	0.400	6.400	
						11.200 cum	

Example 2.11 Estimation in centre line method

Item no.	*Description of item*	*No.*	*Measurements*			*Contents*	*Waste*
			Length	*breadth*	*Height*		
1.	Earthwork in excavation Centre line 2 × 7.5 = 15.00 3 × 4.25 = 12.75 27.75 Less 0.80 26.95 m	1	26.95	0.80	0.675	14.553 cum	
2	Single brick flat soling in foundation [illegible] line 26.95 m	1	26.95	0.80		21.56 sqm	
	[illegible] 1 : 3 : 6 in foundation	1	26.95	0.80	0.15	3.234 cum	

4.	Brickwork in cement mortar 1 : 6 in foundation and plinth						
	Footing I						
	Centre line 27.75 – 0.50 = 27.25 m	1	27.25	0.50	0.15	2.044 cum	
	Footing II						
	Centre line 27.75 – 0.375 = 27.375 m	1	27.375	0.375	0.15	1.54 cum	
	Footing III						
	Centre line 27.75 – 0.25 = 27.50 m	1	27.50	0.25	0.15	1.031 cum	
	Plinth	1	27.50	0.25	0.575	3.953 cum	
5.	D.P.C. 25 mm thick with cement concrete 1 : 2 : 4						
	Centre line 27.50						
	Less 2.00						
	25.50						
		1	25.00	0.25		6.375 sqm	
6.	Earthwork in back filling of foundation trenches						
	Volume of earthwork in excavation					14.553 cum	
	Less vol. of soling		21.56 (Area)		0.75	1.617	
	Less vol. of concrete					3.234	
	Less vol. of brickwork					4.615	
						(–) 9.466	
						5.087 cum	
7.	Earthwork in plinth filling	1	3.00	0.40	0.40	4.80	
		1	4.00	4.00	0.40	6.40	
						11.20 cum	

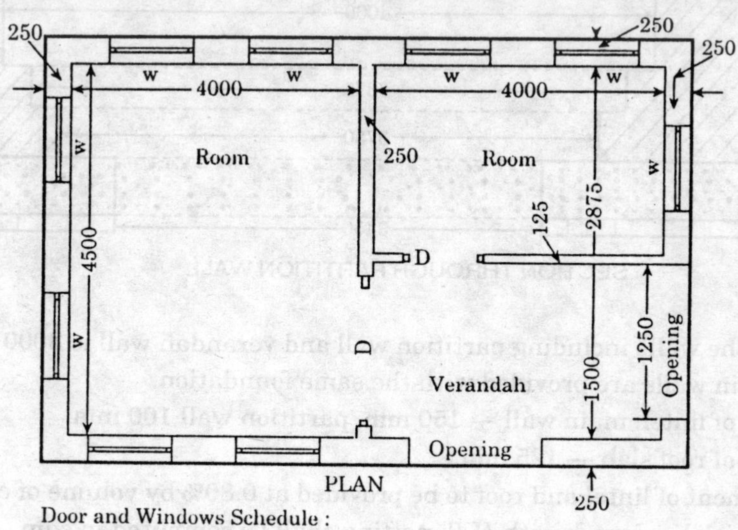

PLAN

Door and Windows Schedule :
Door, D : 1200 × 1200
Window, W : 1000 × 1500

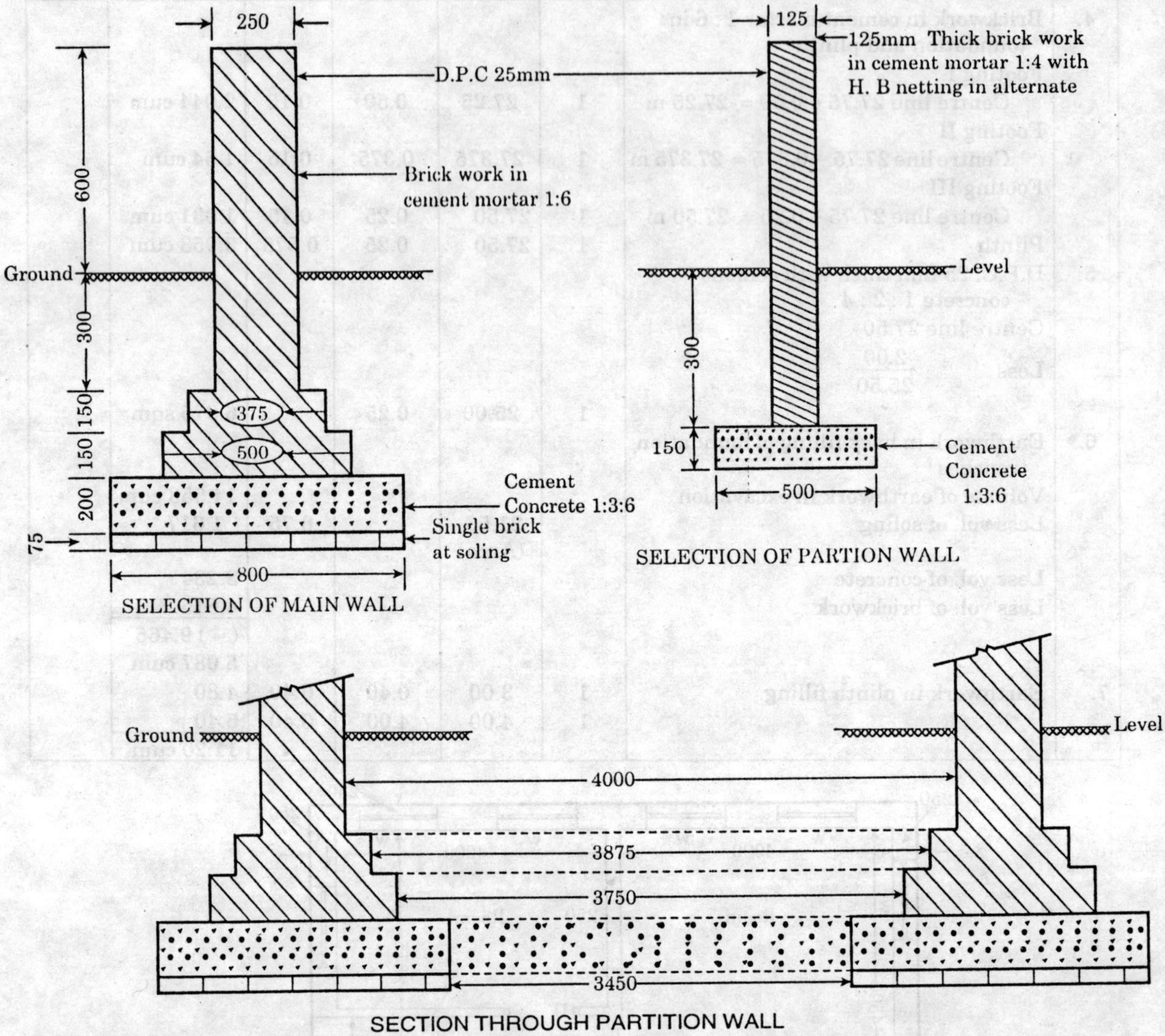

Note:

1. Height of the walls including partition wall and verandah wall is 3000 mm.
2. All the main walls are provided with the same foundation.
3. Thickness of lintel: main wall — 150 mm, partition wall 100 mm.
4. Thickness of roof slab — 125 mm.
5. Reinforcement of lintel and roof to be provided at 0.80% by volume of concrete.
6. 125 mm thick brickwork with *H.B.* netting shall be computed in sqm.

Figure 2.12 Plan and Section.

Example - 12 *Estimation of the quantities of works of the building as shown in the Figure 2.12.*

Estimate

Item no.	*Description of items*	*No.*	*Measurements*			*Content*	*Waste*
			Length	*Breadth*	*Height*		
1.	Earthwork in excavation in foundation						
	Long walls	2	9.30 =	18.60			4.0 + 4.0 + 3 × 0.25 + 2 × 0.275 = 9.30
	Short walls	3	3.95 =	11.85			4.5 − 2 × 0.275
			30.45	0.80	0.875	21.32	= 3.95
	Partition wall	1	3.45	0.50	0.60	1.035	4.0 − 2 × 0.275 = 3.45
						22.355 cum	
2.	Single brick flat soling						
	Main walls	1	30.45	0.80		24.36 sqm	
3.	Cement concrete 1 : 3 : 6 in foundation						
	Main walls	1	30.45	0.80	0.20	4.87	
	Partition wall	1	3.75	0.50	0.15	0.28	3.45 + 2 × 0.15 = 3.75 cum
						5.15	
4.	Brickwork in cement mortar 1 : 6 in foundation						
	Main walls	2	9.0 =	18.00			9.30 − 2 × 0.15 = 9.00
	1st. footing						
	Long walls						
	Short walls	3	4.25 =	12.75			3.95 + 2 × 0.15
			30.75	0.50	0.15	2.31	= 4.25
	2nd footing						
	Long walls	2	8.875 =	17.75			9.00 − 2 × 0.0625 = 8.875
	Short walls	3	4.375 =	13.125			4.25 + 2 × 0.0625 = 4.375
			30.875	0.375	0.15	1.74	
	3rd. footing up to Gr. level						
	Long walls	2	8.625	= 17.25			8.75 − 2 × 0.0625 = 8.625
	Short walls	3	3.875	= 11.625			4.375 − 2 × 0.25 = 3.875
			28.875	0.25	0.30	2.17	
						6.22	
	Gr. level to plinth level	1	31.00	0.25	0.575	4.46	0.600 − 0.025 = 0.575 cum
						10.68	
5.	125 mm thick brickwork in cement mortar with						
	H.B. netting in partition wall	1	5.000		0.15	0.75	3.75 + 2 × 0.625 = 5.00
	up to gr. level	1	4.00		0.30	1.20	3.875 + 2 × 0.0625
						1.950	= 4.00 sqm
	Gr. level to plinth level	1	4.00		0.575	2.30	
						4.250	

Item no.	Description of items	No.	Measurements			Content	Waste
			Length	Breadth	Height		
6.	Damp proof course, 25 mm thick with cement concrete $1:1\frac{1}{2}:3$ with admixture of water proofing compound						
	Main walls	1	31.00	0.25		7.75	
	Partition walls	1	4.00	0.125		0.50	
						8.25	
	Less for doors	1	1.20	0.25		0.30	
		1	1.20	0.125		0.15	
	Verandah opening	1	1.25	0.25		0.31	
		1	2.00	0.25		0.50	
						(–) 1.26	
						6.99	
7.	Earthwork in back filling in foundation					22.10	
	Volume of excavation as per item no. 1						
	Less volume of soling area as per item no. 2	1	× 24.36		0.075	1.83	
	Volume of concrete as per item no. 3					5.15	
	Volume of brickwork as per item no. 4					6.22	
	up to gr. level partition wall item no. 5	1	× 1.2		0.125	0.15	
	area				(–)	13.35	
						8.75	cum
8.	Brickwork in cement mortar 1 : 6 in superstructure						
	Main walls	1	31.00	0.25	2.85	22.09	3.00 – 0.15 = 2.85
	Less for openings						
	Door	1	1.20	0.25	2.10	0.63	
	Windows	9	1.00	0.25	1.50	3.38	
	Verandah	1	1.25 =	1.25			
		1	2.00 =	2.00			
			3.25	0.25	2.10	1.71	
						(–)5.72	
						16.37 cum.	
9.	125 mm thick brickwork in cement mortar 1 : 4 with H.B. netting	1	4.00		2.90	11.60	
	Less for door	1	1.20		2.10	(–)2.52	
						9.08 sqm.	
10.	Cement concrete 1 : 2 : 4 for R.C.C. work in lintel and roof.						
	Lintel						

Item no.	Description of items	No.	Measurements			Content	Waste
			Length	Breadth	Height		
	Main walls	1	31.00	0.25	0.15	1.16	
	Partition wall	1	4.00	0.125	0.10	0.05	
	Roof slab	1	8.75	5.00	0.125	5.47	
						6.68	
11.	Reinforcement 0.8% volume of concrete as per item 10.		6.68 cum				
	0.8% volume of steel		0.05344 cum				
	7850 kg/cum					420 kg	
12.	Shuttering and centering for R.C.C. work						
	Lintel sides	2	8.75	= 17.50			
	Main walls	2 × 2	4.00	= 16.00			
				33.5	0.15	5.03	
	Partition walls	2	4.00		0.10	0.80	
	Sides of main walls	2	5.00	= 10.00			
		2	4.50	= 9.00			
		2	4.375	= 8.75			
				27.75	0.15	4.16	
	Opening bottom	1	1.20	0.25		0.30	
	Doors						
		1	1.25	0.125		0.16	
	Verandah opening	1	1.25	0.25		0.31	
		1	2.00	0.25		0.50	
	Windows	9	1.00	0.25		2.25	
	Slab						
	Sides	2	8.75	= 17.50			
		2	5.00	= 10.00		3.44	
			27.50	0.125		36.00	
	Bottom	2	4.50	4.00		52.95 sqm	

Example 2.13 *Estimate Estimation of the quantities of works of the building as shown in Figure 2.13.*

Item	Description of items	No.	Measurements			Contents	Waste
			L	B	H		
1.	Earthwork in excavation in foundation.						$L = 5.00 + 6.00 + 0.25 + 0.25 + 0.125 + 2 \times \frac{(0.80 - 0.25)}{2}$
	Main walls	3	12.175	= 36.525			$= 12.175$
	Long walls	2	3.450	= 6.900			$L = 4.00 - 2 \times \frac{(0.80 - 0.25)}{2}$
		2	1.950	= 3.900			$= 3.450$
			47.325	0.800	0.775	29.342	$L = 2.50 - 2 \times \frac{(0.80 - 0.25)}{2}$ $= 1.950$ $H = 0.700 + 0.075 = 0.775$
	Partiton wall	1	3.450	0.300	0.575	0.595	$H = 0.50 + 0.075 = 0.575$

	Step	1	6.175	0.025	0.175	0.027	$L = 0.725 + 2.00 + 0.725 + 2.0 + 0.725 = 6.175$ $B = 0.30 - 0.275$ $d = 0.025$ $H = 0.10 + 0.075 = 0.175$
						29.964	cum
2.	Single brick flat soling.	1	47.325	0.800		37.860	
	Partition wall	1	3.450	0.300		1.035	$L = 4.00 - 2 \times \frac{0.125}{2} - 2 \times \frac{0.125}{2} - 2 \times 0.150$
	Steps	1	6.175	0.300		1.853	
						40.748	
3.	Cement concrete 1:3:6 in foundation.	1	47.325	0.800	0.200	7.572	
	Partition wall	1	3.750	0.300	0.150	0.169	$L = 4.00 - 2 \times \frac{0.125}{2} - 2 \times \frac{0.125}{2} = 3.750$
	Steps	1	6.175	0.300	0.100	0.185	
						7.926 cum	
4.	Brickwork in cement mortar 1 : 4 in foundation and plinth.						
	Main walls						
	1st. footing						
	Long walls	3	11.875	= 35.625			$L = 12.175 - 0.300 = 11.875$
	Short walls	2	3.750	= 7.500			$L = 3.450 + 0.300 = 3.750$
	Short walls	2	2.250	= 4.500			$L = 1.950 + 0.300 = 2.250$
			47.625	0.500	0.150	3.572	
	2nd. footing						
	Long walls	3	11.750	= 35.250			
	Short walls	2	3.875	= 7.750			
	Short walls	2	2.375	=4.750			
			47.750	0.375	0.150	2.686	
	3rd. footing						
	Long walls	3	11.625	= 34.875			$L = 11.875 - 0.125 = 11.750$
	Short walls	2	4.000	= 8.000			$L = 3.750 + 0.125 = 3.875$
	Short walls	2	2.500	= 5.000			$L = 2.250 + 0.125 = 2.375$
	up to G.L.		47.875	0.250	0.200	2.394	$L = 11.750 - 0.125 = 11.625$
	Above G.L.		47.875	0.250	0.275	3.291	$L = 3.875 + 0.125 = 4.00$ $L = 2.375 + 0.125 = 2.500$ $H = 0.300 + 0.700 - 0.200 - 0.150 - 0.150 - 0.025 = 0.475$ $= 0.200 + 0.275$
	Partition wall						
	Up to G.L.	1	3.875	0.125	0.150	0.073	$L = 4.00 - \frac{2 \times 0.125}{2}$ $= 3.875$

Item	Description of items	No.	Measurements L	B	H	Contents	Waste
		1	4.000	0.125	0.200	0.100	
	Do above G.L.	1	4.000	0.125	0.275	0.138	
	Step	1	6.175	0.300	0.150	0.278	
						12.532 cum,	
5.	Damp proof course 25 mm thick in cement concrete 1 : 2 : 4						
	Main walls	1	47.875				
	Less openings						
	Doors	2	1.200	= 2.400			
	Front openings	4	2.000	= 8.000			
	Side openings	2	2.025	= 4.050			$L = 2.50 + 0.25 - 0.725 = 2.025$
		(–)	14.450				
			33.425	0.250		8.356	
	Partition walls	1	4.000	0.125		0.500	
						8.856 sqm	
6.	Earthwork in backfilling of foundation trenches						
	Earthwork in excavation as per item no. 1					29.964 cum	
	Less volume of foundation work soling as per item no. 2	1	40.748		0.075	3.056	
	Cement concrete as per item no. 3					7.926	
	Brickwork as per item no. 4						
	1st. footing					3.572	
	2nd. footing					2.686	
	3rd. footing up to G.L.	1	47.875	0.250	0.200	2.394	$H = 0.70 - 0.20 - 0.15 - 0.15 = 0.20$
	Partition wall						
	Lower portion					0.073	
	Upper portion	1	4.00	0.125	0.200	0.100	
						(–) 19.807	
						10.157 cum	
7.	Earthwork in plinth filling						
	Rooms	1	5.000	4.000	0.100	2.000	
		1	6.000	4.000	0.100	2.400	
	Verandah	1	11.125	2.500	0.100	2.781	
						7.181 cum	

Item	Description of items	No.	Measurements			Contents	Waste
			L	B	H		
8.	Brickwork in superstructure in cement mortar 1 : 6						
	Main walls	2	11.625	= 23.250			
	Long walls	2	4.000	= 8.000			
			31.250	0.250	2.850	22.266	$H = 3.00 - 0.15 = 2.85$
	Verandah gable	2 × 1/2	2.50	0.250	0.750	0.469	
	Partition wall	1	4.00	0.125	2.775	1.388	$H = 3.00 - 0.225 = 2.775$
						24.123	
	Less for						
	Doors	2	1.200	0.25	2.100	1.260	
	Windows	8	1.000	0.25	1.200	2.400	
	R.C.C. beam ends	2	0.250	0.20	0.225	0.023	
	Beam bearings	3 × 2	0.250	0.250	0.150	0.056	Including ends of R.S.J
						(–)3.739	
						20.384 cum	
9.	Brickwork in pillars in cement mortar 1 : 4	5	0.725	= 3.625			
		2	0.475	= 0.950			
			4.575	0.250	2.100	2.400 cum	H = up to lintel
10.	Single brick flat soling in flooring						
	Main rooms	1	5.00	= 5.000			
		1	6.00	= 6.000			
			11.00	4.000		44.000	
	Verandah	1	11.125	2.500		27.810	
						71.810 sqm	
11.	Cement concrete 1 : 3 : 6 Area same as item no. 10		71.810		0.100	7.181 cum	
12.	Casting, hoisting and fixing cement concrete bearing blocks for joists and beams of size 250 × 250 × 150 mm	6				6 nos.	
13.	Supplying, hoisting and fixing in position R.S.J. 200 × 100 mm @ 25.4 kg per m	2	4.450			8.900 m	
						226.060 kg	
14.	Shuttering and centering for R.C.C. work						
	Lintel bottoms						
	Doors	2	1.200	= 2.400			
	Windows	8	1.000	= 8.000			
	Verandah	4	2.000	= 8.000			
	"sides	2	2.025	= 4.050			

Item	Description of items	No.	Measurements L	B	H	Contents	Waste
			22.450	0.250		5.613	
	Lintel sides	2	11.625	=23.250			
		2	7.250	= 14.500			
		4	11.125	= 44.500			
		2	4.000	= 8.000			
		2	2.500	= 5.000			
			95.250		0.150	14.288	
	Chajja bottom	6	1.200	0.500		3.600	
	Chajja sides	2 × 6	0.500	$\frac{0.075 + 0.050}{2}$		0.375	
		6	1.200	0.050		3.600	
	Slab bottom	1	11.125	4.000		44.500	
	Slab sides	2	11.625	= 23.250			
	Slab sides	2	4.500	= 9.000			
			32.250	0.100		3.225	
	Beam sides	2	4.000	0.225		1.800	
		2	0.225	0.200		0.090	
						73.851 sqm	
15.	Cement concrete 1 : 2 : 4 in R.C.C. work						
	Lintel	1	47.875	0.250	0.150	1.795	
	Slab	1	11.625	4.500	0.100	5.231	
	Beam	1	4.500	0.200	0.225	0.203	
	Chajjas over windows	6	1.20	$\frac{0.075 + 0.050}{2} \times 0.500$		= 0.225	
						7.454 cum	
16.	M.S. Reinforcement in R.C.C. work Lintel, slab and chajja. Cement concrete as per item no. 15					7.454 cum	
	Less beam				(–)	0.203	
						7.251 cum	
	@ 0.8%					0.058 cum	
	Beam 0.203 cum @ 1.0%					0.002 cum	
						0.060 cum	
	@ 7850 kg per cum					471 kg	
17.	Brickwork in cement mortar 1 : 4 in blocking course on roof.	2	11.625	= 23.250			
		2	4.000	= 8.000			
			31.250	0.250	0.250	1.953	
		2	11.625		23.250		
		2	30.750	0.375	0.125	1.441	
						3.394 cum	

Item	Description of items	No.	Measurements			Contents	Waste
			L	B	H		
18.	Lime terracing over roof 100 mm thick - 7 : 2 : $1\frac{1}{2}$	1	11.125	4.000		44.50	
		2	11.125	= 22.250			
		2	3.800	= 7.600			
			29.850	0.150		4.48	
						48.98 sqm	
19.	Supplying and fixing door and window frames.						
	Doors	2	2 × (2.100 + 1.200)				
				0.100	0.050	0.054	
	Windows	8	2 × (1.200 + 1.00)				
				0.075	0.050	0.132	
						0.186 cum	
20.	Supplying and fixing fan hooks including painting two coats	2				2 Nos.	
21.	Supplying and fixing M.S. clamps 25 × 6 mm for fixing door and window frames						
	i. 225 mm long	2 × 2 × 3				12 nos.	
	ii. 150 mm long	8 × 2 × 2				32 nos.	
22.	Supplying and fixing door and window shutters						
	i. Door shutters 40 mm thick, panelled, double leaf.		2	2.050	1.125	4.613 sqm	
	ii Window shutters 25 mm thick 2/3 panelled and 1/3 glazed.	8	1.125	0.925		8.325 sqm	
23.	Supplying and fixing iron mongeries.						
	a. Doors - 2 numbers						
	i. 100 mm iron hinges	2 × 2 × 3				12 nos.	
	ii. Door handle 150 mm	2 × 2				4 nos.	
	iii. Tower bolt 300 mm long (iron)	2 × 1				2 nos.	
	iv. Hasp bolt (iron)	2 × 1				2 nos.	
	v. Door rings (Brass)	2 × 1				2 nos.	
	vi. Rubber door stops	2 × 2				4 nos.	
	vii. Sand block						
	Window 100 × 50 × 40 mm	2 × 2				4 nos.	

Item	Description of items	No.	Measurements L	Measurements B	Measurements H	Contents	Waste
	b. Windows — 8 numbers						
	i. 75 mm iron hinges	8 × 2 × 2				32 nos.	
	ii. Window handle 100 mm	8 × 2				16 nos.	
	iii. Tower bolt 150 mm (iron)	8 × 2				16 nos.	
	iv. Catch hook (iron)	8 × 2				16 nos.	
24.	Supplying and fixing ventilators 150 × 225 mm size. Including painting two coats.	8				8 nos.	
25.	Salwood work rough dressed in roof truss						
	Wall plate and post plate	2	11.575	0.075	0.050	0.087	
	Rafter	15	3.15	0.050	0.035	0.083	
	Purlins	5	11.575	0.035	0.035	0.071	
						0.241 cum	
26.	Asbestos sheet roofing	1	11.925	3.250		38.760	sqm
27.	Water proofing the junction of Asbestos roofing and wall	1	11.25			11.625m	sqm
28.	Sand and cement plaster 1 : 6						
	a. 15 mm thick (external) walls	1	11.625	= 11.625			
		2	4.500	= 9.000			
			20.625		3.875	79.922	$H = 3.00 + 0.30 + 0.375 + 0.100 + 0.100 = 3.875$
	Varandah plinth	2	2.750	= 5.500			
		1	11.625	= 11.625			
			17.125		0.400	6.850	$H = 0.300 + 0.100 = 0.400$
	Pillars	7	0.725		2.100	10.658	
	Lintel over pillars	1	11.625		0.150	1.744	
	Chajja top and bottom	6 × 2	1.200	0.500		7.200	
	Chajja sides	6 × 2	0.500	$\frac{0.075 + 0.050}{2}$		0.375	
	Window sills	6	1.200	0.050		0.360	
	and jambs	6	4.400	0.075		1.980	$L = 2 \times 1.20 + 2 \times 1.00 = 4.40$
	Step top	1	6.175	0.300		1.853	
		1	6.175	0.150		0.926	
		2	0.300	0.150		0.090	
	End gables	2 × 1/2	2.750	0.750		2.063	
	Blocking course tops	2	11.625	= 23.250			

Item	Description of items	No.	Measurements L	B	H	Contents	Waste
		2	4.000	= 8.000			
			31.250	0.375		11.719	
		2	10.875	= 21.750			
		2	3.375	= 6.750			
			28.500	0.150		4.275	
						131.015	
	Less for window openings	6	1.200	1.000		(–) 7.200	
						122.815 sqm	
	b. 20 mm thick (internal) Rooms	2	5.000	= 10.000			
		2	6.000	= 12.000			
		4	4.000	= 16.000			
			38.000		3.000	114.000	
	Verandah	1	11.625	2.100		24.413	
		1	11.125	0.900		10.013	
	Gable ends	2	2.500	$\frac{0.150 + 0.750}{2}$		2.250	
	Pillars	10	0.250	= 2.500			
		4	0.475	= 1.90			
		3	0.725	= 2.175			
			6.575		2.100	13.808	
	Lintel sides	1	11.125		0.15	1.669	
	" bottom	2	2.500	= 5.000			
	" bottom	4	2.000	= 8.000			
			13.000	0.250		3.250	
	Jams and sills						
	Doors	2	5.400	0.150		1.620	$L = 2 \times 2.1 + 1.2 = 5.40$
		8	4.400	0.075		2.640	$B = 0.075 + 0.075 = 0.15$
		2	4.400	0.075		174.320	$L = 2 \times 1.2 + 2 \times 1.0 = 4.4$
	Deduct for openings.						
	Doors	2 × 2	2.100	1.200		10.080	
	Windows	8 + 2	1.200	1.000		12.000	
						(–) 22.080	
						152.240	sqm
29.	Sand and cement plaster 1 : 4 10 mm thick.						
	Ceiling	1	5.000	4.000		20.000	
		1	6.000	4.000		24.000	
						44.000	
	Deduct for joists	2	4.000	0.100		0.800	
						43.200 sqm	
30.	25 mm thick I.P.S in flooring.						
	Area same as item no. 10					71.810	

Item	*Description of items*	*No.*	*Measurements L*	*B*	*H*	*Contents*	*Waste*
	Add for openings						
	Doors	2	1.200	= 2.400			
	Front openings	4	2.00	= 8.000			
	Side "	2	2.025	= 4.050			
			14.450	0.250		3.613	
						75.423 sqm	
31.	Neat cement finishing on plaster.						
	Skirtings of rooms	2	5.000	= 10.000			
		2	6.000	= 12.000			
		4	4.000	= 16.000			
			38.000	0.100		3.800	
	Verandah	1	11.625	0.100		1.163	
	Pillars	10	0.250	= 2.500			
		3	0.725	= 2.175			
		4	0.475	= 1.900			
			6.575	0.100		0.658	
	Plinth	2	11.625	= 23.250			
		2	7.250	= 14.500			
			37.750	0.400		15.100	
	Step	1	6.175	0.300		1.853	
	ends	2	0.300	0.400		0.240	
						22.814 sqm	
32.	White washing, two coats over a coat of priming						
	Area same as item no. 28 *b*					152.24	
	Area same as item no. 29					43.20	
						195.44	
	Less quantity as per item no. 31 *i*, *ii* and *iii*					(–) 5.62	
						189.82 sqm	
33.	Decorative cement based paint to external walls, two coats over a coat of primer.						
	Same as item no. 28 *a*					116.954	
	Less for item no. 31 *iv* and *v*					(–) 17.193	
						99.761 sqm	
34.	*a.* Painting to wood works, two coats over a coat of priming						
	Doors	1.3 × 2 × 2	2.050		1.125	11.993	Multiplication factor 1.3
	Windows	1.0 × 8 × 2	1.125		0.925	16.650	Multiplication factor 1.0
						28.643 sqm	

Item	Description of items	No.	Measurements			Contents	Waste
			L	B	H		
	b. Painting to wood works, one coat over a coat of priming						
	Wall plate	1	11.575	0.250		2.894	
	Rafters	15	3.150	0.170		8.033	
	Purlins	5	11.575	0.140		8.103	
						19.030 sqm	
	c. Painting over wood work, one coat						
	Doors	13 × 2	5.400	0.100		1.80	Multiplication factor 1.3
	Windows	10 × 8	4.400	0.075		2.640	Multiplication factor 1.0
						3.720 sqm	
35.	Painting to steel surfaces-two coats						
	R.S.J.	2	4.000	0.600		4.800	
	M.S. grills	1.5 × 8	1.100	0.900		11.880	Multiplication factor 1.5
						16.680 sqm	
36.	Supplying and fixing m.s. grill to windows made of 12 mm wide 6 mm thick flats	8	1.100	0.900		7.920 sqm	

SPECIFICATION [Fig. 2.13(*a*)] :

1. Brickwork in foundation and plinth in cement sand mortar 1 : 4
2. Brickwork in superstructure in cement sand mortar 1 : 6
3. Reinforcement to be provided 0.8% in roof slab and lintel, 1% in beam by volume of concrete
4. Brickwork in superstructure in pillars in cement sand mortar 1 : 40.
5. Painting to wood and steel works–two coats over a coat of priming
6. External finishing—cement based paint two coats over a coat of priming
7. Internal finishing—white washing two coats over a coat of priming.

Note :

Data or dimension not furnished may be assumed suitably.

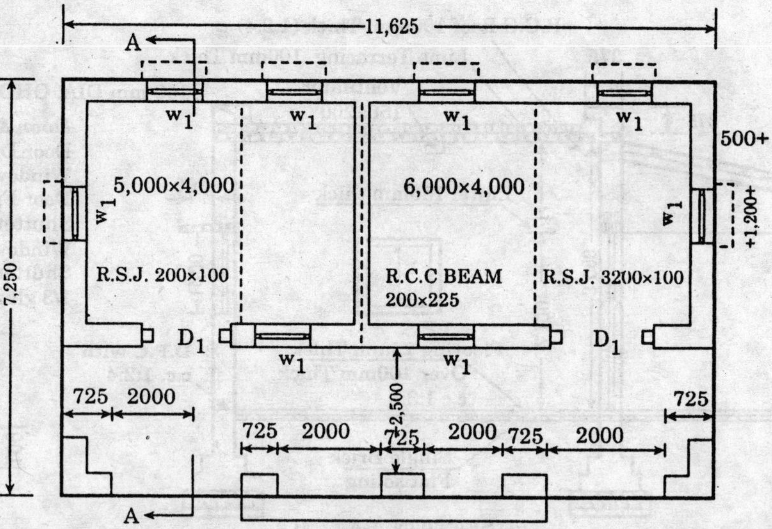

(*a*) PLAN

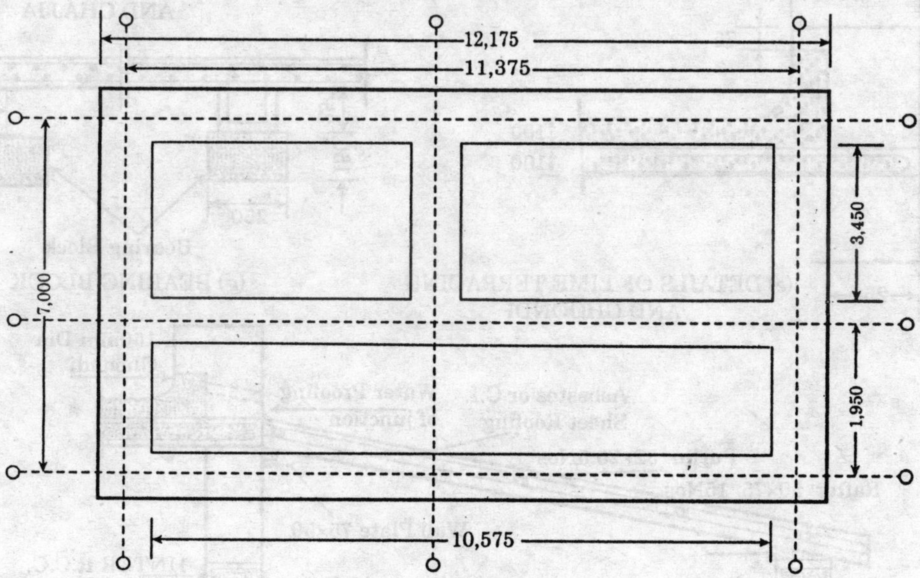

(*b*) FOUNDATION PLAN

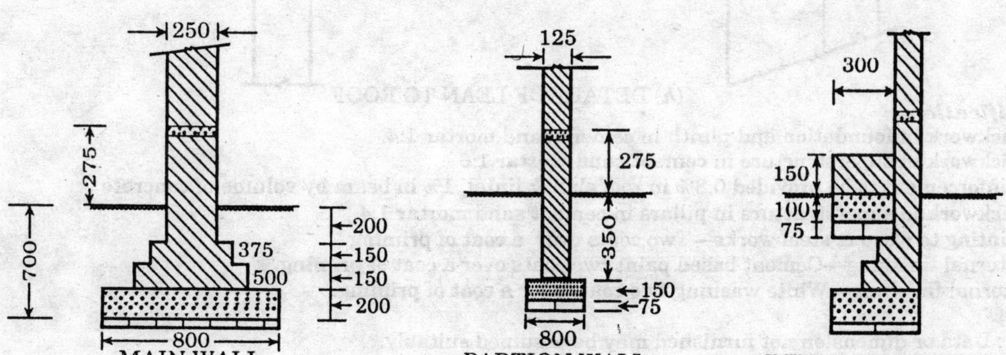

(*c*) DETAIL OF FOUNDATION

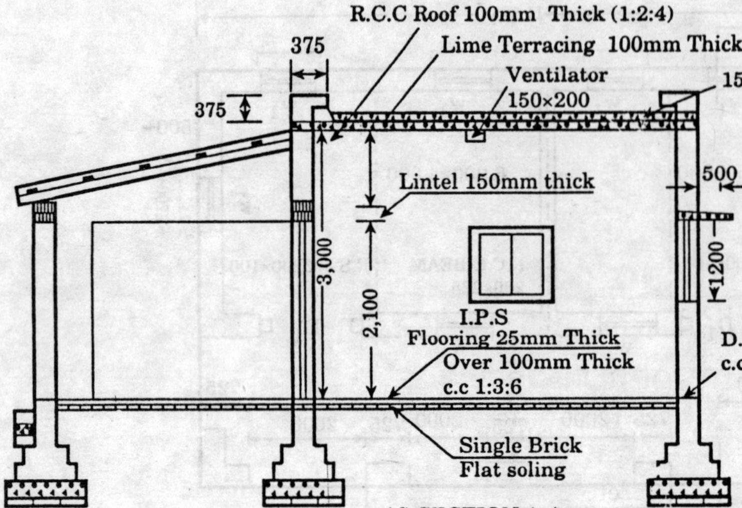

(*d*) SECTION A-A

Door & Windows Schedule
Door D1 — 2,100 × 1,200
Window W1 — 1,000 × 1,200
Door Frame, Salwood — 100 × 50
Shutter, 40 mm thick panelled
Window frame, Salwood 75 × 50
Shutter 25 mm Thick Panelled
1/3 glazed

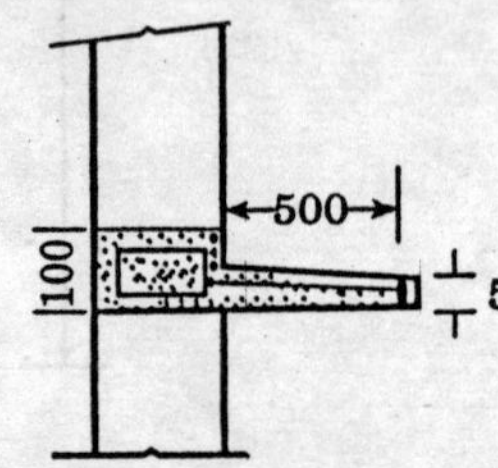

(*f*) DETAILS IN OF LINTEL AND CHAJJA

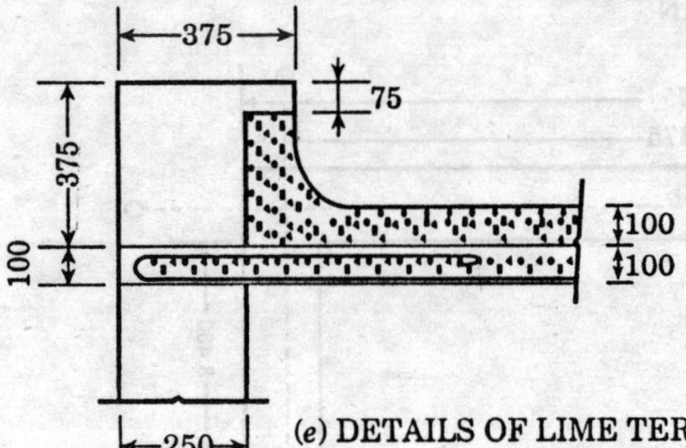

(*e*) DETAILS OF LIME TERRACING AND GHOONDI

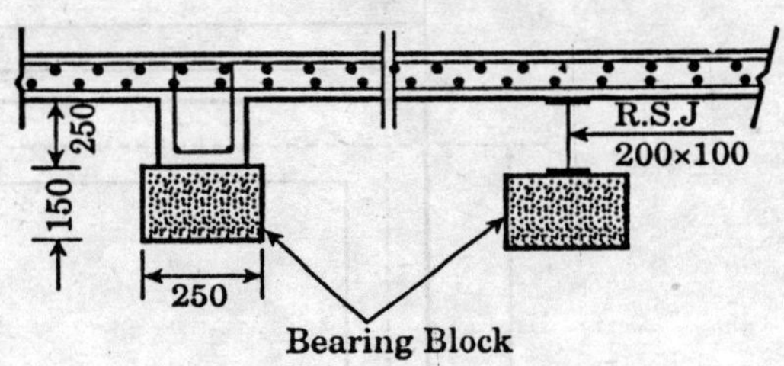

(*g*) BEARING BLOCK

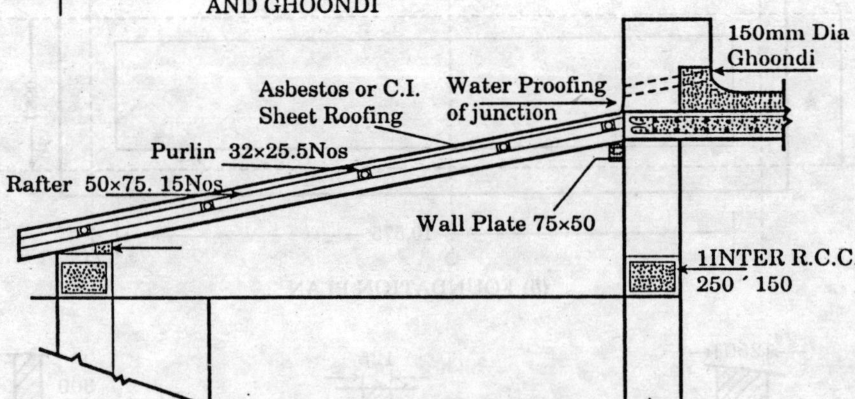

(*h*) DETAIL OF LEAN TO ROOF

Specifications :

1. Brickwork in foundation and plinth in cement sand mortar 1:4.
2. Brickwork in superstructure in cement sand mortar 1:6
3. Reinforcement to be provided 0.8% in roof slab & lintel, 1% in beam by volume of concrete
4. Brickwork in superstructure in pillars in cement sand mortar 1:4.
5. Painting to wood & steel works—Two coats over a coat of priming
6. External finishing—Cement based paint two coats over a coat of priming.
7. Internal finishing—White washing two coats over a coat of priming.

Note : Data or dimension not furnished may be assumed suitably.

Fig. 2.13(*a*) Single Storey Building

3

ESTIMATION OF REINFORCEMENT

3.1.0 ESTIMATION OF QUANTITY OF REINFORCEMENT

In reinforced concrete work, apart from concrete and shuttering, the quantity of reinforcement need be placed is required to be estimated.

The designer of the reinforced concrete structure prepares the Reinforcement Drawing, from which the lengths of the reinforcing bars of different diameters are computed. In the reinforcement drawing, the details of the reinforcement bars – number, diameter, cranking position, etc. are furnished. A Bar-Schedule is prepared furnishing all the details of each category of bar and tabulated.

The length of the bar is calculated from the length of the concrete member with due deduction for the concrete cover.

Standard form of Reinforcement Schedule

Schedule no. ....

Location	*Mark designation*	*Size and type*	*Number of sets*	*Number per set*	*Total number*	*Length in mm*	*Shape (All dimensions are in accordance with the standard, unless otherwise stated)*
Column	C5 6P 35 N	M.S. round 20 mm	6	6	36	3,000	Straight

3.1.1 Hooks and Bends Forming and End Anchorage

The bars are provided with necessary hooks or bends for end anchorage. These are provided according to necessity and conforming to I.S. Code as shown in Figure 3.1.

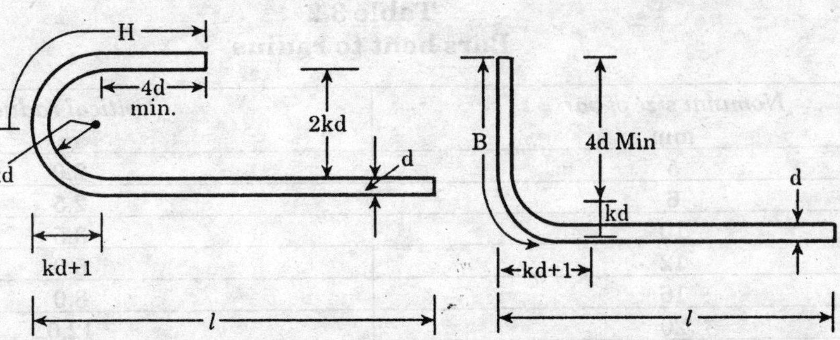

Figure 3.1 Hooks and Bends.

The value of k depends upon the strength of steel bars used. For ordinary m.s. (140 N/mm^2) the value is taken as 2, for medium tensile steel (190 N/mm^2), it is taken as 3 and in cases of cold twisted bar, k value is taken as 4. In cases of bars of diameter above 25 mm, it is desirable to increase the k value to 3, 4, and 6 respectively.

H and B are the Hook and Bend allowance and can be found in Table 3.1.

Table 3.1
Hook and 90° Bend allowance

	Hook allowance						*90° Bend allowance*					
Nominal size of Bar	*Mild steel IS : 432-1960*		*Medium Tensile steel IS : 432-1960*		*Cold worked steel bars IS : 1786-1961*		*Mild steel*		*Medium Tensile steel*		*Cold Worked Steel bars*	
	Min. mm	*Reco-mended mm*	*Min. mm*	*Recomen-ded mm*	*Min. mm*	*Recomen-ded mm*	*Min. mm*	*Recomen-ded mm*	*Min. mm*	*Recomen-ded mm*	*Min. mm*	*Recome-nded mm*
5	75	–	75	–	75	–	75	–	75	–	75	–
6	75	–	75	–	75	–	75	–	75	–	75	–
8	75	–	90	–	105	–	75	–	75	–	75	–
10	90	–	110	–	130	–	75	–	75	–	75	–
12	110	–	130	–	155	–	75	–	75	–	75	–
16	145	–	175	–	210	–	80	–	90	–	95	–
20	180	–	220	–	260	–	100	–	110	–	120	–
22	200	–	240	–	285	–	110	–	120	–	130	–
25	225	–	275	–	325	–	125	–	140	–	150	–
28	250	310	310	365	365	475	146	155	155	170	170	195
32	290	350	350	415	415	545	160	175	175	190	190	225
36	325	395	395	470	470	610	180	200	200	215	215	250
40	360	440	440	520	520	680	200	220	220	240	240	280
45	405	495	495	585	585	765	225	250	250	270	270	315
50	450	550	650	650	850	250	275	275	275	300	300	350

H = Hook allowance taken as 9d, 11d, 13d and 17d for k values 2, 3, 4 and 6 respectively and rounded off to nearest 5 mm, but not less than 75 mm.

B = Bond allowance taken as 5d, 5.5d, 6d and 7d for k values 2, 3, 4 and 6 respectively and rounded off to nearest 5 mm but not less than 75 mm.

3.1.2 Bars Bent to a Radius

When the bars are required to be bent to a radius, the limitations as shown in the Table 3.2 need be followed.

Table 3.2
Bars bent to radius

Nominal size of bar mm	*Critical radius* m
5	2.0
6	2.5
10	3.5
12	5.0
16	8.0
20	12.0
22	18.0
25	24.0
28	34.0
32	40.0

3.1.3 Permissible Bending and Cutting Tolerance

While cutting or bending a bar, it may not be possible to cut or bend it to the exact size and some tolerance need be provided.

Table 3.3
Permissible bending and cutting tolerance

	Dimensions		*Tolerance*	
	Over	*up to and including*	*Plus*	*Minus*
	cm	cm	mm	mm
For bent bars	–	75	3	5
	75	150	5	10
	150	250	6	15
	250	–	7	25
For straight bars	All lengths		25	25

3.1.4 Measurement of Bending Dimensions of Bars of Reinforced Concrete

Ref. No.	*Method of measurement of Bending Dimensions*	*Approximate total length of Bar (L) measured along centre line*	*Sketch and dimensions to be given in schedule.*
1	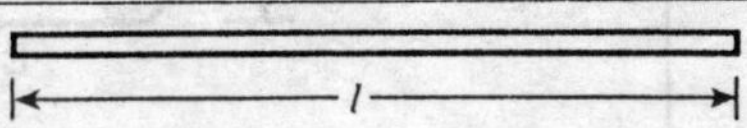	l	Straight
2	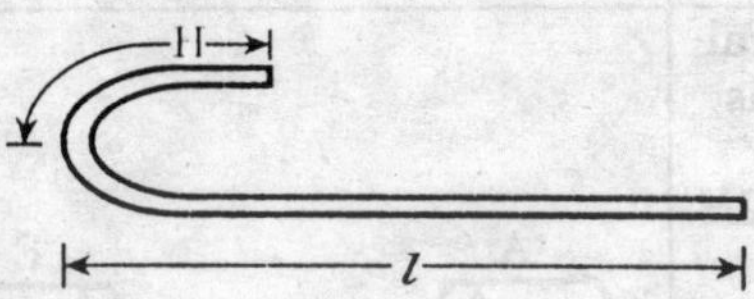	$l + H$	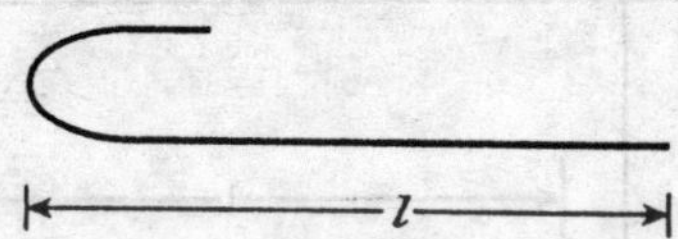
3	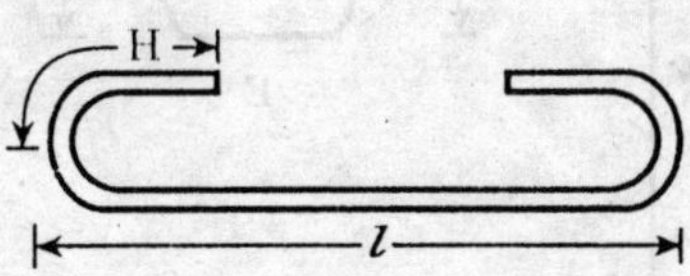	$l + 2H$	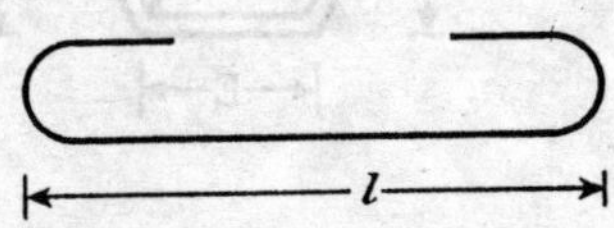
4	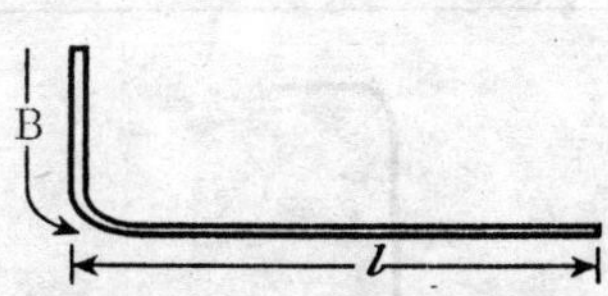	$l + B$	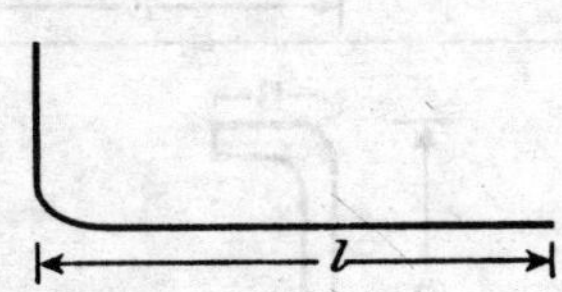

Ref. No.	*Method of measurement of Bending Dimensions*	*Approximate total length of Bar (L) measured along centre line*	*Sketch and dimensions to be given in schedule.*
5		$l + 2B$	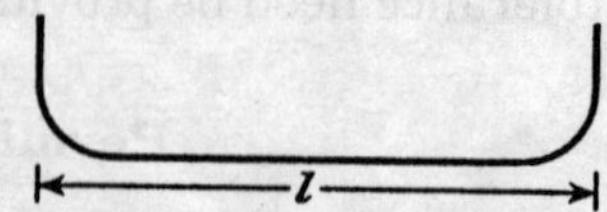
6	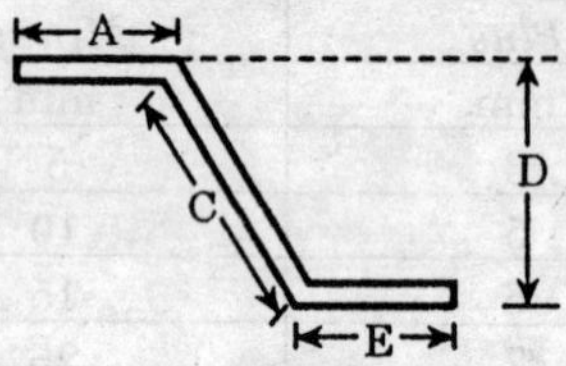	Where C is more than $3D$. $A + C + E$	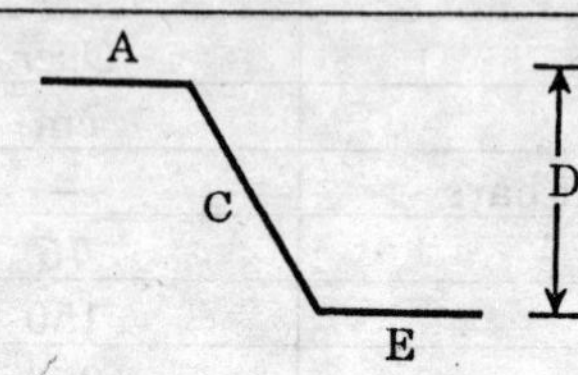
7	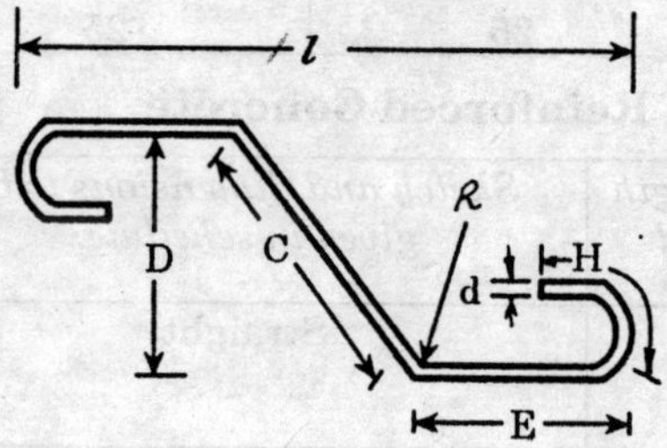	If angle with horizontal is 45° or less, and R is 12 or less. $A + C + E + 2H$ or $l + 2H + C - \sqrt{C^2 - D^2}$ If l is specified, A or E is omitted.	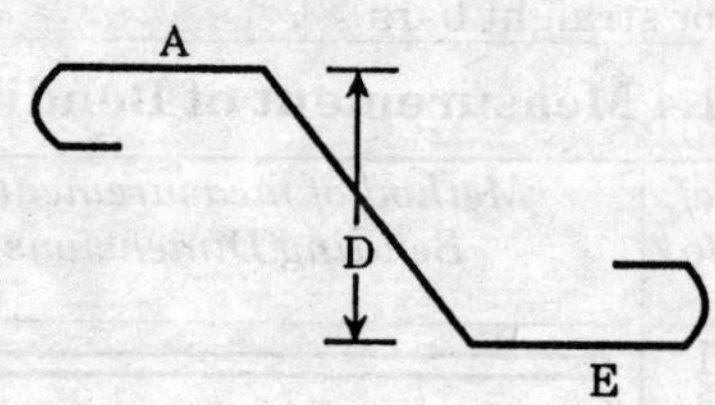
8	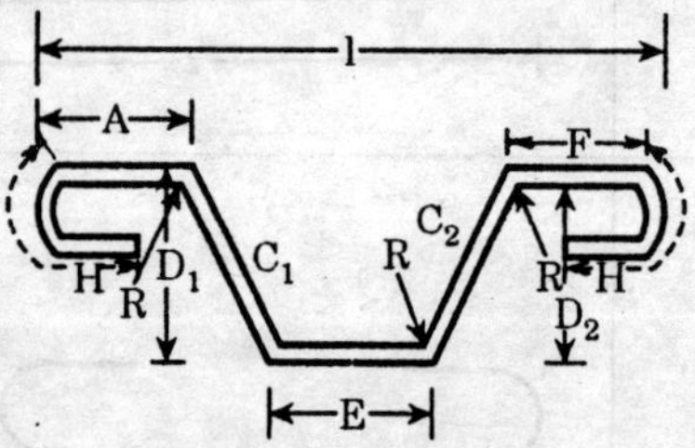	If angle with horizontal is 45° or less, and R is $12d$ or less $A + C_1 + C_2 + E + F + 2H$ or $l + C_1 + C_2 + E + 2H - \sqrt{C_1^2 - D_1^2} - \sqrt{C_2^2 - D_2^2}$ If l is specified, A, E or F is omitted.	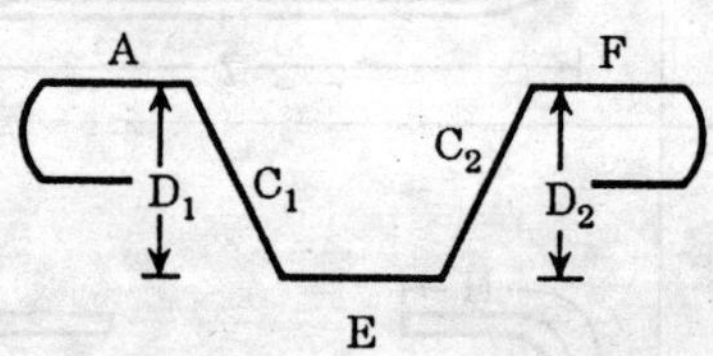
9	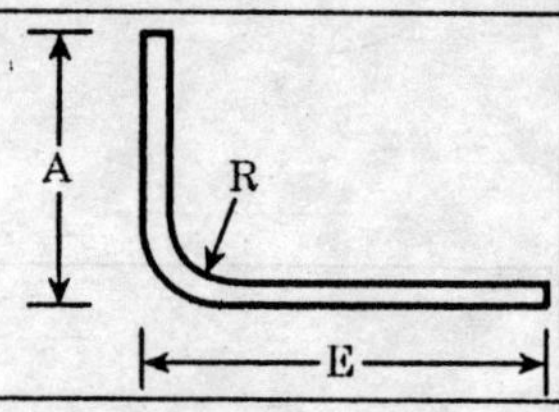	$A + E + 1/2R - d$	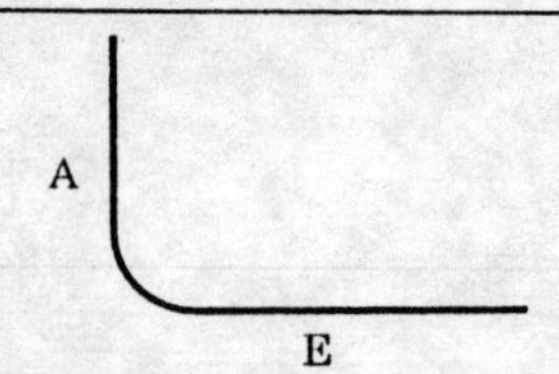
10	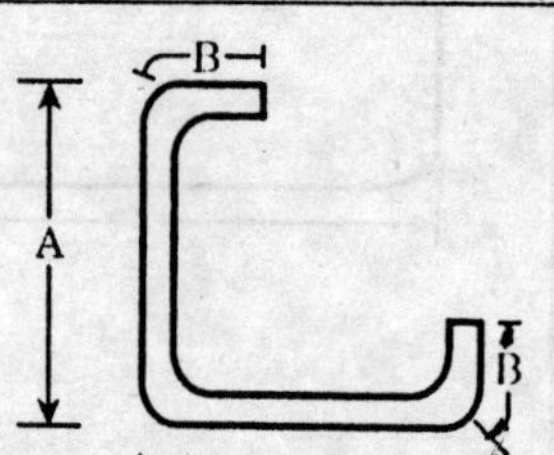	$A + E + 1/2R - d + 2B$	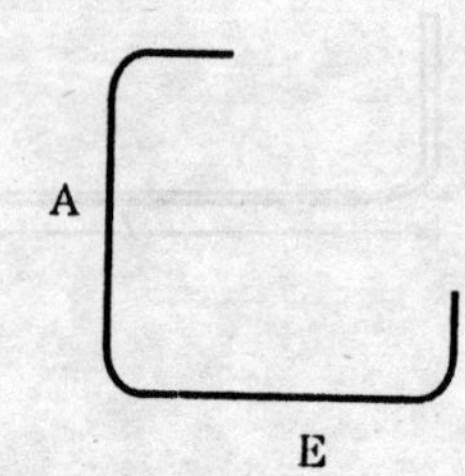

Ref. No.	*Method of measurement of Bending Dimensions*	*Approximate total length of Bar (L) measured along centre line*	*Sketch and dimensions to be given in schedule.*
11	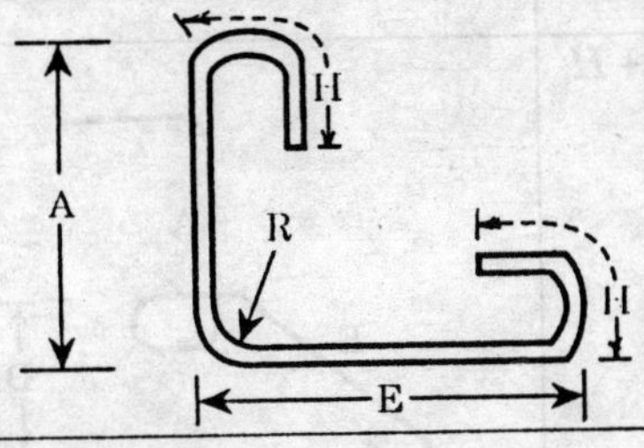	$A + E - 1/2R - d + 2H$	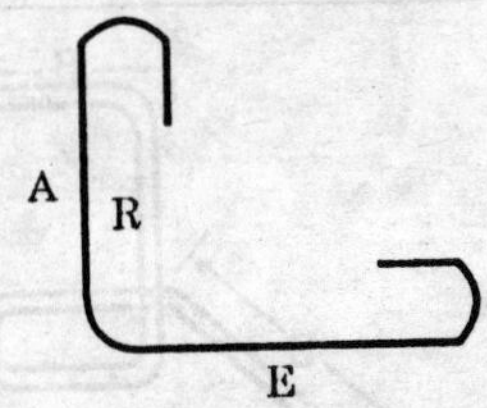
12	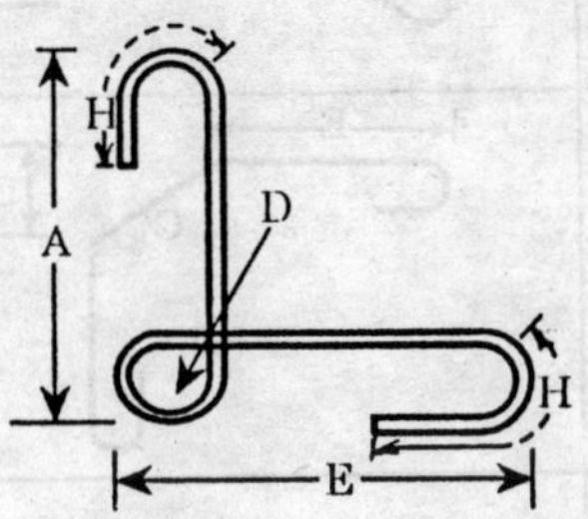	$A + E + 1\frac{1}{3} D + 2H$	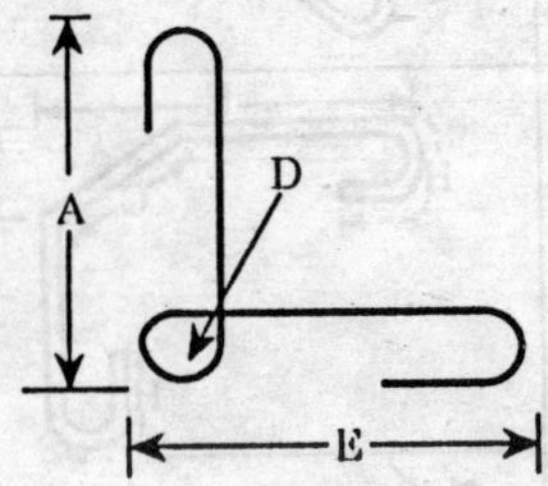
13	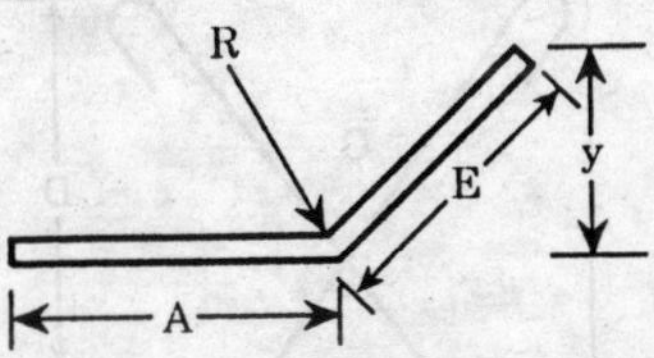	If angle with horizontal is 45° or less $A + E$	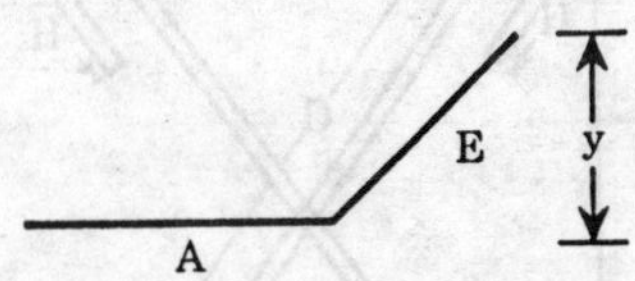
14	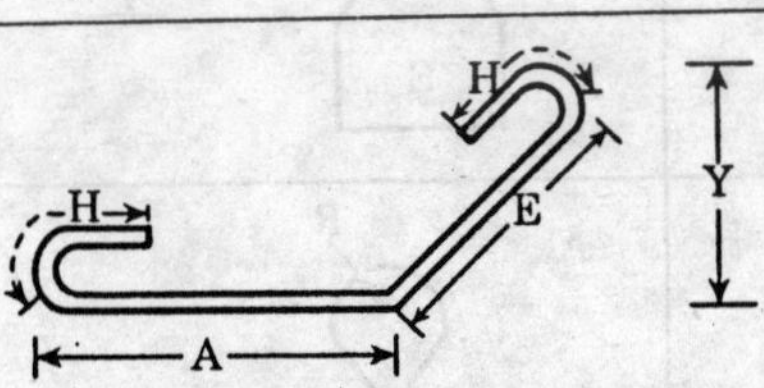	If angle with horizontal is 45° or less and R is 12 or less, $A + E + 2H$. If angle is greater than 45° and R exceeds 12, L to be calculated	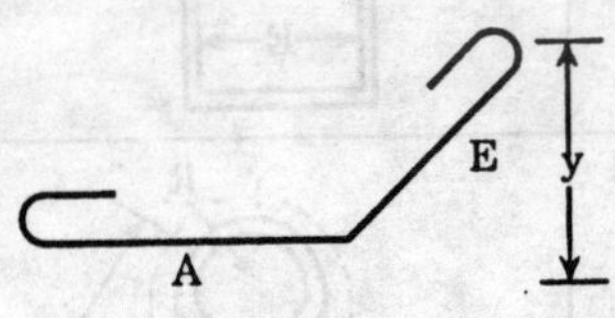
15	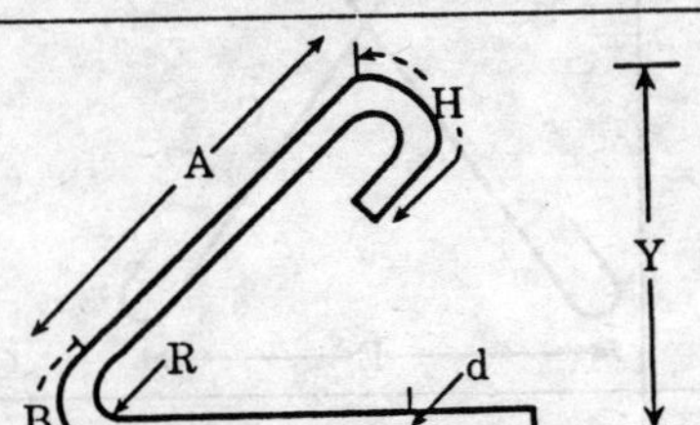	If angle with horizontal is 45° or less $A + B + C + H - 2(R + D)$ If angle is greater than 45° and R exceeds 12d, L to be calculated.	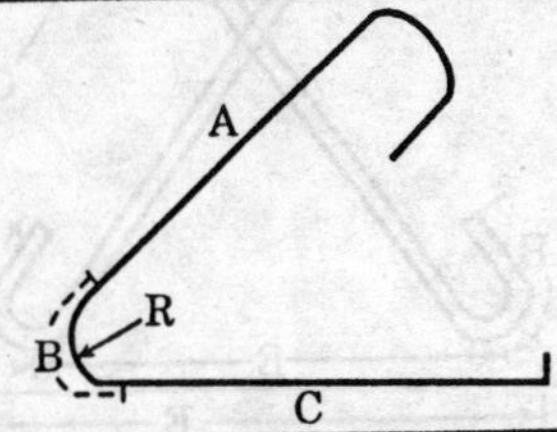
16	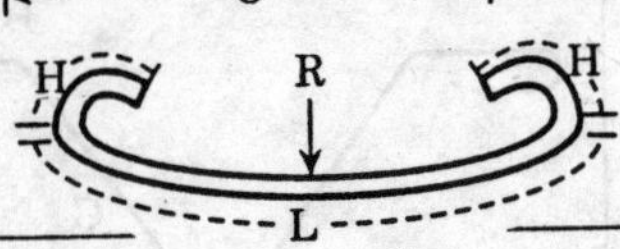	$l + 2H$	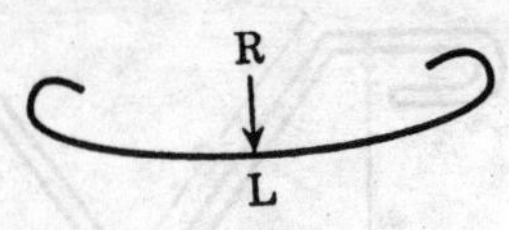
17	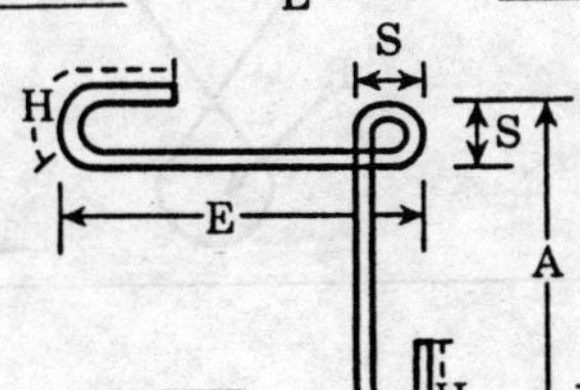	$A + E + 2S + 2H + d$	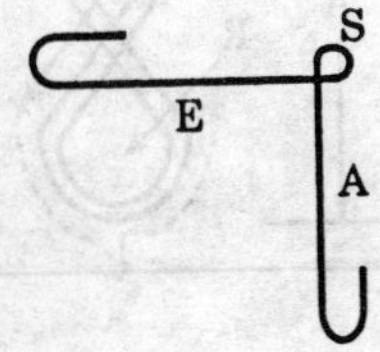

Ref. No.	Method of measurement of Bending Dimensions	Approximate total length of Bar (L) measured along centre line	Sketch and dimensions to be given in schedule.
18	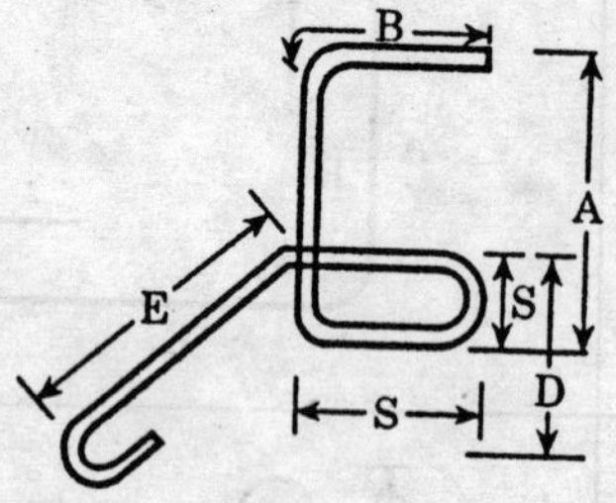	$A + E + 3S + 2d + B + H$	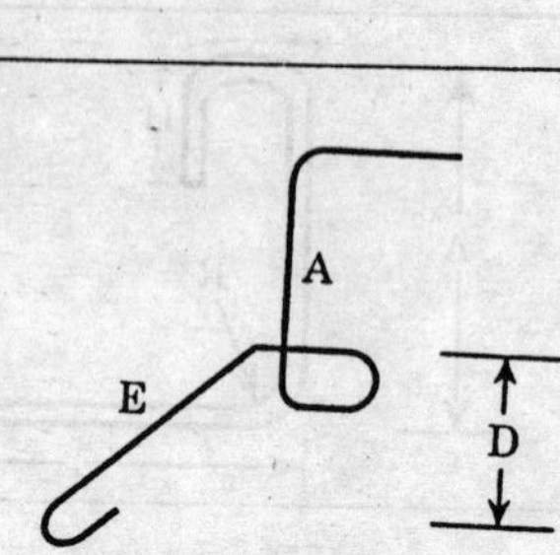
19	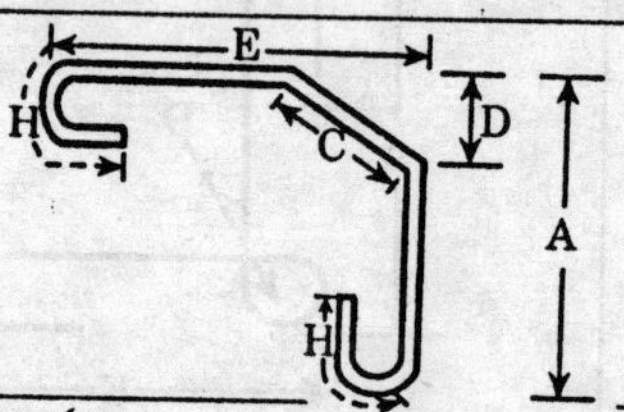	$A + E + C + 2H - \sqrt{C^2 - D^2} - D$	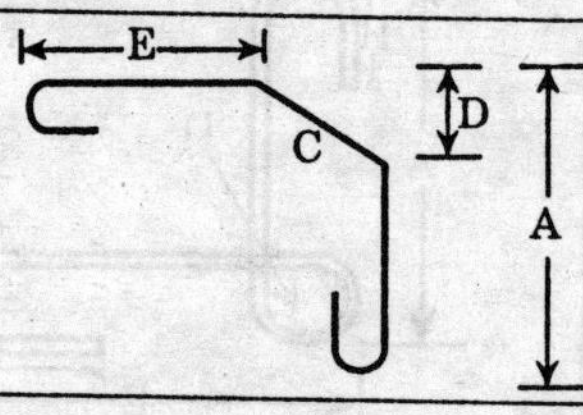
20	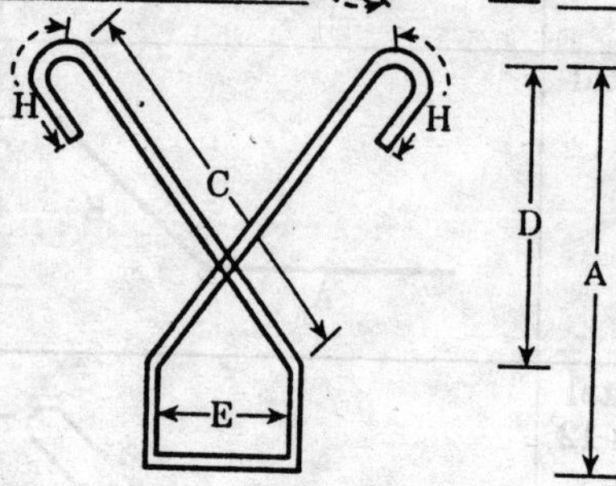	$E + 2(A - D + C + H)$	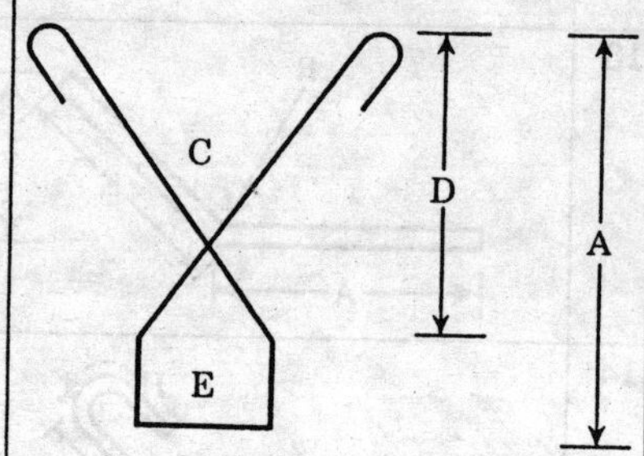
21	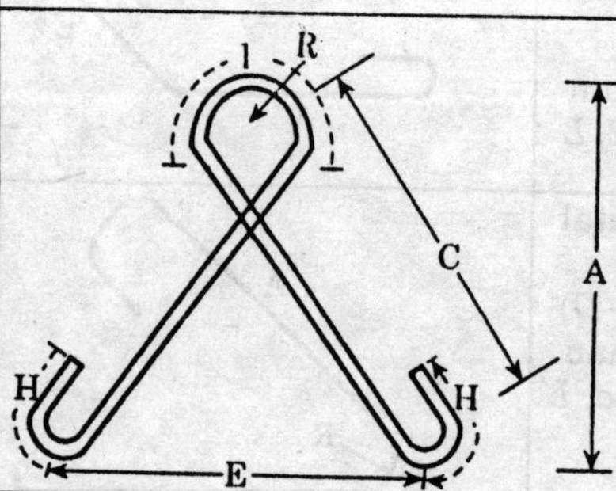	$l + 2C + 2H$	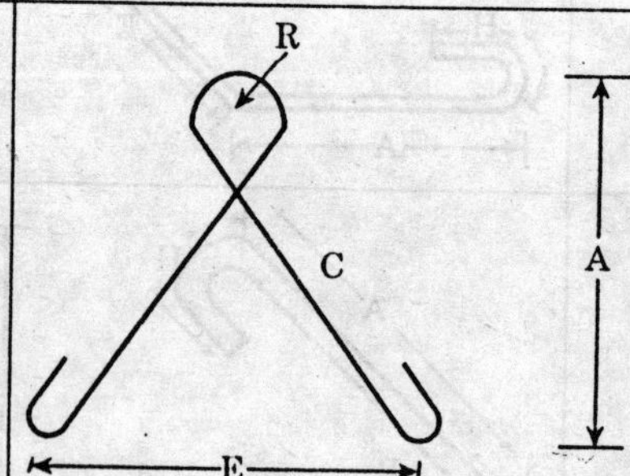
22	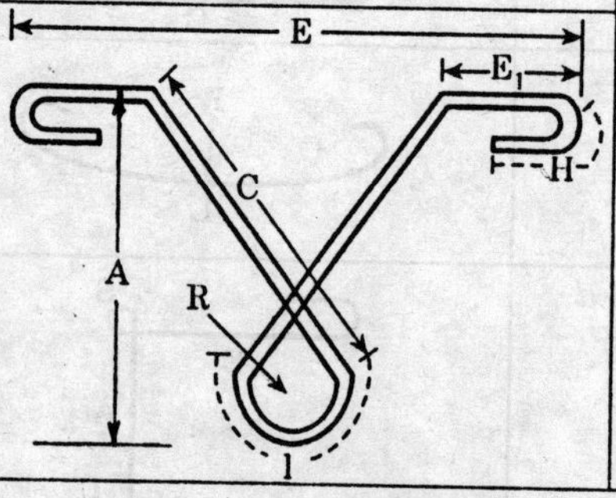	$2C + 2E_1 + l + 2H$	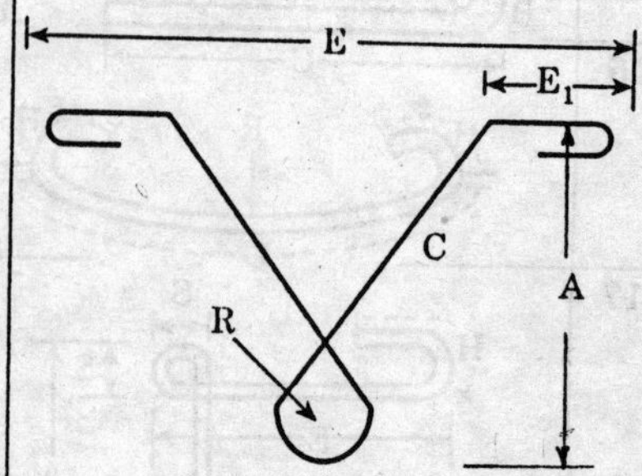

Ref. No.	*Method of measurement of Bending Dimensions*	*Approximate total length of Bar (L) measured along centre line*	*Sketch and dimensions to be given in schedule.*
23	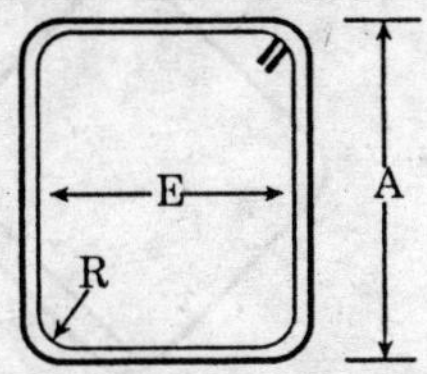	$2(A+E)+24d$	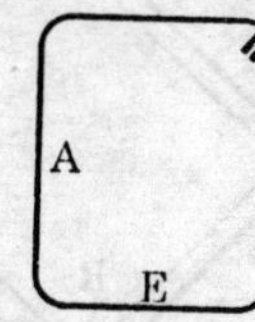
24	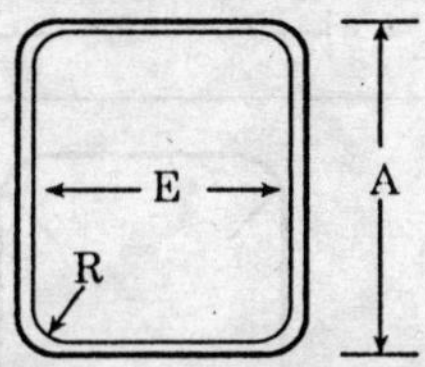	$2(A+E)+20d$	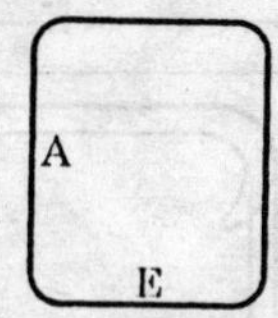
25	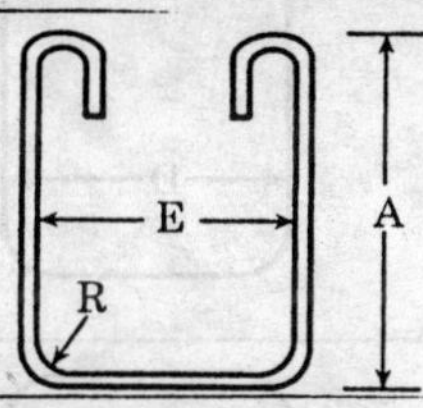	$2A+E+28d$	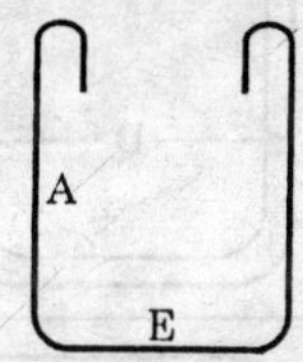
26	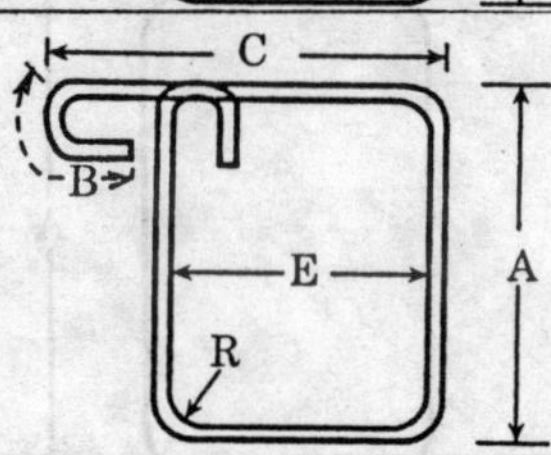	$2A+E+C+12d+B$	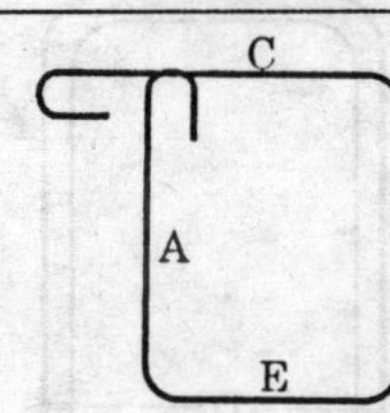
27	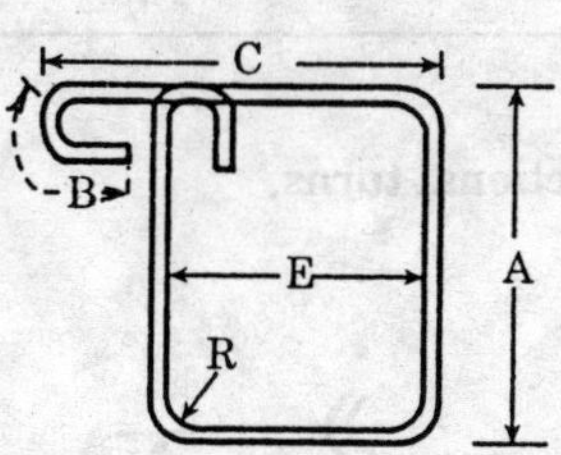	$2A+E+C+9d+B$	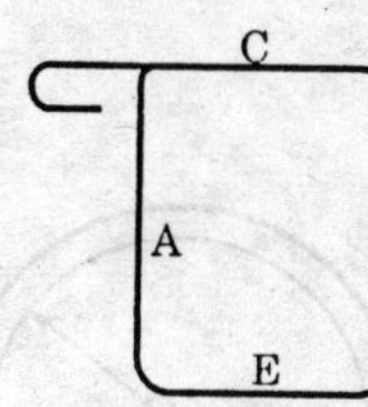
28	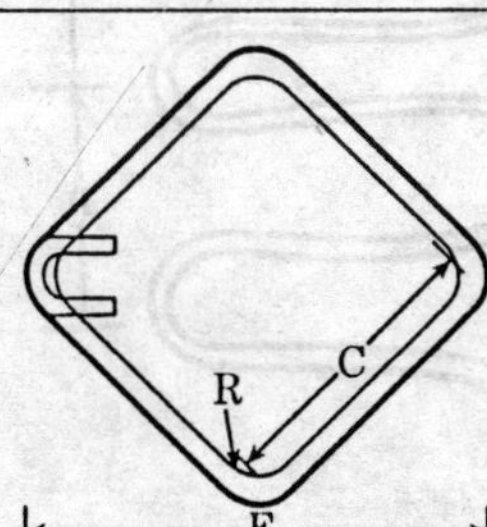	$4C+24d$	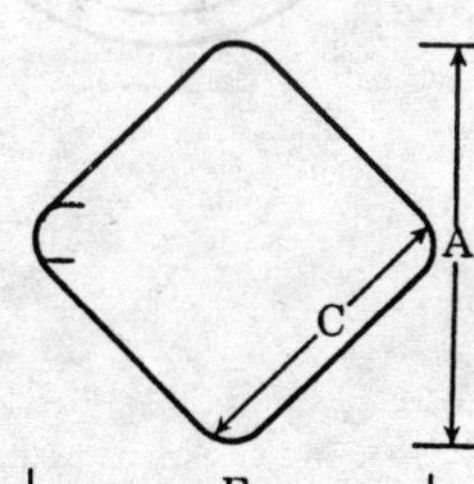

Ref. No.	*Method of measurement of Bending Dimensions*	*Approximate total length of Bar (L) measured along centre line*	*Sketch and dimensions to be given in schedule.*
29	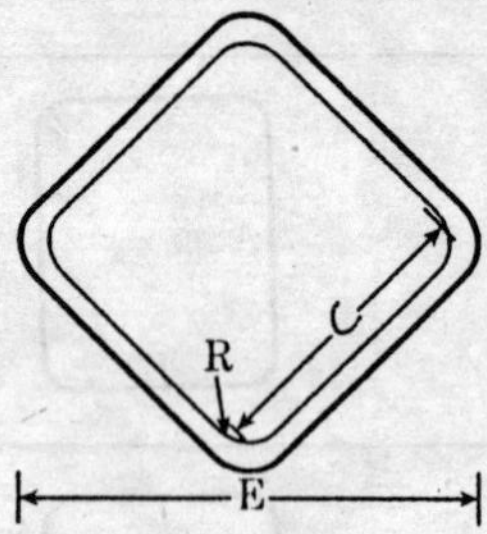	$4C + 20d$	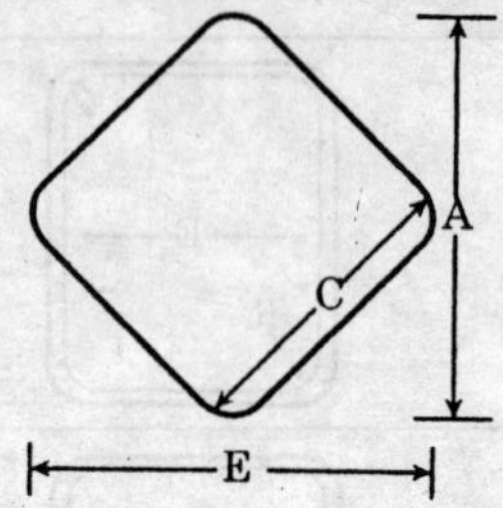
30	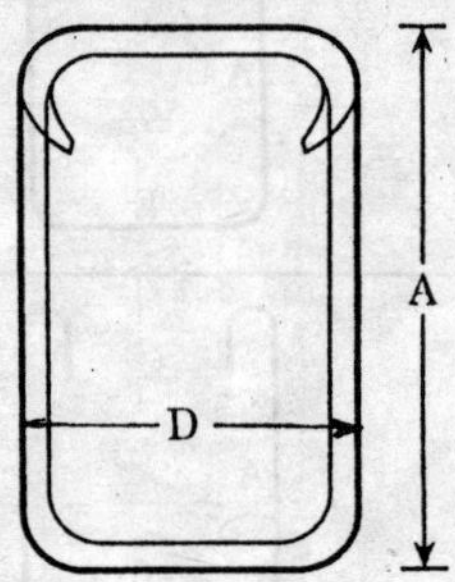	$2A + 3D + 22d$	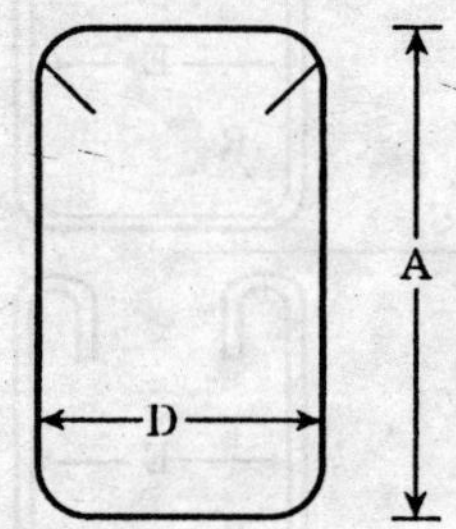
31	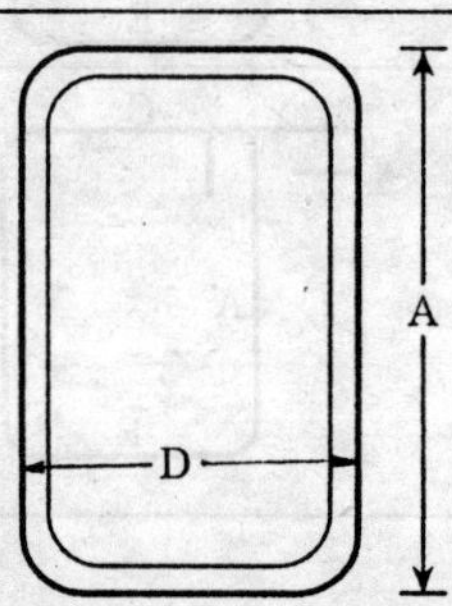	$2A + 3D + 22d$	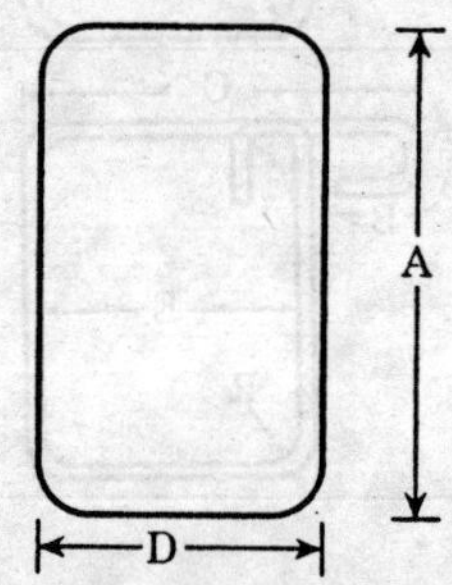
32	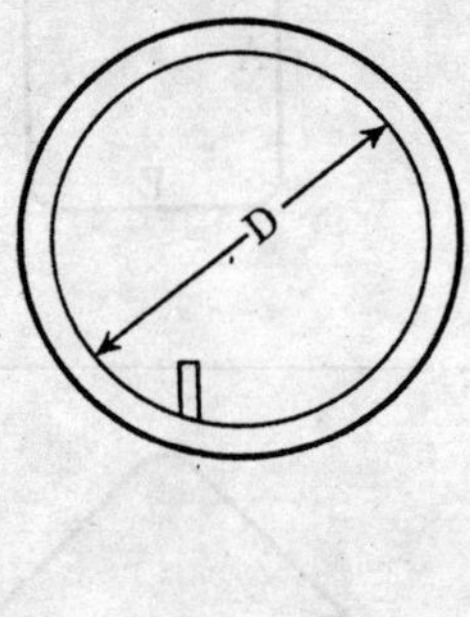	Where p is not greater than $D/5$ $N(D + d) + 8d$ N = Number of complete and fractional turns, D = Internal diameter, p = Pitch of the helix, d = Size of bar.	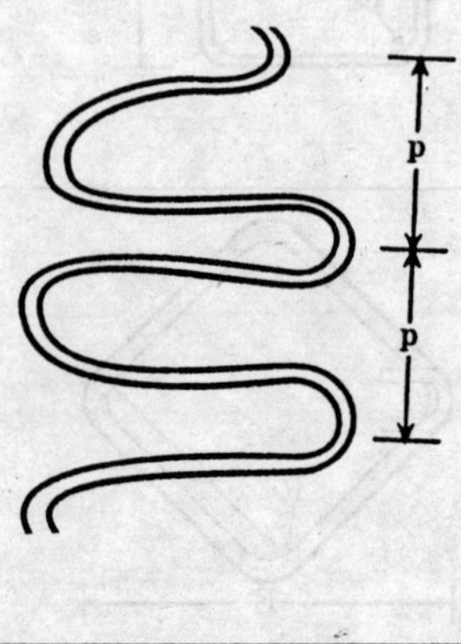

3.1.5 Arrangement of Tying Reinforcement Bars in Column Sections of Different Sizes and Shapes

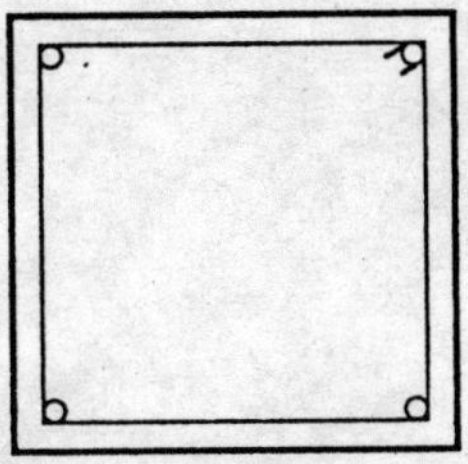

4 Bars with single ties

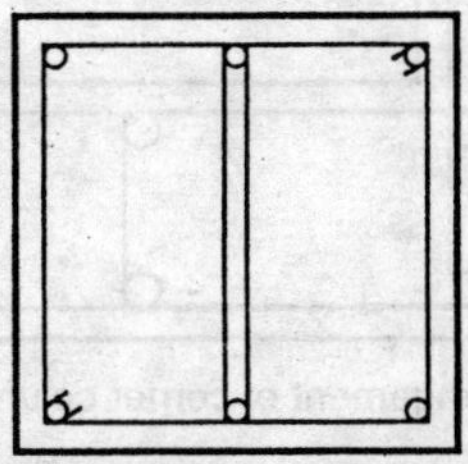

6 Bars with 2 ties per set

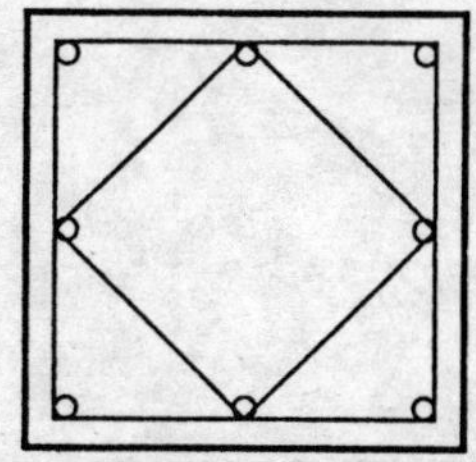

8 Bars with 2 ties per set

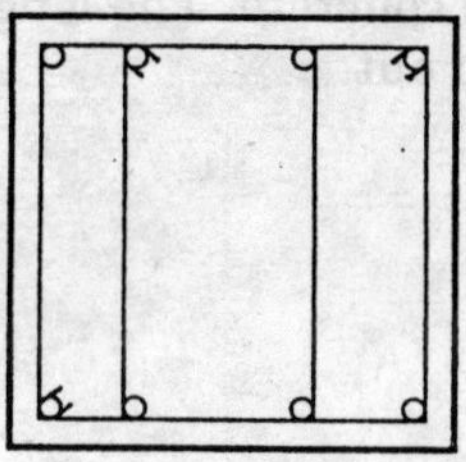

10 Bars with 3 ties per set

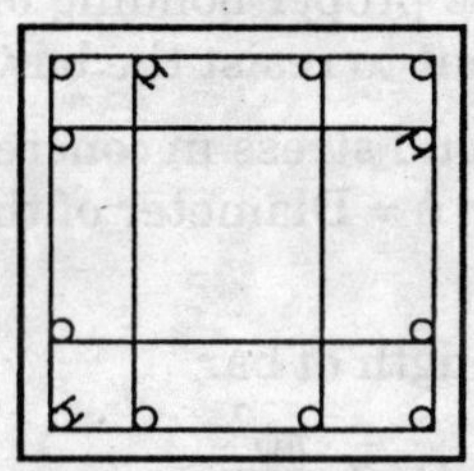

12 Bars with 3 ties per set

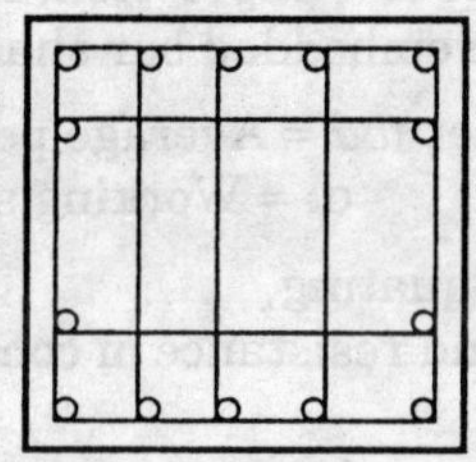

14 Bars with 4 ties per set

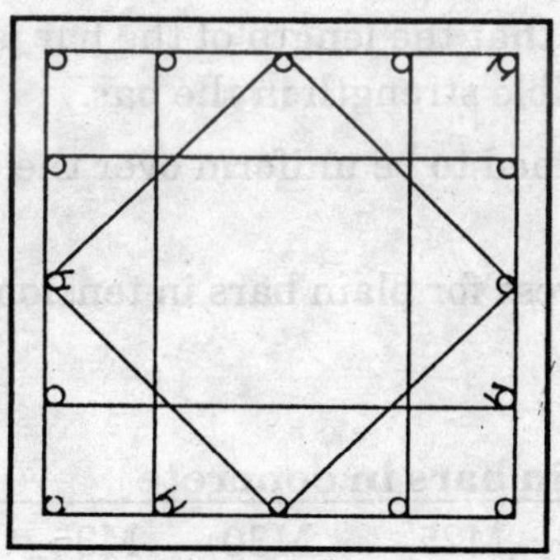

16 Bars with 4 ties per set

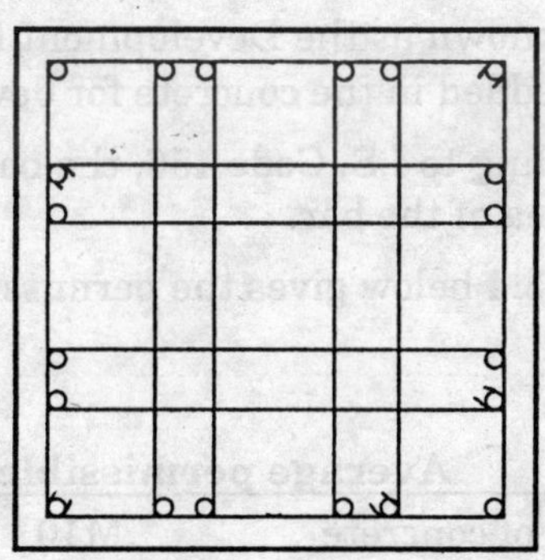

18 Bars with 5 ties per set

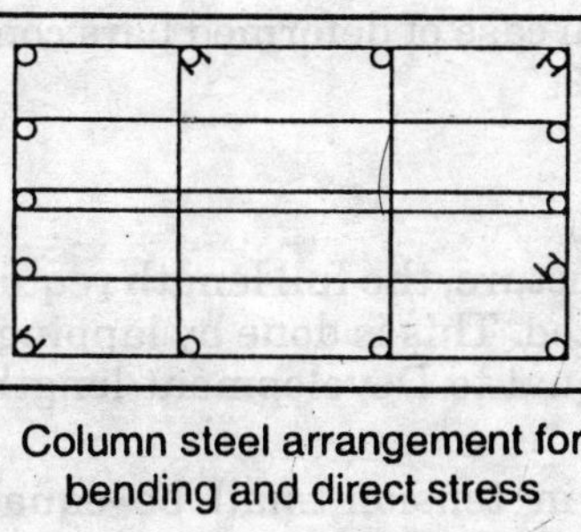

Column steel arrangement for bending and direct stress

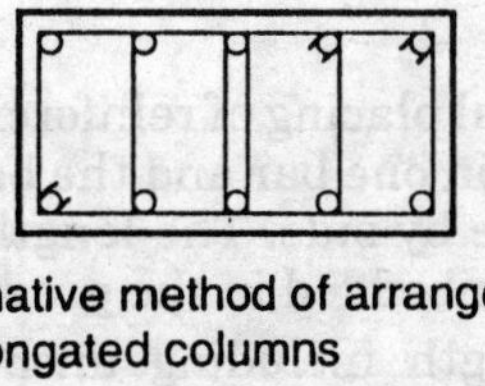

Alternative method of arrangement for elongated columns

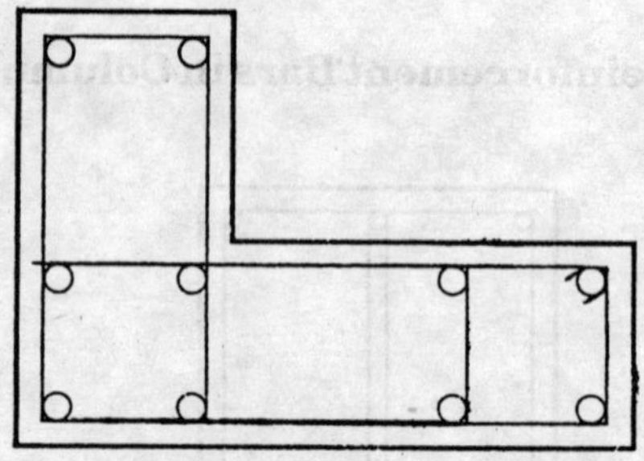

Typical arrangement of corner column

3.2.0 DEVELOPMENT LENGTH AND LAP LENGTH

When a reinforcing bar is embedded in concrete and is subjected to certain stress either tensile or compression, there shall be proper bonding of the bar with the concrete. The length of the embedded bar shall be sufficient to resist the bar from being pulled out.

Let τbd = Average permissible bond stress in concrete,

σ_s = Working stress in bar, ϕ = Diameter of the bar.

Equating,

Bond resistance of concrete = Strength of bar

$$\tau bd \times \pi \phi \times L_d = \sigma_s \frac{\pi\phi^2}{4}$$

$$L_d = \frac{\phi\sigma_s}{4\tau bd}$$

L_d is known as the Development length, which means that the length of the bar is needed to be embedded in the concrete for developing full permissible strength in the bar.

According to I.S. Code 456, the bond stresses are assumed to be uniform over the effective surface area of the bar.

Table 3.4 below gives the permissible average bond stress for plain bars in tension.

Table 3.4

Average permissible bond stress of plain bars in concrete

Grade of concrete	M10	M15	M20	M25	M30	M35	M40
τbd N/mm^2	—	0.6	0.8	0.9	1.0	1.1	1.2

τbd shall be increased by 25% for bars in compression. In case of deformed bars conforming to I.S. 1786-1985, the value of τbd shall be increased by 40%.

Lap length

During actual placing of reinforcing bars in concrete structure, the full length required may not be available in one bar and the bars may have to be spliced. This is done by lapping the two bars placing side by side. The length of lapping shall be equal to Development length for the particular bar embedded in the grade of concrete.

The lap length including anchorage value of hooks in tension shall be equal to the development length in tension. The straight length shall not be less than 15*d* or 200 mm.

The lap length in compression shall be equal to the development length in compression, calculated but not less than 24*d*.

When two bars of different diameters are spliced, the lap length shall be on the basis of the smaller diameter bar. Lap splices shall be considered as staggered if the centre to centre distance of the splices is not less than 1.3 times the lap length.

Table 3.5
Development length for Plain and Deformed Bars

Working stress of plain bars in tension = 140 N/mm² *for bars up to 20 mm dia.* = 130 N/mm² *for bars over 20 mm dia.*	*Grade of concrete*	*For plain bars*		*For deformed bars*	
		Tension	*Compression*	*Tension*	*Compression*
Working stress in compression = 130 N/mm² for all dia.	M15	58*d*	43.5*d*	68.5*d*	45.25*d*
	M20	44*d*	32.5*d*	51.5*d*	34 *d*
Working stress for deformed bar in tension = 230 N/mm²	M25	39*d*	29*d*	46*d*	30.20*d*
In compression = 190 N/mm²	M30	35*d*	26*d*	41*d*	27.20*d*

3.2.1 Cranking of the Bars

Cranking or bending up of the bars is needed for taking a bar in the lower layer where they are not required and bringing those to upper layer where required or vice versa.

Again, cranked bars help in taking shear in the member.

Bending of the bars are generally done at 45° angle and some times at 30° or 60° angle. Due to bending up or down some extra length of the bar is required. This has to be calculated for finding out the total length of the bar.

Let d be the effective depth of the bar,

$$\text{Length of Crank} = \frac{d}{\sin 30°} = 2d$$

$$\text{Length of Crank} = \frac{d}{\sin 45°} = \frac{d}{0.707}$$

$$= 1.41d$$

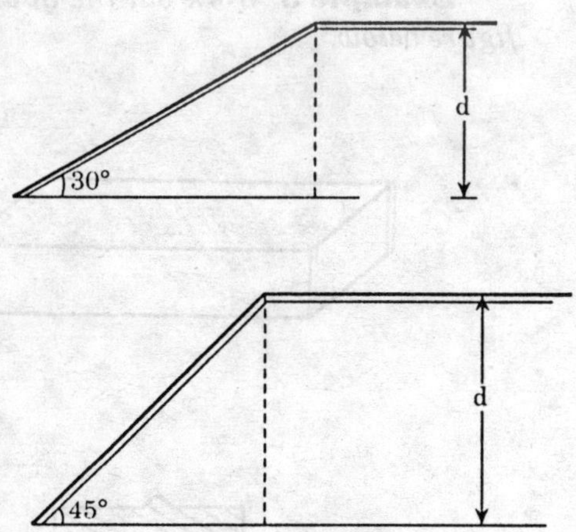

Figure 3.2 Cranking of bar.

3.2.2 Bending of Bars

Bars shall be bent cold except bars larger than 25 mm in size which may be bent hot at temperature not exceeding 850°C, excepting those bars which depend for their strength on cold working. Hot bars shall not be cooled by quenching.

Any type of equipment may be used for bending of bars with prior approval of the Engineer in Charge.

3.2.3 Tying of Reinforcement Bars

Precautions shall be taken to prevent displacement of reinforcement during shuttering and concreting.

Bars crossing each other, where required, shall be secured by binding with annealed wire of size not less than 0.90 mm and shall conform to I.S. 280 – 1962, Specification for Mild steel wire. In such case, a manner that they will not slip over each other at the time of fixing and concreting should be chosen.

Every compression bar shall be tied at least in two perpendicular directions.

Stirrups may be staggered, provided it is ensured that the corresponding stirrups form a uniform pattern in elevation.

Three methods of tying reinforcing bars are shown below. Of the three methods, the method illustrated at *A* should be preferred to method *B*, and that *B* to *C*.

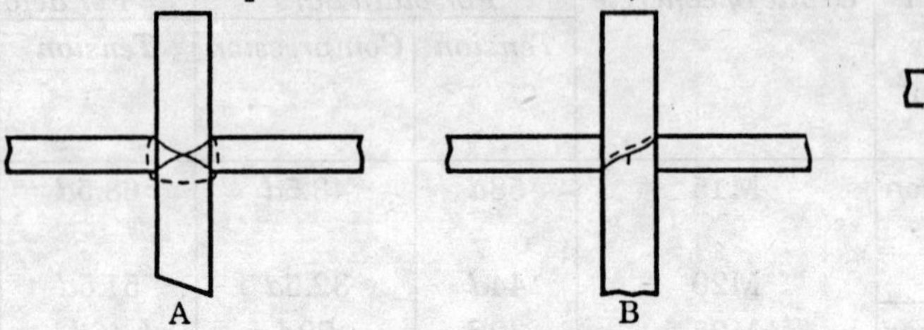

Figure 3.3 Tying of reinforcing bars.

3.2.4 Cover Blocks

Cover blocks which are generally of cement concrete mortar, shall be used to ensure the required cover for the reinforcement.

Cover blocks are generally square or rectangular in plan with or without binding wire embedded in them which will be tied to the reinforcement at the time of placing. Rings with suitable hole at the centre may also be used.

Reinforcement seats made of plastic have also been innovated which are very convenient to use and keep the bar in correct position.

Example 3: *Work out the quantities of steel in R.C.C. lintel over a door opening from the figure below.*

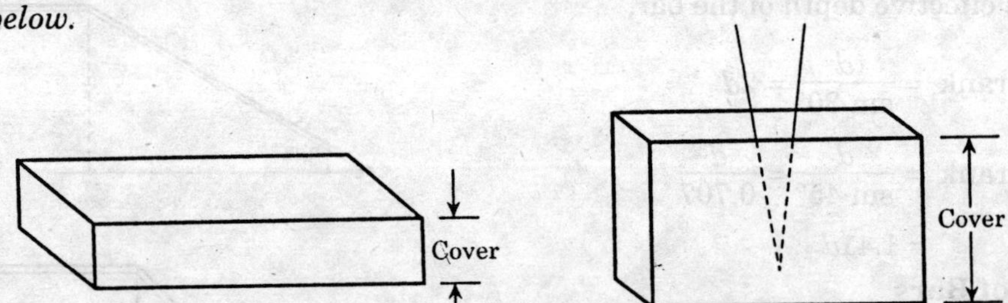

Figure 3.4 Cover Block.

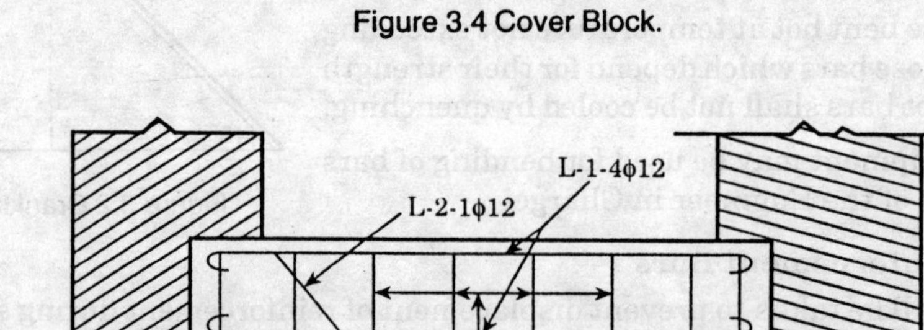

Figure 3.5 Lintel over door.

A Bar-Schedule shall be prepared, from which the quantity of steel of different sizes can be found out.

Bar-Schedule

Location	*Mark / Designation*	*Size & Type*	*No. of set*	*No. per set*	*Total no.*	*Length*	*Shape*
Lintel	L-1	12 mm dia.	1	4	4	1,635	
Lintel	L-2	12 mm dia.	1	1	1	1,720	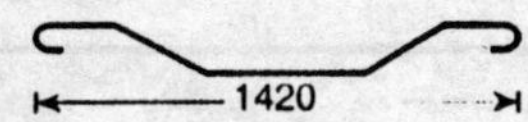
Lintel	L-3	6 mm dia.	1	12	12	700	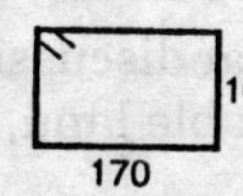

(*i*) $L = 1{,}200 + 300 - 80 + 18 \times 12 = 1{,}635$ mm = 1.64 m

(*ii*) $L = 1{,}200 + 300 - 80 + 18 \times 12 + 2 \times 0.42 \times 100 = 1{,}720$ mm = 1.72 m

(*iii*) $L = 2 \times 170 + 2 \times 100 + 24 \times 6 = 685$ mm = 0.69 m

Quantity of steel

12 mm dia. m.s. bar $4 \times 1.64 + 1 \times 1.72 = 8.28$ m @ 0.89 kg/m = 7.37 kg

6 mm dia. m.s. bar $12 \times 0.69 = 8.28$ m @ 0.22 kg/m = 1.82 kg

9.19 kg

4

ESTIMATION OF SPECIAL SECTIONS AND STRUCTURES

4.1.0 ESTIMATION OF MULTISTOREY BUILDING

So far discussions have been limited to single storey building ; but now a days due to scarcity of buildable land, buildings with more than one storey are mostly built.

Cost of construction of building of more than one storey is not economical. Cost of construction per sqm of floor area of a two storey building is economical than that of a single storey building. This is due to sharing of cost of construction of foundation and plinth by the two floors. Cost of construction of foundation and plinth of a two storey building does not increase or the increase is insignificant in comparison to the cost of construction of single storey building.

However, after two storeys, cost of construction increases with the increase in number of storey. The rate of increase in cost per sqm of floor area is steep up to sixth floor. But after that the rate of increase is not very high. This will be evident from the graph 4.1.

4.1.1 Mode of estimation

Quantities of multistoreyed building is estimated floorwise. It is easier to compute the items floorwise, otherwise, the quantities would be mixed up and make things complicated.

Moreover, rate of construction of different items vary floorwise. The labour component increases as the output of item per labourer decreases due to increase in cost of lifting.

In multistoreyed building construction, some special implements and appliances are required. Special technique may have to be adopted. Materials of increased strength may be needed. All these increase the cost of construction of multistoreyed buildings.

In standard schedule of rates, the rates of items are available floorwise. This is applicable in cases of all the items of work.

4.2.0 METHOD OF ESTIMATION

Estimation of such tall structures comprising of more than one floor is not difficult and formidable. Estimation of different parts are taken separately and then added together.

When the multistoreyed building is a R.C.C. framed structure. On columns and beams, estimation is done for the R.C.C. frame. The frame starts from the foundation.

The foundation may be of isolated footing or combined footing or may be of Raft foundation.

The section of the column is generally not varied; but kept the same from ground to any upper floor. The strength of the column section is maintained according to requirement by varying the quantity of steel. The columns are numbered, which is done generally during the structural design and the same number marks in the drawing is maintained while estimating also.

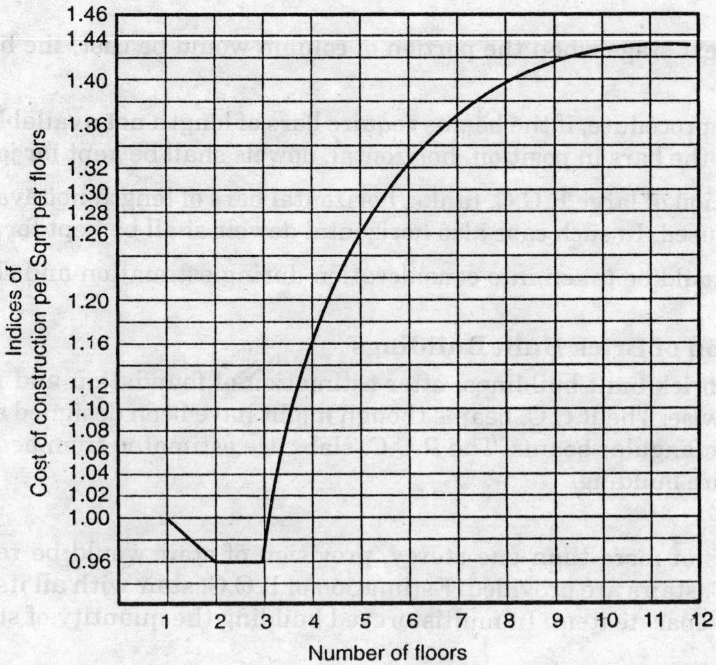

Graph 4.1. Trend of rise in cost of construction in relation to number of floors.

Numbers are also allotted to beams during design. The section and reinforcement are varied according to requirement. During estimating the numbers allotted are maintained and quantities estimated floorwise. The beams may have haunches at the support. These are also taken care of with the beams. Though the beams may be designed as flanged beams, during estimation these are taken as rectangular sections.

The slabs are estimated as rectangles from beam to beam.

There may be other R.C.C. members, which are estimated separately.

4.2.1 Bar Schedule

In each case of estimation of R.C.C. structure or part thereof, preparation of Bar Schedule is essential for assessing the quantity of steel. Bar Schedule may be prepared for all items together, but should be shown separately in tabular form for easy understanding of the Quantity Surveyor.

In a multistoreyed building, the columns may be very tall according to the height of the building. The vertical reinforcement may be through and of the same height. But such long reinforcing bars may not be available in the market. Reinforcing bars available are generally of 6.00 m long, excepting the coils available for smaller diameter bars. Lapping and splicing of the bars would be required. Moreover, there would be difficulty in keeping such tall bars in vertical position. Splicing of the bars would require provision of lap length of the bars.

The quantity required for lap length is not generally indicated in the estimate, but provided on percentage basis. This is not proper. The quantities as required should be incorporated and should be shown in the Bar Schedule also. Development length and Lap length have been discussed in details under paragraph 3.2.0.

During construction of the foundation whether isolated footing or combined footing, dowels for the vertical reinforcement should be provided keeping the length of lapping for splicing in future. In the next stage when the portion of column would be cast, the bars would be lapped with the dowels.

In the same procedure, if the beams require bars of length not available in the market or is difficult to keep the bars in position, horizontal, dowels shall be kept for joining in future.

In construction of large R.C.C. tanks, horizontal bars of length not available in the market may have to be used. In such case also horizontal dowels shall be kept for joining in future.

All these should be taken into consideration during estimation and shall be shown in the Bar Schedule.

4.2.2 Estimation of Brick Built Buildings

In cases of brick built buildings, after estimation of foundation and plinth, the walls are estimated floorwise. The R.C.C. beams though might have been designed as flanged beams are estimated as rectangular beams. The R.C.C. slabs are estimated from beam to beam or as one slab for the entire building.

4.2.3 Stair

In buildings of more than one storey, provision of stair would be required. Now a days generally R.C.C. stairs are provided. Estimation of R.C.C. stair with all its necessary items are computed as a separate item. In multistoreyed building the quantity of stair is also estimated floorwise.

4.2.4 Brick Filler Wall or Panels

Brick filler walls or panels and partition walls are generally made of bricks. The filler walls when outer walls, are generally made of bricks, the filler walls when used as outer enclosure of building are generally 200 mm or 250 mm thick. These are measured in volume and floor wise. The item should include all necessary bonding materials.

Partition walls are either 125 mm or 75 mm thick and are measured in superficial unit—sqm and floorwise. The walls are provided with hoop reinforcement in the form of iron strips or wire nets and are provided at alternate or at suitable layers. The rates of the items should take care of such provisions.

Example 4.1 *Estimate the quantities of R.C.C. frame-work, including the isolated footing of a ground plus three storey structure as shown in Figure 4.1. All the floors have the same height-3,000 mm.*

Estimation

Item No.	*Description of item*	*No.*	*Measurement*			*Contents*	*Waste*
			Length	*Breadth*	*Height*		
1	Earthwork in excavation in foundation.						
	Bases of						
	Column C 1	2	1.80	1.80	2.075	13.446	
	Column C 2	10	1.50	1.50	2.075	46.688	
						60.134	cum
2	Mat cement concrete in foundation 1 : 3 : 6.	2	1.80	1.80	0.075	0.486	
		10	1.50	1.50	0.075	1.688	
						2.174	cum
3	Cement concrete 1 : 2 : 4 for R.C.C. work in foundation and superstructure. Foundation footing						

(Contd..)

Item No.	Description of item	No.	Length	Breadth	Height	Contents	Waste
	Column C 1	2	1.80	1.80	0.225	1.458	
		2 ×	$\frac{L}{6}(A_1 + A_2 + 4A_m)$				$L = 0.775$
		2 ×	$\frac{0.775}{6}(0.36 + 3.24 + 4 \times 1.44)$			2.418	$A_1 = 0.6 \times 0.6 = 0.36$ $A_2 = 1.8 \times 1.8 = 3.24$ $A_m = 1.2 \times 1.2 = 1.44$
	Column C 2	10	1.50	1.50	0.225	5.063	
		10 ×	$\frac{L}{6}(A_1 + A_2 + 4A_m)$			9.07	$L = 0.775$ $A_1 = 0.6 \times 0.6 = 0.36$
		10 ×	$\frac{0.775}{6}(0.36 + 2.25 + 4 \times 1.103)$				$A_2 = 1.5 \times 1.5 = 2.25$ $A_m = 1.05 \times 1.05 = 1.103$
	Columns C 1 & C 2	12	0.25	0.25	15.138	11.354	
	Tie beams	17 × 1	3.55	0.25	0.20	3.018	
	Beams B_1 & B_2	17 × 4	3.55	0.25	0.30	18.105	
	Lintel	17 × 4	3.55	0.25	0.10	6.035	
	Slab	4	11.65	7.85	0.125	45.726	
						102.247	cum
4	Shuttering and centering including staging						
	Base of Column C 1	2 × 4	1.80	0.225		3.24	
	Base of column C 2	10 × 4	1.50	0.225		13.50	
	Columns C 1 & C 2	12 × 4	0.25		14.265	171.18	
	Beams B1 & B2						
	Sides	17 × 4 × 2	3.55	0.30		144.84	
	Bottoms	17 × 4	3.55	0.25		60.35	
	Slab bottom	6 × 4	3.55	3.55		302.46	
	Slab sides	4 × 2	(11.65 + 7.85)		0.125	19.50	
	Lintels	17 × 4	3.55	(0.25 + 0.10 + 0.10)		108.63	
						823.70	
	Less for junctions						
	Beam & columns		4 × (16 + 18) × 0.30		0.225	9.18	
	Tie beams and columns	34	0.25	0.20		1.70	
	Lintels and Columns	4 × 34	0.25	0.10		3.40	
						(−)14.28	
						809.42	sqm
5	Earthwork in backfilling of foundation trenches						
	Volume of Earthwork as per item no. 1					60.134	cum
	Less						
	Volume of Mat concrete as per item No. 2					2.174	
	Volume of cement concrete in foundation Ref. item No. 3					5.063	
						9.070	
						1.458	
						2.418	
	Column portions	12	1.275	0.25	0.25	0.956	
					(−)	21.139	
						38.995	cum
6	M.S. reinforcement for R.C.C. works	As per bar schedule					

ABSTRACT OF COST

Item No.	Description of item	Quantity	Unit	Rate	Amount	Remarks
1	Earthwork in excavation in foundation with all lead and lift	60.134	%cum	2,973.00	1,788.00	
2	Mat cement concrete 1 : 3 : 6 in foundation	2.174	cum	1,931.00	4,198.00	
3	Cement concrete 1 : 2 : 4 for R.C.C. work in foundation and superstructure	102.247	cum	2,373.00	2,42,632.00	
4	Shuttering and centering including staging	809.42	sqm	105.00	84,569.00	
5	Earthwork in back filling of foundation trenches	38.995	%cum	1,738.00	678.00	
6	M.s. reinforcement including cutting to size, bending and binding and placing in position	14,951.62	kg			
		149.5162 (Vide page 51)	qtl.	2,083.10	3,11,457.00	
		Total			6,45,322.00	
		Add contingency @ 5%			32,266.00	
					6,77,588.00	
		Add work establishment @ 5%			33,879.00	
					7,11,467.00	

Item No.	Description of item	No.	Measurements			Content	Waste
			Length	Breadth	Height		
	Abstract of M.S. Reinforcement			Ref. Bar schedule No. 4.1			
	16 mm dia bars	16	6.000			96.000	
		16	6.000			96.000	
		16	6.000			96.000	
		40	6.000			240.000	
		40	6.000			240.000	
		40	6.000			240.000	
		120	5.895			707.400	
		60	4.530			271.800	
		24	1.690			40.560	
		24	0.990			23.760	
		160	5.070			811.200	
		16	1.690			27.040	
		32	0.980			31.360	
						2921.120 m	
		1.56 kg/m				4,556.95 kg	
	12 mm dia. bars						
		48	1.915			91.920	
		200	1.615			323.000	
		40	6.000			240.000	
		40	6.000			240.000	
		32	4.685			149.920	
		24	3.935			94.440	
		12	6.000			72.000	
		32	4.335			138.720	
		24	3.605			86.520	
		12	6.000			72.000	
		1,700	1.465			2,490.500	
		312	4.335			1352.520	
		312	4.335			1352.520	
		104	5.885			612.040	

(Contd..)

Item No.	Description of item	No.	Measurements			Content	Waste
			Length	Breadth	Height		
		104	5.965			612.040	
		96	4.335			416.160	
		64	4.335			277.440	
		48	3.580			171.840	
						8793.58 m	
		24	6.000			144.00	
		64	3.580			229.120	
		32	6.000			192.00	
		308	1.615			497.420	
		440	0.915			402.600	
						10,258.72 m	
		0.888 kg/m				9,109.74 kg	
	10 mm dia. bars						
		16	1.730			31.680	
		6	4.580			28.80	
		80	1.580			150.400	
		30	3.940			125.400	
		1,272	0.980			1,246.560	
						1,581.76 m	
		0.62 kg/m				981.05 kg	
	6 mm dia. bars						
		425	0.810			344.250	
		1,700	0.610			1,037.000	
						1,381.25 m	
		0.22 kg/m				303.88 kg	
						14,951.62 kg	

Plinth area $= 4 \times 11.65 \times 7.85$

$= 365.81$ sqm

Steel reinforcement required = 14,951.62 kg

Steel reinforcement required per sqm $= \dfrac{14,951.62}{365.81}$

$= 40.87$ kg

Over all percentage of steel with reference to volume of structural concrete.

Concrete = 102.247 cum.

Steel = 1,4951.62 kg

$$\text{Volume of steel} = \frac{1,491.62}{7850} = 1.90466 \text{ cum}$$

$$\text{Percentage of steel} = \frac{1.90466}{102.247} \times 100 = 1.86$$

Percentage of steel according to diameter of bars.

16 mm	diameter	Torsteel	4,556.95 kg	=	30%
12 mm	diameter	Torsteel	9,109.74 kg	=	61%
10 mm	diameter	Torsteel	981.05 kg	=	7%
6 mm	diameter	Torsteel	303.88 kg	=	2%
			14,951.62 kg		100%

Calculation of requirement of steel as per Table 8.5 and 8.7

$A = 91.45$ sqm per floor.

Requirement of steel

(*a*) Super structure

$$= 1491 + 92.0\,A - 0.36\,A^2$$

$$= -\ 1491 + 92.0 \times 91.45 - 0.36 \times 91.45^2$$

$$= -\ 1491 + 8413.4 - 3010.72$$

$$= 3{,}911.68 \text{ kg}$$

For 4 floors = 15,646.73 kg

(*b*) Substructure

$$-\ 171 + 10.47\,A - 0.041\,A^2$$

$$= -\ 171 + 10.47 \times 91.45 - 0.041 \times 91.45^2$$

$$= 171 + 956.57 - 342.89$$

$$= 442.68 \text{ kg}$$

Total for superstructure and substructure

$$= 15{,}616.73 + 442.68$$

$$= 16{,}059.41 \text{ kg}$$

$$\text{Steel required per sqm} = \frac{16{,}059.41}{91.45 \times 4}$$

$$= 43.90 \text{ kg}$$

Bar schedule No. 4.1

Ref. Example 4.1

Location	*Mark / Designation*	Size and Type	*No. of set*	*No. per set*	*Total no.*	*Length in mm*	*Shape of the bar*
Founda-tion Base F_1	f_1	12 mm dia.	2 × 2	12	48	1,915	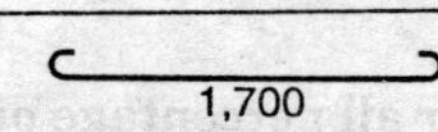
	f_2	10 mm dia.	2	4 × 2	16	1,980	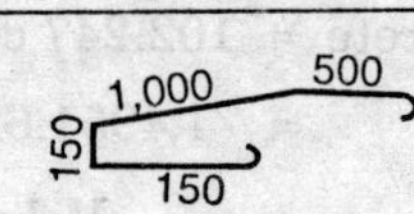
	f_3	10 mm dia.	2	3	6	4,680 (av)	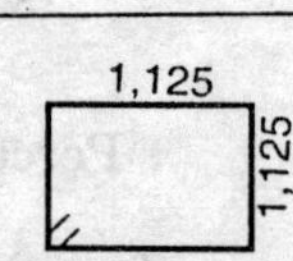
F_2	f_4	12 mm dia.	10 × 2	10	200	1,615	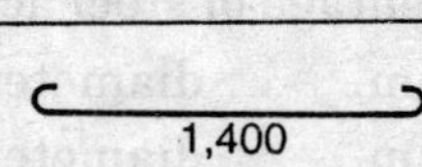
	f_5	10 mm dia.	10	4 × 2	80	1,880	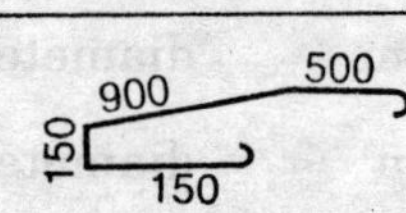

(Contd..)

Location	*Mark/ Designation.*	*Size and Type*	*No. of set*	*No. per set*	*Total no.*	*Length in mm*	*Shape of the bar*
	f_6	10 mm dia.	10	3	30	4,180 (av)	1,000 × 1,000
Column C_1	c_1	16 mm dia.	2 2 2	8 8 8	16 16 16	6,000 6,000 6,000	5,325 / 530 6,000 5,855
C_2	c_2	16 mm dia.	10 10 10	4 4 4	40 40 40	6,000 6,000 6,000	5,325 / 530 6,000 5,855
	c_3	12 mm dia.	10 10	4 4	40 40	6,000 6,000	5,325 / 530 5,855
Both C_1 and C_2	c_4	10 mm dia.	106	12	1,272	980	200 × 200
Tie beams	t_1	12 mm dia.	4	4 × 2	32	4,685	4,225 / 350
Tie beam	t_2	12 mm dia.	4 4	3 × 2 3 × 1	24 12	3,935 6,000	3,475 / 350 6,000
	t_3	6 mm dia.	17	25	425	810	
Lintel	l_1	12 mm dia.	4 4 4	4 × 2 3 × 2 3 × 1	32 24 12	4,335 3,605 6,000	4,225 3,495 6,000

(*Contd..*)

Location	Mark / Designation.	Size and Type	No. of set	No. per set	Total no.	Length in mm	Shape of the bar
	l_2	6 mm dia.	17 × 4	25	1,700	610	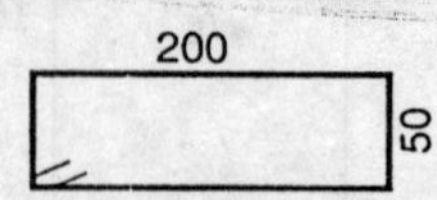
Beam B_1 main bars	b_1	16 mm dia.	3 × 4 3 × 4	5 × 2 5 × 1	120 60	5,895 4,530	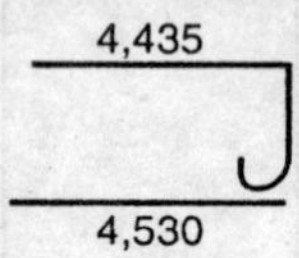
	b_2	16 mm dia.	6 × 4	1	24	1,690	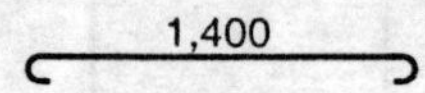
top bars	b_3	16 mm dia.	3 × 2 × 4	1	24	990	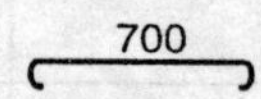
Beam B_2 main bars	b_4	16 mm dia.	4 × 4	5 × 2	160	5,070	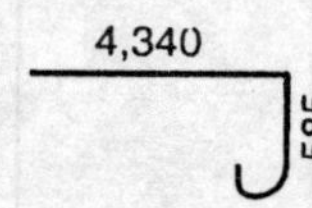
top bars	b_5	16 mm dia.	4 × 4	1	16	1,690	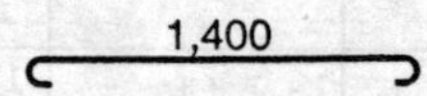
	b_6	16 mm dia.	4 × 2 × 4	1	32	980	
Stirrups for both B_1 & B_2	b_7	12 mm dia.	17 × 4	25	1,700	1,465	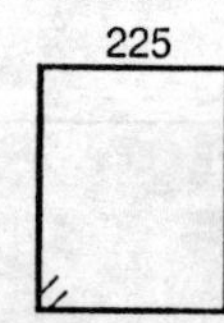
Slab Main bars	s_1	12 mm dia.	1 × 4	39 × 2	312	4,335	
	s_2	12 mm dia.	1 × 4	39 × 2	312	4,375	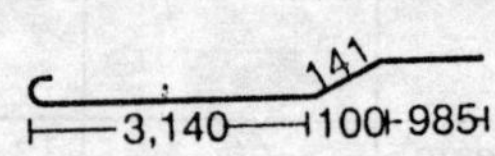
	s_3	12 mm dia.	1 × 4	26 × 2	104	5,885	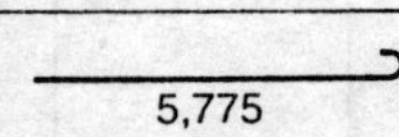
	s_4	12 mm dia.	1 × 4	26 × 2	104	5,965	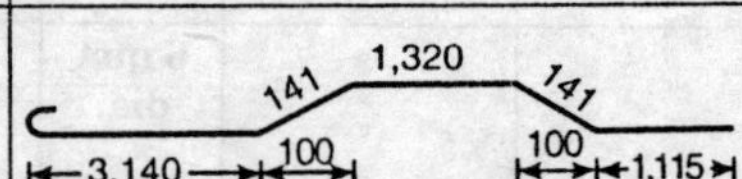
Top bars	s_5	12 mm dia. "	2 × 4 2 × 4	6 × 2 4 × 2	96 64	4,335 4,335	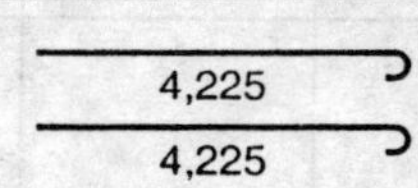

(Contd..)

Location	*Mark / Designation.*	*Size and Type*	*No. of set*	*No. per set*	*Total no.*	*Length in mm*	*Shape of the bar*
	s6	12 mm dia.	1 × 4	6 × 2	48	3,580	3,470
		"	1 × 4	6 × 1	24	6,000	6,000
	s7	12 mm dia.	2 × 4	4 × 2	64	3,580	3,470
			2 × 4	4 × 1	32	6,000	6,000
	s8	12 mm dia.	7 × 4	11	308	1,615	1,400
	s9	12 mm dia.	10 × 4	11	440	915	700

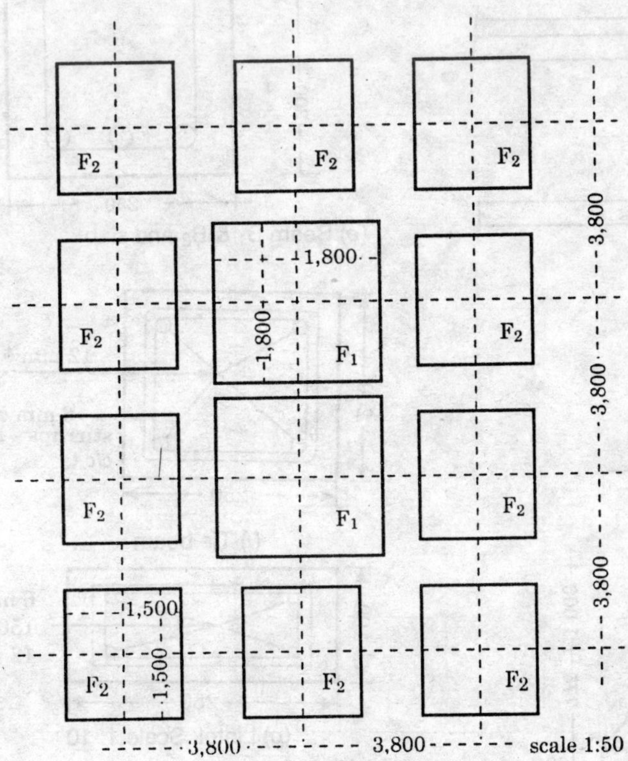

(*a*) Foundation plan isolated footings

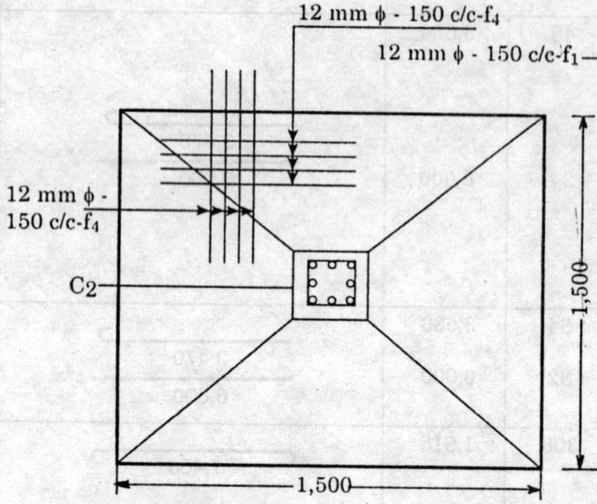

(*b*) Foundation - F_2

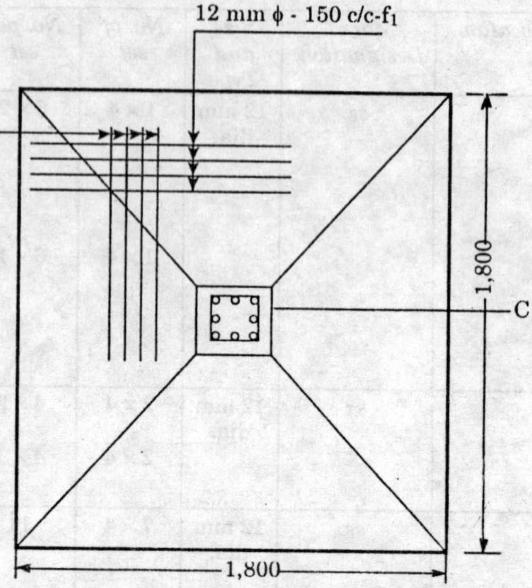

(*c*) Foundation - F_1 Scale 1: 25

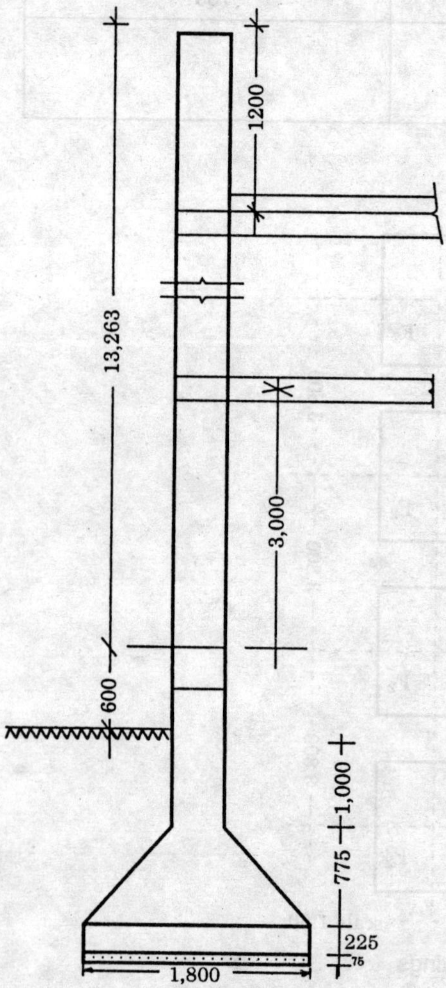

(*d*) Section thro. column

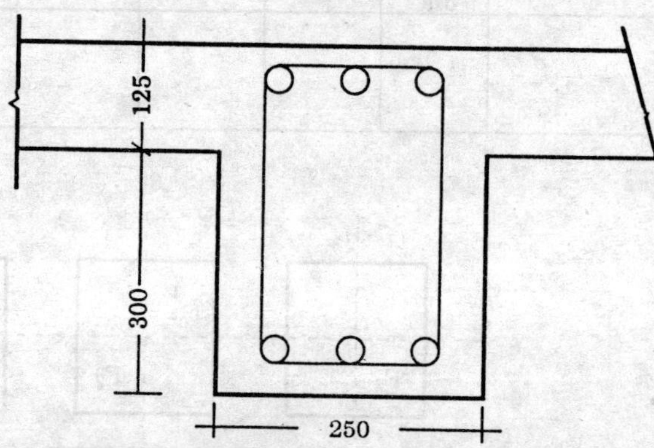

(*e*) Beam B_1 & B_2 and slab

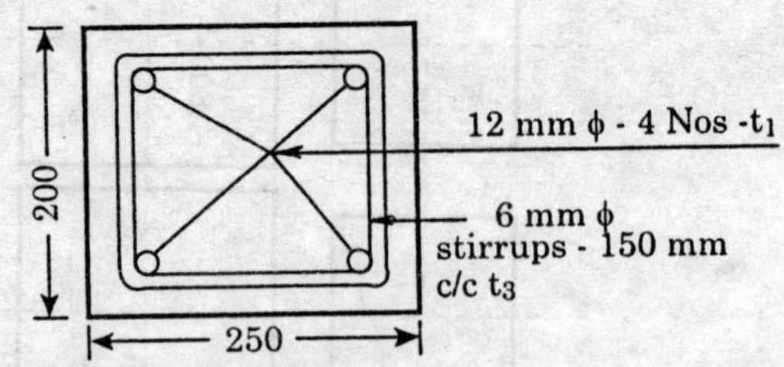

(*f*) Tie beam

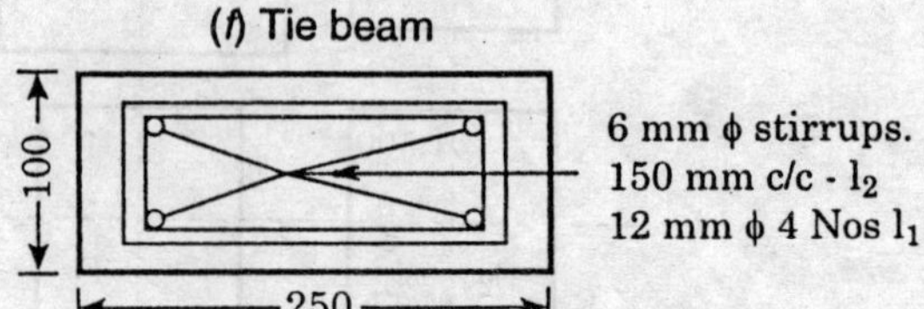

(*g*) Lintel, Scale 1: 10

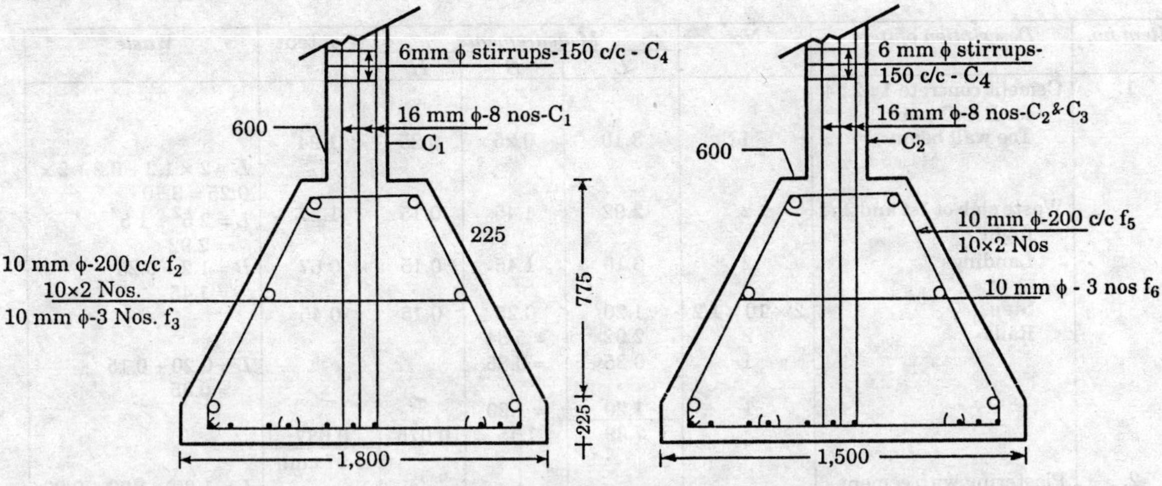

(*h*) Details of foundation's column

Example 4.2 *Detailed estimate of reinforced cement concrete stair*

Ref : Drawing no. 4.3

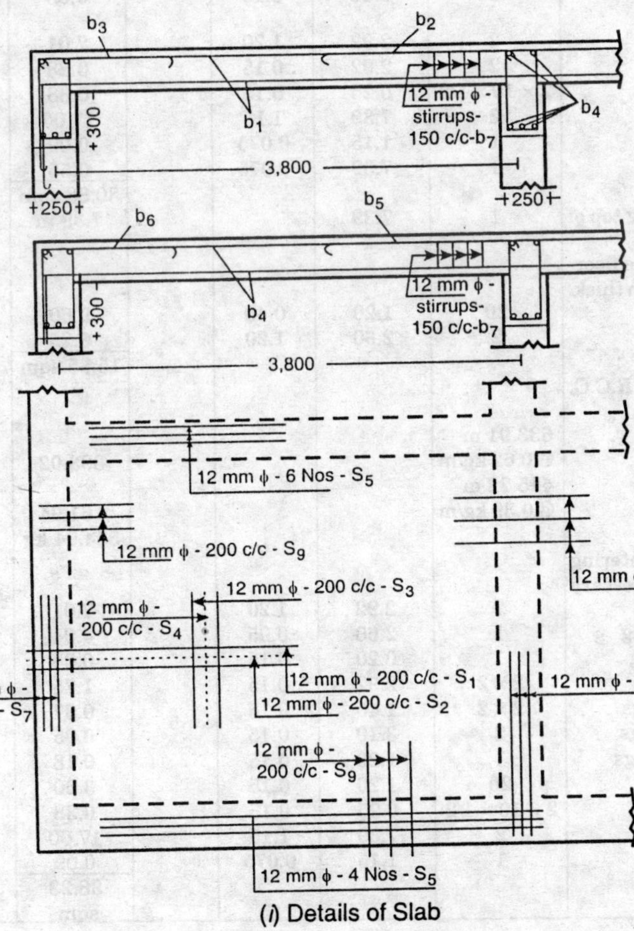

(*i*) Details of Slab

Figure 4.2 Details of R.C.C. Framed Structure

Item no.	Description of item	No.	Measurements L	B	H	Content	Waste
1.	Cement concrete 1 : 2 : 4 for R.C.C work						
	Toe wall beam	1	3.10	0.25	0.25	1.94	$L = 2 \times 1.2 + 0.2 + 2 \times 0.25 = 3.10$
	Waste slab of 1st and 2nd flight	2	2.92	1.45	0.15	1.27	$L = 2.5^2 + 1.5^2 = 2.92$
	Landings	2	3.10	1.45	0.15	0.67	$B = 1.2 + 0.25 = 1.45$
	Steps	2 × 10 × 1/2	1.20	0.25	0.15	0.45	
	Rails	2	2.92	= 5.84			
		1	0.35	= 0.35			$L = 0.20 + 0.15 = 0.35$
		1	1.20	= 1.20			
			7.39	1.15	0.075	0.637	
						4.97 cum	
2.	Plastering with cement sand mortar 1 : 4, 10 mm thick						$L = 1.20 + 1.20 + 0.20 = 2.60$
	Soffit of landings	2	2.60	0.95		4.94	
	Landing edges	1	0.20	0.15		0.03	$H = 1.20 - 0.25 = 0.95$
	Soffit of flights	2	2.92	1.20		7.01	
	Flight edges	2	2.92	0.15		0.88	
	Steps	2 × 10 × 1/2	0.25	0.15		0.38	
	Rails	2	7.39	1.15		17.00	
	Rail front	1	1.15	0.075		0.09	
	Rail top	1	7.39	0.075		0.55	
						30.88 sqm	
3.	Extra for moulding top of rail	1	7.39			7.39 m	
4.	Indian patent stone flooring on steps, 25 mm thick.						
	Steps	20	1.20	0.40		9.60	
	Landings	2	2.60	1.20		6.25	
						15.85 sqm	
5.	Reinforcement for R.C.C. work - Tor steel.						
	10 mm dia.	633.91 m @0.62 kg/m				393.02	
	8 mm dia.	415.22 m @0.39 kg/m				161.94	
						554.94 kg	
6.	Shuttering and centering with staging as necessary						
	Soffit of flights	2	2.92	1.20		7.01	
	Soffit of Landing	1	2.60	0.95		4.94	
	Sides of landing	1	0.20	0.15		0.03	
	Sides of flights	2 × 2	2.92	0.15		1.75	
	Ends of landings	2 × 2	1.45	0.15		0.87	
	Sides of landings	2	3.10	0.15		0.95	
	Sides of lan dings	1	1.20	0.15		0.18	
	Steps - sides	20	1.20	0.15		3.60	
	Steps ends	2 × 10 × 1/2	0.25	0.15		0.38	
	Rail sides	2	7.39	1.15		17.00	
	Rail ends	1	1.15	0.075		0.09	
						38.23 sqm	

ABSTRACT OF COST

Item no.	*Description of item*	*Quantity*	*Unit*	*Rate*	*Amount*	*Remarks*
1.	Cement concrete	4.97	cum	2,373.00	11,793.00	
2.	Cement sand plastering. 1 : 4—10 mm thick.	30.88	sqm	42.00	1,297.00	
3.	Extra for moulding rail top.	7.39	m	19.00	140.00	
4.	Indian patent stone flooring 25 mm thick	15.85	sqm	71.00	1,125.00	
5.	Reinforcement with Tor steel	544.33 = 5.44	kg Qtl.	2,083.10	11,320.00	
6	Shuttering and centering for cement concrete work with staging	38.23	sqm	105.00	4,014.00	
					29,689.00	
	Add contingency @ 5%				1,484.00	
					31,173.00	
	Add work establishment @ $2\frac{1}{2}$ %				779.00	
					31,952.00	

Abstract of reinforcement

Ref : Bar Schedule no. 1

1. 10 mm dia. Tor steel $4 \times 3.000 = 12.00$
$14 \times 4.360 = 61.04$
$28 \times 1.500 = 42.00$
$14 \times 5.400 = 75.60$
$14 \times 1.740 = 24.36$
$14 \times 1.500 = 21.00$
$104 \times 1.425 = 148.20$
$52 \times 3.000 = 156.00$
$4 \times 1.440 = 5.76$
$28 \times 1.500 = 42.00$
$18 \times 1.425 = 25.65$
$14 \times 1.450 = 20.30$
633.91 m

2. 8 mm dia. Tor steel $13 \times 1.140 = 14.82$
$14 \times 2.900 = 40.60$
$7 \times 1.400 = 9.80$
$38 \times 1.400 = 53.20$
$260 \times 0.680 = 176.80$
$100 \times 1.20 = 120.00$
415.92 m

Detailed estimate of reinforced concrete stair - Drawing no. 4.2

Reinforcement Schedule No. 1

Location	*Mark/ Designation*	*Size and type*	*Number of set*	*Number per set*	*Total number*	*Length m*	*Shape of bar*
Toe beam main bars	s-1	10 mm dia.	1	4	4	3.000	Straight
Toe beam stirrups	s-2	8 mm dia.	1	13	13	1.140	
1st. flight and landing main bar bottom	s-3	10 mm dia.	1	14	14	4.360	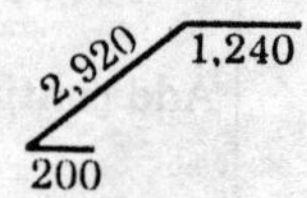
1st. & 2nd flight top main bars	s-4	10 mm dia.	2	14	28	1.500	
2nd flight main bars	s-5	10 mm dia.	1	14	14	5.400	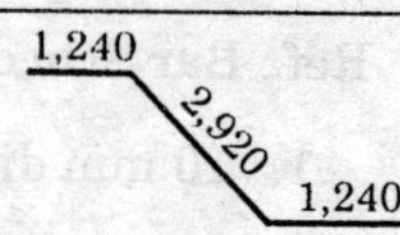
Bottom main bars 2nd flight	s-6	10 mm dia.	1	14	28	1.740	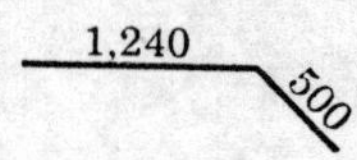
Top bar main, 2nd flight	s-7	10 mm dia.	1	14	14	1.500	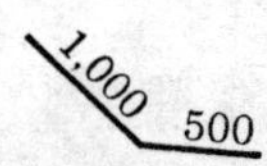
Cross bars 1st. & 2nd flight	s-8	10 mm dia.	2 4	30 11	104	1.425	Straight
Cross bars landing top & bottom	s-9	10 mm dia.	2 × 2	13	52	3.000	Straight
Railing horizontal bars, 1st. & 2nd flight	s-10	8 mm dia.	2	7	14	2.900	Straight
Railing 1st. floor	s-11	8 mm dia.	1	7	7	1.400	Straight
Railing verticals	s-12	8 mm dia.	1 1 1	16 16 6	38	1.400	
Extra main bar in landing, jn. of flights top & bottom main bars	s-13	10 mm dia.	2	2	4	1.440	Straight
Top bar flights	s-14	10 mm dia.	2	14	28	1.500	Straight

(Contd..)

Location	*Mark / Design-ation*	*Size and type*	*Number of set*	*Number per set*	*Total number*	*Length m*	*Shape of bar*
Distribution bars top flights	s-15	10 mm dia.	2	9	18	1.425	Straight
Step	s-16	8 mm dia.	20	13	260	0.680	
Top tie	s-17	8 m m dia.	20	5	100	1.200	Straight
Top bar main 1st. flight bottom	s-18	8 mm dia.	1	14	14	1.450	

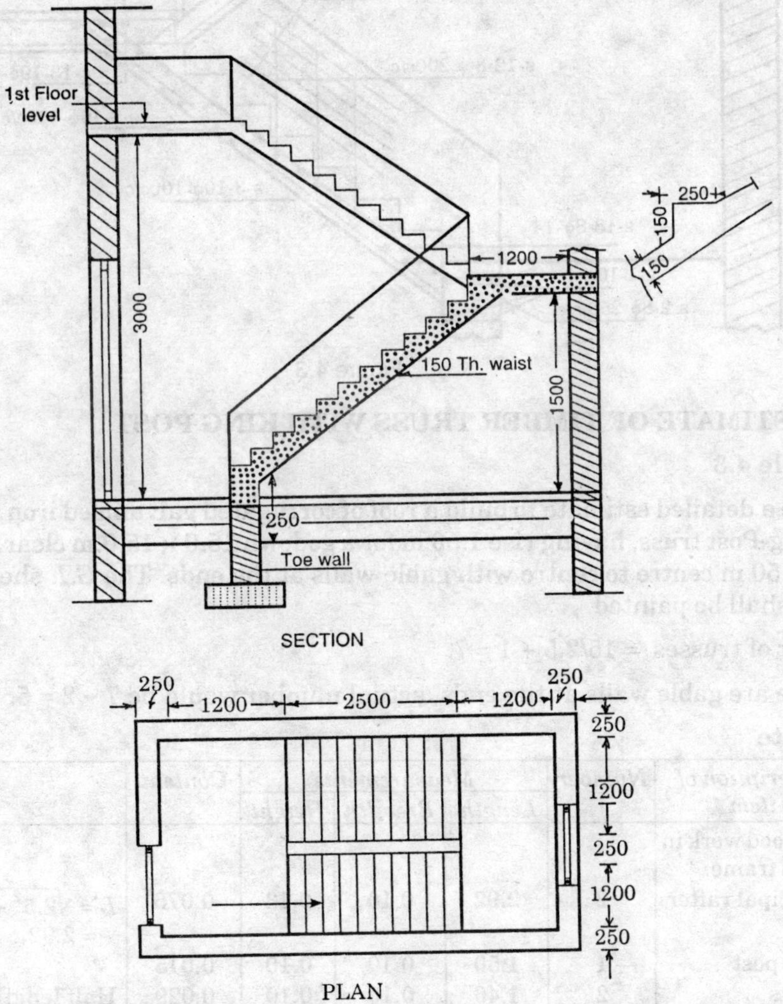

Figure 4.3 R.C.C. Stair.

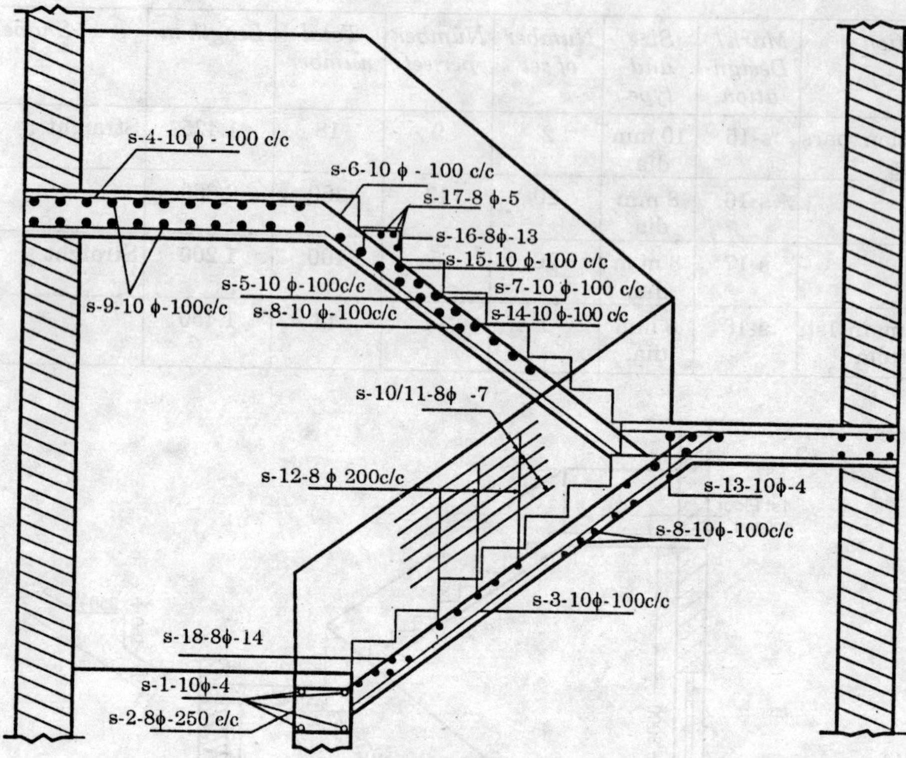

Figure 4.3

4.3.0 ESTIMATE OF TIMBER TRUSS WITH KING POST

Example 4.3

Prepare a detailed estimate to build a roof of corrugated galvanised iron sheet supported on wooden King-Post truss, having rise 1.50 m for a godown 15.0 × 15.0 m clear. The spacing of the trusses is 2.50 m centre to centre with gable walls at the ends. The *G.I.* sheets are of 24 G. All wood work shall be painted.

Number of trusses = 15/2.5 + 1 = 7.

As there are gable walls at the ends, actual number would be 7 – 2 = 5.

Estimate

Item no.	*Description of item*	*Number*	*Measurements*			*Content*	*Waste*
			Length	*Breadth*	*Height*		
1	Salwood work in truss frame.						
	Principal rafter	2	2.92	0.10	0.13	0.076	$L = \sqrt{2.5^2 + 1.5^2}$ = 2.92,
	King post	1	1.50	0.10	0.10	0.015	
	Struts	2	1.46	0.10	0.10	0.029	Half length of principal rafter
	Tie beam	1	5.50	0.10	0.15	0.83	
	Wooden cleats for purlins	2	0.15	0.08	0.08	0.009	
						0.2049	cum

(*Contd..*)

Item no.	Description of item	Number	Measurements			Content	Waste
			Length	Breadth	Height		
	Quantity for 5 such trusses 5 × 0.2049					1.0245	cum
	Purlins	2	15.30	0.08	0.12	0.300	
	Ridge board	1	15.30	0.04	0.15	0.092	
	Common rafters 600mm center	2 × 26	3.40	0.05	0.10	1.326	No. $= \frac{15}{0.60} + 1 = 26$ $L = \sqrt{1.5^2 + 3.05^2}$
	Eaves board	2	15.30	0.025	0.18	0.140	2.5 + 0.30 + (0.50 – 0.25) = 3.05
	Battens	2 × 5	15.30	0.06	0.08	0.734	
	Wall purlins	2	15.30	0.10	0.08	0.248	
						3.865	cum
2	Iron works in one truss.						
	(*a*) Straps 50 × 10 mm three way strap at ridge	2	0.90			1.80	
	U-shape at central bottom	1	1.30			1.30	L = 2 × 0.60 + 0.10 = 1.30
	U-strap at heel	2	0.70			1.40	L = 2 × 0.30 + 0.10 = 0.70
						4.50 m	
				@ 3.91 kg/m		17.60 kg	
	(*b*) Anchor bolts 20 mm diameter	2	0.30			0.60 m	
				@ 2.47	kg/m	1.48 kg	
	(*c*) 8 mm thick washer for U-heel straps.	2	0.20	0.08		0.032	
	For anchor bolts	2	0.08	0.08		0.013	
						0.045 sqm	
	(*d*) Bolts and nuts.		@ 62.8	kg/sqm		2.83 kg	
	For heel straps	2 × 4				8 nos.	
	For anchor bolts	1 × 2				2 nos.	
						10 nos.	
			@ 0.25 kg each			2.50 kg	
	(*e*) Gibs and Cotters for fixing and tighten-ingcentral strip			L.s.		1.00 kg	
		Total for one truss				25.41 kg	
		Total for five truss				127.05 kg	
3	Corrogated G.I. sheet roofing fitted and fixed with all fittings, bolts and nuts and bitumen washers etc.	2	15.30	3.50		107.10 sqm	
4	Galvanised iron sheet ridging with necessary lap, fitted and fixed with necessary fittings, etc.	1	15.30			15.30 m	

(*Contd..*)

Item no.	Description of item	Number	Measurements			Content	Waste
			Length	Breadth	Height		
5	Painting two coats over a coat of priming.						
	(*a*) Iron works C.I. sheet roofing	2 × 2 × 1.14	15.30	3.50		244.188	
	G.I. ridge	2	15.30	0.45		13.770	
						257.958	sqm
	(*b*) Wood works.						
	Principal rafter 100 × 130	2	2.92	0.46		2.686	
	King post 100 × 100	1	1.50	0.40		0.600	
	Struts 100 × 100	2	1.46	0.40		1.168	
	Tie beam 100 × 150	1	5.50	0.50		2.750	
	Cleats 80 × 80	1	0.15	0.32		0.048	
						7.252	
		For 5 such trusses 5 × 7.252 =				36.26 sqm	
	Common rafter 50 × 100	2 × 26	3.40	0.30		53.04	
	Purlin 80 × 120	2	15.30	0.40		12.40	
	Battens 60 × 80	2 × 5	15.30	0.28		42.84	
	Ridge board 40 × 150	1	15.30	0.38		5.81	
	Eve board 25 × 180	2	15.30	0.41		12.55	
	Wall purlin 80 × 100	2	15.30	0.28		8.57	
						171.47 sqm	

Absrtact of cost

Item no.	Description of item	Quantity	Unit	Rate	Amount	Remarks
1	Salwood work rough dressed in roof truss, rafter, purlin, batten, etc. fitted and fixed complete, excluding the cost fittings.	3.865	cum	39,200.00	1,51,508.00	
2	Iron work including fitting and fixing.	127.05	kg	35.00	4,447.00	
3	24 gauge (0.5mm thick) corrogated G.I, sheet work (excluding the supporting frame work) including fitting and fixing with all necessary fittings, lap to be provided 150 mm.	107.10	sqm	290.00	31,059.00	
4	G.I. sheet ridging with 24 gauge sheets 250 mm lap and fitted and fixed with all necessary fittings	15.30	m	105.00	16,065.00	
5	(*a*) Painting two coats over a coat of priming on iron works (with any shade excepting white)	257.96	sqm	34.90	9,003.00	
	(*b*) Painting one coat over a coat of priming on timber works (with any shade except white).	171.47	sqm	24.70	4,235.00	
					2,16,317.00	
		Add contingency @ 5%			10,816.00	
					2,27,133.00	
		Add work establishment @ 2.5 %			5,678.00	

(*Contd..*)

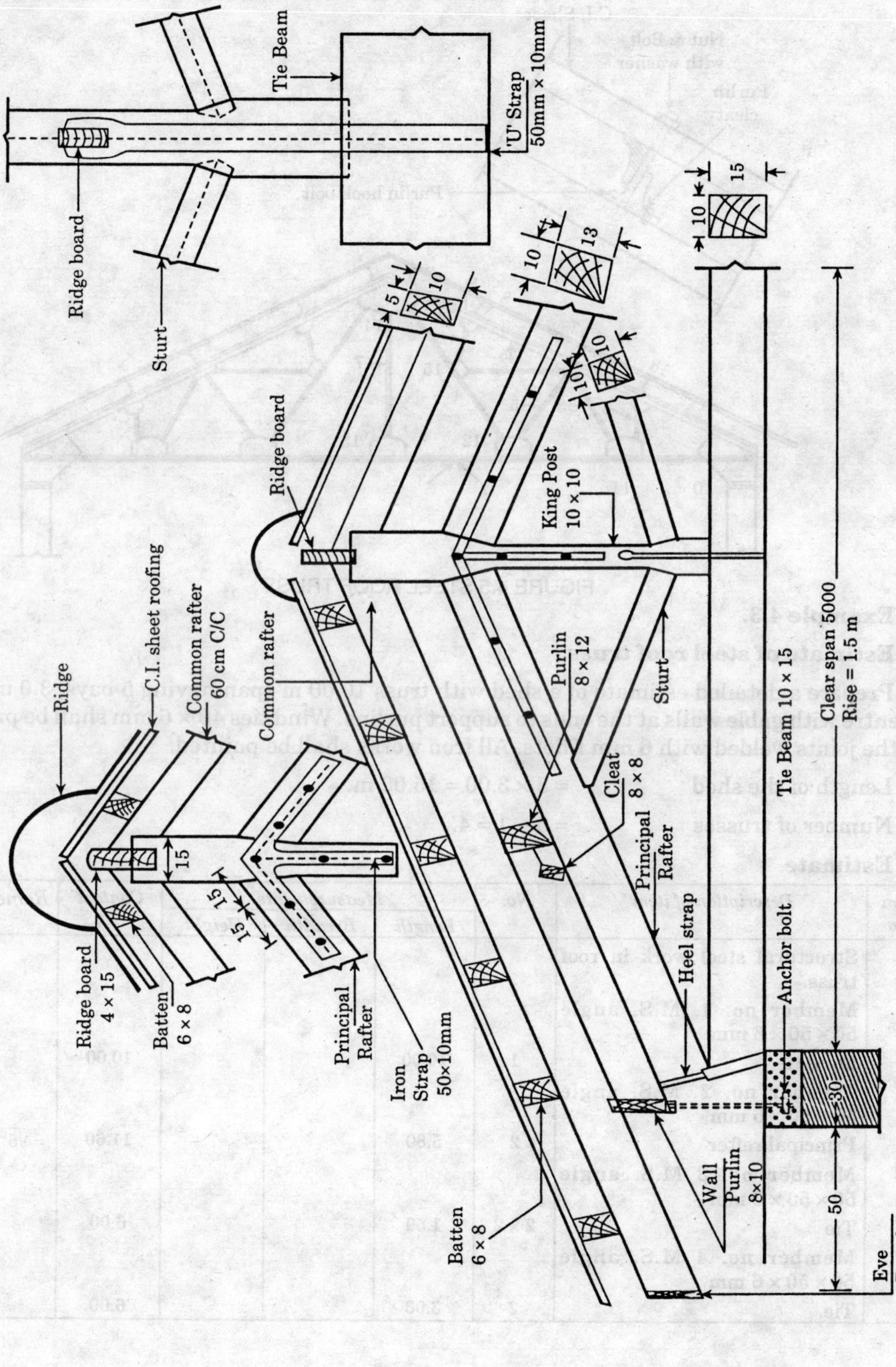

Fig. 4.4 TIMBER ROOF TRUSS WITH KING POST

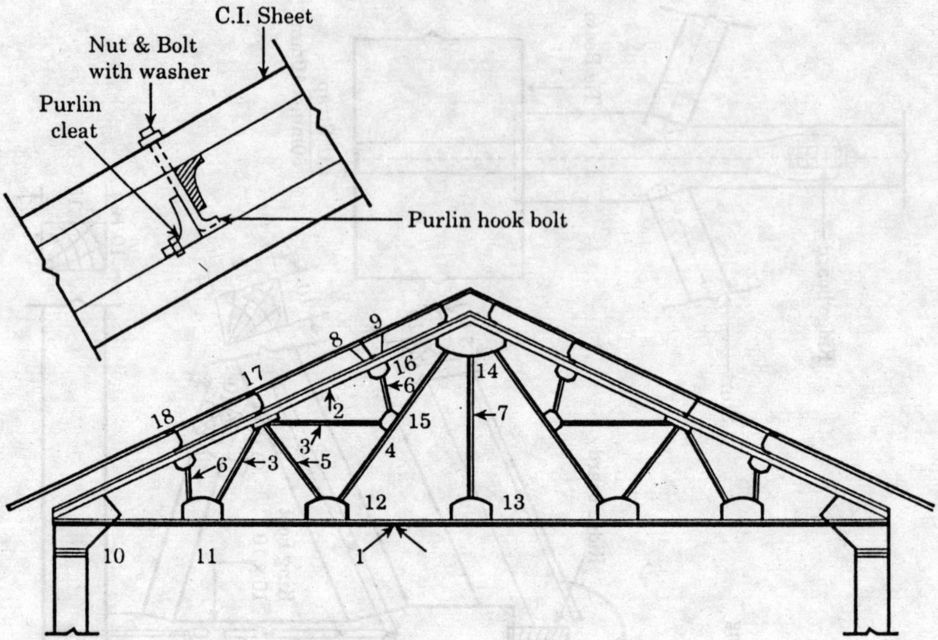

FIGURE 4.5 STEEL ROOF TRUSS

Example 4.3.

Estimate of steel roof truss.

Prepare a detailed estimate of a shed with truss 10.00 m span having 5 bays, 3.0 m centre to centre with gable walls at the ends to support purlins. Wind ties 40 × 6 mm shall be provided. All the joints welded with 6 mm fillets. All iron works shall be painted.

Length of the shed = 5 × 3.00 = 15.00 m.

Number of trusses = 5 – 1 = 4.

Estimate

Item no.	*Description of item*	*No.*	*Measurements*			*Content*	*Remarks*
			Length	*Breadth*	*Height*		
1.	Structural steel work in roof truss.						
	Member no. 1. M.S. angle 50 × 50 × 6 mm						
	Main tie.	1	10.00			10.00	
	Member no. 2. M.S. angle 50 × 50 × 6 mm						
	Principal refter	2	5.80			11.60	$= \sqrt{5^2 + 2.94^2}$
	Member no. 3 M.S. angle 50 × 50 × 6 mm						
	Tie	2 × 2	1.50			6.00	
	Member no. 4 M.S. angle 50 × 50 × 6 mm						
	Tie	2	3.00			6.00	

(Contd..)

	Member no. 5 M.S. angle 50 × 50 × 6 mm						
	Strut	2	1.50			3.00	
	Member no. 6 M.S. angle 50 × 50 × 6 mm						
	Strut	2 × 2	0.60			2.40	
	Member no. 7 M.S. angle 50 × 50 × 6 mm						
	Suspender	1	2.50			2.50	
						41.50	
	For 4 such trusses	4 × 4	1.50			166.00 m	
	Member no. 8 M.S. angle 50 × 50 × 6 mm						
	Purlin	5 × 2	15.25			152.50 m	
	Member no. 9 M.S. angle 50 × 50 × 6 mm						
	Purlin cleats	5 × 2 × 4	0.05			2.00	
						320.50 m	
		@ 4.5	kg/m			1442.25 kg	
	Gusset plate 6 mm thick						
	Member no. 10	2	0.50	0.25		0.25	
	" " 11	2	0.30	0.30		0.18	
	" " 12	2	0.30	0.30		0.18	
	" " 13	1	0.30	0.30		0.09	
	" " 14	1	0.50	0.30		0.15	
	" " 15	2	0.30	0.30		0.18	
	" " 16	2	0.20	0.20		0.08	
	" " 17	2	0.60	0.20		0.24	
	" " 18	2	0.20	0.20		0.08	
						1.43	
	For 4 such trusses	= 4 × 1.43				5.72	sqm
	@ 47.1	kg/sqm				= 269.41	kg
						1,711.66	kg
2.	24 gauge G.I. sheet corrugated roofing including all fittings, nuts, bolts and washers.	2	15.50	6.10		189.10	sqm
3.	24 gauge G.I. sheet ridging	1	15.50			15.50	sqm
4.	Painting two coats over a coat of priming.						
	One truss						
	Length of M.S. angle 50 × 50 × 6 = 166.00 m						
	Perimeter = 2 (50 + 50) = 200 mm	1	166.00	0.20		33.20	
	Purlins	1	154.50	0.20		30.90	
	Gusset plates	1 × 2	5.72			11.44	

	G.I. roofing Corrugated	2 × 1	14 × 189.10			431.15	
	Ridging	1 × 2	15.50	0.45		13.95	
						520.64	sqm

ABSTRACT OF COST

Item no.	*Description of item*	*Quantity*	*Unit*	*Rate*	*Amount*	*Remarks*
1.	Structural steel works in roof truss.	1711.66 = 17.117	Qtl.	2,468.00	42,245.00	
2.	24 gauge G.I. sheet corrugated roofing including all fittings, nuts, bolts and washers	189.10	sqm	290.00	54,839.00	
3.	24 gauge G.I. sheet ridging	15.50	m	105.00	1,628.00	
4.	Painting two coats over a coat of primer	520.64	sqm	36.40	18,951.00	
					1,17,663.00	
		Add contingency @ 5%			5,883.00	
					1,23,546.00	
		Add work establishment @ 2.5%			3,089.00	
					1,26.635.00	

5

WATER SUPPLY AND SANITARY ENGINEERING

5.1.0 PROVISION FOR WATER SUPPLY AND SANITATION

Buildings after construction need be provided with water supply and sanitation for its proper use. Building without these provisions cannot serve the purpose of its construction.

Provisions need be made for :

(*i*) Potable water for drinking and other than household purposes,

(*ii*) Drainage for proper removal of the used water for keeping the premises hygienic, and

(*iii*) Sanitation of the environment by removal of solid and liquid waste produced by the inhabitants of the premises and keeping the area pollution free.

5.1.1 Water Supply

Water supply in the premises can be provided by various means :

(*i*) Where there is no town water supply system, it may be necessary to instal tube-well or digging open well. Where there is existing piped water supply, water may be drawn from the system by a ferrule connection.

Requirement of water

As per National Building Code 1983, requirement of water for different types of buildings are as below :

	Types of building	*Requirement of water per head per day in liter*
1.	Residential (with flushing system)	200
2.	Residential (without flushing system)	135
3.	Factories	45
4.	Hospitals	340 (per bed)
5.	Hostels	135
6.	Offices	45
7.	Day schools	45
8.	Restaurants	70 (per seat)
9.	Hotels	180 (per bed)
10.	Cinema, Theatre	15 (per seat)

5.1.2 Tube-Well

Tube-well may be of two types–Deep tube-wells and shallow tube-wells.

Water from shallow tube-well is not considered fit for drinking.

Shallow tube-wells are sunk directly by sinking the pipes to be used for drawing water. Deep tube-wells are sunk, sinking larger diameter casing pipes and then lowering the pipes for drawing water. After lowering of the pipes, the casing is withdrawn.

Water from the shallow tube-wells are drawn by mounting a hand pump on the top of the pipes lowered, while water from deep tube-well is drawn by installation of a suitable pump capable of drawing water from a greater depth.

Tube-well consists of different parts :

(*i*) Plug at the lowest point,

(*ii*) Blind pipe - above the plug, a short piece of pipe of the same diameter is joined to reach the water bearing strata level,

(*iii*) Filter or strainer for drawing water from the water bearing strata,

(*iv*) Main tube-well pipe from the strainer to the top,

(*v*) Pump base, and

(*vi*) Hand pump.

In case of deep tube-well, the length of the main pipe is of two different diameters. The lower length with strainer is for drawing water as usual. On the top of it, the length of the pipe has greater diameter for housing a submersible pump for lifting water. The pump machine is installed on top of the tube-well at ground level and the pump unit is hung from the tube-well pipe at the bottom by a pipe column through which the water is lifted.

Example 5.1 *Prepare an Estimate for sinking a tube-well 40 mm diameter having a strainer of length 2 × 1.80 m long. The total length of the pipe including the strainer is 60.00 m.*

Item no.	*Description of item*	*No.*	*Measurements*			*Content*	Waste
			Length	*Breadth*	*Height*		
	A. Supply of materials						
1.	C.I. plug 40 mm dia.	1				1 No.	
2.	40 mm dia. Strainer.	1 × 2	1.80			3.60 m	
3.	40 mm dia. G.I. pipe	1	56.40			56.40 m	60.0 – 3.60 = 56.40
4.	Hand pump No. 6	1				1 No.	
	B. Labour						
1.	Sinking of 40 mm dia. G.I. pipe by Jet method system and withdrawing the same	1	60.00			60.00 m	
2.	Fitting, fixing, joining and lowering 40 mm dia. pipes with strainer and plug in the bore hole including supply of necessary sockets	1	60.00			60.00 m	
3.	Supplying, filling and packing the gap of the pipe and the bore hole by sand	L.s.					
4.	Fitting fixing and erecting the hand pump in position, including supply of necessary bolts.	1 No.				1 No.	

(Contd..)

Item no.	Description of item	No.	Measurements			Content	Waste
			Length	Breadth	Height		
	C. Miscellaneous						
1.	Construction of 1.20 × 1.20 m masonry platform with pump base of cement concrete 1 : 2 : 4, 100 mm thick over a single brick flat soling including construction of 125 × 75 mm brick band around the platform, plastering with cement sand mortar 1 : 3, 12 mm thick and finishing by neat cement, complete.	1 No.				1 No.	
2.	Construction of brick masonry surface drain 150 mm wide and 100 mm deep with cement concrete 1 : 3 : 6 base, 100 mm thick, plastering with sand and cement mortar, 12 mm thick 1 : 3 and finishing with neat cement, complete	1	2.00			2.00 m	

ABSTRACT OF COST

Item No.	Description of item	Quantity	Unit	Rate	Amount	Remarks
	A. Supply of materials					
1.	G.I. Plug 40 mm dia.	1 No.	Each	10.00	10.00	
2.	40 mm dia. strainer, I.S. mark	3.6 m	m	545.00	1,962.00	
3.	40 mm dia. G.I. pipe of approved quality	56.4 m	m	130.00	7,332.00	
4.	Hand pump No. 6 of approved quality. Supplying, fitting, and fixing in position including supply of necessary bolts.	1 No.	Each	407.00	407.00	
	B. Labour					
1.	Sinking of 40 mm dia. G.I. pipe by Jet method and withdrawing the same and fitting, fixing, joining and lowering 40 mm dia. G.I. pipe with strainer and plug in the bore hole, including supply of necessary sockets	60 m	m	49.50	2,970.00	
2.	Supplying and filling and packing the gap of the pipe and the bore hole by sand	1 No.	Each L.S.	50.00	50.00	
	C. Miscellaneous					
1.	Construction of 1.20 × 1.20 m masonry platform of cement concrete 1 : 2 : 4 with cement concrete base for the pump over a single brick flat soling, construction of 125 × 75 mm brick band around Plastering with sand and cement mortar 1 : 3, 12 mm and neat cement thick complete	1 No.	Each L.S.	300.00	300.00	

(Contd..)

Item No.	*Description of item*	*Quantity*	*Unit*	*Rate*	*Amount*	*Remarks*
2.	Construction of brick masonry surface drain 150 mm wide 100 mm deep with cement concrete 1 : 3 : 6 base, 100 mm thick, plastering 12 mm thick with cement sand mortar 1 : 3, neat cement finishing, complete	2.00 m	m	100.00	200.00	
					13,231.00	
	Add contingency @ 5%				662.00	
					13,893.00	
	Add work establishment @ $2\frac{1}{2}\%$				347.00	
					14,240.00	

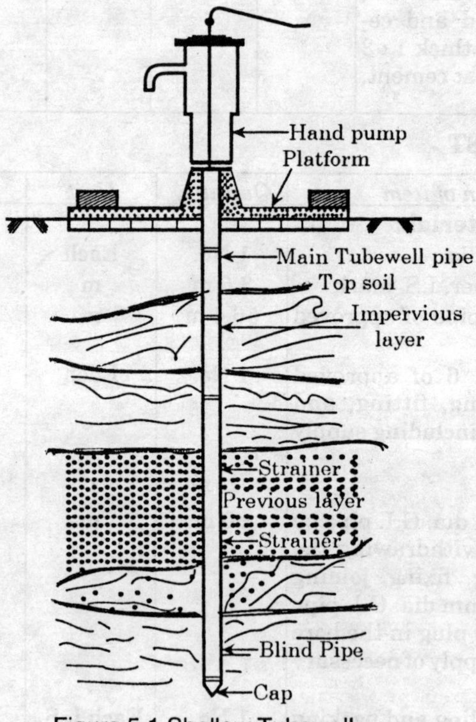

Figure 5.1 Shallow Tubewell.

5.1.3 Deep Tube Well

Deep tube-well is constructed in the same method as shallow tube wells. The only difference is the larger diameter housing pipe is sunk by sinking a casing pipe. The pipes are lowered. The two different diameter pipes are joined by a Bell-Socket. The pump machine is installed on the pump base on the top of the housing pipe and located in a pump house. The pump is hung from the pump machine. Verticality of the housing pipe is essential.

Construction of small pump house the locating for pump and also other electrical installations is necessary.

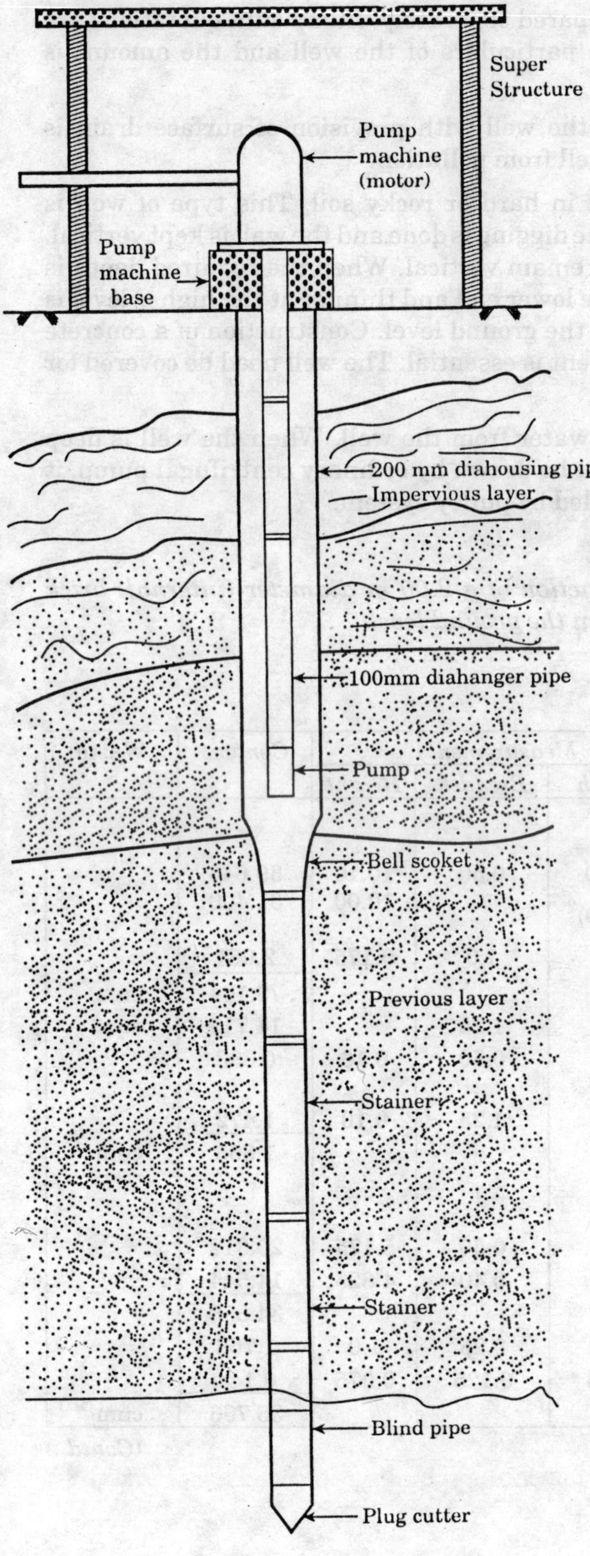

Figure 5.2 Deep Tubewell.

Drilling of wells

Drilling may be done by Percussion or by Rotary tools or by Jetting. The excavated materials are brought up by means of a bailer or hollow drill tool or by some hydraulic process in which water or mud-laden fluid is pumped down the hole which carries up the excavated material as it returns to the surface.

Reverse Circulation Method

In this method circulation of mud-slurry in the drill is effected by hydraulic process from the bottom of the hole instead of forcing the slurry from the top.

Rotary Boring

Rotary or churn drills are frequently employed for drilling wells in almost all sorts of hard or soft soils. Power driven machines are used with tripod or legged derick. Drilling is accomplished by rapidly rotating a pipe fitted with a toothed cutting shoe drills or shot drills.

Rotary method is quicker. Hole of greater diameter may be made in a shorter time. It is useful for greater depths and for penetrating hard and solid rocks.

It is obvious that drilling of deep well would require operation of a good number of machines for different purposes—Rotary Rig, Derick, Compressor, Pump, Motor, etc. While estimating, consideration need be made in the analysis of rates of items for the hire charges or depreciation of the machineries and also for the skilled labourers required for operation of those.

Estimate for sinking of the deep tube-well, pump and its installation and construction of necessary pump house for housing the pump is prepared in the same line as in case of sinking small diameter tube-well.

5.1.4 Wells

Wells for supply of water are of various types and are constructed in different ways.

In rural areas, wells are generally constructed of burnt clay rings of diameter 900 mm to 1,200 mm and 500 mm high. These are sunk by well diggers. The ring is placed on the ground and soil from inside the ring is scupped out. The process is continued till water bearing strata is reached.

Estimate for such well construction is not prepared separately. Lump sum quotations are obtained from the well diggers, giving them the particulars of the well and the amount is incorporated in the building estimate.

Construction of a concrete platform around the well with provision of surface drain is essential on hygienic ground and protecting the well from pollution.

The other type of well is masonry well built in hard or rocky soil. This type of well is constructed on selected place by digging the soil. The digging is done and the wall is kept vertical. As the soil is hard or clayee, the walls generally remain vertical. When the required depth is reached, brick or stone masonry wall thicker at the lower end and thinner at the higher level is built. The wall is taken about 1.00 m higher than the ground level. Construction of a concrete platform around the well with drainage arrangement is essential. The well need be covered for protection against external pollution.

Sometimes, pumps are installed for drawing water from the well. When the well is deep enough, and pump cannot be fixed or water cannot be drawn by ordinary centrifugal pump, it is drawn from the well by hanging bucket and pulled by pulley system.

Example 5.2 *Prepare an estimate for construction of a 2.00 m diameter (internal) brick masonry well. The well would be 10.00 m deep from the ground level.*

Estimate

Item no.	*Description of item*	*No.*	*Measurements*			*Content*	Waste
			Length	*Breadth*	*Height*		
1.	Earthwork in excavation in digging of well and platform.						
	Steining portion	$1 \times \pi$	2.500	0.50	10.10	39.643	
	Central shaft	$1 \times \pi$	$\frac{1}{4}(2.00)^2$		10.00	31.400	
	Platform	$1 \times \pi$	3.75	1.0	0.175	2.061	
						73.104	cum
2.	Single brick flat soling	$1 \times \pi$	3.75	1.25		14.719	sqm
3.	Cement concrete 1 : 3 : 6 below the wall steining	$1 \times \pi$	2.50	0.50	0.10	0.393	
	Platform	$1 \times \pi$	3.75	1.25	0.10	1.472	
		$1 \times \pi$				1.865	cum
4.	Brickwork in cement mortar 1 : 3 Steining wall						
	Lower course	$1 \times \pi$	2.50	0.50	5.175	20.312	
	Upper course	$1 \times \pi$	2.40	0.40	4.825	14.544	
						34.856	
	Above ground level	$1 \times \pi$	2.25	0.25	1.0	1.766	
	Band around platform	$1 \times \pi$	4.875	0.125	0.075	0.144	
						36.766	cum

(*Contd..*)

Item no.	*Description of item*	*No.*	*Measurements*			*Content*	*Waste*
			Length	*Breadth*	*Height*		
5.	Cement sand plaster 1 : 3, 15 mm thick, finished with neat cement						
	Inside including parapet	$1 \times \pi$	2.00		11.00	69.080	
	Outside parapet	$1 \times \pi$	3.00		1.00	9.420	
	Top of parapet	$1 \times \pi$	2.25	0.25		1.766	
	Platform	$1 \times \pi$	3.75	1.25		14.719	
	Platform sides	$1 \times \pi$	5.00	0.15		2.355	
						97.340	sq m
6.	Supplying and fixing M.s. cat ladder	40				40	Nos.
7.	Earthwork in back filling.						
	Volume of Earthwork in excavation Item no. 1					39.643	cum
	Less						
	Volume of concrete item no. 3					1.865	
	Central shaft						
	Volume of steining item no. 4					34.856	
					(–)	36.721	
						2.922	cum
8.	Top covering, installation of pump or pulley system for lifting water	Lump sum					

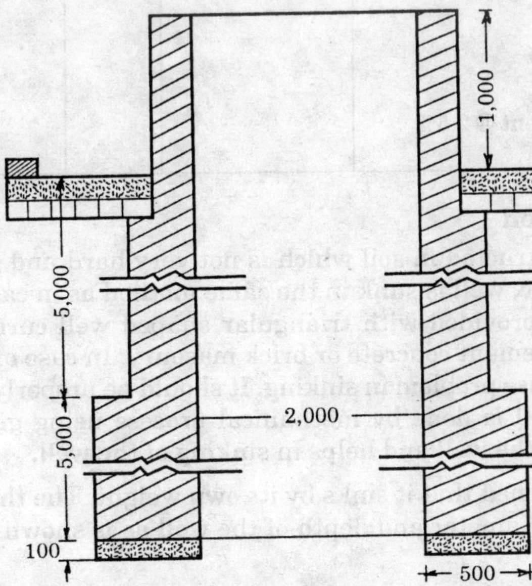

Fig. 5.3 Well

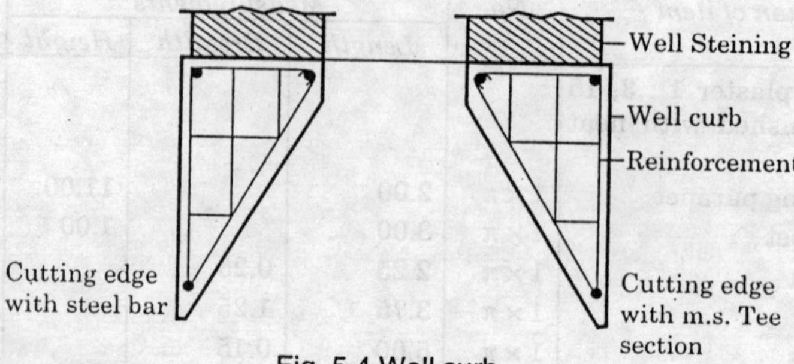

Fig. 5.4 Well curb.

Abstract of cost

Item no.	*Description of item*	*Quantity*	*Unit*	*Rate*	*Amount*	*Remarks*
1.	Earthwork in excavation in digging of well and platform base	73.104	%cum	5,497.00 (av)	4,019.00	
2.	Single brick flat soling	14.719	sqm	95.00	1,398.00	
3.	Cement concrete 1 : 3 : 6	1.865	cum	1,623.00	3,027.00	
4.	Brickwork in cement mortar 1 : 4	36.766	cum	1,760.00	67.708.00	
5.	Cement and sand plaster 1 : 3, 15 mm thick with neat cement finishing	97.340	sqm	76.00	7,398.00	
6.	Supplying and fixing cat ladder made of 12 mm dia. m.s bar, U-shaped.	40 Nos.	Each	10.00	400.00	
7.	Earthwork in back filling	2.922	%Cum	1,738.00	51.00	
8.	Top covering, installation of pump or pulley system for lifting water	L.S.			5,000.00	
					89,001.00	
	Add contingency @ 5%				4,450.00	
					93,451.00	
	Add work establishment @ 2.5%				2,336.00	
					95,787.00	

5.1.5 Well Sinking Method

When the well is constructed in soil which is not very hard and keeping the side vertical after digging is not possible, well is sunk in the same method as in case of well sunk below the bridge piers. The well is provided with triangular shaped well curb over cutting edge. The steining is built either of cement concrete or brick masonry. In case of brick masonry steining, the lighter steining may pose problem in sinking. It should be properly designed. Excavation of soil from inside of the well is done by mechanical process using grabbing excavator which scuppes earth from inside the well and helps in sinking of the well.

The steining is so designed that it sinks by its own weight. The thickness of the steining is varied with the proposed diameter and depth of the well as is shown in the tabulated form in the Table 5.1.

However, when the well does not sink by its own weight, weight as required is placed on the steining by constructing a temporary platform over it for expediting the sinking.

While estimating, all these factors need be taken care of in the analysis of rate of different items of the work to make the estimate realistic.

Table 5.1
Thickness of steining of wells

Depth of well from ground level in mtr.	*Suggested thickness in centimeter for diameter for diameter of well in metre*					
	1.5 m	*3.0 m*	*4.5 m*	*6.0 m*	*9.0 m*	*12.0 m*
3.00	40	40	40	50	50	50
6.00	40	50	50	50	60	70
9.00	50	50	50	60	70	90
12.00	50	60	60	70	80	100
18.00	60	60	70	80	90	110
24.00	60	70	80	90	—	—
30.00	70	80	90	110	—	—
36.00	70	90	100	—	—	—

5.2.0 DRAINAGE

A system need be developed for drainage, removal and disposal of waste water and storm water from the houses and the locality.

5.2.1 Surface Drain

Generally, surface drains of different sections as necessary are provided for collection and removal of waste water from the households and storm water from the locality.

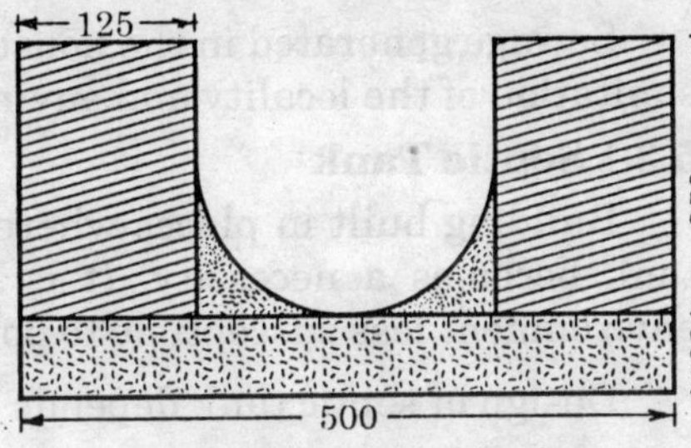

Figure 5.5 Surface Drain.

Example 5.3 *Prepare a cost estimate of a surface drain as shown in the Figure 5.5.*

Estimate

Estimate is prepared for 1.0 m length of the section and then provision is made in the main estimate as required by multiplying the cost of 1.00 m by the required length.

Quantity considered for 10.0 m

Item No.	*Description of item*	*No.*	*Measurements Length*	*Breadth*	*Height*	*Content*	*Waste*
1.	Earthwork in excavation.	1	10.00	0.50	0.35	1.750	cum
2.	Cement concrete 1 : 3 : 6.	1	10.00	0.50	0.10	0.500	cum
3.	Brickwork in cement mortar 1 : 4 for cheeks.	2	10.00	0.125	0.25	0.625	
4.	Cement concrete 1 : 2 : 4 for shaping the invert.	1	10.00	0.250	0.125	0.313	
	Less	$\frac{1}{2}.\pi$	$\frac{0.25^2}{4} \times 10.00$		(–)	0.245	
						0.068	cum
5.	Cement and sand plaster 1 : 3, 15 mm thick with neat cement finishing.	2	10.00	0.375		7.500	0.125 + 0.125 + 0.125 = 0.375
		1	$10.00 \times \pi \times \frac{0.25}{2}$		3.925	3.925	
						11.425	sqm

ABSTRACT OF COST

Item no.	*Description of item*	*Quantity*	*Unit*	*Rate*	*Amount*	*Remarks*
1.	Earthwork in excavation.	1.750	cum	2,973.00	52.00	
2.	Cement concrete 1 : 3 : 6.	0.500	cum	1,931.00	966.00	
3.	Brickwork in cement mortar 1 : 4.	0.625	cum	1,760.00	1,100.00	
4.	Cement concrete 1 : 2 : 4	0.068	cum	2,373.00	161.00	
5.	Cement and sand plaster 1 : 3, 15 mm thick with neat cement finishing	11.425	sqm	76.00	868.00	
					3147.00	
	Add contingency @ 5%				157.00	
					3304.00	
	Add work-establishment @ 2.5 %				83.00	
	Total cost for 10.00 m Length				Rs. 3,387.00	

Cost per meter length Rs. 339.00

5.3.0 SEWAGE DISPOSAL

Sewage generated in the household need be collected and disposed of safely for keeping the sanitation of the locality and environment clean and pollution free.

5.3.1 Septic Tank

Building built in places where there is no public sewerage system, construction of Septic tank becomes a necessity. It is a simple and cost-optimised sanitation system providing environment less susceptible to pollution.

Design of septic tank depends on the volumes required for :

(*a*) Settling of the heavier particles,

(*b*) Digestion of effluent, and

(*c*) Storage of digested sludge.

Space required for settling

The volume required for accomodation of the effluent and settling of the heavier particles during the detention period depends upon the average flow of fluid per capita per day which is taken as 45 liters when only the effluent of latrine flows into the septic tank. If waste water is also allowed in the septic tank, per capita per day flow ranges from 90—115 litre.

Space for digestion

Volume required for digestion is taken as 42.5 liter or 0.0425 cum per capita per day.

Space required for storage of digested sludge is taken as 0.213 liter per capita per day.

The storage volume depends upon the frequency of cleaning.

In 6 months, the quantity of digested sludge per capita

$$= 6 \times 30 \times 0.213 = 38.3 \text{ liter or}$$

28 liter compact.

Period of sludging and storage capacity

Period of sludging	*Storage capacity required*
6 months	28 liter
1 year	50 liter
2 year	70 liter
3 year	85 liter

Example 5.4 *Design a septic tank for 100 users, assuming rated water supply 50 liter per head per day.*

Assuming detention period = 24 hours

Cleaning frequency = 3 years

The following values are assumed.

Volume required for settling—50 liter per capita,

Volume required for digestion—0.425 cum per capita,

Volume required for storage :

One year	– 0.049 cum
Two year	– 0.078 cum
Three year	– 0.085 cum

Design

(*a*). Space required for settling $= \dfrac{50 \times 100}{1000} = 5.00$ cum

(*b*). Space required for digestion $= 100 \times 0.0425 = 4.25$ cum

(*c*). Space required for storage of sludge $= 100 \times 0.085 = 8.50$ cum
(assuming cleaning frequency 3 year)

Total space required = 5.00 + 4.25 + 8.50 = 17.75 cum

Providing 300 mm free board above the fluid level in the tank, the dimensions of the tank needed are :

Depth	1.70 + 0.30 = 2.00 m
Breadth	2.00 m
Length	5.50 m
Volume	= 5.50 × 2.00 × 2.00 = 22.00 cum

Example 5.5 *Estimate the cost of a septic tank for use of 100 users as per drawing no. 5.3.*

100 users' septic tank require a net liquid volume of 18.7 cum as per Table.

Septic tank as per drawing no. 5.3 will provide the required net liquid volume.

$1 \times 5.50 \times 2.00 \times 1.70 = 18.70$ cum.

Estimate

Ref. Drawing No. 5.3.

Item no.	*Description of item*	*No.*	*Measurements*			*Contents*	*Waste*
			Length	*Breadth*	*Height*		
1.	Earthwork in excavation	1	6.30	2.80	2.40	42.336	cum
2.	Cement concrete 1 : 3 : 6	1	6.30	2.80	0.15	2.646	cum
3.	Cement concrete 1 : 2 : 4	1	5.75	2.20	0.15	1.898	cum
4.	Brickwork in cement mortar 1 : 4						
	Long walls	2	6.30	0.40	1.00	5.04	
	Short walls	2	2.00	0.40	1.00	1.60	
	Long walls	2	5.90	0.20	1.15	2.714	
	Short walls	2	2.00	0.20	1.15	1.113	
	Partition wall	1	2.00	0.075	1.70	0.255	

(*Contd..*)

Item no.	Description of item	No.	Measurements			Contents	Waste
			Length	Breadth	Height		
						10.722	cum
5.	Cement concrete 1 : 2 : 4 in R.C.C. work	1	5.90	2.40	0.10	1.416	cum
6.	M.S. reinforcement for R.C.C. work						
	10 mm dia. bars	60	2.72	= 163.2 m			
				@ 0.62 kg per m		101.184	
	6 mm dia. bars	25	5.985	= 149.625 m			
				@ 0.22 kg per m		32.918	
						134.102	kg
7.	Shuttering and centering Ceiling	1	5.50	2.00		11.00	
	Sides	2	5.90	= 11.80			
		2	2.40	= 4.80			
				16.60	0.10	1.66	
						12.66	sqm
8.	Cement and sand plastering 1 : 4, 15 mm thick	2	5.50	= 11.00			
	Internal surface of wall	2	2.00	= 4.00			
				15.00	2.00	30.00	
	Partition wall	2	2.00	1.70		6.80	
	Partition wall top	1	2.00	0.075		0.15	
	External surface of wall	2	6.30	= 12.60			
		2	2.80	= 5.60			
			18.20	1.00		18.20	
		2	5.90	= 11.80			
		2	2.40	= 4.80			
			16.60	1.25		20.75	
		2	6.30	= 12.60			
		2	2.80	= 5.60			
			18.20	0.20		2.64	
						78.54	sqm
9.	Cement and sand plaster 1 : 3, 10 mm thick with neat cement finished same as item no. 8 ceiling	1	5.9	2.00		78.54	
						11.80	
						90.34	sqm
10.	Cement and sand plaster 1 : 3, 15 mm thick Top of slab	1	5.90	2.40		14.16	
	Floor	1	5.50	2.00		11.00	
						25.16	sqm
11.	Supplying and fixing S.W. Tee 100 mm dia.	2				2	Nos.
12.	Supplying and fixing 450 mm dia. C.I mainhole cover	2				2	Nos.
13.	Supplying and fixing C.I. vent pipe 100 mm dia. with cowl, 2.00 m long	1 No				1 No.	
14.	Supplying and fixing C.I. cat ladder	24 Nos.				24 Nos.	

ABSTRACT OF COST

Item no.	*Description of item*	*Quantity*	*Unit*	*Rate*	*Amount*	*Remarks*
1.	Earthwork in excavation	42.336%	cum	2,973.00	1,259.00	
2.	Cement concrete 1 : 3 : 6	2.646	cum	1,931.00	5,109.00	
3.	Cement concrete 1 : 2 : 4	1.898	cum	2,373.00	4,504.00	
4.	Brickwork in cement mortar 1 : 4	10.722	cum	1,760.00	18.871.00	
5.	Cement concrete 1 : 2 : 4 in R.C.C work	1.416	cum	2,373.00	3,360.00	
6.	M.S. reinforcement for R.C.C. work	134.102	kg	20.831	2,793.00	
7.	Shuttering and centering	12.66	sqm	35.00	443.00	
8.	Cement and sand plastering 1 : 4, 15 mm thick	78.54	sqm	53.00	4,163.00	
9.	Cement and sand plastering 1 : 3, 10 mm thick with neat cement Finished	90.34	sqm	63.00	5,691.00	
10.	Cement and sand plastering 1 : 3, 15 mm thick	25.16	sqm	61.00	1,535.00	
11.	Supplying and fixing S.W. Tee 100 mm dia.	2	Nos.	95.00	190.00	
12.	Supplying and fixing 450 mm dia. C.I. manhole cover	2	Nos.	290.00	580.00	
13.	Supplying and fixing vent pipe 100 mm dia. with cowl, 2.00 m long	1	No.	575.00	575.00	
14.	Supplying and fixing C.I. cat ladder	24 Nos.	Each	10.00	240.00	
					49,313.00	
	Add contingency @ 5%				2,466.00	
					51,779.00	
	Add work establishment @ 2.5%				1,294.00	
				Rs.	53,073.00	
	Cost per capita = Rs. 531.00					

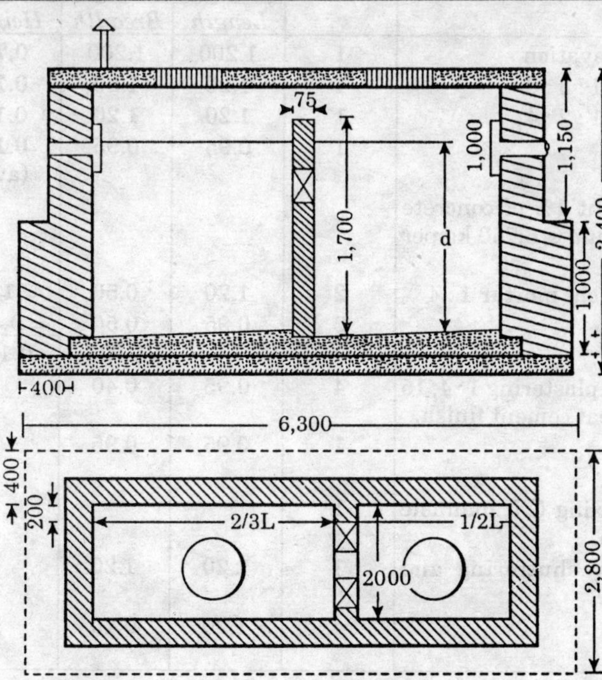

Fig. 5.6 Septic Tank.

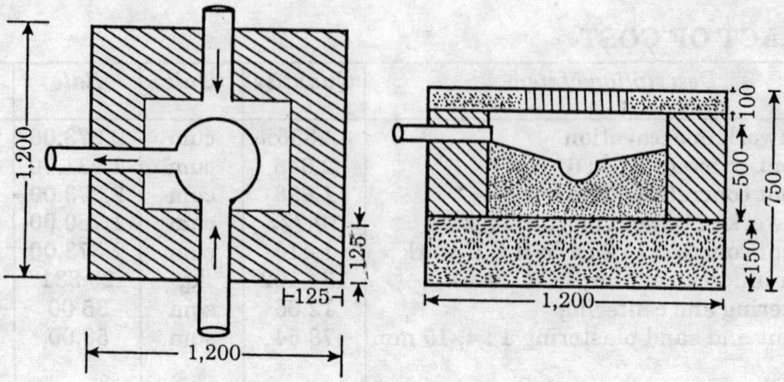

Fig. 5.7 Inspection Pit.

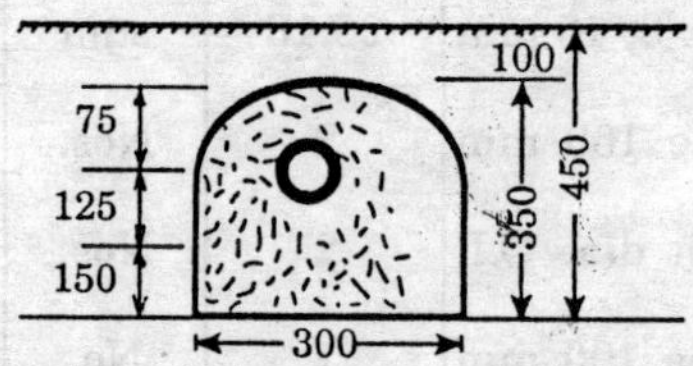

Fig. 5.8 Laying of S.W. Pipe.

5.3.2 Inspection Pit

Example 5.6 *Estimate the cost of construction of a* 1.200 × 1.200 *m inspection pit as shown in Figure 5.7.*

Estimate

Item no.	*Description of item*	*No.*	*Measurement*			*Content*	*Waste*
			Length	*Breadth*	*Height*		
1.	Earthwork in excavation	1	1.200	1.200	0.75	1.08	cum
2.	Cement concrete 1 : 3 : 6	1	1.20	1.20	0.15	0.216	cum
3.	Cement concrete 1 : 2 : 4	1	1.20	1.20	0.10	0.144	
		1	0.95	0.95	0.10 (av.)	0.099	
						0.234	cum
4.	M.S. reinforcement 1% of concrete 0.144 = 0.00144 cum @ 8,750 kg per cum					12.60	kg
5.	Brickwork in cement mortar 1 : 4	2	1.20	0.50	= 1.20		
		2	0.95	0.50	= 0.475		
				1.675	0.125	0.209	cum
6.	Cement and sand plastering 1 : 4, 15 mm thick with neat cement finish.	4	0.95	0.40		1.52	
		1	0.95	0.95		0.903	
						2.423	sqm
7.	Supplying and fixing C.I. manhole cover 450 mm dia.	1				1 No.	
8.	Hire charges for shuttering and centering.	1	1.20	1.20		1.44	
		4	1.20	0.10		0.48	
						1.92	sqm

ABSTRACT OF COST

Item no.	Description of item	Quantity	Unit	Rate	Amount	Remarks
1.	Earthwork in excavation	1.08	%cum	2,973.00	32.00	
2.	Cement concrete 1 : 3 : 6	0.216	cum	1,931.00	417.00	
3.	Cement concrete 1 : 2 : 4	0.234	cum	2,373.00	555.00	
4.	M.S. reinforcement	12.60	kg	20.831	262.00	
5.	Brickwork in cement mortar 1 : 4	0.209	cum	1,760.00	368.00	
6.	Cement and sand plastering 1 : 4, 15 mm thick with neat cement finish	2.423	sqm	68.00	165.00	
7.	Supplying and fixing manhole cover 450 mm dia.	1 No.	each	290.00	290.00	
8.	Hire charges for shuttering and centering	1.92	sqm	35.00	67.00	
					2,156.00	
	Add contingency @ 5%				108.00	
					2,264.00	
	Add work establishment @ 2.5%				57.0	
					2,321.00	

5.3.3. Laying of S.W. Pipe

Laying of S.W. pipe 100 mm dia.

Example 5.7 *Estimate the cost of laying S.W. pipe 100 mm dia. 1.00 m length. as shown in Figure 5.5*

Estimate

Considering 10.00 m length.

Item no.	Description of item	No.	Measurements Length	Breadth	Height	Content	Waste
1.	Earthwork in excavation	1	10.00	0.30	0.45	1.35	cum
2.	Cement concrete 1 : 3 : 6 with Jhama Khoa	1	10.00	0.30	0.35	1.05	
	Less	1	$10.00 \times \frac{\pi \times 0.125^2}{4}$		(–)	0.123	
						0.927	cum
	(Reduction in volume of concrete due to shape is neglected as it balances the cost of labour for shaping)						
3.	Supplying and laying S.W. pipe 100 mm dia.	1	10.00			10.00	m
4.	Earthwork in back filling.						
	Volume of excavation					1.35	cum
	Less volume of concrete without deduction				(–)	1.05	
						0.30	cum

ABSTRACT OF COST

Item no.	Description of item	Quantity	Unit	Rate	Amount	Remarks
1.	Earthwork in excavation	1.35	%cum	2,973.00	40.00	
2.	Cement concrete 1 : 3 : 6 with Jhama Khoa	0.927	cum	1,623.00	1,505.00	
3.	Supplying and laying S.W. pipe	10.00	m	76.00	760.00	
4.	Earthwork in back filling	0.30%	cum	1,738.00	5.00	
					2,310.00	
	Add contingency @ 5%				116.00	
					2,426.00	
	Add work establishment @ 2.5%				61.00	
	Total cost of 10.00 meter				2,487.00	
	Cost per meter	= Rs. 249.00				

Abstract of cost of construction of Septic tank 100 users complete with Inspection pit, S.W. pipes, etc.

Item no.	*Description of item*	*Quantity*	*Unit*	*Rate*	*Amount*	*Remarks*
1.	Construction of septic tank 100 users	1 No.	Each	53,073.00	53,073.00	
2.	Construction of Inspection pit	2 Nos	Each	2,321.00	4,642.00	
3.	Supplying and fixing C.I. 100 dia. siphon in inspection pit	1 No.	Each	390.00	390.00	
4.	Supplying and laying S.W. pipe 100 mm dia. on cement concrete bed and protected by cement concrete 0.075 mm thick	5.00	m	249.00	1,245.00	
					59,350.00	
	Cost per capita	Rs. 594.00				

5.3.4 Yard Gully

Yard gully is made of stone ware and is available in the market. The size of the Yard gully is mentioned by the measurement of the entry mouth which is closed by C.I. grating. The size of the pipe is generally 150 mm. These are placed on the sides of the road or in the yard for collection of storm water and draining the same in the sewerage system. The S.W. yard gully pieces are placed in the inspection pit like masonry chamber for keeping those in position and for protection against breakage. The yard gully has 60 to 75 mm water seal for preventing obnoxious gasses coming out through it.

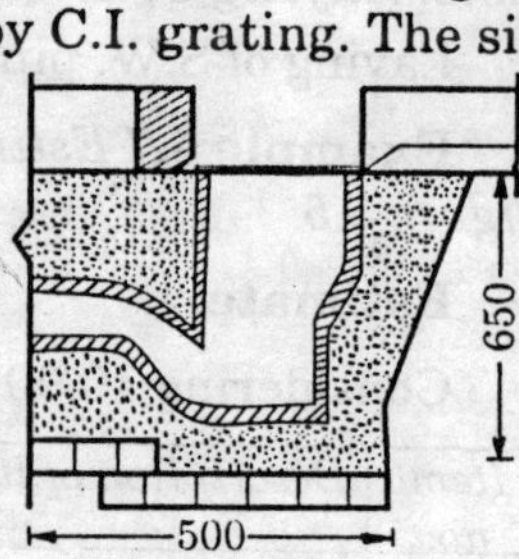

Figure 5.9 Gully Pit.

Example 5.8 *Estimate the cost of providing a yard gully with masonry chamber as shown in Figure 5.9.*

Estimate

Item no.	*Description of item*	*No.*	*Measurements*			*Content*	*Waste*
			Length	*Breadth*	*Height*		
1.	Earthwork in excavation	1	0.500	0.500	0.875	0.219	cum
2.	Single brick flat soling	1	0.500	0.500		0.25	
		1	0.500	0.150		0.075	
						0.325	sqm
3.	Cement concrete 1 : 3 : 6 with Jhama khoa	1	0.500	0.500	0.650	0.163	cum
	Less volume of yard gully which is neglected					nil	
						0.163	cum
4.	Supplying and fixing in position S.W. yard gully piece with cement sand mortar 1 : 4 and also including supplying and fixing of C.I. grating	1 No.				1 No.	

ABSTRACT OF COST

Item no.	*Description of item*	*Quantity*	*Unit*	*Rate*	*Amount*	*Remarks*
1.	Earthwork in excavation.	0.219	%cum	2,973.00	7.00	
2.	Single brick flat soling.	0.325	sqm	95.00	31.00	
3.	Cement concrete 1 : 3 : 6 with Jhama khoa.	0.163	cum	1623.00	265.00	

(Contd..)

Item no.	Description of item	Quantity	Unit	Rate	Amount	Remarks
4.	Supplying and fixing in position S.W. Yard gully piece with cement and sand mortar 1 : 4 including the C.I. grating 230 × 230 mm and S.W. pipe 150 mm dia.	1 No.		334.00	334.00	
					637.00	
	Add contingency @ 5%				32.00	
					669.00	
	Add work establishment @ 2.5%				17.00	
					686.00	

5.3.5 Master Trap or Intercepting Trap

Master trap or Intercepting trap is made of S.W. and are available in the market. The size of the trap is denoted by diameter of the pipe which is generally 150 mm. The function of the Master trap is important. The sewage from the houses generally contain unwanted solid materials which may choke the sewer. These are intercepted and are collected in the U-shaped portion of the trap for removal. Water or fluid matter flows into the sewer. The trapped solid materials are collected through the cleaning eye and removed.

The Master trap or the incepting trap is installed in masonry chamber like yard gully and is located at the end of the domestic sewer line before entering the main public sewer.

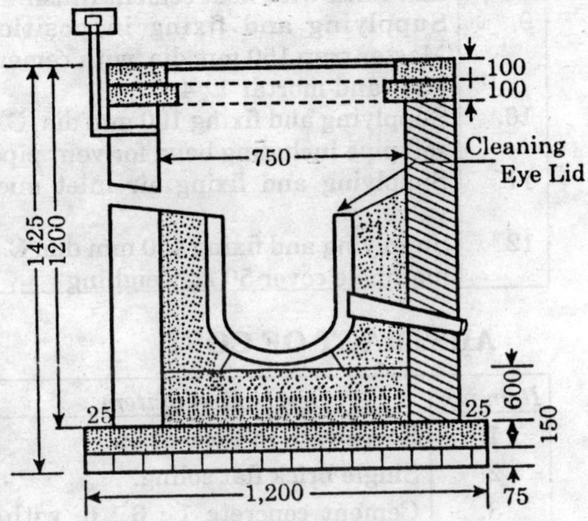

Figure 5.10 Master/intercepting Trap.

Example 5.9 *Estimate the cost of installation of a Master trap of size 150 mm as shown in Figure 5.10.*

Estimate

Item no.	Description of item	No.	Measurements Length	Breadth	Height	Content	Remarks
1.	Earthwork in excavation	1	1.20	1.20	1.425	2.052	cum
2.	Single brick flat soling	1	1.20	1.20		1.44	sqm
3.	Cement concrete 1 : 3 : 6	1	1.20	1.20	0.15	0.216	
		1	0.75	0.75	0.60	0.338	
						0.554	cum
4.	Brickwork in cement mortar 1 : 4	2	1.15	= 2.30			
		2	0.75	= 1.50			
			3.80	0.200	1.00	0.760	cum
5.	Cement concrete 1 : 2 : 4 for R.C.C. work						
	Top cover	1	1.15	1.15	0.10	0.132	
	Base	1	1.15	1.15	0.10	0.132	
						0.264	cum
6.	M.S. reinforcement 1% of the volume of concrete 1% of 0.264 = 0.00264 cum 7850 kg per cum					20.724	

(Contd..)

Item no.	Description of item	No.	Measurements Length	Breadth	Height	Content	Remarks
	Add 5% for wastage					1.036	
						21.760	kg
7.	Hire and labour charges for shuttering and centering	1	0.75	0.75		0.563	
		4	1.15	0.20		0.920	
		$1 \times \pi$	0.50	0.10		0.157	
		$1 \times \pi$	0.40	0.10		0.126	
						1.766	sqm
8.	Cement and sand plastering 1 : 4, 12 mm thick with neat cement finish.	4	0.75	0.60		1.80	sqm
9.	Supplying and fixing in position Master trap 150 mm dia. with cement and sand mortar 1 : 4	1 No.				1 No.	
10.	Supplying and fixing 100 mm dia. C.I. soil pipe including bend for vent pipe	3 m				3 m	
11.	Supplying and fixing air inlet mica valve.	1 No.				1 No.	
12.	Supplying and fixing 450 mm dia. C.I. mainhole cover 50 kg weighing	1 No.				1 No.	

ABSTRACT OF COST

Item no.	Description of item	Quantity	Unit	Rate	Amount	Remarks
1.	Earthwork in excavation.	2.052	%cum	2,973.00	61.00	
2.	Single brick flat soling.	1.44	sqm	95.00	137.00	
3.	Cement concrete 1 : 3 : 6, with Jhama Khoa.	0.554	cum	1,623.00	899.00	
4.	Brickwork in cement mortar 1 : 4.	0.760	cum	1,760.00	1,338.00	
5.	Cement concrete 1 : 2 : 4.	0.264	cum	2,373.00	626.00	
6.	M.S. reinforcement	21.760	kg	20.831	453.00	
7.	Hire and labour charges for shuttering and centering	1.766	sqm	35.00	62.00	
8.	Cement and sand plastering 1 : 4, 15 mm thick	1.80	sqm	53.00	95.00	
9.	Supplying and fixing in position with cement mortar 1:4 Master trap 150 × 150 mm	1 No.	Each	390.00	390.00	
10.	Supplying and fixing 100 mm dia. C.I. soil pipe including bend for vent pipe	3	m	76.00	228.00	
11.	Supplying and fixing C.I. inlet for 100 mm dia. mica valve	1 No.	Each	73.00	73.00	
12.	Supplying and fixing 450 mm dia. C.I. manhole cover	1 No.	Each	290.00	290.00	
					4,652.00	
	Add contigency @ 5%				233.00	
					4,885.00	
	Add work establishment @ 2.5%				122.00	
					5,007.00	

5.3.6 Manhole

Mainholes are required to be provided in the sewer lines for the purposes as mentioned below:

(*i*) Providing connection of lateral sewer, feed sewer, domestic sewer or branch sewer.

(*ii*) At every bend, junction in the sewer line for easy flow of the effluent.

(*iii*) In straight lengths also, manholes need be provided at every 80 m interval, even if there be no bend or angle.

These are constructed in masonry and provided with manhole cover for easy entry of labour inside for cleaning.

Manhole may be shallow or deep as required according to the depth of the sewer line.

Example 5.10. *Estimate the cost of a masonry manhole, square in shape, 1.0 × 1.0 m, the total depth up to the invert of the sewer 3.150 mm.*

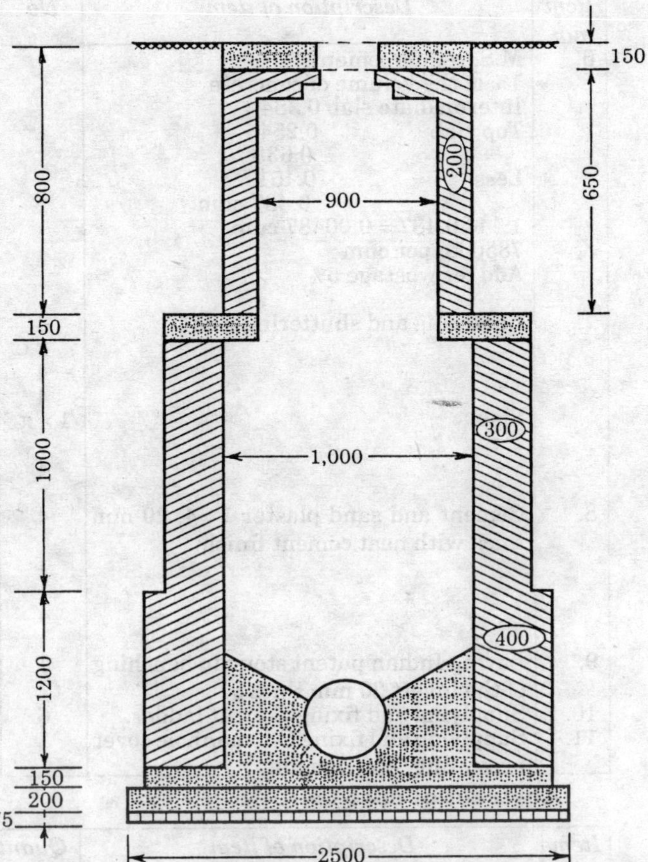

Figure 5.11. Manhole

Estimate

Item no.	Description of item	No.	Measurements Length	Breadth	Height	Content	Remarks
1.	Earthwork in excavation	1	2.50	2.50	3.575	22.344	cum
2.	Single brick flat soling.	1	2.50	2.50		6.25	sqm
3.	Cement concrete 1 : 3 : 6 with Jhama Khoa.	1	2.50	2.50	0.20	1.25	cum
4.	Brickwork in cement mortar 1 : 4.	4	1.40	0.40	1.20	2.688	
		4	1.30	0.30	1.00	1.560	
		4	1.10	0.20	0.650	0.572	
	Corbel	4	0.70	0.20	0.20	0.112	
						4.932	cum
5.	Cement concrete 1 : 2 : 4	1	1.80	1.80	0.15	0.486	
		1	1.00	1.00	0.15	0.15	
					(av.)		
	Intermediate slab	1	1.60	1.60	0.15	0.384	
	Top slab	1	1.30	1.30	0.15	0.254	
						1.274	cum
	Less	1	0.90	0.90	0.15	0.122	
		$1 \times \pi \times \frac{0.50^2}{4} \times 0.15$				0.029	
					(–)	0.151	
						1.123	cum

(*Contd..*)

Item no.	Description of item	No.	Measurements Length	Breadth	Height	Content	Remarks
6.	M.S. reinforcement.						
	1% of the volume of concrete						
	Intermediate slab 0.384						
	Top slab 0.254						
	0.638						
	Less 0.151						
	0.487 cum						
	1% of 0.487 = 0.00487 cum						
	7850 kg per cum				38.23		
	Add for wastage 5%				1.911		
					40.141	kg	
7.	Centering and shuttering Band.	4	1.80	0.15		1.08	
		2	1.00	0.10		0.20	
		4	0.90	0.15		0.54	
		4	1.60	0.15		0.96	
	Slab	1 × π	.50	0.50		1.96	
			4				
		4	1.30	0.15		0.78	sqm
						5.52	
8.	Cement and sand plaster 1 : 4, 20 mm thick with neat cement finish.	4	1.0	2.05		8.20	
		1	0.90	0.10		0.09	
		1	1.00	0.10		0.10	
		4	0.90	0.95		3.42	
						11.81	sqm
9.	Laying Indian patent stone in benching of the invert 20 mm thick.	1	1.00	1.00		1.00	sqm
10.	Supplying and fixing C.I. cat ladder.	6				6 Nos.	
11.	Supplying and fixing C.I. manhole cover heavy duty 450 mm dia.	1				1 No.	

Abstract of cost

Item No.	Description of item	Quantity	Unit	Rate	Amount	Remarks
1.	Earthwork in excavation.	22.344	%cum	2973.00	664.00	
2.	Single brick flat soling.	6.25	sqm	95.00	594.00	
3.	Cement concrete 1 : 3 : 6 with Jhama khoa.	1.25	cum	1623.00	2,029.00	
4.	Brickwork in cement mortar 1 : 4.	4,932	cum	1,760.00	8680.00	
5.	Cement concrete 1 : 2 : 4.	1,123	cum	2,373.00	2,665.00	
6.	M.S. reinforcement.	40.141	kg	20.831.00	836.00	
7.	Centering and shuttering.	5,52	sqm	35.00	193.00	
8.	Cement and sand plaster 1 : 4, 20 mm thick.	11.81	sqm	62.00	732.00	
9.	Laying Indian patent stone in benching of the invert 20 mm thick with neat cement finish	1.00	sqm	73.00	73.00	
10.	Supplying and fixing C.I. cat ladder	6 Nos.	Each	10.00	60.00	
11.	Supplying and fixing C.I. manhole cover heavy duty 450 mm dia.	1 No.	Each	1040.00	1040.00	
					17,566.00	
	Add contingency @ 5%		Rs.		845.00	
			Rs.		18,411.00	
	Add work establishment @ 2.5%		Rs.		460.00	
					18,871.00	

5.4.0 INTERNAL PLUMBING AND WATER SUPPLY ESTIMATE

Estimation of internal plumbing and water supply lines require preparation of drawing superimposing on the building drawing in plan and in elevation, showing the necessary lines and location of the different sanitary and plumbing installations.

Mode of measurement

The soil and the waste water lines are provided with C.I. pipes of required diameter varying from 75 mm to 150 mm and are measured linearly in meters. These lines may be provided with P.V.C. pipes also. Waste water lines may be of C.I./P.V.C/Asbestos cement pipes. These are measured linearly.

Water supply lines are provided with G.I. pipes or hard P.V.C. pipes. These are also measured linearly in meters.

In both the cases, some fittings are required. The lengths are measured of the pipe's lengths and the fittings are added separately in numbers according to their size and type. However, in both the cases, the lengths may be measured including the fittings in position. In such case cost of the lines with fittings shall have to be analysed before.

The sanitary fittings—Indian type or commode type pan, wash-basin, sink, flushing cistern, flush pipe, valves, bibcock, etc. are measured in numbers. These may be traditional variety of C.I. or G.I. or porcelain. However, now a days other varieties of pipes and fittings of the materials — polythene, fibre glass, stainless steel are available. These also may be used as convenient and suitable.

Drawing for sanitary and plumbing lines should be prepared carefully, so that the length of the pipes needed may be minimum.

It may be necessary to lay the pipes above ground level or may have to be laid below ground. While laying soil pipe below ground level, it should be protected by covering with cement concrete. G.I. pipe laid underground should be laid over sand bed of minimum 150 mm thick. The pipes laid underground should be given a coat of painting over a coat of anticorrosive paint. When the pipe above crosses a wall, sleeve should be provided, through which the pipe should be laid.

The vertical pipes should be perfectly vertical and fixed with strong clamps and bobins as required.

In water supply lines, long screw shall be provided suitably for easy taking out of the pipes as required.

The polythene pipes may be joined either by special fittings meant for the purpose or may be joined by ordinary plain G.I. fittings.

Example 5.11: *Prepare a cost estimate of internal plumbing and water supply of a two storeyed building having of Indian type W.C. in the ground floor and a commode type W.C. in the first floor with one water supply tab in each bath and kitchen as shown in drawing No. 5.12.*

Estimate

Item no.	Description of item	No.	Measurements			Content	Waste
			Length	Breadth	Height		
	A. **Indian type W.C.**						
1	Supplying and fixing Indian type porcelain pan 450 mm long in ground floor, fixed with cement and sand mortar 1 : 4.	1				1 No.	

(*Contd..*)

Item no.	Description of item	No.	Measurements Length	Breadth	Height	Content	Waste
2	Supplying and fixing porcelain foot-rest, 250 × 150 mm, set in cement and sand mortar 1 :4.	1				1 pair	
3	Supplying and fixing C.I. P-trap 100 mm dia. with horn	1				1 No.	
4	Supplying and fixing C.I. extension piece 100 mm dia. 225 mm long for connection with the vertical stack	1				1 No.	
5	Cutting chase hole in 250 mm thick wall for soil pipe 100 mm dia. and making good to damages and fixing pipe	1				1 No.	
6	Supplying and fixing 10 lt capacity flushing cistern on a pair of C.I. bracket including painting two coats	1				1 set	
7	Supplying and fixing 32 mm dia. 2.00 m long G.I. flush pipe including joining with porcelain pan at one end and with cistern at the other end.	1				1 set	
8	Supplying and fixing 50 mm dia. vent pipe (antisyohonage pipe) joining with horn of C.I. trap and C.I. vent pipe including cutting chase in 250 mm thick wall as necessary 1 m long.	1				1 No.	

Item No.	Description of item	No.	Measurements Length	Breadth	Height	Content	Waste
	B. **Commode type W.C.**						
1	Supplying and fixing Commode type W.C. of Porcelain 460 mm long including trap with horn.	1				1 set	
2	Supplying and fixing C.I. extension piece 100 mm dia. 225 mm long	1				1 No.	
3	Supplying and fixing 50 mm dia. C.I. antisyphonage pipe joining with horn of commode trap and vertical vent pipe including cutting chase in 250 mm wall	0.50				0.50	m
4	Supplying and fixing lowdown porcelain flushing tank 15 lt. capacity including 32 mm flush pipe	1				1 No.	
	C. **External pipe lines**						
1	Supplying and fixing C.I. soil pipe (light) 100 mm dia. including supply of C.I. bobins, hooks, etc. as required and C.I. fittings, bends, junctions with door for vertical stack	1	8.00			8.00	m
2	Supplying and fixing 100 mm dia. cowl	2				2 Nos.	
3	Supplying and fixing C.I. pipes for waste water including supply of bends, junctions with door, bobins and hooks, etc. as required	1	8.00			8.00	m
4	Supplying and laying C.I. soil pipe under ground	1	1.00			1.00	m

(*Contd..*)

Item No.	Description of item	No.	Measurements			Content	Waste
			Length	Breadth	Height		
	D. Water supply						
1	Construction of R.C.C. water storage tank 1,000 lt. capacity keeping provision for C.I. water tight cover with locking arrangement, 40 mm dia. over flow and 20 mm dia. outlet	1				1 No.	
2	Supplying and fixing 20 mm dia. supply pipe above ground including painting two coats	1	7.00			7.00	
		1	5.00			5.00	
						12.00	m
3	Supplying and fixing 15 mm dia. G.I. pipe for distribution system including painting two coats	2	2.00			4.00	
		1	1.00			1.00	
						5.00	m
4	Supplying and fixing gunmetal fullway valve						
	32 mm dia.	1				1 No.	
	20 mm dia.	2				2 Nos.	
5	Supplying and fixing bibcock 15 mm dia. brass chromium plated.	4				4 Nos.	
6	Construction of masonry ground reservoir of capacity 10,000 lts.	1				1 No.	
7	Supplying and fixing porcelain wash basin 550 × 400 mm including waste and waste water drainage pipe 1.50 m long.	1				1 No.	
8	Supplying and fixing sink including fixing waste and waste water drainage G.I. pipe extention up to 1.50 m long fixing on C.I. bracket complete	1				1 No.	
9	Supplying and fixing chromium plated shower rose 150 mm dia. including bend, etc. as necessary complete	1				1 No.	
10	Supplying and fixing centrifugal pump 1.5 H.P for lifting water from Ground reservoir to house-top storage tank	1				1 No.	

ABSTRACT OF COST

Item no.	Description of item	Quantity	Unit	Rate	Amount	Remarks
	A. Indian type W.C.					
1	Supplying and fixing Indian type porcelain pan 450 mm long in ground floor, fixed with cement and sand mortar 1 : 4	1 No.	Each	325.00	325.00	
2	Supplying and fixing porcelain foot-rest, 250 × 150 mm, set in cement and sand mortar 1 : 4	1 Pair	Each Pair	99.00	99.00	
3	Supplying and fixing C.I. P-trap 100 mm dia. with horn	1 No.	Each	298.00	298.00	
4	Supplying and fixing C.I. extension piece 100 mm. dia. 225 mm long for connection with vertical stack	1 No.	Each	178.00	178.00	

(Contd..)

Item no.	Description of item	Quantity	Unit	Rate	Amount	Remarks
5	Cutting chase-hole in 250 mm thick wall for soil pipe 100 mm dia. and making good to damages and fixing pipe	1	Each	25.00	25.00	
6	Supplying and fixing 10 lt. capacity flushing cistern on a pair of C.I. bracket, including painting two coats	1 Set	Set	652.00	652.00	
7	Supplying and fixing 32 mm dia. 2.00 m long G.I. flush pipe including joining with porcelain pan at one end and with cistern at the other end	1 Set	Set	236.00	236.00	
8	Supplying and fixing 50 mm dia. vent pipe (antisyphonage pipe) joining with horn of C.I. trap and C.I. vent pipe including cutting chase in 250 mm thick wall as necessary, 1 m long.	1 No.	Each	147.00	147.00	
					1,960.00	
	B. **Commode type W.C**					
1	Supplying and fixing Commode type W.C. of porcelain 460 mm long with trap and horn	1	Set	697.00	697.00	
2	Supplying and fixing C.I. extension piece 100 mm dia. 225 mm long	1	Each	178.00	178.00	
3	Supplying and fixing 50 mm dia. C.I. antisyphonage pipe joining with horn of commode trap and vertical vent pipe including cutting chase in 250 mm wall	0.50	m	147.00	74.00	
4	Supplying and fixing lowdown porcelain flushing tank 15 lt. capacity including 32 mm flush pipe	1	No.	1,895.00	1,895.00	
					2,844.00	
	C. **External pipe lines**					
1	Supplying and fixing C.I. soil pipe line (light) 100 mm dia. including supply of C.I. bobins, hooks, etc. as required and C.I. fittings, bends, junction with door for vertical stack.	8.00 m	m	244.00	1,952.00	
2	Supplying and fixing 100 mm dia. cowl.	2 Nos.	Each	87.00	174.00	
3	Supplying and fixing C.I. pipes for waste water including supply of bends junctions with door, bobins and hooks, etc. as required.	8.00 m	m	206.00	1,648.00	
4	Supplying and laying C.I. soil pipe under ground.	1.00	m	244.00	244.00	
					4,018.00	
	D. **Water supply**					
1	Construction of R.C.C. water storage tank 1,000 lt. capacity keeping provision for C.I. water tight cover with locking arrangement, 40 mm dia. over flow and 20 mm dia. outlet.	1 No.	Each	5,000.00	5,000.00	

(*Contd..*)

Item no.	*Description of item*	*Quantity*	*Unit*	*Rate*	*Amount*	*Remarks*
2	Supplying and fixing 20 mm dia. supply pipe above ground including painting two coats.	12.00 m	m	94.00	1,128.00	
3	Supplying and fixing 15 mm dia. G.I. pipe for distribution system including painting two coats.	5.00 m	m	90.00	450.00	
4	Supplying and fixing gunmetal fullway valve.					
	32 mm dia.	1 No.	Each	526.00	526.00	
	20 mm dia.	2 Nos.	Each	220.00	440.00	
5	Supplying and fixing bibcock 15 mm dia. brass chromium plated.	4 Nos.	Each	222.00	888.00	
6	Construction of masonry reservoir of capacity 10,000 lts.	1 No.	Each	25,000.00	25,000.00	
7	Supplying and fixing porcelain wash basin 550 × 400 mm including waste and waste water drainage pipe 1.50 m, complete.	1 No.	Each	947.00	947.00	
8	Supplying and fixing sink including fixing waste and waste water drainage G.I. pipe extension up to 1.50 long fixing on C.I. bracket, complete 600 mm × 450 mm × 200 mm.	.1 No.	Each	275.00	275.00	
9	Supplying and fixing chromium plated shower rose 150 mm dia. including bend, etc. as necessary	1 No.	Each	114.00	114.00	
10	Supplying and fixing centrifugal pump 1.50 H.p. for lifting water from ground reservoir to housetop storage tank	1 No.	Each	986.00	986.00	
					35,754.00	

General Abstract of Cost

Item no.	*Description of item*	*Quantity*	*Unit*	*Rate*	*Amount*	*Remarks*
A	Indian type W.C.			Rs.	1,960.00	
B	Commode type W.C.			Rs.	2,844.00	
C	External pipe lines			Rs.	4,018.00	
D	Water supply			Rs.	35,754.00	
	Total				44,576.00	
	Add contingency @ 5%			Rs.	2,229.00	
					46,805.00	
	Add work establishment @ 2.5%			Rs.	1,170.00	
					47,975.00	

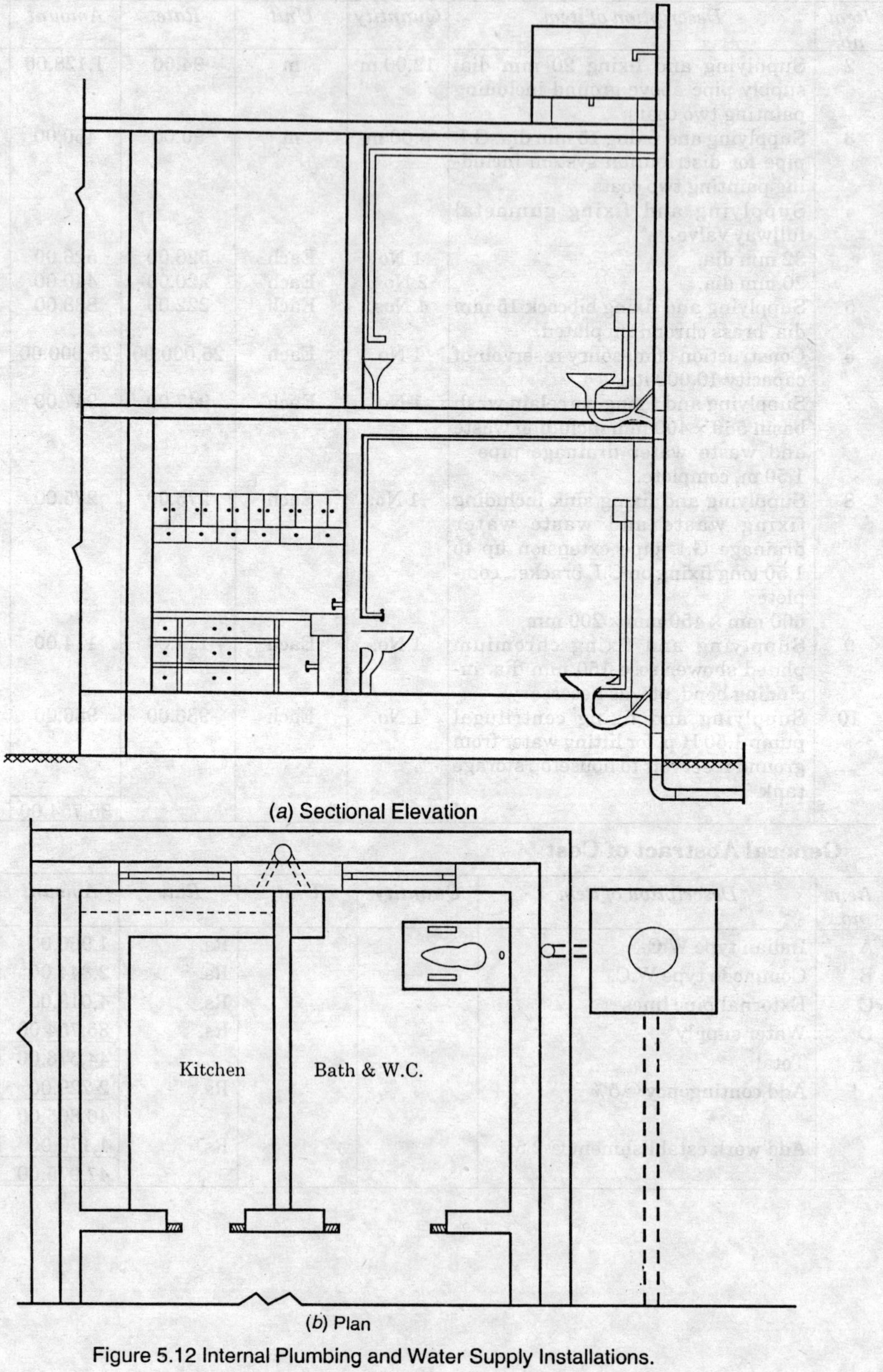

(*a*) Sectional Elevation

(*b*) Plan

Figure 5.12 Internal Plumbing and Water Supply Installations.

6

ELECTRIFICATION

6.1.0 ELECTRIFICATION OF BUILDING

Prior to preparation of an estimate for electrification of a building the following points need be clarified :

(*i*) Type of wire to be used,

(*ii*) Provision of light, fan and power points required,

(*iii*) Number of circuits to be built, and

(*iv*) Requirement of total power.

6.1.1 Electrification of Building Comprises of Different Parts

(*a*) ***Service connection.*** Service connection of a building is done by the Electric supply authority on requisition for which certain fees are required to be paid by the applicant.

(*b*) ***Electric wiring.*** Electric wiring is laid in the building for required distribution of electric power within the premises from the supply point to different points, like—light, power, etc. through the meter.

Types of wiring

Electric wire drawn in the premises may be of various systems :

(*a*) Batten wiring system where electric wire is laid on wooden battens. P.V.C. battens are also used in wiring, now-a-days.

(*b*) Surface conduit system — where electric wire is drawn through steel tube fixed on the wall.

(*c*) Concealed conduit wiring — Electric wire is drawn through conduit of steel tube or P.V.C. pipe laid concealed in wall or ceiling during construction.

Provision of light, fan and power points

Requirements of different number of points for light, fan and power shall be assessed according to the necessity. The requirement may be tabulated for assessing actual requirement of power.

6.1.2 Requirement of Electric Power on Area Basis

(*i*)	Normal lighting.	20 watts per sq m
(*ii*)	Lighting with lifts, pumps but without air conditioning.	30 watts per sq m
(*iii*)	Additional capacities for technical building like laboratories, hospitals, etc.	11 watts per sq m
(*iv*)	Additional capacity for air conditioning (of air conditioned area)	100 watts per sqm

6.1.3 Rating of Lamp, Fan and Socket — Outlet Points

While estimating the current to be carried by any conductor for loading of circuits, the figures as indicated in I.S. 732 - 1963 shall be assumed unless otherwise specified.

Wattage of each illuminating body and other equipments are mentioned on the body of the article.

Example 6.1. *Prepare a detailed estimate for electrification of a two storeyed building as shown in the plan of ground floor assuming that electrification of the first floor shall be the same as that of ground floor. The wiring shall be with P.V.C., Aluminium wire on wooden batten. Provision for electric points shall be as below.*

Drawing room — One ceiling fan, one tube light, two bracket lights, and a power plug 5 amp.

Each bed room — One tube light, one bracket light, one ceiling fan, one bed light, and a power plug 5 amp.

Dining space — One tube light, one bracket light, one fan, and a power plug.

Kitchen — One bracket light, one tube light, one fan, one power plug - 5 amp, and a power plug 15 amp.

W.C. and bath each — One bracket light.

Stair case — One bracket light with twin control light and one under side of the landing.

Main gate — One bracket light and one calling bell.

Schedule of points

Sl. no.	*Particulars of location*	*Light no.*	*Tube no.*	*Fan no.*	*Plug No. 5 amp*	*Power Plug no. 15 amp*	*Bell no.*	*Remarks*
1	Drawing room	2	1	1	1	–	–	
2	Bed room 3.1 × 3.1 m	2	1	1	1	–	–	
3	Bed room 4.1 × 3.5 m	2	1	1	1	–	–	
4	Dining space	1	1	1	1	–	–	
5	Kitchen	1	1	–	1	1	–	
6	W.C. & bath (2 Nos.)	2	–	–	–	–	–	
7	Store	1	–	–	–	–	–	
8	Stair case	2 + 1	–	–	–	–	–	
9	Main gate	1	–	–	–	–	1	
		15	5	4	5	1	1	

Total number of points = 15 + 5 + 4 + 5 + 1 + 1 = 30 plus 1 power plug.

Connected load (assuming wattage per point according to I.S. 732)

Wattage of light points 15 × 60	= 900 watt
Wattage of tube light points 5 × 40	= 200 watt
Wattage of fan points 4 × 60	= 240 watt
Wattage of plug points 5 amp. 5 × 60	= 300 watt
Wattage of power plug 15 amp. 1 × 2,000	= 2,000 watt
Wattage of calling bell 1 × 60	= 60 watt
	3,700 watt

The power supply authority will provide meter for power in accordance with the connected load.

No. of circuits :

Separate circuit will be provided for the 15 amp power plug. So total wattage excluding the circuit for the power plug = 1,700 watt

Supply voltage available = 230 volt

Total load permitted in a circuit = 500 watt

Number of circuits required $= \frac{1700}{500} = 3$

Number of points 30 and number of circuits = 3

So number of points per circuit = 30/3 = 10

Total number of circuits = 3 + 1 = 4

Total number of points per circuit does not exceed 10.

Main switch: The line current in the main switch $= \frac{3,700}{230} = 16.09$ amps

Main switch to be provided of capacity 30 amps, 230 volts.

Provision for future alterations for the main board and for 4 circuit, provide 4-way Distribution board.

Estimate

Item no.	*Description of item*	*Quantity*	*Unit*	*Rate*	*Amount*	*Remarks*
1	Supplying and fixing metal clad 30 amp Grade I main switch I.S.I mark brand with all necessary kit kat inside the premises	1 No.	Each	120.00	120.00	
2	Supplying fitting and fixing 4 - way 15 amp metal distribution box (concealed type) approved brand with necessary cutting in the walls and finishing the same	1 No.	Each	150.00	150.00	
3	Drawing internal circuit lines with 2.5 Sq mm two single core P.V.C. Aluminium wire in 20 mm dia. alkathene conduit with 14 s.w.g. G.I. earthing attachment from distribution box of different switch boards	10 × 6.00 = 60.00	m	12.00	720.00	
4	Supplying 2.50 Sq mm two single core P.V.C. Aluminium wire of approved brand (length 3 times the length of travel)	180	m	75.00	13,500.00	
5	Supplying and fixing metal concealed switch boxes with milk white paste cover for					
	(*a*) One regulator and 5 piano type switch for one plug point	3 Nos.	Each	60.00	180.00	
	(*b*) For one piano type switch and one for plug	3 Nos.	Each	25.00	75.00	

(Contd..)

Item no.	Description of item	Quantity	Unit	Rate	Amount	Remarks
	(*c*) For one piano type switch only	5 Nos.	Each	75/-	375.00	
	(*d*) Switch board for 15 amp power plug	1 No.	Each	25/-	25.00	
6	Providing and drawing cables for lights, fans, calling bell, 5 amp plug points with $2 \times 1 \times 1.40$ single core P.V.C. insulated and sheathing wire in 19 mm in black stone enamelled conduit/G.I. conduit to light/fan/call bell point and painting conduit and piano type anchor switches or any other approved brand including cutting necessary chases on wall surface and laying in R.C.C. wherever required before casting and mending good damages, complete (av. 6.0 m run)	30 points	Each	175/-	5,250.00	
7	Providing and drawing cables for 2-way staircase light point as in item No. 6	2 points	Each	160/-	320.00	
8	Providing and laying cables for 15 amp plug points with 2×6 sq mm P.V.C Aluminium stranded wire of approved brand as in item no. 6	1 point	Each	160/-	160.00	
9	Supplying fitting and fixing fan clamps of 12 mm dia. M.S. rod before casting of concrete	4 Nos.	Each	15/-	60.00	
10	Earthing with 50 mm dia. G.I. pipe class B medium quality driven in ground for a length of 3.0 m with top end 30 cm below G.L. connected with G.I. wire no. 6 S.W.G. or copper conductor as per drawing and in accordance with I.S. 3043 Code of practice for Earthing	1 Set	Each	300/-	300.00	
11	Charges for service connection payable to power supply authority for meter, main fuse, earthing, drawing cables, etc.	1 Item	Each	800/-	800.00	
12	Charges payable to the Electric supply authority for temporary service connection	1 Item	Each	400/-	400.00	
13	Supplying and fixing in position 122 cm (48 inch) ceiling fan with regulator and fitting complete	4 Nos	Each	750/-	3,000.00	
14	Supplying and fixing Fluorescent lamps (Tube) 1,200 mm long with fittings of approved quality and make	5 Nos.	Each	250/-	1,250.00	
15	Supplying light bulbs including fixing	15 Nos.	Each	10/-	150.00	
16	Supplying and fixing call bell of approved quality and make including fixing the same in position with necessary fittings	1 No.	Each	100/-	100.00	
	Total for one floor				26,935/-	
	For two floors				53870.00	
	Add contingency @ 5%				2,694.00	
					56,564.00	
	Add work establishment @ 2.5%				1,414.00	
					57,978.00	

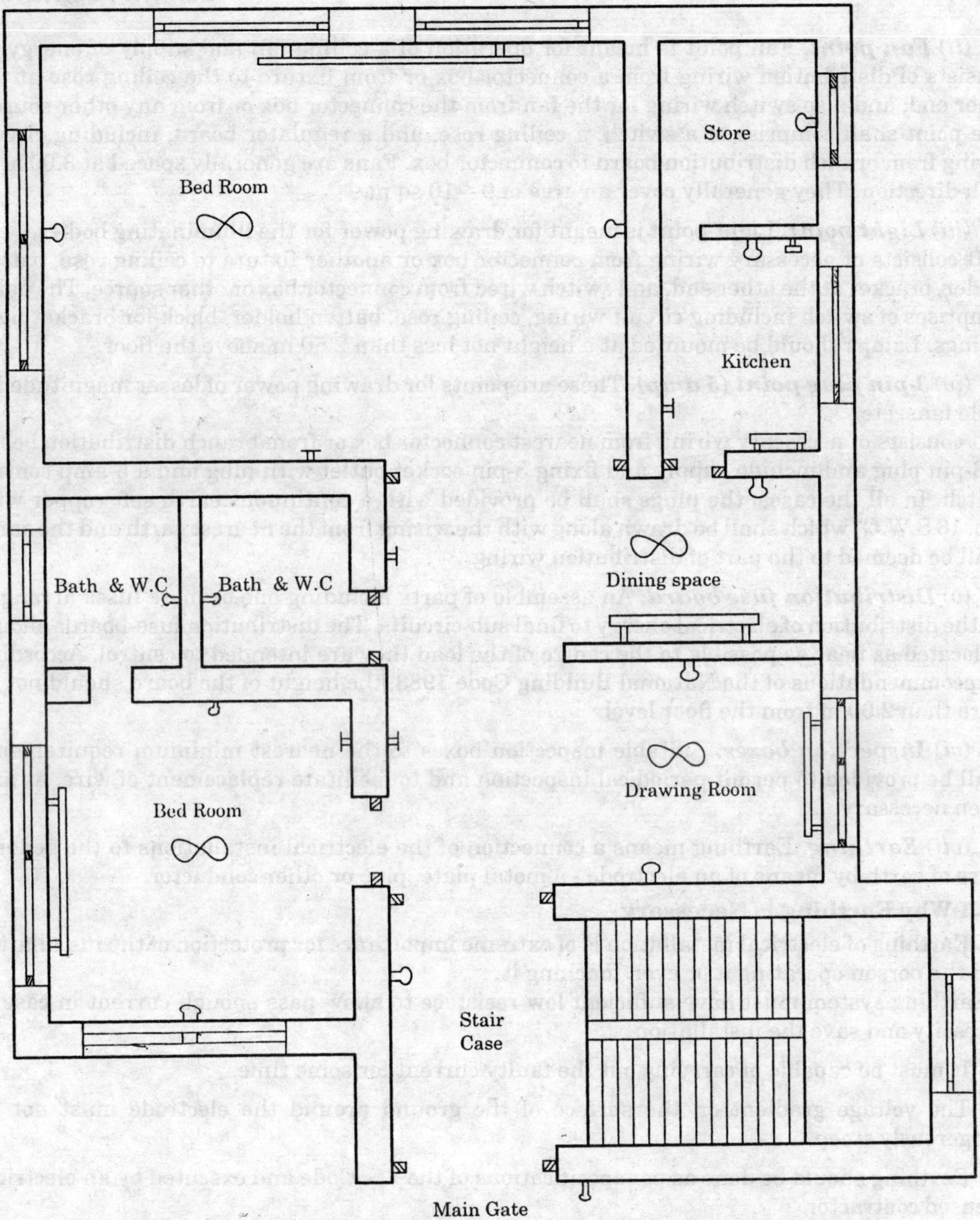

Figure 6.1 PLAN SHOWING DISTRIBUTION OF ELECTRICAL INSTALLATIONS.

6.2.0 DESCRIPTION OF ITEMS

(*i*) *Points.* A point means a power point for supplying energy to illuminating body or fan or a plug point. It consists of the branch wiring from distribution board, switch as required, ceiling rose when required, socket-outlet or suitable termination. A three pin socket-outlet shall include in addition, the connecting cable or wire from earth pin of the socket to the earth stud of the branch distribution board.

(*ii*) ***Fan point.*** Fan point is meant for operation of a ceiling fan and supply of energy. It consists of distribution wiring from a connector box or from fixture to the ceiling rose at the other end; and also switch wiring for the fan from the connector box or from any other source. The point shall comprise of a switch, a ceiling rose, and a regulator board, including circuit wiring from branch distribution board to connector box. Fans are generally spaced at 3.00 m in both direction. They generally cover an area of 9 – 10 sq m.

(*iii*) ***Light point.*** Light point is meant for drawing power for the illuminating bodies.

It consists of necessary wiring from connector box or another fixture to ceiling rose, batten holder, bracket at the other end, and switch wired from connector box or other source. The point comprises of switch including circuit wiring, ceiling rose, batten holder, block for bracket light fittings. Lamps should be mounted at a height not less than 2.50 m above the floor.

(*iv*) ***3-pin plug point (5 amp).*** These are points for drawing power of lesser magnitude for table fans, etc.

It consists of necessary wiring from nearest connector box or from branch distribution board to 3-pin plug and include supply and fixing 3-pin socket outlet with plug and a 5-amp control switch. In all the cases, the plugs shall be provided with a continuous earth soft copper wire (No. 16 S.W.G) which shall be drawn along with the wiring from the nearest earth and the same shall be deemed to the part of distribution wiring.

(*v*) ***Distribution fuse board.*** An assemble of parts including one or more fuses arranged for the distribution of electrical energy to final sub-circuits. The distribution fuse-boards should be located as near as possible to the centre of the load they are intended to control. According to recommendations of the National Building Code 1983, the height of the board should not be more than 2.00 m from the floor level.

(*vi*) **I*nspection boxes.*** Suitable inspection boxes to the nearest minimum requirements shall be provided to permit periodical inspection and to facilitate replacement of wire, as and when necessary.

(*vii*) ***Earthing.*** Earthing means a connection of the electrical installations to the general mass of earth by means of an electrode - a metal plate, pipe or other conductor.

6.2.1 Why Earthing is Necessary

Earthing of electrical installation is of extreme importance for protection of the installation and the person operating it or even touching it.

Earthing system must have sufficient low resistace to allow pass enough current in case of necessity and save the installation.

It must be capable of carrying out the faulty current for some time.

The voltage gradient on the surface of the ground around the electrode must not be dangerously steep.

Earthing should be done as per specifications of the I.S. Code and executed by an electrical licensed contractor.

6.2.2 Circuit Breaker

It is a device installed in each circuit. The device consists of a fuse which melts at a certain point when the temperature in the wire exceeds that limit and breaks the circuit and saves the electrical installation and prevents fire in the premises.

6.2.3 Fire Resisting Paints

Paints are available which can resist high temperature in cases of emergency and protect the electrical installation and the wiring. This paint need be applied on the wiring.

7

IRRIGATION WORKS

7.1.0 IRRIGATION WORKS

Irrigation works comprise of various structures.

The structures are canals of different types and forms for carrying water from the source for distribution to different places where the same will be utilised.

Earthen Dams across a water way are built for storing water during rainy season or during flood and are then used during the lean season for irrigation purpose or for generating hydro-electric power.

Weirs are constructed across a flowing channel for controlling the flow of the channel.

Sluice gates are provided in the path of a flowing channel with gate for controlling the flow as desired or for completely closing the flow when required.

Aqueduct

Aqueduct is provided for channelising two different kinds of flows crossing each other. It is like viaduct in Road Works. Viaduct is provided for channelising the flow of two different categories of traffic crossing without interruption of flow of any. Similarly, aqueduct is provided for channelising two different flows *e.g.* irrigation water and fowl drainage water without mixing the two. The two different channels flow uniterrupted one above the other.

Hume pipe and hume pipe siphon

Simple hume pipe channels are provided for the passage of water across an embankment. Hume pipe siphon is provided when the level of invert of hume pipe below the embankment does not permit natural easy flow. In such case, the hume pipe invert below the embankment is lowered and then after crossing the embankment the invert is raised. The flow is affected due to siphonic action of the closed pipe section.

7.2.0 CANAL WORKS

Canals for irrigation work is important and constitute a major part of it. Canals are generally of different types and mostly constructed of earth and on ground.

7.2.1 Three Types of Canals

There are three types of canal sections.

(*i*) Canals partly in excavation,

(*ii*) Canals partly in excavation and partly in embankment, and

(*iii*) Canal fully in embankment.

7.2.2 Canals Fully in Excavation (Figure 7.1)

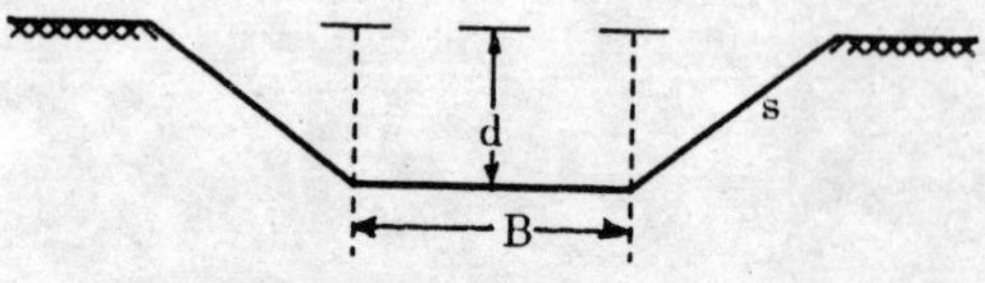

Figure 7.1 Canal Fully Excavated

B = Bed width,

d = Depth of excavation,

s = Side slope, 3 : 1 meaning horizontal 3 and vertical 1, and is referred as $s = 3$,

Sectional area $= B.d + s.d^2$.

Quantity of earthwork = Sectional area × length.

The quantity of earthwork is calculated either by mid section formula or by Average end area formula applying Simpson's Rule as explained in the Chapter on Road Works.

7.2.3 Land Width Required

Permanent land width required $= B + 2sd$.

In addition to the permanent land width, some additional land width may be required for the spoil bank or other purpose. The same also should be taken into consideration.

Area of permanent land = Width of permanent land × length.

7.2.4 Canals Partly in Embankment and Partly in Excavation (Figure 7.2)

B = Bed width of the canal,

d = Depth of excavation,

h = Height of embankment,

H = Height of banking from bed of the canal,

$h = H - d$

Free board is the extra depth of the embankment over the designed level of the canal water.

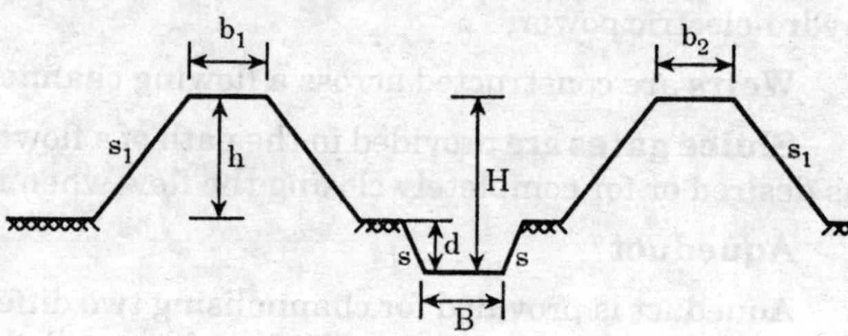

Figure 7.2 Canal Partly Excavated and partly in Embankment

b_1 and b_2 are the top widths of the banking. These are generally the same; but may be different, if any service road is provided for inspection of the canal, it is generally provided on the left bank.

Sectional area of excavation $= Bd + sd^2$

Sectional area of banking $= (b_1 + b_2)\, h + 2s_1 h^2$

Quantity of excavation and banking are calculated on the same method as mentioned in case of canal fully in excavation.

Balanced depth of digging or economical section

When the quantities of earthwork in excavation and banking are equal, the section is termed economical and the depth of digging is termed 'balanced'.

Quantity of digging = Quantity of banking

i.e. Sectional area of digging = Sectional area of two banks

or, $$Bd + sd^2 = (b_1 + b_2)\, h + 2s_1 h^2$$

When the quantity of earthwork in excavation is more than the quantity of banking, the surplus earth is utilised to form spoil bank.

When the quantity of earthwork in excavation is less than the earth required for banking, the extra quantity of earth required is taken from the borrow pits dug along the bank in extra width of land.

While making provision in estimate for banking, the quantities of extra earth required from borrow pit is taken into consideration.

If Q_1 and Q_2 are the quantities of earthwork in excavation and banking respectively, the quantity of earthwork in banking $= Q_2 - Q_1$.

If Q_2 is less than Q_1, no earthwork is banking is considered in estimate.

7.2.5 Canal Fully in Embankment (Figure 7.3)

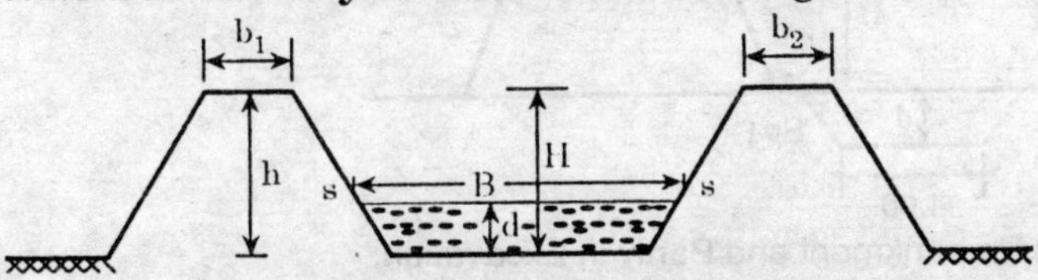

Figure 7.3 Canal Fully in Embankment

B = Bed width,

H = Height of banking from the bed of the canal,

d = depth of filling below the bed of canal up to the ground level,

d is denoted as + ve for cutting and – ve for filling

h = Height of banking $= H - (-d)$

Sectional area of banking $= (b_1 + b_2)\, h + 2s_1\, h^2$,

In the estimate no earthwork need be provided for the depth $(-d)$ between ground level and canal bed. This depth will be filled up in due course by silting.

But in case, the canal is fully in embankment for the entire down stream side and the bed level is above ground level then provision for earthwork for this portion need be made. The quantity is found considering the whole area as solid first and then deducting the canal area.

Sectional area

= Central area + (Outside slope areas) – area of canal.

$= (xh + 2s_1h^2) - (BH + s_1H^2)$

Where, $x = B + b_1 + b_2 + 2s_1\, H^2$

Obtaining the net sectional area, the same need be multiplied by the length as mentioned before.

Example 7.1 *Calculate the quantity of earthwork of a portion of channel with the following data:*

Bed width = 4 m,

Free board = 500 mm

Slope of excavation = 1 : 1

Slope of banking = 2 : 1

Fully supply depth = 1.0 m

Top width of both embankment = 2.00 m

Ground levels and bed levels at distances of every 30.00 m are as below :

Chainage	*Ground level*	*Proposed bed level*
0.00 m	210.20	210.00
30.00 m	210.80	209.80
60.00 m	209.80	209.60
90.00 m	209.60	209.40
120.00 m	209.50	209.20
150.00 m	209.30	209.00

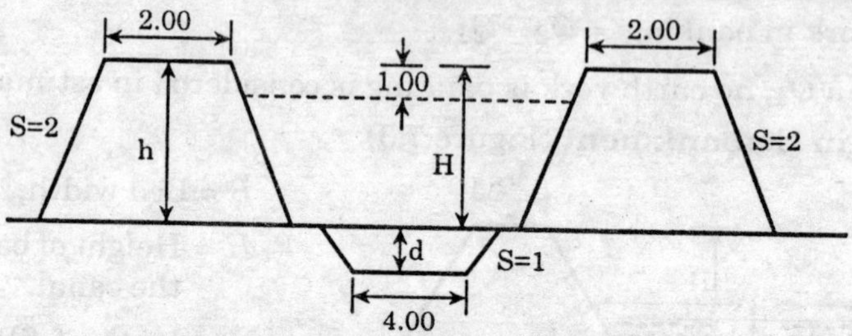

Figure 7.4 Canal Partly in Embankment and Partly in Excavation.

Volume of earthwork is calculated in tabular form as follows :

Example 7.2 *An irrigation canal has the following details :*

Bed width	5.00 m
Top width of left bank	3.00 m
Top width of right bank	1.50 m
Side slopes in cutting	1 : 1
Side slopes in banking (both)	$1\frac{1}{2}:1$
Height of banks from bed	2.55 m
Longitudinal slope of the bed	1 in 5000

There is no transverse slope of the bed and the ground. Ground levels at 6 consecutive sections at 50 m intervals are as under.

Station	1	2	3	4	5	6
G.L (m) R.L.	100.00	100.31	100.52	100.57	99.68	99.21

Bed level at station 1 (m), R.L. 98.50.

Estimate the quantity of earthwork in cutting and banking.

Longitudinal slope of the bed = 1 : 5000

Stations at intervals of 50 m. So there would be level difference between the stations of $\frac{50}{5000} = 0.01$ m

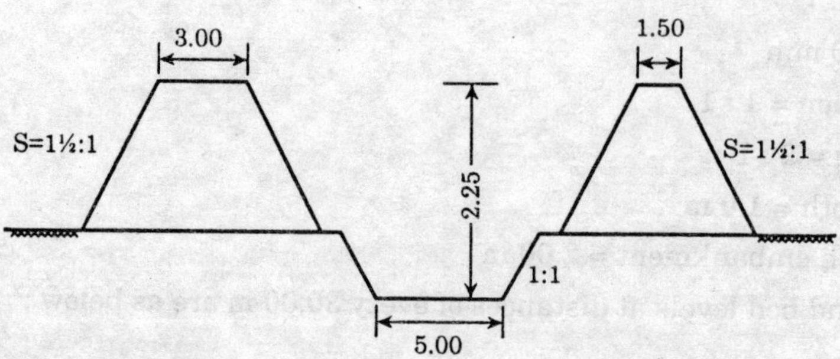

Figure. 7.5 Canal in cutting and banking.

Cutting: Bed width, $B = 4.00m$; Side slopes, $s = 1$								Banking: Height of banks from bed, $H = 1.0+0.50 = 1.50m$; Top width of left bank $b_1 = 2.0$ m; Top width of right bank, $b_2 = 2.0$ m						Side slopes $s_1 = 2$	
Station of Chainage	Depth of cutting, d	Area of central portion $B \times d$	Area of sides sd^2	Total sectional area $Bd + Sd^2$	Total mean area	Distance between stations D	Quantity, Q_1 Total mean area $\times D$	Height of above bed H	Height of bank above G.L. $h = H - d$	Area of central portion $= (b_1 + b_2)\ h$	Area of sides $2s_1h^2$	Total sectional area Col (11 + 12)	Total mean sectional area	Total quantity Q_2 = Total mean area $\times D$	Balance quantity $Q_2 - Q_1$ from borrow pit
	m	m^2	m^2	m^2	m^2	m	m^3	m	m	m^2	m^2	m^2	m^2		m^3
1	0.20	0.80	0.04	0.84	–	–	–	1.50	1.30	5.20	6.76	35.20	–	–	–
2	1.00	4.00	1.00	5.00	2.92	30.00	87.60	1.50	0.50	2.00	1.00	2.00	18.58	557.40	469.80
3	0.20	0.80	0.40	0.84	2.92	30.00	87.60	1.50	1.30	5.20	6.76	35.15	18.58	557.40	469.80
4	0.20	0.80	0.40	0.84	0.84	30.00	25.20	1.50	1.30	5.20	6.76	35.15	35.15	1054.50	1029.30
5	0.30	1.20	0.09	1.29	1.07	30.00	32.10	1.50	1.20	4.80	4.80	23.04	29.10	873.00	840.90
6	0.30	1.20	0.09	1.29	1.29	30.00	38.70	1.50	1.20	4.80	4.80	23.04	23.04	691.20	652.50
					Total	=	271.20							3733.50	3462.30
							Cum							Cum	Cum

Quantity of earthwork in excavation = 271.20 Cum

Quantity of earthwork in embakment to be taken from borrow pit = 3733.50 Cum

Total = 3462.30 Cum

Cutting — *Bed width, B = 5.00 m, Side slopes, s = 1*								*Banking* — *Height of Banks from bed H = 2.55 m*; *Top width of left bank b_1 = 3.00 mm*; *Top width of right bank b_2 = 1.50 m*; *Side slopes, s1 = 1½*						
Station or chainage	*Depth of cutting, d*	*Mean depth d_m*	*Area of central portion Bd_m*	*Area of sides sd^2 m*	*Total area $Bd_m + sd_m$ (A_m)*	*Distance between stations D*	*Quantity $Q_1 = A_m \times D$*	*Height of bank above bed, H*	*Height of bank above G.L. (mean) $h = H - d_m$ Col. 9 – 3*	*Area of central portion $(b_1 + b_2)\ h$*	*Area of sides (mean) $2s_1\ h^2$*	*Total mean area col. 11 + 12*	*Quantity Q_2 col. 13 × D*	*Balance quantity for banks from borrow pit $Q_2 - Q_1$*
	m	*m*	*m^2*	*m^2*	*m^2*	*m*	*m*	*m*	*m*	*m^2*	*m^2*	*m^2*	*m^2*	*m^2*
1	1.50	–	–	–	–	–	–	–	–	–	–	–	–	–
2	1.82	1.66	8.30	2.756	11.056	50	552.80	2.55	0.89	4.005	2.376	6.381	319.05	–
3	2.04	1.93	9.65	3.725	13.375	50	668.75	2.55	0.62	2.790	1.153	3.943	197.15	–
4	2.10	2.07	10.35	4.285	14.635	50	731.75	2.55	0.48	2.160	0.691	2.851	142.55	–
5	1.22	1.66	8.30	2.756	11.056	50	552.80	2.55	0.89	4.005	2.376	6.381	319.05	–
6	0.76	0.99	4.95	0.98	5.930	50	296.50	2.55	1.56	7.020	7.301	14.321	716.05	419.55
							2802.60 Cum						1693.85 Cum	419.55 Cum
								Quantity of earthwork in cutting = 2802.60						
								Quantity of earthwork in banking = 419.55						

Bed level of station 1 is 98.50

Bed level of station 2 is 98.50 – 0.01 = 98.49 m

Bed level of station 3 is 98.49 – 0.01 = 98.48 m

Bed level of station 4 is 98.48 – 0.01 = 98.47

Bed level of station 5 is 98.47 – 0.01 = 98.46

Bed level of station 6 is 98.46 – 0.01 = 98.45

Tabulating the R.L. at ground level and proposed bed level, the depth of cutting at different stations are found out.

Station	1	2	3	4	5	6
G.L. (m) R.L.	100.00	100.31	100.52	100.57	99.68	99.21
Proposed bed level (m) R.L.	98.50	98.49	98.48	98.47	98.46	98.45
Depth of cutting	1.50	1.82	2.04	2.10	1.22	0.76

Volume of earthwork will now be worked out in tabular form.

7.2.6 Estimation of Dam

Dam is generally made of earth. Dam is provided with a hearting section and is built of clayee soil to make it impervious to water percolation. A lining of bricks or boulder is provided on the upstream side of the dam.

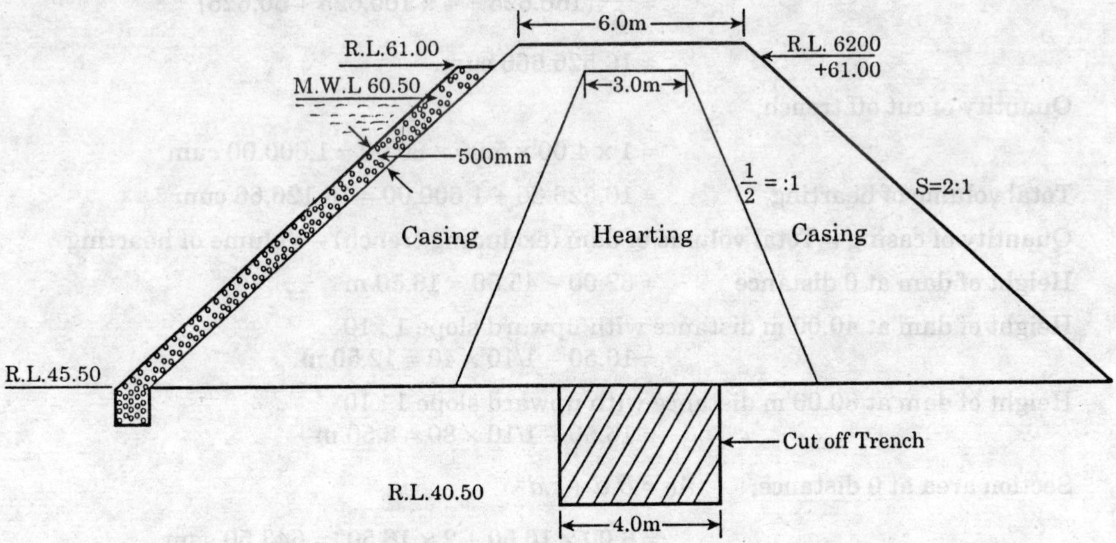

Fig. 7.6 Cross section of earthen dam.

Example 7.3. *Cross section of an earthen dam is shown in the Figure 7.6. The hearting embankment is specified to be built of fine clay and that the casing with morrum. A 500 mm thick dry rubble pitching is provided on the up stream face of the dam. The ground slopes upwards uniformly at the rate of 1 in 10 in the direction parallel to the centre line of the dam. The lateral slope at the site is assumed to be level.*

Determine the quantities of materials that would be required for the hearting, casing and pitching for a length of 80 meter of the dam.

Hearting excluding cut off trench

Height of the dam at 0 distance = 61.00 – 45.50 = 15.50 m

Height of the dam at 40 m distance when the ground slopes upwards at

1 : 10 = 15.50 – 1/10 × 40 = 11.50 m

Height of the dam at 80 m distance = 15.5 – 1/10 × 80 = 7.50 m

Top width B = 3.00 m, Side slope s = 1/2 : 1

Sectional area at $A_0 = B.d + s.d^2$

$= 3.00 \times 15.50 + 0.5 \times 15.5^2$

$= 166.625$ sqm

Sectional area at 40 m distance $= 3.00 \times 11.50 + 0.50 \times 11.50^2$

$A_{40} = 100.625$ sqm

Sectional area at 80 m distance $= 3.00 \times 7.50 + 0.50 \times 7.50^2$

$A_{80} = 50.625$ sqm

Volume of hearting $= \frac{L}{3}(A_0 + 4\,A_{40} + A_{80})$

$= \frac{80}{3}(166.625 + 4 \times 100.625 + 50.625)$

= 16,526.666 cum.

Quantity of cut off trench,

$= 1 \times 4.00 \times 5.00 \times 80.00 = 1{,}600.00$ cum

Total volume of hearting = 16,526.66 + 1,600.00 = 18,126.66 cum

Quantity of casing = Total volume of dam (excluding trench) – Volume of hearting

Height of dam at 0 distance = 62.00 – 45.50 = 16.50 m

Height of dam at 40.00 m distance with upward slope 1 : 10

= 16.50 – 1/10 × 40 = 12.50 m

Height of dam at 80.00 m distance with upward slope 1 : 10

= 16.50 – 1/10 × 80 = 8.50 m

Section area at 0 distance, $A_0 = B.d + s.d^2$

$= 6.00 \times 16.50 + 2 \times 16.50^2 = 643.50$ sqm

Section area at 40 m distance, $A_{40} = 6.00 \times 12.50 + 2 \times 12.50^2 = 387.50$ sqm

Section area at 80 m distance, $A_{80} = 6.00 \times 8.50 + 2 \times 8.50^2 = 195.50$ sqm

Total volume of the dam (excluding trench)

$= \frac{80}{3}(643.50 + 4 \times 387.50 + 195.50)$

= 63,706.67 cum

Quantity of casing = 63,706.67 – 16,526.67 = 47,180.00 cum

Pitching

Area of 50 mm thick boulder pitching on one side,

$$= L \times d_m \sqrt{1 + s^2}$$

where, L = 80.00 m

$$d_m = 1/2\,(16.50 + 8.50) = 12.50 \text{ m}$$

$$s = 2$$

Area of pitching above G.L. $= 80 \times 12.50 \sqrt{1 + 2^2}$

$= 80 \times 12.50 \times 2.236079 = 2{,}236.07$ sqm

Area of pitching below G.L. $= 80.00 \times (45.50 - 44.50) = 80.00$ sqm

Total area of 50 mm thick pitching $= 2{,}236.07 + 80.00 = 2{,}316.07$ sqm

Quantity of dry rubble, $= 2{,}316.07 \times 0.5 = 1{,}158.04$ cum

Abstract of cost of materials

Item no.	*Description of item*	*Quantity*	*Unit*	*Rate*	*Amount*	*Remarks*
1	Materials for hearting (dry clay)	18,127	cum	12.00	2,17,524.00	
2	Materials for casing local ordinary earth	47,180	cum	8.00	3,77,440.00	
3	Dry rubble	1,158	cum	40.00	46,320.00	
					6,41,284.00	
	Add contingency @ 5%				32,064.00	
					6,73,348.00	
	Add work establishment @ 2.5%				16,834.00	
					6,90,182.00	

7.3.0 OTHER STRUCTURES

Apart from the canals, various other structures are constructed for irrigation works. These structure are designed as per necessity and detailed drawings are prepared. Estimates are prepared on the basis of the detailed drawings. Estimates of these structures are framed like estimates of structures required for buildings, roads, bridges, and culverts, etc.

The structures are Weirs, Tank weirs, Sluices, Aqueducts, Siphon aqueducts or Drainage siphons. Hume pipe conduits are also constructed for irrigation purpose.

Irrigation works often require some mechanical structures also — Sluice gate, Water lifting arrangement, Large pumps, Small pumps. These are available in the market. Manufacturers are available who also instal those at site on request. These are provided in the estimates as complete items.

7.3.1 Lining of Canals

Canals often require lining on the surface. Purpose of lining the canal surface is to achieve economy. Lining facilitates increase in velocity of flow of water and thus helps in reducing the cross section of the canal. It considerably reduces loss of fluid due to seepage. Lining also stabilises the canal section and reduce maintenane cost of the structure.

Example 7.4. *Prepare an estimate for providing lining on the exposed surface of a canal as shown in the Figure 7.7.*

The lining shall be done by laying cement concrete tiles of proportion 1 : 3 : 6, size 30 × 150 × 53 mm laid on 20 mm thick layer cement sand mortar 1 : 5. A layer of cement sand mortar 1 : 3, 25 mm thick shall be provided on top of lining for sealing the joints.

The length of the canal is 1,000 m.

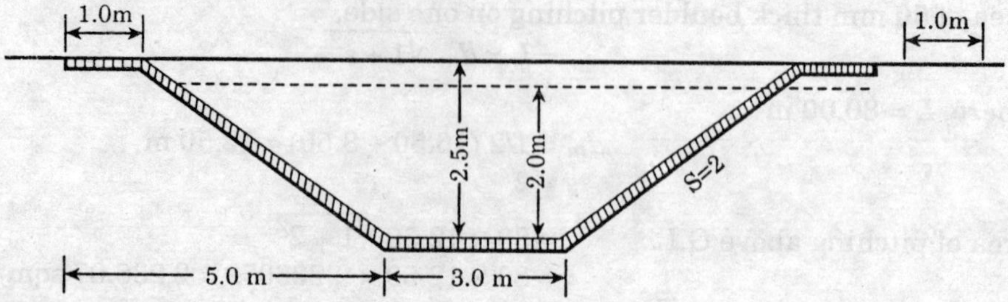

Figure 7.7 Single lining of canal surface.

Perimeter of the canal before lining

$$= 3.00 + 2\sqrt{5.00^2 + 2.50^2} + 1.00 + 1.00$$

$$= 3.00 + 2 \times 5.60 + 2.00 = 16.20 \text{ m}$$

Area of lining $= 1{,}000.00 \times 16.20 = 16{,}200$ sqm

Estimate

Item no.	*Description of item*	*No.*	*Measurement*			*Content*	Waste
			Length	*Breadth*	*Height*		
1.	Earthwork in excavation 195 mm deep.	1	16,200	sqm		16,200	sqm
2.	Preparation of sub-grade including dressing ramming and wetting.	1	16,200	sqm		16,200	sqm
3.	Laying cement sand mortar 1 : 5, 20 mm thick.	1	16,200	sqm		16,200	sqm
4.	Supplying and laying cement concrete 1 : 3 : 6 tile of size 30 × 150 × 53 mm on mortar bed and filling the joints with cement sand mortar 1 : 3.	1	16,200	sqm		16,200	sqm
5.	Laying cement sand mortar 1 : 3 on top of tiles.	1	16,200	sqm		16,200	sqm

ABSTRACT OF COST

Item no.	*Description of item*	*Quantity*	*Unit*	*Rate*	*Amount*	*Remarks*
1.	Earthwork in excavation 195 mm deep.	16,200	sqm	2.00	32,400.00	
2.	Preparation of sub-grade including dressing ramming and wetting.	16,200	sqm	1.50	24,300.00	
3.	Laying 20 mm thick cement sand mortar 1 : 5 on the sub-grade.	16,200	sqm	42.00	6,80,400.00	
4.	Supplying and laying cement concrete 1 : 3 : 6 tiles including filling the joints with cement sand mortar 1 : 3.	16,200	sqm	60.00	9,72,000.00	
5.	Laying cement sand mortar 1 : 3, 25 mm thick on top of laid tiles.	16,200	sqm	50.00	8,10,000.00	
					25,19,100.00	

Add contingency @ 5%	1,25,955.00
	26,45,055.00
Add work establishment @ 2 ½%	66,126.00
	27,11,181.00

Rate per meter of lining = 2,711

Rate per sqm of lining = 167

8

BUILDING ECONOMICS

8.1.0 STUDY OF ECONOMICS OF A BUILDING

Before launching a Building Project, the manager of the project should examine the project in all aspects, *e.g.* planning, design, construction technology, materials to be used and economics of the building prior to deciding upon the management technique to be adopted. This detailed study of the project is necessary to ensure completion of the project without wastage of time, materials, manpower and finance. For optimising economy, attention must be given from the planning and design stage. Deciding upon the shape and size of the building is important as these influence the cost of the structure.

8.1.1 Construction Technology

Construction technology adopted is still the old traditional one. The technology is selected in consideration of suiting the masons, carpenters and other tradesmen. The trades have passed from generation without adoption of any innovation and new idea. The tradesman are averse to adoption of any new technology.

A manager should give serious thought over all these and should not hesitate to adopt new technology, new substitute materials to achieve his goal. In doing so, he will have to examine the scheme and shall have to evaluate the cost of the building as accurately as possible.

8.2.0 ASSESSMENT OF COST OF CONSTRUCTION AND REQUIREMENT OF MATERIALS

These are the vital information required by a manager for efficient management of a Project. The cost of a structure (building) is assessed on the basis of its plinth area or the volume contents which is again based on plinth area. The first hand information received from the client does not furnish the required plinth area as the client may not have any idea about it. The client may furnish the information in terms of rooms or at best the size of the rooms (carpet area), from which the plinth area of the proposed building shall have to be calculated. Again there is no hard and fast rule for computation of plinth area from the carpet area of a building. The ratio of plinth area to carpet area varies widely for different buildings. The ratio depends on the types of the building *i.e.* masonry building or framed structure building. Again it depends upon the efficiency of planning which depends upon the capability of the planner. As for example, efficiency of planning for an appartment building 80% would be considered satisfactory while that for a public building or school or market building 65% may be considered a high efficiency.

Carpet area is the useable area whereas plinth area is the area covered by the building at the plinth level. To get plinth area from the carpet area, other ancilliary areas shall be added *i.e* the area of verandah, balcony, corridor, kitchen, bath, thickness of the walls, stair case, etc. according to the type and nature of the building. These areas vary according to the type and nature of building. Wall areas vary according to shape of the building and the method of design. Hence no definite formula can be developed establishing the relation. However, some approximate ratio may be used for ready calculation.

Percentage of wall area	R.C.C. framed structure	Other building in masonry
With respect to carpert/Floor area	8%	15% to 17%

Example 8.1 *An office building is proposed to be constructed. The building would house rooms for officers 4 nos., clerical staff 50 nos., other service staff 10 nos., store 120 sqm, record room 120 sqm. Find the cost on the plinth area basis, if cost of construction is Rs. 4,000.00 per sqm.*

Floor area required

Officers 25 sqm each

Clerical staff 5 sqm each

Service staff 2 sqm each

Floor area = (4 × 25 + 50 × 5 + 10 × 2 + 120 + 120) + (10 % corridor + 10 % Lobby + 5 % stair.)

= (100 + 250 + 20 + 240) + 10% + 10% + 5%

= 610 + 61 + 61 + 31 = 763 sqm.

$$\text{Plinth area} = 763 + \frac{8}{100} \times 763 = 763 + 61 = 824 \text{ sqm}$$

The building would be two storeyed, 412 sqm in each floor.

Cost = 824 × Rs. 4,000.00 = Rs. 32,96,000.00

Cost of the building may be computed on volume basis. The plinth area is multiplied by the floor height including the thickness of the slab and the volume is found out. The volume is multiplied by the rate per unit volume and the cost is found out.

Example 8.2 *Referring to example 8.1,*

Plinth area of the building = 824 sqm

Let the floor height be 3.0 m including the thickness of the slab,

Volume = 824 × 3.0 = 2,472 cum,

Cost at Rs. 1,300.00 per cum = Rs. 32,13,600.00

8.3.0 BREAKUP OF TOTAL COST OF BUILDING ON PERCENTAGE BASIS

Total cost of the building may be divided into different sub-heads and components of the structure on percentage basis of the total cost to facilitate finding out of approximate cost involved in item and of different materials that would be required.

Table 8.1

Breakup of cost of item on percentage basis of costs

	Major items	*Single storey masonry wall*	*Two storey masonry wall*	*Ground plus two R.C.C. frame*	*Ground plus three R.C.C. frame*
	1	2	3	4	5
1.	Foundation and plinth	32.00%	25.00%	15.00%	16.00%
2.	Superstructure including finishing works	49.75%	57.00%	65.00%	62.00%
3.	(*a*) Electrical installation	4.00%	4.00%	4.00%	4.00%
	(*b*) Sanitary, plumbing and drainage	12.25%	12.00%	14.00%	16.00%
4.	Tube-well and pump house	2.00%	2.00%	2.00%	2.00%
		100.00%	100.00%	100.00%	100.00%

Table 8.2
Breakup of cost (a) foundation and plinth as percentage of total cost

(*a*)	*Foundation and plinth*	*Single storey with masonry wall*	*Two storey with masonry wall*	*Ground plus two R.C.C. frame*	*Ground plus three R.C.C frame*
	1	2	3	4	5
1.	Earthwork in excavation and back felling	2.00%	3.00%	13.00%	5.00%
2.	Brick soling and Jhama concrete	61.00%	60.00%	15.00%	7.00%
3.	Cement concrete for structural work	–	–	30.00%	56.00%
4.	Shuttering and centering for R.C.C. work	–		9.00%	9.00%
5.	Reinforcement for R.C.C. work	–	–	24.00%	11.00%
6.	Brickwork and D.P.C.	37.00%	37.00%	9.00%	12.00%
		100.00%	100.00%	100.00%	100.00%

Table 8.3

(*b*)	*Superstructure*	*Single storey masonry wall*	*Two storey masonry wall*	*Ground plus two R.C.C. frame*	*Ground plus three R.C.C. frame*
	1	2	3	4	5
1.	Brickwork	24.00%	25.00%	12.50%	12.00%
2.	Cement concrete	15.00%	15.00%	18.00%	19.00%
3.	Shuttering and centering for R.C.C. work	4.50%	4.50%	4.00%	4.00%
4.	Reinforcement for R.C.C. work	9.00%	11.00%	18.00%	18.00%
5.	Flooring	5.00%	6.00%	12.00%	12.00%
6.	Finishing works	3.00%	2.50%	2.00%	2.00%
7.	Plastering	9.00%	8.50%	8.00%	8.00%
8.	Door and window frame	2.60%	3.00%	3.00%	3.00%
9.	Door and window shutter	13.00%	12.00%	8.50%	8.50%
10.	Painting to wood works	2.00%	2.00%	2.00%	2.00%
11.	Internal wall painting	1.50%	1.50%	2.00%	2.00%
12.	Decorative cement based paint to external wall.	2.00%	2.00%	4.00%	4.00%
13.	Lime terracing	6.00%	5.00%	4.00%	3.50%
14.	Miscelleneous	3.40%	2.00%	2.00%	2.00%
		100.00%	100.00%	100.00%	100.00%

8.4.0 ASSESSMENT OF QUANTITY OF MATERIALS AND LABOUR

Assessment of quantity of different materials and labour of different categories of buildings is made on percentage basis on the total cost of construction as detailed, is very approximate. Cost differs widely as cost of construction differs widely from place to place and the price of materials and labour do not follow any rationality and do not bear any proportion.

To obviate the difficulty and to arrive at reasonably correct quantities of different materails and number of different categories of labour required, Central Building Research Institute has worked out certain statistical based equations for building portion, which relate to consumption of each materials/labour to plinth area of the building. For services portion, the norms/requirements have been given in tabular form. Statistical relations have been worked out for residential and office buildings—both load bearing and framed structure.

The equations developed by the Central Building Research Institute are represented which can be very fruitfully used for assessing the quantities of materials for different types of buildings.

Statistical relations are furnished in tabular form. These are based on specifications of the structures.

Table 8.4
Specifications adopted in residential building

Element	*Single and double storey construction*	*Four storey (RCC Framed Building)*
1	2	3
Foundation	Plain cement concrete foundation 1:5:10 with stone ballast, brickwork in cement mortar 1:6, 38 mm thick DPC with cement concrete 1:2:4 and a bitumen coating on top @1.7 kg/sqm, sand filling 100 mm in plinth.	RCC 1:2:4 column footing on lean concrete (1:4:8) mat with stone ballast, RCC 1:2:4 plinth beams finished smooth with 6mm cement mortar 1:3, brickwork in cement mortar 1:6, sand filling 100mm in plinth.
Frame		RCC 1:2:4 Columns and beams finished smooth with 6mm mortar 1:3.
Walling	Brick work in cement mortar 1 : 6, load bearing walls one brick wide and partition walls half brick thick, RCC work 1 : 2 : 4 in lintels, beams and chajjas finished smooth with 6 mm thick cement mortar 1 : 3.	Brick work in cement mortar 1 : 6 RCC work 1 : 2 : 4 in lintels, beams and chajjas finished smooth with 6 mm thick cement mortar 1 : 3.
Floor	38 mm thick cement concrete 1 : 2 : 4 laid over cement concrete 115 mm thick 1 : 5 : 10 with stone ballast	38 mm thick cement concrete 1 : 2 : 4 laid over 115 mm thick cement concrete 1 : 5 : 10 with stone ballast in ground floor and over RCC slab in upper floors.
Roof	RCC slab with lime terracing avg. 110 mm thick with bitumen coating underneath @ 1.7 kg/sqm.	RCC slab with lime terracing av. 110 mm thick with bitumen coating under neath @ 1.7 kg/sqm and top finished with 40mm cement concrete. Brick work in cement morter 1 : 6 in parapet finished with cement concrete 1 : 2 : 4 coping. Timber frames 100 × 75 mm, 38 m thick timber panelled shutters for doors and fully glazed shutters for doors and fully glazed shutters for windows.
Joinery	Timber frames 100 × 75 mm, 38mm thick panelled shutters for doors and fully glazed shutters for windows.	
Finishes	Sand and cement plaster on the wall 1 : 6, 12 mm thick on smooth sides and 20 mm thick on rough sides, cement plaster 1 : 3 in skirting and dado, internally white washed, externally colour washed, painting wood-work with oil paint.	12 mm thick cement paster 1 : 4 on internal faces of the walls, and 20 mm thick cement plaster 1 : 3 on external faces of walls including neeru finish internally white washed and externally colour washed, painting wood-work with oil paint.
Stair	RCC stairs in double storey.	RCC stair.
Fittings & Fixtures.	Precast RCC shelves, M.S. round bar in window grating, raised cooking platform.	Precast RCC 1 : 2 : 4 shelves, M.S. round bars in window gratings, timber cup- boards, raised cooking platform.

TABLE 8.5

Equations for materials requirement (A is the plinth area in m^2) in residential buildings

	Equations Single Storey	Double Storey	Four Storey (RCC Framed)
1	2	3	4
Bricks (% nos.)	$2.26A + 66.8$	$2.15A + 63$	$-26.2 + 2.56A - 0.0096A^2$
Cement (Tonne)	$0.153A + 0.57$	$0.145A + 0.54$	$0.182A - 0.35$
Steel (kg)	$21.3A - 314$	$21.97A - 305$	$-1491 + 92.0A - 0.36A^2$
Sand (m^3)	$0.47A - 7$	$0.43A - 5.6$	$0.361A - 0.38$
Coarse aggregate:			
(i) 20 mm down (m^3)	$0.176A - 0.21$	$0.178A - 0.21$	$0.295A - 0.75$
(ii) 40 mm down (m^3)	$0.145A + 1.5$	$0.075A + 0.78$	$0.45 + 0.0027A + 0.0001A^2$
Brick aggregate (m^3)	$0.113A - 0.83$	$0.056A - 0.42$	$0.021A + 0.01$
Timber Frames and shutters (m^3)	$0.019A + 0.23$	$0.019A + 0.23$	$0.02A + 0.11$
Timber shuttering (m^3)	$0.0042A$	$0.0042A$	$0.009A - 0.03$
Ballies (m)	$0.504A$	$0.504A$	$0.009A + 0.14$
Lime (Quintal)	$0.045A + 0.35$	$0.073A - 0.17$	$0.063A - 0.08$
Surkhi (m^3)	$0.052A - 0.37$	$0.026A - 0.18$	$0.01A$
Glass (m^2)	$0.064A - 0.73$	$0.064A - 0.73$	$0.056A - 0.06$
Bitumen (kg.)	$1.836A - 9$	$0.918A - 4$	$0.357A - 2.41$
Primer (lt.)	$0.048A$	$0.048A$	$0.045A + 0.56$
Paint (lt.)	$0.08A + 0.27$	$0.08A + 0.27$	$0.075A + 0.93$

* Equations for superstructure only. For sub-structure, refer Table-8.7

TABLE 8.6

Equation for labour requirement (A is the plinth are in m^2) in residential buildings

Labour	Equations Single Storey	Double Storey	Four Storey (RCC framed)
1	2	3	4
Mason (days)	$1.335A + 28$	$1.355A + 26$	$1.57A - 2$
Carpenter (days)	$1.184A - 9$	$1.194A - 9$	$1.61A$
Painter (days)	$0.19A$	$0.19A$	$0.19A$
Blacksmith (days)	$0.269A - 4$	$0.274A - 4$	$-16 + 1.01A - 0.004A^2$
Mazdoor (days)	$4.769A + 32$	$4.91A + 33$	$5.49A - 9.2$

* Equations for super-structure only: For sub-structure, refer Table 8.7

Equations for Materials and labour requirement of sub-structure in 4-Storeyed (RCC Framed) Residential Building

Table 8.7

Materials / Labour	Equations
Materials	
Cement (tonne)	$0.0204A - 0.014$
Sand m^3	$0.036A$
Coarse Aggregate 20mm. and down m^3	$0.071A - 0.01$
Steel (kg)	$-171 + 10.46A - 0.041A^2$
Timber shuttering m^2	$0.0007A$
Ballies (m)	$0.036A + 0.06$

Materials / Labour	*Equations*
Labour	
Mason (days)	0.023 A
Carpenter (days)	0.05 A
Blacksmith (days)	$-1.6 + 0.1A - 0.0003A^2$
Mazdoor (days)	0.343 A

Table 8.8
Equations for Materials/Labour requirements for Office Buildings

Materials / Labour	*Equations*
Cement (tonne)	0.1925A + 18.52
Fine sand (m^3)	0.08A + 105.5
Coarse sand (m^3)	0.2592A – 80.94
Coarse aggregate (m^3) 20 mm nominal size	0.2728A – 48.5
Coarse aggregate (m^3) 10 mm nominal size	0.1164A – 20.74
Coarse aggregate (m^3) 40 mm nominal size	0.0151A + 73.91
Brick ballast 25 mm nominal size (m^3)	0.0426A – 38.37
Timber for form work (m^3)	0.005A + 11.19
Timber for joinery (m^3)	0.0024A – 0.53
Ballies (m)	0.5507A + 797.5
Bricks % Nos.	1.1829A – 524.23
Deformed bars (tonne)	0.0479 A
Door shutters (m^2)	0.0636A – 17.07
Window shutters (m^2)	0.1117A + 93.26
Glass (m^2)	0.1407A + 55.99
Primer (lt)	0.0256A + 9.7
Paint (lt)	0.0322A + 7.24
Lime (Qtl)	0.0754A – 51.21
Surkhi (m^3)	0.0204A – 18.39
Marble chips (Qtl)	0.1338A – 48.52
Marble powder (m^3)	0.0012A – 0.36
Mason (Days)	1.1314A – 407.4
Carpenter (Days)	0.7094A + 449.09
Glazier (Days)	0.0122A + 10.31
Painter (Days)	0.0905A + 37.26
Blacksmith (Days)	0.479A
Beldar (Days)	6.055A – 2024.87

Note: (*i*) A is the total plinth area (m^2) of all the floors of the building.

(*ii*) The relations are applicable for a range of 1,600 m^2 to 26,000 m^2 plinth area.

(*iii*) The type of foundation considered is column footing.

(*iv*) The relation for reinforcement has been given in terms of deformed bars, 10 to 20% of this reinforcement may be taken as mild steel.

(*v*) In case of raft foundation, additional quantities of 10 m^3 of R.C.C. 1 : 2 : 4 work along with 1.2 tonnes of reinforcement per 100 m^2 of plinth area may be added.

8.5.0 OVERALL ECONOMY OF A BUILDING

The overall economy is required to be assessed for studying the economic viability of the project. The overall economy of building is generally assessed on the basis of cost of construction of the building; no cognizance is given on the cost-in-use of the structure. The cost-in use of a building includes the capital cost of the building, its renewal cost after expiry of the estimated life, cost of maintenance and repairs of the building during the period under calculation and any other charges or taxes likely to be incurred for the structure.

If the economy of the structure is evaluated taking cost-in-use in consideration, the structure apparently appearing to be economical on the basis of capital cost may ultimately prove to be uneconomical.

While working out the economics of a building, only on the basis of capital investment would not provide a realistic picture. The parameters life and operation and maintenance costs are very much interconnected as timely and adequate maintenance very much influence the length of life. Inadequate and ill-timed maintenance may shorten the life of a building and thus would affect its economy. Again, life of a building depends upon the specifications of items adopted in the construction. Proper and better specification and adequate precautionary measures for improving the durability of the structure not only extends the life of a building, but also reduce the maintenance cost and thus improves the economics.

Example 8.3 *Compare the economics of the three types of buildings, the particulars are given below.*

Type	*Cost of contruction per sqm*	*Life in years*	*Rate of increase in cost p.a.*
A	Rs. 5,000.00	60	15%
B	Rs. 2,000.00	40	10%
C	Rs. 1,500.00	20	10%

The comparison of the economics would be made on per sqm basis of each type.

(*i*) The maximum life cycle of type A building is 60 years, the pattern of replacement during the period would be as below:

Type A	nil
Type B	40th year
Type C	20th and 40th year

(*ii*) The cost of construction of the buildings and the cost of replacement may be calculated on the basis of formula, taking into account of the present cost and the rate of increase in cost.

$P = (1 + i)^n$ where, P = cost of construction at the nth year,
n = number of years,
i = rate of increase in cost.

The cost of replacement would as below:

Type A			nil
Type B	at 40th year	45.25 × 2,000.00	90,500.00
Type C	at 20th year	6.73 × 1,500.00	10,095.00
	at 40th year	45.25 × 1,500.00	67,875.00

(*iii*) Operation, maintenance and repairs and tax cost of the buildings in 60 years would be as below:

Type A Rs. 24/- p.a. with rate of increase at 5% p.a.

$$353.584 \times 24.00 = \text{Rs. } 8,486.00$$

Type B Rs. 24/- p.a. with rate of increase at 5% p.a.

$$353.584 \times 24.00 = \text{Rs. } 8,486.00$$

Type C Rs. 30/- p.a. with rate of increase at 5% p.a.

$$353.584 \times 30.00 = \text{Rs. } 10,608.00$$

The present values of the costs at 5% are:

Type A	Rs. 8,486.00 × 0.05354	= Rs. 454.00
Type B	Rs. 8,486.00 × 0.05354	= Rs. 454.00
Type C	Rs.10,608.00 × 0.05354	= Rs. 568.00

(*iv*) The present values of the renewal costs at 8% per p.a. of the types are:

Year	*Present values of the types*			
	A	B	C	
0	Rs. 5,000.00	2,000.00		Rs. 1,500.00
20	-	-	Rs. 10,095.00 × 0.215	= Rs. 2,170
40	-	Rs.90,50.00 × 0.046 = Rs. 4,163.00	Rs. 67,875.00 × 0.046	= Rs.3,122.00
	Rs. 5,000.00	Rs. 6,163.00		Rs. 6,792.00

(*v*) The total cost in use of the types inclusive of all charges would be as below:

Type	*Cost of construction including cost of renewal at present value*	*O.M.R. charges at present value*	*Total*
A	Rs. 5,000.00	Rs. 454.00	Rs. 5,454.00
B	Rs. 6,163.00	Rs. 454.00	Rs. 6,617.00
C	Rs. 6,792.00	Rs. 568.00	Rs. 7,360.00

It is seen that the type C building which apparantly appeared economical when only the costs of construction were compared; but when all the charges were taken into consideration at present value, the type A building becomes most economical. This is due to durability of the building and the low operation, maintenance and repair charges.

8.6.0 ELEMENTAL COST ANALYSIS (ECA)

The manager in charge of building construction project has to assess the cost of the building prior to construction and even prior to framing of a detailed estimate. To facilitate quick assessment of cost of the building or its element (part) in a more realistic manner he can take the help of Elemental Cost Analysis as developed by the Central Building Research Institute (CBRI).

Elemental Cost Analysis (ECA) is a systematic breakdown of cost data of different elements or parts of building. The building is divided into different elements—foundation, walls, roof, floors, reinforcement, finishes, door and window frames, water supply, electrical installations, etc. Cost of the elements are ascertained with respect to unit plinth area of the building. ECA helps is making primary comparison of cost of building. It attempts to isolate points of difference so that variations in specification and functions can be properly evaluated.

In normal practice, the cost of the elements is evaluated either on percentage basis of plinth area cost or on the basis of absolute cost. But cost of construction varies from time to time and from place to place. It is difficult to arrive at an acceptable standard. Central Building Research Institute (CBRI) has developed a method of elemental cost analysis in terms of consumption of basic materials and labour per unit plinth area of building. The data of basic materials consumed had been collected from a set of final bills of different construction agencies for a set of common specifications. After making adjustments, the consumption of materials and labour was worked out with the help of average materials and labour constants for each element.

The consumption of materials/labour for 10 sqm of plinth area for two and four storeyed residential buildings (load bearing construction) were tabulated and are given in Table-8.9. With this data, elemental cost analysis for any place at any time can be worked out from the rates of materials and labour prevailing in the particular place at the particular time.

TABLE 8.9.1

Material and labour inputs for various elements and sub-elements for two and four-storeyed residential buildings (load bearing walls)

	For 10 m^2 plinth area							Figs. in lines 'a' are for four-storeyed dwellings. Figs. in line 'b' for two -storeyed dwellings.						
Sl. No.	Materials or Labour	Elements		(i) Foundation and Plinth				(ii) Walling			(iii) Structural Floor			
		Sub-element unit	Excavation	Earth filling	Sand filling	Bed concrete	Brick work	Damp proof course	Brick work	RCC in lintel chajja, beams tc	Reinforcement.	RCC concrete work	Form work.	Slab reinforcement
1.	Cement	a. ton	–	–	–	0.09	0.08	0.005	0.3	0.133	–	0.44	–	–
		b.	–	–	–	0.13	0.09	0.01	0.3	0.122	–	0.44	–	–
2.	Sand	a. m^3	–	–	0.2	0.32	0.34	0.007	1.3	0.19	–	0.64	–	–
		b.	–	–	0.4	0.46	0.39	0.013	1.3	0.18	–	0.64	–	–
3.	Coarse Aggregate	a. $m.^3$	–	–	–	0.61	–	0.013	–	0.34	–	1.113	–	–
		b.	–	–	–	0.87	–	0.03	–	0.31	–	1.113	–	–
4.	Steel	a.kg	–	–	–	–	–	–	–	–	51.0	–	–	100.0
		b.	–	–	–	–	–	–	–	–	46.0	–	–	100.0
5.	Timber	a. m^3	–	–	–	–	–	–	–	0.0144	–	–	0.0304	–
		b.	–	–	–	–	–	–	–	0.0137	–	–	0.0304	–
6	Ballies	a.m	–	–	–	–	–	–	–	1.20	–	–	3.71	–
		b.	–	–	–	–	–	–	–	1.13	–	–	3.71	–
7.	Bricks	a.No.	–	–	–	–	627	–	2371	–	–	–	–	–
		b.	–	–	–	–	716	–	2371	–	–	–	–	–
8	Bitumen	a. kg	–	–	–	–	–	0.66	–	–	–	–	–	–
		b.	–	–	–	–	–	1.33	–	–	–	–	–	–
9.	Mason	a. day	–	–	–	0.07	0.9	0.035	5.6	0.24	–	0.93	–	–
		b.	–	–	–	0.1	1.01	0.07	5.1	0.22	–	0.93	–	–
10.	Carpenter	a. day	–	–	–	–	–	–	–	0.72	–	–	4.18	–
		b.	–	–	–	–	–	–	–	0.68	–	–	4.18	–
11.	Blacksmith	a. day	–	–	–	–	–	–	–	–	0.50	–	–	0.95
		b.	–	–	–	–	–	–	–	–	0.45	–	–	0.95
12.	Painter	a. day	–	–	–	–	–	0.008	–	–	–	–	–	–
			–	–	–	–	–	0.016	–	–	–	–	–	–
13.	Beldar	b. day	1.10	0.51	0.05	1.20	1.9	0.035	10.62	2.19	0.50	5.85	4.2	0.95
			0.99	0.94	0.091	1.73	2.18	0.07	10.08	1.87	0.45	5.25	4.2	0.95

TABLE 8.9.2
Materials and labour inputs for various elements and sub-elements for two and four-storeyed residential buildings (load bearing walls)

Sl. No.	*Materials or labour*	*Element*	*(iv) Stair case*			*(v) Doors*			*(vi) Windows*			
		Sub element unit	*RCC (concwork only)*	*Form work*	*Reinforcement*	*Frame*	*Shutter*	*Hold fast*	*Frame*	*Shutter*	*Hold fast*	*Windows grill.*
1.	Cement	a. tonne	0.019	–	–	–	–	0.007	–	–	0.006	–
		b.	0.019	–	–	–	–	0.007	–	–	0.006	–
2.	Sand	a. m^3	0.028	–	–	–	–	0.014	–	–	0.013	–
		b.	0.028	–	–	–	–	0.014	–	–	0.013	–
3.	Coarse aggregate	a. m^3	0.049	–	–	–	–	0.027	–	–	0.025	–
		b.	0.049	–	–	–	–	0.027	–	–	0.025	–
4.	Steel	a. kg	–	–	7.5	–	–	2.4	–	–	2.3	22.4
		b.	–	–	7.5	–	–	2.4	–	–	2.3	22.4
5.	Timber	a. m^3	–	0.0012	–	0.038	0.052	–	0.04	0.021	–	–
		b.	–	0.0012	–	0.038	0.052	–	0.04	0.021	–	–
6.	Ballies	a. m	–	0.03	–	–	–	–	–	–	–	–
		b.	–	0.03	–	–	–	–	–	–	–	–
7.	Glass	a. m^2	–	–	–	–	–	–	–	0.47	–	–
		b.	–	–	–	–	–	–	–	0.47	–	–
8.	Mason	a. day	0.11	–	–	–	–	0.19	–	–	0.17	–
		b.	0.11	–	–	–	–	0.19	–	–	0.17	–
9.	Carpenter	a. day	–	0.12	–	0.04	2.5	–	0.42	1.23	–	0.13
		b.	–	0.12	–	0.4	2.5	–	0.42	1.23	–	0.13
10.	Blacksmith	a. day	–	–	0.07	–	–	0.18	–	–	0.17	0.65
		b.	–	–	0.07	–	–	0.18	–	–	0.17	0.65
11.	Beldar	a. day	0.27	0.07	0.07	0.2	0.68	0.23	0.21	0.37	0.22	0.20
		b.	0.23	0.07	0.07	0.2	0.68	0.23	0.21	0.37	0.22	0.20

TABLE 8.9.3
Materials and labour inputs for various elements and sub-elements for two and four storeyed residential buildings (Load bearing walls)

Sl. No.	*Element*		*(vii) Flooring*		*(viii) Flooring*		*(ix) Finishes*			
	Material or labour	*Sub-element unit*	*40 mm PCC layer*	*Skirting*	*Lime conc.*	*Bitumen Painting*	*15mm plaster*	*12 mm plaster*	*White/colour wash*	*Painting*
1.	Cement	a. tonne	0.13	0.025	0.014	–	0.086	0.072	–	–
		b.	0.13	0.025	0.028	–	0.092	0.077	–	–
2.	Sand	a. m^3	0.155	0.049	0.029	0.013	0.366	0.306	–	–
		b.	0.155	0.049	0.058	0.026	0.394	0.33	–	–
3.	Coarse aggregate	a. m^3	0.31	–	–	–	–	–	–	–
		b.	0.31	–	–	–	–	–	–	–

(Contd...)

Sl. No.	Element		(vii) Flooring			(viii) Flooring		(ix) Finishes		
	Material or labour	*Sub-element unit*	*40 mm PCC layer*	*Skirting*	*Lime conc.*	*Bitumen Painting*	*15mm plaster*	*12 mm plaster*	*White/colour wash*	*Painting*
4.	Brick aggregate.	a. m^3	–	–	0.21	–	–	–	–	–
		b.	–	–	0.42	–	–	–	–	–
5.	Lime	a. qtl.	–	–	0.33	–	–	–	0.153	–
		b.	–	–	0.66	–	–	–	0.176	–
6.	Surkhi	a. m^3	–	–	0.10	–	–	–	–	–
		b.	–	–	0.20	–	–	–	–	–
7.	Brick Tiles	a. no.	–	–	74	–	–	–	–	–
		b.	–	–	148	–	–	–	–	–
8.	Glass	a. m^3	0.46	–	–	–	–	–	–	–
		b.	0.46	–	–	–	–	–	–	–
9.	Bitumen	a. kg	–	–	–	3.55	–	–	–	–
		b.	–	–	–	7.10	–	–	–	–
10.	Primer	a. ltr	–	–	–	–	–	–	–	0.44
		b.	–	–	–	–	–	–	–	0.44
11.	Paint	a. ltr	–	–	–	–	–	–	–	0.85
		b.	–	–	–	–	–	–	–	0.85
12.	Mason	a. day	1.45	0.33	0.40	–	1.81	1.61	–	–
		b.	1.45	0.33	0.80	–	2.01	1.73	–	–
13.	Painter	a. day	–	–	–	0.03	–	–	–	0.53
		b.	–	–	–	0.06	–	–	–	0.53
14.	White washer	a. day	–	–	–	–	–	–	0.92	–
		b.	–	–	–	–	–	–	1.06	–
15.	Beldar	a. day	2.15	0.47	2.22	0.08	2.86	2.41	0.92	0.53
		b.	2.15	0.47	4.44	0.16	3.07	2.59	1.06	0.53

Table 8.9.4.

Materials and labour inputs for various elements and sub-elements for two and four-storeyed residential buildings (load bearing walls)

Sl.No	*Materials/labour*	*Element*	*(x) Water Supply and Sanitary Services*		
		Sub-element unit	*Fittings*	*Soil/Waste vent/drainage pipes.*	*Water Supply*
1.	W.C. Seat (complete with all accessories and fittings)	no.	0.18	–	
2.	Wash basin-do-	no.	0.18	–	–
3.	Sand cast iron pipe				
	a. 100 mm	m	–	1.04	–
	b. 50 mm	m	–	1.46	–
4.	Cement	tonne	–	0.065	–
5.	Sand	m^3	–	0.19	–
6.	Coarse aggregate	m^3	–	0.32	–
7.	Paint	ltr.	0.15	0.47	0.04
8.	Primer	ltr.	–	0.020	0.02
9.	Bricks	no.	–	38	–
10.	M.S. Holder Bat Clamp	no.	–	1.5	–

(Contd...)

Sl.No	Materials/labour	Element	(x) Water Supply and Sanitary Services		
		Sub-element unit	Fittings	Soil/Waste vent/drainage pipes.	Water Supply
1	2	3	4	5	6
11.	Floor trap	no.	–	0.54	–
12.	G.I. Pipe 15 mm	m	–	–	2.5
13.	G.I.Pipe 20 mm and above	m	–	–	3.3
14.	Bib Cock 15 mm	no.	–	–	0.54
15.	Stop Cock 15 mm	no.	–	–	0.54
16.	Pig lead	kg	–	4.2	–
17.	Spun yarn	kg	–	0.61	–
18.	Lead connector 30 cm	no.	–	–	0.18
19.	Shower rose 100 mm	no.	0.18	–	–
20.	Tank (RCC) 270 ltr	No.	–	–	0.10
21.	S.W.Pipe 100 mm–150 mm	m	–	1.7	–
22.	Gully Trap 100 mm × 100 mm	no.	–	0.7	–
23.	Fitter	day	0.28	0.57	0.69
24.	Mason	day	0.15	0.73	–
25.	Painter	day	0.045	0.30	0.07
26.	Beldar	day	0.39	2.00	0.56

Computation based on medium size tenement (plinth area 56 m^2) double Storeyed construction.

TABLE 8.9.5

Materials and labour inputs for various elements and sub-elements for two and four-storeyed residential buildings (load bearing walls)

Sl. No.	Materials/Labour	Element	(xi) Internal Electrification		
		Sub-element unit.	Wiring	Fittings	L.C. Boards Switches and distribution boards.
1	2	3	4	5	6
1.	5 Amp. Tumbler switch (single Pole)	no.	2.4	–	–
2.	5 Amp. Tumbler Switch (double Pole)	no.	0.1	–	–
3.	15 Amp. Tumbler Switch (double Pole)	no.	0.19	–	–
4.	5 Amp. socket	no.	0.47	–	–
5.	15 Amp. socket	no.	0.19	–	–
6.	PVC insulated Al Conductor single core cable:				
	a. 1.5 sqmm	m	26.3	–	–
	b. 2.5 sqmm		2.6	–	–
	c. 4.6 sqmm		5.0	–	–
7.	Conduit 15mm (H.G.)	m	11.0	–	–
8.	Conduit 25mm (H.G.)	m	1.33	–	–
9.	Socket for 19mm & 25mm conduit	no.	4.7	–	–
10.	Inspection bends 19mm & 25mm	no.	3.1	–	–
11.	Saddles or Stapplers	no.	30.00	–	–
12.	I.C. Box 75 × 75 × 60 mm (deep)	no.	2.9	–	–
13.	I.C. Box 200 × 150 × 100 mm (deep)	no.	5.4	–	–
14.	Phenolic laminated sheet	m^2	0.04	–	–

(Contd...)

15.	Junction Box	no.	2.2	–	–
16.	Ceiling rose (2 Plate)	no.	2.1	–	–
17.	"L" type cast Al. anodised wall bracket brass socket (complete)	no.	–	1.41	–
18.	Circular ceiling fitting (complete)	no.	–	0.24	–
19.	Bulk Head Fitting (complete)	no.	–	0.19	–
20.	15 Amp S.P. & N. Switch Fuse Unit	no.	–	–	0.47
21.	2 way M.C.D.B. 15 Amp./Way	no.	–	–	0.24
22.	Wireman	day	1.19	0.07	0.04
23.	Mason	day	2.24	–	–
24.	Painter	day	0.03	–	–
25.	Khalasi	day	3.71	0.07	0.04

Computation is based on tenement of 70 m^2 plinth area.

Example 8.4 *Calculate the approximate quantity of (a) Bricks, (b) Cement, (c) Steel, (d) Coarse aggregate 20 mm down, (e) Coarse aggregate 40 mm down, and (f) Sand required for a single storey building of plinth area 100 sqm.*

(*a*) *Bricks*

Refer Table 8.5 $A = 100$ sqm

Requirement of Bricks

$= 2.26A + 66.8 = 2.26 \times 100 + 66.8 = 226 + 66.8$ %nos $= 292.8 \times 100 = 29{,}280$nos.

(*b*) *Cement*

Refer Table 8.5 $A = 100$ sqm

Requirement of Cement

$= 0.153A + 0.57 = 0.153 \times 100 + 0.57 = 15.3 + 0.57 = 15.87$ Tonne

(*c*) *Steel*

Refer Table 8.5 $A = 100$ sqm

Requirement of steel

$= 21.3A - 314 = 21.3 \times 100 - 314 = 2130 - 314 = 1{,}816$ kg

(*d*) *Coarse aggregate 20 mm down*

Refer Table 8.5 $A = 100$ sqm

Requirement of coarse aggregate 20 mm down

$= 0.176A - 0.21 = 0.176 \times 100 - 0.21 = 17.6 - 0.21 = 17.39 \text{ m}^3$

(*e*) *Coarse aggregate 40 mm down*

Refer Table 8.5 $A = 100$ sqm

$= 0.145A + 1.5 = 0.145 \times 100 + 1.5 = 14.5 + 1.5 = 16.0 \text{ m}^3$

(*f*) *Sand*

Requirement of Sand

$= 0.47A - 7 = 0.47 \times 100 - 7 = 47 - 7 = 40 \text{ m}^3$

Example 8.5 *Calculate the approximate quantity of (a) Bricks, (b) Cement, (c) Steel, (d) Coarse aggregate 20 mm down, (e) Coarse aggregate 40 mm down, and (f) Sand for a two storey building having 4 dwelling units each 100 sqm of plinth area built in load bearing construction.*

(*a*) *Bricks*

Refer Table 8.5 $A = 100$ sqm

Requirement of Bricks for one unit of 100 sqm.

$= 2.15A + 63 = 2.15 \times 100 + 63 = 215 + 63$ %nos. $= 278 \times 100. = 27{,}800$ Nos.

For 4 such units

$= 4 \times 27{,}800. = 1{,}08{,}000$ Nos.

(*b*) *Cement*

Refer Table 8.5 $A = 100$ sqm

Requirement of cement for 1 unit of 100 sqm

$= 0.145A + 0.54 = 0.145 \times 100 + 0.54 = 14.5 + 0.54 = 15.04$ Tonne

For 4 such dwellings

$= 4 \times 15.04 = 60.16$ Tonne

(*c*) *Steel*

Refer Table 8.5 $A = 100$ sqm.

Requirement of steel for one unit of 100 sqm.

$= 21.97A - 305 = 21.97 \times 100 - 305 = 2{,}197 - 305 = 1{,}892$ kg

For 4 such dwellings

$= 4 \times 1{,}892 = 7{,}568$ kg.

(*d*) *Coarse aggregate 20 mm down*

Refer Table 8.5 $A = 100$ sqm

Requirement of coarse aggregate 20 mm down for 1 unit of 100 sqm

$= 0.178A - 0.21 = 0.178 \times 100 - 0.21 = 17.8 - 0.21 = 17.59\ m^3$

For 4 such dwellings

$= 4 \times 17.59 = 70.36\ m^3$

(*e*) *Coarse aggregate 40 mm down*

Refer Table 8.5 $A = 100$ sqm.

$= 0.075A + 0.78 = 0.075 \times 100 + 0.78 = 7.5 + 0.78 = 8.28\ m^3$

For 4 such dwellings

$= 4 \times 8.28 = 33.12\ m^3$

(*f*) *Sand*

Requirement of sand for 1 dwelling $A = 100$ sqm

Refer Table 8.5

$= 0.43A - 5.6 = 0.43 \times 100 - 5.6 = 43.0 - 5.6 = 37.4\ m^3$

For 4 such units

$= 4 \times 37.4 = 149.60\ m^3$

Example 8.6 *Calculate the approximate quantities of (a) Bricks, (b) Cement, (c) Steel, (d) Coarse aggregate 20 mm down, (e) Coarse aggregate 40 mm down and f Sand required for a four* *storey building in R.C.C. framed construction comprising of 2 dwellings per floor of 100 sqm each.*

(*a*) *Bricks*

Refer Table 8.5 $A = 100$ sqm

Requirement of Bricks per dwelling of 100 sqm.

$$= -26.2 + 2.56A - 0.0096A^2 = -26.2 + 2.56 \times 100 - 0.0096 \times 100 \times 100$$
$$= -26.2 + 256 - 96 = 256 - 122.2\% \text{ Nos} = 133.8 \times 100 = 13{,}380 \text{ Nos.}$$

For 2×4 such dwellings = $8 \times 13{,}380$ = 1,07,040 nos.

(*b*) *Cement*

Refer Table 8.5 $A = 100$ sqm

Requirement of cement per dwelling of 100 sqm

Super structure

$$= 0.182A - 0.35 = 0.182 \times 100 - 0.35 = 18.2 - 0.35 = 17.85 \text{ Tonne}$$

For 2×4 such dwellings = 8×17.85 = 142.80 Tonne

Add for substructure

Refer Table 8.7

$$= 0.0204A - 0.014 = 0.0204 \times 100 - 0.014 = 2.04 - 0.014 = 2.026 \text{ Tonne}$$

For 2×1 such units = 2×2.026 = 4.052 Tonne

Total for superstructure and substructure

$$= 142.80 + 4.052 = 146.852 \text{ Tonne}$$

(*c*) *Steel*

Superstructure

Refer Table 8.5

Requirement of steel per dwelling of 100 sqm $A = 100$ sqm

$$= -1{,}491 + 92.0A - 0.36A^2 = -1{,}491 + 92.0 \times 100 - 0.36 \times 100 \times 100$$
$$= -1{,}492 + 9{,}200 - 3{,}600 = 9{,}200 - 5{,}091 = 4{,}209 \text{ kg.}$$

For 2×4 such dwellings

$$= 8 \times 4{,}209 = 33{,}672 \text{ kg}$$

Add for substructure

Refer Table 8.7

$$= -171 + 10{,}46A - 0.041A^2 = -171 + 10.46 \times 100 - 0.041 \times 100 \times 100$$
$$= -171 + 1{,}046 - 410 = 1{,}046 - 581 = 465 \text{ kg}$$

For 2×1 such units = 2×465 = 930 kg

Total for superstructure and substructure

$$= 33{,}672 + 930 = 34{,}602 \text{ kg}$$

(*d*) *Coarse aggregate 20 mm down*

Superstructure

Requirement of coarse aggregate 20 mm down per dwelling

Refer Table 8.5 $A = 100$

$= 0.295A - 0.75 = 0.295 \times 100 - 0.75 = 29.5 - 0.75 = 28.75 \text{ m}^3$

For 2×4 such dwellings

$= 8 \times 28.75 = 230.0 \text{ m}^3$

Add for substructure

Refer Table 8.7 $A = 100$ sqm

$= 0.171A - 0.01 = 0.171 \times 100 - 0.01 = 7.1 - 0.01 = 7.09 \text{ m}^3$

For 2×1 such units

$= 2 \times 7.09 = 14.18 \text{ m}^3$

Total for substructure and superstructure

$= 230.0 + 14.18 = 244.18^3$

(*e*) *Coarse aggregate 40 mm down*

Superstructure

Coarse aggregate 40 mm down per dewlling

Refer Table 8.5 $A = 100$ sqm

$= 0.45 + 0.0027A - 0.0001A^2 = 0.45 + 0.0027 \times 100 - 0.0001 \times 100 \times 100$

$= 0.45 + 0.27 - 1.00 = 0.72 - 1.00 = \text{nil}$

(*f*) *Sand*

Superstructure

Requirement of sand per dwelling of 100 sqm

Refer Table 8.5 $A = 100$ sqm

$= 0.361A - 0.38 = 0.361 \times 100 - 0.38 = 36.1 - 0.38 = 35.72 \text{ m}^3$

For 2×4 such dwellings

$= 8 \times 35.72 = 285.76 \text{ m}^3$

Add for substructure

Refer Table 8.7

Requirement of sand per unit

$= 0.036A = 0.036 \times 100 = 3.60 \text{ m}^3$

For 2×1 such units

$= 2 \times 3.6 = 7.2 \text{ m}^3$

Total for superstructure and substructure

$= 285.76 + 7.2$

$= 292.96 \text{ m}^3$

8.7.0 FINANCIAL CONTROL

A project need be efficiently controlled by the management. Responsibility of the management does not end with planning and execution of the work. Management includes financial planning and control of it during the entire process of execution, so that the operation ends successfully without any fund problem which would otherwise hamper the physical progress. Physical progress of a project cannot be ensured without proper financial inflow of fund required at different stages as planned. This part of the management is better controlled by a Cash-Flow Chart. The cash-flow chart will indicate the flow of fund required, expenditure, return, if any, expected from the project at different stages. It shows the expected financial benefit that may accrue at the completion of the project.

Example 8.7. *project costing Rs. 500 lac is proposed to be financed by borrowing from a financial institution. The loan will be drawn as required. The borrowed amount will bear an interest at the rate of 10% per annum. The project is expected to yield Rs. 700 lac in a span of 8 years starting from the third year.*

Draw a Cash-Flow Chart.

CASH-FLOW CHART

All figures are in Rs. lac

Year	*Expenditure*	*Loan during the year*	*Return from the project*	*Return of loan with interest*	*Interest on loan during the year 10%*	*Total loan & interest at the end of the year Cumulative*	*Remarks*
0	50.00	50.00	–	–	2.5	52.50	
1	100.00	100.00	–	–	10.25	162.75	
2	100.00	50.00	50.00	–	18.78	231.53	
3	100.00	–	100.00	–	23.15	254.68	
4	100.00	–	100.00	–	25.47	280.15	
5	50.00	–	100.00	50.00	28.02	258.17	
6	–	–	100.00	100.00	25.82	183.99	
7	–	–	100.00	100.00	18.40	102.39	
8	–	–	100.00	100.00	10.24	12.63	
9	–	–	50.00	13.89	1.26	36.11	Surplus
	500.00	200.00	700.00	363.89			

(*i*) It would be seen from the Cash-Flow Chart that the project was self financing.

(*ii*) Borrowed amount would be returned fully with interest in 10 years.

(*iii*) The project would yield Rs. 36.11 lac as surplus after meeting all the liabilities.

If the actual financial inflow from the project *i.e* return from the project goes wrong, the net surplus at the end of the 9th year Rs. 36.11 lac would be eroded partly or fully. In the event of such occurrence, the manager foreseeing that the final yield might be eroded and/or there is possibility of loss, might suggest ways and means for enhancing the return from the project much ahead to counter the possibility of any loss in the future and keep the project financially viable.

8.8.0 FINANCIAL VIABILITY ANALYSIS

Before finally deciding upon a project, it should be examined in all respects whether the project is economically viable to justify if taking of the project would be economically beneficial for the client. This is done by undertaking a financial viability analysis of the project.

Financial viability is a quantitative technique to decide the financial prospect of a project on a rational basis. It is not a Cash-Flow Chart which furnishes the inflow and outflow of fund only; but does not indicate anything about viability of the project. Whereas, Financial viability analysis provides a comprehensive statement of development and return in terms of figures and justifies the viability of the project. The financial viability provides comparison of financial benefits likely to be accrued against the cost to be incurred. It explains clearly whether the project would be financially viable and profitable or the project would be worthwhile and financially beneficial.

Financial viability analysis should be undertaken for each and every project for appraising the client about the financial prospect in clear terms. In conducting such analysis all the probable costs likely to be incurred for the project should be taken into account including the interest, if any likely to be paid, outgoings on account of maintenance and operation, tax, etc. as the financial viability study period would continue beyond the project duration period; it may even be for the total life span of the structure. On the benefit side also, all the financial incomes, premiums, rents, etc. shall be taken into account during the same period.

In financial viability analysis, only the direct financial benefits shall be taken into account. There may be other benefits which cannot be quantified and accounted for financially. These would be left out. There is tendency to show the projects financially viable anyhow by incorporating distorted information. These should be avoided.

Economic cost

Economic cost of project is different from that of the financial cost. These two are not the same. In working out the economic cost of the project, it may be necessary to apply shadow wage rate for unskilled labour and also shadow pricing for foreign exchange component. As regards the benefits, it is often not possible to quantify the indirect benefits. It would be sufficient to consider for Cost-Benefit Analysis, only the direct quantifiable benefits. Benefits may be considered taking into view either of the two:

(*a*) Before and after situation

(*b*) With or without situation

Analysis on the before and after situation is suitable for projects of curative nature that means the projects which tries to cure a problem whereas with and without approach will be appropriate for projects of preventive nature, *i.e.* project which would try to prevent a future crisis. In estimating the costs and in quantification of the benefits, it is often necessary to make a number of assumptions. In some cases, consideration of the future condition has to be made. If the conditions change from that assumed, the results of the Cost-Benefit Analysis would also change substantially. In order to understand the degree of uncertainty, a sensitivity analysis should be undertaken where the assumed factors would be varied within a range and their effects on Benefit-Cost ratio or on Internal Rate of Return (IRR) would be studied.

8.8.1 Benefit Cost Ratio (B/C)

Benefit Cost Ratio of probable benefits and costs of project which can conveniently be used as a technique developed for expressing profitability in terms of a single number or index. The index can be used as a basis for judging whether a project is profitable enough to be acceptable and also to compare the economics of one project with another.

The costs and benefits in connection with a project is generally spread out in a number of years. All these future values should be converted to the present values which is called discounting. Once the financial costs and benefits of a project have been identified and measured, the ratio may be found out. The ratio would be a single digit figure and is termed 'Benefit-Cost Ratio.' If the ratio is more than unity, the project is economically viable. Alternative projects may be framed, and Benefit-Cost Ratio of each may be studied and the most suitable one may be taken up.

8.8.2 Social Benefit-Cost Analysis

A private individual or a Real Estate Developer is interested in direct financial gain and does not take interest in other human aspects. Hence, it is a straight-forward exercise to decide whether the project is justified or not.

But in a public sector project, aspects other than financial need be taken into consideration. A housing project when undertaken by a private agency, his sole aim is to have some profit margin, but in a public-sector, a housing project for a Economically Weaker Section or Low Income Group may have to be undertaken even with subsidy. It is therefore, necessary to apply some different yardstick for justification of such projects. The social benefits likely to be achieved need be taken into account in addition to financial benefits.

8.8.3 Internal Rate of Return (IRR)

Internal Rate of Return is another method of appraising the economic justification of a project. In this method the discounted cost streams are compared with the discounted benefit streams. The rate at which the discounted cost would be equal to the discounted benefits, has to be worked out on trial and error basis. This rate *i.e.* the IRR is a clear indication about the justification for the project because it can be compared with the opportunity cost of the capital.

Example 8.8. *A builder intends to build a commercial project. Preliminary exercise indicates that the cost of the project would be Rs. 500 lac, inclusive of cost of land, Rs. 50 lac. The expenditure planning indicates that the project would take 6 years for completion. It would yield Rs.700 lac from the third year of starting. Calculate the index of financial viability of the project.*

The cost and benefit schedule would be as below:

Year	*Cost Rs. lac*	*Benefit Rs. lac*
0	50	–
1	100	–
2	100	50
3	100	100
4	100	100
5	50	100
6	–	100
7	–	100
8	–	100
9	–	50
	500 lac	700 lac

Commutation of Benefit-Cost Analysis and Internal Rate of Return (IRR)

	Direct finan-cial cost in lac	*Discounted costs*				*Direct financial benefits in lac*	*Discounted Benefits*			
		11%	12%	12.5%	13%		11%	12%	12.5%	13%
0	50.00	50.00	50.00	50.00	50.00	–	–	–	–	–
1	100.00	90.09	89.29	88.89	88.50	–	–	–	–	–
2	100.00	81.16	79.72	79.01	78.32	50.00	40.58	39.86	39.50	39.16
3	100.00	73.12	71.18	70.23	69.31	100.00	73.12	71.18	70.23	69.31
4	100.00	65.87	63.55	62.43	61.33	100.00	65.87	63.55	62.43	61.33
5	50.00	29.68	28.37	27.74	27.14	100.00	59.35	56.74	55.49	54.28
6	–	–	–	–	–	100.00	53.46	50.66	49.33	48.03
7	–	–	–	–	–	100.00	48.17	45.24	43.85	42.51
8	–	–	–	–	–	100.00	43.39	40.39	38.97	37.62
9	–	–	–	–	–	50.00	19.54	18.03	17.32	16.69
	500.00	389.92	382.11	378.30	374.60	700.00	403.48	385.65	377.12	368.93

B/C Ratio at 11% = 1.06 12% =1.03 12.5% = 1.00 13% = 0.98 IRR = 12.5%

9

COMPREHENSIVE STATUS REPORT

9.1.0 INTRODUCTION

Project manager before commencing a building work would like to know the comprehensive status of the project to enable himself equipped for all possible difficulties he may have to face during execution of the work.

9.1.1 Information Required by a Project Manager

Quantity surveyor may be of great help in this respect. He may help the project manager in all respects and acquaint him with all possible information he (the project manager) may like to have. The information required may be obtained from the sources :

9.1.2 Detailed Estimate

The quantities of different materials that would be required may be worked out from the estimated quantities of items of work and multiplying those by the index of requirement per unit provided in the appendix 7.

Requirement of labour

The approximate number of different categories of labour may be obtained with the help of Section 13.4.0 and 13.5.0 in which estimation of requirement of labour and their standard combination for different items of work has been furnished. In this respect the analysis of different items of work may be of help. However, all possible items of Civil Engineering works cannot be brought in a nut shell. Some of the items may have to be worked out from the idea provided and method as indicated. This method is generally adopted and commonly used. The quantities of materials and labour obtained are broad based and more reliable as those are obtained by working out the quantities of different items of work. The quantities obtained are useful datas for framing Bar-Chart and Network Construction Management.

9.1.3 Approximate Quantities on Plinth Area Basis

Approximate quantities of materials and labour may be obtained with the help of Tables as provided in Section 8. The method has been developed by the Central Building Research Institute, Roorkee. The method is based on plinth area of the building. It provides for working out approximate quantities on Statistical basis. It is not as reliable as the former.

9.1.4 Comprehensive Status Report

In both the methods, the project manager shall have to do a lot of work for finding out the quantities of materials and labour as he would like to have. Hence, there is a pressing demand for development of a comprehensive method of working out the Status Report of the project which will speak for instantaneously the quantities of different materials and labour.

Thus, the necessity of developing such a comprehensive status report was felt from which the project manager can readily have his desired information.

The statement provides break up of quantities of labour and materials in detail of the items.

The abstract of the statement furnishes the total quantity of each kind of material and each category of labour. The project manager on obtaining the information may be able to plan as he would desire. The scheduling of the materials and labour required would be easy. As the quantities are obtained from the detailed estimate, the figures are reliable and more correct.

9.2 ABSTRACT OF QUANTITIES AND AMOUNT

Refer Exercise 2.13.

Item no.	*Description of item*	*Quantity*	*Unit*	*Rate*	*Amount*
1.	Earthwork in excavation in foundation	29.984	% cum	2,973.00	891.00
2.	Single brick flat soling	40.748	sqm	95.00	3,871.00
3.	Cement concrete 1 : 3 : 6 in foundation.	7.926	cum	1,623.00	12,864.00
4.	Brickwork in cement mortar 1 : 4 in foundation.	12.532	cum	1,760.00	22,056.00
5.	Damp proof course 25 mm thick	8.856	sqm	70.00	620.00
6.	Earthwork in back filling	10.157	% cum	1,738.00	177.00
7.	Earthwork in plinth filling	7.181	% cum	1,738.00	125.00
8.	Brickwork in superstructure in cement mortar 1 : 6	20.384	cum	1,602.00	32,655.00
9.	Brickwork in pillars in cement mortar 1 : 4	2.400	cum	1,760.00	4,224.00
10.	Single brick flat soling in floor	11.810	sqm	95.00	1,122.00
11.	Cement concrete 1 : 3 : 6	7.181	cum	1,931.00	13,867.00
12.	Casting, hoisting cement concrete bearing blocks	6	Nos.	100.00	600.00
13.	Supplying hoisting and fixing R.S.J.	226.060 kg = 2.261	Qtl.	110.00	249.00
14.	Shuttering and centering	73.851	sqm	105.00	7,754.00
15.	Cement concrete 1 : 2 : 4	7.454	cum	2,373.00	17,688.00
16.	M.S. reinforcement	471	kg	20.831	9,811.00
17.	Brickwork in cement mortar 1 : 4	3.394	cum	1,760.00	5,973.00
18.	Lime terracing 7 : 2 : 2, 100 mm thick	48.98	sqm	142.00	6,955.00
19.	Supplying and fixing door and window frame	0.186	cum	2,898.00	5,390.00
20.	Supplying and fixing fan hook	2 Nos.	Each	25.00	50.00
21.	Supplying and fixing m.s. clamp 25 × 6 mm				
	i. 225 mm long	12 Nos	Each	12.00	144.00
	ii. 150 mm long	32 Nos	Each	8.00	256.00
22.	Supplying and fixing door and window shutters				
	i. Door shutter 40 mm thick panelled double leaf	4.163	sqm	3445.00	15,892.00
	ii. Window shutter 25 mm thick 2/3 panelled and 1/3 glazed.	8.325	sqm	1,977.00	16,459.00
23.	Supplying and fixing iron mongeries				
	a. Door 2 Nos.				
	i. 100 mm iron hinge	12 Nos.	Each	16.60	199.00
	ii. Door handle 150 mm	4 Nos.	Each	17.35	69.00
	iii. Tower bolt 300 mm long (iron)	2 Nos	Each	52.20	104.00
	iv. Hasp bolt (iron)	2 Nos.	Each	80.00	160.00
	v. Door rings (brass)	2 Nos.	Each	10.00	20.00
	vi. Rubber door stop	4 Nos.	Each	25.00	100.00
	vii. Sand block 100 × 50 × 40 mm	4 Nos.	Each	12.00	48.00

(Contd...)

Item no.	Description of item	Quantity	Unit	Rate	Amount
	b. Window 4 Nos.				
	i. 75 mm iron hinge.	32 Nos.	Each	7.75	248.00
	ii. Window handle 100 mm	16 Nos.	Each	8.15	130.00
	iii. Tower bolt 150 mm (iron)	16 Nos.	Each	35.85	574.00
	iv. Catch hook (iron)	16 Nos.	Each	39.00	624.00
24.	Supplying and fixing ventilators 150 × 225 mm	8 Nos.	Each	26.50	215.00
25.	Salwood work rough dressed in roof truss	0.241	cum	39,200.00	9,447.00
26.	Asbestos sheet roofing	38.760	sqm	170.00	6,589.20
27.	Water proofing the junction of asbestos roofing and wall	11.625	m	50.00	581.00
28.	Sand and cement plaster 1 : 6				
	i. 15 mm thick	122.815	sqm	45.00	5,527.00
	ii. 20 mm thick	152.240	sqm	73.00	11,114.00
29.	Sand and cement plaster 1 : 4, 10 mm thick	43.200	sqm	42.00	1,814.00
30.	25 mm I.P.S. in flooring	75.423	sqm	91.00	6,863.00
31.	Neat cement finishing on plaster	22.814	sqm	15.00	342.00
32.	White washing two coats over a coat of priming	189.82	% sqm	466.00	885.00
33.	Decorative cement based paint two coats over a coat of priming	99.761	sqm	19.00	1,895.00
34.	*a*. Painting to wood works, two coats over a coat priming	28.643	sqm	40.00	1,146.00
	b. Painting to wood works, one coat over a coat of priming	19.030	sqm	25.10	478.00
	c. Painting to wood works one coat	3.720	sqm	14.90	55.00
35.	Painting to steel surface two coats	16.680	sqm	32.20	538.00
36.	Supplying and fixing m.s. grill made of 12 mm × 6 mm flats	7.920	sqm	360.00	2,851.00
	Plinth area =11.625 × 7.25 = 84.281 sqm Rate per sqm = Rs. 2,699.00			Rs.	2,27,458.00

(Contd...)

9.3.0 Labour Output Constants (Items of Work)

S. No.	Description of work	Unit	Labour	Recommended constant (Days)	Remark
1.	**Excavation and Earthwork**	cu. m.	Mate Mazdoor	0.06 0.62	Extra refilling in layer
	(a) Excavation over areas upto 1.5 m and removal	cu. m.	Mate Mazdoor	0.06 0.60	Mate 0.20 Mazdoor 0.25
	(b) Excavation in trenches.	cu. m.	Mate Mazdoor	0.06 0.5	Bhisti 0.02
2.	**Concrete**				
	(a) Hand mixed C.C.	cu. m.	Mason Mazdoor Bhisti	0.1 2.13 0.7	
	(b) Hand mixed L.C.	cu. m.	Mason Mazdoor Bhisti Bullock with Driver	0.1 2.65 0.8 0.15	
	(c) R.C.C.Work	cu. m.	Mason Mazdoor Bhisti Mixer operator Mixer Vibrator	0.24 0.25 0.90 0.07 0.07 0.07	
3.	**Mortars**				
	(a) Cement mortar any mix. By hand.	cu. m.	Mazdoor Bhisti	0.75 0.07	
	(b) Cement, lime, sand and mix.	cu. m.	Mazdoor Bhisti Bullock with driver	1.33 0.1 0.33	
4.	**Brick work (walls)**				Labour for mixing will be extra in all types of lime work
	(a) Exceeding one brick thick. Cement : Lime mortar	cu. m.	Mason Mazdoor Bhisti	0.94 1.8 0.2	
	(b) One brick thick. Cement : Lime mortar	sq. m.	Mason Mazdoor Bhisti	0.25 0.4 0.1	
	(c) Hall brick in 'Cement mortar'	sq. m.	Mason Mazdoor Bhisti	0.12 0.2 0.07	
	(d) Tile work in Superstructure in cement mortar	sq. m.	Mason Mazdoor Bhisti	1.8 1.8 0.2	
5.	**Form work Fabrication and erection**				
	1. Columns and walls	cu. m.	Carpenter	0.25	

(Contd...)

S. No.	Description of work	Unit	Labour	Recommended constant (Days)	Remark
			Mazdoor	0.20	
	2. Suspended floors/roofs	sq. m.	Carpenter	0.23	
			Mazdoor	0.20	
	3. Sides and soffits of beams	sq. m.	Carpenter	0.30	
6.	Reinforcement Bar reinforcement complete	Quintal	Bar bender	1.0	
			Mazdoor	1.0	
7.	**Plastering and Pointing**				
	(*a*) 15 mm thick cement plaster	Quintal	Mason	0.08	
			Mazdoor	0.1	
			Bhisti	0.1	
	(*b*) Struck pointing to brickwork cement mortar	Quintal	Mason	0.08	
			Mazdoor	0.1	
			Bhisti	0.1	
8.	**Paving and floor finish**				Labour for mixing concrete will be each for (*a*) and (*b*)
	(*a*) 40 mm thick floor finish, P.C.C.	Quintal	Mason	0.08	
			Mazdoor	0.12	
			Bhisti	0.1	
	(*b*) 40 mm thick terrazo flooring (*i*) Laying	Quintal	Mason	0.22	
			Mazdoor	0.22	
			Bhisti	0.01	
	(*ii*) Cutting, grinding and polishing	Quintal	Mazdoor	0.5	
			Machine	0.4	
9.	**Damp proof course**				
	(*a*) 40 mm thick P.C.C.	sq. m.	Mason	0.1	
			Mazdoor	0.1	
			Bhisti	0.01	
	(*b*) 20 mm thick P.C.C.	sq. m.	Mason	0.1	
			Mazdoor	0.1	
			Bhisti	0.01	
10.	**Joinery**				
	(*a*) Door and window chaukhats	cu. m.	Carpenter	20.0	
			Mazdoor	2.0	
	(*b*) 40 mm thick door or window shutters	sq. m.	Carpenter	0.9	
			Mazdoor	0.1	
	(*c*) Fixing ready made shutters	sq. m.	Carpenter	0.25	
			Mazdoor	0.25	
11.	Glazing Fixing glass panes on steel or wood	sq. m.	Glazier	0.2	
			Mazdoor	0.01	
12.	Painting and Polishing	sq. m.	Painter	0.35	
13.	**White washing and colour washing**				
	(*a*) Three coats on new surface	sq. m.	Washer	0.02	
			Mazdoor	0.01	

(*Contd...*)

S. No.	Description of work	Unit	Labour	Recommended constant (Days)	Remark
	(b) Two coats colour washing over one under coat white wash on new work	sq. m.	Washer Mazdoor	0.03 0.01	
	(c) White wash one coat on old or new work.	sq. m.	Washer	0.02	
	(d) Distempering with dry distemper 3 coats on new surface including a priming coat.	sq. m.	Painter Mazdoor	0.08 0.04	
14.	**Terraced roofing**				
	(a) 10 cm thick mud phuska including one layer of tile and gobar leeping	sq. m.	Mason Mazdoor Bhisti	0.13 0.36 0.11	
	(b) 10 cm thick lime concrete terracing	sq. m.	Mason Mazdoor Bhisti	0.1 0.37 0.15	

9.3.1. Labour Output Constants (Quantity of Work per day)

S. No.	Description of item	Quantity of Work per day	Remarks
1.	**Mason**		
	(i) Lime concrete	10 cu. m.	20 to 30 sq. m.
	(ii) Cement concrete 1 : 5 : 10	10 cu. m.	
	(iii) c.c. in R.C.C. 1 : 2 : 4	3 cu. m.	
	(iv) Brick work in foundations	2 cu. m.	
	(v) Brick work in superstructure	1.5 cu. m.	
	(vi) Brick work in arches	1 cu. m.	
	(vii) Half brick work in partitions	8 sq. m.	
	(viii) Tile work in superstructure	0.5 cu. m.	
	(ix) 40 mm thick D.P.C.	10 sq. m.	
	(x) Stone work ashlar type	0.25 cu. m.	
	(xi) Stone work random rubble	1.0 cu. m.	
	(xii) Marble work	0.05 cu. in.	
	(xiii) Brick flooring	15 sq. m.	
	(xiv) P.C.C. flooring	8 to 10 sq. m.	
	(xv) Terrazo flooring	4 to 5 sq. m.	
	(xvi) Marble flooring	1 to 2 sq. m.	
	(xvii) Stone flooring	4 to 5 sq. m.	
	(xviii) Mud phuska	8 sq. m.	
	(xix) Lime concrete terracing	10 sq. m.	
	(xx) 15 mm thick plaster	10 sq. m.	
	(xxi) Pointing	10 sq. m.	
	(xxii) Punning	20 sq. m.	

(Contd...)

S. No.	Description of item	Quantity of Work per day	Remarks
	(xxiii) R. B. Work	4 to 5 sq. m.	
	(xxiv) Tile roofing	5 sq. m.	
	(xxv) Three coats white or colour washing on new surface	50 sq. m.	
	(xxvi) Two coats white washing on new surface	100 sq. m.	
2.	**Carpenter**		
	(i) Timbering in trenches open type	300 to 400 sq. m.	
	(ii) Centring and shuttering	4 to 8 sq. m.	
	(iii) Door and window chaukhat	0.05 cu. m.	
	(iv) Door and window shutter	1 sq. m.	
	(v) Jafri work	1 sq. m.	
	(vi) Pelmets	5 sq. m.	
	(vii) Jali work	5 sq. m.	
	(viii) Wooden floors	0.5 sq. m.	
	(ix) A.C. sheet roof	8 sq. in.	
	(x) Ceiling work	2 sq. m.	
	(xi) Fixing shutters	4 sq. m.	
	(xii) Fixing glass panes	5 sq. m.	
	(xiii) Wooden marking	2 to 4 sq. m.	
3.	**Painter**		
	(i) Distempering on new surface	20 sq. m.	
	(ii) Wood preservative on new wood work	50 sq. m.	
	(iii) Painting wood work with priming coat	20 sq. m.	
	(iv) Painting new wood work with two coats along with priming coat	10 sq. m.	
	(v) Painting old wood work with one coat	30 sq. m.	
	(vi) Varnishing new wood work complete	20 sq. m.	
	(vii) Polishing new wood work complete	5 sq. m.	
	(viii) Applying one coat of bitumen on D.P.C.	50 sq. m.	
4.	**Blacksmith**		
	(i) M.S. Bars, bending, binding and placing in position	100 kg.	
	(ii) Structural steel work	200 kg.	
5.	**Labourer**		
	(i) Earthwork in trenches	2 to 3 cu.m.	
	(ii) Earthwork in filling.	5 to 10 cu. m.	
	(iii) Concrete work in foundations	0.4 cu. m.	
	(iv) Concrete work in R.C.C.	0.3 cu. m.	
	(v) Mixing cement mortar	3 cu. m.	
	(vi) Delivering bricks	4000 No.	
	(vii) Breaking brick ballast 25 mm size	0.8 cu. m.	
	(viii) Breaking stone ballast 40 mm size	0.5 cu. m.	
	(ix) Excavation in rock	1 cu. m.	
	(x) Delivering mortar	5 cu. m.	

9.4.0 ABSTRACT OF MATERIALS AND LABOUR

		Quantity	Unit	Rate	Amount
	A. Materials				
1.	Bricks	17.117	% Nos.	2,800.00	47,928.00
2.	Stone chips 20 mm down	22.542	cum	825.00	18,593.00
3.	Sand	30.536	cum	35500	10,840.00
4.	Cement	8.031	cum		
		= 231 bags	bag	140.00	32,340.00
5.	Stone chips 6 mm down	0.195	cum	760.00	148.00
6.	R.S.J.	2.261	Quintal	2,000.00	4,522.00
7.	Water proofing compound	4.65	kg	70.00	326.00
8.	Hard wood	1.527	cum	10,000.00 (Reduced rate)	15,270.00
9.	Steel reinforcement	495	kg	10.00	4,950.00
10.	Stone lime (slaked)	1.515	cum	2,785.00	4,219.00
11.	Surkhi	1.420	cum	400.00	568.00
12.	Brick khoa	5.00	cum	350.00	1,750.00
13.	Salwood	0.448	cum	29,750.00	13,328.00
14.	Teak wood	0.433	cum	67,000.00	29,011.00
15.	Cement based paint	50 kg			
		= 1 bag	bag	600.00	600.00
16.	High gloss oil paint	10.474	Liter	100.00	1,047.00
17.	Primer oil paint	4.296	Liter	60.00	258.00
18.	M.S. flat	95.04	kg	12.00	1,140.00
19.	Asbestos sheet corrugated	40.70	sqm	50.00	2,035.00
20.	Miscellaneous items with lump sum provision		L.S.		10,108.00
					1,99,985.00
	B. Labour				
1.	Head mason	5.304	Mandays	95.00	504.00
2.	Mason	61.393	Mandays	85.00	5,218.00
3.	Carpenter	37.642	Mandays	85.00	3,200.00
4.	Mazdoor	220.579	Mandays	65.00	14,338.00
5.	Beater	31.846	Mandays	65.00	2,070.00
6.	Painter	15.429	Mandays	95.00	1,466.00
7.	Blacksmith	7.920	Mandays	80.00	634.00
					27,419.00
					22,7404.00

Materials 88%

Labour 12%

9.5.0 PERCENTAGE OF COST OF MAJOR MATERIALS

1. Bricks	Rs. 47,928.00	23.97%
2. Stone chips 20 mm down	18,597.00	9.30%
3. Sand	10,840.00	5.42%
4. Cement	32,340.00	16.57%
5. Salwood	13,328.00	6.66%
6. Teakwood	29,011.00	14.51%
7. Hard wood	15,270.00	7.64%

9.6.0 QUANTITY OF MATERIALS AS PER TABLE 8.5

(*i*) Bricks

Refer Table 8.5 $A = 84.281$ sqm

Requirement of bricks

$$= 2.26A + 66.8 = 2.26 \times 84.281 + 66.8$$

$$= 190.48 + 66.80 = 257.28\% = 257.28 \times 100 = 25{,}728 \text{ Nos.}$$

(*ii*) *Cement*

Refer Table 8.5 $A = 84.281$ sqm.

Requirement of cement

$$= 0.153A + 0.057 = 0.153 \times 84.281 + 0.057$$

$$= 12.89 + 0.057 = 12.95 \text{ Tonnes}$$

(*iii*) *Stone chips 20 mm down*

Refer Table 8.5 $A = 84.281$ sqm

Requirement of coarse aggregate 20 mm down

$$= 0.176\, A - 0.21 = 0.176 \times 84.281 - 0.21$$

$$= 14.83 - 0.21 = 14.62 \text{ Tonnes}$$

(*iv*) *Sand*

Refer table 8.5 $A = 84.281$ sqm

Requirement of sand

$$= 0.47\, A - 7 = 0.47 \times 84.281 - 7$$

$$= 39.61 - 7 = 32.61 \text{ cum}$$

(*v*) *Steel*

Refer table 8.5 $A = 84.281$ sqm

Requirement of steel

$$= 21.3A - 314 = 21.3 \times 84.281 - 314$$

$$= 1{,}795.19 - 314 = 1481 \text{ kg}$$

(*vi*) *Timber for frames and shutters and shuttering*

Refer Table 8.5 $A = 84.281$ sqm

Requirement of timber

$$= 0.019A + 0.23 = 0.019 \times 84.281 + 0.23$$

$$= 1.60 + 0.23 = 1.83 \text{ cum}$$

9.7.0 COMPARISON OF REQUIREMENT OF MATERIALS

	Materials	*Requirement for 84.281 Sqm plinth area unit*	
		As per detailed estimate	*Approximate quantity as per Table 8.5*
1.	Bricks	17,117 Nos.	25,728 Nos.
2.	Cement	11.55 Tonnes	12.95 Tonnes
3.	Stone chips 20 mm down	22.542 cum	14.62 cum
4.	Sand	30.536 cum	32.61 cum
5.	Steel	495 kg	1,481 kg
6.	Timber	2.408 cum	1.83 cum

Note : The formulae under Table are based on statistical basis. For further comparison also refer Table 8.2 and 8.3 under Chapter 8.

9.8.0 AVERAGE NUMBER OF MANDAYS OF LABOUR PER SQM OF PLINTH AREA

Plinth area = 84.281 sqm

Total number of mandays of labour required = 380.113

Average number of mandays of labour required

Per sqm of plinth area $= \dfrac{380.113}{84.281} = 4.51$ number of mandays

10

ROAD WORKS

10.1.0 ESTIMATION OF ROAD WORKS

Estimation of road works consists of three parts.

(*i*) **Earthwork in embankment or cutting.** This involves working out the quantities of earthwork required for building the embankment or earthwork in cutting for laying the road pavement. Estimation of quantities depend upon the existing ground condition, its level and level of the proposed formation. The embankment sides or the sides of the cutting are always kept in slope. This slope also need be known. A longitudinal section along the proposed alignment is drawn and cross-sections at regular intervals are drawn showing the ground and formation levels, on the basis of the longitudinal section and cross-sections, the volume of earthwork in embankment or cutting is worked out.

(*ii*) **Construction of bridges and culverts.** Bridges and culverts of different sizes, magnitudes and different types may be used to bridge over the gaps for the waterways across the road. The culverts may be box-type bridge, arch culverts, plain slab culverts, R.C.C. piped culverts, and also minor bridges and major bridges. These structures may be built by using various materials—stone-rubble masonry, concrete, brick masonry or steel. The commonly used materials are brick masonry and cement concrete and reinforced concrete. Though method of estimation of the quantities is the same in all the cases, but due to special shapes adopted and according to the situation, technique of estimation may have to be varied.

(*iii*) **Pavement portion of the road.** Pavement portion of the road also vary according to the load and volume of the traffic. It also depends upon the climatic condition and also on the materials available. Except in special cases of important roads, materials available locally are used. Cost of imported materials increase the cost of construction. However, for the wearing course, materials may have to be brought from a distance in spite of its cost, as wearing course has to sustain the wear and tear and abrasion on the surface due to the traffic moving on it.

10.2.0 EARTHWORK IN EMBANKMENT OR CUTTING

Road pavement is laid on embankment or cutting depending on the ground condition. Generally, in the plains, embankments are built on which the pavements are laid. In hilly areas, cutting is required to be done for fixing the alignment of the roads. In irrigation works for fixing the alignment of canals, cutting may also be necessary.

The volume of earthwork in embankment or cutting is worked out by using formulae suitable for easy and quick calculation.

10.2.1 Embankment

Cross section of road or flood embankment is usually in the form of trapezium and the quantity or earthwork can be worked out with the help of prismoidal formula.

Quantity or volume = Cross sectional area × length.

Sectional area $= 2b \times h + 2 \times \frac{sh \times h}{2}$

$= 2bh + sh^2$

Volume for length, $L = L \times$ Cross-sectional area

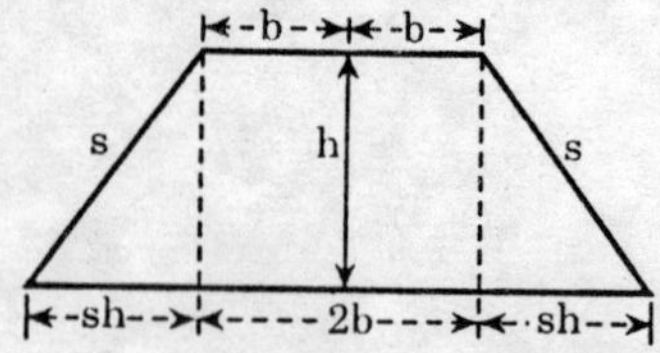

Figure 10.1 Embankment.

The cross-sectional area of two ends generally vary, the volume is calculated on the basis of mean cross-sectional area.

10.2.2. Prismoidal Formula

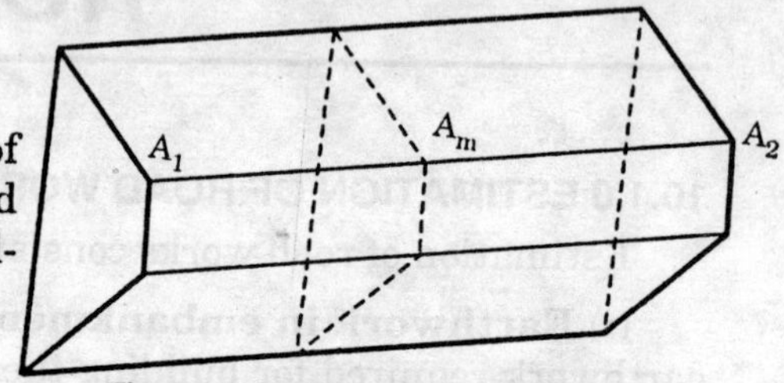

Figure 10.2 Prismoidal Formula.

Prismoidal formula for calculation of the volume of embankment is applied when the length is appreciable and the variation of cross-section at the ends and the mid-length is substantial.

$$\text{Volume} = \frac{L}{6}(A_1 + A_2 + 4A_m)$$

Where, L = Length of the section,

A_1 = Cross-sectional area at one end,

A_2 = Cross-sectional area at the other end,

A_m = Cross-sectional area at the mid-length.

Example 10.1. *Calculate the volume of an embankment 20 m long having 10 m wide crest and the slope 1 : 4, the height at one end is 4 m and at the other end is 6 m.*

Here, $L = 20$ m, $h = 4$ m and 6 m, $2b = 4$ m

$$A_1 = 2bh + sh^2 = 10 \times 4 + 4 \times 4^2$$

$$= 40 + 64 = 104 \text{ sqm}$$

$$A_2 = 2bh + sh^2 = 10 \times 6 + 4 \times 6^2$$

$$= 60 + 144 = 204 \text{ sqm}$$

$A_m = 2bh + sh^2$ height at mid section

$$= \frac{4+6}{2} = 5 \text{ m},$$

$$= 10 \times 5 + 4 \times 5^2 = 50 + 100 = 150 \text{ sqm}$$

$$\text{Volume} = \frac{L}{6}(A_1 + A_2 + 4\,A_m)$$

$$= \frac{20}{6}(104 + 204 + 4 \times 150)$$

$$= \frac{20}{6} \times 908 = 3{,}026.67 \text{ cum.}$$

10.2.3 Simpson's Rule

Prismoidal formula is applicable when the total length is not very long and the embankment has three sections ; but when the total length is long enough, calculation of volume with three sections only does not give fair result. In such case, Simpson's Rule gives comparatively better result.

Simpson's rule for computation of approximate value of area under a curve or of a definite integral

Simpson's rule is based on the assumption that any curve can be built from the area of parabola which have axes vertical. Simpson's rule does not give the correct result ; but provides approximate results very close to the correct results.

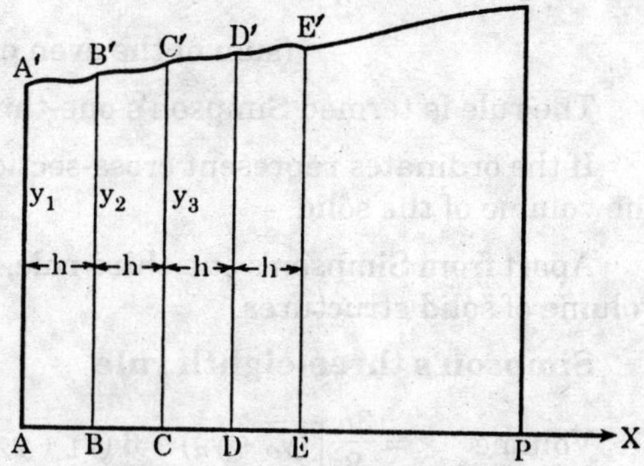

Figure 10.3. Simpson's Rule.

Let $A'\ B'\ C'$........ P' be any curve and let equidistant ordinates y_1, y_2, y_3 .... be drawn at intervals equal to h.

Consider the part of area that lies between y_1 and y_2 and let the portion $A'\ B'\ C'$ of the curve be replaced by a parabolic arc.

Since the area is to be expressed in terms of ordinates, we may work from the origin any where on the x axes.

Let the origin be taken at B, the foot of the ordinate y_2. x co-ordinates of A and C will be $-h$ and h respectively.

The equation $y = ax^2 + bx + c$ represents any parabola with its axis vertical. The area of the double strip $A\ C\ C'A'$.

$$= \int_{-h}^{h} y\, dx = \int_{-h}^{h} (ax^2 + bx + c)\, dx$$

$$= \int_{-h}^{h} \frac{a\,x^3}{3} + b\,\frac{x^2}{2} + cx = \frac{2\,h}{3}\,(a\,h^2\ 3c) \qquad ...(1)$$

Also $A'\,(-h, y_1)$, $B'\,(0, y_2)$, $C'\,(h, y/3)$ lies on the parabola.

$$Y_1 = a\,h^2 - bh + c,\ Y_2 = c,\ Y_3 = a\,h^2 + bh + c$$

We get, $\qquad 2\,ah^2 = y_1 + y_3 - 2y_2$

Hence, from (1), the area of the double strip $A\ C\ C'A'$

$$= \frac{h}{3}\,(y_1 + y_3 + 4\,y_2)$$

Similarly, the area of the next double strip

$$= \frac{h}{3}\,(y_3 + y_5 + 4\,y_4) \text{ and so on}$$

Now, let the number of such double strips be n, so that the total number of ordinates are $(2\,n + 1)$.

$$\text{Whole area} = \frac{h}{3}\,[(y_1 + y_3 + 4\,y_2) + (y_3 + y_5 + 4\,y_6) + \ (y_{2n-1} + y_{2n+1} + 4\,y_{2n})]$$

$$= \frac{h}{3}\,(y_1 + y_{2n+1}) + 2\,(y_3 + y_5 + \text{.......}y_{2n-1}) + 4\,(y_2 + y_4 + \text{......}y_{2n})$$

$$= \frac{h}{3} [(\text{sum of the first and the last ordinates}) + (\text{sum of the odd ordinates}) + (\text{sum of the even ordinates})].$$

The rule is termed Simpson's one-third rule.

If the ordinates represent cross-sectional areas at equal intervals, the simpson's rule gives the volume of the solid.

Apart from Simpson's one-third rule, there are other rules also for computation of area and volume of solid structures.

Simpson's three-eighth rule

$$\text{Volume} = \frac{3h}{8}\left[(y_o + y_n) + 3\,(y_1 + y_2 + y_4 + y_5.....) + 2\,(y_3 + y_6 + y_{n-3})\right].$$

Trapezoidal rule

$$\text{Volume} = \frac{h}{2}\left[(y_o + y_n) + 2\,(y_1 + y_2 + ...y_{n-1})\right].$$

Where, h = length of individual strips,

y_0, y_1, y_2, y_3 .... y_n are the ordinates at the stations 0, 1, 2, 3, ... n

The rule shall be selected and applied for computation of area or volume according to suitability and situation.

Comparison of the results computed by different rules

Example. *Find the volumes by using (i) Trapezoidal rule, (ii) Simpson's one-third rule, and (iii) Simpson's three-eighth rule.*

Divide the interval (0, 6) into six parts each of h = 1.

The values of co-ordinates at the situation are furnished as below :

Stations	0	1	2	3	4	5	6
Cross-sectional area	1	0.5	0.2	0.1	0.0588	0.0385	0.027
	y_0	y_1	y_2	y_3	y_4	y_5	y_6

(*i*) **Trapezoidal rule**

$$\text{Volume} = \frac{h}{2} [(y_0 + y_6) + 2\,(y_1 + y_2 + y_3 + y_4 + y_5)]$$

$$= 1/2\,(1 + 0.027) + 2\,(0.5 + 0.2 + 0.1 + 0.588 + 0.0385)$$

$$= 1.4108 \text{ cubics.}$$

(*ii*) **Simpson's one-third rule**

$$\text{Volume} = \frac{h}{3} [(y_0 + y_6) + 4\,(y_1 + y_3 + y_5) + 2\,(y_2 + y_4)]$$

$$= \frac{1}{3} [(1 + 0.027) + 4\,(0.5 + 0.1 + 0.0385) + 2\,(0.2 + 0.0588)]$$

$$= 1.3662 \text{ cubics.}$$

(*iii*) **Simpson's three-eighth rule**

$$\text{Volume} = \frac{3h}{8} [(y_0 + y_6) + 3\,(y_1 + y_2 + y_4 + y_5) + 2\,y_3]$$

$$= \frac{3}{8} [(1 + 0.027) + 3\,(0.5 + 0.2 + 0.0588 + 0.0385) + 2\,(0.1)]$$

$$= 1.3571 \text{ cubics.}$$

It is seen that the rules do not give the same result as the results are approximates.

Example 10.2. *Calculate the volume of road embankment 120 m long, having crest width 8.0 m at height of embankment at 30 m intervals starting from 0 is 0.60 m, 1.10 m, 1.60 m, 2.0 m and 1.3 m. The slope of the bank is 1 : 2.*

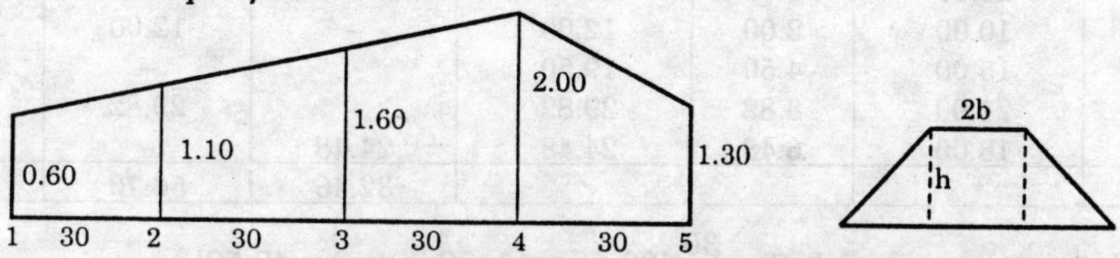

Figure 10.4 Longitudinal Section of Embankment.

Section	*HT. at Stn.*	*Area of central portion 2bd*	*Area of sides* sh^2	*Total sectional area*	*Total sectional area of 1st & last sections*	*Total sectional area of int. even sections*	*Total sectional area of int. odd sections*
1.	0.60	4.80	0.72	5.52	5.52	–	–
2.	1.10	8.80	2.42	11.22	–	11.22	–
3.	1.60	12.80	5.12	17.92	–	–	17.92
4.	2.00	16.00	8.00	24.00	–	24.00	–
5.	1.30	10.40	3.38	13.78	13.78	–	–
					19.30	35.22	17.92

$$\text{Volume between stations 1 \& 5} = \frac{30}{3} [19.30 + 4 \times 35.22 + 2 \times 17.92]$$

$$= 10\,[19.30 + 140.88 + 35.84] = 1{,}960.20 \text{ cum.}$$

Example 10.3. *Estimate the quantity of earthwork required in a road embankment having 10 m formation width, 2 : 1 side slope in a length of 7 chains, each chain being 30 m long. The central difference of formation and ground is 0.70 m, 1.2 m, 2.0 m, 1.0 m, 1.5 m, 2.1 m 1.8 m and 1.5 m at 0 to 7th chain respectively. Assume the ground is level in a direction transverse to the centre line.*

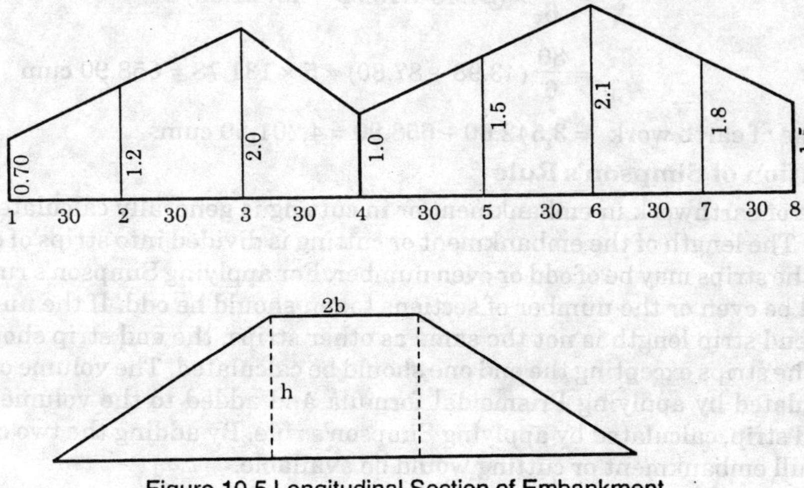

Figure 10.5 Longitudinal Section of Embankment.

Since there are eight sections which is even in number, it would be necessary to calculate the volume of end strip separately.

Stns	*Hts. of stns. d*	*Area of central portion 2 bd*	*Area of sides sh^2*	*Total sectional area*	*Total sect. area of 1st & last sect.*	*Total sect. area of int. even sects.*	*Total sect. area of int. odd sects.*
1.	0.70	7.00	0.98	7.98	7.98	–	–
2.	1.20	12.00	2.88	14.88	–	14.88	–
3.	2.00	20.00	8.00	28.00	–	–	28.00
4.	1.00	10.00	2.00	12.00	–	12.00	–
5.	1.50	15.00	4.50	19.50	–	–	19.50
6.	2.10	21.00	8.82	29.82	–	29.82	–
7.	1.80	18.00	6.48	24.48	24.48	–	–
					32.46	56.70	47.50

Volume between section 1 & 7 $= \frac{30}{3}[32.46 + 4 \times 56.70 + 2 \times 47.50]$

$= 10\,[32.46 + 226.80 + 95.00] = 10 \times 354.26 = 3{,}542.60$ cum.

Volume of the end strip between stations 7 & 8.

Area of section at station $8 = 2bh + sh^2 = 10 \times 1.5 + 2 \times 1.5^2$

$= 15 + 4.5 = 19.50$ sqm

Sectional area at station 7 = 24.48 sqm

Mean depth $h_m = \frac{1.8 + 1.5}{2} = 1.65$ m

Area at mid section $A_m = 10 \times 1.65 + 2 \times 1.65^2$

$= 16.5 + 5.45 = 21.95$ sqm

Volume of end strip

$$V_e = \frac{L}{6}(A_7 + A_8 + 4A_m)$$

$$= \frac{30}{6} \times (24.48 + 19.50 + 4 \times 21.95)$$

$$= \frac{30}{6}(43.98 + 87.80) = 5 \times 131.78 = 658.90 \text{ cum}$$

Total volume of earth work $= 3{,}542.60 + 658.90 = 4{,}201.50$ cum.

10.2.4 Application of Simpson's Rule

The volume of earthwork in embankment or in cutting is generally calculated by applying Simpson's rule. The length of the embankment or cutting is divided into strips of equal lengths. In dividing so, the strips may be of odd or even number. For applying Simpson's rule the number of strips should be even or the number of sections taken should be odd. If the number of strips is even, or the end strip length is not the same as other strips, the end strip should be left out and volume of the strips excepting the end one should be calculated. The volume of the end strip should be calculated by applying Prismoidal formula and added to the volume of the length without the end strip, calculated by applying Simpson's rule. By adding the two quantities, the volume of the full embankment or cutting would be available.

So long, it has been assumed that the ground on which the embankment would be built is level. But in practice, it may not be so. The ground may have transverse slope. The parameter has to be taken into consideration.

There may be various other ground conditions. In each case, the area of the section shall have to be calculated, then Simpson's rule shall be applied.

In case of cutting, the area of sections shall have to be found out, then either by applying prismoidal formula or Simpson's rule the volume of cutting shall be evaluated.

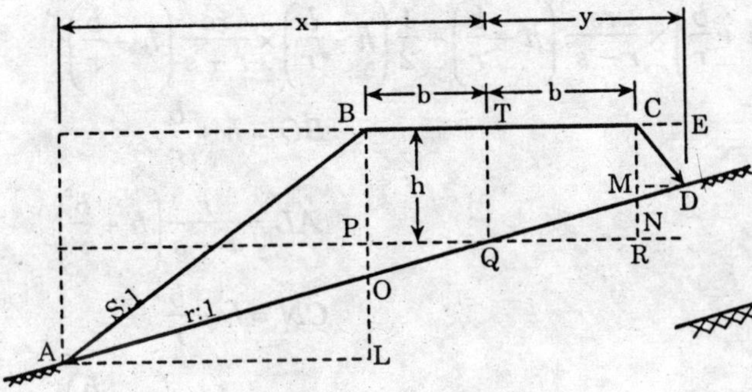

Figure 10.6 Section in Embankment.

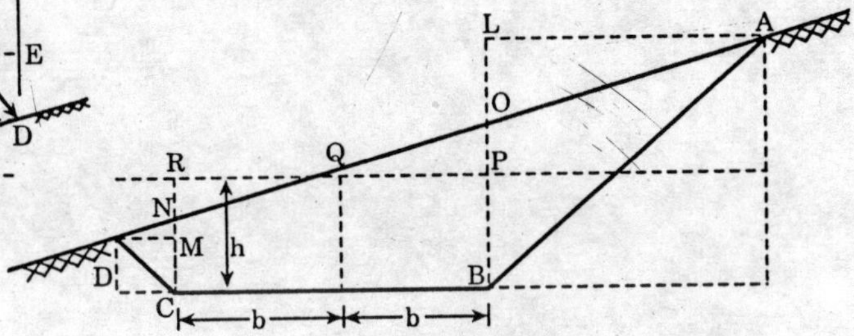

Figure 10.7 Section in Cutting.

Referring to Figure 10.6 which represents a section of embankment and Figure 10.7 which represents a section in cutting, in both the cases, the sections have side slopes, *s* and transverse slope, *r*. From the figures, the values required from finding the lengths *X* and *Y* and cross-sectional areas of embankment or cutting can be found out with the help of geometry.

Referring to Figures 10.6 and 10.7.

$$\frac{OL}{Al} = \frac{1}{r} \quad \therefore \quad \frac{OL}{OP} = \frac{Al}{r}$$

$$\frac{QP}{PQ} = \frac{1}{r} \quad \therefore \quad \frac{PQ}{r} = \frac{b}{r}; \quad \frac{Bl}{AL} = \frac{1}{s} \quad \therefore \quad Bl = \frac{AL}{s}$$

$$BL = BP + OP + OL = h + \frac{b}{r} + \frac{AL}{r}$$

$$\frac{AL}{s} = h + \frac{b}{r} + \frac{AL}{r} \text{ or } \frac{AL}{s} - \frac{AL}{r} = h + \frac{b}{r}$$

or $$Al\left(\frac{r-s}{rs}\right) = h + \frac{b}{r} \text{ or } AL = \frac{rs}{r-s}\left(h + \frac{b}{r}\right)$$

Side width, $$x = AL + b = \frac{rs}{r-s}\left(h + \frac{b}{r}\right) + b \qquad \text{...(1)}$$

Similarly,

$$\frac{NR}{QR} = \frac{1}{r} \qquad NR = \frac{QR}{r} = \frac{b}{r} \qquad \frac{MN}{DM} = \frac{1}{r} \qquad MN = \frac{DM}{r} \qquad \frac{CM}{DM} = \frac{1}{s} \qquad CM = \frac{DM}{s}$$

$$CR = NR + NM + CM = \frac{b}{r} + DM\left(\frac{1}{s} + \frac{1}{r}\right) = h$$

or $$h - \frac{b}{r} = DM\left(\frac{r+s}{rs}\right) \qquad DM = \frac{rs}{r+s}\left(h - \frac{b}{r}\right)$$

Side width, $Y = CT + CE = CT + DM$

$$= b + \frac{rs}{r+s}\left(h - \frac{b}{r}\right) \quad \text{...(2)}$$

Area, $ABCD$ = Area $OBCN$ + Triangle ABO + Triangle NCD,

= Area $PBCN$ + Area ABO + Area NCD

$$= 2bh + \frac{1}{2} BO \times AL + \frac{1}{2} CN \times DM$$

$$= 2bh + \frac{1}{2}\left(h + \frac{b}{r}\right) \times \frac{rs}{r-s}\left(h + \frac{b}{r}\right) + \frac{1}{2}\left(h - \frac{b}{r}\right) \times \frac{rs}{r+s}\left(h - \frac{b}{r}\right)$$

$$BO = h + \frac{b}{r}$$

$$AL = \frac{r}{r-s}\left(h + \frac{b}{r}\right)$$

$$CN = h - \frac{b}{r}$$

$$DM = \frac{rs}{r+s}\left(h - \frac{b}{r}\right)$$

$$= 2bh + \frac{1}{2}\left[\frac{rs}{r-s}\left(h + \frac{b}{r}\right)^2 + \frac{rs}{r+s}\left(h - \frac{b}{r}\right)^2\right]$$

$$= \frac{sb^2 + 2br^2 h + r^2 sh^2}{r^2 - s^2} = \frac{sb^2 + r^2 (2b + sh^2)}{r^2 - s^2} \quad \text{...(3)}$$

The formulae thus obtained are :

Side width, $X = b + \frac{rs}{r-s}\left(h + \frac{b}{r}\right)$ Side width, $Y = b + \frac{rs}{r+s}\left(h - \frac{b}{r}\right)$ and

Cross-sectional area, $ABCD = \frac{sb^2 + r^2 (2bh + sh^2)}{r^2 - s^2}$

Example 10.4. *Estimate the quantity of earthwork in cutting 60 m long for a road section with crest width at the formation 10 m, side slope 1:2, depth of centre at every 20 m is 2.0 m, 2.4 m, and 3.0 m. Cross slopes at every 20 m are 1 in 10, 1 in 8 and 1 in 12.*

Solution :

Distance in m	*Depth at centre*	*Cross slope*
0	2.0	1 in 10
30	2.4	1 in 8
60	3.0	1 in 12

Cross sectional area, $A = \frac{sb^2 + r^2 (2bh + sh^2)}{r^2 - s^2}$

(*i*) **Cross sectional area at 0 m**

$$A_0 = \frac{2 \times 5^2 + 10^2 (2 \times 5 \times 2.0 + 2 \times 2^2)}{10^2 - 2^2}$$

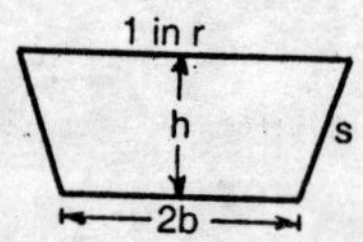

$$= \frac{50 + 100\,(20 + 8)}{100 - 4} = \frac{50 + 2{,}800}{96} = 29.69\ \text{m}^3$$

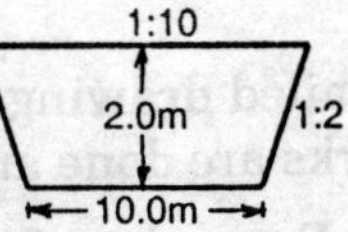

(*ii*) **Cross sectional area at 30 m**

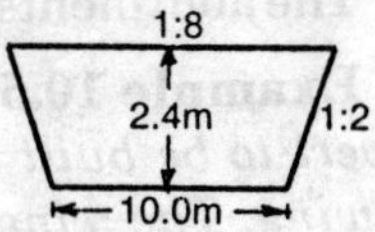

$$A_{30} = \frac{2 \times 5^2 + 8^2\,(2 \times 5 \times 2.4 + 2 \times 2.4^2)}{8^2 - 2^2}$$

$$= \frac{50 + 64\,(24 + 11.52)}{60} = \frac{50 + 2{,}273.28}{60} = 38.72\ \text{m}^3$$

(*iii*) **Cross sectional area at 60 m**

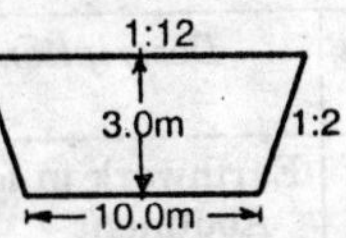

$$A_{60} = \frac{2 \times 5^2 + 12^2\,(2 \times 5 \times 3 + 2 \times 3^2)}{144 - 4}$$

$$= \frac{50 + 144\,(30 + 18)}{140} = 49.73\ \text{m}^3$$

Using prismoidal formula,

Volume of earthwork $= \dfrac{30}{3}\,(29.69 + 49.73 + 4 \times 38.72)$

$= 10 \times 234.21 = 2{,}342.1\ \text{m}^3$

Quantity of earthwork in embankment or cutting is calculated from the survey map and longitudinal section along the proposed alignment and cross sections at regular intervals.

The height of the embankment or depth of cutting is available from the longitudinal and cross sections. The heights of embankment and corresponding ground level is furnished in R.Ls. (Reduced level). The difference of the two R.Ls. gives the height of embankment or cutting.

In hilly areas, the road is generally provided with a longitudinal slope or gradient. This may be provided in percentage basis with reference to length or on ratio basis. This shall have to be converted into height in metre per regular and equal interval for calculation of the quantity of earthwork as per formulae.

Slope given on percentage basis – 2% slope means rise or fall of 2 m in 100 m. If the regular interval is 30 m, then for each 30 m,

$$\text{rise or fall} = \frac{2}{100} \times 30 = 0.6\ \text{m}$$

Transverse slope of ground is measured by Tangent Clinometer and the value found in terms of tan θ is then converted into slope ratio.

For example $\tan\theta = 0.083$

$$\therefore \quad \frac{1}{\tan\theta} = \frac{1}{0.083} = 12 \quad \therefore\ r : 1 = 12 : 1$$

10.3.0 CULVERTS AND BRIDGES

Culverts and bridges, minor or major are properly designed, taking into consideration of the width of the waterway, velocity of the flowing water, scour depth, etc.

After design of the structure including finalisation of the specifications of the different items, detailed drawings are prepared, on the basis of which, estimate of the quantities of items of works are done and the cost estimate prepared.

Examples of two culverts, one with brick-masonry abutment and R.C.C. slab and another with cement concrete abutment and R.C.C. slab are given below.

The abutments may be of stone boulders also. The technique of estimation remains the same.

Example 10.5. *Estimate the quantities of item of works and prepare a cost estimate of the culvert to be built with brick-masonry and R.C.C. slab of clear span 2.50 m as shown in the drawing. The wing walls are at right angles to the abutment with curtain and drop wall and flooring. Depth of foundation of abutment from the channel bed is 1.0 m.*

Estimate

Item no.	*Description of item*	*No*	*Measurements*				*Waste*
			Length	*Breadth*	*Height*	*Content*	
1.	Earthwork in foundation						
	Abutment	2	8.70	1.0	1.0	17.4	8.0 + 2 × 0.15 + 2 × 0.2 = 8.7
	Wing walls	2 × 2	2.50	1.0	1.0	10.0	
	Curtain and drop wall	2	1.8	0.5	1.0	1.8	2.5 – 2 × (0.2 + 0.15) = 1.8
	Floor	1	7.25	1.8	0.25	3.26	8.0 – 2 × 0.375 = 7.25
							2.5 – 2 × 0.350 = 1.80
						32.46	cum
2.	Cement concrete 1 : 3 : 6 in foundation						
	Abutment	2	8.70	1.0	0.4	6.96	
	Wing walls	2 × 2	2.50	1.0	0.4	4.00	
	Curtain and drop walls	2	1.80	0.5	0.4	0.72	
	Floor	1	1.80	0.80	0.1	0.14	
						11.82	cum
3.	Brickwork in abutment and wing walls (1:4)						
	Abutment	2	8.40	0.70	0.60	7.06	
		2	8.00	0.50	1.30	10.40	1.5 – 0.2 = 1.30
	Wing walls	2 × 2	2.35	0.70	0.60	3.95	2.50 – 0.15 = 2.35
		2 × 2	2.35	0.50	1.80	8.46	1.5 + 0.30 = 1.80
	Parapet	2	8.0	0.25	0.675	2.70	0.60 + 0.075 = 0.675
	String course	2	8.0	0.10	0.075	0.12	
	Curtain and drop wall	2	1.80	0.25	0.60	0.54	
						33.23	cum
4.	Cement concrete 1 : 2 : 4 in plain and RCC works						
	Bed block	2	8.00	0.50	0.20	1.60	
	Slab	1	8.00	3.50	0.30	8.40	
	Wheel guard	2	8.00	0.45	0.20	1.44	
						11.44	cum
5.	Floor with double brick flat	1	7.5	2.1		15.75	sqm
6.	Earthwork in back filling Volume of earthwork in excavation.						
	Item no. 1					31.01	cum

(*Contd...*)

Item no.	Description of item	No	Measurements				Waste
			Length	Breadth	Height	Content	
	Less volume Cement concrete 1 : 3 : 6 item no. 2					13.03	
	Brickwork in abutment					7.06	
	Wing wall					3.95	
	Curtain & drop wall					0.63	
	Floor, item 5		15.75 sqm × 0.15			2.36	
						(–) 27.03	
						3.98	cum
7.	Flush pointing to brickwork with cement sand mortar 1 : 4						
	Inner face of abutment	2	8.00	1.3		20.80	
	Wing walls	2 × 2 × 1/2	3.0	2.00		12.00	
	Floor	1	8.00	2.50		20.00	
						52.80	sqm
8.	Cement sand plaster 15 mm thick, 1 : 4						
	Ceiling	1	8.00	2.50		20.00	
	Bed block	2	8.00	0.20		3.20	
	Slab ends	2	3.50	3.00		21.00	
	Bed block ends	2 × 2	0.50	0.20		0.40	
						44.60	sqm
9.	Cement sand plaster (1 : 4) 15 mm thick on brickwork						
	Wing wall top	2 × 2	3.00	0.50		6.00	
	Parapet	2 × 2	8.00	0.675		21.60	
	Sides	2 × 2	0.25	0.675		0.675	
	Ends	2	8.00	0.35		5.60	
	Top	2	8.00	0.175		2.80	
	String course	2 × 2	0.10	0.075		0.03	
						36.705	sqm
10.	Wearing course with cement concrete $1 : 1\frac{1}{2} : 3$	1	8.00	2.60	0.075	1.56	cum
11.	Tarred paper on bed block	2	8.00	0.50		8.00	sqm
12.	Mild steel reinforcement for RCC work						
	As per bar schedule						
	Bar a 16 mm dia.		107 × 4.96			530.72	
	Bar b 16 mm dia.		107 × 3.72 m			398.04	
						928.76	m
	Bar c 10 mm dia.		29 × 8.12			235.48	
	Bar c 10 mm dia.		29 × 8.12			235.48	

(Contd...)

Item no.	Description of item	No	Measurements				Waste
			Length	Breadth	Height	Content	
	Bar d 10 mm dia.		54 × 1.50			81.00	
	Bar e 10 mm dia.		8 × 8.12			64.96	
						616.92	m
	16 mm dia. bar 928.76		1.58 kg/m = 1467.44 kg				
	10 mm dia. bar 616.92		0.617 kg/m = 380.64 kg				
						1,848.08	kg
13.	Shuttering and centering for concrete work						
	Foundation	2	8.70	0.4		6.96	
	Abutment	2 × 2	1.00	0.4		1.60	
	Wind walls	2 × 2 × 2	2.50	0.4		8.00	
		2 × 2	1.00	0.4		1.60	
	Curtain and drop walls	2 × 2	1.80	0.4		2.88	
		2 × 2	8.00	0.2		6.40	
	Bed block	2 × 2	0.50	0.2		0.40	
	Slab	1	8.00	2.50		20.00	
	Bottom	2	8.00	0.30		4.80	
	Sides	2	3.50	0.30		2.10	
	Wheel guard	2 × 2	8.00	0.20		6.40	
		2 × 2	0.45	0.20		0.36	
						61.50	sqm

Abstract

Item No.	Description of item	Quantity	Unit	Rate	Amount	Remarks
1.	Earthwork in excavation in foundation	32.46	% cum	2,973.00	965.00	
2.	Cement concrete 1 : 3 : 6 in foundation	11.82	cum	1.623.00	19,184.00	
3.	Brickwork in abutment and wing walls (1 : 4)	33.23	cum	1,760.00	58,485.00	
4.	Cement concrete 1 : 2 : 4 in plain and RCC work	11.44	cum	2,640.00	30,202.00	
5.	Floor with double brick flat (1 : 6)	15.75	sqm	250.00	3,938.00	
6.	Earthwork in back filling	3.98	% cum	1,738.00	69.00	
7.	Flush pointing with cement sand mortar 1 : 4	52.80	sqm	26.00	1,373.00	
8.	Cement sand (1 : 6) plaster 15 mm thick	44.60	sqm	45.00	2,007.00	
9.	Cement sand (1 : 4) plaster 15 mm thick on brickwork	36.705	sqm	53.00	1,945.00	
10.	Wearing course with cement concrete $1:1\frac{1}{2}:3$	1.56	cum	2,690.00	4,196.00	
11.	Tarred paper on bed block	8.00	sqm	300.00	2,400.00	
12.	Mild steel reinforcement for RCC work	1.848	Tonne	20831.00	38,496.00	
13.	Shuttering and centering for concrete work	61.50	sqm	110.00	6,765.00	
					1,70,025.00	

Rate per metre of span Rs. 68,010.00

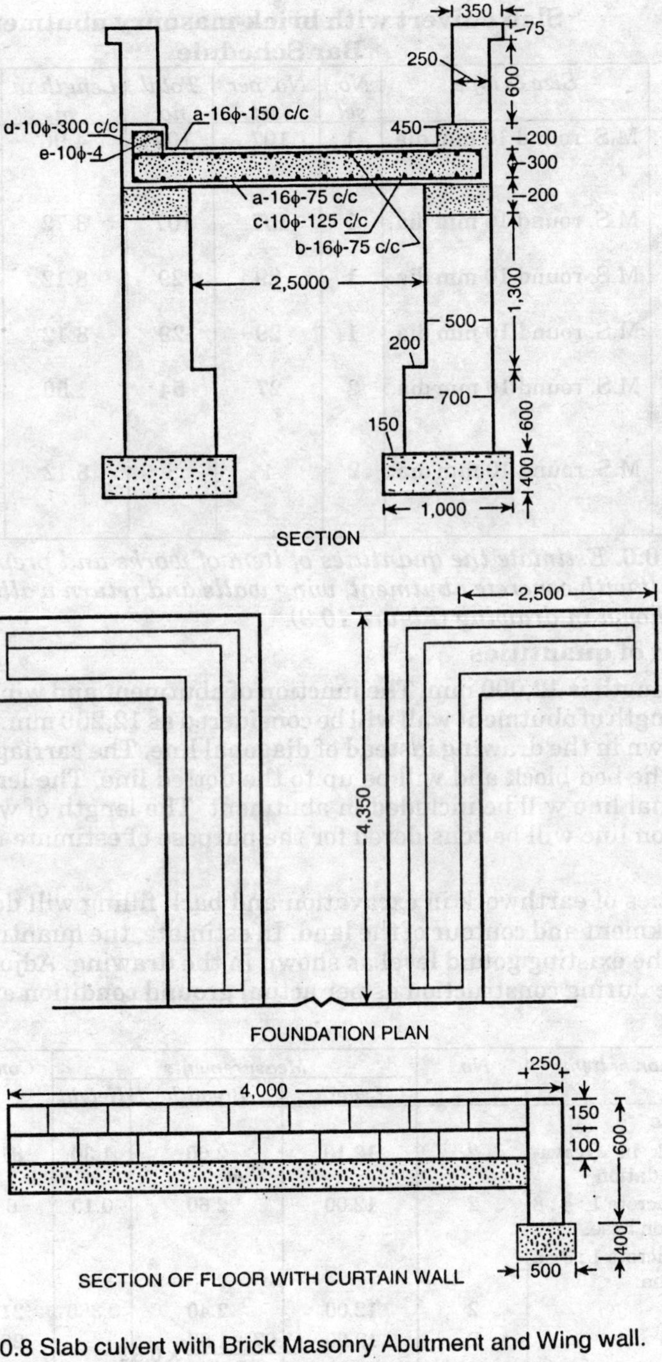

Figure 10.8 Slab culvert with Brick Masonry Abutment and Wing wall.

Slab culvert with brick-masonry abutment
Bar Schedule

Location	*Bar mark*	*Size & type*	*No. set*	*No. per set*	*Total no.*	*Length in m*	*Shape (All dimensions are in mm)*
Slab	a	M.S. round 16 mm dia.	1	107	107	4.96	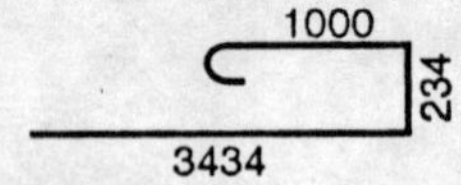
Slab	b	M.S. round 16 mm dia.	1	107	107	3.72	
Slab	c	M.S. round 10 mm dia.	1	29	29	8.12	
Slab	c	M.S. round 10 mm dia.	1	29	29	8.12	
Wheel guard	d	M.S. round 10 mm dia.	2	27	54	1.50	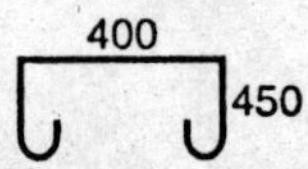
Wheel guard	e	M.S. round 10 mm dia.	2	4	8	8.12	

Example 10.6. *Estimate the quantities of item of works and prepare a cost estimate of the culvert to be built with concrete abutment, wing walls and return walls and R.C.C. slab of clear span 3.0 m as shown in drawing (Figure 10.9).*

Estimation of quantities

Abutment length is 12,000 mm. The junction of abutment and wing wall may be seen in the drawing. The length of abutment wall will be considered as 12,200 mm. The shape of the junction would be as shown in the drawing instead of diagonal line. The carriage way slab length 12,000 mm will be on the bed block and will be up to the dotted line. The length from the dotted line up to the diagonal line will be included in abutment. The length of wing wall though actually up to the junction line will be considered for the purpose of estimate up to the dotted diagonal line.

The quantities of earthwork in excavation and back filling will depend upon the profile of the road embankment and contour of the land. In estimate, the quantities have been calculated on the basis of the existing gound level as shown in the drawing. Adjustment as necessary will have to be made during construction as per actual ground condition at site.

Estimate

Item no.	*Description of item*	*No.*	*Measurements*			*Content*	*Waste*
			Length	*Breadth*	*Height*		
	Abutments						
1.	Earth work in excavation in foundation	2	12.10	2.60	1.30	81.80	cum
2.	Cement concrete 1 : 4 : 8 in foundation base.	2	12.00	2.60	0.10	6.24	cum
3.	Cement concrete 1 : 3 : 6 in foundation.						
	Base	2	12.00	2.40	0.380	21.89	
	Foundation	2	12.00	$\frac{1.07 + 1.87}{2} \times 0.82$		28.93	
	Abutment	2	12.00	$\frac{0.60 - 1.07}{2} \times 2.00$		48.00	
	Triangular shape at the end to meet the wing wall	2 × 2 × 1/2	0.20 × 0.60 × 0.35			0.084	cum
						98.90	

(Contd...)

Item no.	Description of item	No.	Measurements			Content	Waste
			Length	Breadth	Height		
4.	Cement concrete 1 : 2 : 4 in bed block	2	12.00	0.60	0.22	3.17	cum
5.	Earthwork in back filling of foundation trenches.						
	Volume of earth-work in excavation item no. 1					81.80	cum
	Volume of concrete 1 : 4 : 8 Foundation				6.24		
					21.89		
					28.93		
				(–)	57.06		
						24.74	cum
6.	Shuttering and centering						
	Foundation base	2 × 2	12.00		0.38	18.24	
		2 × 2	2.40		0.38	3.65	
	Abutment	2	12.00		1.091	26.18	$\sqrt{0.82^2 + 0.72^2} = 1.091$
		2	12.00		1.868	20.83	$\sqrt{0.82^2 + 0.285^2} = 0.868$
		$2 \times 2 \times \frac{1.87 + 0.945}{2} \times 0.82$				4.62	
		$2 \times 2 \times \frac{0.945 + 0.60}{2} \times 2.0$				6.18	
		2	12.00		2.0	48.00	
		2	12.00		2.017	48.41	$\sqrt{2^2 + 0.265^2} = 2.017$
	Bed block	2 × 2	12.00		0.22	10.56	
		2 × 2	0.60		0.22	0.53	
						187.20 sqm	
7.	Providing tarred paper on bed block	2	12.00	0.30		7.20	sqm
8.	Providing expansion joint with bituminous felt	2 × 2	2.40		0.38	3.65	
		$2 \times 2 \times \frac{1.87 + 0.945}{2} \times 0.082$				4.62	
		$2 \times 2 \times \frac{0.945 + 0.60}{2} \times 2.00$				6.18	
		2 × 2	0.60		0.22	0.53	sqm
						14.98 sqm	
9.	Providing weep holes 100 mm dia. including packing at the back with shingles	2 × 2 × 4				16	Nos.

Reinforced Cement Concrete Slab

Item no.	Description of item	No.	Measurements			Content	Waste
			Length	Breadth	Height		
1.	Cement concrete 1 : 2 : 4						
	Slab	1	12.00	3.60	0.305	13.18	3.0 + 2 × 0.3 = 3.60
	Parapet	2	3.60	0.40	0.50	1.44	cum
						14.62	
2.	Shuttering and centering for R.C.C. work						

(Contd...)

Item no.	Description of item	No.	Measurements			Content	Waste
			Length	Breadth	Height		
	Slab bottom	1	12.00	3.00		36.00	
	Slab ends	2	3.60	0.305		2.20	
	Slab sides	2	12.00	0.305		7.32	
	Parapet sides	2 × 2	3.60	0.50		7.20	
	Parepet ends	2 × 2	0.40	0.05		0.08	
						52.80	
3.	Wearing course av. 75 mm thick with cement concrete 1:1 $\frac{1}{2}$:3	1	3.60	11.20	0.075	3.02	
4.	M.S. reinforcement including bending binding and placing As per bar-schedule						
	Bar a 16 mm dia.	80 × 4.020 = 321.60					
	Bar b 16 mm dia.	80 × 3.820 = 305.60					
	Bar e 16 mm dia.	29 × 12.225 = 354.53					
		981.73			m @ 1.58 kg/m = 1,551.13 kg		
	Bar c 10 mm dia.	40 × 4.150 = 166.00					
	Bar d 10 mm dia.	12 × 12.115 = 145.38					
	Bar f 10 mm dia.	24 × 2.155 = 51.72					
	Bar g 10 mm dia.	10 × 3.720 = 37.20					
	Bar h 10 mm dia.	24 × 1.280 = 30.72					
	Bar j 10 mm dia.	8 × 3.720 = 29.76					
		460.78			m @ 0.617 kg /m = 284.30 kg		
					11,835.43 kg		
	Add 5% for laps and wastage				91.77		
					1,927.20 kg = 1.927 Tonne		

Slab Culvert with Cement Concrete Abutment

Bar Schedule

Location	Bar mark	Size type	No. of set	No. per set	Total no.	Length in m	Shape (All dimensions are in mm)
Slab	a	M.S. round 16 mm dia.	1	80	80	4.020	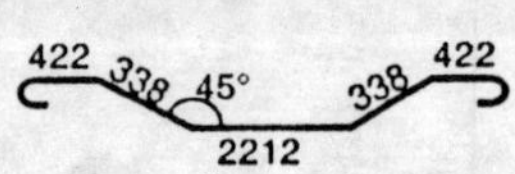
Slab	b	M.S. round 16 mm dia.	1	80	80	3.820	
Slab	c	M.S. round 10 mm dia.	1	40	40	4.150	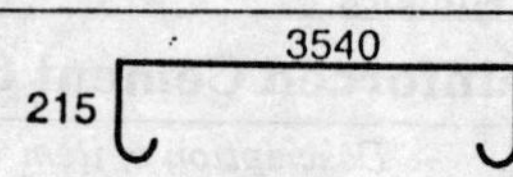
Slab	e	M.S. round 16 mm dia.	1	29	29	12.225	
Slab	d	M.S round 10 mm dia.	1	12	12	12.115	

(Contd...)

Location	Bar mark	Size type	No. of set	No. per set	Total no.	Length in m	Shape (All dimensions are in mm)
Wheel guard	f	M.S. round 10 mm dia.	2	12	24	2.155	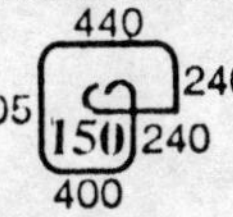
Wheel guard	g	M.S. round 10 mm dia.	2	5	10	3.720	
Parapet	h	M.S. round 10 mm dia.	2	12	24	1.280	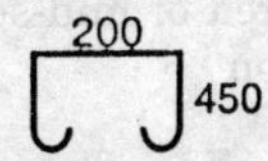
Parapet	j	M.S round 10 mm dia.	2	4	8	3.720	

Wing walls

Four wing walls at 45° angle with the abutment have been provided. Length of each is 4,000 mm.

Length of the wing wall depends upon the height of the embankment. The height of the wing wall at the upper end is equal to height of the abutment plus the thickness of the slab. The height at the lower end and the height of the return wall would be the same and depends upon the height of the embankment and the situation.

Estimation

Item no.	Description of item	No.	Measurements Length	Breadth	Height	Content	Waste
1.	Earthwork in excavation in foundation	1	4.00	2.40 (av)	1.30	12.48	1/2 (2.6 + 2.2) = 2.4 m
	Such 4 walls	4 × 12.48				49.92	cum
2.	Cement concrete 1 : 4 : 8 in foundation	1	4.00	2.40 (av)	0.1	0.96	
	Such 4 walls		4 × 0.96			3.84	cum
3.	Cement concrete 1 : 3 : 6 in foundation and above						
	Cross-sectional area at top end						
	Base	1	2.40 (av)	0.38		0.912	
	Foundation	1 ×	$\frac{1.87 + 1.07}{2} \times 0.82$			1.21	
		1 ×	$\frac{0.60 + 1.07}{2} \times 2.00$			1.67	
		1 ×	0.60 × 0.525			0.315	
						4.107 sqm	
	Cross-secti-onal area at lower end.	1	2.00	0.30		0.60	

(Contd...)

Item no.	Description of item	No.	Measurements Length	Breadth	Height	Content	Waste
		1 ×	$\frac{1.55 + 0.852}{2} \times 0.90$			1.081	
		1 ×	$\frac{0.852 + 0.60}{2} \times 0.80$			1.581	
		1	0.60	0.505		0.303 3.565	
	Area of mid-section						
		1	2.40	0.30		0.72	
		1 ×	$\frac{1.75 + 0.925}{2} \times 0.90$			1.204	
		1 ×	$\frac{0.925 + 0.60}{2} \times 1.28$			0.976	
		1	0.60	0.525		0.315 3.215 sqm	
	Volume as per prismoidal formula Volume $V = L/6\ (A_1 + 4A_m + A_2)$ Volume = 4.0/6 (4.107 + 4 × 3.215 + 3.565)						L = Length A_1 & A_2 Area of end sections A_m = Area of mid section
						= 13.688	
	4 such wing walls = 4 × 13.02					54.75	
3.	Earthwork in back filling. Volume of excavation					49.92	
	Less Volume of concrete 1 : 4 : 8 Concrete 1 : 3 : 6 up to Gr. level					3.84	
		$\frac{4.0}{6}$ (2.122 + 4 × 1.681 + 1.924)					$A_1 = 0.912 + 1.21 = 2.122$ $A_m = 0.60 + 1.081 = 1.681$ $A_2 = 0.72 + 1.204 = 1.924$
				$= \frac{4}{6}$ (2.122 + 6.724 + 1.924)			
				$= \frac{4}{6} \times 10.77$			
				= 7.18		7.18	
	4 such wing walls					28.72	

(Contd...)

Item no.	Description of item	No.	Measurements: Length	Breadth	Height	Content	Waste
					(–)	32.56	
	Volume of back filling					17.36	cum
4.	Shuttering and centering for concrete work						
	Base	2	4.00 ×	$\frac{0.38 + 0.3}{2}$		2.72	
	Foundation	1	4.0	$\frac{1.091^2 + 1.030}{2}$		4.242	$\sqrt{820^2 + 720^2} = 1.092$
							$\sqrt{900^2 + 500^2} = 1.030$
		1	4.00 ×	$\frac{0.835 + 0.930}{2}$		3.53	$\sqrt{820^2 + 160^2} = 0.835$
							$\sqrt{900^2 + 238^2} = 0.930$
	Superstruc-ture	1	4.0 ×	$\frac{2.00 + 1.280}{2}$		= 6.56	
		1	4.0 ×	$\frac{2.04 + 0.834}{2}$		= 5.75	$\sqrt{2000^2 + 390^2} = 2.04$
						22.80 sqm	$\sqrt{800^2 + 238^2} = 0.834$
	4 such wing walls		4 ×	22.80		91.20	sqm
5.	Weep holes	4 × 2 × 3				24 Nos.	

Return Walls 4 Numbers – Length 1.00 each

Section Uniform Throughout

Item no.	Description of item	No.	Measurements: Length	Breadth	Height	Content	Waste
1.	Earthwork in excavation in foundation	4	1.00	2.20	1.30	11.44	cum
2.	Cement concrete 1 : 4 : 8 Below base	4	1.00	2.00	0.10	0.80	
3.	Cement concrete 1 : 3 : 6 in foundation						
	Base	4	1.00	2.00	0.30	2.40	
	Foundation	4	1.00 ×	$\frac{1.55 + 0.852}{2}$ ×	0.90	= 4.32	
	Breast	4	1.00 ×	$\frac{0.60 + 0.852}{2}$	× 0.80	= 2.32	
	Top	4	1.00	0.60	0.505	1.21	
						10.25 cum	
4.	Shuttering and centering for concrete work Foundation						

(*Contd...*)

Item no.	Description of item	No.	Measurements Length	Breadth	Height	Content	Waste
	Base	4 × 2	1.00		0.30	2.40	
		4	2.00		0.30	2.40	
	Foundation	4	1.00		1.01	4.04	$\sqrt{460^2+900^2}$ = 1.01
		4	1.00		0.924	3.70	$\sqrt{210^2+900^2}$ = 0.924
	Ends	4 ×	1.0	$\times \frac{0.878+1.55}{2} \times 0.90$		= 4.37	
	Breast	4 × 1.00			0.802	3.21	$\sqrt{801^2+40^2}$ = 0.802
		4	1.00		0.835	3.34	$\sqrt{808+238^2}$ = 0.835
	Ends	$4 \times \frac{0.60+0.878}{2} \times 0.80$				2.36,	
	Top	4 × 2	1.00		0.505	4.04	
	Ends	4	0.60		0.505	1.21	sqm
						31.07	
5.	Earthwork in back filling					11.44	
	Earthwork in excavation						
	Less volume of structures						
	Concrete below base			0.80			
	Concrete base			2.40			
	Concrete foundation			4.32			
					(–)	7.52	cum
						3.92	
6.	Weep holes	4 × 2				8	Nos.

Curtain Wall and Drop Wall

Item no.	Description of item	No.	Measurements Length	Breadth	Height	Content	Waste
1.	Earthwork in excavation in foundation	2	0.60	1.00	1.28	1.54	cum
2.	Cement concrete 1 : 4 : 8 in foundation.						
	Below base	2	0.60	1.00	0.10	0.12 cum	3.00 − 2.40 = 0.60
3.	Cement concrete 1 : 3 : 6 in foundation.						
	Base	2	0.60	1.00	0.38	0.456	
		$2 \times \frac{0.50+0.80}{2} \times$ 1.82 × 0.65			1/2		(2840 + 800)
						$= \frac{1.538}{1.994}$ cum	= 1.82 0.60 + 0.20 − 0.15 = 0.65

(Contd...)

Item no.	Description of item	No.	Measurements Length	Breadth	Height	Content	Waste
4.	Shuttering and centering						
		2 × 2	0.80		0.38	1.216	
		2	1.82		0.65	2.366	
		2	1.82		0.734	2.672	
						6.254 sqm	
5.	Earthwork in back filling						
	Volume of Excavation					1.54	cum
	Less volume structure						
	Cement concrete 1 : 4 : 8					0.12	
	Cement concrete 1 : 3 : 6	2	0.60	1.00	0.38	0.456	
		$2 \times \frac{0.50 + 0.80}{2} \times 0.60 \times 0.65$				= 0.507	
					(–)	1.083	
						0.457	cum
	Flooring						
1.	Earthwork in excavation	1	10.20	0.60	0.25	1.53	cum
2.	Cement concrete 1 : 4 : 8	1	11.00	2.84	0.10	3.12	cum
3.	Cement concrete 1 : 3 : 6	1	12.00	2.84	0.15	5.112	cum

Appron

Item no.	Description of item	No.	Measurements Length	Breadth	Height	Content	Waste
1.	Earthwork in excavation in box cutting for appron 300 mm deep.	1 ×	$\frac{3.0 + 8.66}{2} \times$	2.83× 0.30		= 4.95	cum
2.	Supplying and laying stone boulders of min. size 200 mm in the box cutting, packing and setting					4.95	cum
3.	Filling cement and sand mortar 1 : 6 from top in the inter spaces and finishing the top. 35 % of the volume of boulder filling					1.73	cum

(*a*) Wing Wall Section upper end

(*b*) Wing Wall Mid-section

(*c*) End-Section of Wing Wall & Return Wall

(*d*) Junction of Abutment Wing & Return Wall

(*e*) Section of Abutment

(*f*) Longitudinal Section

(*g*) Cross Section

(*h*) Drop Wall & Floor

Slab Culvert with Cement Concrete Abutment Absrtact

Item No.	Description of item	Quantity	Unit	Rate	Amount	Remarks
1.	Earthwork in excavation in foundation					
	Abutment	81.80				
	Wing walls	49.92				
	Return walls	11.44				
	Curtain & drop walls	1.54				
	Flooring	1.53				
	Appron	1.95				
		151.18%	cum	2,973.00	4,495.00	
2.	Cement concrete 1:4:8 in foundation					
	Abutment	6.24				
	Wing walls	3.84				
	Return walls	0.80				
	Curtain & drop walls	0.12				
	Flooring	3.12				
		14.12	cum	1,340.00	18,921.00	
3.	Cement concrete 1:3:6 in foundation and above					
	Abutment	98.90				
	Wing walls	54.75				
	Return walls	10.25				
	Curtain & drop walls	1.99				
	Flooring	5.11				
		171.00	cum	1,623.00	2,11,533.00	
4.	Cement concrete 1:2:4 in bed block and R.C.C. work					
	Abutment	3.17				
	Slab	14.62				
		17.79	cum	2640.00	46,,966.00	
5.	Earthwork in back filling					
	Abutment	24.74				
	Wing walls	17.29				
	Return walls	3.92				
	Curtain & drop walls	0.46				
		46.48%	cum	1,738.00	80,782.00	
6.	Shuttering and centering					
	Abutment	187.20				
	Slab	52.80				
	Wing walls	91.20				
	Return walls	31.07				
	Curtain & drop walls	6.25				
		368.42	m^2	110.00	40,526.00	
7.	Providing tarred paper on bed block					
	Abutment	7.20	m^2	300.00	2,160.00	
8.	Providing expansion joint					
	Abutment	14.98	m^2	200.00	2,996.00	
9.	Providing weep holes					
	Abutment	16				
	Wing walls	24				
	Return walls	8				
		48	Each	30.00	1,440.00	

10.	M.S. reinforcement Slab	1.927	Tonne	2,0831.00	40,141.00
11.	Wearing course av. 75 mm thick with cement concrete 1:1½:3	3.02	m^3		
12.	Supplying and laying stone boulders of min. 200 mm in the box cutting, packing and setting, Appron	4.95	cum	200.00	990.00
13.	Filling with cement and sand mortar 1:6 from top in the inner spaces and finishing the top. Appron	1.73	cum	175.00	303.00
					5,17,253.00
		Add contingency @5%			25,863.00
		Add work-establishment @2.5%			12,931.00
		Rate per meter Rs.			1,85,349.00

10.4.0 PAVEMENT PORTION OF THE ROAD

Pavement portion or hard crust of road consists of :

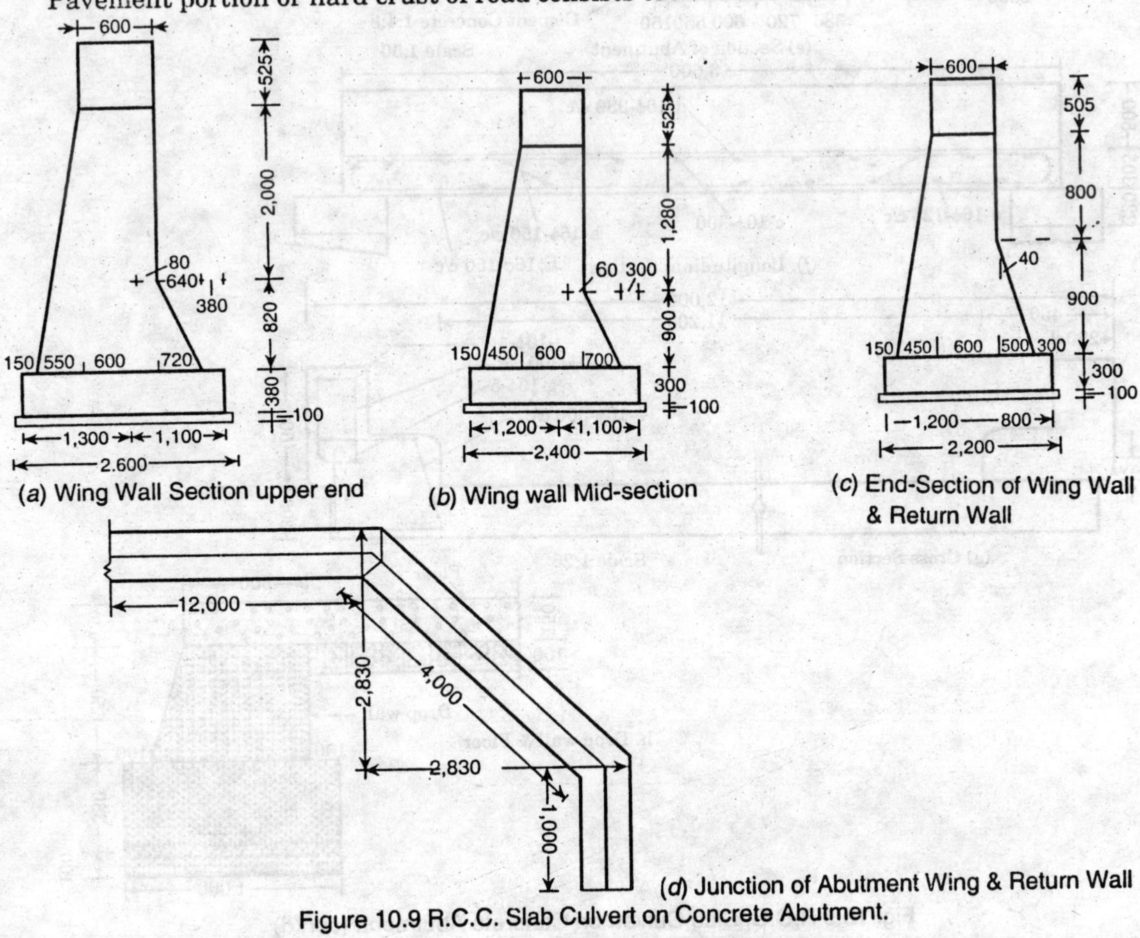

(a) Wing Wall Section upper end (b) Wing wall Mid-section (c) End-Section of Wing Wall & Return Wall

(d) Junction of Abutment Wing & Return Wall

Figure 10.9 R.C.C. Slab Culvert on Concrete Abutment.

(*a*) **Base course or soling :** The course is laid on the prepared earth surface. Earth surface is prepared by box-cutting to a depth required for putting the hard crust. It is measured in sqm of the item laid.

(*b*) **Bearing course :** It is the course which actually bears the wheel load of the traffic. The depth of the course is determined according to the load of the volume of the traffic and its velocity of movement. This course may consist of more than one layer of different materials. The item is measured in cubic meter of the volume of material used.

(*c*) **Wearing course:** This course is laid over the bearing course and protects the bearing course from the wear and tear due to traffic moving on it. The thickness of the wearing course

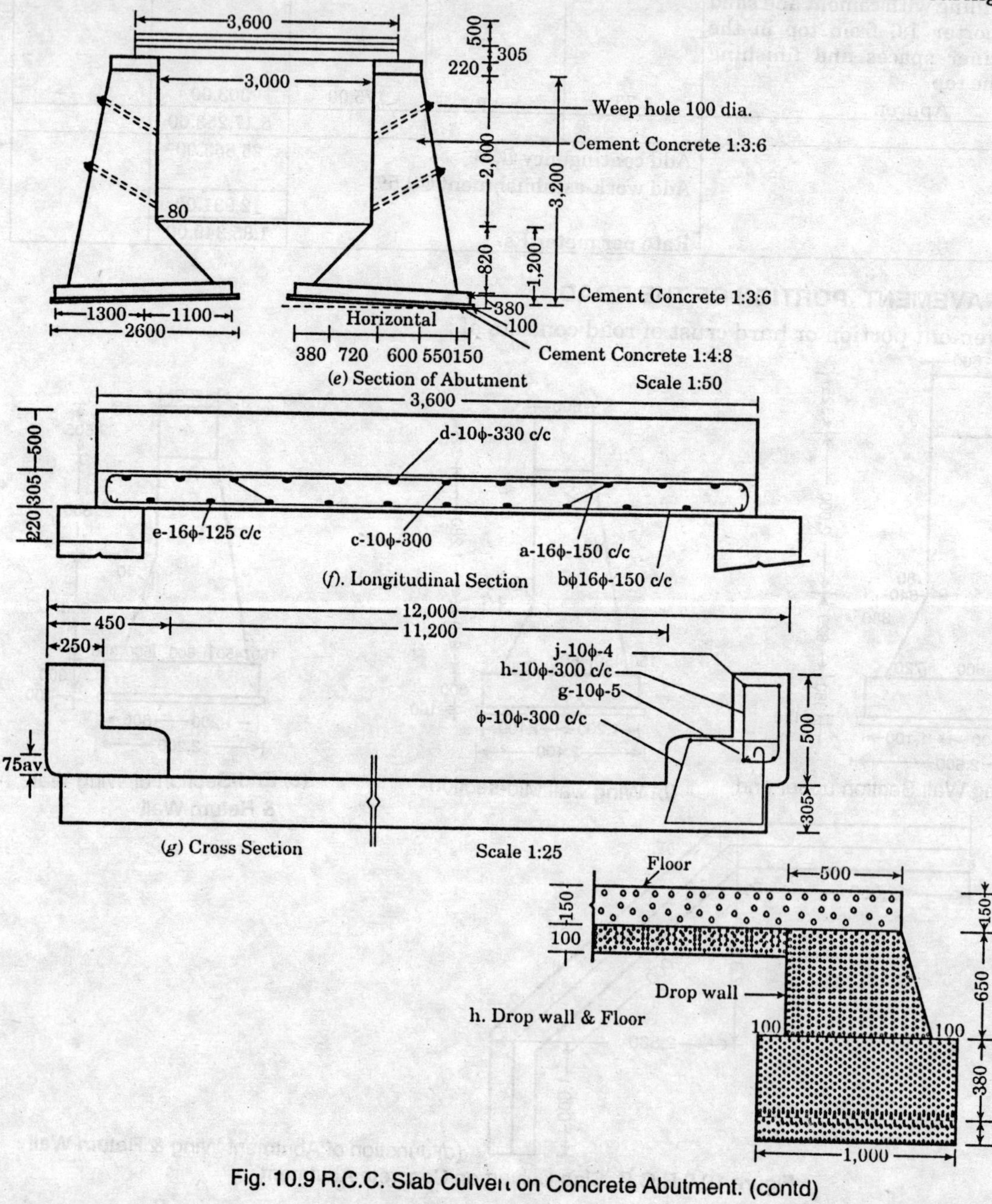

Fig. 10.9 R.C.C. Slab Culvert on Concrete Abutment. (contd)

also add to the thickness of the hard crust. The course is generally a bituminous one. The item is measured in sqm of the surface area covered.

Apart from the above course, edging at the edge of the hard crust for protection of the bearing course is provided.

Alternatively, shouldering may be provided along the edge of the bearing course for the same purpose. Edging provided is generally brick on end edge and shouldering provided is generally single brick flat soling or a layer 100 or 150 mm thick, provided with stone boulders or shingles or brick khoa.

Example 10.7. *Calculate the quantities of works to be done for 1 km length of road as shown in section in Figure 10.10.*

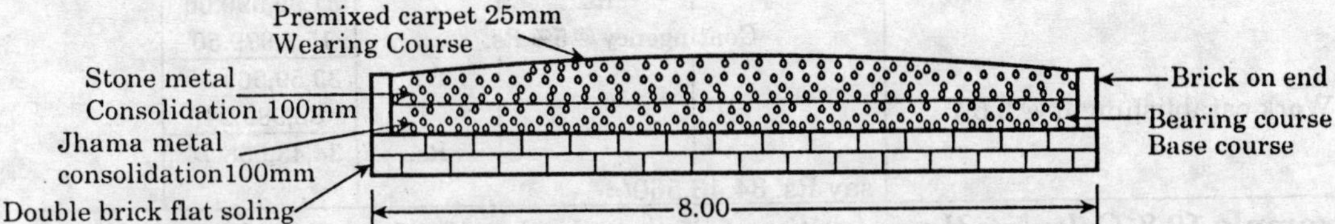

Figure 10.10 Road Pavement.

Estimation

Item no.	*Description of item*	*No.*	*Measurements*			*Content*	*Waste*
			Length	*Breadth*	*Height*		
1.	Box-cutting 350 mm deep including dressing, and rolling the surface and providing camber as necessary	1	1,000.00	8.00		8,000.00	sqm
2.	Laying double brick flat soling with picked jhama bricks including filling the gaps of bricks with powered earth available from box cutting.	1	1,000.00	8.00		8,000.00	sqm
3.	Brick on end edging with 1st. class bricks	2	1,000.00			2,000.00	m
4.	Supplying, spreading and consolidating picked jhama brick khoa 50 mm —65 mm size	1	1,000.00	7.85	0.10	785.00	cum
5.	Supplying spreading and consolidating trap stone metal 40 mm — 25 mm size	1	1,000.00	7.85	0.10	785.00	cum
6.	Premixed carpet 25 mm thick with bitumen 80/100 and stone chips 12 mm down @ 3.38 cum per 100 sqm including blinding by sand @ 0.5 cum per 100 sqm.	1	1,000.00	7.85		7850.00	sqm

Absrtact

no.	*Description of item*	*Quantity*	*Unit*	*Rate*	*Amount*	*Remarks*
1.	Box-cutting 350 mm deep including dressing, rolling and cambering	8,000.00	sqm	15.00	1,20,000.00	
2.	Suppling & laying double brick flat soling with picked jhama bricks, including filling the gaps of bricks with powdered earth available from box-cutting	8,000.00	sqm	189.00	15,12,000.00	

(Contd...)

3.	Brick on end edging with 1st. class bricks	2,000.00	%m	2,470.00	49,400.00	
4.	Supplying, spreading and consolidating picked jhama metal	785.00	cum	600.00	4,71,000.00	
5.	Supplying, spreading and consolidating trap stone metal	785.00	cum	800.00	6,28,000.00	
6.	Premixed carpet 25 mm thick with bitumen 80/100 and stone chips 12 mm down 3.38 cum per 100 sqm, including blinding by sand 0.5 cum per sqm.	7,850.00	sqm	53.40	4,19,190.00	
			Rs.		31,99,590.00	
			Contingency @ 5% Rs.		15,9,979.50	
				Rs.	33,59,569.50	
	Work establishment @ 2.5%				83,989.24	
				Rs.	34,43,558.74	
		say Rs. 34,43,560/=				

Example 10.8. *Calculate the quantities of works to be done for 1 km length of road as shown in the section (Figure 9.11).*

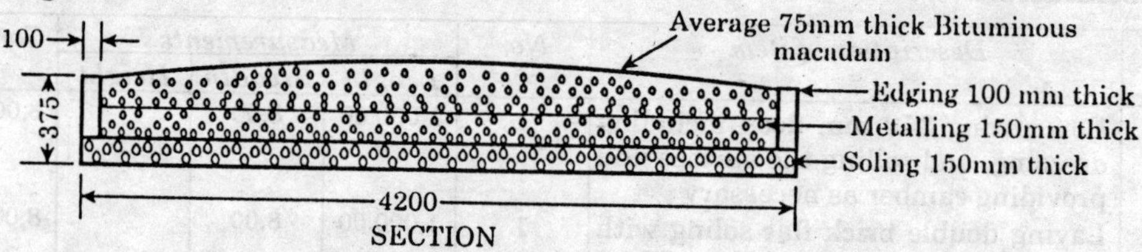

Figure 10.11 Road Pavement.

Estimation of Quantities

Item no.	*Description of item*	*No.*	*Measurements*			*Content*	*Waste*
			Length	*Breadth*	*Height*		
1.	Box cutting and dressing and consolidating the sub-grade, depth up to 375 mm	1	1,000.00	4.20		4,200.00	sqm
2.	Supplying boulder up to 100 mm size at road side	1	1,000.00	4.20	0.15	630.00	cum
3.	Labour for laying boulder soling 150 mm average thick including packing and rough dressing Quantity same or item 2					630.00	cum
4.	Supplying boulder at road side in stacks for edging	2	1000.00	0.10	0.300	60.00	cum
5.	Labour for laying stone edging laid to correct line and level 100 mm wide	2	1000.00			2000.00	m
6.	Supplying trap stone metal 40 mm to 25 mm size, stacked at road road side	1	1000.00	4.00	0.15	600.00	cum
7.	Labour for spreading and consolidating stone metal Quantity same as item 6					600.00	cum
8.	Laying of bituminous macadam *a*. Supplying stone chips 25 mm – 6 mm size for 75 mm thick bituminous macadam	1	1000.00	4.00		= 4000.00	sqm
	@ 8.5 cum per 100 sqm.					340.00	cum

	b. Sand	1	1000.00	4.00	= 4000	sqm
	@ 1.5 cum per 100 sqm				60.00	cum
	c. Matrix	1	1000.00	4.00	= 4000	sqm
	@ 665 kg per 100 sqm				26.60	tonne
9.	Labour for Bituminous macadam 75 mm thick including thorough cleaning of the surface, dressing, etc.	1	1000.00	4.00	4000.00	sqm

Abstract

Item No.	*Description of item*	*Quantity*	*Unit*	*Rate*	*Amount*	*Remarks*
1.	Box cutting, dressing and consolidating the sub-grade depth up to 300 mm	4,200.00	sqm			
2.	Supplying boulder up to 100 mm size in stacks at road side.	630.00	cum			
3.	Labour for laying 150 mm av. thick boulder soling including packing and rough dressing	630.00	cum			
4.	Supplying boulder 100 mm size at road side for edging.	60.00	cum			
5.	Labour for laying stone edging laid to correct line and level, 100 mm wide.	2,000.00	m			
6.	Supplying trap stone metal 40 mm to 25 size stacked at road side.	600.00	cum			
7.	Labour for spreading and consolidating stone metal.	600.00	cum			
8.	Laying Bituminous macadam.					
	a. Supplying stone chips 25 mm down up to 6 mm	340.00	cum			
	b. Supplying sand	60.00	cum			
	c. Supplying Bitumen 70/80 grade.	26.60	Tonne			
9.	Labour for laying Bituminous macadam 75 mm thick including thorough cleaning and dressing of the surface.	4,000.00	sqm			
	Contingency @ 5%					
	Work establishment @ $2\frac{1}{2}$%					

11

TENDERING, CONTRACTUAL PROCEDURE, DRAFTING OF TENDER AND CONTRACT DOCUMENTS

11.1.0 TENDERING AND CONTRACTUAL PROCEDURE

On receiving the administrative approval and Technical sanction of the detailed estimate, the Executive agency or the Executive Engineer who have been entrusted with the work is entitled to proceed with the work provided there is adequate provision in the budget estimate and Expenditure sanction of the Finance Department of the Government.

When all the above pre-requisitions are existing, the Executive Engineer or the Engineer in Charge begins to do the formalities of calling tenders for the work which is the first step towards actual commencement of the work.

11.2.0 TENDERING PROCEDURE

The department entrusted with execution of the project is entitled to commence execution after inviting tenders in proper method, processing them and finalising the tender found suitable. This part of the procedure is also time consuming. Generally, some actions which could be standardised are taken before hand. Similar other actions regarding the particular project which are possible to be taken in anticipation are also taken to curtail delay.

Preparation of tender documents

Tender document generally comprises of four/five parts :

Part I Contains description of the work, general rules and directions, standard terms and conditions of contract, schedule of materials with prices, proposed to be issued by the department.

Part II Contains standard technical specifications of materials and workmanship.

Part III Contains schedule of items with quantity, unit, estimated rates and amounts.

Part IV Contains complete set of drawings furnishing details of work as far as possible. These drawings are marked 'meant for tendering and not for execution.'

Part V Apart from the above four parts, in some cases, another part is added which contains technical specification of any special item or items of work which would require any particular technology or material or any special tools and plants.

Parts I and II are standard and are always kept ready in printed form for saving time and are specified by form number. Part III, IV and V are prepared as required for each individual tender separately and are added to the document.

All these parts make the tender document complete. Complete set of document is bound in a book form and is priced for sale to the intending tenderers.

11.2.1 Tender Notice

Notices are issued to various departments and organisations and also released through newspapers for wide publicity of the tender. A specimen of tender notice is given below. This tender notice is generally termed as short tender noticelar abridged tender notice and the documents complete with all the parts is termed as detailed notice.

SPECIMEN TENDER NOTICE

Notice

Office of the ....

Tender number ....

Sealed tenders are invited from the experienced, bonafide and resourceful contractors of appropriate class of enlisted contractors and also from the outside reputed contractors for the undermentioned work :

1. Name of the work : Here title of the project and the part for which the tender has been called for is to be mentioned.
2. Short description of the work : Brief description of the work intended to be executed is to be mentioned.
3. Estimated cost of the work : Rs.
4. Earnest money : As per terms and conditions.
5. Time for completion of the work : As desired
6. Manner of depositing earnest money : As mentioned in the terms and conditions.
7. Source of receiving tender documents : As suitable and in practice.
8. Person to whom the tenders are to be deposited : As desired

Any other information in connection with the tender may be had from the .... on all working days during office hours up to the date of tendering.

....

Person inviting tender

11.3.0 QUOTING OF RATES BY THE TENDERERS OR OFFERING TENDER RATES

There are different methods of tendering.

(*a*) **Two parts tender:** Tenders may be invited in two parts.

Part I would contain all technical matters without any indication about the rate, the contractor proposes to quote. Sometimes, in this part contractors are asked to submit alternative design of structure, if they liked. Contractors are asked to submit their terms and conditions, if they so desired.

In the second part, contractors are asked to offer their proposed rates or the financial proposal.

The first part of the tender is opened in presence of the tenderers who have submitted tenders and desired to be present. Tenders are then scrutinized, and analysed after getting clarification. The tenders which are found to be technically sound and acceptable are selected and their other part *i.e.* the second part or the financial part is opened in presence of the selected contractors. Their rates are disclosed. These are then scrutinized and evaluated and finally the tender which is found technically sound and financially favourable is selected for acceptence.

This method of tendering is adopted for very large and complicated works.

(*b*) **Item rate tender.** In cases of tenders of moderate value, the general method is to furnish the estimated rates and amount in the schedule of items or 'Bill of Quantities' and the contractors are asked to quote their contractual percentage on the schedule which shall be applicable on all the items.

The method has been found to be suitable for tenders of moderate value and having no complication.

11.4.0 BID CAPACITY

The capacity of an intending tenderer need be assessed prior to issuing the tender documents to him for participation in the tender. The financial capacity is assessed by Bid Capacity *i.e.,* his estimated capacity to bid.

Bid capacity of a tenderer

Bid capacity of tenderer means the financial capability of an intending tenderer for permitting him to participate in tendering for a work. This clause is generally incorporated in cases of tenders for large amounts.

The bid capacity is estimated on the basis of his performance in the passed five years.

Bid Capacity = 1.5 times the average turnover of five years multiplied by duration of the project less the value of the work at hand in next two years.

Example 11.1. *Annual turnover of an intending tenderer is as below :*

Year	*Turnover*
1992 - 93	Rs. 7.80 crore
1993 - 94	Rs. 12.40 crore
1994 - 95	Rs. 16.67 crore
1995 - 96	Rs. 14.86 crore
1996 - 97	Rs. 17.20 crore. Account not submitted to Registrar of companies

Updating the amounts to current year.

Rs. 7.80 × 1.46 = Rs. 11.39
Rs. 12.40 × 1.33 = Rs. 16.49
Rs. 16.67 × 1.21 = Rs. 20.17
Rs. 14.86 × 1.10 = Rs. 16.35

Rs. 64.40 crore

Average of 4 years = 64.40/4 = Rs. 16.10 crore

As the accounts of 1996 – 97 has not been submitted to the Registrar of companies, the turnover of the year is left out. If the amount of turnover is taken into account, the total would be Rs. 81.16 crore and the average turnover for 5 years would be Rs. 16.32 crore.

Let the duration of the working period for the proposed work be 2 years.

The tenderer need declare the value of work at hand. Let the value of work at hand be 36.72 crore.

∴ Bid capacity of the tenderer at present would be

$$= (1.5 \times 16.10 \times 2) - 36.72$$

$$= \text{Rs. } 11.58 \text{ crore.}$$

This is based on the assumption that the tenderer would be capable of executing 1.5 times the average value of work per annum. Duration is two years. So the average value is multiplied by 1.5. Again, when it is multiplied by 2. The value of the work at hand is deducted. The net value would be the probable capacity of the tenderer.

The tenderer's bid capacity for further work is Rs. 11.58 crore.

In all cases, the estimated value of the work is declared.

In consideration of the nature of the work, and other parameters, a percentage is fixed. The amount obtained by multiplying the estimated value of the work by the percentage should not exceed the bid capacity of the tenderer.

In the present case, let the estimated value of the work be Rs. 16.00 crore and the percentage factor be 60.

The value of the work up to which the tenderer can bid is Rs. 9.60 crore.

So the tenderer is capable of bidding for the tender of the work valued Rs. 16.00 crore.

Question arises, if the turnover of the tenderer should include the cost of materials issued by the department.

When the materials are issued against some price, the turnover should be inclusive of the cost of materials issued by the department. However, if the materials are issued by the department without realising any cost, the value of the materials issued by the department need not be taken into the turnover.

11.5.0 SUBMISSION OF TENDERS

Tender documents complete in all respects and accompanied by evidence of deposit of requisite earnest money are submitted by the tenderers within the specified date and time to the officer inviting tender as mentioned in the notice.

11.6.0 ACCEPTANCE OF THE TENDER

After scrutiny and evaluation, when a tender has been selected for acceptance, the matter is conveyed to the selected tenderer with the request to deposit the balance earnest money and submit the formal tender for formal acceptance of it or is asked to enter into an agreement.

In the public works system, the acceptance of the selected tender on behalf of the Governor of the state is considered as agreement. On receipt of the letter of selection of the tender, the tenderer has to deposit the balance security deposit and submit additional copies of tender for duplicate and triplicate copies of the accepted tender. In cases of statutory bodies a formal agreement is entered into by the parties on stamp paper enclosing all the papers of the documents and other clarifications or any other terms agreed upon by both the parties.

11.7.0 SUPERVISION AND EXECUTION OF THE WORK

On receipt of the work order, the contractor commences the work and proceed with it. The responsibility of the department is to exert proper supervision to ensure the quality control of the work so that no dispute arises in future, specially for the portions which would be concealed or covered up. Although the primary responsibility of the contractor is to ensure the quality by exercising strict supervision, still the responsibility of the department or the client is no less, as ultimately he is the owner of the structure and shall have to pay for the work on being satisfied with the quality. Department or the client shall have to check the work and on being satisfied, his representative would measure up the work and record the same in the measurement book for payment.

In case of large works, one or more representatives of the client should be stationed at site. They shall check the materials collected, whether those conform to the specification and as per sample submitted by the contractor earlier and duly approved by the authority. The quality of the work at all stages shall be controlled by testing the works done and cheking the lines and levels. If any material collected or work done is found to be underspecified, the contractor should be asked to remove the material from the site forthwith and the underspecified work shall be asked to demolish.

11.8.0 ACCOUNTING OF THE WORK

With the progress of work, the quantities of the items shall be measured and recorded and interim payments made. On completion of the work, the representative of the client shall record final measurement and being satisfied, would arrange for final payment of all works.

Accounts of materials issued by the department and cost thereof already realised shall be finalised. When all these accounts are finalised, a clear picture regarding all the aspects of the work would be clear.

11.9.0 MAINTENANCE

On completion of the construction and when the structure is in use, maintenance and operation would start to keep the structure use worthy during its life cycle and to maintain the supply of essential items necessary for using the structure *e.g.* water supply, power supply, etc.

Occasional and regular repairs and replacement of parts of the structure under maintenance would also be required for proper upkeeping of the structure and for prevention against early decay of the members of the structure.

11.10.0 SYSTEM OF CARRYING OUT CONTRACT

The recognised system for carrying out work other than by the employment of daily labour are 'piece work' and 'contract work'. Piece work is that for which only the rate is agreed upon without reference to the total quantity of work to be done in a given period.

All other works done under agreement is termed 'contract work' and in agreements for such work, which should invariably be in writing. There should generally be a stipulation as to the quantity of work to be done and the time within which it is to be completed.

11.10.1. Contract

Contract is an agreement between two persons declaring their common intention to do or not to do an act. All agreements are contracts, if they are made with free consent of the parties competent to make contract for lawful consideration with a lawful object as defined under Section 2 (k) of Indian Contract Act of 1872.

11.10.2. Basis of Contract

Variation of cost is expected, according to the basis on which a contract is placed, and this must be taken into account when estimating and decided upon the form of contract. Studies carried out by the CBRI have shown that lump sum contract performs the best in respect of completion time, completion cost and time and cost overruns for repititive type of construction.

Competitive tenders based on bill of quantities is also likely to produce keen competition, resulting reduction in cost. Negotiated contract on a 'bill of quantities' will not be economical when compared with the lowest tender obtained in a competitive method. Sometimes 'cost plus' contracts are entered into, where actual cost plus an agreed percentage is paid to the contractor. A higher cost of work will give a higher amount to the contractor. Consequently, the cost of construction is likely to be higher in this type of contract.

11.10.3. Time Factor

The cost of a project depends on its completion time. Overhead costs of a contractor per unit time is usually constant. Delay in the completion of the project, delays return on the investment, consequently results in increased cost to the contractor and to the owner. Optimum completion time for a project depends upon the quantum of work, infrastructural facilities and availability of materials and labour. When a project is asked to be completed before the optimum time, over-time working at enhanced overtime rates has to be adopted. This would increase the cost of the project.

11.10.4. Ingredients of Contract

An agreement should contain the following :

(*i*) Proposal,
(*ii*) Communication of proposal,
(*iii*) Consideration,
(*iv*) Consent,
(*v*) Competency to contract,
(*vi*) Communication when complete, and
(*vii*) Revocation of proposal and acceptance.

11.10.5. Contract Document

Contract document consists of :

(*i*) A complete set of drawings with details explaining the work,
(*ii*) Complete specifications of items of works, including any special specification for any item,
(*iii*) Schedule of quantities of various items of works,
(*iv*) Complete set of terms and conditions including any special terms and conditions, and
(*v*) All correspondences and clarifications made and agreed upon.

11.10.6. Different Types of Contracts

Contracts may be of different types,

(*i*) **Lumpsum contract.** In lumpsum contract, contractor is engaged to execute the work with all its contingencies for a fixed sum.

(*ii*) **Schedule contract or item rate contract or Unit price contract.** Schedule contract or item rate contracts are those in which the contractor undertakes to execute the work at fixed rates ; the sum he is to receive depending upon quantities and kind of work done or material supplied. In this system, the contractor has the advantage to manipulate the rates of items. He can quote higher rates for the items to be executed at the early stage and compensate the same by quoting lower rates for items to be executed at the later stage. Thus keeping the total amount competitive.

(*iii*) **Percentage contract.** It is identical in all respects with the item rate contract. In this system, the bill of quantities with rates and amount is provided. The contractor is asked to quote his percentage on the schedule given, which would be applicable on all the items. Thus the draw-back of the item rate contract is eliminated

(*iv*) **Labour contract.** Contract in which the tenderer is asked to quote rates only of the labour portion of the work, all materials required are supplied by the department.

The tenderers may be asked to quote rate of labour only for the items of work or mandays of labourer.

(*v*) **Materials supply contract or contract for supply of materials.** Contract in which the tenderer is asked to quote rates of different kinds of construction materials to be supplied to the godown or at site including stacking. No rate for labour or execution of the work is asked for.

(*vi*) **Piece-work agreement.** In case of small works and in which assessment of quantity of work is time consuming, rates of probable items of works are agreed upon without reference to the total quantity of work to be done or the quantity of work to be done in specified time.

(*vii*) **Cost plus percentage rate contract.** Contract entered into in which the tenderer quotes rate for the work and also a percentage towards his profit component. This type of contract is generally adopted when conditions are such that labour and material rates are liable to fluctuate. In this type of contract no bill of Quantities or Schedule of Rates are incorporated.

(*viii*) **Cost plus fixed fee contract.** In this type of contract, the contractor is paid an agreed fixed Lump-sum amount over and above the actual cost of the work. The fee covers the over-heads and profit of the contractor.

(*ix*) **Cost plus sliding or fluctuating fee scale contract.** In this type of contract, the tenderer quotes the actual cost of construction plus an amount of fee inversely variable according to the increase or decrease of the estimated cost of construction agreed first by both the parties. Thus higher the actual cost, the lower will be the value of the fee and vice versa.

(*x*) **Progressive Rate contract.** The contract is the same as percentage contract. The deviation is that the quantities and rate of the items provided in the schedule are divided into three or more parts with rates of the items progressively increasing. Contractor on timely completion of the first part of an item is automatically entitiled to get higher rate for the same item in the second part and so on.

The procedure encourages the contractor in completion of the work timely and thus completing the work as per programme and time schedule.

(*xi*) **Target contract.** Contract where the contractor is paid on a cost-plus percentage basis for work performed under the contract and in addition he receives a percentage plus or minus on the savings or excess effected against either or prior agreed estimate of total cost or a target value arrived at by measuring the work on completion and valuing at prior agreed rates.

Advantage of the contract is the contractor feels encouraged to use his skill and experience in keeping the cost low. However, the contractor may show higher cost of construction and thus he may gain more amount even after covering the penalty for excess expenditure.

(*xii*) **Measured contract or Schedule contract.** Except lump-sum contract all other types of contracts are measured contracts. In this type, the total cost of a work is worked out by detailed measurement of different items of work after its completion. A bill is then prepared by multiplying the measured quantities by their respective rates. Item of rate contract, percentage contract, cost plus type contract, material supply contract, etc. are examples of measured contract.

(*xiii*) **Negotiated contract.** In this contract, the work is awarded on contract by mutual negotiation between the parties without inviting tenders. It may be of any form mentioned in (*i*), (*ii*), (*iii*) and (*v*).

The contract is entered into to obtain reasonable rates or in case of emergency when time may not be available for going through the normal process of tendering.

Advantage of this system is that it brings some economy in expenditure. The parties selected being always reliable and financially sound, the work is done uninterrupted and with less chances of dispute.

(*xiv*) **Rate contract.** Director General of Supplies and Disposal of Central Government invites tender and fixes rates of such articles and makes Rate Contract with the manufacturer or supplier to supply the articles or materials for a certain period. The prices of the materials or articles remain firm and fixed during the currency of the Rate Contract except for the price variation conditions. The different departments of the central and State Government and Statutory bodies are entitled to avail the Rate Contract.

(*xv*) **Turn-key job or Combined Engineering and Construction Contract.** It sometimes happens that construction of project is desired to be dealt with only one party for all services, both engineering and construction. This is achieved by this type of contract. Offers are invited from specialised contractors for all planning, design, plans, specifications, preparation of estimates and construction services under one contract on competitive basis. The contract may be drawn either on a firm price or cost-plus basis.

11.10.7 Comparative Performance of Different Contract Systems

As the system of contract affects the completion time and cost of the project to a great extent, study of the comparative performance of various systems is needed for effective economy of the work. Lumpsum contracts are based on a fixed price including profit margin of the contractor and is agreed upon in advance and the contractor has to complete the work in accordance with the plans, specifications, construction details and other contract documents which are supplied to him in advance.

In item rate contract and percentage contract, 'bill of quantities' are prepared for all the anticipated items. In item rate contract, items are priced by the contractor and payments are made for the amount of work actually executed. In percentage rate contract the contractor quotes on precentage basis on the rates provided in the 'bill of quantities'. The percentage quoted is applicable on all the items. Payment is made itemwise on the basis of quantities of work actually executed.

11.10.8 Merits and Demerits of Different Contract Systems

Lumsum contract is preferred for traditional and repetitive type of construction. The nature and extent of work is indicated on the drawings and specifications, with or without 'bill of quantities'. The significant attributes of this type of contract system are :

(*i*) Commitments are known in advance,

(*ii*) Better and easier cost control can be exercised by the contractor as he has more independence in the matter.

(*iii*) Reduction in administrative work of the owner/client is possible during construction period, resulting in better supervision as much of the works are done by the contractor.

(*iv*) Higher efficiency and speed in construction can be effected by the contractor leading to his increased profit.

(*v*) Preparation of plans, construction details and specifications are possible in advance as in general, these are done by the contractor.

(*vi*) Contractor can quote better rates based on new techniques and/or innovation.

Works which entail large estimates using relatively few methods of construction and where the volume of work cannot be exactly determined in advance, item rate or percentage rate contracts are preferred. The significant attributes of these systems are :

(*i*) A reasonably accurate estimate is a prerequisite ;

(*ii*) The system provides for more variations ;

(*iii*) Complete drawings and specifications are generally not required in advance. These are generally prepared and supplied with the progress of the work ;

(*iv*) Possibility of over-payment to contractor due to computation and book keeping is reduced ;

(*v*) Overrunning of time and cost due to delayed decision on drawings, details and specifications is a common phenomenon.

11.10.9. Performance of Different Contract Systems (Statistical Basis)

Statistical relationships of performance of different contract systems with regard to time and cost and total plinth area of buildings of projects are established. Comparison of the systems was done with respect to the following parameters.

(*i*) **Completion time**

Lumpsum contract — least time,

Item rate contract — 45 — 75 per cent more time,

Percentage rate contract — 45 — 55 per cent more time.

(*ii*) **Completion cost**

Apart from the normal variations like specifications, number of storey, execution sites, design features, construction year and degree of tender competition or bidding, volume of work influence greatly the completion cost in different contract system.

Buildings with plinth area up to 1,870 sqm, performance of percentage rate contract is comparatively better.

Buildings with plinth area above 1,870 sqm, performance of lumpsum contract is better than percentage rate or contract.

(*iii*) **Variation in time**

Projects completed within variation of time up to 50% from the stipulation time :

Lumpsum contract — 79%

Precentage rate contract — 36%

Item rate contract — 30%

In rest of the projects, the time variation was more than 50% the comparative performance of lumpsum contracts was better.

(iv) **Variation in cost**

Variation on completion cost remaining within 5% of contract cost:

Lumpsum contract — 85%

Percentage rate contract — 46%

Item rate contract — 45%

(*v*) **Disputes**

Incidence of disputes leading to arbitration;

Lumsum contract — 10%
Percentage contract — 47%
Item rate contract — 19%

Performance of lumpsum contract is better than percentage rate contract and item rate contract for projects like housing. Difference in performance of percentage rate contract and its rate contract is very little.

11.10.10 Some Standard Terms and Conditions which Need be Incorporated in the Tender Document Part I

(*i*) **Earnest Money.** Earnest money is the amount, the contractors are asked to deposit prior to tendering, demonstrating their earnestness for the tender. This is generally 1% - 2% of the estimated value of the tender and is asked to deposit atleast one day prior to tender date. The earnest money of the unsuccessful tenders are refunded without any interest.

(*ii*) **Security deposit.** Security deposit is the amount which the tenderer whose tender has been selected for acceptance, is asked to deposit prior to formal acceptance of the tender or execution of agreement. This amount varies from 5% to 8% of the value of the tender, after consideration of the contractual percentage inclusive of the amount already deposited as earnest money. This security deposit is taken in two parts — one part about 2% including the earnest money is asked to deposit prior to acceptance or execution of the agreement and the balance is recovered from progressive bills proportionately.

(*iii*) **Supplementary items.** The schedule of items or 'bill of quantities' shows the details of items of works to be executed. Any item of work not appearing in the schedule but required to be executed by the contractor under the contract is called supplementary item. Procedure for finalisation of the rate of the supplementary item of work should be indicated.

(*iv*) **Compensation.** When a contractor fails to complete the work within the specified period for no fault of the client, he is liable to pay compensation for the loss and/or damages suffered by the client. Procedure for realisation of compensation for the loss should be specified in the tender.

(*v*) **Liquidated damages.** Liquidated damage is an amount of compensation payable by a contractor to the owner due to delayed construction having no relationship with the actual damage. If the contractor fails to complete the work within the time period prescribed in the tender, then, the contractor shall have to pay to the owner the sum stated in tender as liquidated damage for such default and not as a penalty, for everyday for the excess period taken between the date of completion as specified in the tender or the extended time as the case may be and the date of actual completion of the work. The payment or deduction of such damage shall not relieve the contractor from his obligations and liabilities under the contract. If, before the completion of the whole work, any part of the work is occupied or used by the owner and is duly certified by the Engineer in Charge, the liquidated damages for delay shall be reduced in the proportion in which the value of the part so certified bears to the value of the whole of the work. The security money deposited and deducted from the contractor is held up in full or part from the contractor during this period.

(*vi*) **Extension of time.** The contract is made for execution of the work within a specified period. When the work is not completed within the period and the period is extended on agreement of both the sides, the extended period of time is called extension of time.

(*vii*) **Escalation of prices.** Due to wide variation of prices of materials and labour in large works, provision need be made for price contingency of materials and labour. There are various formulae for calculating the amount on account of price variation. The most acceptable formula is based on R.B.I. price indices for materials and labour.

Formula for price escalation/de-escalation

(*a*) **Materials**

$$V_m = (0.60\ W - M_d) \times \frac{I_m - I_{mo}}{I_{mo}}$$

Where, V_m = Escalation/de-escalation on account of variation of prices of materials.

W = Total gross value of the work done at tendered rate.

M_d = Value of the materials issued by the department at fixed rate.

I_m = Wholesale price index number for all commodities as ruling during the period under consideration as published in the R.B.I. Bulletin.

I_{mo} = Wholesale price index number for all materials other than issued by the department ruling at the time of tendering and as published in the R.B.I. bulletin.

(*b*) **Labour**

$$V_l = 0.25\ W \times \frac{L_L - L_{L0}}{L_{L0}}$$

Where, V_l = Escalation/de-escaration on account of variation of price of labour.

W = Total gross value of the work at the tendered rate.

L_l = Consumer price index number for industrial labour applicable for the region of the site of work as ruling during the period under consideration as published in R.B.I. Bulletin.

L_{l0} = Consumer price index number for industrial labour applicable for the region of the site of work as ruling in the month of submitting tender as published in the R.B.I. Bulletin.

Procedure for computation of price escalation shall be indicated in clear terms in the tender.

(*vii*) **Termination of the contract.** When a contractor fails to fulfil the terms of the contract and the work is incomplete, the contract may be terminated. Prior to termination, the contractor shall be served with a show cause notice asking him to explain why he would not be made liable to pay compensation for non-fulfilment of the contract. On receiving his reply and after due consideration, the contract may be terminated by the authority spelling out the mode of payment or realisation of the compensation. Procedure for termination of the contract where such situation arises shall be delineated clearly.

(*ix*) **Defects liability period.** After the work is complete, the contractor remains responsible for making good to any defect observed in the work for a specified period. This period is called defects liability period. The security money deposited or deducted from the contractor is held up in full or part during this period.

(*x*) **Completion certificate.** On completion of the work in all respects including removal of all surplus materials, contractor's godown, etc., clearance of site and being satisfied that there is no liability due from the contractor, the Engineer in Charge would inspect the work and issue a completion certificate. This should be recorded in the measurement book.

(*xi*) **Refund of Security Deposit.** There are two systems of refund of security deposit;

(*i*) The total security deposit lying at the credit of the contractor is refunded in full on recommendation of the Engineer in Charge and on certified by him that there was no liability due from the contractor after expiry of the defect liability period or maintenance period.

(*ii*) The security deposit is sometimes refunded in two stages. 50% of the total security is refunded along with the final bill and the balance 50% after expiry of the defect liability period or the maintenance period. In both the cases, the Engineer in Charge certifies that the work has been completed satisfactorily and there is no liability due from the contractor.

(*xii*) **Ceiling on the security deposit.** Ceiling on the total secuirity deposit has been introduced. The quantum of ceiling varies in different organisations from Rs. 2.00 lac to Rs. 5.00 lac. Recovery of the part security would be effected till the ceiling amount is reached.

(*xiii*) **Work Order.** On completion of the contractual formalities or on formal acceptance of the tender, the Engineer in Charge issues order to commence the work allowing a short period for preparation, mobilization and any other preparatory work.

(*xiv*) **Mobilization period.** Certain period of time according to the nature and value of work is allowed before reckoning the date of commencement of the work. A clause mentioning the period for preparation should be incorporated in the tender document. Engineer in Charge mentions the same again in the work order. Actual period of work is reckoned after the date of mobilization.

(*xv*) **Work programme.** During the mobilization period, the contractor prepares a work programme and schedule of materials that would be required to be issued by the department. The programme is finalised after mutual discussion and a Bar-Chart or CPM network is drawn and agreed upon by the both. The programme is followed through out the period of work. The contractor is bound by the time limit *i.e.* the total period of work. He is also bound to produce proportionate progress of the work in proportionate time. He is also bound to follow the programme. The department is also bound to deliver the site of work immediately after the work order and extend all assistance in persuance of the terms and conditions of the contract, specially the issue of the materials of good quality as and when indented by the contractor as per programme.

(*xvi*) **Arbitration.** With increase in volume of the construction work and with increase in knowledge of one's democratic rights and eligibility, disputes in the contract works have increased. In spite of all possible care taken in drafting the tender and contract documents, lapses, errors, flaws and ambiguity may remain in the contract document which would subsequently give rise to disputes. Misinterpretation of the provisions in the contract documents may also give rise to disputes. All these cannot be resolved by the Engineer in Charge, he being a party to the contract. There is always an air of grudge and mistrust. In the situation a person like umpire is required who can deliver justice to both the parties.

Provision of an 'Arbitration' clause in persuance of 'Arbitration and Conciliation Ordinance, 1996' in the tender is desired to solve the problems arising in the future. Necessary provision of such clause should be made in the tender document to create confidence of the tenderers and contractors.

12

PROCEDURE OF TAKING MEASUREMENTS OF WORK AND PREPARATION OF BILL

12.1.0 PROCEDURE FOR EXECUTION OF WORK

Procedure for execution of a work need systematic approach from the initial stage to the completion. The initiation of a work begins with the request of the requisitioning department or the client stating his necessities or requirements regarding the work or the project. On receipt of the demand, the Executive department prepares a detailed estimate or project report with a cost estimate. The requisitioning deparment or the administrative department *i.e.* the client accords his approval. The estimate or the project report is then examined by the Technical department of the Executive agency and the competent authority in the department accords Technical sanction.

The Executive department is now in a position to take up the work for execution, provided there is provision in the budget for the work.

12.2.0 PREPARATION OF TENDER DOCUMENT

After the detailed estimate has been technically sanctioned, tenders are invited provided there is provision of fund in the budget for the work. Tender documents are prepared for inviting tenders.

Relevant tender papers with clauses both standard and special are to be incorporated in the tender document. Clauses regarding manner of depositing earnest money and security deposit and other important clauses need be included.

Specifications of standard items shall be referred to in the tender documents and those of any special items shall be drawn and incorporated in the part II of the document.

Part III of the tender document shall contain schedule of items with quantity, unit and estimated rates. While preparing the schedule of Rates or sometimes termed 'Bill of Quantities' every care shall be taken to make the items of work as explicit as possible. However, the description shall be brief. The specifications of the items incorporated shall supplement the information not clear enough from the description of the item and also supplement the drawings of the work.

12.3.0 INVITATION OF TENDER

When the tender documents are prepared, tenders shall be invited from the eligible contractors with publicity through the news papers. The minimum time gap between the date of publication of the notice and the date of receipt of the tenders shall be atleast two weeks. Copies of such tender notice shall be sent to various Engineering Offices, and other offices of importance for wide publicity.

12.4.0 POWERS OF ACCEPTING TENDERS

In Public Works Department system, the powers of acceptance of the tenders are as below:

(*a*) Assistant Engineer - Works valued up to Rs. 25,000/-

(*b*) Executive Engineer - Works valued up to Rs. 3,00,000/-

(*c*) Superintending Engineer - Works valued above Rs. 3,00,000/- and up to Rs. 15,00,000/-

Tenders valued above Rs. 15,00,000/- shall be referred to the tender committee.

12.5.0 CLASSIFICATION OF CONTRACTORS

There are four categories of enlisted contractors in the Public Works Department system of works.

Class I — above Rs. 2.00 lac up to Rs. 5.00 lac.

Class II — above Rs. 1.00 lac up to Rs. 2.00 lac.

Class III — above Rs. 50.00 thousand up to Rs. 1.00 lac.

Class IV — up to Rs. 50.00 thousand.

Besides these enlisted contractors, there are bonafide outside contractors also. These outside contractors can submit tender on production of their credentials and proof of their financial capability and bonafide, for all original works. These tenders are termed open tenders.

The classified contractors are entitled to submit tenders for maintenance and repair works valued according to their classification. They can submit tenders in response to open tenders for original works also, but within their financial limits of classification.

The outside contractors have to deposit earnest money each time of their tendering, the classified contractors need not deposit earnest money at the time of submission of the tender as they have to keep in deposit a sum of money at the time of their enlistment.

12.6.0 SUBMISSION OF TENDERS

Tenders are submitted at a specific place as mentioned in the notice, observing all the formalities. The tenders are dropped in a sealed tender box and are allowed to be dropped up to a specific time of a specific date.

12.7.0 QUOTING OF RATES

The tenderers are asked to follow the procedure and quote their rates as mentioned in the tender document.

12.8.0 OPENING OF THE TENDERS

Unless otherwise mentioned, all the tender documents and related papers together with evidence of deposition of earnest money should be packed in one sealed cover with name of the work and addressed to whom to be submitted. The tenders are opened in presence of the tenderers who may like to be present at the specified place and time. The rates quoted by each of the tenderer is announced. The tenderers are entitled to examine the documents submitted, if they so desired.

12.8.1. Register of Tenders Received

A register is maintained for recording the particulars of the tenders received wherein a column exists for number of corrections in the tenders. After entering the records of the tenders, register is signed by the officer opening the tenders and the tenderers present.

12.8.2. Evaluation of Tenders

The tenders are then scrutinized, the tenders which are considered informal are rejected forthwith. The remaining tenders are examined in cosideration of the rates quoted and special conditions, if there be any. A comparative statement is prepared showing details of all the tenders.

12.8.3. Selection of the Tender

The tender found favourable taking into consideration of all the aspects is selected for acceptance and the tenderer is intimated accordingly for depositing the balance security deposit money and entering into an agreement. The earnest money deposited by other unsuccessful tenderers is refunded.

12.9.0. WORK ORDER

Formal work order is issued by the Engineer in Charge to the contractor when the tender has been accepted or who has entered into an agreement. Copy of the work order is forwarded to the Subordinate Engineer.

The work is now to be executed and completed within the stipulated time period. The work has to be executed progressively – proportionate work in proportionate time.

12.10.0 MEASUREMENT OF THE WORK

The contractor is generally entitled to Running On Account Bills with the progress of the work. The work as done is measured and recorded in measurement book.

The Executive Engineer is the Engineer in Charge and is responsible for proper execution of the work and payment of the work on execution. He himself can measure up the work; but as it is not possible in most cases, the Assistant Engineer and the Subordinate Engineer who are the Executive staff records the measurements in the measurement book.

12.10.1. Measurement Book

Measurement book is considered as the most important record of works as it is the basis of all accounts in the Public Works system of works, whether the work is done by engaging labour in Muster Roll or as piece work or by contract. Even the supply of materials including local petty purchases for works are recorded in the measurement book. The description of the work must be lucid, so that the nature of work can be identified without difficulty and check can be undertaken easily. Payments of all works including that done by daily labours and for supplies should be made on the basis of detailed measurements recorded in the measurement book.

To facilitate the preparation of estimates and bill for periodical repairs, Standard Measurement Books are prepared for all such repair works which are usually undertaken for renewal works as routine items.

12.10.2. Recording Measurements in Measurement Book

Measurement book shall be written carefully. The particulars regarding the contract and works must be furnished at the commencement of recording in the form as shown in the specimen below. Measurement of works shall be written down following the sequence of the progress of work and reference must be entered of the contract item numbers. The description of the items of works must be entered in details as in the contract. If there is any deviation, the same must be mentioned for reducing the rates for payment for the portion of the work less done. Any additional work done must also be recorded for payment as supplementry item. The measurement of the item which would be covered up subsequently *e.g.* reinforcement, etc. must be entered earlier before being covered up.

Measurement for works done shall be taken just after completion of the work. If necessary, line sketch or shape of the work done may be drawn to explain the method of measurement taken. If any standard formula of mensuration has been applied for calculation of the quantity, the same must be furnished in the measurement book.

Too many correction of dimension of measurements is not desired. However, if there be any, the cancellation must be done neatly and the wrong and correct entries must be legible. Each correction must be initialed separately. No overwriting must be done in the measurement book.

All entries in the measurement book must be done only by the person who is authorised to write it and the measurement book has been duly issued to him by the competent authority.

After entering the measurement, the same must be signed by the person recording the measurement with his office stamp indicating his designation.

Sample of Measurement Book

(First page)

1. Name of the work:
2. Name of the contractor:
3. Situation of the work:
4. Number and date of agreement:
5. Date of written order to commence work:
6. Date of actual completion of work:
7. Date of recording measurement:
8. Reference of previous measurements:

Item no.	*Description of item of works*	*No.*	*Length*	*Breadth*	*Height*	*Contents*

12.10.3 Standard Measurement Book

Detailed measurement may be dispensed with in the case of periodical repair works when the quantities are recorded in the efficiently maintained Standard Measurement Books.

To facilitate the preparation of estimates and bill of quantities for periodical repair works, a Standard Measurement Book should be prepared and maintained showing the detailed measurements of each kind of repair which is usually subjected to renewal in each year or periodically.

12.11.0 IMPREST

Impress is a standing advance of a fixed amount of money given to an individual to enable him to make certain category of disbursements entrusted to his charge by the authority according to such rules.

Imprest may be temporary or permanent.

12.11.1 Temporary Imprest

Temporary imprest is the advance given for meeting disbursement of some specific work. On completion of the work and disbursement of the amount, accounts with the balance amount, if any, shall be submitted to the authority.

12.11.2 Permanent Imprest

Permanent imprest is the advance of a fixed amount given permanently to the authorised individual for meeting the outgoings of some recurring items. After spending a considerable portion of the advance, and on submission of the account, the amount spent is recouped to restore the full sanctioned permanent amount.

12.12.0 PREPARATION OF BILL

When the detailed measurement have been recorded in the measurement book, the Subordinate Engineer or the Executive staff does the calculations and works out the quantities of each item of the work as per units mentioned in the schedule of items.

12.12.1 Running on Account Bill

When the quantities have been worked out, the Subordinate Engineer or the Executive staff draws and abstract of the quantities of the work done. The abstract is drawn in the measurement book by adding the quantities of the same item together. While drawing the abstract, the number of items as appear in the 'Schedule of Quantities' or in the 'Bill of Quantities' in the contract is maintained. He then adds the amounts of the items and finds out the amount payable after taking into consideration of the percentage above and below as the quoted by the contractor.

He then shows separately a statement of recoveries, if there be any, on any account, from the contractor, may it be for materials issued or any machinery given on hire or on any other account.

If there be any item not done as per specification and the rate of payment has to be reduced, the analysis of the reduced rate shall be shown and should be mentioned as part rate.

When all these are done, the bill is considered as complete. He signs the bill and makes out copy of the same in the standard form. He then submits the bill to the Senior Engineer. The Senior Engineer checks the bill, compares the items, quantities, rates and amount with schedule of quantities. He verifies the part rates, if there be any. He may check the measurements at site, if he so desire. He then signs the bill and the Measurement Book and forwards the same to the Executive Engineer or the Engineer in Charge recommending payment.

The measurements in the measurement books and bill are checked in the Executive Engineer's office together with the terms and conditions of the contract, specially the completion period. Executive Engineer may check the measurements entered in the Measurement book, if he so desire. The bill is then passed for payment by order of the Executive Engineer. The requisite security deposit is deducted and the amount is paid to the contractor by an "account payee" cheque.

When the bill is a First Running on Account one, there is less problem. But when it is a second or third or any subsequent running on account bill, the procedure of carrying over of the previous quantity of work done and amount paid arises. The work done after the previous running on account bill is recorded and the quantity worked out. These are then brought forward in the abstract as the quantity 'since previous' bill. To this the quantity shown up to previous bill is added and work done up to date is arrived at and the amount of the same is calculated. All the items are calculated in this procedure. The total shows the total amount payable inclusive of the previous payments. When this amount has been found out, the amount paid up to the previous bill is deducted and amount payable for the present bill is found out.

In case of recoveries, this practice is not followed. The entries are done in each bill separately without any carry over.

12.12.2 Final Bill

In all respects, it is like Running on account bill having a previous running on account payment. The amount calculated as since previous is the amount of the final bill.

The senior Engineer and executive staff certify separately that the works have been done as per specification and there is no liability due from the contractor.

Final bills are drawn in the measurement book and then copied in the bill form "Final payment". There may be cases, in which conditions may be to refund 50% of the security due to the contractor with the final bill. This amount is added on receipt of a report from the senior Engineer in the form specified for the purpose.

12.12.3 First and Final Bill

There may be cases, when the work is small, the full amount payable is paid in one bill without any Running on Account payment. The recording of measurements and drawing of the abstract of the bill in the measurement book is done in the same manner. The bill copy is done in a separate bill form known as 'First and Final Bill' form. All the certificates necessary for the final bill need be furnished with this bill.

12.12.4 Supply Bills

Measurements for supply of any materials are recorded in the measurement book in the same procedure at that of the work. Immediately on receipt of any supply a Purchase Account is drawn in the specified form with reference to the measurement book where the supply has been recorded. The purchase account is forwarded to the Executive Engineer for advance booking of the expenditure against the supply. An abstract of the bill is drawn in the measurement book. Copy of the same is done in 'Supply bill form' in the same manner as 'Running on account' and 'Final' or 'First and Final' bills as in the case of works.

12.13.0 COMPLETION CERTIFICATE

On completion of each work satisfactorily, the Executive Engineer on the basis of the recommendation of the senior Engineer and after verification of the office records that there is no liability due from the contractor, issues a completion cretificate to the contractor.

P. W. Accounts Form 27 - Running Account Bill - C

Cash book Voucher No. .... Dated ....

Name of ....

Purpose of supply ....

Serial No. of this bill ....

No. & date of his last bill for this work ....

Reference to agreement...

Date of written order to commence work ....

Date of actual completion of work ....

I. Account of work done or supplies made

Unit	*Quantity executed or supplied to date as per measurement book*	*Items of work or supplies (Grouped under "sub-head" and "sub-works" of estimate)*	*Rate*		*Amount*				*Remarks*
					up to date		*Since previous bill (total for each sub-head)*		
1	2	3	4		5		6		7
			Rs.	p.	Rs.	p.	Rs.	p.	
		Carried over	...	..	...	..	...	...	
Last page position Total value of work done or supplies made to date (A)... Deduct Value of work done or supplies shown on previous bill.... Net value of work or supplies since previous bill (F) Figure (F) in words, Rupees									....

II. Certificate and Signature

The measurements were made by .... on ....

and recorded at page .... of Measurement Book No. ....

No advance payment has been made previously without detailed measurements.

Signature of officer (Rank) Sub-Divisional Officer preparing bill.

......Sub-Division

....

Dated signature of Contractor

Dated signature of Officer ....

authorising payment ....

Final payments
P.W. Accounts form 26 - Running Account Bill - B
Cash book Voucher No.......... dated..........
Name of Contractor..................
Name of work.......................
Serial No. of this bill ....
No. and date of his previous bill for this work........
Reference to agreement ....
Date of written order to commence work................
Date of actual completion of work.....................

I. Accounts of Works Executed

Advance payment for work not yet maesured			*Item of work (grouped under "sub-heads" and "sub-works" of estimate*	*Unit*	*Rate*	*Quantity executed up to date as per measure-ment book*	*Payment on the basis of actua: measure-ments*		*Remarks (with reasons for delay in adjusting payments shown in columns)*
Total as per pre-vious bill	*Since pre-vious bill*	*Total up to date*					*Up to date*	*Since previous*	
1	2	3	4	5	6	7	8	9	10
					Rs. P.		Rs. P.	Rs. P.	

Total value of work done to date (*A*)
Deduct value of work shown in pre. bill
Net value of work since pre. bill (*F*)
Figure (*F*) in words - Rupees

Final Payments

II - Amount of "Secured Advances" allowed on the security of

Quantity outstanding from previous bill	*Deduct quantity of work measured since previous bill*	*Quantity outstanding including quantity brought to site since previous bill*	*Full rate as assessed by the Divisional Officer*	*Description of Materials*	*Unit*	*Reduction at which advance is made*	*Up to date amount of advance*	*Reference to Divisional Officer's written orders authorising the advance*	*Reasons for non-clearance of advance when outstanding more than three months.*
1	2	3	4	5	6	7	8	9	10
	Total amount outstanding as per this account ... Deduct amount outstanding as per entry (*C*) prev. bill.. Net amount since previous bill (in words) Rupees								(*C*) (*E*)

II. Certificates and Signatures

Dated signature of Officer preparing the bill

(Rank) Sub-Divisional Officer

.... Sub-Division.

.... Division

Dated Signature of Contractor Officer authorising payment

....

(Rank)........................ ....

13

SPECIFICATION

13.1.0 WHAT IS SPECIFICATION

Specification is a separate description of a particular item of work and contains detailed description of all workmanship and materials which are required to complete the item of work in accordance with its drawings and details. In most cases it is not possible to furnish all the information on the drawings, regarding the quality of materials to be used and the quality of workmanship to be achieved during construction. These information regarding the materials and the workmanship are conveyed through 'specification' for the work. Thus the drawings with specifications describe the item of work completely.

13.1.1 Necessity of Specifications

Necessities of drawing specifications of work are :

(*i*) It ascertains with reasonable accuracy the cost of an unit quantity of work.

(*ii*) It conveys the desired description of the work as correctly as possible.

(*iii*) It specifies the workmanship and method of work as desired.

(*iv*) It specifies the equipments, tools and plants that may be required to execute the work.

(*v*) It helps in verifying and checking the strength of materials for the work.

(*vi*) In case of any non-standard item of work, specification is more important as it can provide full guidance for execution of the work.

(*vii*) Spefication identifies as far as possible correctly the materials required, manner of execution, and the strength desired of the finished item of work.

(*viii*) Specification supplements the information furnished in the drawing.

(*ix*) Specification is an important ingredient of the tender document and the contract.

(*x*) Specification helps to avoid or resolve any dispute arising during execution of the work. When any dispute actually arises, it helps the arbitrator in arriving at the judgement/award.

13.1.2 How to Write Specification

While drafting specification, the following points need be taken into consideration.

(*i*) Description of the materials — Quality, size, strength, cheking up at site, proportion of mixing, etc.

(*ii*) Workmanship — Complete description of workmanship, the method of mixing, laying, preparation of base or surface, compaction, finishing, curing, i.e. all stages shall be clearly and carefully stated.

(*iii*) Tools and Plants to be engaged shall be mentioned as may be necessary.

(*iv*) Protection of the green work after laying — if any special method to be adopted shall be described.

(*v*) Expression — the specification shall be concise, but be clear without any ambiguity or vagueness.

(*vi*) Care should be taken regarding site condition, nature of work to present a clear picture of the work and as desired to be executed.

13.1.3 Types of Specifications

(*i*) **Types of specifications.** Detailed specifications for different works are drawn up for standard and mostly used items of works and printed to save time and labour in drawing those every time. The standard specifications are attached to tender documents.

(*ii*) **Special specification.** These are drawn separately for items of works those are not covered in the standard specifications and for items having deviation from the standard specification.

13.2.0 SPECIFICATIONS

(*i*) **Bricks — first class.** Bricks should conform to I.S. 1077 of 1957 and should be table moulded, well burnt, copper coloured, free from cracks and with sharp and angular edges. It should be of uniform shape and standard size. It should give ringing sound when struck with each other. When broken should show a bright homogeneous and compact structure free from voids. It should not absorb water more than 20% by weight when soaked in cold water for a period of 24 hours. It should be sufficiently hard. No impression should be left on brick surface, when scratched with finger-nail. It should not break when dropped flat on hard ground from a height of about one meter. It should have low thermal conductivity and should be sound proof. When soaked in water for 24 hours and kept in shade for drying, should not show deposits of white salts. It should have crushing strength not below 55 kg per sq cm.

(*ii*) **Fine/Coarse aggregate for cement concrete.** These are inert or chemically inactive materials which form the bulk of cement concrete. The aggregates are bound together by means of cement.

(*a*) The materials which passes through 4.7625 mm size B.S. test sieve and conform to I.S. 383 of 1963 is termed as fine aggregate or sand. Usually natural river or pit sand is used as fine aggregate. Sand as fine aggregate shall be coarse, consisting of sharp angular grains. It shall be clean and free from dust, dirt and organic matters. Sea sand shall not be used without specific permission.

(*b*) The materials which is retained on 4.7625 mm size B.S. test sieve and conforms to I.S. 383 of 1963 is termed as coarse aggragete. Broken or crushed hard stone is generally used as coarse aggregate. The nature of the work decides the maximum size of the coarse aggregate. It shall be hard, strong, dense, clean and free from soft, friable, thin, flat, elongated or laminated, flaky pieces and shall be roughly cubical in shape. It must be clean and free from dirt and any foreign matter. The broken edges shall be sharp and angular.

(*iii*) **Brickwork in cement mortar 1 : 6**

Bricks to be used must be first class, well burnt, regular in shape and size, copper colour and sound ringing clearly. The bricks shall be properly saturated in water for atleast 12 hours. While laying, the bricks shall be thoroughly bedded and flushed with mortar. The joints shall be properly filled with mortar and grouted at every fourth layer.

The bricks shall be laid in proper bonds as specified. The work must be finished in all face-work and the joints raked out properly to receive the rendering. The brickwork should be carried out regularly in all cases. No part shall be left one meter lower than another part. Where it would be necessary to carry on the same section of a building in uneven course, the end bricks shall be raked so as to maintain a uniform and effectual bond. Not more than 1.0 metre height of wall shall be built in a day.

(*iv*) **Lime concrete in foundation.** Proportion of ingredients used for the concrete is 18 : 36 : 100 or 1 : 2 : 5½

The concrete shall consist of broken jhama khoa of size 12 mm — 25 mm obtained by breaking 1st. class bricks or brick bats. Surkhi shall be made of 1st. class bricks or brick bats and shall be coarse. Lime shall be slaked stone lime screened so as not to contain any small lump. Lime shall be fully in powder condition. Mixing of the concrete shall be made on a platform to keep it clear and free from any foreign material. The mixed concrete in wet condition shall be kept in pile for 24 – 48 hours and the mixture turned once or twice a day to ensure thorough mixing of the ingredients. The mixed concrete shall be carried to the foundation bed which has been properly cleaned and concrete must not be thrown in the trench from the ground. The concrete shall be laid in thickness of not more than 150 mm. After laying of the concrete, it shall be well rammed with wooden mallet or iron rammer. The surface of each layer shall be scrapped before laying of next layer. When thicker layer is laid, each layer laid in one operation shall not be more than 150 mm thick.

(*v*) **Cement concrete 1 : 2 : 4.** The concrete shall have four parts of coarse aggregate of hard stone of nominal size 20 mm, sharp edge, clean and graded. Sand shall constitute two parts which shall be coarse, clean and free from any dust or foreign material. If necessary, the ingredients shall have to be washed before use. Cement shall be one part which shall be of fresh quality. Water for mixing and curing shall be potable and free from injurious and deleterious material.

The aggregates shall be batched by volume with respect to a bag of cement of 50 kg. Measurement of the batches shall be by wooden boxes of same size. Bulkage of the sand shall be measured and necessary allowance shall be made. Water shall be measured either by volume in calibrated vessels or by weighing. The specified water cement ratio shall have to be maintained.

The mixing of concrete shall be made in a mechanical mixer. Mixing shall be continuous and uniform consistency shall be maintained. In case due to exigency and to keep the concreting continuous hand mixing has to be resorted to, 10% extra cement shall have to be used.

Concrete shall be transported from the place of mixing to the place of final deposit quickly. Ramming, tamping, levelling, vibrating all these operations shall be completed before the initial setting of concrete starts. Concrete must not be dropped from a height greater than 1.0 m.

Prior to laying of concrete, the mould shall be cleaned and the inside of the mould shall be properly protected to resist absorption of water. The mould shall be made water tight. The reinforcement laid shall be in correct position and during concreting all care shall be taken so that the reinforcing bars are not displaced. Concrete shall not be laid in layers of thickness more than 300 mm.

Concrete after laying shall be thoroughly compacted by mechanical vibration or hand rodding or both. In case of reinforced concrete, care must be taken to ensure packing of concrete around the reinforcing bars specially at the junctions.

Concreting shall be carried out continuously up to the predetermined position of construction joint. The concrete shall be cured by pounding water over it or by keeping the surface damp for a mimimum period of 14 days or as specified.

During concreting random samples of concrete shall be taken in test moulds to ascertain the strength of concrete after 7 days and 28 days. During the process of concreting slump tests shall be carried out at regular intervals to ensure consistency of the concrete.

(*vi*) **Damp proof course.** Damp proof course usually a layer of cement concrete is laid in between the plinth and the superstructure wall to prevent the rise of moisture by capillary action from the ground and thereby creating a barrier against ingress of damp effectively.

The brickwork of the plinth is completed up to the desired height less by the thickness of the Damp proof course which is generally 25 mm to 40 mm. The top level of the brickwork is checked. If there be any deficiency in level, it shall be corrected by concrete. However, the thickness of the Damp proof course shall not be less than the desired thickness as specified. The surface of the brickwork shall be thoroughly cleaned and roughened for receiving the concrete layer. It is then thoroughly wetted. The cement concrete of mix 1 : 1½: 3 with 5% admixture of water proofing compound by weight of cement is laid on it, compacted thoroughly by wooden mallet and trowel. When the laying and compaction is complete, but before starting of initial setting of the concrete, the top surface of the layer shall be chequered for providing better bonding with the brick layer which shall be laid later. The concrete layer shall then be cured by water as usual in case of cement concrete for atleast a week and brickwork shall not be done over it till the cement concrete of the Damp proof course attains sufficient strength.

To improve the quality of Damp proof course two layers of bitumen of grade 30/40 or 60/70 are laid, one over the brickwork prior to laying of cement concrete layer and the other over the cement concrete layer.

(*vii*) **Interior plaster on brickwork.** The joints of the masonry are to be raked out to a depth of 15 – 20 mm and the wall shall be washed with fresh water and shall be thoroughly wetted. A rendering of plaster sufficiently thick to cover by 6 mm minimum all the projections shall be applied in an even and uniform coat. In case of lime sand plaster the mortar shall be well beaten with hand tappers and wetted occasionally with fresh water while beating. Over the surface a mixture of fat lime and shell lime in the proportion of 2 : 1 shall be laid and made smooth with wooden rubbers and very lightly beaten.

In case of sand cement plaster — rendered surface shall be smoothened by trowel. Mortar mixed must be used up prior to starting of initial setting of cement. The finished plaster shall be cured by sprinkling water.

(*viii*) **Grey artificial stone flooring (Indian patent stone flooring).** The flooring may be laid either on the under base of lime concrete or cement concrete in the ground floor or on R.C.C. slab in the upper floor.

Prior to laying of the artificial stone flooring of specified thickness varying from 25 mm to 50 mm, the base shall be properly levelled, raked, cleaned and washed to remove all foreign materials. The bed of the flooring shall be checked for level and slope as desired with top marks of concrete or mortar. A layer of cement slurry of medium consistency shall be spread over the prepared bed. The flooring shall be laid in alternate panels separated by glass or aluminium strips.

The concrete mix for the flooring shall be 1 : 2 : 4 or 1 : 1½: 3 with stone chips 12 mm down and coarse sand. Concrete mixed in a concrete mixer shall be laid properly and uniformly and compacted by tampering and levelled. After laying of the flooring concrete and before it has hardened the top shall be finished with cement paste of thick consistency of 3 mm to 6 mm thickness and top finished smooth with trowel. The finished floor shall be cured by pounding water of 75 mm depth for a period of 7 days, minimum.

This type of flooring is left unpolished. However, if desired the flooring may be polished by hand grinding with pumic stone or may be machine polished.

(*ix*) **Terrazo tile flooring.** Terrazo tile flooring may be laid on a prelaid lime concrete or cement concrete base in ground floor or on R.C.C. slab in upper floor.

Prior to laying of the terrazo tiles, the base shall be checked for level and slope and properly raked out and cleaned. If necessary, the top may be corrected as required by cement concrete 1 : 2 : 4 with 6 mm down stone chips.

Terrazo tiles may be laid in either of the ways on the base course:

(*a*) with cement concrete backing, or

(*b*) with lime surkhi mortar backing.

(*a*) *With cement concrete backing.* The backing is of cement concrete of proportion 1 : 2 : 4 with stone chips of 6 mm down and coarse sand. The backing concrete is laid in uniform thickness of 20–25 mm over which the terrazo tiles of finished shape and size are laid. The joints kept are very thin and filled with cement sand mortar.

After 24 hours of laying the tiles, the surface shall be cured by sprinkling water. At least after 7 days the top shall be ground by stones and polished. At least three polishing shall be applied to get a moderately smooth surface. The top shall then be cleaned by removing all slurry. The surface shall again be polished either by wax or oxalic acid powder by rubbing with clean cloth.

(*b*) *With lime surkhi mortar backing.* In this method with backing of lime surkhi mortar, the backing, materials are changed and all other operations are the same. The top of the joints are finished with cement prior to grinding.

In both the methods, design of laying pattern of the tiles need be prepared and got approved by the authority. Design should be such that the pattern of laying and the colour of the tiles shall be the same in the rooms when the doors are closed. They are not laid for entire length and breadth of the rooms. Dividing strips are introduced at 500 mm or at suitable intervals to avoid development of cracks in the floor. Dividing strips shall be provided at the door junctions or at change of pattern of laying tiles.

(*x*) **Terrazo flooring cast in situ.** Terrazo flooring consists of two layers— one is the screed of cement concrete backing of thickness varying from 20 mm to 30 mm laid uniformly. The screed is cement concrete of proportion 1 : 2 : 4 with stone chips 6 mm down and coarse sand. Prior to laying of the screed, the base shall be properly checked for level and slope. If there be any defect in level, it shall be corrected by concrete of screed. The minimum thickness of the screed shall be maintained. The base shall be properly raked and cleaned before laying of the screed. After laying of the screed and allowing it for hardening, the terrazo finish shall be laid with ordinary portland cement or white cement mixed with two parts of crushed marble chips 3 mm to 8 mm of white, black or any other colour as desired. Coloured cement of approved manufacture may be used in lieu of mixing pigment with cement. Marble chips shall be mixed dry thoroughly with the mixture of cement and pigment and then mixed wet into a fairly stiff workable plastic consistency and laid in position in thickness varying from 10 mm to 20 mm.

Terrazo finish is laid generally in panels of desired size separated by dividing strips of aluminium or glass. Panels are laid alternatively. At junctions of terrazo flooring of different shade or pattern or at the door junctions, dividing strips are invariably fixed. The depth of the strips is the same as that of the thickness of terrazo finish with the screed. Within 24 hours of laying of the screed but after it has hardened sufficiently, it should be cleaned washed and brushed with neat cement slurry. The terrazo mixture shall then be laid in position slightly proud of the finished level to allow for cutting and polishing. Before taking its initial set, it shall be trowelled to bring the maximum number of marble chips on the surface.

The surface shall then be kept wet for 14 days. Curing and polishing shall be carried out by machine or by hand grinding after 36 hours of laying and shall be followed by two more cuttings at intervals of 2 to 4 days. The grain of carburundum stone shall be finer in each case. Pin-holes if any after each cut shall be made good.

Terrazo and Mosaic flooring are the same, only difference is, in mosaic flooring a definite pattern is formed with the marble chips and in terrazo flooring no such pattrn is developed.

(*xi*) **Lime terracing on roof.** Lime terracing shall be laid on the roof with lime concrete of proportion 1½ parts of slaked lime, 2 parts of 1st. class surkhi and 7 parts of 1st. class brick khoa of size passing through 25 mm ring. Porous brick ballasts showing signs of saltpetre shall not be used. The volume of wet mortar of lime and Surkhi should be 50 percent of stacked volume of brick aggregate.

The ingredients shall be thoroughly mixed and matured in damp condition for 72 hours so that all traces of unslaked lime is removed during this period, the mixture shall be turned over and mixed thoroughly. During the operations of mixing khunji water shall be added and allowed to soak in.

Prior to laying of the terracing, the roof surface should be properly levelled with desired slope towards the drain-mouth and washed clean. Minimum slope of the roof 1 in 48 shall be provided. The surface of the slab should be thoroughly cleaned with a rag soaked in kerosine oil and treated with two coats of bitumen. Lime water shall be sprinkled and then the matured concrete shall be laid at specified thickness. The laid concrete shall be checked for slope and levelled properly. Any depression shall be filled in by addition of concrete or mortar only. The surface shall than be beaten by wooden mallets for atleast a week with three beaters per 10 sqm till the roof emits ringing sound. A solution of methi, lime, molasses, catechu water in lime water shall be added to the concrete while mixing and ramming. During compaction by beating, the surface shall be liberally sprinkled with lime water and a mixture of gur (jaggery and boiled solution of bael fruit boiled in 100 litre of water). The mortar carried on the surface due to beating shall be rendered smooth and finished off with lime rubbing. Afterwards the finished surface shall be smoothened by trowel with mustard oil. The finished surface shall be kept wet by covering with paddy straw and sprinkling water. The straw covering shall be retained on the surface till it is decayed. Ghoondies (cove) 100 mm minimum radius shall be formed all along the edge of the terracing at the junction with the parapet walls. The top edge of the junction with parapet wall shall be proptected by a brick or concrete oversailing course and top finished smooth and sloped inwards. The mouth of rain water pipes shall be properly finished with added slope.

(*xii*) **Half terracing.** Half the thickness of the existing damaged terracing shall be picked up carefully and removed. The loose materials shall be removed and the surface cleaned and washed. The surface shall then be checked for slope and level. The Ghoondies (cove) shall be carefully cut and removed.

Lime concrete of proportion 1½ : 2 : 7 shall be prepared in the same process as in case of lime terracing and with same ingredients and admixtures. The mixed concrete in damp condition shall be laid in the same manner only excepting that a layer of lime surkhi mortar 1 : 1 shall be laid over the old surface. The other operations are the same as in lime terracing including keeping the surface wet and preparation of Ghoondies.

(*xiii*) **Tarfelting on roof.** Tarfelting is a water proofing course. It is laid on the roof to make it water proof. It is a specialised job and shall be executed by specially trained skilled labours only.

The surface of the roof shall be properly checked for slope and level. Necessary correction of slope shall be made if necessary with cement concrete 1 : 2 : 4 with 6 mm down stone chips. The surface shall then be cleaned and washed and allowed to dry up.

Bitumen 30/40 or 60/70 or 80/100 shall be melt and raised to the required temperature in tar boiler. The hot bitumen shall be spread evenly over the surface at the rate of 15 kg per 10 sqm of surface. Bitumen is poured by perforated can on the roof surface and the thickness is made even by the rubber squeezer. After/certain portion has been covered with bitumen, the sheets of tarfelt available in rolls shall be laid over the bitumen surface. The junctions of the sheets shall be overlapped by a minimum width of 100 mm. At the edges of roof at the junction with the parapet, the felt should be taken atleast 150 mm high into the parapet by cuting a chase atleast 50 mm deep. The top of the felt at the junction in the chase shall be sealed properly by sealing compound like mastic asphalt and then covered by cement mortar. After the surface has been fully covered with felt again a layer of hot bitumen shall be spread over the felt evenly with the rubber squeezer.

The top of the felt shall then be covered by spreading sand or protected by spreading gravel of 12 mm or by setting clay tiles or cement or terrazo tiles. In case of tiling the top joints shall be filled with cement sand mortar or bitumen to seal against entry of water.

Tarfelting consists of six layers :

(*a*) Bitumen – first layer on the roof surface,

(*b*) Felt – which itself consists of three layers *e.g.* bitumen, hessian and bitumen,

(*c*) Bitumen – top layer, and

(*d*) Protective layer of gravel or sand or tile.

(*xiv*). **Decorative waterproof cement coating.** Decorative water proof cement coating is applied over sand and cement plaster and finished with red oxide to give a decorative finish.

Materials — Cement shall be fresh portland cement and sand shall be of medium quality, clean, free from organic matter and salts. Red oxide shall be of approved quality.

Thickness — The average thickness shall be regulated at the time of plastering by keeping suitable thickness of gauges.

Preparation of the surface — The joints shall be raked out to a depth of at least 15 mm in masonry walls while laying on the masonry surface. In case of concrete walls, the surface shall be roughened by hacking. The surface shall be cleaned thoroughly, washed with water and kept wet before commencement of the work.

Application of undercoat — The undercoat shall be of cement plaster of thickness and mix as described in the item and shall be laid immediately after preparation of the mix. The undercoat shall be finished rough with scratching tool to form a key for the top coat. Mortar for top coat which shall consist of uniform and smooth layer of plaster of specified thickness and of mix 1 : 3 (1 cement and 3 coarse sand) or as specified. Unless specified 3.5 kg of red oxide to 50 kg of cement shall be mixed thoroughly with cement and then sand shall be added and mixed. The full quantity of dry mortar required for a room shall be prepared in one pot in order to ensure uniform colour. Wet mortar shall be prepared in usual manner as and when required.

Application of top coat - The top coat shall be done in the next day after the under coat has been applied. The plastering shall be done to the thickness specified and finished smooth by application of cement red oxide mix at the rate of 1.0 kg per sqm. of the surface. The ratio shall be 3.5 kg of red Oxide to 50 kg of cement if not otherwise mentioned. When the surface has hardened sufficiently it shall then be brought to a fine polish by use of polishing stones.

Curing - Curing shall commence on the next day of plastering when the plastering has hardened sufficiently and shall be continued for a minimum period of 7 days.

***(xv)* White washing.** White washing slurry shall be prepared from 5 parts of stone lime and 1 part of shell lime. The lime shall be dissolved in a tub with sufficient quantity of water (about 4 – 5 litre per kg of lime) and the whole shall be thoroughly mixed and stirred until it attains the consistency of thin cream. The wash shall be taken out in small quantities and strained through clean coarse cloth. Clean gum dissolved in hot water shall then be added in suitable proportion of 2 kg of gum arabic per cum of lime cream, alternatively Fevicol may be used to prevent the white wash coming off easily when rubbed. Indigo up to 3 gm per kg of lime dissolved in water or as necessary shall be mixed as per standard practice.

Scaffolding shall be double or single according to requirement. If ladder is used, pieces of old gunny bags or cloth rags shall be tied on their tops to avoid damage or scratches to the plastered surfaces, etc. proper stage scaffolding shall be erected while white washing the ceiling.

The surface shall be prepared by removing all mortar droppings and foreign matter and thoroughly cleaned with hair or fiber brush or other means as may be required to produce a clean and even surface. All loose pieces and scales shall be scrapped off and holes, cracks, etc. stopped with mortar to match with surrounding finish. The slurry should be cured sufficiently and the surface shall be washed with clean water. In case where the surface has been previously white washed or colour washed, the old white wash or colour wash shall be entirely removed and the surface broomed down before the new wash is applied ; the surface shall be cleaned by scrapping and washed with clean water prior to application of wash.

On the surface so prepared, white wash shall be laid on with a brush. The first stroke of the brush shall be from right to left, another from left to right. Over the first stroke, in a similar manner another stroke from the top downwards and from bottom upwards over the first stroke shall be applied before the previously applied strokes. This will form one coat; each coat must be allowed to dry and shall be subjected to inspection and approval before the next coat is applied. When dry, the surface shall show no sign of cracking. It shall present a smooth and uniform finish free from brush marks and it should not come of easily when rubbed with finger.

***(xvi)* Colour washing.** Colour wash slurry shall be prepared by adding approved colouring matter to the white wash (prepared for white washing) according to the shade required. Application shall be made after cleaning the surface in the same process and workmanship and specification as applicable to white washing.

***(xvii)* Distemper.** Distempering is application of cheap, durable and easily applicable decorative final finishing coat on the plastered or concrete surface.

Distemper is composed of base — whiting or chalk, carrier — water or oil, colouring pigment and size. Distempers are of two kinds based on the medium or carrier used - water or oil.

Distemper may be prepared at site by mixing the ingredients. It is available ready-mixed in the form of paste in sealed buckets of different capacity. Water need be added in proportion as advised by the maker and stirred properly for even mixing. It can then be applied on the surface. Distemper is available in dry powder form. The powder distemper of approved colour and shade and of approved manufacture shall be mixed with water as per guidance of the manufacturer and liquid applicable slurry is formed.

Distemper should not be mixed in a larger quantity than is actually required for a day's work and should be kept well stirred and applied with proper distempering brush.

Application to different surfaces. New plastered surface should be allowed to dry atleast for two months before application.

New lime plastered surface should be washed with a solution of vinegar and water 1 : 12 or sulphuric acid solution 1 : 50 and left for 24 hours. The wall should then be thoroughly washed with clean water.

Cement plastered surface should be washed with a solution of 1 kg of zinc sulphate in 10 litre of water and then allowed to dry.

Before distempering, the surface should be wiped with clean cloth to remove any efflorescence. No distempering shall be done till after 12 months of the walls having been plastered or white washed. Distemper gives poor results in wet locations; it should be applied in dry weather.

Applications. Scaffolding shall be double or single as required or directed.

The surface for distemper shall be cleaned and all cracks set right. All irregularities shall be sand papered smoothened and wiped clean. The surface so prepared shall be washed, cleaned and allowed to dry. It must be free from dust completely before application of distemper. In case of new walls special care shall be taken to see that it was completely dry. For old walls which had earlier been distempered, the surface shall be cleaned of grease, dust, etc. The flakings of previous coating, if any, shall be taken off. All cracks, holes and surface defects shall be repaired with gypsum and allowed to set hard. Priming coat shall be applied over the complete dry surface in the manner as recommended by the maker in the case of patent distemper. When no primer is applied a finely powered chalk mixed with a thin solution of glue shall be applied to prepare a good, hard back ground. The coating when dry shall be sand papered cleaned and smoothened as far as possible.

Distemper shall be applied in dry weather with broad stiff brush in long parallel strokes. The treated surface shall be allowed to dry and harden. Second or succeeding coats shall not be applied until the preceeding coat has dried and has been approved. More coats of distemper shall be applied if required in exactly the same manner as the first one but only after the earlier coat applied has thoroughly dried.

On newly lime plastered surface distemper shall be applied in two coats over a coat of priming. On the old lime plastered surface covered with one or two coats hard dry white wash, one coat of distemper without priming can be applied, but a coating of warm glue is considered useful.

(*xviii*) Form work. Form work for concrete is a mould for holding the concrete in position and giving it the shape required. It shall be made of timber, plywood or steel. The timber used shall be hard and of strong quality and light in weight. The size and thickness of the timber scantling and planks shall be as per design and as shown in the drawing.

The form work shall be made as per drawing and true to the dimensions. It shall be supported on staging as required. The staging shall be strong enough to support the form work with live and dead weight without undergoing any deflection or bulging. It shall be perfectly water tight. The joints shall be tounge and groove and nailed properly and then covered by polythene sheets on top to make it water tight. Polythene sheet shall be laid in a perfect manner without any folding.

The propping of the form work shall be with steel, timber section posts or ballies. These shall have minimum 100 mm least dimension in section. The supporting props shall rest on wooden base and then on a pair of wedges. The props shall be properly braced horizontally and diagonally.

The surface of the shuttering shall be smooth, cleaned and coated with soap solution or raw linseed oil.

When the concrete has gained its strength expected after 28 days, the formwork with staging may be removed. The striking out of the shuttering shall be made very carefully and systematically without causing any damage to the concrete. Special care shall be taken while stripping the form work at the edges. The stripping of the vertical sides shall be done first then the under sides.

(*xix*) **Wood work for door and window frames.** Door and window frames are made of timber like teak, sal, sisoo, deodar or as specified. The timber used must be of good quality and not having any defect or desease like knots, holes, fungi-infection. It shall be well seasoned and treated. It shall have been swan in the direction of the grains. Sawing of the timber shall be truly straight and square. The scantling selected shall be cut to proper size and planed smooth and according to the full dimensions, rebate, rounding and moulding as per drawing. Repair to the timber of any kind like patching or plugging shall not be made.

The joints of the frame shall be mortice and tenon type, simple, and neat and shall fit in full without any wedge or filling. Prior to final fixing, the joining shall be glued with synthetic resin and then pinned by inserting bamboo pins of 6 mm diameter.

The surface of the frame shall be smoothened by sand paper. The surface which would be in contact with wall shall be painted with creosote oil or primer paint or boiled coal tar. The exposed surface shall be applied with primer or painted as directed only after inspection of the frame in position.

The fixing of the frame shall be by coach screws at least three in case of door frames and two in case of window frames on each vertical side. The screws shall be 12 mm sunk in the frame and the top of the screw shall be covered by wooden chip fixed and glued. the screws shall be at least 100 mm long inside the masonry wall. Alternatively, the frames shall be fixed by m.s clamps, in which case the clamps shall be embedded in the wall during construction of the wall or the clamps shall be embedded in concrete blocks separately and then the blocks with clamps placed in position during construction of the wall.

(*xx*) **Wood work for door and window shutters.** The timber used shall be as specified, well seasoned, free from any defect or desease like, rot, sap, etc. The timber shall be dry and free from any kind of patch or plugging.

(*a*) Panelled shutters - The timber shall be of correct section and well planed faces at right angles. The grooves should be made as shown in the drawing. The panel shall be framed into the grooves properly and fully having only 1.5 mm air space. The styles and rails must be made into frame with correct mortice and tenons and fitted well. While fitting, the tenons shall pass at least 1/4 of the width of the styles. After assembly, the styles shall be projecting as horn. The styles and rails shall have 12 mm groove for receiving the panels. While fixing the frame, the contact surface of the mortice and the tenon shall be smeared with synthetic glue.

The depth of the rebate in the frame for housing the shutters shall not be less than 12 mm. The joints of the frames shall be pressed and secured by bamboo pins of about 6 mm diameter. While finishing, the horns of the styles shall be removed and the ends smoothened.

(*b*) *Batten Shutters*. The planks for the battens shall be 20 mm thick unless otherwise specified and the width shall be 125 mm to 150 mm. The battens shall be joined by tongue and groove or rebated 12 mm minimum. The edges of the joint shall be chamferred. The ledges and the braces shall be thicker than the battens and shall be fixed on the back with screws at least two numbers in each batten. The ledges and braces shall be 100 mm to 250 mm wide.

(*xxi*) Supplying and fixing Indian pattern water-closet including flushing cistern, complete. The Indian pattern water-closet shall be white glazed earthenware of first class quality and with approved I.S.I. mark. The size shall be as specified and make, design, approved by the Engineer in Charge. The pan shall have an integrated flushing rim and also shall have inlet or supply horn for connecting flush pipe. The flushing rim and inlet shall be of self-draining with weep holes at the flushing inlet to the pan. The pan shall be connected with 100 mm C.I. trap '*P*' or '*S*' type, heavy quality, 50 mm diameter vent pipe shall be connected with the horn as necessary.

The flushing cistern shall be a manually operated one, C.I. high level, pull and let go type I.S. approved with removable cover, 15 liter capacity. The cistern shall be fixed on C.I. brackets and fitted with 40 mm diameter flush pipe made of G.I. pipe and fitted to the pan. The cistern shall be mosquito proof and shall operate smoothly and efficiently.

The pan shall be placed on the floor at the specified space kept for the purpose. The pan and the surrounding area shall be 150 mm raised so that water from the floor cannot flow into the pan. The fixing of the pan shall be by cement concrete 1 : 2 : 4 and cement mortar 1 : 1. The joints shall be water proof. A pair of porcelain foot rest, 25 × 13 × 3 cm, shall be fixed and set in cement mortar 1 : 3.

All sanitary and plumbing works shall be carried through licensed plumber. On completion of the work, the area shall be cleaned and all stain marks in the pan removed so that the droppings of mortar, etc. do not choke the pipe later. The functioning and water tightness of the installation shall be tested, specially the joints - flush pipe and pan, short piece and pan, short piece and trap and trap and soil pipe line. The joints of C.I. pipe and trap and trap and short piece shall be lead caulked. The C.I. pipe, trap, Cistern, Flush pipe shall be painted two coats over a primer coat.

14

ANALYSIS OF RATES

14.1.0 ANALYSIS OF RATES

The method of arriving at a probable cost per unit quantity of work or supply in accordance to its specification including cost of materials required, labour, equipment, etc. based on the prevailing rates is called analysis of rate.

14.1.1 Composition of Unit Rate

The unit rate of an item comprises of the following:

(*i*) Cost of materials required including cost of carriage and all taxes.

(*ii*) Cost of labour necessary to execute the work depending upon the nature of work.

(*iii*) Cost of tools and plants that may be required. It is generally taken as percentage of the cost of materials and labour.

(*iv*) Sundries/contingencies to cover the cost of unforeseen expenditure that may be required during the process of execution.

A provision of water charges @ 1% of the total cost is generally added where water is not available at site.

(*v*) Contractor's profit and overhead charges @ 10% is added to the analysis to cover his profit on the capital invested and for his other tax liabilities and establishment charges.

14.2.0 RATES OF MATERIALS AND LABOUR

	Materials	*Unit*	*Rates (Rs.)*
1.	1st class bricks	%0 Nos.	2,800.00
2.	2nd. Class bricks	%0 Nos.	2,750.00
3.	1st. class picked jhama bricks	%0 Nos.	2,850.00
4.	Flyash bricks	%0 Nos.	2,300.00
5.	Jhama bats	cum	385.00
6.	Jhama metal (50 mm to 65 mm)	cum	445.00
7.	1st class bats	cum	350.00
8.	Ordinary bats	cum	275.00
9.	Sand coarse (fineness modulus not less than 2)	cum	355.00
10.	Medium sand (fineness modulus 1.8 to 2)	cum	290.00
11.	Fine sand	cum	215.00
12.	Silver sand	cum	180.00
13.	1st class Raniganj pattern tiles	% Nos	400.00
14.	Surkhi	cum	400.00
15.	Lime	cum	2,785.00
16.	Trap stone metal 63 mm size	cum	650.00
17.	Trap stone metal 50 mm size	cum	670.00
18.	Trap stone metal 40 mm size	cum	700.00

19.	Trap stone metal 25 mm size	cum	735.00
20.	Trap stone chips 20 mm size	cum	825.00
21.	Trap stone chips 12 mm size	cum	720.00
22.	Trap stone chips 10 mm size	cum	690.00
23.	Trap stone chips 6 mm size	cum	600.00
24.	Tor steel bars	Tonne	15,000.00
25.	Mild steel bars	Tonne	10,000.00
26.	Sal wood	cum	29,750.00
27.	Teak wood	cum	67,000.000
28.	Hard wood seasoned and treated	cum	15,000.00
29.	G.I pipe 25 mm diameter, medium	Meter	70.00
30.	G.I pipe 100 mm diameter, medium	Meter	750.00

	Labour	*Unit*	*Rate (Rs.)*
1.	Mason (head)	Each per day	95.00
2.	Mason (ordinary)	Each per day	85.00
3.	Mazdoor (male, female Bhistee)	Each per day	65.00
4.	Carpenter (head)	Each per day	95.00
5.	Carpenter (ordinary)	Each per day	85.00
6.	Carpenter (helper)	Each per day	65.00
7.	Beater (women)	Each per day	65.00
8.	Gharamee (head)	Each per day	90.00
9.	Gharamee (ordinary)	Each per day	70.00
10.	Stone cutter	Each per day	90.00
11.	Santras	Each per day	90.00
12.	Blacksmith (head)	Each per day	90.00
13.	Blacksmith (ordinary)	Each per day	80.00
14.	Blacksmith (helper)	Each per day	65.00
15.	Fitter mechanic	Each per day	95.00
16.	Fitter mechanic (helper)	Each per day	85.00
17.	Hammer man	Each per day	70.00
18.	Khalasi	Each per day	65.00
19.	Tarman	Each per day	70.00
20.	Painter	Each per day	95.00
21.	Plumbing mistri	Each per day	95.00
22.	Spray painter	Each per day	95.00
23.	Plumbing mazdoor (helper)	Each per day	70.00
24.	Mathor mistri	Each per day	95.00
25.	Mathor labour	Each per day	70.00
26.	Welder	Each per day	90.00
27.	Welder helper	Each per day	70.00
28.	Rod binder (head)	Each per day	95.00
29.	Rod binder (ordinary)	Each per day	85.00
30.	Rod binder (helper)	Each per day	70.00
31.	Mosaic mistri	Each per day	95.00

14.3.0 METHOD OF FINDING OUT THE REQUIREMENT OF MATERIALS

(*i*) **Cement concrete 1 : 2 : 4 with stone chips**

Dry volume of the mix per cubic metre of finished concrete varies from 1.54 to 1.57 cum in case of stone used as coarse aggregate and in case of Jhama chips whose void percentage is more, the dry volume varies from 1.57 to 1.60 per cum.

Cement concrete 1 : 2 : 4 with stone chips

Considering 10 cum of concrete,

Summation of the proportion is 1 + 2 + 4 = 7

Requirement of cement = 15.4/7 = 2.2 cum = 63.4 bags

(1 bag of cement = 0.0347 cum)

Requirement of sand = 2.2 × 2 4.4 cum

Requirement of stone chips = 2.2 × 4 8.8 cum

(*ii*) **Cement concrete 1 : 2 : 4 with Jhama chips**

Summation of the proportion is 7

Considering 10 cum of concrete,

Requirement of cement = 15.8/7 = 2.25 cum = 64.54 bags

Requirement of sand = 2.25 × 2 = 4.50 cum

Requirement of Jhama chips 2.25 × 4 = 9.00 cum

Note :

Volume of cement

1 cum of ordinary portland cement = 1440 kg

1 bag of cement = 50 kg

Volume of 1 bag of cement = 50/1440 = 0.0347 cum

1 cum of cement = 28.82 bags

(*iii*) Lime concrete 18 : 36 : 100 or 1 : 2 : 5.5

Summation of the proportion = 1 + 2 + 5.5 = 8.5

Dry volume varies from 15.4 – 15.7 cum per cum of finished concrete

Requirement of lime = 15.5/8.5 = 1.8 cum

Requirement of Surkhi = 1.8 × 2 = 3.6 cum

Requirement of Jhama chips = 1.8 × 5.5 = 9.9 cum

= 10.0 cum say

(*iv*) **Single brick flat soling**

Using modular bricks,

Overall size of bricks = 200 × 100 × 100 mm

Flat surface area = 200 × 100 mm = 0.02 sqm

Requirement of bricks per 10 sqm = 10/0.02 = 500 Nos.

Due to irregularity in shape and due to space left between the bricks, requirement is reduced by 15%.

Requirement of bricks = 500 – 500 × 15/100 = 425 Nos.

(*v*) **Brickwork in cement mortar 1 : 6**

Requirement of bricks

Volume of 1 brick = 200 × 100 × 100 mm^3

No. of bricks required per cum of brickwork = $\dfrac{1}{0.20 \times 0.10 \times 0.10}$

= 500 Nos.

Net size of brick = 190 × 90 × 90 mm

Requirement of mortar = 1 – (500 × 0.19 × 0.09 × 0.09)

= 0.23 cum

The quantity shall be increased by 15% due to filling of frogs

Volume $= 0.23 + 0.23 \times 15/100 = 0.264$ cum

The volume of mortar thus obtained is that in wet condition.

Dry volume will be obtained by increasing the volume by 1/3.

Volume of dry mortar $= 0.264 + 0.264 \times 1/3 = 0.35$ cum.

Summation of the proportion of the mortar = 1 + 6 = 7

Requirement of the cement = 0.35/7 = 0.05 cum $0.05 \times 28.82 = 1.44$ bag

Requirement of sand $= 1.44 \times 6 = 8.65$ cum.

(*vi*) **Sand and cement plaster 12 mm thick 1 : 6**

Volume of plaster 100 sqm $= 100 \times 0.012 = 1.20$ cum

Add extra for irregularity in shape of surface, filling of raked joints and wastage 20%

$= 1.20 + 1.20 \times 20/100 = 1.44$ cum.

Increase for dry volume by 1/3 $= 1.44 + 1.44 \times 1/3 = 1.92$ cum

Summation of the proportion = 7

Volume of cement = 1.92/7 = 0.274 cum = 7.90 bags

Volume of sand $= 0.274 \times 6 = 1.64$ cum

In similar principle, requirement of different materials for various items of works can be calculated.

Requirement of materials for different items have been tabulated in Appendix - 1.

14.4.0 ESTIMATION OF REQUIREMENT OF LABOUR

Standardisation of output of different labour for various items of work is difficult as the output of labour depends upon various factors, e.g. helping hand, quality of materials, weather condition, work site, location of item of work. Output of work of labour further depends upon the place, area, district or state he comes from.

However, some standards have been fixed.

Output of labourers

	Description of work	*Quantity of output per day of 8 hours*
(*i*)	Earthwork in excavation with normal lead and lift	2.27 cum per mazdoor
(*ii*)	Earthwork in filling	4.00 cum per mazdoor
(*iii*)	Single brick flat soling	9.00 sqm per mazdoor
(*iv*)	Lime concrete in foundation	10.00 cum per mazdoor
(*v*)	Cement concrete	5.00 cum per mazdoor
(*vi*)	Cement concrete (R.C.C.)	3.25 cum per mazdoor
(*vii*)	Brickwork in foundation and plinth	1.25 cum per mazdoor
(*viii*)	Brickwork in superstructure	1.10 cum per mazdoor
(*ix*)	Lime terracing in roof 100 mm thick	5.00 sqm per mazdoor
(*x*)	White washing 2 coats over a coat of priming	66.70 sqm per Painter

Similar estimation for other items of work also can be made.

14.5.0 STANDARD COMBINATIONS OF LABOUR FOR OPTIMUM OUTPUT

Output of work depends upon various factors of which combination of worker is important. Sometimes, a mason with one helper may produce maximum output, while in some other case, 2 helpers may be required with 1 mason for producing optimum output. Thus for different items of work, different combinations of labourers may produce optimum output.

	Description of work	*Unit*	*Labour in days (8 hours)*
(i)	Earthwork in excavation	10 cum	Mazdoor 4 ¼
(ii)	Earthwork in filling	10 cum	Mazdoor 2 ½
(iii)	Lime concrete in foundation	10 cum	Head mason 1/2 Mason 1 Mazdoor 18 Bhistee 2
(iv)	Cement concrete in foundation	10 cum	Head mason 1/2 Mason 2 Mazdoor 12 Bhistee 2
(v)	Reinforced cement concrete	10 cum	Head mason 1/2 Mason 3 Mazdoor 18 Bhistee 4
(vi)	Brickwork in foundation and plinth	10 cum	Head mason 1/2 Mason 8 Mazdoor 14 Bhistee 2
(vii)	Brickwork in superstructure	10 cum	Head mason 1/2 Mason 9 Mazdoor 15 Bhistee 2
(viii)	15 mm thick plastering	10 sqm	Head mason ½ Mason 1 Mazdoor 1.4 Bhistee 0.1
(ix)	White washing/colour washing 2 coats over a coat of priming	100 sqm	Painter 1 ½ Mazdoor 2 ½
(x)	Lime terracing 100 mm thick	10 sqm	Head mason 1/20 Mason 2 Mazdoor 1.7 + 1.9 = 3.6 Bhistee 0.3 + 0.3 = 0.6 Beater 6 ½
(xi)	125 mm thick brickwork	10 sqm	Head mason 1/2 Mason 1.40 Mazdoor 1.0
(xii)	10 mm thick plaster 1 : 4 in ceiling	10 sqm	Head mason 1/2 Mason 1.0 Mazdoor 1.50
(xiii)	One coat white wash over old white washed surface	100 sqm	Painter 1.4 Helper 1.0
(xiv)	Snow-cem one coat	100 sqm	Painter 1/5 Helper 1/8
(xv)	Breaking over-burnt bricks to Ballast 40 mm down	cum	Mazdoor 1 ⅓
(xvi)	Breaking over-burnt bricks to chips	cum	Mazdoor 2

14.6.0 ANALYSIS OF RATES

A. Building Works

(i) Earthwork in excavation, depth not exceeding 1.5 m with normal lead and lift of 50 m and 1.5 m respectively.

Considering quantity of 10 cum.

(*a*) Labour

Mazdoor 4 ¼ Nos. @ 65.00	276.25
Mason 1/22 No. @ 85.00	3.86

	280.11
(*b*) Water charges @ 1%	2.80
(*c*) Sundries and T & P @ 1/2 %	1.40

	284.31
(*d*) Profit & overhead @ 10%	28.43

	312.74

Rate per cum = Rs. 31.00

(*ii*) Earthwork in back filling with consolidation in layers of 200 mm lead 50 m and lift up to 1.5 m.

Considering quantity of 10 cum

(*a*) Labour

Mazdoor $2\frac{1}{2}$ Nos. @ 65.00	162.50
(*b*) Water charges @ 1%	1.63
(*c*) Sundries and T & P @ 1/2%	0.82

	164.95
(*d*) Profit and overhead @ 10%	16.50

	181.45

Rate per cum = Rs. 18.00

(*iii*) Single brick flat soling

Considering quantity of 10 sqm.

(*a*) Materials	
Bricks 425 Nos. @ 2,800.00% Nos.	1,190.00
(*b*) Labour	
Mazdoor 1 no. @ 65.00	65.00

	1,255.00
(*c*) Water charges @ 1%	12.55
(*d*) Sundries and T & P @ 1/2%	6.28

	1,273.83
(*e*) Profit and overhead @ 10%	127.38

	1,401.21

Rate per sqm = Rs. 140.00

(*iv*) Lime concrete in foundation with 25 mm down Jhama chips, Surkhi and lime 100 : 36 : 18.

Considering quantity of 10 cum.

(*a*) Materials		
Jhama chips	10 cum @ 445.00	4,450.00
Surkhi	3.6 cum @ 400.00	1,440.00
Lime	1.8 cum @ 2,785.00	5,013.00
(*b*) Labour		
Head mason	1/2 No. @ 95.00	47.5
Mason	1 No. @ 85.00	85.00
Mazdoor (including Bhistee)	20 Nos.@.65.00	1,300.00
		12,335.5
(*c*) Water charges @ 1%		123.36
(*d*) Sundries and *T* and *P* @ 1/2%		61.68
		12,520.54
(*e*) Profit and overhead @ 10%		1,252.05
		13,772.59

Rate per cum Rs. 1,377.00

(*v*) Cement concrete 1 : 3 : 6 with stone chips

Considering quantity of 10 cum

(*a*) Materials		
Stone chips	9.24 cum @ 825.00	7,623.00
Sand	4.62 " @ 355.00	1,640.10
Cement	1.55 cum @ 140.00 = 44.67 bags	6,253.80
(*b*) Labour		
Head mason	1/2 Nos. @ 95.00	47.50
Mason	2 Nos. @ 85.00	170.00
Mazdoor (including Bhistee)	14 Nos. @ 65.00	910.00
		16,644.40
(*c*) Water charges @ 1%		166.44
(*d*) Sundries and T & P @ 1/2%		83.22
		16,894.06
(*e*) Profit and overhead @ 10%		1,689.41
		18,583.47

Rate per cum = Rs. 1858.00

(*vi*) Cement concrete 1 : 2 : 4 with stone chips.

Considering quantity of 10 cum

(*a*) Materials

Stone chips	8.8 cum @ 825.00	7,260.00
Sand	4.4 cum @ 355.00	1,562.00
Cement	2.2 cum	
	= 63.4 bags @ 140.00	8,876.00

(*b*) Labour

Head mason	1/2 No. @ 95.00	47.50
Mason	3 Nos. @ 85.00	255.00
Mazdoor	22 Nos. @ 65.00	1430.00
		19,430.5
(*c*) Water charges @ 1%		194.31
(*d*) Sundries and *T* & *P* @ 1/2%		97.15
(*e*) Profit and overhead @ 10%		19,721.96
Rate per cum = Rs. 21,694.00		1,972.20
		21,694.16

(*vii*) Brickwork in cement mortar 1 : 6.

Considering quantity of 10 cum.

(*a*) Materials

Bricks (modular) 5,000 Nos. @ 2,500.00%. Nos.		12,500.00
Mortar 3.5 cum		
Cement 3.5/7 = 0.5 cum = 14.41 bags @ 140.00 bag		2,017.40
Sand 0.5 × 6 = 3.0 cum	@ 355.00 cum	1,605.00

(*b*) Labour

Head mason	1/2 No.	@ 95.00 Ea.	47.50
Mason	9 Nos.	@ 85.00 Ea.	765.00
Mazdoor (including Bhistee)	17 Nos.	@ 65.00 Ea.	1,105.00
			18,039.90
(*c*) Water charges @ 1%			180.40
(*d*) Sundries and *T* & *P* @ 1/2%			90.20
			18,310.50
(*e*) Profit and overhead @ 10%			1,831.05
Rate per cum Rs. 2,014.00			20,141.55

(*viii*) Sand and cement plaster 1 : 6, 12 mm thick.

Considering quantity of 100 sqm.

(*a*)	Materials			
	Sand	1.64 cum	@ 290.00	475.60
	Cement	0.274 cum = 7.96 bags @ 140.00		1,114.40
(*b*)	Labour			
	Head mason	1/2 No.	@ 95.00	47.50
	Mason	10 Nos.	@ 85.00	85.00
	Mazdoor	15 Nos.	@ 65.00	975.00
	(including Bhistee)			200.00

(*c*)	Scaffolding *L.S.*			2,897.50
(*d*)	Water charges	@ 1%		28.98
(*e*)	Sundries and T & P @ 1/2%			14.49

				2,940.97
(*f*)	Profit and overhead	@ 10%		294.10

				3235.07

Rate per sqm = Rs. 32.00

(*ix*) Steel reinforcement for R.C.C. work including bending, binding and placing in position.

Considering 1 quintal quantity of reinforcement.

(*a*)	Materials			
	Tor steel	1.00 quintal		
	Wastage 5%	0.05 quintal		

		1.05 quintal	@ 1,500.00	1,575.00
	Black annealed wire 1 kg		@ 20.00	20.00
(*b*)	Labour			
	Mason cum Black smith 1 No.		@ 80.00	80.00
	Mazdoor	1 No.	@ 65.00	65.00

				1,740.00
(*c*)	Water charges @ 1%			17.40
(*d*)	Sundries and T & P @ 1/2%			8.70

				1,766.10
(*e*)	Profit and overhead @ 10%			176.61

				1,942.71

Rate per quintal = Rs. 1,943.00

(*x*) White washing 2 coats over old white washed surface.

Considering quantity of 100 sqm.

(*a*) Materials			
Stone lime (unslaked)	30.00 kg	@ 2.05	61.50
Gum	0.16 kg	@ 50.00	8.00
Blue *L.s.*			10.00
(*b*) Labour			
Painter	$1\frac{1}{2}$ Nos.	@ 95.00	142.50
Mazdoor	$2\frac{1}{2}$ Nos.	@ 65.00	162.50
			384.50
(*c*) Scaffolding	*L.s.*		50.00
			434.50
(*d*) Water charges	@ 1%		4.35
(*e*) Sundries and *T* & *P*	@ 1/2%		2.18
			441.03
(*f*) Profit and overhead @ 10%			44.10
			485.13

Rate per sqm. = Rs. 5.00

(*xi*) **Terrazo flooring 10 mm thick over 20 mm cement concrete 1 : 2 : 4 base. Dark shed with grey cement.**

Considering quantity of 100 sqm.

Materials required

Concrete for base	= 0.02 × 100 = 2.0 cum (wet)
Dry volume	= 1.58 × 2.0 = 3.16 cum
Cement required	= 3.16/7 = 0.46 cum = 12.97 bag
Sand required	= 2 × 0.45 = 0.90 cum
Stone chips required	= 2 × 0.90 = 1.80 cum
Volume of terrazo	= 0.01 × 100 = 1.0 cum. (wet)
Dry volume	= 1.58 × 1.0 = 1.58 cum
Volume of cement	= 1.58/3 = 0.53 cum = 15.27 bag
Marble chips	= 0.53 × 2 = 1.06 × 16.5 = 17.49 qtl.
Marble powder = 1/3 by weight of cement	= 15.27 × 50 × 1/3
	= 254 kg = 2.55 qtl.
Pigment 3.5 kg per bag of cement	= 3.5 × 15.27 = 53.2 kg

Cost

(*a*) Materials

Cement concrete base		
Stone chips 1.80 cum @ 600.00		1,080.00
Sand 0.90 cum @ 355.00		319.50
Cement 12.97 bags @ 140.00		1,815.80
Terrazo		
Marble chips 17.49 qtl. @ 260.00		4,547.40
Cement 15.27 qtl @ 140.00		2,137.80
Marble powder 2.55 " @ 270.00		688.50
Pigment 53.20 kg @ 50.00		2,660.00
(*b*) Labour		
Head Mason	1 No. @ 95.00	95.00
Mason	20 Nos. @ 85.00	1700.00
Mazdoor	30 Nos. @ 65.00	1,950.00
(including Bhistee)		
		16,994.00
Polisher	98 Nos. @ 65.00	6,370.00
Carburundum stone	*L.s.*	150.00
Oxalic acid	*L.s.*	150.00
		23,664.00
(*c*) Water charges	@ 1%	236.64
(*d*) Sundries and T & P	@ 1/2%	118.32
		24,018.96
(*e*) Profit and establishment @ 10%		2,401.90
		26,420.86

Rate per sqm. = Rs. 264.00

(*xii*) Terrazo flooring 10 mm over 20 mm thick cement concrete 1 : 2 : 4 base. Light shade with white cement.

Considering quantity of 100 sqm.

Same as *a*. and *b*. of item *xi*.		23,664.00
Add difference in cost of white cement and grey cement for terrazo layer only 15.27 bags	@ 160.00	2,443.20
		26,107.20
(*c*) Water charges @ 1%		261.07

(*d*) Sundries and T & P @ 1/2% 130.53

26,498.80

(*e*) Profit and establishment @ 10% 2,649.88

29,148.68

Rate per sqm 291.00

(*xiii*) Providing aluminium strip 40 mm wide and 1.5 mm thick.

Considering 100 sqm of flooring.

Length of strip required = (5 + 5) 10 = 100 m

Area of strip = 100 × 0.04 = 4.00 sqm

Wastage @ 5% 0.02 sqm

4.20 sqm

@ 4.1 kg/sqm = 17.2 kg

Cost

Material

Aluminium strip 17.2 kg @ 25.00 430.00

Labour

Mason	1/4 No. @ 85.00	21.25
Mazdoor	1/4 No. @ 65.00	16.25

		467.50

Rate per sqm of flooring = Rs. 5.00

This rate is to be added as extra with the cost of Terrazo flooring, if strips are desired to be provided.

(*xiv*) Sal wood work in door and window frame.

Details of door frame :

Door size 2.10 × 1.20 m

Section of the frame pieces 0.10 × 0.10 m

(*a*) Material

Wood 2 × 2.10 = 4.20

1 × 1.20 = 1.20

5.40 × 0.1 × 0.1 = 0.054 cum

Wastage 5% = 0.003

0.057 cum

@ 29,750.00 1,695.75

(*b*) Labour

Carpenter	1 No. @ 85.00	85.00
Helper	1/2 No. @ 65.00	32.50

(*c*) Water charges @ 1%		1,813.25
(*d*) Sundries and T & P @ 1/2%		18.13
		9.07
		1840.45
(*e*) Profit and establishment @ 10%		184.05
		2,024.50

Rate per cum = Rs. 68,894.00

In case of frame with other variety of timber, cost of timber shall be modified.

(*xv*) Door and window shutters of C.P. teak wood.

Door shutter 40 mm thick panelled, with 20 mm thick panels.

(*a*) Materials

Styles	$2 \times 2.01 \times 0.10 \times 0.04 = 0.0161$		
Rails	$1 \times 1.03 \times 0.10 \times 0.04 = 0.0041$		
	$2 \times 1.03 \times 0.20 \times 0.04 = 0.0165$		
Panels	$1 \times 0.875 \times 0.875 \times 0.02 = 0.0153$		
	$1 \times 0.735 \times 0.875 \times 0.02 = 0.0129$		
		0.0649	
	Wastage 15%	0.0097	
		0.0746 cum	
		@ 67,000.00	4,998.20
(*b*) **Labour**			
Carpenter	4 Nos. @ 85.00		340.00
Helper	1 No. @ 65.00		65.00
			5403.20
(*c*) Water charges @ 1%			54.03
(*d*) Sundries and T & P @ 1/2%			27.02
			5,484.25
(*e*) Profit and establishment @ 10%			548.43
			6,032.68

Rate per sqm (2.01 × 1.03)
of finished shutter = Rs. 2,914.00

(*xvi*) 100 mm thick lime terracing over R.C.C. roof.
Considering quantity of 10 sqm.
Proportion of lime concrete used $7 : 2 : 1\frac{1}{2}$
Requirement of materials
Summation of proportion = $11\frac{1}{2}$
Volume of concrete $100 \times 0.10 = 10.00$ cum (wet)
Dry volume = 15.5 cum
Requirement of lime $= 15.5 \times 1.5/10.5 = 2.22$ cum
Requirement of Surkhi $15.5 \times 2/10.5 = 2.95$ cum
Requirement of Jhama chips $= 15.5 \times 7/10.5 = 10.33$ cum
(25 mm down)
Molasses = 10.00 kg
Methi = 2.00 kg
Catechu = 1.00 kg
Mustard oil = 2.00 kg

Cost

(*a*) Materials			
Jhama chips	10.33 cum @ 445.00		4,598.85
Surkhi	2.95 cum @ 400.00		1,180.00
Lime	2.22 cum @ 2,785.00		6,182.70
Molasses	10.00 kg @ 15.00		150.00
Catechu	1.00 kg @ 50.00		50.00
Methi	2.00 kg @ 50.00		100.00
Mustard oil	2.00 kg @ 56.00		112.00
Misc. Bael fruit solution and straw		L.s.	50.00
(*b*) Labour			
Head mason	1/2 No.	@ 95.00	47.50
Mason	1 + 10 = 11 Nos.	@ 85.00	935.00
Mazdoor (including Bhistee)	20 + 22 = 42 Nos.	@ 65.00	2,730.00
Beater (female)	65 Nos.	@ 65.00	4,225.00
			20,361.05
(*c*) Water charges		@ 1%	203.61
(*d*) Sundries and T & P		@ 1/2%	101.80
			20,666.46
(*e*) Profit and establishment		@ 10%	2,066.65
			22,733.11

Rate per sqm = Rs. 2,273.00

(*xvii*) White washing 2 coats over a coat of priming over new work.

Considering quantity of 100 sqm.

(***a***)	**Materials**			
	Stone lime	25 kg	@ 5.00 kg	125.00
	Shell lime	5 kg	@ 7.00 kg	35.00
	Blue	200 gm	@ 5.00 per 100 gm	10.00
	Adhesive	3.0 kg	@ 50.00 kg	150.00
	Sand paper	L.s		10.00
(***b***)	**Labour**			
	Painter	$1\frac{1}{2}$No.	@ 95.00 Ea.	142.50
	Mazdoor	$2\frac{1}{2}$Nos.	@ 65.00 Ea.	162.50
	Staging and platform		L.s.	50.00
				685.00
(*c*)	Water charges		@ 1%	6.85
(*d*)	Sundries and T & P		@ 1/2%	3.43
				695.28
(*e*)	Profit and establishment		@ 10%	69.53
				764.81

Rate per sqm = Rs. 8.00

(*xvii*) Painting to wood works 2 coats over a coat of primer.

Considering 100 sqm area.

(*a*)	Materials			
	Primer	7.50 liters	@ 80.00 lt.	600.00
	Putty	L.s.		100.00
	Paint	12.0 liters	@ 115.00 lt.	1,380.00
(*b*)	Labour			
	Painter	8.0 number	@ 95.00	760.00
	Mazdoor (helper)	8.0 Number	@ 65.00	520.00
				3,360.00
(*c*)	Water charges	1%		33.60
(*d*)	Sundries, T & P	1/2%		16.80
				3,410.40

Rate per sqm = Rs. 34.00

(*xviii*) Decorative cement base painting two coats

Considering 100 sqm area

(*a*) Materials

Snowcem or Durocem			
1st coat			30.00 kg
2nd coat			20.00 kg
			50.00 kg
@ 25.00 kg =			1,250.00
(*b*) Labour			
Painter	5 Numbers	@ 95.00 Ea	475.00
Mazdoor/helper	5 Numbers	@ 65.00 Ea.	325.00
			2050.00
(*c*) Water charges	1%		20.50
(*d*) Sundries & T & P	1/2%		10.25
			2,080.75
(*e*) Profit and Over head	10%		208.08
			2,288.83

Rate per sqm = Rs. 23.00

(*xviv*) Damp proof course 25 mm thick with cement concrete $1 : 1\frac{1}{2} : 3$ with admixture of water proof compound 5% by weight of cement.

Considering quantity of 10 sqm

(*a*) Materials

Stone chips 6 mm down	0.22 cum	@ 600.00 cum	132.00
Sand	0.11 cum	@ 355.00 cum	39.05
Cement	0.073 cum		
	= 2.10 bag	@ 140.00 bag	294.00

Water proofing compound 5% of cement 105 × 0.05 = 5.25 kg Rs. 80.00 = 420.00

(*b*) Labour

Head mason	1/80 Number @ 95.00		1.19
Mason	3/40 Number @ 85.00		63.75
Mazdoor	1/2 Number @ 65.00		32.50
			982.44
(*c*) Water charges	1%		9.82
(*d*) Sundries and T & P	1/2%		4.91
			997.17

(*e*) Profit and Over head 10% 99.71

1,096.88

Rate per sqm. = Rs. 110.00

(*xx*) Stone masonry

Random Rubble masonry in cement mortar in foundation and plinth.

Considering 10 cum

Quantity of materials required.

Volume of mortar per 10 cum = 4.2 cum

Cement $= \frac{4.2}{7} = 0.60$ cum = 17.29 bags

Sand $= 0.6 \times 6 = 3.60$ cum

(*a*) Materials

Stone (undressed) = 11.7 cum @ 200.00 cum =	2,340.00
Through stone or headers = 0.80 cum @ 225.00 cum =	180.00
Cement 0.60 cum = 17.29 bags @ 140.00 bag	2,420.60
Sand 3.60 cum @ 355.00	1,278.00

(*b*) Labour

Head mason 0.50 No. @ 95.00	47.50
Mason 10.0 Nos. @ 85.00	850.00
Mazdoor including Bhisti 19 Nos. @ 65.00 p.d.	1,235.00
	8,351.10
(*c*) Water charges 1%	83.51
(*d*) Sundries and T & P 1/2%	41.75
	8,476.36
(*e*) Profit and Overhead 10%	847.64
	9324.00

Rate per cum Rs. 932.40

(*xxi*) Coursed Rubble stone masonry in cement mortar 1:6 in Foundation and plinth.

Considering 10 cum

Volume of mortar per 10 cum = 4.0 cum

Cement = 4.0/7 = 0.57 cum = 16.47 bags

Sand $= 0.57 \times 6 = 3.42$ cum

(*a*) Materials:

Stone	11.7 cum @ 200.00 cum	=	2,340.00
Through stone or Headers 0.8 cum @ 225.00 cum		=	180.00
Cement 16.43 bags @ 140.00 bag =		=	2,300.20
Sand (coarse) 3.42 cum @ 355.00 cum =		=	1,214.10

(*b*) Labour:			
Head mason	1/2 No.	@ 95.00 p.d. =	47.50
Mason	13 Nos.	@ 85.00 p.d. =	1,105.00
Mazdoor including Bhisti 20 Nos.		@ 65.00 p.d. =	1,300.00
			8,486.80
(*c*) Water charges	1%		84.87
(*d*) Sundries and T & P	1/2%		42.43
			8,614.10
(*e*) Profit and overhead	10%		861.41
			9,475.51

Rate per cum = 947.50

(*xxii*) Ashlar masonry in cement mortar (1 : 6) in superstructure ground floor.

Considering 10 cum

Requirement of materials:

Volume of mortar per 10 cum = 2.5 cum

Cement 2.5/7 = 0.36 cum, Sand = 0.36 × 6 = 2.2 cum

(*a*) Materials:		
Stone (undressed)	12.5 cum @ 200.00	= 2,500.00
Cement 0.36 cum = 10.38 bags @ 140.00 bag		= 1,453.20
Sand (medium) = 2.20 cum @ 290.00 cum		= 638.00
Scaffolding	L.s.	= 50.00
(*b*) Labour:		
Head mason	1/2 No. @ 95.00 p.d.	= 47.50
Mason	25 Nos. @ 85.00 p.d.	= 2,125.00
Mazdoor including Bhisti 35 Nos. @ 65.00		= 2,275.00
		9,088.70
(*c*) Water charges	1%	90.89
(*d*) Sundries and T & P	1/2 %	45.44
		9,225.03
(*e*) Profit and overhead	10%	922.50
		10,147.53

Rate per cum = Rs. 1,014.75

Calculation of mortar for Random Rubble Stone Masonry

Considering 10 cum of volume of work

Dry lime mortar of 4.4 cum and cement mortar 4.2 cum per 10 cum volume of work will be required. Dividing these quantities of mortars by summation of proportions and multiplying the result by the respective strength of proportion quantities and ingredients have been shown below.

Lime mortar	*Lime*	*Sand or Surkhi*
Proportion 1 : 2	1.5 cum	3.0 cum
" 1 : 3	1.1 cum	3.3 cum
" 1 : 4	0.9 cum	3.6 cum

Cement mortar	*Cement*	*Sand*
Proportion 1 : 3	1.00 cum = 28.82 bags	3.00 cum
" 1 : 4	0.84 cum = 24.21 "	3.36 cum
" 1 : 5	0.70 cum = 20.17 "	3.50 cum
" 1 : 6	0.60 cum = 17.29 "	3.60 cum

(*xxiii*) Rule pointing in cement mortar 1 : 3 on brickwork.

Considering 100 sqm of area.

Calculation of materials:

An approximate quantity of 0.63 cum (dry) mortar is required per 100 sqm of Rule and Tuck pointing. In case of flush pointing, 75% of the above quantity is considered adequate.

Cement required $= \frac{0.63}{4} = 0.16$ cum

Sand $= 0.16 \times 3 = 0.48$ cum.

(*a*) Materials:				
Cement 0.16 cum = 4.61 bags		@ 140.00 per bag	Rs.	645.40
Sand (medium) = 0.48 cum		@ 290.00 cum	Rs.	139.20
Scaffolding	L.s.		Rs.	20.00
(*b*) Labour:				
Head mason	0.50 No.	@ 95.0 p.d.		47.50
Mason	10.00 Nos.	@ 85.00 p.d.		850.00
Mazdoor including Bhisti	1.00 No.	@ 65.00 p.d.		65.00
				1,767.10
(*c*) Water charges	1%			17.67
(*d*) Sundries and T and P 1/2 %				8.84
				Rs. 1,793.61
(*e*) Profit and Overhead	10%			179.36
				1,972.97

Rate per sqm = Rs. 19.75

(*xxiv*) Supplying and fixing m.s ornamental grill, joints continuously welded and fixing with necessary screws.

Grill weighing 12 kg pers sqm.

Considering 1 sqm of grill

(*a*) Materials

M.s. flat	12 kg	Rs. 12.00 per kg	=	144.00

(*b*) Labour

Blacksmith 1 No.	Rs. 80.00	= 80.00
Helper 1 No.	Rs. 65.00	= 65.00
Misc charges for transport welding hoisting and fixing		= 50.00
		339.00
(*c*) Water charges	1%	3/50
(*d*) Sundries and T & P	1/2 %	1/75
		354/25
Profit and overhead	10%	35/43
		389/68

Say Rs. 380.00 per sqm.

B. Water Supply, Drainage and Sanitation

(*i*) Supplying, fitting and fixing 15 mm diameter G.I. pipe with G.I. fittings and M.S. clamps including cutting holes in walls and mending good the same complete for internal works.

Considering 100 m length

(*a*) Materials:

15 mm diameter pipe (medium) 100 m @ 68.00 m =		Rs.	6,800.00
Fittings and wastage 5% of pipe cost		Rs.	340.00
White lead, oil, hemp L.s.		Rs.	20.00
Cement, sand, grit (for mending wall) L.s.		Rs.	50.00

(*b*) Labour:

Fitter	3 Nos. @ 95.00 p.d. =	285.00
Assistant fitter	4 Nos. @ 85.00 p.d. =	340.00
Mazdoor	6 Nos. @ 65.00 p.d. =	390.00
		Rs. 8,225.00
(*c*) Water charges	1%	82.25
(*d*) Sundries and T & P	1/2 %	41.12
		8,348.37
(*e*) Profit and overhead	10%	834.84
		Rs. 9,183.21

Rate per m = Rs. 91.80.

(*ii*) Supplying fitting and fixing 100 mm diameter C.I. pipe provided with tight on joint including testing of joint and trench cutting for pipe laying up to a depth of invert 900 mm with a sand layer of 150 mm below and rectifying, dressing, etc. complete.

(Length of each pipe is 4.0 m and supplied from the departmental store within 10 km.).

Considering 20 m of pipe length.

Number of joints with 4.0 m length of pipe = 20/4 = 5 Numbers.

(*a*) Materials:

Carriage of materials weighing approximately
450 kg within 10 km distance L.s Rs. 50.00

5 nos. tighton joint

Rubber gusket 100 mm diameter 4 Nos. 10.00 each 40.00

Sand (fine) 1.2 cum 215.00 258.00

(*b*) Labour:

Trench cutting $1 \times 20.0 \times 1.15 \times 0.40 = 9.20$ cum @ 10.00 cum = 92.00

Trench filling

Sand filling $1 \times 20.0 \times 0.4 \times 0.15 = 1.20$ cum @ 8.00 cum = 9.60

Earth filling $1 \times 20.0 \times 0.40 \times 1.00 = 8.00$

Less $\pi d^2/4 \times 20.0 = \pi\ 0.1^2/4 \times 20.0 = 0.157$

7.84 cum @ 10.00 = 78.40

Pipe laying

Fitter	1/2 no.	95.00	= 47.50
Fitter helper	1 No.	85.00	= 85.00
Mazdoor	4 No.	65.00	= 260.00
			920.50
(*c*) Water charges	@ 1%		9.21
(*d*) Sundries and T & P	@ 1/2 %		4.65
			934.36
(*e*) Profit and Overhead		10%	93.44
			Rs. 1,027.88

Rate per meter = Rs. 51.40

(*iii*) Supplying laying and joining 150 mm diameter glazed stoneware pipe with cement mortar (1 : 1) in trench with 150 mm bed and with protective concrete over the pipe.

Considering 15 m length

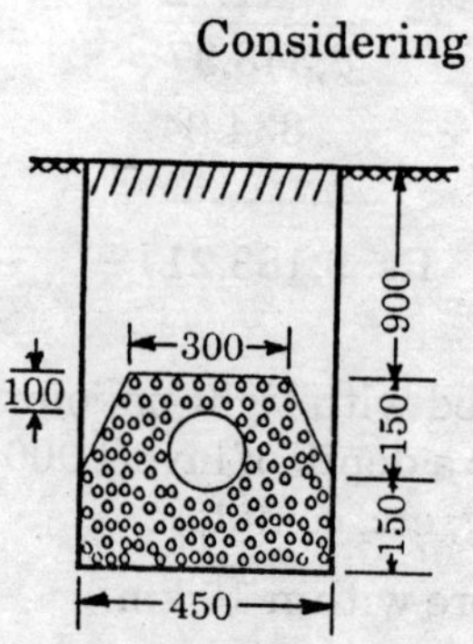

(*a*) Materials:

150 mm diameter S.W. pipe 600 mm long each 25 Nos.

40.00 each = Rs. 1,000.00

Allowance for breakage 5% 50.00

Cement for joining 1.02 bag Rs. 140.00 per bag = 142.80

Concrete for embedding pipe:

Volume of concrete

$$\frac{0.30 + 0.45}{2} \times 0.25 \times 15.0 = 1.41$$

$1 \times 15.0 \times 0.45 \times 0.15 = 1.01$

2.42

Less $1/4\ (\pi \times 0.15^2) \times 15.0 = 0.265$

2.16 cum

Stone chips $0.88 \times 2.16 = 1.90$ cum @ 825.00			= 1,567.50
Sand	0.95 cum @ 355.00		= 337.25
Cement	1.90/6 = 0.32 cum = 9.12 bags @ 140.00 =		1,277.24

(*b*) Labour:

Mazdoor for cutting trench $1.20 \times 0.45 \times 15.0 = 8.10$ cum

Mazdoor 4.0 Nos.

Filling Volume = 8.10 cum Less 2.42 = 5.69 cum

Mazdoor 2.0 Nos. / 6.0 Nos.	@ 65.00 Each		Rs.	390.00
Head mason	0.50 No.	95.00 each		47.50
Mason	1.50 Nos.	85.00 each		127.50
			Rs.	4,938.95
(*c*) Water charges	1%			49.39
(*d*) Sundries and T & P	1/2 %			24.69
				5,013.03
(*e*) Profit and Overhead	10%			501.30
			Rs.	5514.33

Rate per meter = Rs. 367.50

(c) **Road works**

Average out put of a Steam Roller (working 8 hours a day).

(*i*)	Embankment compaction	370 sqm
(*ii*)	Stone boulders compaction	90 sqm
(*iii*)	Stone ballast consolidation for macadam	20 cum
(*iv*)	Brick ballast consolidation for macadam	28 cum
(*v*)	Laterite ballast consolidation for macadam	34 cum

Approximate hire charges of roller 8 to 10 tonnes excluding

wages of driver, cleaner and night-guard	Rs. 500.00 per day
and including staff	Rs. 1,200.00 per day
Hire charges of Tar boiler	Rs. 400.00 per day

(*i*) Earthwork in excavation from borrow pits and depositing the soil in layers of 230 mm including rough dressing within a lead of 30.0 m and lift of 900 mm.

Considering 10 cum

(*a*) Labour:

Mazdoor (Beldar) for cutting earth and placing the same in busket.	1.50 Nos.
Mazdoor for carrying and unloading the earth	2.00 Nos.
Mazdoor for rough dressing	0.20 Nos.

	3.70 Nos.
@ 65.00 p.d. =	240.50
(*b*) Water charges 1%	2.41
(*c*) Sundries and T & P 1/2%	1.20

Rs.	244.11
(*d*) Profit and overhead 10%	24.41

Rs.	268.52

Rate per cum = Rs. 269.00

(*ii*) Laying Jhama khoa ballast and over-burnt brick ballast true to camber including consolidation with power roller, carrying the metal from road side within a lead of 150m, thickness 75 mm to 100 mm (complete).

Considering 10 cum

(*a*) Labour :

Mazdoor for			
Spreading and carrying	10.5 Nos.		
Hand picking and rectifying defects	3.5 Nos.		
Watering and blinding	7 Nos.		
Shouldering at the edges	3.5 Nos.		

	24.5 Nos.	65.00	1,592.50
Hire charges of Roller @ 28 cum per day including pay of its staff @ 1,200.00 p.d.			428.57
Diesel for Road Roller @ 18 lts per day 6 liters @ 17.00 per liter			102.00

			2,123.07
(*b*) Water charges 1%			21.23
(*c*) Sundries and T & P 1/2%			10.62

			2,154.92
(*d*) Profit and Overhead 10%			215.49

			2,370.41

Rate per cum Rs. 237.00

(*iii*) Surface dressing or Bituminous painting one coat
Considering 100 sqm of surface area.

(*a*) Materials :
Stone chips 12 mm @ 1.52 cum per 100 sqm 1.52 cum
Bitumen (transported to work site) @ 825.00 cum = 1,254.00
194 kg per 100 sqm + $2\frac{1}{2}$ % wastage = 0.199 tonne
@ 2,000.00 tonne = 398.00

(*b*) Labour:
Mazdoor (Beldar) for
(*i*) brushing off road surface 4.50 Nos.
(*ii*) Heating and spraying bitumen 2.5 Nos.
(*iii*) Spreading chips 2.0 Nos.

9.00 Nos. @ 65.00
585.00

(*c*) Plant:
Hire charges of Tar boiler including sprayer
1/6 day @ 400.00 per day = 66.67

(*d*) Roller:
Hire charges @ 600 sqm per day 1/6 day @ 1,200.00 = p.d. 200.00

(*e*) Fuel:

Fire wood for heating bitumen @ 4 quintal
per tonne of bitumen = 796 kg @ 250.00 quintal = 199.00
Diesel for Roller 18 lt. per day = 3 lt. @
Rs. 17.00 per Lt. = 51.00

Rs. 2,753.67

(*f*) Water charges 1% 27.54

(*g*) Sundries and T & P 1/2% 13.77

2,794.98

(*h*) Profit and overhead 10% 279.50

3,074.48

Rate per sqm. = Rs. 30.75

(*iv*) Surface dressing or Bitumen painting second coat.
Considering 100 sqm

(*a*) Materials:
(*i*) Stone chips 12 mm 1 cum per 100 sqm = 1 cum @ 720.00 cum = 720.00

(ii) Bitumen 120 kg% sqm + 2.5% wastage = 0.123 tonne
@ 2,000.00 tonne 246.00

(b) Labour
Mazdoor for

(i) brushing off road surface 2.0 Nos.
(ii) heating and spraying of bitumen 1.5 Nos.
(iii) Spreading stone chips 1.5 Nos.

5.0 Nos. @ 65.00 = 325.00

(c) Plant
Hire charges of Tar boiler including sprayer
800 sqm per day = 1/8 day @ 400.00 p.d = 50.00

(d) Rolling
Hire charges of Roller 800 sqm per day = 1/8 day @ 1,200.00 p.d. = 150.00

(e) Fuel
Fire wood for heating Bitumen @ 4 quintal per tonne of
Bitumen = 0.492 quintal @ 250.00 quintal = 123.00
Diesel for Roller 18 liter per day = 6 liter @ 17.00 per liter = 107.00

1,721.00

(f) Water charges 1% 17.21
(g) Sundries and T & P 1/2% 8.60

1,746.81

(h) Profit and Overhead 10% 174.68

1,921.49

Rate per sqm = Rs. 19.20

(v) Providing Seal coat with paving bitumen S-90 and stone chips 10 mm nominal size.
Considering 100 sqm of surface area.

(a) Materials
Bitumen S-90 150 kg @ Rs. 2,000.00 per tonne = 300.00
Stone chips 10 mm nominal 1.05 cum @ 720.00 cum = 756.00

(b) Labour for cleaning, brushing, heating and spraying 4.5 Nos. @ 65.00 Ea. 292.50

(c) Plant
Hire charges of Road Roller and Tar boiler including
attendant staff 900 sqm per day = 1/9 day
Road Roller @ 1,200.00 p.d. = 133.33
Tar boiler @ 400.00 p.d. = 44.44

(*d*) Fuel

Steam coal for heating 2 quintal per tonne of Bitumen

0.150 × 2.0 = 0.30 Quintal @ 350.00 per Quintal = 105.00

Diesel for Roller 18 liter per day = 2 liter @ 17.00 per liter = 34.00

1665.27

(*e*) Water charges 1% 16.65

(*f*) Sundries and T & P 1/2 % 8.32

(*g*) Profit and overhead 10% 1,690.24

169.02

1,859.26

Rate per sqm = Rs. 18.59

(*vi*) 25 mm thick premixed carpet or premixed Bituminous Road surface.

Considering 100 sqm.

(*a*) Materials

Bitumen 73 kg for tack coat per% sqm + wastage 2.5 % = 75 kg = 0.075 Tonne @ 2000.00 Per Tonne 160.00

For premix carpet

(*i*) Stone chips 12 mm standard 3.38 cum per% sqm = 3.38 cum @ 720.00 cum = 2,433.60

(*ii*) Bitumen 64 kg per cum of stone + 2.5 percentage wastage = 0.192 + 2.5 percent = 0.197 tonne @ 2,000.00 tonne = 394.00

(*iii*) Sand (coarse) for flushing 0.50 cum per% sqm = 0.50 cum @ 355.00 cum = 177.50

(*b*) Labour (Beldar) for

(*i*) Brushing off old surface 4 Nos.

(*ii*) Heating and applying tack coat 2 Nos.

(*iii*) Heating mixing and spreading chips 9 Nos.

(*iv*) Flushing sand 1 No.

16 Nos. @ 65/– each = 1040.00

(*c*) Plant

Hire charges of Tar boiler including sprayer 560 sqm per day = 1/6 day Rs. 400.00 per day = –66.67

(*d*) Rolling

Hire charges of Roller including attendant staff 560 sqm per day = 1/6 day Rs. 1,200.00 per day = 200.00

(*e*) Fuel

Fire wood for heating Bitumen = 0.75 + 0.197 = 0.272 Tonne @ 4 quintal per Tonne

= 1.088 quintal @ 250.00 per Quintal = 272.00

Diesel for Roller 18 liter per day = 3 liters @ 17.00 per liter = 51.00

Rs. 4,784.77

(*f*) Water charges 1% 47.85

(*g*) Sundries and T and P 1/2% 23.92

Rs. 4,856.54

(*h*) Profit and overhead 10% 485.65

Rs. 5,342.19

Rate per sqm Rs. 53.40

(D). Analysis of rate for carriage of materials.

Carriage of materials depends upon the factors:

1. Cost of capital investment on vehicle and wages of driver cleaner etc. This includes the probable hire charges of the vehicle per day including cost of the friver, but excluding the cost of fuel.
2. Cost of fuel

Cost of oil consumption per kilometer.

3. The capacity of the vehicle and loading unloading time. This varies according to the material as given below

Sl. No.	*Materials to be carried*	*Capacity per trip*	
		Bullock cart	***Diesel truck***
(*i*)	Bricks		
	(*a*) Modular or standard	400 Nos.	2,000 nos.
	(*b*) Traditional	300 Nos.	1,800 Nos.
(*ii*)	Sand, lime, Surkhi, Moorum, Earth, Ballast, Rubbish, Boulders, etc.	0.90 cum	4.20 cum
(*iii*)	Cement, Stone block, steel or other heavy material	1.5 tonnes	8.0 tonnes
(*iv*)	Timber	1.4 cum	3.5 cum
(*v*)	S.W. pipe *a*. 100 mm diameter	75.0 m	350.0 m
	b. 150 mm diameter	45.0 m	180.0 m
(*vi*)	Tar, Bitumen, etc.	1.5 T	5.0 T

4. Labour cost for loading, unloading and delay per trip.
5. Speed of the vehicle,
6. Number of trips in working day during working hours. This again depends upon the factors – lead, speed of the vehicle.

$$N = \frac{H}{\frac{2L}{S} + W}$$

Where, H = Working hours per day, L = Lead in kilometer, S = Speed in kilometer,

W = The time allowed for loading and unloading per trip in hours.

7. Lead of the materials,
8. Allowance for movement of truck from parking place to duty spot and back.

Example 14.1. *Analysis of rate for carriage of materials like Sand, Lime Moorum, Earth, Ballast, Boulders, Rubbish, etc. for a lead of 5 km.*

$$\text{No. of trips} = \frac{H}{\frac{2L}{S} + W} \qquad \text{Here, } H = 8, L = 5, S = 4 \ \& \ W = 3/4$$

$$\text{No. of trips} = \frac{8}{\frac{2 \times 5}{4} + \frac{3}{4}} = 2.46$$

Adopting local rate for hiring charges of Bullock cart 200.00 per day

Cost per trip = 200.00 / 2.46 = Rs. 81.30

Volume of materials to be carried = 1 cum, carrying capacity = 0.90 cum No. of trips required = 1/0.9 = 1.11

Materials	*Unit of rate*	*Quantity per trip*	*No. of trip*	*Rate per trip*	*Amount*
Sand, lime, Moorum, Earth, Ballast, Boulder, etc.	cum	0.90	1.11	81.30	Rs. 90.24
Add 10% for profit and over-head					9.02
			Total		Rs. 99.26

The carrying rate of 1 cum of any of the materials above by Bullock cart for a lead of 5 kilometer = Rs. 99.26.

Example 14.2. *1,000 Number of bricks to be transported to a distance of 8 km from the site of manufacture in a cart or diesel truck. By rate analysis find out which one will be cheaper with the following. Cart charges = Rs. 200.00 per day (8 hours) with carrying capacity 300 Nos. of bricks; hire charges of diesel truck = Rs. 1,200.00 per day (8 hours) with a carrying capacity of 1,800 Nos. of bricks, cost of diesel = Rs. 17.0 per liter; Mobile oil = Rs. 80.00 per liter; Mazdoor Rs. 65.00 each per day. Average speed = 20 km per hour. The rate should be analysed to standard practice.*

Case 1.

By cart:

$$\text{Number of trips per day} = \frac{H}{\frac{2L}{S} + W}$$

Where, H = Working hours per day,

L = Lead in km

S = Speed in hour

W = Hour allowed for loading and unloading

H = 8, L = 8 km.

S = 4 km. per hour

W = 3/4 hour.

$$\text{Number of trips} = \frac{8}{\frac{2 \times 8}{4} + 3/4} = 1.68$$

Cost per trip $= \dfrac{200}{1.68} =$ Rs. 119.05

Adding 10% for profit and overhead Rs. 119.05 + 11.91 = Rs. 130.96

For 300 Numbers of bricks, carrying cost = Rs. 130.96

For 1,000 numbers of bricks, carrying cost $= \dfrac{130.96}{300} \times 1{,}000$ = Rs. 436.53

Case 2. By diesel truck.

Number of trips per day,

$$N = \frac{H}{\frac{2L}{S} + W}$$

Where, H = Working hours = 8

L = Lead = 8 km.

S = Average speed per hour = 20 km

W = Hour required for loading and unloading = 1.0 hour

$$N = \frac{8}{\frac{2 \times 8}{20} + 1} = 4.44$$

Total kilometerage done per day = 2 N L + 6 (6 km is from parking place to duty spot)

$= 2 \times 4.44 \times 8 + 6 = 77.04$ km.

(*a*) Diesel oil consumed at the rate of 5 liters per 5 km

$= \dfrac{77.04}{5} = 15.41$ liters

Cost of diesel oil at the rate of Rs. 17.0 per liter

$= 15.41 \times 17.0 =$ Rs. 261.97

(*b*) Mobil oil consumed at the rate of 8 liters per 140 km

$= \dfrac{77.04}{140} = 0.55$ liters

Cost of mobil oil at the rate of Rs. 80.00 per liter

= Rs. 0.55×80.00 = Rs. 44.00

(*c*) Labour charges of 6 Mazdoor Rs. 65.00 Each per day = Rs. 390.00

(*d*) Hire charges of diesel truck per day = Rs. 1,200.00

Rs. 1,895.97

Cost per trip $= \dfrac{1{,}895.97}{4.44} =$ Rs. 427.02

Add 10% profit and overhead 427.02 + 42.70

= Rs. 469.72

For 1,000 number of bricks carrying cost $= \dfrac{469.72}{1800} \times 1{,}000$

= Rs. 260.96

Carrying cost by diesel truck is cheaper by Rs. 436.53 – 260.96

= Rs. 175.57 per % Nos. of bricks.

15

ARBITRATION

15.1.0 INTRODUCTION

Construction operations involve about half of our all outlays. The quantum of outlay is increasing rapidly. As per report, the outlay in 1989 – 90 was about Rs. 38.305 crore against Rs. 12.941 crore in 1980 – 81.

With the increase in volume of construction work number of disputes in the contracts has increased. At the end of April, 1989 about 2,07,086 cases were pending in the Supreme Court only. Chief Justice of Supreme Court, Hon' ble E.S. Venkatramaiah said,

"People have become conscience of their rights conferred under various constitutions. Therefore, the situation should be met in a positive way and not by culminating the avenues for the enforcement of legitimate rights or redressing of grievances according to laws."

With the rising in number of disputes, there was a tendency to resolve them by adopting unfair approach towards settlement.

15.1.1 Reasons for Increase in Disputes

The inherent nature of the Engineering contracts is such that arising dispute cannot be totally ruled out. Moreover, the eroding powers of the Engineering Officers to take a decision according to their conscience seems to have contributed to the situation.

The reasons for increase in number of disputes are many. Some of them are as below:

(*i*) The nature of Engineering contracts is such that all the contingencies cannot be covered while tendering.

(*ii*) Preparation of drawings, tender documents, etc. involve voluminous works. These are generally completed in a hurry, leaving rooms for disputes in future.

(*iii*) Issuing work order hurriedly without complete possession of the site of work with access, causes delay in commencing the actual work leading to dispute.

(*iv*) Incomplete information and drafting of specifications without taking much care cause disputes in future.

(*v*) Delay in arranging removal of underground services, if there be any, cause delay in commencement of work, which ultimately result in dispute in future.

(*vi*) Failure to provide essential services like — water supply, power, etc. at site.

(*vii*) Delay in collection of scarce materials — cement, steel or any other material proposed to be issued by the department and stipulated in the tender document.

(*viii*) Delay in preparation and issuance of detail working drawing.

(*ix*) Incomplete, unrealistic and ambiguous specifications causing confusion and delay.

(*x*) Delay in settlement of rate for items of works not provided in the 'Bill of Quantities' i.e. supplementary items.

(*xi*) Delay in taking measurement of works done, preparation and submission of running on account and final bills.

(*xii*) Delay in issuing of completion certificate.

(*xiii*) Delay in preparation of snag list for correction of the same by the contractor.

(*xiv*) Levy of compensation for alleged delay in completion.

(*xv*) Claim of compensation for increased cost of construction during overrun period due to delay attributed to the department.

15.1.2 Origin of disputes

The common origin of disputes in building and Engineering contracts may be classified in two categories namely,

(*i*) disputes which arise due to improper management of contract and are independent of the terms of the contract, and

(*ii*) the disputes which arise in connection with or related to the terms of the contract.

15.2.0 ORIGIN OF ARBITRATION ACT

The observation of the Supreme Court in A.I.R. 1981, S.C.—2075 "Interminable time consuming, complex and expensive court procedures impelled jurists to search for an alternative forum, less formal, more effective and speedy for resolution of disputes avoiding procedural claptrap".

This led to the enactment of Arbitration Act, 1940. The law of Arbitration in India substantially contain in three enactments — Arbitration act 1940, the Arbitratory (protocol and convention) Act 1937, and Foreign Awards (Recognition) Act 1961. The Arbitration Act 1940 containing general law of arbitration was felt to become outdated. This has been replaced by the Arbitration and Conciliation Ordinance, 1996.

15.2.1 Arbitration—the Oldest Method for Settlement of Disputes

Arbitration is one of the oldest method for settlement of disputes in India and rest of the world. It is being used traditionally for a long time for settlement of disputes in Engineering contracts.

15.3.0 ARBITRATION

Arbitration is the process for settlement of dispute in a contract. It is an adjunct to the litigation. In a contract system, there shall be the possibility of either of the parties disputing any provision of the contract either during execution of a work or after completion of it.

Arbitration really means setting up, and going to, a private court sometimes called 'domestic court' — instead of the usual Civil Court. Arbitration often substitutes litigation because forum for speedy and substantial justice untrammelled by legal technicalities by getting the disputes resolved by a person in whom the parties have full faith.

The forum of arbitration has been established in the hope that it would enable the parties to settle the disputes with speed, economy and privacy. The subject matter is better considered by an experienced, technically qualified arbitrator — observing formality of the Award.

The essence of arbitration is that it is a substitution by consent of the parties by a tribunal of their choice. The arbitration is a voluntary act of the parties. The judge in the case is not a judge who is forced upon by the process of law. Selection of a judge is as per the choice of the parties.

15.3.1 Arbitration Agreement

Arbitration agreement is an agreement by the parties to submit to arbitration all or certain disputes which have arisen or which may arise between them in respect of a defined relationship whether contractual or not.

Essential requirements of an arbitration agreement

An arbitration agreement shall be in writing.

It may be contained in a document signed by the parties, or an exchange of letters, telex, telegrams or other means of communication which provides a record of the agreement or an exchange of statements of claim and defence in which the existence of the agreement is alleged by one party and not denied by the other.

An arbitration clause may be incorporated in the contract, mentioning the procedure of arbitration. In Public Works system of contract, a clause (clause 25) is provided for arbitration.

15.3.2 Arbitrator

In Public Works system of contract, clause 25 provides for that the Chief Engineer would be sole arbitrator. In Central Public Works contracts, clause 25 provides for that the Director General, Works would be the sole arbitrator. In Municipal Corporation contract, generally, Deputy Mayor is mentioned as the sole arbitrator. They generally delegate their power as arbitrator to some other efficient and competent person, not below the rank of Superintending Engineer to act as arbitrator.

In other cases, clauses are provided mentioning the method of appointing arbitrator or arbitration tribunal. The arbitration tribunal may consist of one person or more persons agreed by the parties, but in any case the number should not be even.

15.3.3 Power to Refer the Parties to Arbitration When There Is An Arbitration Agreement

(*i*) When there is an agreement in existence, a party applies to a judicial authority in a matter which is the subject of agreement, the authority shall refer the parties to arbitration.

(*ii*) In spite of an application has been made to a judicial authority by a party, the arbitration shall continue.

15.3.4 Arbitrator Should Be Independent

A person appointed as an arbitrator should be independent; he shall disclose in writing any circumstances likely to give rise to justifiable doubt as to his independence.

15.3.5 Engineer Arbitrator

The points of disputes in the Engineering contracts are generally of technical nature or arising out of claims of the technical persons.

It is therefore, expected that such disputes would be better understood and adjudicated upon by the Engineer-arbitrator.

15.3.6 Place of Arbitration

The parties are free to select a place for arbitration. In case, the parties cannot agree, the tribunal shall determine the place for arbitration it considers appropriate, in consideration of the circumstances, including convenience of the parties, their representatives, witnesses, experts, inspection of documents, goods or other property.

15.3.7 Language of Arbitration

The parties are free to agree upon the language or languages to be used in arbitral proceedings.

Failing to agree, the arbitral tribunal shall determine the language or languages to be used in the arbitral proceedings.

15.4.0 JURISDICTION OF ARBITRAL TRIBUNAL

(*i*) The arbitral tribunal may rule on its own jurisdiction, including ruling on any objection with respect to the existence or validity of the arbitration agreement, and for that purpose, –

(*a*) an arbitration clause which forms part of a contract shall be treated as an agreement independent of the other terms of the contract; and

(*b*) a decision by the arbitral tribunal that the contract is null and void shall not entail ipso jure the invalidity of the arbitral clause.

(*ii*) A plea that arbitral tribunal does not have jurisdiction shall be raised not later than the submission of the defence statement; however, a party shall not be precluded from raising such plea merely because that he has appointed or participated in appointment of an arbitrator.

(*iii*) A plea that arbitral tribunal is exceeding the scope of its authority shall be raised as soon as the matter alleged to be beyond the scope of its authority is raised during the arbitral proceedings.

(*iv*) The arbitral tribunal may, in either of the cases referred to admit a later plea that if it considers the delay justified.

(*v*) The arbitral tribunal shall decide on a plea referred to, where the arbitral tribunal takes a decision rejecting the plea, continue with the arbitral proceedings and make an arbitral award.

(*vi*) A party agrieved by such an arbitral award may make an application for setting aside such an arbitral award.

15.4.1 Interim Measures Ordered by An Arbitral Tribunal

The arbitral tribunal may order a party to take any interim measure of protection as the tribunal may consider necessary, unless otherwise agreed by the parties.

15.4.2 Removal of Arbitration Tribunal by the Court

The court has the power to remove arbitration tribunal under the circumstances:

(*i*) The court may, on application of any party to a reference, remove an arbitration tribunal who fails to use all reasonable despatch in entering on and proceeding with the reference and make an award.

(*ii*) The court may remove an arbitrator who has misconducted himself of the proceedings.

15.4.3 Power of Court to Appoint Arbitrator

Court can appoint an arbitrator in any of the following cases:

(*i*) When the parties cannot agree or concur in the appointment, or

(*ii*) When an arbitrator neglects or refuses to act, or is incapable of acting or dies.

15.5.0 DIFFERENT FORMS OF ARBITRATION AGREEMENT

At present different forms of arbitration agreements are in existence which raises confusion. With a view to reduce the ambiguities in the arbitration agreements in various contracts, efforts are being made and are done by organisations to rationalise the agreements. The planning commission had formulated a draft standard agreement as early as 1968, but till now rationalisation of arbitration agreement has not materialised.

Engineering bodies like Institution of Engineers, Builders association are also working in the matter.

15.6.0 CONDUCT OF ARBITRATION PROCEEDINGS

The arbitral tribunal shall treat the parties equally and shall give each equal opportunity to present his case. He shall not be bound by the code of civil procedure and evidence act. The parties are free to agree on the procedure to be followed by the tribunal.

In case the parties fail to an agreement, the tribunal may conduct the proceedings in the manner it considers appropriate in determining the admissibility, relevance, materiality and weight of any evidence.

15.6.1 Statement of Claims and Defence

(*i*) Within the period of time as agreed upon by the parties or determined by the arbitral tribunal, the claimant shall state the facts supporting his claims, the points at issue and relief or remedy sought and the respondent shall state his defence in respect of these particulars, unless the parties have otherwise agreed as to the required elements of those statements.

(*ii*) The parties may submit all documents they consider to be relevant or may add a reference to the documents or other evidence they will submit.

(*iii*) Parties may amend or supplement his claim or defence during the course of the arbitral proceedings, unless the arbitral tribunal considers it inappropriate to allow the amendment having regard to the delay in making it.

15.6.2 Hearing and Written Proceedings

The arbitral tribunal shall decide the nature of the hearing and presentation of evidence. The tribunal may decide upon oral hearing or submission of written hearing.

The tribunal shall give sufficient advance notice to the parties of any hearing and of any meeting for the purpose of inspection of any document or goods or other property.

The copies of the documents submitted by the party shall be made available to the other party.

15.6.3 Expert Appointment by Arbitral Tribunal

The tribunal may if it desires appoint one or more expert to report to it on specific issues as determined by the tribunal and the parties shall have to co-operate with such expert as necessary by furnishing relevant information.

15.6.4 Court Assistance in Taking Evidence

The arbitral tribunal or a party with the approval of the arbitral tribunal, may apply to the court for assistance in taking evidence, specifying the names and addresses of the parties and the arbitrators, general nature of the claim and relief sought and evidence to be obtained.

The court may in such case take evidence, and execute the request by ordering that the evidence be provided directly to the arbitral tribunal.

15.6.5 Decision Making by Panel of Arbitrators

In arbitral proceedings with more than one arbitrator, the decision of the tribunal shall be made by a majority of all its members.

15.6.6 Settlement

The arbitration may encourage settlement of all disputes and, with agreement of the parties, may use mediation, conciliation or other procedures at any time during the arbitral proceedings to encourage settlement.

If during arbitral proceedings a settlement is agreed by the parties, the tribunal shall terminate the proceedings and record the same in the form of an award on agreed terms.

An arbitral award on agreed terms shall have the same status and effect as any other arbitral award.

15.7.0 ARBITRAL AWARD

An arbitral award shall be made in writing and signed by the members of the arbitral tribunal with date and place of arbitration.

The arbitral award shall state the reasons upon which the award is based.

If however, the parties have agreed, no reason may be furnished.

A signed copy of the award shall be delivered to each party.

The arbitral tribunal may, at any time during the arbitral proceedings, make an interim award on any matter with respect to which it may make a final award.

The arbitral tribunal may include in the sum awarded, interest at such rate as it deems reasonable, on the whole or any part of the money, for the whole or part of the period between the date on which the cause of action arose to the date on which the award is made.

The sum awarded by the arbitral tribunal shall carry an interest at the rate of eighteen per cent per annum from the date of award to the date of payment.

15.7.1 Power of the Court to Modify Award

The court may modify or correct an award,

(*a*) when court finds that award was beyond the scope of arbitration agreement, or

(*b*) when the award is imperfect in form or contains any obvious error which can be amended without amending such decision, or

(*c*) where the award contains clerical mistake, or accidental slip or omission.

15.7.2 Finality and Enforcement of Arbitration Award

An arbitral award shall be final binding on the parties and persons claiming under them respectively.

When the time for making an application to set aside the arbitral award has expired, or such application having been made, it has been refused, the award shall be enforced in the manner as if it was a decree of the court.

15.7.3 Arbitration Agreement not to be Discharged by Death of Party There To

An arbitration agreement shall not be discharged by the death of any party there to either as respects the deceased or as respects any other party, but shall be in such event be enforceable by or against the legal representative of the deceased.

The mandate of an arbitration shall not be terminated by the death of any party or by whom he was appointed.

15.7.4 Cost of Arbitration

The cost of award shall be fixed by the arbitral tribunal. The arbitral tribunal shall mention the party entitled to costs and who shall pay the costs. The amount of costs and method of determining the amount and the manner in which the costs shall be paid shall also be mentioned.

The costs means, reasonable costs relating to fees and expenses of the arbitrators and witnesses, legal fees, and expenses, administrative fees of the institution supervising and any other expenses incurred in connection with the arbitral proceedings and the arbitral award.

15.8.0 RECOURSE AGAINST ARBITRAL AWARD

Application can be made to judicial authority against an arbitral award for setting aside such award.

(*a*) Arbitral award may be set aside by the court only, if party making the application furnishes proof that –

(*i*) a party was under some incapacity, or

(*ii*) the arbitration agreement is not valid under the law to which the parties have subjected to, or failing any indication there on, or

(*iii*) the party making the application was not given proper notice of the appointment of an arbitrator or of the arbitration proceedings or was otherwise unable to present his case, or

(*iv*) the arbitral award deals with a dispute which does not fall within the terms of submission to arbitration, or

(*v*) the composition of the arbitral tribunal or the proceedings was not in accordance with the agreement of the parties.

(*b*) If the court finds that –

(*i*) the subject matter of the dispute is not capable of settlement by arbitration, or

(*ii*) the arbitral award is in conflict with the public policy of India.

15.8.1 Power of the Court to Remit Award

(*i*) The court may from time to time remit the award or any matter referred to arbitral tribunal for consideration upon such terms as it thinks fit.

(*a*) Where the award left undetermined any of the matter referred to arbitration, or it determines any matter beyond the scope of arbitration agreement and such matters cannot be separated without affecting the determination of the matters referred; or

(*b*) where the award is so indefinite as to be incapable of execution, or

(*c*) where an objection to the legality of the award is apparent upon the face of it.

(*ii*) Where an award is remitted under any of the above item, the court shall fix the time within which the arbitration tribunal shall submit its decision to the court.

15.9.0 TERMINATION OF PROCEEDINGS

The arbitration proceedings shall be terminated by the final award or by an order of the arbitral tribunal when

(*i*) the claimant withdraws his claim,

(*ii*) the parties agree on termination of the proceedings, or

(*iii*) the arbitral tribunal finds continuation of the proceedings unnecessary.

15.9.1 Power to Refer Parties to Arbitration

(*i*) When an arbitration agreement exists, a party bring the matter to a judicial authority, the authority has the power to refer the dispute to arbitration.

15.9.2 Interim Measures by the Court

A party may, before or during arbitral proceedings or at any time after an arbitral award but before it has become a decree, apply to the court:

(*i*) for appointment of a guardian for a minor or a person of unsound mind for the purpose of arbitral proceedings, or

(*ii*) for an interim measure pertaining in respect of any of the following:

(*a*) the preservation, interim custody or sale of any goods which are the subject matter of the arbitration agreement,

(*b*) securing the amount in dispute in the arbitration,

(*c*) detention, preservation or inspection of any property or thing which is the subject matter of dispute in arbitration,

(*d*) interim injunction or the appointment of a receiver,

(*e*) such other interim measure of protection as may appear to the court to be just and convenient.

15.10.0 CONCILIATION

Application and scope

Parties having agreed upon may apply for conciliation of disputes arising out of legal relationship, whether contractual or not and to all proceedings relating there to.

15.10.1 Conciliation Proceedings

The party initiating conciliation shall send to the other party a written invitation to conciliate, briefly identifying the subject of the dispute. The conciliation proceedings shall commence when the other party accepts in writing the invitation to conciliate. If the other party rejects the invitation, there will be no conciliation proceeding. The invitation for conciliation shall be accepted within 30 days of its initiation, otherwise it will be treated as rejected.

15.10.2 Conciliator

Generally there shall be one conciliator. However, if the parties agree, there may be two or three conciliators. The conciliators shall act jointly.

Appointment of conciliators

(*i*) When one conciliator is agreed, the parties may agree on the name of a sole conciliator.

(*ii*) When two conciliators are agreed, each party shall name one conciliator.

(*iii*) When three conciliators are agreed, each party shall name one conciliator and the third conciliator shall be an agreed name and he shall act as the presiding conciliator.

The parties may seek assistance of suitable institution for appointment of conciliators, if necessary.

15.10.3 Submission of Statements to Conciliator

The conciliator, upon his appointment shall request the parties to submit a brief statement describing the general nature of the dispute.

The conciliator may request the parties to submit further statement mentioning the grounds supported by documents, evidence, etc. The party shall send copies of such documents and other evidences to the other party.

15.10.4 Role of Conciliator

The conciliator shall assist the parties in an independent and impartial manner in his attempt to reach an amicable settlement of the dispute.

The conciliator may, at any stage of the conciliation proceedings, make proposals for a settlement of the dispute. Such proposals need not be in writing and need not be accompanied by a statement of the reasons therefor.

15.10.5 Administrative Assistance

In order to facilitate the conduct of the conciliation proceedings, the parties, or the conciliator with the consent of the parties, may arrange for administrative assistance by a suitable institution or person.

15.10.6 Communication between Conciliator and Parties

The conciliator may invite the parties to meet him or may communicate with them orally or in writing. He may meet or communicate with the parties together or with each of them separately.

The conciliator shall determine the place of meetings of the parties with the conciliator.

15.10.7 Settlement of Agreement

When the conciliator feels that elements of settlement acceptable to the parties exist, he shall formulate the terms of a possible settlement and ask the parties for their observations. On receiving their reaction, the conciliator shall formulate the terms of a possible settlement in the light of observations by the parties.

If the terms of agreement drawn by the conciliator is agreed by the parties, a settlement agreement shall be drawn by the conciliator or he shall assist the parties in drawing up the settlement agreement.

When the parties sign the settlement agreement, it shall be final and binding on the parties.

The conciliator shall authenticate the settlement agreement and furnish a copy thereof to each of the parties.

The settlement agreement shall have the same status and effects as it is an arbitral award on agreed terms on the substance of the dispute rendered by an arbitral tribunal.

The conciliation proceedings shall be terminated by signing of the settlement agreement, or by a written declaration of the conciliator, after consultation with the parties, or by a written declaration of a party to the other party and the conciliator, or by a written declaration of the parties addressed to the conciliator to the effect that the conciliation proceedings are terminated.

15.10.8 Resort to Arbitral or Judiciary Proceedings

During the conciliation proceedings, the parties shall not resort to any arbitration or judicial proceedings in respect to a dispute that is the subject-matter of the conciliation proceeding.

15.10.9 Costs

Upon termination of the conciliation proceedings, the conciliator shall fix the costs of conciliation and give written notice thereof to the parties. The costs shall include fees and expenses of the conciliator, witnesses, any expert advice, assistance provided by any institution or person, any other expenses incurred in connection with the conciliation proceedings and settlement agreement.

The costs shall be borne equally by the parties, unless agreed otherwise.

The conciliator may direct each party to deposit an equal amount as advance for the costs.

15.11.0 PRECAUTIONARY MEASURES TO BE TAKEN BY THE ENGINEER IN CHARGE TO AVOID ARBITRATION

Arbitration case against a contract arises from the disputes, probable causes of which have been listed under the paragraph 14.1.1. It is not exhaustive, but indicative. There may be other reasons also. The objective of the Engineer in charge should be to avoid dispute. If there be any, he should try to remove the cause of dispute not by appeasing the contractor, but by offering justice.

In the tender and contract document some vague terms are used which may ultimately result into dispute. These should be avoided, and if possible should be totally avoided.

It has been held by the Supreme Court that expressions e.g. 'arising out of' or 'in respect of' or 'in connection with' or 'in relation to' or 'in consequence of' or 'concerning' or 'related to' in the contract are of the widest amplitude and contain and even include questions as to the existence, validity and effect of the arbitration agreement. It has been further held that the test to determine whether the claim fell within the scope of the phrases such as one 'arising out of' or 'related to' or 'concerning' the contract is whether it becomes necessary to have recourse to the contract by which the parties are bound to settle the disputes one or other. If so, then the dispute arises out of the contract.

Vagueness in the specification is often a source of dispute. The terms often used 'to the satisfaction of the Engineer in Charge' is in no way acceptable. Again, 'as directed by the Engineer in Charge' is untenable. In case of issue of materials by the department, it is generally mentioned 'to be issued from the departmental godown within the jurisdiction of ....' This does not specify the kilometerage, the contractor shall have to carry the materials. About specification of stone chips, it is sometimes mentioned 'percentage of size 6 mm shall be up to 25%' and so on. This 'up to 25%' does not specify any firmness on which a correct rate can be quoted.

Absence of any clause regarding price contingency gives rise to dispute. In the present day market price of materials and labour are increasing rapidly. In view of that a price contingency clause is a must in the tender which is likely to continue for more than six months.

In view of the above, the Engineer in Charge should draft the tender documents carefully and try to avoid the vagueness of the clauses and specifications and make the documents transparent.

15.12.0 COMMENTS ON SOME CLAUSES OF CONTRACT

(*i*) **Time period** (delay or extension of time). Clause 5 of the Public Works Department contract form mentions that if found necessary, the contractor may apply for extension of time period within 7 days of its expiry.

In clause 2 of the same contract form, it is mentioned that 'time is the essence of the contract'. The two provisions are contradictory. Clause 2 again says that the contractor has to perform proportionate work in proportionate time. The contents of the clause is vague as it does not clarify, how the proportions shall be worked out, on the basis of the value of the work done or otherwise. An item of work may have less monitary value, but may require more time for execution. Hence, the assessment depends upon the whims of the Site Engineers.

All such disputable clauses should be modified to make the contracts void of ambiguity, and make it effective and transparent.

Issue of the essential materials by the department

The essential materials are issued by the department as those may not be readily available in the market and also to guarantee the quality. The issue rates of the materials are generally lower than the market rates and are generally not updated. The issuance of the materials is an indirect financial help to the contractor. A contractor can reap advantage by receiving more materials than required at an early stage, sale the excess materials in the market and continue the work investing the money in the work. Later, he would purchase the quantity of materials sold and complete the work.

The worst case may be, the contractor may leave the work incomplete and earning profit by selling the materials which he would have earned by executing the work. The contract provision for guarding the malpractice is recovering the cost of unutilised quantity of materials at double the issues rate.

Clause 3 of the contract specifies process of termination of contract. Clause 3*a*, states that when the contractor has left the work incomplete and has rendered himself liable to pay compensation, the contract would be rescind and the whole of the security deposit shall stand forfeited.

In an arbitration case of a contract for construction of a few culverts, the contractor left the job after executing hardly 20% of the work. There was excess quantity of steel and cement issued. The department rescind the contract and claimed forfeiture of the security deposit and claimed recovery of cost of materials taken in excess of requirement for the portion of work done at double the issue rate as was stipulated in the contract.

The claimant submitted–as the department had not submit any statement of financial loss suffered by it due to non-completion of the work, it was assumed that no financial loss was suffered by the department and as such question of compensation did not arise. A reference of Hon'ble Patna High Court judgement was cited, where the Hon'ble High Court upheld return of the security deposit as no financial loss was suffered by the Government in the particular case.

As regards double rate recovery of the cost of excess materials received by the contractor, a Tripura High Court case was cited, where the Hon'ble High Court opened that materials once issued to the contractor at a price is sold to him and is his property. The department has no further right over the same.

All these are the lacunae of the existing contract form. These need be amended.

15.13.0 LIMITATION PERIODS

(*i*) Period of limitation for application of arbitration. While examining the request for application of arbitration from a contractor or supplier or any claim in a litigation case, the Engineer in Charge should examine whether the claim of the contractor is time-barred in accordance to the provisions of Limitation Act 1908 or 1963 as the case may be. If the claim has not been preferred in writing within 90 days of receiving intimation from the Engineer in Charge that the final bill is ready for payment, the claim will be deemed to have been waived and absolutely barred and the Engineer in Charge shall be discharged as released of all liabilities under the contract in respect of those claims. The period of limitation should be reckoned from the intimation of the final bill.

(*ii*) Period of limitation for appointment of arbitrator. When a contractor applies for arbitration to the Chief Engineer according to arbitration clause, he should appoint an arbitrator within 30 days from the date of receipt of the application.

(*iii*) Period of limitation to appoint an arbitrator after receiving notice from the court. If the appointment is not made within 15 clear days after the service of the said notice, the court may, on the application of the party who gave the notice and after giving the other parties an opportunity of being heard, appoint an arbitrator.

16

VALUATION

16.1.0 VALUATION

Valuation is the art of assessing the present fair value of a property at a stated time. Valuation of anything is an estimation of the value of it in terms of money. It only attempts at suggesting the fair prices of properties. Yet valuation is not an arbitrary process. It is based on certain facts and only after judicious processing of such facts and indications, fair price of a property at a stated time can be suggested.

16.1.1 Cost

The actual amount incurred in producing a commodity which has some value is called cost.

16.1.2 Prime Cost

Expenditure incurred or charges involved directly in production of a commodity is called prime cost.

16.1.3 Supplementry Cost

Expenditures like rental charges, establishment charges, management cost, salaries, services which are indirectly involved in production is termed supplementary cost.

16.1.4 Price

Price of a produce is the actual cost of production plus the profit expected.

16.1.5 Value

The term value has got a wide spectrum. Value of a commodity is not its price. Price is a materialistic measure while value includes something more than that. Price is fact and value is an estimate of what it should be. It is a measure of:

(*i*) Utility,

(*ii*) Scarcity, and

(*iii*) Transferability or marketability.

16.1.6 Market Value

Market value of a commodity is the value at which it can be exchanged in the market. It indicates the marketability or transferability of the commodity.

16.1.7 Depreciation

The term depreciation is derived from the Latin word 'depreciatum' measuring the fall in value or becoming less in worth. There are many ways in which a property can loose its value. Whenever a building is newly constructed, its value does not remain the same due to wear and tear of the property. With the passing of time the usefulness period of life of the structure becomes less and less due to wear and tear of the property or building in addition to the decay or decline due to any natural cause, building is ultimately of no use and is abandoned.

The gradual decrease in the value of the usefulness of a property is known as depreciation.

Loss of value on account of use, wear and tear, structural deterioration, life span calculated on the percentage rates of the total life also depends upon maintenance, type of structure and life, etc. Thus the value of the structure reduces gradually due to use and life, continuous wear and tear and a certain depreciation may be allowed to fix the present value. The gradual annual decrease in the value of a property is known as annual depreciation.

Loss of value of the property is called depreciation. Loss of value of the property may be due to normal wear and tear and/or may be due to some other cause like -

(*i*) Physical condition,
(*ii*) Functional obsolescence,
(*iii*) Economic obsolescence.

16.1.8 Discounting

Conversion of future value of a property to its present value or the base year or to any other year with respect to the year of future value and the particular year considered as base year on an assigned rate is called discounting.

16.2.0 PURPOSE OF VALUATION

Valuation of properties are done to serve various purpose, some of them are as below:

(*i*) **Levying betterment charges**. When a property falls under an improvement scheme of the area, its value increases consequently. Revised valuation of the property becomes necessary for ascertaining the quantum of additional charges payable.

(*ii*) **Preparation of balance-sheet.** Valuation of the premises is needed for preparation of balance sheet of the company.

(*iii*) **Buying and selling of property**. Valuation of property is necessary in cases of buying or selling of property for knowing the realistic value of the property by the buyer or purchaser.

(*iv*) **Acquisition**. Valuation of a property is necessary when it is proposed to be acquired by Government or Semi-Government organisation.

(*v*) **Court fees/Stamp duty.** Valuation of the property is required for assessing the amount of court fees or stamp duty.

(*vi*) **Insurance.** Valuation of the property is necessary for taking out an insurance policy against it.

(*vii*) **Rent determination.** Valuation of the property is required for finding out the probable rent of the premises.

(*viii*) **Security of loans.** Valuation of the property is required for granting a loan against it.

(*ix*) **Taxation.** Valuation of property is required for assessing municipal or other taxes.

(*x*) **Rehabilitation of dilapidated building.** Valuation of the premises is necessary when the owner desires to rehabilitate it.

(*xi*) Valuation of a property is required for proper economic appraisal of it to the client.

16.3.0 DIFFERENT FORMS OF VALUE

There are different forms of value which are used in connection with the value of properties and to suit the purpose.

(*i*) **Accomodation value**. With the increase in population and rapid urbanisation, demand for accomodation land increases. Agricultural land is converted into accomodation land for which permission need be taken. The surrounding area of township is converted into accomodation land. Value of accomodation land is greater than agricultural land and less than building land.

(*ii*) **Assessed value**. The value of a property which is recorded in the register of the local authority for determining the tax payable is called assessed value.

(*iii*) **Book value.** Book value is the cost that was invested for acquiring a property less the depreciation for the period.

(*iv*) **Salvage value.** Salvage value is the value realised by sell of a structure or machinery which has outlived its span of life.

(*v*) **Scrap value.** Scrap value is the value of a structure or machinery which has outlived its span of life and is proposed to be sold as scrap, less the cost of demolition.

(*vi*) **Replacement value**. Replacement value indicates the value of a structure or portions thereof if the same is proposed to be replaced at current rates.

(*vii*) **Earning value.** Earning value is the present value of a property which will start yielding an income in future.

(*viii*) **Annual value.** Annual value is the percentage of the assessed value of a property on the basis of which taxes are calculated by the local authority.

(*ix*) **Distress value.** Distress value is the value of a property when it has to be sold under reason of unusual character.

The reasons may be,

(*a*) fear of war, riots, earthquake, etc.

(*b*) financial difficulties of seller,

(*c*) intention to favour the purchaser,

(*d*) court decree,

(*e*) insufficient knowledge of the seller,

(*f*) quarrel among the partners, etc.

(*x*) **Monopoly value.** Monopoly value is the value which is demanded by a seller who is in a position to dictate the sale price, may be due to shape, size, location of the property or due to any other reason. It may also be that the purchaser is in a commanding position to dictate the price.

(*xi*) **Potential value**. Potential value of a property is the value when the property has some potential importance e.g. an agricultural land adjacent to a township has potential of building land.

(*xii*) **Sentimental value**. Sentimental value is the value of a property when the owner attaches some sentiment to it. He does not want to sell it even at a high rate due to sentimental ground.

(*xiii*) **Speculative value.** Speculative value is the value of a property when the purchaser wants to acquire the property and sell it after a period at a high premium. The purchaser speculates with the property and earns more. Speculation depends upon the economic rule of demand and supply. When the demand increases and supply is less, price of the commodity increases. Conversely, when demand is less and the supply is more price of the commodity is lowered. In a competitive market, the price is determined neither by the demand alone nor by the supply alone. But it is determined by the forces of demand and supply working together. Such a price is known as an equilibrium price.

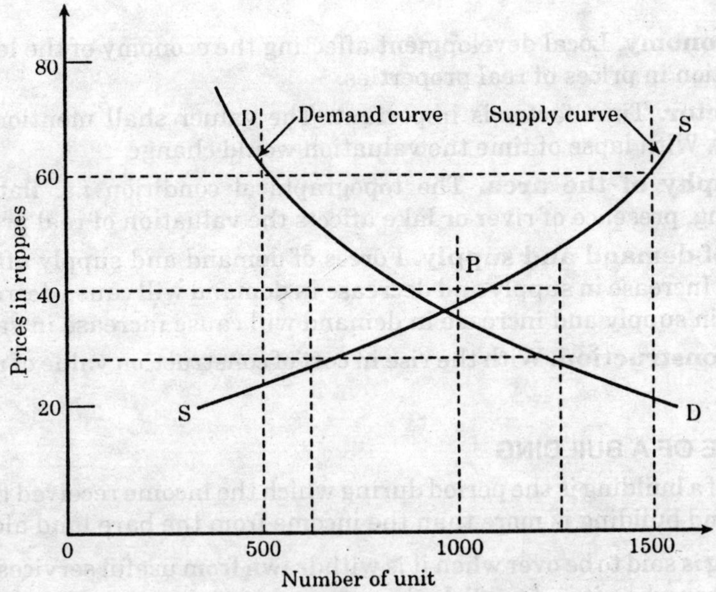

Fig. 16.1 Force of Supply and Demand.

16.4.0 FACTORS AFFECTING THE VALUE OF A PROPERTY

There are various factors affecting the value of a real property. Following are some of them which affect the property market.

(*i*) **Climatic condition.** The climatic condition of the place affects the value of the property. In some particular climate certain plants grow or certain industry develops which affects the value of the property, e.g. Tea grows in hill slopes, Timber industry is suitable in the neighbourhood of forest, etc.

(*ii*) **Communications.** Communication is an important factor affecting the value of property. Area having good surface communication is suitable for growth of industry, consequently the value of property in the area increases.

(*iii*) **Local demand and fashion.** Local demand affects the value of property. The fashion or elevation of structure also influences the value of the property greatly.

(*iv*) **Government policies.** The policies of Union and State adopted from time to time affect the interest of the investors and growth of industry which consequently affect the value of real property.

(*v*) **Individual aspect of property.** Individual choice of any area affects the real property market; but its effect is more in case of residential area. A person may have choice for any particular area or a particular house and he may be willing to shell higher price for it.

(*vi*) **Potentiality.** Potential value of a property influences the value of it in the market.

(*vii*) **Services.** The intending purchaser prior to making final negotiation regarding purchasing a property enquires about availability of the essential services like water supply, sewerage and drainage. The availability of the services affects the value of the real property.

(*viii*) **State of repairs.** A well maintained property will have longer life span and will fetch higher price.

(*ix*) **Lack of market information.** The intending purchaser may not have correct information about the prevailing market price and may offer higher price.

(*x*) **Local economy**. Local development affecting the economy of the locality may cause appreciation in prices of real properties.

(*xi*) **Time factor.** Time factor is important. The valuer shall mention the time of his reporting. With lapse of time the valuation would change.

(*xii*) **Topography of the area.** The topographical condition *i.e.* flat, level, or hilly, undulating, presence of river or lake affects the valuation of real property.

(*xiii*) **Forces of demand and supply.** Forces of demand and supply affects the value of property. Increase in supply and decrease in demand will cause decrease in value and decrease in supply and increase in demand will cause increase in value.

(*xiv*) **Cost of construction.** With the rise in cost of construction value of real property will increase.

16.5.0 FUTURE LIFE OF A BUILDING

The future life of a building is the period during which the income received from the property consisting of land and building is more than the income from the bare land alone.

Life of a building is said to be over when it is withdrawn from useful services or it gets retired from usefulness either when it is demolished or when out used.

16.5.1 Economic life

The economic life or service life of a property is that period during which the income from the land and building taken as one unit is more than the income from bare land alone and moreover the said income remains constant during the said economic period. It is usually adopted at 60 to 70 years for an R.C.C. framed residential building.

Life of a building depends on the following factors:

(*i*) Materials of construction,

(*ii*) Repairs and maintenance,

(*iii*) Sub-soil conditions,

(*iv*) Climatic conditions,

(*v*) Use of building, i.e. building used for residential purpose or used as a godown.

(*vi*) Vibration due to any activity in the vicinity,

(*vii*) If the structure is in a precarious condition, a shorter life would be adopted as compared to its normal life.

16.5.2 How to Ascertain the Future Life of a Building

Ascertaining the future life of a building is a complex job. The building shall require thorough inspection. All possible data having any bearing to its life shall have to be collected and the same shall be studied carefully and in the light of practical experience one can estimate the approximate future life of a building.

The building shall be inspected in the light of the following:

(*i*) Mode of construction,

(*ii*) Settlement of foundation,

(*iii*) Cracks in walls,

(*iv*) Construction of roof and sanitary blocks,

(*v*) Condition of flooring, joists, beams and posts,

(*vi*) Decay due to other reasons like attack of white ants, fungi infection causing dry rot, etc.

(*vii*) Capital repair works executed and those required at present.

16.5.3 Ascertaining the Approximate Year of Construction

For valuation purpose, it becomes necessary to ascertain the present age of the structure. This can be ascertained either from the cadestal survey map or 'as built drawing or completion drawing', if available. In absence of both, the age of a building can be ascertained by inspection and verification of the Architectural mode of the structure, local information, plagues installed on the body of the structure or from materials used in construction.

Approximate life of buildings is adopted as below:

(*i*) Permanent structures – R.C.C. framed, R.S.J, framed or timber framed, masonry structures with R.C.C. roof -60 -70 years.

(*ii*) Semi-permanent structures – Masonry structures with tile or A.C. or C.I. roof -30 -35 years.

(*iii*) Temporary structures – C.I. sheet wall and roofing, split bamboo walls and tile, A.C. or C.I. sheet roofing –10 years.

Future life of a building can be estimated by deducting the age of the structure from its estimated life.

16.5.4 Obsolescence

Obsolescence of a building is defined as when its functional utility comes to an end and there is no other alternative but to pull it down as the returns from the bare site will be more than the returns from the building with the land.

16.6.0 METHOD OF VALUATION

Where it is not possible to obtain fair and maintainable rent which is a comparable one or where there is no direct evidence of rent, physical method of valuation of such property is made to obtain the market value.

16.6.1 Valuation of Land

Systems available for valuation of land only are:

(*i*) Comparative method,

(*ii*) Residual value technique, and

(*iii*) Belting system.

(*i*) **Comparative method.** In this method, the piece of land whose valuation is to be obtained is directly compared with comparable pieces of land which have been sold recently. Necessary allowances for 'plus and minus' factors are made for making the properties comparable. The technique aims at utilising local information available. However, it is next to impossible to find pieces of land having identical size and characteristics. The method gives an approximate indication of valuation.

(*ii*) **Residual value technique.** The technique involves systems like:

(*a*) **Development method of valuation.** When comparison with large extents of land is not possible or not available, the large area of land is subdivided into small plots and those are compared with similar other small plots. This technique is generally adopted by the developers. The value of a small plot cannot be straight away integrated for obtaining the value of large plot. The values of the small plots can be integrated and after deducting the cost of infrastructure, value of the large plot can be obtained.

(*b*) **Flat rate technique.** This is modification of the development method of valuation. The difference between the two is that while aggregating the cost of sub-divided small plots for obtaining the value of large plot, the area required for the infrastructure shall be deducted.

(*c*) **Hypothetical building scheme.** The origin of the method or the technique of valuation is based on the well defined principles of valuation "he market value should be determined not necessarily according to its present disposition, but laid out in the most lucrative and advantageous way in which the owner can dispose of it."

In accordance with the above principle the potential future value of the land in constructing is added to the present value and the valuation of the land is obtained.

(*iii*) **Belting system.** It is generally known that value of the land decreases as its depth from the frontage increases reaching up to a point of saturation, whereby further reduction will not be applicable. The front land is more valuable than the back land. So it has to be found out till what depth the value of the land will not decrease further and that would be the 'standard depth'. The method is nothing but 'Zoning theory'. In abiding by the 'Zoning theory' large area of land is divided into different Zones or Belts. In belting system, the depth and frontage play important role. There may be other factors also influencing the value of land in zoning system, e.g. land belonging to a particular belt, but located at the junction of two roads, land belonging to the same belt, but having South or East facing shall have extra advantage and shall fetch higher value.

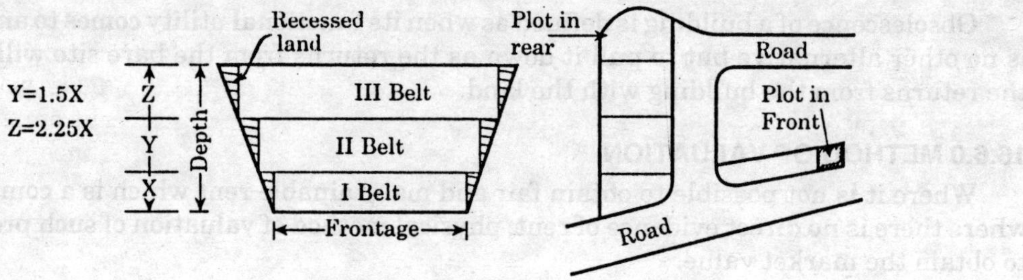

Fig. 16.2 Belting System.

Recess land. Recess land is that portion of land (which lies between the plot boundary which makes an obtuse angle with the road lines; zero frontage point) and a perpendicular drawn from the junction of the said boundary with the road line.

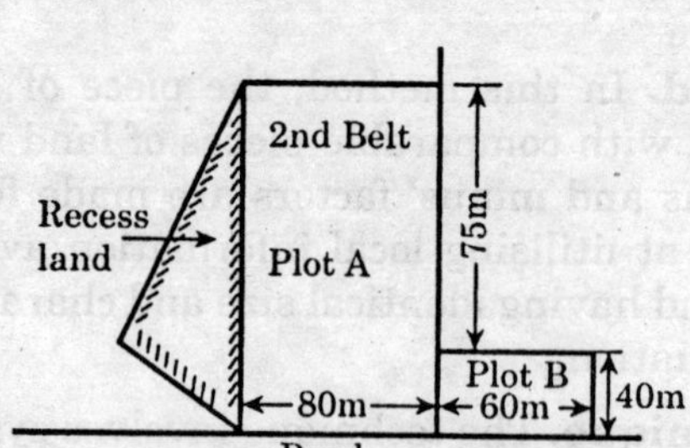

Fig. 16.3 Recess Land.

Land-locked land. Land-locked land is the land having no means of access and as such it is not possible to develop the same. Land-locked land will have much less value and it will be useful to the neighbours only and no outside person will like to purchase it.

While planning for development of an area cases of land-locked land may arise. The piece of land is made marketable by making it a tandem plot of land.

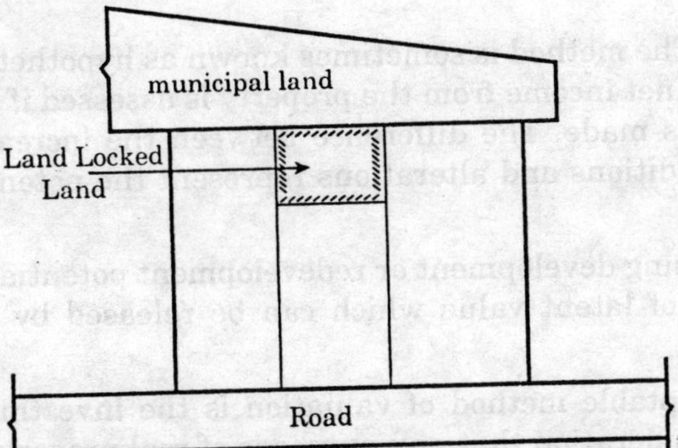

Fig. 16.4 Land Locked Land.

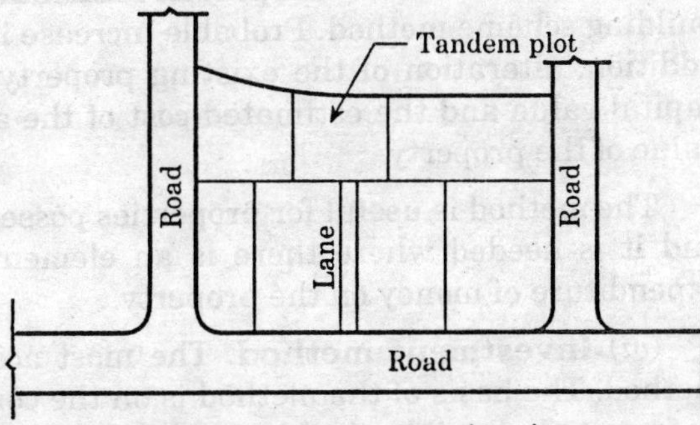

Fig. 16.5 Tandem Land.

16.6.2 Methods of Valuation for Lands with Buildings

Valuation of land with building is done by adopting any of the following methods.

(*i*) **Rental method.** Rental method of valuation is important and is mostly adopted.

The gross income from the property by way of rent received is ascertained. The usual outgoings to which the property is subjected to is deducted from the gross income. The net income from the property is thus obtained. Depending upon the rate of interest on gilt-edged securities and bank rate, suitable rate of interest is estimated for the property under consideration. The Y.P. is worked out. If the income is to continue for perpetuity, the Y.P. is worked out in perpetuity; But if it is to continue for a shorter duration, Y.P. is worked out on single or dual rate basis up to the useful life of the structure. Multiplying the net annual income by Y.P., the capitalised value of the property is found out.

(*ii*) **Direct comparison of the capital value method.** In this method valuation of a property is arrived at by comparison with the known value of another property. In reality the characteristics make properties extremely heterogeneous from one another. A property may have characteristics like building characteristics, site characteristics, neighbourhood characteristics, etc. All these are very much variable from property to property. However, in this method a very rough idea of the value of the property may be obtained. For conveniency the value of a property is reduced to an unit basis for comparison purpose e.g. per square metre or cubic metre, etc.

(*iii*) **Profit basis method.** This method is often used for valuation of commercial premises. In this method, the profit earned from the property is estimated. This is generally the rent received by the landlord. When the premises is used by the owner himself a hypothetical tenant is assumed to run the trade and a probable rent is assumed. From this gross profit, the net profit is obtained by deducting the outgoings which is considered as net surplus from the profit and the landlord's share as owner of the property, and may be capitalised to its value.

(*iv*) **Cost method.** The present cost of construction of the property is estimated and then the present cost is reduced by allowing depreciation according to the age of the property. The price of the site is aggregated to the depreciated value of the property to arrive at the real valuation of the property.

This method is widely used; but it has some drawbacks. The setting of depreciated value from the present cost of the property does not depend on the age of the property and its structural condition, but the value may fall due to other reasons like – economic, social, functional obsolescence. However, this would give a fairly satisfactory result.

(*v*) **Residual or development method.** The method is sometimes known as hypothetical building scheme method. Probable increase in net income from the property is assessed if any addition, alteration of the existing property is made. The difference between the increased capital value and the estimated cost of the additions and alterations represent the potential value of the property.

The method is useful for properties possessing development or redevelopment potentiality and it is needed where there is an element of latent value which can be released by the expenditure of money on the property.

(*vi*) **Investment method.** The most acceptable method of valuation is the investment method. The basis of the method is on the consideration that any purchase of real property is an investment and hence is capable of generating income. Even when a property is purchased for own occupation the estimated income is considered to be the net saving in rent.

The net annual income to be received or receiveable is found out and the rate of interest at which should the income be capitalised is assessed.

On assuming the rate of interest, the ratio of Year's Purchase, Y.P. is found out.

$$\text{Y.P.} = \frac{100}{\text{rate percent}}$$

On finding out the Y.P., the capital value can be foundout.

Capital value = Net income per annum × Y.P.

Example 16.1. *If a house earns a net income of Rs. 10,000.00 p.a. and the approximate rate of return is 10%, what sum will an investor would like to pay for acquiring the property?*

Capitalised value = Net income per annum × Y.P.

$$\text{Y.P.} = \frac{100}{\text{rate percent}} = \frac{100}{10} = 10$$

Capitalised value = 10,000 × 10 = Rs. 1,00,000.00

16.7.0 OUTGOINGS

Outgoings are the normal expenditures required to be incurred against a premises let out on rental basis. The expenditures are municipal taxes and rates, Insurance premiums, collection and management charges, cost of services and amenities provided, Repairs and maintenance charges, special increamental value of the property payable to the lessors on aleanation as per lease terms, etc.

16.8.0 SINKING FUND

The capital in a property can be divided into two parts. One for the land which does not depreciate and does not lose value. The other part is the building. The building is subjected to the natural process of decay and thereby lose the capital value till a time comes when the physical life of the building is zero and the owner is left with the land only. The owner's share of capital invested in the building is lost. To overcome such a situation, the owner need invest some portion of the return from the property in the form of security so that when the life of the building has expired, the money thus invested in securities or otherwise with interest will be intact and the capital required for rebuilding the structure is available. The amount, the owner is required to invest in securities per annum for growing with interest to the required amount for meeting the cost of rebuilding the structure is termed as Annual Sinking Fund. The amount can be utilised for any major repair or rehabilitation of the structure to regain the life of the structure after lapse of a definite period.

However, in practice the acqusition of a property may not be perpetual, but may be for a fixed period and the person acquiring the property would like that the capitalised value is redeemed in the period of possession of the property and that too at the present value. Simultaneously he would like that the capital invested should earn some profit by way of interest.

In the first case only one rate of interest was involved and is termed Single Rate. In the second case two rates of interests are involved e.g. (*i*) for earning against the capital invested and (*ii*) for redemption of the capital.

(*i*) Rate of interest for capital – which may be termed as remunerative rate of interest.

(*ii*) Rate of interest for redemption of capital for sinking fund – which may be termed as accumulative rate of interest.

The sinking fund rates are generally lower. When the rates on both the accounts are the same, the Y.P. calculated is called on Single Rate. When the rates adopted for the two purposes are different, the Y.P. calculated is called Double Rate.

16.9.0 LEASEHOLD PROPERTY

The best form of ownership namely freehold tenure entitles the freeholder the right to utilise and deal with the land as the freeholder pleases subject to rules and regulations of the local authority and the Government.

The full right of the freehold tenure may be subdivided by a lease or leases so as to create two or more interests in the property like lessor's interest, lessee's interest, etc.

The lessor surrenders some of his rights to possess, occupy and use for terms and conditions as stated in the lease, retaining the right to repossess the property at the end of the lease term called reversion.

The lessee having acquired some rights by virtue of the leasedeed may create a sub-lease or he may assign his interest in the lease to some one else.

16.9.1 Types of Lease

Lease may be of two types (*i*) building lease and (*ii*) occuption lease.

Building lease

Open land is leased out on payment of periodic consideration known as 'Ground Rent'. The lessee shall improve the land at his own cost. Period of lease is usually 50, 98, 99, or 999 years.

Covenants and conditions setting forth the rights and obligations of each part to the lease, including covenant on the part of the lessee to deliver up the premisess on the determination of the term.

Occupation lease

Complete property consisting of the land and building is given on lease on payment of periodic consideration known as 'Rack Rent' that is full rent of the property which is not outside the orbit of the Rent Control Act, except for exempted properties.

16.9.2 Value of Lessor's Interest

The lessor's interest in a property leased out will consist of:

(*i*) Capitalised value of the lease rent for the unexpired period of lease.

(*ii*) Present value of reversion to the property at the expiry of the lease period.

16.9.3 Lessee's Interest

Lessee's interest in the property leased out consists of:

(*i*) Profit rental for the unexpired period of the lease (for valuation purpose standard rent should be considered), and

(*ii*) Interest on the cost of improvement if any as per the covenant of the lease.

16.10.0 MORTGAGE

The owner of a freehold or leasehold property interested to have a loan, grants an interest in his property to other person as a security against the loan advanced by that person. The owner of the property is said to perform a mortgage.

The person granting such interest is known as the mortgagor and the person advancing loan for such interest is known as the mortgagee.

In the mortgage deed, the mortgagor agrees to repay the loan, and when the loan is fully repaid, the owner of the property has got a power to recover his property from the mortgagee. This is termed as equity of redemption.

16.11.0 ANNUAL REPAIRS AND MAINTENANCE

Annual repairs and maintenance falls under 'outgoings' in respect of a structure. The amount spent on this account depends upon various factors— age of the structure, situation of it with respect to climatic conditions, specification of the works, nature of use, nature of maintenance, etc.

Repairs and maintenance directly affects the age of the sturcture. Adequate maintenance and repairs prolong the life of the structure which means indirect increase in real value. A building constructed with improved specification and with quality control will have longer life and minimum cost in use. As the outgoings of such a structure will be less, there will be increase in the capitalised value.

16.11.1 Capital Invested for Repair Works

In cases of repairs and rehabilitation of old structures, economics of the cost involved and the capital to be invested for the work arises. The owner would like to know if the redemption of the capital invested at a rate and at interest on capital would be possible in specified period of time. If the owner is satisfied and considers that the capital would be fully safe guarded, only then he would be interested in investing in such venture.

16.12.0 METHODS OF ESTIMATING COST DEPRECIATION

There are various methods of ascertaining the cost depreciation of a property. Some of them are:

(*i*) **Straight line method.** This is the simplest method for working out the depreciation of a property.

In this method, it is assumed that property loses its value at uniform rate yearly. A salvage or scrap value is assumed.

$$D = \left(\frac{C - S}{n}\right)$$

where, D = annual depreciation, C = original cost, S = salvage or scrap value, and n = life of the property in years.

(*ii*) **Constant percentage method.** The method is also known as declining balance method or written down value or equal percentage method. In this method, the value of the property reduces yearly by a constant percentage of the residual value of the preceeding year.

Let C = original cost, S = salvage or scrap value,

n = number of years and p = constant percentage.

Then the value of the property at the end of first year

$$= C - pC = C - (1 - p)$$

Value of the property at the end of the second year

$$= C\,(1 - p\,C) - C\,(1 - p\,C)\,p = C\,(1 - p)^2$$

Value of the property at the end of n years

$$= C(1 - p)^n$$

Which is the salvage or scrap value

The formula will fail when the value of $S = 0$

(*iii*) **Quantity survey method.** This is widely used and is a reasonable method.

The building whose depreciated value is to be ascertained is surveyed in details and loss in value owing to physical deterioration is worked out. A detailed estimate is prepared adopting approximate reduced rates of items and the value is worked out. The cost of repairs or restoration of the building is also estimated. These shall have no relation to some fixed percentage to the cost of the property. The basis of this method is observation and not assumption.

(*iv*) **Sinking fund method**. In this method, the depreciation of a property is assumed to be equal to the annual sinking fund set aside by the owner and investing the same every year at compound rate of interest so that after a specified period, the amount accumulated would be sufficient to meet the cost of restoration of the building.

(*v*) **Unit cost method.** This method of calculating depreciation is applicable to machines and other equipments where it is possible to work out the cost per unit out put. In this method, it is assumed that a machine after n years of use will give the same unit cost of out put during its remaining years.

16.13.0 COST OF CONSTRUCTION

In calculating depreciation or ascertaining the valuation of a building, it becomes necessary to assume the cost of construction.

The recognised methods of calculating the cost of construction for the purpose are:

(*i*) Area of building,

(*ii*) Cubical content of building, and

(*iii*) Detailed or itemwise method.

These have been explained in paragraph 2.2.0 and of Chapter 2.

16.14.0 VALUATION FORMULAE AND TABLES

Efficient computation is needed for valuation of property and ascertaining the probable interest that the capital could earn in a certain period, the present value of the sum to be invested at a deferred date, the amount to be set aside annually for replacement of a part or major repairs of building to be undertaken at a later date or at the end of its estimated life, the capital that could be invested on property, the net income from which one would be able to capitalise the value of the property, etc.

Detailed calculation of these is laborious and time consuming. Formulae for different computations have been developed and in order to save time and reduce chances of error in computation, valuation tables have been developed on the basis of first principles and mathematical formulae.

16.14.1 Finding Out the Amount Accumulated at the Given Term

To find the amount accumulated on Rs. 1.00 at the rate of interest i after n years.

$P = (1 + i)^{n)}$, Where, P = Amount at the end of the term,

i = Rate of interest p.a. compound,

n = Number of years.

See Table 16.1 in Appendix I

Example 16.2. *It is estimated that the cost of repairs of a house would be Rs. 50,000.00. The tenant agreed to pay 50% of the amount without any other condition and paid his share. The owner fails to repair the house in two years and the cost of repairs rises to Rs. 65,000.00 and as agreed earlier, the tenant again agreed to share 50% of the cost. Calculate what balance amount the tenant would have to pay? The prevailing rate of interest being 10%.*

The amount of Re. 1.00 at 10% interest will grow to,

$P = (1 + i)^n$, Where, $i = 0.10$, $n = 2$

$= (1 + 0.10)^2$

$= 1.1^2 = 1.21$

The amount paid by the tenant was Rs. 25,000.00 has grown to

$= 1.21 \times 25{,}000.00$

= Rs. 30,250.00

The sum payable now by the tenant, 50% of Rs. 65,000.00

= Rs. 32,500.00

The balance amount payable = Rs. 32,500.00 − Rs. 30,250.00

= Rs. 2,250.00

16.14.2 Finding Out The Present Value, P.V.

To find the present value, P.V. of Re. 1.00 receivable at the end of a given term, n with rate of interest, i.

$$\text{P.V.} = \frac{1}{(1+i)^n}$$ Where, i = Rate of interest p.a. compound

n = Number of years.

The formula is actually the reverse of formula 16.14.1.

See Table 16.2 in Appendix I

Example 16.3. *A tank has an area of 200 sqm and is 3m deep. The price of the adjoining solid land is Rs. 100.00 per sqm, 10 years hence. If the cost of consolidated earth filling inclusive*

of all costs is Rs. 10.00 per cum, find out the value of the tank portion of the land assuming that it would require 10 years for the made up soil to be solid land. A rate of interest of 6% may be adopted to work out the present value of the land.

The cost of filling of the tank = 200 × 3 × 10.00 = Rs. 6,000.00

The cost of filling per sqm $= \frac{6,000}{200} =$ Rs. 30.00

The price of adjoining solid land, 10 years hence = Rs. 100.00 per sqm

P.V. pf Re.1.00 in 10 years at 6% interest $= \frac{1}{(1+0.06)^{10}} = 0.56.$

as here, $i = 0.06$ and $n = 10$.

P.V. of the land after filling = 100.00 × 0.56 = Rs. 56.00

Deducting the cost of filling Rs. 30.00

Rate of the tank portion = Rs. 26.00 per sqm

The formula can be used for finding the discounted value of an amount payable or receivable in future to the present value, when such valuation becomes necessary for finding the present value.

Example 16.4. *Find out the discounted value of Rs. 100.00 lac receivable in the 9th year hence to the present value at discount rate of 13%.*

$$\text{P.V. of Re. } 1.00 = \frac{1}{(1+i)^n} \quad \text{here, } i = 0.13, \; n = 8$$

$$= \frac{1}{(1+0.13)^8}$$

$$= 0.3762$$

∴ P.V. of 100.00 lac = 100 × 0.3762

= Rs. 37.62 lac.

16.14.3 Finding out the amount to which the Invested Amount will grow in given terms

$$\text{Amount, } A = \frac{(1+i)^n - 1}{i}$$

Where, A = Amount to which Re. 1.00 p.a. invested at the end of each year will accumulate in a given time,

i = Rate of interest, compound,

n = Number of years.

See Table 16.3 in Appendix I

The following three points are to be noted:

(*i*) Re. 1.00 becomes due to be invested at the end of the year,

(*ii*) Re. 1.00 gets added at the end of each year,

(*iii*) Re. 1.00 will be added at the end of the period.

Example 16.5. *A tenanted house is required to be repaired at a cost of Rs. 50,000.00. The tenants ask the landlord to repair the house investing his fund and agree to pay the amount required for repairs without any obligation after 10 years. What amount will have to be deposited by the tenants yearly in a bank, if the prevailing rate of interest was 12% for the recurring deposit.*

The amount of Re. 1.00 p.a. at 12% interest in 10 years would be,

$$= \frac{(1+i)^n - 1}{i} = \frac{(1+0.12)^{10} - 1}{0.12} \qquad \text{here, } i = 0.12$$

$$= 17.55 \qquad n = 10$$

For growing Rs.17.55, amount to be deposited p.a. is Re. 1.00 for 10 years.

Hence, for growing 50,000.00 amount to be deposited p.a. to the bank $= \dfrac{\text{Rs. } 50{,}000.00}{17.55}$

= Rs. 2,849.00

The tenants shall have to deposit Rs. 2,849.00 p.a to the bank at the rate of interest 12% to pay Rs. 50,000.00 to the landlord after 10 years.

16.14.4 Annual Sinking Fund

Annual Sinking Fund is the fund set aside annually out of the annual income from the capital invested which at the compound rate of interest will grow by the end of the term to replace the capital invested or for a major repair or replacement of an important part after expiry of its life.

In case of a building, a sinking fund may be created to replace the building after expiry of its calculated life fully or for major rehabilitation and renovation work after a lapse of a definite period.

The formula for sinking fund is the reverse of the formula of the amount of Rs. 1.00 per annum as in 15.13.3. The amount set aside for sinking fund is deposited in bank to carry an interest and grow to the required amount in a definite period.

Sinking fund, $S = \dfrac{i}{(1+i)^n - 1}$ where, S = Amount of sinking fund,

i = Compound rate of interest p.a. on the amount deposited,

n = Number of years.

See Table 16.4 in Appendix I

Example 16.6. *A person purchases a building at a cost of Rs. 2,00,000.00, it is anticipated that the building would require a thorough repair and renovation after 25 years at an estimated cost of Rs. 1,00,000.00 at that time. What amount should the person set aside in a bank at an interest of 4% to meet the future renovation cost.*

$$S = \frac{i}{(1+i)^n - 1} \qquad \text{here, } i = 0.40,\ n = 25$$

$$= \frac{0.04}{(1+0.04)^{25} - 1} = 0.024$$

For Re. 1.00, the annual sinking fund should be Rs. 0.024,

For Rs. 1,00,000.00, the annual sinking fund would be

1,00,000 × 0.024 = 2,400.00.

16.14.5 Year's Purchase

Year's purchase is the figure or multiplier which when multiplied by the net income gives the capitalised value of a property on the material date of valuation, Y.P.

It indicates how many times the annual income is secured for its value.

Capitalised value = Net income × Y.P.

$$\therefore \quad \text{Y.P.} = \frac{100}{i} \text{ or } \frac{1}{i} \qquad \text{Where, } i = \text{Rate percentage of net income.}$$

Example 16.7. *A person acquires a property at a cost of Rs. 10,000.00 which is expected to yield 5% net profit (exclusive of all outgoings). What is the year's purchase?*

$$\text{Capitalised value} = \text{Net income} \times \text{Y.P.}$$

$$10{,}000 = 500 \times \text{Y.P.}$$

$$\therefore \quad \text{Y.P.} = \frac{10{,}000}{500} = 20$$

$$\text{Again} \quad \text{Y.P.} = \frac{100}{i} \text{ or } \frac{1}{i} \qquad \text{where, } i = \text{rate of profit (interest)}$$

$$= \frac{100}{5} = 20 \text{ or } \frac{1}{5} = 0.20$$

This is the case of perpetuity i.e. without any definite time limit.

In practice the cases are not so simple as the acquisition of a property may not be perpetual, but may be for a fixed period and the person acquiring the property would like that the capitalised value is redeemed in the period of possession of the property and that too at the present value.

This may be calculated by the use of the formula for finding out the amount to which Rs. 1.00 p.a. invested at the end of each year will accumulate in a given time at compound rate of interest, and the dividing by the amount of Re. 1.00 accumulated for the same number of years, i.e. $(1 + i)^n$

$$\text{Y.P.} = \frac{(1+i)^n - 1}{i} \Big/ (1+i)^n = \frac{(1+i)^n - 1}{i\,(1+i)^n}$$

Referring back to the previous example, where $i = 0.05$ and considering for a period of 10 years.

$$\frac{(1+i)^n - 1}{i} = \frac{(1+0.05)^{10} - 1}{0.05} = 12.58$$

$$\text{and} \quad (1+i)^n = (1+0.05)^{10} = 1.63$$

$$\therefore \quad \text{Y.P.} = \frac{12.58}{1.63} = 7.723$$

The capitalised value of Rs. 500.00 p.a after 10 years

= 500.00 × 7.723

= Rs. 3861.50

Or it may be stated that the net income of Rs. 500.00 with Year's Purchase 7.723 would produce a capitalised value of the property Rs. 3,861.50.

Capitalised value = Net income × Y.P.

Rs. 3,861.50 = Rs. 500 × 7.723

This is known as Year's Purchase – Single rate.

An investor is still not satisfied, he may like his investment to be safe guarded by setting aside a sum as sinking fund at a rate of interest which will be able to replace the property after the expiry of the period.

Now, to find out the present value of Re.1.00 per annum for given number of years, allowing simple interest at i per annum on capital and accumulation of annual sinking fund at 's' rate of interest per annum, let the assumed value to be V.

In this case, the two values are to be added.

Let the present value = V,

Each annual instalment would be $V \times i$ and the sinking fund instalment

$$= V \times \frac{s}{(1+s)^n - 1}$$

$$\therefore \quad 1 = Vi + V\frac{s}{(1+s)^n - 1} \quad \text{or} \quad 1 = V\left[i + \frac{s}{(1+s)^n - 1}\right]$$

$$V = \frac{1}{i + \dfrac{s}{(1+s)^n - 1}} = \frac{1}{i+s}$$

Where, $$S = \frac{s}{(1+s)^n - 1}$$

Table 16.5

V is the present value or Year's purchase at dual rate.

$$= \frac{1}{\text{Rate of simple interest on capital} + \text{Accumulation of amount of sinking fund per annum}}$$

It is seen that in case of income of short duration, consideration has to be made of the following types of interest while fixing the value of Y.P.

(*i*) Rate of interest for capital – which may be termed as remunerative rate of interest (*i*)

(*ii*) Rate of interest for redemption of capital for sinking fund — which may be termed as accumulative rate of interest (*s*).

Sinking fund rates are generally lower. When the rates on both the accounts are the same, the Y.P. is called on Single Rate. When the rates are different, the Y.P. is termed on Duel Rate.

Single rate Y.P. at 12% for 10 years is 5.65 and Duel rate Y.P. at 12% and 3% for 10 years is 4.83. The difference is due to adoption of different rates for the sinking funds.

The Year's purchase Y.P. may be defined as the present value of the net income of a property after a certain period with due consideration of the remunerative rate of interest on the capital and the accumulative rate of interest for redemption of the capital.

16.14.6 Finding Out Y.P. of Reversion to a Perpetuity After a Given Number of Years

Single rate of Y.P. is used for income produced by freehold properties and the role of sinking fund in the case would be to make arithmatical asjustment to the Y.P. merely to permit valuation to be made for terminal incomes. As a matter of fact, the annual sinking fund is a reducing agent in the formula and it devalues Y.P. to such an extent that no value is attached to the period during which there is no income flow.

To find Y.P. of reversion to a perpetuity after a given number of years.

In this case, the Y.P. for incomes continue up to the perpetuity, but starts at some future date. Such incomes are known as deferred incomes and as Y.P. for non-income period is not available, Y.P. for deferred income can be worked out from the following equation.

$$\begin{bmatrix}\text{Y.P. for deferred income}\\ \text{of a reversion to perpetuity}\end{bmatrix} = \begin{bmatrix}\text{Y.P. in}\\ \text{perpetuity}\end{bmatrix} - \begin{bmatrix}\text{Y.P. for the non-income}\\ \text{period on single rate basis.}\end{bmatrix}$$

or $\dfrac{1}{i} - \dfrac{1}{i + \dfrac{i}{(1+i)^n - 1}}$ Where, i = Rate of interest

n = Number of years for the non-income period.

Table 15.6

Example 16.8. Net income from a property is Rs. 1,200.00.

Calculate the capitalised value at the rate of 12% p.a. (a) in perpetuity and (b) verify the value by calculating the same in two parts

(*i*) for 10 years and (*ii*) reversion to perpetuity.

(*a*) Y.P. in perpetuity at the rate of 12% = 100/12 = 8.33.

Capitalised value = 8.33 × 1,200.00 = Rs. 10,000.00

(*b*) The above result may be verified by addition of the two parts

(*i*) **First 10 years.** Y.P. on the single rate basis according to formula 15.13.5

As per Table Y.P. is 5.65,

Capitalised value = 5.65 × 1,200.00 = 6,780.00

(*ii*) **Reversion to perpetuity at the rate.** of 12% = 8.33 – 5.65 =2.68

Capitalised value = 2.68 × 1,200.00 = 3,216.00

Rs. 9,996.00

say Rs. 10,000.00

16.14.7 Finding the Annuity Re. 1.00 Will Purchase on the Single Rate Principle

Annuity = Return on capital + Return of capital

$$A = i + s$$

$$A = i + \frac{i}{(1+i)^n - 1}$$

$$= \frac{i + (1+i)^n}{(i+i)^n - 1}$$

w here, i = Rate of interest p.a.

s = Annual sinking fund

n = Number of years

This formula is useful in calculation of annual equal instalments with capital and interest and amortisation cost with interest. Again annuity is the inverse of Year's Purchase.

Example 16.9. *A person purchases a house at Rs. 20,000.00 on hire purchase basis. The amount is payable in 15 equal annual instalment at 6% interest. Calculate the annual instalment payable.*

Annual instalment, $A = \dfrac{i\,(1+i)^n}{(1+i)-1}$ Here, $i = 0.06$
$n = 15$

$$A = \frac{0.06\,(1+0.06)^{15}}{(1+0.06)^{15}-1}$$

$$= 0.10296$$

Annual instalment of Rs. 20,000.00 is $0.10296 \times 20{,}000.00$

= Rs. 2,059.20

16.14.8 Finding the Depreciation Percentage Based on Sinking Fund Method

Depreciation percentage = $(S \times A)\,100$

Where, S = Annual sinking fund, A = Amount invested.

As per formula 16.14.4, sinking fund at given rate of interest for the total life of a building,

Sinking fund, $S = \dfrac{i}{(1+i)^n - 1}$ Where, n = Age of the building

i = Rate of interest of investment in S.F. (compound)

As per formula 16.14.3, amount of Rs. 1.00 p.a invested at the end of each year will accumulate in a given time at compound rate of interest

$$A = \frac{(1+i)^n - 1}{i}$$

Example 16.10.

(*i*) *Calculate the depreciation percentage based on sinking fund method for a building having a life of 50 years and of age 16 years at the rate of 4%.*

(*ii*) *What would be the depreciation percentage for the above building at the age of 40 years at the rate of 9%.*

(*iii*) *Calculate the depreciation replacement cost of the building, if the cost of the building is estimated at Rs. 4,80,000.00 as if new in both the cases.*

(*i*) $S = \dfrac{i}{(1+i)^n - 1} = \dfrac{0.04}{(1+0.04)^{50} - 1} = 0.007$ Here, $i = 0.04$
$n = 50$ (life)
$n = 16$ (age)

$$A = \frac{(1+i)^n - 1}{i} = \frac{(1 = 0.04)^{16} - 1}{0.04} = 21.82$$

$\therefore$ Depreciation percentage = $(S \times A)\,100$

$= (0.007 \times 21.82)\,100 = 15.27\%$

(*ii*) $S = \dfrac{i}{(1+i)^n - 1} = \dfrac{0.05}{(1+0.05)^{50} - 1} = 0.005$ Here, $i = 0.05$
$n = 40$ (age)

$$A = \frac{(1+i)^n - 1}{i} = \frac{(1+0.05)^{40} - 1}{0.05} = 120.80$$

$\therefore$ Depreciation percentage $= (S \times A)\ 100$

$= (0.005 \times 120.80)100 = 60.4\%$

The building cost as if newly constructed is Rs. 4,80,000.00

In the first case, depreciation at the rate of 4% for life 50 years and age 16 years is 15.27%

Depreciation = 15.27 × Rs. 4,80,000.00 = Rs. 73,296.00

$\therefore$ Depreciated cost of the building

= Rs.4,80,000.00 – Rs. 73,296.00

= Rs.4,06,704.00

In the second case,

Depreciation at the rate of 5% for life 50 years and age 40 years = 60.40%

Depreciation = 60.40% of Rs. 4,80,000.00 = Rs. 2,89,920.00

$\therefore$ Depreciation value of the building = Rs. 4,80,000.00 – Rs. 2,89,920.00. = Rs. 1,90,080.00

16.14.9 Miscellaneous Examples

Example 16.11. *The tenants of a building have agreed to return a sum of Rs. 37,500.00 to the owner of the building which he has spent on repairs. It is agreed that the amount should be returned in 25 regular yearly instalments with 8% interest. Work out the yearly instalment. The present value of Re.1.00 per annum allowing interest on capital at 8% (adding for redemption of capital at 8%) is 10,675.00 I.S. 82. Annuity of Rs. 37,500.00 payable in 25 years at 8% interest is to be found out.*

The present value of Rs. 1.00 per annum as per condition is 10.675.00

$\therefore$ Annuity of Rs. 37,500.00 $= \dfrac{37{,}500}{10{,}675}$

= Rs. 3,513.00.

Example 16.12. *The tenants of a building have agreed to give an annual increment in rent of Rs.1,200.00 for twenty years, if the owner had agreed to secure and repair the building. What amount should the owner spend on repair now, allowing interest at 8%. The present value of an annuity of Rs.1.00 per annum at 8% for 20 years is 9.818.* I.S. '83

Annual instalment, annuity is Rs. 1,200.00

The present value of annuity of Rs. 1.00 per annum at 8% for 20 years is 9.818.

Capitalised value = annual instalement × annuity of Re. 1.00

= 1,200 × 9.818

= Rs. 11,782.00

Example 16.13. *An old building is to be let out on lease for 10 years at a monthly rent of Rs. 1,000.00. The tenants pay an advance for execution of repairs to the landlord a sum of Rs. 50,000.00 as loan to be recovered in 10 years at the rate of interest at 8% per annum. Determine the amount of rent to be reduced per month for such loan.*

Loan amount, *i.e.* the capital invested = Rs. 50,000.00 repayable in equal monthly instalments with 8% interest in 10 years.

Annual instalment, annuity of Re. 1.00 p.a.

$$1 + \frac{i}{(1+i)^n - 1}$$

where, i = annual interest rate 0.08

n = number of years, 10

Annuity of Re. 1.00 p.a. $= 0.08 + \frac{0.08}{(1+0.08)^{10} - 1}$

$$= 0.08 + \frac{0.08}{1.08^{10} - 1} = 0.08 + \frac{0.08}{2.59 - 1}$$

$$= 0.08 + \frac{0.08}{1.59} = 0.08 + 0.069 = 0.149$$

Annual instalment of Rs. 50,000.00 = 50,000 × 0.149 = Rs. 7,450.00

∴ Monthly instalment = 7450/12 = Rs.621.00

Monthly rent to be reduced = Rs.621.00.

17

COMPUTERISED ESTIMATION OF QUANTITIES OF WORK

17.1.0 INTRODUCTION

The present age is termed as computer age. Computer is being introduced in all spheres of life, in all sorts of works—small and large, simple and complicated, difficult and easy. Introduction of computer saves enormous time in calculation of complicated arithmetic and solving difficult problems. It produces results error-free. In Engineering works, various calculations are required to be performed which are not only complicated and time consuming, but also many a time boring and susceptible to human error. Repetitive calculations are prone to error and an incorrect calculation may result severe consequences. The calculations of Engineering matters need to be error-free. This can be achieved to a very high degree by introduction of computer.

Computer has already made its presence felt in the design of structures and planning. Computer is being used in these fields gainfully and has shown justification of introduction.

Estimating is a subject involving numerous calculations which are time consuming and subject to human error. The computer can be suitably used for saving time and obtaining error-free results in Estimation.

17.2.0 COMPUTER PROGRAMME

A programme solves a particular problem with the help of a computer. A programme writes the instructions and data in a subset of English like language called the programming language. A computer is basically a series of statements conveying instructions to get a certain job done. The statements of an estimation job are framed on the basis of input information obtained from the drawing sheets of the structure.

The instructions are arranged serially according to the sequence of operations. While arranging the information serially, these are coded according to the computer language.

17.2.1 Estimation Programme

A Demo programme is written in *Q* basic language and can be run in any Personal Computer— supporting the language.

17.2.2 Assumptions

It is assumed from the basic drawing that the walls are straight line constructions and the connecting walls are always perpendicular to each other.

17.2.3 Inputs

The following inputs are required. All the dimensions are in millimetre. The variable names used in the programme for each input is shown as below:

Input	Variable names
Breadth of single brick flat soling	bsbfsol
Height of single brick flat soling	hsbfsol
Breadth of cement concrete	bccon
Height of cement concrete	hccon
Breadth of first footing	bffoot
Height of first footing	hffoot
Breadth of second footing	bsfoot
Height of second footing	hsfoot
Breadth of third footing	btfoot
Height of third footing	htfoot
Breadth of wall	bwall
Height of wall	hwall
Breadth of DPC	bdpc
Height of DPC	hdpc
Number of walls	nwall
Length of walls	wl(i)

For each wall, the programme asks whether it is connected to any other wall so as to take care of the overlap volume.

The following out puts are obntained.

Earthwork in excavation, Single brick flat soling, Volume of cement concrete base, first, second and third footing lengths, DPC area, Earthwork in back filling of the foundation trenches and Earthwork in plinth filling.

17.3.0 TEST CASE. Ref. Example –2.10

A test case data is built in the programme. These get displayed to the user in the beginning. Any volume can be changed selectively by the user.

The programme is simple demonstration of the effective use of computer calculation and design. The features of this programme shows how to frame the programme for the inputs from the drawing and how to arrange those effectively, quickly and also to get more accurate results.

17.4.0 PROGRAMME

```
DIM wl (20)
CLS
PRINT "All dimensions to be put in millimeter only"
PRINT : PRINT
PRINT "Press any key to continue"
1 IF INKEYS = " " THEN 1
REM INPUT "Breadth of single brick flat soil          ", bsbfsoil
REM INPUT "Height of single brick flat soil           ", hsbfsoil
REM INPUT "Breadth of cement concrete                 ", bscon
REM INPUT "Height of cement concrete                  ", hscon
REM INPUT "Breadth of first footing                   ", bffoot
```

```
REM INPUT "Height of first footing                ", hffoot
REM INPUT "Breadth of second footing              ", bsfoot
REM INPUT "Height of second footing               ", hsfoot
REM INPUT "Breadth of third footing               ", btfoot
REM INPUT "Height of third footing                ", htfoot
REM INPUT "Breadth of wall                        ", bwall
REM INPUT "Height of wall                         ", Hwall
REM INPUT "Breadth of DPC                         ", Bdpc
REM INPUT "Height of DPC                          ", hdpc
REM INPUT "Number of walls                        ", nwall
3
RESET
READ bsbfsoil
READ hsbfsoil
READ bscon
READ hscon
READ bffoot
READ hffoot
READ bsfoot
READ hsfoot
READ btfoot
READ htfoot
READ bwall
READ hwall
READ bdpc
READ hdpc
READ nwall
4
CLS
LPRINT " 1 ...Breadth of single brick flat soil   ", bsbfsoil
LPRINT " 2 ...Height of single brick flat soil    ", hsbfsoil
LPRINT " 3 ...Breadth of cement concrete          ", bscon
LPRINT " 4 ...Height of cement concrete           ", hscon
LPRINT " 5 ...Breadth of first footing            ", bffoot
LPRINT " 6 ...Height of first footing             ", hffoot
LPRINT " 7 ...Breadth of second footing           ", bsfoot
LPRINT " 8 ...Height of second footing            ", hsfoot
LPRINT " 9 ...Breadth of third footing            ", btfoot
```

```
LPRINT " 10 ...Height of third footing                    ", htfoot
LPRINT " 11 ...Breadth of wall                            ", bwall
LPRINT " 12 ...Height of wall                             ", hwall
LPRINT " 13 ...Breadth of DPC                             ", bdpc
LPRINT " 14 ...Height of DPC                              ", hdpc
LPRINT " 15 ...Number of walls                            ", nwall
LPRINT
LPRINT
LPRINT " Dimensions are in millimeter "
LPRINT : LPRINT
5
INPUT "Want to change any value ? ", a$
IF a$ = "n" OR a$ = "N" THEN GOTO 20
INPUT " type the item number you would like to change", num
IF num = 1 THEN INPUT "Breadth of single brick flat soil", bsbfsoil
IF num = 2 THEN INPUT "Height of single brick flat soil ", hsbfsoil
IF num = 3 THEN INPUT "Breadth of cement concrete ",bscon
IF num = 4 THEN INPUT "Height of cement concrete ", hscon
IF num = 5 THEN INPUT "Breadth of first footing ", bffoot
IF num = 6 THEN INPUT "Height of first footing ", hffoot
IF num = 7 THEN INPUT "Breadth of second footing", bsfoot
IF num = 8 THEN INPUT "Height of second footing ", hsfoot
IF num = 9 THEN INPUT "Breadth of third footing ", btfoot
IF num = 10 THEN INPUT "Height of third footing ", htfoot
IF num = 11 THEN INPUT "Breadth of wall ", bwall
IF num = 12 THEN INPUT "Height of wall ", hwall
IF num = 13 THEN INPUT "Breadth of DPC ", bdpc
IF num = 14 THEN INPUT "Height of DPC ", hdpc
IF num = 15 THEN INPUT "Number of walls ", nwall
GOTO 5
20 evol = 0
totleng = 0 : totfleng = 0 : totsleng = 0 : tottleng = 0
FOR i = 1 TO nwall
LPRINT "Length of wall "; i;
PIRNT "length of wall ", i
a$ = "n"
```

```
n = 0
INPUT wl (i)
LPRINT wl (i)
REM READ wl (i)
IF i > = 2 THEN 25 ELSE 30
2F INPUT "is the wall connected to any wall already described ?" , a$
n = 0
30 IF a$ = "Y" OR a$ = "Y" THEN 35 ELSE 40
35 INPUT "Number of sides connected to walls described ? ", n
40 leng = wl (i) – n * ((bsbfsoil – bwall) / 2)
fleng = wl (i) – n * ((bffoot – bwall) / 2)
sleng = wl (i) – n * ((bsfoot – bwall) / 2)
tleng = wl (i) – n * ((btfoot – bwall) / 2)
IF n = 1 THEN leng = wl (i) : fleng = wl (i) : sleng = wl (i) : tleng = wl (i)
IF a$ = "n" OR a$ = "N" THEN leng = wl (i) + (bsbfsoil – bwall)
IF a$ = "n" OR a$ = "N" THEN fleng = wl (i) + (bffoot – bwall)
IF a$ = "n" OR a$ = "N" THEN sleng = wl (i) + (bsfoot – bwall)
IF a$ = "n" OR a$ = "N" THEN tleng = wl (i) + (btfoot – bwall)
PRINT "Base length =" ; leng; "mm"
PRINT "First footing length = "; fleng ; "mm"
PRINT "Second footing length = "; sleng ; "mm"
PRINT "Third footing length = "; tleng ; "mm"
totleng = totleng + leng
totfleng = fleng + totfleng
totfsleng = totsleng + sleng
tottleng = tottleng + tleng
evol = evol + leng * bsbfsoil * (hsbfsoil + hscon + hffoot + hsfoot + htfoot)
PRINT
a$ = "n"
NEXT i
LPRINT : LPRINT
LPRINT " The Volume of Earth work = "; evol; "cu mm"
LPRINT : LPRINT
LPRINT " Single brick flat soling in foundation "; totleng * bsbfsoil ; " sq mm
LPRINT " Cement concrete in foundation " ; totleng * bacon * hscon; " cu mm"
LPRINT " Brick work in cement morter in foundation and footing "
```

```
f1 = totfleng * bffoot * hffoot
LPRINT : LPRINT
LPRINT "Footing 1 "; f1 : " cu mm"
f2 = totsleng * bsfoot * hsfoot
LPRINT "Footing 2 "; f2 ; "cu mm"
f3 = tottleng * btfoot * htfoot
LPRINT "Footing 3 "; f3; " cu mm"
LPRINT "Plinth "; tottleng * bwall * (hwall - hdpc) ; " cu mm"
LPRINT : LPRINT
INPUT "Number of doors please ", numdo
LPRINT "D.P.C Area =" ; (tottleng - numdo * 1000) * bdpc ; " sq mm"
LPRINT : LPRINT
x2 = totleng * bsbfsoil * hsbfsoil
x3 = totleng * bscon * hscon
f = f1 + f2 + f3
x = evol – x2 – x3 – f
LPRINT "Earthwork in back filling of trench"; x; "cu mm"
LPRINT : LPRINT
INPUT " Number of rooms ? ", nroom
pfill = 0
INPUT "Height of Hard crust in mm ", hh
FOR i = 1 TO nroom
PRINT " length of room in mm "; i;
INPUT room
PRINT "breadth of room in mm "; i;
INPUT broom
pfill = pfill = lroom * broom * hh
NEXT i
LPRINT : LPRINT
LPIRNT "Earth work in plinth filling = "; pfill; " cu mm"
INPUT "More Calculations ? ", cal$
IN cal$ = "Y"  OR cal$ = "Y" THEN GOTO 3
DATA 800, 75, 800, 150, 500, 150, 375, 150, 250, 150, 250, 600, 250, 25, 5
REM DATA 7750, 7750, 4000, 4000, 4000
```

Press any key to continue

1 ...Breadth of single brick flat soil	800
2 ...Height of single brick flat soil	75
3 ...Breadth of cement concrete	800
4 ...Height of cement concrete	150
5 ...Breadth of first footing	500
6 ...Height of first footing	150
7 ...Breadth of second footing	375
8 ...Height of second footing	150
9 ...Breadth of third footing	250
10 ...Height of third footing	150
11 ...Breadth of wall	250
12 ...Height of wall	600
13 ...Breadth of DPC	250
14 ...Height of DPC	25
15 ...Number of walls	5

Dimensions are in millimeter

Length of wall 1 7750

Length of wall 2 7750

Length of wall 3 4000

Length of wall 4 4000

Length of wall 5 4000

The Volume of earth work = 1.4553E+10 cu mm

Single brick flat soling in foundation 2.156E+07 sq mm

Cement concrete in foundation 3.234E+09 cu mm

Brick work in cement morter in foundation and footing

Footing 1 2.04375E+09 cu mm

Footing 2 1.539844E+09 cu mm

Footing 3 1.03125E+09 cu mm

Plinth 3.953125E+09 cu mm

D.P.C. area = 6375000 sq mm

D.P.C. Area = 6375000 sq mm

Earthwork in back filling of trench 5.087156E+09 cu mm

Earthwork in plinth filling = 1.12E + 10 cu mm

17.5.0 REDUCING THE UNITS

The unit in programming was millimeter. The units of the results are obviously in millimeter, sq. millimeter or cubic millimeter. These need to reduced to conventional units of meter, sq meter or cubic meter as used in practice.

Earthwork in excavation in foundation

$$1.4553E + 10 \text{ cu mm} = 1.4553 \times \frac{10^{10}}{10^9} = 14.553 \text{ cum.}$$

Single brick flat soling

$$2.156E + 07 \text{ sq.mm} = 2.156 \times \frac{10^7}{10^6}$$

$$= 21.56 \text{ sq.mm}$$

Cement concrete in foundation

$$3.234E + 09 \text{ cu mm} = 3.234 \times \frac{10^9}{10^9} = 3.234 \text{ cum}$$

Brickwork in cement mortar in foundation and plinth

$$\text{Footing 1 } 2.04375E + 09 \text{ cu mm} = 2.04375 \times \frac{10^9}{10^9} = 2.04375 \text{ cum}$$

$$\text{Footing 2 } 1.539844E + 09 \text{ cu mm} = 1.539844 \times \frac{10^9}{10^9} = 1.539844 \text{ cum}$$

$$\text{Footing 3 } 1.03125E + 09 \text{ cu mm} = 1.03125 \times \frac{10^9}{10^9} = 1.03125 \text{ cum}$$

$$\text{Plinth } 3.953125E + 09 \text{ cu mm} = 3.953125 \times \frac{10^9}{10^9} = 3.953125 \text{ cum}$$

$$\text{DPC area } 6375000 \text{ sq.mm} = 6375000 \times \frac{1}{10^6} = 6.375 \text{ sqm}$$

Earthwork in back filling = 5.087156E + 09 cu mm

$$= 5.087156 \times \frac{10^9}{10^9}$$

$$= 5.087156 \text{ cum}$$

Earthwork in plinth filling = 1.12E + 10 cumm

$$= 1.12 \times \frac{10^{10}}{10^9}$$

$$= 11.2 \text{cum}$$

17.6.0 COMPARISON OF THE QUANTITIES WITH THE MAUALLY CALCULATED QUANTITIES

Referring to example at page 20, Example 2.10

	Item of work	*Quantity as manually calculated*	*Quantity as per computer*
1.	Earthwork in excavation in foundation	14.553 cum	14.553 cum
2.	Single brick flat soling	21.56 sqm	21.56 sqm
3.	Cement concrete in foundation (1 : 3 : 6)	3.234 cm	3.234 cum
4.	Brickwork in foundation and plinth (1 : 6)		
	Footing I	2.044 cum	2.044 cum
	Footing II	1.54 cum	1.54 cum
	Footing III	1.031 cum	1.031 cum
	Plinth	3.953 cum	3.953 cum
5.	DPC	6.375 sqm	6.375 sqm
6.	Earthwork in back filling	5.087 cum	5.087 cum
7.	Earthwork in plinth filling	11.20 cum	11.20 cum

18

CONSTRUCTION MANAGEMENT

18.1.0 CONSTRUCTION MANAGEMENT

In a developing country, volume of construction activity goes on increasing. So has construction component increased in many folds in recent times in our country.

The primary goal of a project is a quality product within budget, on time and with little or no litigation. To achieve such goal it is essential that the project is managed properly and effectively. Due to increase in volume of construction activity, its diversity and input of modern techniques and innovations, the traditional concept of project management is becoming obsolete. This is becoming more and more difficult on account of rising expectations of the decision makers and the beneficiaries — people, to complete the construction in tight time schedule. All these facts of the day call for adoption of available modern Management Techniques in the field of construction.

It is not correct that only the big projects need modern Management Technique. Projects — big or small equally need adoption of Management Technique for its systematic construction and completion as desired.

18.2.0 WHAT IS MANAGEMENT

During construction process many difficult and complex management problems generally arise. To overcome them and to ensure judicious allocation and efficient use of resources, improved management techniques need be adopted. The objective of the management is to make the best use of all the available resources. One of the most serious problems faced by construction industry is related to time and consequent cost over runs. Modern management techniques available are vital tools for tackling those problems and ensure timely and economical completion of projects.

MANAGEMENT

Management is a scientific tool for organising the methodical approach of planning, programming and execution of a project and also monitoring the progress of the work including quality control, scheduling of materials, labours and plants and machineries that would be required for the project.

A project is composed of various activities and they are interrelated. The activities or functions need be coordinated and monitored for timely completion with quality control, so that the total project is completed in the time frame specified. During this process, other functions also get into the process;

(*i*) **Material management.** Material of various categories and in large quantities are required for execution of the project. These need be procured timely so that there may not be any delay of the item due to non-availability or shortage of materials or any particular material.

(*ii*) **Labour management.** Different categories of labourers are required at different stages of construction. This also has to be looked before and planned properly so that there may not be any hindrance due to shortage of any category of labour at any stage.

(*iii*) **Plants and Equipments.** Various plants and equipments (machineries) may be needed at different stages of construction project. These need be planned properly so that they are available at the right time. Any of the plants and machineries may break down during progress of work. Suitable standby should be kept so that the same may be put into service to keep the execution schedule as per programme and maintain its normal progress.

18.2.1 Objectives of Project Management

Project management is a highly specialised job. It becomes more complicated as the process involves human factor at all stages. The involvement of human factor need be taken into account to achieve the objectives of the project management.

The objectives are:

(*i*) Completion of the project allowing for minimum duration of time,

(*ii*) The project should be completed without delay using the available manpower and other resources,

(*iii*) The project should be completed without any delay and with minimum capital investment and without compromising with the quality.

18.3.0 PHASES OF PROJECT MANAGEMENT

Project management comprises of three phases which are to be taken care of:

(*i*) Planning and programming—

The project should be planned properly and the different activities programmed according to sequence of operation.

(*ii*) Scheduling—

Scheduling of the activities, scheduling of the materials required and scheduling of the plants and machineries that would be necessary.

(*iii*) Control

Project controlling or monitoring i.e., keeping observation on the performance so that no over running of time occurs.

18.4.0 PROJECT PLANNING AND PROGRAMMING

On conceiving a project, the concerned Engineering department need be intimated of the relevant requirements to enable them to prepare preliminary plans and estimates for obtaining administrative approval of the project. Study of the requirements need be made for achieving optimum construction costs. Selection of site and acquisition of land and its development also need be started simultaneously. These take considerable time and necessitate proper planning and phasing of the work. Programming of all the operations for execution of the work is essential and should be done with all possible care. The various operations in a construction programme are to be so synchronised in such a manner that the expenditure incurred at each stage does not remain idle for long. The programme should include the quickest and most economical methods of execution of work, consistent with the different operations of the construction. The programming should ensure continuous productive work in optimum time.

The planning part of management is followed by programming:

(*a*) **Planning.** Planning of a project means formulation of the project and sanctioning of it by the appropriate authorities. The procedure comprises essentially of the following activities.

(*i*) Investigation for preparing the preliminary project report,
(*ii*) Preparation of preliminary project report,
(*iii*) Administrative approval of the project by the concerned Administrative department,
(*iv*) Initiation of the land acquisition proposal,
(*v*) Investigation for the detailed project report,
(*vi*) Preparation of the detailed plans and estimates and preparation of the detailed project report,
(*vii*) Technical sanction of the project by the competent authority in the technical department to whom the job has been assigned,
(*viii*) Budget allotment,
(*ix*) Tendering procedure,
(*x*) Acceptance of the tender,
(*xi*) Supervision and execution of the work,
(*xii*) Accounting work, and
(*xiii*) Maintenance of the works in operation.

(*i*) **Investigation for preparation of the preliminary report.** On the basis of the request and requirement of the client or the department, information are to be collected for preparation of the project and a preliminary or a rough cost estimate. Although detailed investigations are not undertaken at this stage as it may involve heavy cost, but it should be taken care of that on the basis of the preliminary investigation, preliminary project report with cost estimate would be prepared and administrative approval would be sought for on it. The preliminary cost estimate should not fall far off from the detailed cost estimate necessitating revised administrative approval.

(*ii*) **Preparation of preliminary project report.** Preliminary project report with preliminary or rough cost estimate shall be prepared furnishing an idea and the financial aspects of the project. The client or the department after study of the project report will ask for next stage work, i.e., a detailed project report. Administrative approval of the project may sometimes be accorded on the basis of preliminary report, but rationally it should be accorded on the basis of the detailed report.

(*iii*) **Administrative approval by the concerned Administrative Department of the client.** The concerned department or the client on receipt of the project report will go through it and examine the information and analysis furnished, examine the physical and financial viability and specially the availability of the fund in the department. They may require clarification on various point and the report may have to be modified or adjusted to suit the desire and interest of the client. Obviously, the project belongs to them. When the project report is found acceptable and the fund or the source of it is available, the concerned department or the client shall accord Administrative approval of the Project.

Administrative approval of project is normally accorded on the basis of detailed project report supported by a detailed cost estimate. Preparation of detailed project report and cost estimate require considerable time. For saving time and expediting the project, Administrative approval is often accorded on the basis of preliminary project report and rough cost estimate.

If the project is proposed to be funded by taking loan from any financial institution in stages for a fixed period with a rate of interest, the same shall have to be taken into consideration in the financial analysis. Dialogue may have to be made with the institution to convince them regarding repayment of the loan.

(*iv*) **Initiation of land acquistition proposal.** On conceiving a project, proposal for acquisition of land required for the project should be initiated without any delay. The process of acquisition of land is a long drawn one and in most cases causes inordinate delay due to various litigations, etc., resulting not only delay in completion of the project but increasing the cost of the project. Land acquisition proceedings should be initiated along with other actions regarding planning of the project so that possession of the land is available as soon as the project is sanctioned.

(*v*) **Investigation for the detailed project report.** On receipt of the approval of the preliminary report, detailed survey of the site is undertaken, detailed investigation and studies are undertaken for preparation of the detailed project report. The investigation and studies shall cover wide range — analysis of the requirement and finalisation of the provisions, study of soil, study of environment, ecology, transport, communication, weather, specially rainfall, seismic effect, flood levels, etc. All possible information shall be collected and incorporated in the report. The report shall consist of an index plan with reference to some important object nearby so that the location may be identified without any difficulty. The report should indicate the distances of the important places and public utility services and a cost estimate based on unit area basis-rates based on similar project executed currently in the area or obtained by analysing it. A cost benefit ratio shall be shown justifying the economic viability of the project.

A report on physical viability of the project shall also be incorporated. A report on amortisation of the cost of the project together with a cash flow chart showing the in-flow and out-flow of fund shall be furnished. In conclusion a report shall be incorporated justifying why the project shall be taken up and what would happen if the same was not taken up.

The detailed project report shall cover all possible technical, financial and social information and remarks on their implication on the project. All possible analysis of the information shall be incorporated. In a housing project, calculation of requirement of water, power and sewage disposal shall be included. The areas provided for dwelling or other purpose shall be justified. In the case of any road project involving large volume of traffic, the road width and depth of hard crust provided shall be justified by proper and acceptable calculations.

Detailed information regarding availability of construction materials like bricks, stone, stone chips, sand, timber and specially water need be collected and supplied to the planning and estimating section of the project deparment. Information regarding availability of local labours both skilled and unskilled with their wages need be collected. A regular flow of these information is desired by the planning and design branch for preparation of an authentic document, 'Project Report' and Detailed Estimate.

(*vi*) **Preparation of detailed plans and estimates.** When the project report has been approved by the concerned Administrative department and the same has been communicated, detailed plans and estimate of the project shall be prepared. This shall be preceeded by design of the project and its component parts. While designing, rapport must be kept with the conncerned department who will be in charge of execution, regarding the design and technical matters, so that there may not be any dispute at any later stage. This will have to be done through discussions time to time which will eliminate controversies and save much time.

All references and authorities and code shall be furnished for ready reference of the client's technical department regarding design and construction technology.

Preparation of complete detailed plans and estimates may take substantial time. However, some of the detailing and construction drawings which will not affect the cost may be left for furnishing later and a cost estimate may be drawn. The rates of the cost estimate shall be adopted from a standard schedule of rates with consent of the client. The cost estimate shall be prepared carefully and as far as correctly. If the cost of construction varies more than 5% of the estimated cost, a revised estimate shall have to be prepared for Administrative and Technical sanction of the concerned authorities. To ensure guard against increase in cost due to price contingency, provision for escallation of cost year-wise shall be made. This shall be made in accordance to the R.B.I. price indices for both labour and materials as available and then projecting the same for the proposed construction period.

Materials and Labour Requirements

On completion of estimate of work, an estimate of manpower and material requirements is generally required to be prepared. This is required for various purposes such as budgeting and procurement of materials, specially the scarce materials, computation of cost indices, justification of tenders, preparation of schedule of materials for project management, etc. The estimation may be done in various ways.

(*a*) Approximate requirements may be obtained on percentage basis of the cost of the structure. This is a very approximate method. Tables for approximate estimation of materials and labour are generally maintained by the estimating branch.

(*b*) The most dependable method is to compute the requirements from the quantities of the detailed estimate. The computation can be readily done on the basis of charts and tables available in all the 'Schedule of Rates'.

(*c*) C.B.R.I. has established quicker method based on statistical equations which relate computation of materials/labour with the plinth area of buildings.

(*vii*) **Technical sanction of the Project with cost estimate.** When all the above procedures have been complied with and the technical department of the client is satisfied and the cost estimate is within 5% of the preliminary/detailed cost estimate on which administrative approval had been accorded by the appropriate authority in the clients technical department shall accord technical sanction of the project. If the detailed estimate varies more than 5% of the preliminary cost estimate, revised Administrative approval would be required.

The technical sanction together with a set of plans and estimate shall be forwarded to all concerned including the department entrusted for the execution.

(*viii*) **Budget allotment.** Technical Department entrusted for execution shall wait for provision of the full amount of the project or part in the budget estimate. Generally, token provision is kept in the budget in anticipation to avoid delay. When the detailed cost estimate is ready and the total amount with the duration of construction is known, appropriate amount is provided in the revised budget estimate generally at the later part of the financial year.

(*ix*) **Tendering procedure.** After technical sanction of the project preceeded by the Administrative approval and having provision of appropriate amount in the Budget, the department entrusted for execution of the project is entitled to commence execution after inviting tenders in proper method, processing them and finalising the tender found suitable. This part of the procedure is also time consuming. Generally, some actions which can be standardised are taken before hand. Similar other actions regarding the particular project which are possible to be taken in anticipation are also taken to curtail delay.

18.5.0 PROGRAMMING

Planning and programming part of the management are the activity of the project effected prior to commencement of the actual work which are required for proper implementation of a project. Planning and programming are therefore, essential prerequisites.

Programming of a project is most important for its proper implementation. Management of a project becomes difficult if the programming of it is not done carefully and consideration of its different components were not taken into account. Estimation of times that would be required for implementing the same also cannot be made properly. A detail work programme shall be prepared and submitted by the contractor in consultation with the client, but programming for the whole project including preliminary and planning activities need be made by the agency responsible for planning.

There are various methods of programming of a work; however, Bar-chart and CPM are most effective methods and are widely applied.

Programming by bar-chart not only helps in proper and systematic approach of the project, but it helps in exercising control over it during its implementation. Bar-chart may be used in exercising control of the financial progress also.

18.6.0 SELECTION OF MANAGEMENT TECHNIQUE

The primary objectives of construction management are to utilise human, financial and material resources usefully and effectively. With the growing complexity and increasing volume of construction activities traditional methods of construction management have failed to deliver the desired results. Improved, modern and effective method of management is needed for achieving the objectives. Bar-chart, PERT, CPM, Line of balance (LOB) Integrated Management System (IMS) as developed by the CBRI are the techniques or tools for effective and efficient management control. The systems have their advantages and draw backs. Selection of a particular system would depend upon the nature of work, whether indoor factory line production or outdoor field construction, specific purpose and suitability. Management by these modern tools require adequate training in the field. This also would be a factor for selection of a particular method.

Applying a technique without having adequate knowledge of the subject may lead to disaster instead of offering any potential help. Judging the merit of the method, and its possibility of proper implementation, a particular method shall have to be adopted. All the methods would not serve the same purpose.

Apart from the methods as mentioned, there are other methods also. The latest trend is to introduce management control by computer. In the coming days some other better and precise methods would be available.

Whatever may be the method, the basic aims of management is to optimise the utilisation of the resources available and thus to achieve economy in all respects. When applied properly, management technique is sure to yeild favourable results and prove saving of resources. Thus it would prove economical not only to the owner/client but also would save national resources.

18.7.0 BAR-CHART

In Bar Chart method the project is divided into a number of clear activities which can be identified separately. Each activity denote a complete item of work. A bar-chart is a chart showing the progress of different activities in respect of time. The duration of activities can be read from a Bar-Chart. These activities are presented linearly against vertical axes of a two co-ordinate axes diagram. The horizontal axes represent the duration period of activities, i.e. time required for completion of the activities, which is estimated from the past experience of similar work. Each bar represents one specific item or work or activity of the project. The beginning and the end of each bar represent the time of commencement and the time of finishing of the activity. The lengths of the bar therfore, represents the duration period of the activity.

As the Bar-Chart is represented on two axes, time against activity, probable expenditure and actual financial progress can also be shown on the chart with the help of the two axes. The horizontal axes indicating the time and the vertical axes showing the planned expenditure. The line on the chart obtained from the two co-ordinates generally takes S-shape and is therefore, termed as S-curve. Both planned and actual expenditures can be shown and curves obtained. The curves may be shown in different colours or one in firm line and the other in dotted line.

Thus a Bar Chart can represent both physical and financial planning and progress.

Example 18.1.

	Activities	*Duration*
1.	Earthwork in excavation in foundation	2 weeks
2.	Foundation concrete and Brickwork upto plinth	5 weeks
3.	Brickwork in superstructure	6 weeks
4.	Shuttering and centering for roof slab	4 weeks
5.	Laying of reinforcement	2 weeks
6.	Concreting of roof slab	4 weeks
7.	Releasing shuttering	4 weeks
8.	Fixing door and window frames	2 weeks
9.	Rendering internal and external	4 weeks
10.	Flooring	3 weeks
11.	Fixing door and window shutters	2 weeks
12.	Finishing works	5 weeks

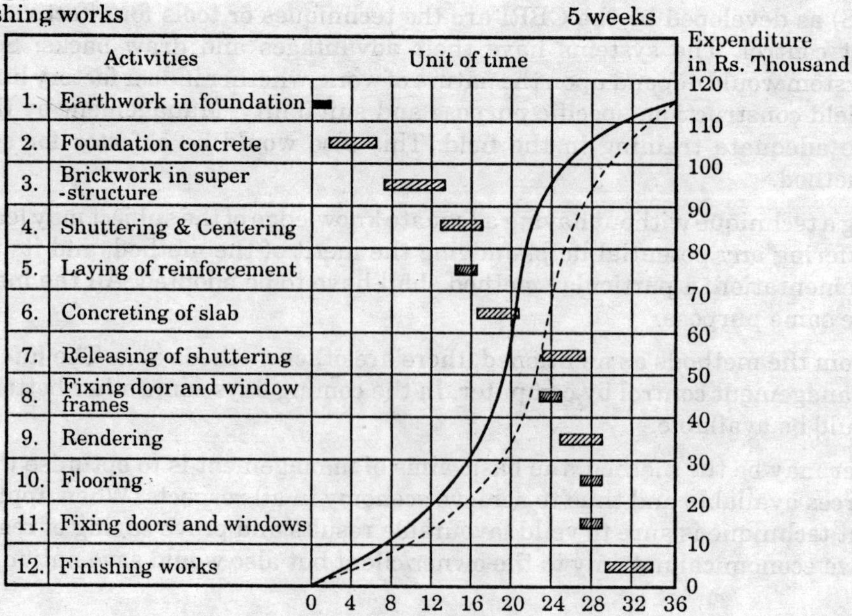

Fig. 18.1 BAR CHART

18.7.1 Shortcomings of Bar-chart and Remedial Measures

A Bar-chart mainly depicts the major items of work and if all the detailed items are shown, the chart would be very clumsy. Moreover, a particular activity whether small or big is shown by a bar without any details of sub-activities which would be required for exercising proper control over the project. Further, the actual commencement or completion of an activity with relation to the other is not clear.

These deficiencies can be overcome by introducing marking stages or 'Mile Stones' and by indicating inter-relationship of the activities.

Example. *Let there be a work comprising of the following activities.*

A. Excavation of foundation trenches	14 weeks
B. Laying of soling	12 weeks
C. Laying of concrete	8 weeks

If the activities were taken one after the other total time required would have been 34 weeks. But the activities can be suitably overlapped and the total duration period can be shortened.

Activity *B* is dependent upon activity *A*, again activity *C* is dependent upon both activities A and *B*. Activity B can start after activity *A* has progressed sufficiently. Again, activity *C* can start when both the activities *A* and *B* have progressed.

Activities *B* has a few stages.

(*i*) Collection of bricks,

(*ii*) Levelling the foundation bed,

(*iii*) Laying of bricks, and

(*iv*) Filling the gaps of bricks laid.

These may be marked by (mile stone)

Activity *C* has a few stages

(*i*) Collection of materials, and

(*ii*) Mixing, laying and compacting of concrete.

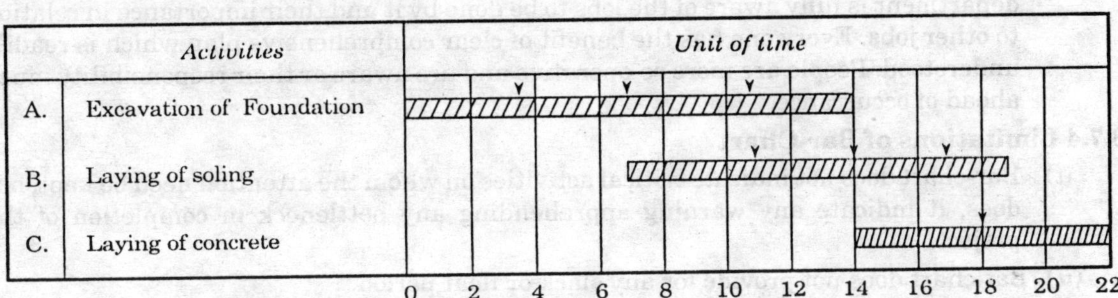

Fig. 18.2 Bar-chart with mile stones

18.7.2 Control

Project controlling or monitoring is a very important part of project management. Controlling of project starts after planning and scheduling and when the project work has actully began. Control on the project would be exercised by following the Bar-Chart digram as has been drawn earlier. Information collected from the field activity wise would be imposed on the Bar-chart or the network diagram periodically and the situation observed if the project is progressing as per programme. If it is observed that the progress is not satisfactory and it is lagging, the cause shall be found out and corrected.

A Bar-Chart as such does not show the progress of work, hence cannot be used for controlling the project; but it can be utilised for controlling by showing the programme of work by bars with hatched lines or colouring the bars and the actual progress by introducing another set of bars with different colour and drawn below the programme bars.

Thus a Bar-Chart can be utilised as a tool for controlling a project. Financial programme and progress may be displayed in the Bar-Chart. Control over collection of materials and plants and machineries may thus be effectively exercised by a Bar-Chart.

The manager finds out the lagging activity in the Bar-Chart and takes action for rectification of the cause. In doing so he may have to reschedule the activities, shorten the duration or change the sequence of activity. He may have to reschedule the planning of Resources and plants and machineries. The manager needs keeping his watchful eyes on the Bar-chart. The Bar-chart will tell the manager, the item of work on which his attention is needed. The action required for rectification shall have to be taken as soon as a snag is detected.

18.7.3 Advantages of Bar-Chart

(*i*) Bar-chart is simple, can be drawn quickly and is understood easily. Much training is not required for drawing and understanding it.

(*ii*) Comparison of planned schedule and performance can be had readily by bars drawn showing performances in different colours.

(*iii*) Effects of delay, changes required in cases of emergency can be identified when the activities involved are comparatively less in number.

(*iv*) Interrelationship of activities can be displayed although to a limited extent by introducing 'Mile stones' or 'marking stages':

(*v*) Requirement of resources in quantity and exact time when required can be known in advance by separate bars.

(*vi*) Financial position, both planned and performed can be displayed by introducing S-curve.

(*vii*) Bar-chart provides for the means of improved communication and co-ordination. Each department is fully aware of the jobs to be done by it and their importance in relation to other jobs. Every one has the benefit of clear comprehensive plan which is readily understood. People are more co-operative and are aware or their responsibility much ahead of occurrance.

18.7.4 Limitations of Bar-Chart

(*i*) Bar-chart does not indicate critical activities on whom the attention need be kept, nor does, it indicate any warning apprehending any bottleneck in completion of the project.

(*ii*) Bat-chart does not provide for any slack or float period.

(*iii*) Bar-chart itself does not take care of cost aspects of the project unless a S-curve is introduced.

(*iv*) Planning cannot be separated from scheduling in the Bar-chart.

(*v*) A large number of activities can be started concurrently, but their interdependence cannot be indicated in the Bar-chart.

(*vi*) The effect of work progressing ahead or lagging of the planned schedule is not indicated.

(*vii*) Reading and reporting on the basis of Bar-chart is done on the basis of approximate percentage of a particular item represented by a Bar. The information obtained is insufficient for providing any comprehensive idea of the situation.

(*viii*) A Bar-chart does not indicate the progress of the project as a whole; hence, it cannot be used as a control device which is necessary in cases of a dynamic programme.

(*ix*) Uncertainty or tolerance in duration times and probability are not displayed.

18.8.0 NETWORK MANAGEMENT

The Network management system uses logical and simple procedures for reducing large volumes of complex information into a graphical or tabular form which can be readily employed in decision making. The technique enables all round co-ordination among various project agencies to complete the project in time. However, the process need regular review and updating along with the progress of the work.

18.9.0 PERT

PERT—Programme Evaluation and Review Technique. It is basically a method of logical, disciplined and analytical concept of evaluation and reviewing of a programme. It is designed as probablistic network of activities and events. The activities and the network do not take into account of the cost involved. However, PERT indicates probable crisis methodology of reporting on the progress.

In this method of programming, the work or the project is divided into a number of clear activities which can be identified separately. Schedule of activities are prepared and represented linearly by short straight lines and are connected with one another by events represented by small circles. The activities are arranged following the sequence of their occurence and are connected by the events and thus a network is formed.

The events either denote starting or ending of an activity. The activities are marked with incoming or outgoing arrow signs from the nodes to indicate their progress direction. Each activity, require some period of duration for its completion. This time period is noted above the activity line at the middle.

The expected time period of duration of an activity is estimated by evaluation of mean of the three times as below:

$$t_e = \frac{1}{6}(a + 4\,m + b)$$

Where, t_e = expected time.

a = optimistic time, the time that would be required for completion of the activity if nothing goes wrong.

b = pessimistic time, the time that would be required for completion of the activity taking into account of all sorts of difficulties and bottlenecks.

m = most likely time, time for completion of the activity which occurs most frequently.

Example 18.2 Where, $a = 3$, $b = 15$ and $m = 6$

$$t_e = \frac{1}{6}(3 + 4 \times 6 + 15) = \frac{1}{6}(3 + 24 + 15) = \frac{42}{6} = 7$$

The activities of example in paragraph 17.7 is reproduced in network.

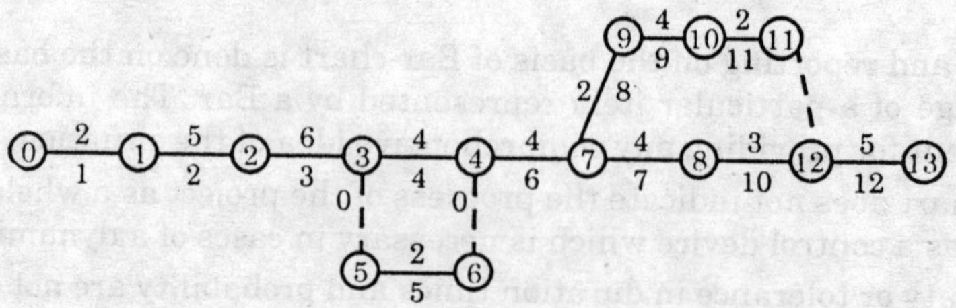

Fig. 18.3 Network Diagram

18.9.1 Advantages of PERT

PERT provides for a number of significant advantage. Some of them are mentioned below:

(*i*) The most important advantage of the technique is the possible anticipation of crisis. Warning can be given sufficient time in advance and enough time is generally available for correction of the process of the work.

(*ii*) PERT also signals need to the completion dates of some activity so that it can be matched with schedule of other activity. Thus it may help in retardation of progress in the department over producing and causing blockage of capital. It can guide the management in deployment of labour according to necessity.

(*iii*) PERT provides for logical and disciplined basis for planning. Breaking the project into activities and finding out their relationship to build a network is much helpful as it clarifies the thinking of the management as to what is involved in the project. The project as a whole could be visualised clearly at any time. This induces possible improvement with the resultant saving of time.

(*iv*) PERT provides for precise reporting of the progress. Delays can be pin-pointed and responsibilities fixed up. Better understanding of the project status and related various departments is possible.

18.10.0 CRITICAL PATH METHOD, CPM

CPM means Critical Path Method. It is synthesising in concept. The network diagram is activity oriented and deterministic in nature. In CPM network, time is related to cost.

Critical Path. A network of activities are drawn for programming of the project for finding out the possible completion time of any intermediate event and to estimate the total project time.

In estimating the total project time, there would be a number of paths leading to the completion event. The path of longest duration is termed 'Critical Path' and the activities lying in the critical path are called 'Critical Activities'.

Any delay occuring in completion of any critical activity will cause in consequential delay in completion of the project. The total time required for completion of the project is calculated starting from the initial event, calling it 'zero time' and then proceeding along the possible paths towards the end event. This method is called 'Method of forward pass'. In this way we can find the critical path of the network. However, for identifying the critical path, another strategy is resorted to. This is known as 'Backword pass method'. In the analysis counting of time begins from the last event whose occurance of earliest time (E) is known. The latest possible occurance times (L) of the events are calculated by substracting the times. The strategy of backward pass may be extended to the entire network. When the exercise is complete, it will be seen that in a critical path E and L values of the tail and head events of all the critical activities are the same and the difference between the E values of the tail and head events and the L values of the head and tail events are the same and equal to the duration period of the activities.

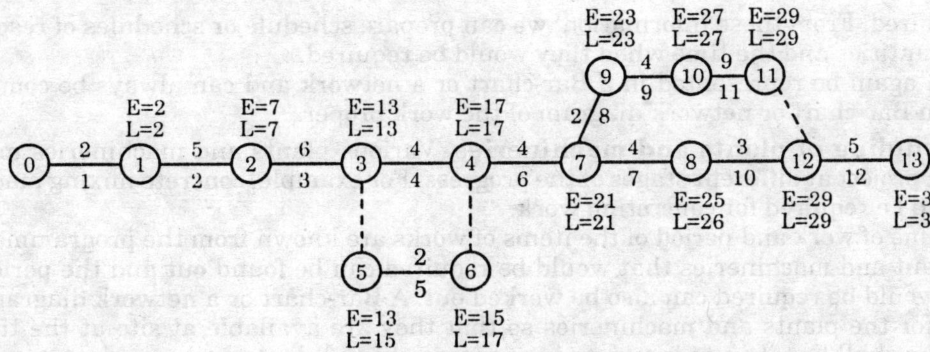

Fig. 18.4 Network Diagram with Critical Path.

The activities of example in paragraph 17.7 is reproduced in network.

PATH-I		PATH-II		PATH-III		PATH-IV		
Activity	*Time*	*Activity*	*Time*	*Activity*	*Time*	*Activity*	*Time*	*Weeks*
0—1	2	0—1	2	0—1	2	0—1	2	"
1—2	5	1—2	5	1—2	5	1—2	5	"
2—3	6	2—3	6	2—3	6	2—3	6	"
3—4	4	5—6	2	5—6	2	3—4	4	"
4—7	4	4—7	4	4—7	4	4—7	4	"
7—8	4	7—9	2	7—8	4	7—9	2	"
8—12	3	9—10	4	8—12	3	9—10	4	"
12—13	5	10—11	2	12—13	5	10—11	2	"
		12—13	5			12—13	5	"
33		32		31		34		Weeks

PATH - (*IV*) is critical.

Programme prepared by a network shall be strictly adhered to for completion of the project in the prescribed time period.

However, in practice it would be seen that due to various reasons there may be delay in completion of a particular activity. In such case changes would occur in the network and the critical path may be altered and some other activities may become critical. These would be dealt in the control of the project.

18.10.1 Scheduling

(*i*) **Scheduling of the activities.** Scheduling of activities involved are required for drawing of the programme, hence it should be drawn prior to programming. Scheduling of activities comprises of list of the activities with activity number and their duration. The list of the activities shall be made following the sequence of the items of works to be done and the numbering also shall be done accordingly so that the same numbers may be used in the network.

A project may contain more than one components which can be executed independently. In such case, the project shall be divided into parts, component wise and separate programme and network developed. These component networks shall be connected to each other by events and a network would be developed. The sub-networks shall be numbered separately and shall be considered as activities of the master network. The duration of the sub-networks shall be considered as duration of the activities of the master network. Thus the master network shall reflect the whole project, while the sub-networks, the programme of the component units.

(*ii*) **Scheduling of resources (material).** When a programme of the project has been drawn either by Bar-chart or by Network diagram, the period and time of execution of a particular activity or item of work is known. The estimate of the project with all details has been prepared earlier; hence, we know the volume of work of the activity and the resources or materials that would be required. From these information, we can prepare schedule or schedules of resources with their quantities and the time when they would be required.

This can again be represented in a Bar-chart or a network and can always be compared with the main Bar-chart or network diagram of the work proper.

(iii) **Scheduling of plants and machineries.** Various plants and machineries may be required for a project at different stages of the progress. For example, concrete mixing machine, vibrator would be required for concreting work.

The volume of work and period of the items of works are known from the programme. The particular plant and machineries that would be required can be found out and the period for which these would be required can also be worked out. A Bar-chart or a network diagram can be prepared for the plants and machineries so that they are available at site at the time of necessity. Care shall be taken to incorporate spare number of plants and machineries so that there may not be any hold up of work during actual execution due to non-availability of the plants and machinery.

18.11.0 CONTROL BY NETWORK/CPM

Network can be used for controlling a project. However, this will not highlight the actual progress of the project. On receving feed information from the field, the manager shall impose them on the network diagram. The length of line of activity does not indicate graphically the time consumed or the actual progress of the activity. Only the position of the activity in terms of lagging or advancing can be obtained. The manager concentrates on the critical path and notes if the activities on the critical path are progressing as planned. If a critical activity is not complete within the duration period, the critical path may change and some other path may become critical and the total duration period would be changed. In that case, he would have to reschedule the activities and redraw the network. On finding the activity lagging, he may take action to improve its progress and restore the original critical path, if possible. In doing so, he may have to crash the particular activity to shorten the duration period. Obviously, crashing an activity would enhance its completion but would involve additional cost which the client may not like to incur. Hence, the manager shall have to decide whether to allow the overrun of time causing consequent delay in completion of the project or to crash the activity or the activities to restore the original work programme. Financial implication of both the alternatives shall have to be evaluated and decision taken in consultation with the client. Thus network with CPM can be effectively used for controlling a project.

As mentioned earlier, a master network may be divided into sub-networks of important and complete items. Considering these as activities master net-work can be drawn. In such case, monitoring shall have to be exercised on each sub-network and then the master network. Financial implication in both the cases shall have to be evaluated.

18.11.1 Difference between PERT and CPM

	PERT	CPM
(i)	It is basically analytic in concept and designed as probabilistic network.	It is basically synthesising in concept and is termed as deterministic network
(ii)	It is formed of event oriented diagrams.	It is formed of activity oriented diagrams.
(iii)	The time estimation of duration is based on three probable times.	Time estimation of duration is based on experience of similar activity without having any allowance for uncertainty.
(iv)	Duration times of activities are not related to cost.	Duration times are related to cost.
(v)	The method is generally used for Research and Development projects, production development, and similar projects involving uncertain factors.	The method can gainfully be used for repetitive work — construction activities, maintenance and repairs and production control, planning and scheduling.

18.11.2 Differences between Network and Bar-Chart

	Network	Bar Chart
(i)	Logical planning of activities can be separated from time scheduling;	Planning cannot be separated from scheduling;
(ii)	Interrelationship of activities is established through out the project;	Very little such relationship is available;
(iii)	Effect of any delay of change is readily available;	Generally a few immediate effects can be identified;
(iv)	Time period may have to be reallocated at any point, but redrawing of the network is rarely required;	Frequently becomes completely out of schedule necessitating redrawal of chart;
(v)	Resource requirements with time are always known in advance;	Very limited indication is available in this respect;
(vi)	Spare times are available e.g. slack, floats etc. systematically calculated and allocated;	There is no spare time in the planning;
(vii)	Critical activities and bottle necks are highlighted;	No such identification of critical activity; consequently crash resources are often wasted on non-critical activities;
(viii)	It helps in maintaining the time schedule as problems can be foreseen and decisions can be taken adequately in advance.	Last minute or late knowledge of problem often upsets target;
(ix)	Overall costs can be minimised constant review and curtailment of overhead cost by decompressing the non-critical activities;	No such possibility exists;

18.11.3 Advantages of Network Analysis

Various advantages can be derived by application of network analysis in capital projects in their execution starting from ab initio to completion stage.

(i) It limits possibility of overlooking any activity in a project;

(ii) It shows interrelationship of all the activities in a project;

(iii) It shows clearly the relationship controlling the order of performance of various activities than any other management tool;

(iv) It helps quick and easy communication of ideas. The pictorial approach helps much than any verbal instruction;

(v) It contributes disciplined thinking. It trends to prevent error, ommission caused due to careless planning and generates confidence in the integrity of the schedule;

(vi) It provides time schedule containing much more information than any other technique;

(vii) It identifies those jobs which are critical in a project. Attention can be put on them;

(viii) It predicts trouble areas, showing the timing and warns against any future problem;

(ix) It gives an accurate forecast of resource requirements—materials /labour, quantity and variety;

(x) It provides method of resource allocation suiting the condition and to maintain or to minimise overall cost;

(xi) It integrates all elements of a programme in detail as desired by the management;

(xii) It relates time to cost, which allows regulating any proposed change;

(xiii) It facilitates reporting and project documentation;

(xiv) It simplifies communication and improves co-ordination through the use of detailed common language i.e. action plan.

18.11.4 Limitations of Network

Following are the main limitations of Network.

(i) Network having large number of activities if analysed properly and in details require large number of mandays for calculation, which is a very monotonous job.

(ii) Repetitive manual calculations are seldom error free and an uncorrected early error can produce an useless programme.

(iii) It is very difficult to indentify the error very precisely enabling correction without undue delay, resulting wastage of analysing efforts.

(iv) It is often necessary and advantageous to analyse different sequences present in large Networks for easy understanding. But this is not possible in a limited time in this method.

(v) It is often difficult to carryout extensive check on the data supplied and the validity of the Network due to its complexity.

18.11.5 Application of Network Analysis

Construction

One of the most widely accepted application of Network analysis is in the area of construction activities in all the disciplines e.g. construction of buildings of any magnitude, Cinema houses, Stadium, cultural halls, dams, roads, bridges, etc.

Repairs and maintenance

In this field of Repairs and Rehabilitation of structures, the technique can be effectively applied. In planned maintenance and preventive maintenance, the conventional approach is mostly found to be quite inadequate in consideration of the narrow time span and limited resource often available. The need for skilled maintenance and manpower necessary can be effectively met by the Network analysis for economy in cost and time.

18.12.0 CONTROL

Bar- chart, CPM, PERT etc. provide for ample control of a project during its execution. Apart from control of execution of work other controls are necessary for efficient management of the project.

18.12.1. Quality Control

Quality control is one of the most important activities of management. Progress of a work without quality control cannot be considered as a work at all. It is the foremost duty of the manager to maintain the quality throughout the duration of the work. This he would do with the help of efficient, experienced and well conversant group of field staff and also with various testing machines and implements. Control of quality shall be exercised on the daily execution of different items of work, specially those which would be covered up.

18.12.2 Quality of Materials

Before using any material in work, the same should be inspected thoroughly to ensure that the material is of quality as specified. If necessary, it may be tested at site or in laboratory.

Cement to be used shall be of fresh stock. This may be tested at site. Cement shall be bluish grey cement colour and on pushing hand inside a bag full of cement, one shall have cool feeling. It may be tested by making briquattes and breaking those after 7 days. These tests do not give very correct results, but are indicative. In case of any doubt, cement sample shall be sent to laboratory for testing its physical and chemical properties.

During concreting, concrete cubes shall be taken random from mixed concrete for testing compressive strength after 7 days and 28 days. Concrete is generally poured for long durations. Throughout the operation, its consistency shall be maintained ensuring the water cement-ratio. This can be done easily by slump test with the help of a slump cone.

The materials like aggregates shall be clean, sharp, hard, free from any dirt or dust. If necessary, those shall be washed and cleaned.

Bricks used shall be of first class quality, shall emit ringing sound when struck together or by observing its breaking pattern from a fall which would indicate the quality. Before use the bricks shall be soaked in water at least for 12 hours.

Timber used shall be checked thoroughly to ensure that it is free from knots, damaged fibre, diseases like rot, fungi attack etc. Timber shall be well seasoned and treated.

Paint or varnish to be used shall be from sealed containers, shall be used properly with brush or spray guns without adding any thinner.

Materials required and used in Civil Engineering works are of different varieties and in large quantites. These are generally handled by human being. Hence, it is difficult to control the quality unless watchful eyes are kept on them.

18.12.3 Quality of Workmanship

Workmanship is again another field of numerous problems and loopholes. Workmanship shall be maintained for quality control. The finishing of the work shall be of A grade. The slope, line, level shall be maintained as specified in the drawing. Possibility of human error and mistakes leading to defects in workmanship are there as human factor exists almost throughout the entire operation. However, careful and watchful manager can still deliver good end production by exerting his control.

Progress and quality control shall proceed side by side. One should not pose problem to other.

18.13.0 FINANCIAL CONTROL

This is another field where control of the management is called upon. Responsibility of the management does not end with planning and execution of the work. Management includes financial planning and control of it during the entire process of execution, so that the operation ends successfully without any fund problem which would otherwise hamper the physical progress. Physical progress of a project cannot be ensured without proper financial inflow of fund required at different stages as planned. This part of the management is better controlled by a Cash-Flow Chart. The cash-flow chart will indicate the flow of fund required, expenditure, and return, if any expected from the project at different stages. It shows the expected financial benefit that may accrue at the completion of the project.

Example 18.3. *A project costing Rs. 500 Lacs is proposed to be financed by borrowing from a financial institution. Loan will be drawn as required. The borrowed amount will bear an interest at the rate of 10% per annum. The project is expected to yield Rs. 700 Lacs in a span of 8 years starting from the third year.*

Draw a Cash-Flow Chart.

Cash-Flow Chart

All figures are in Rs. Lacs.

Year	*Expenditure during the year*	*Loan during the year*	*Return from the project*	*Return of Loan with interest*	*Interest on loan during the year 10%*	*Total loan and interest at the end of the year cumulative*	*Remarks*
1st	50	50	-	-	2.50	52.50	
2nd	100	100	-	-	10.25	162.75	
3rd	100	50	50	-	18.78	231.53	
4th	100	-	100	-	23.15	254.68	
5th	100	-	100	-	25.47	280.15	
6th	50	-	100	50	28.02	258.17	
7th	-	-	100	100	25.82	18.99	
8th	-	-	100	100	18.40	102.39	
9th	-	-	100	100	10.24	12.63	
10th	-	-	50	13.89	1.26	36.11	Surplus
	500	200	700	363.39			

(*i*) It would be seen from the Cash-Flow that the project was self-financing.

(*ii*) Borrowed amount would be returned fully with interest in 10 years.

(*iii*) The project would yield Rs. 36.11 Lac as surplus after meeting all the liabilities.

If the actual financial inflow from the project i.e. return from the project goes wrong, the net surplus at the end of 10th year Rs. 36.11 Lacs would be eroded partly or fully. In the event of such occurrence the manager foreseeing that the final yield might be eroded and/or there is possibility of loss, he might suggest ways and means for enhancing the return from the project much ahead to counter the possibility of any loss in the future and keep the project financially viable.

18.14.0 PROGRESS REPORT

For easy and quick understanding of the status of a project, a periodic progress report need be prepared and submitted to the Client or the Authority for his appraisal. The report should be simple and easily understable without any technicality.

18.14.1 Percentage Progress

Percentage progress report system has been envolved to satisfy the requirement. The Bar-chart, Network Analysis, CPM, are the tools available for better management of the projects and exerting control at various level of the work. But none of the methods can indicate the overall progress of the project which is often necessary for monitoring both financial and physical progress of the project. Client or the authority generally like to know the status of the project at any particular point of time or at regular interval and that in a simple way. A percentage progress report would provide a satisfactory communication from the management of the project.

The percentage progress is a method of exercising overall control of a project as it indicates the percentage of work already done and percentage of work remaining. It is a simple method and can be understood easily. But it does not help much in indicating the particular activity causing any delay in the process, which is better indicate in network. Process depends upon assessment of the physical progress of the elements of the work at site, which is collected on approximate estimation basis by the field staff and is subjected to error. However, the method extends help in ascertaining the overall progress of a project.

In the method, the project is divided into a possible number of sub-heads which can be identified individually. The financial weightage of the sub-heads in relation to the whole project is noted on each sub-head in separate proforma. A project may comprise of many sub-heads.

18.15.0 MANAGEMENT AND QUANTITY SURVEYOR

A Quantity Surveyor plays an important and vital roll in the management of a construction project. He gets himself involved in most of the activities in different stages of management from the very beginning to the completion of a project; although in most cases, he remains in the background.

18.15.1 Planning and Programming

In the planning and programming he extends help in investigation and preparation of the preliminary project report. He furnishes the Rough cost of the items incorporated in the preliminary estimate. Even, he estimates the approximate area that would be required for implementation of the project and calculate the approximate cost of the land.

The detailed estimate for the project report is prepared by him. This a laborious and long drawn process and of vital importance for the management of the project. He prepares the Comprehensive Status Report which is of immenese help of the project manager and helps a lot in planning and programming and Scheduling of materials and labour.

While the project report is in the process of Technical Sanction clarification regarding the cost of items of work are furnished by the quantity surveyor. The approximate amount that should be kept in the budget estimate is also determined by the quantity surveyor.

18.15.2 Estimation of Quantities

As regards estimation of quantities of different materials and the times of their requirement, he is the competent person to furnish those information. In the same way he furnishes the requirement of the plants and machineries those would be required for the project and the exact period of their requirement.

The requirement of labour of different categories required at different times of work is also computed by him and furnished to the authority for feeding the management.

When the work is in progress, the quantities of work done of different items or activities need be found out. Quantity surveyor is the right man to assess the quantities and feed the person reponsible drawing or updating the Bar-Chart or CPM Network with the field information.

18.15.3 Tendering Procedure

Preparation of the tender documents, preparation of the notice inviting tender are the functions of the quantity surveyor. On receipt of the tenders from the intending tenderers, the quantity surveyor's function is to scrutinize those, see if the tenders received were all valid and then making enquiries for the clarification needed. He then compares the tenders and places those to the tender accepting committee or Board with his comments. On selection of the tender and its acceptance, he communicates the acceptance of the particular tender to the tenderer.

18.15.4 Construction Management

During construction management, he plays vital roll. He is the suitable person to divide the item of works into activities. He estimates the probable duration of the activities i.e. the time that would be required to complete the activity and he frames the Bar-Chart or the CPM Network. He extends all possible information required for framing the Bar-Chart or CPM Network.

18.15.5 Final Measurement and Payment

Finally, he takes the measurement of the work done against different items for interim payment and also for final payment.

Even after final payment, if there be any dispute or claim, it is the quantity surveyor who submits an initial report on the dispute or claim if it was justified and to what extend. In case of any Arbitration on any claim, the quantity surveyor helps in all respects the authority to defend the arbitration case.

Thus it is seen the quantity surveyor involves himself in almost all the stages of construction and helps the authority or the persons reponsible for project management from the very initial to the final stage of the process.

19

PREVALENT SCHEDULE OF RATES

(Based on Schedule of Rates of Presidency Circle, P.W.D., Government of West Bengal 2002-2003.)

S. No.	*Description of items*	*Unit*	*Rate*	*Remarks*
	Building - A Earthwork		**Rs. P**	
1.	Earthwork in excavation of foundation trenches or drains in all sorts of soil.	% cum	2,973.00	
2.	Earthwork in filling in foundation trenches or plinth with good earth.	% cum	1,738.00	
3.	Filling in foundation or plinth by siver sand.	% cum	21,900.00	
4.	Earthwork in filling in compound, tank, etc.	% cum	3,130.00	
5.	Hire and labour charges for shoring work.	sqm	38.00	
	B. Dismantling, Cutting chase, Holes, etc.			
1.	Dismantling all types of masonry excepting cement concrete.	cum	114.50	
2.	Dismantling all types of plain cement concrete works	cum	250.00	
3.	Dismantling R.C. floor, roof, beams, etc.	cum	375.00	
	C. Brickwork, concrete work, etc.			
1.	Single brick flat solıng	sqm	95.00	
2.	Cement concrete with graded jhama khoa			
	6 : 3 : 1 proportion	cum	1,623.00	
	8 : 4 : 1 proportion	cum	1,340.00	
3.	Cement concrete 4 : 2 : 1 with graded stone chips	cum	2,373.00	
4.	Cement concrete with graded stone ballast 6 : 3 : 1	cum	1,931.00	
	8 : 4 : 1	cum	1,729.00	
5.	Hire and labour charges for shuttering with centering.	sqm	105.00	
6.	Reinforcement for reinforced concrete work. Tor steel/Mild steel	M.T.	2,0831.00	
7.	Brickwork with first class bricks in lime and surkhi mortar (1 : 2)	cum	1,520.00	
8.	Brickwork with 1st class bricks in cement mortar (4 : 1)	cum	1,760.00	
9.	Brickwork with 1st class bricks in cement mortar (6 : 1)	cum	1,602.00	

S. No.	Description of items	Unit	Rate Rs. P	Remarks
10.	125 mm thick brickwork with 1st class bricks in cement mortar (4 : 1).	sqm	230.00	
11.	125 mm thick brickwork with 1st class bricks in cement mortar (3 : 1)	sqm	247.00	
12.	200 mm thick brickwork with flyash bricks set in sand cement mortar (6 : 1)	cum	1,478.00	
	D. Flooring			
1.	Terraced flooring of lime concrete with jhama khoa, surkhi and stone lime $7 : 2 : 1\frac{1}{2}$.			
	75 mm thick	sqm	114.00	
	100 mm thick	sqm	142.00	
2.	Brick-on-edge floor or pavement with 1st class bricks set close in cement mortar (6 : 1).	sqm	238.00	
3.	Artificial stone in flooring, dado, staircase, etc. with cement concrete 4 : 2 : 1 with stone chips.			
	20 mm thick	sqm	73.00	
	25 mm thick	sqm	91.00	
	35 mm thick	sqm	103.00	
4.	25 mm thick (finished) terrazo work, cast in situ.			
	(*i*) 9 mm thick terrazo topping In ordinary grey colour	sqm	230.00	
	(*ii*) 12 mm thick terrazo topping In ordinary grey colour	sqm	242.00	
5.	25 mm thick damp proof course with cement concrete with stone chips (4 : 2 : 1) and with admixture of water proofing compound.	sqm	70.00	
6.	Supplying, fitting and fixing 20 mm to 37.5 mm thick Chunar (Mirzapur/Dholpur slab to floor set in lime mortar (2 : 1).	sqm	526.00	
7.	Supplying fitting and fixing 1st. quality porcelain tiles of any size in walls and floors. White	sqm	477.00	
8.	Marble flooring 19 to 22 mm thick tiles set in lime mortar (2 : 1) or cement mortar (2 : 1).	sqm	937.00	
9.	Marbulite work in floor, dadoo, skirting, etc.	sqm	367.00	
10.	20 mm to 25 mm thick Kota stone slab set in lime mortar (2 : 1) or cement mortar (4 : 1).	sqm	750.00	
	E. Roofing and Sheet Walling			
1.	Lime terracing on roof with lime concrete (7 : 2 : 2)			
	75 mm thick (average)	sqm	170.00	
	100 mm thick (average)	sqm	201.00	
2.	Roofing of Ranigunge pattern tiles 1st class quality pointing all joints with valamoid or similar bituminous paste.	sqm	91.00	
3.	-Do- With cement mortar (3 : 1)	sqm	84.00	
4.	Asbestos corrugated sheet work.			

S. No.	*Description of items*	*Unit*	*Rate* Rs. P	*Remarks*
	In roof	sqm	170.00	
	In wall	sqm	168.00	
5.	Galvanised corrugated iron sheet work (excluding supporting frame work).			
	In roof with 0.63 mm thick sheet	sqm	290.00	
	In wall with 0.63 mm thick sheet	sqm	284.00	
6.	Galvanised plain sheet works			
	In roof with 0.63 mm sheet	sqm	201.00	
	In wall with 0.63 mm sheet	sqm	188.00	
7.	Asbestos ridging	m	185.00	
8.	Galvanised iron sheet ridging	m	105.00	
	F. Structural Steel Works Grills, Gates, etc.			
1.	M.S. structural works in beams, etc.	Quintal	2,342.00	
2.	M.S. structural works in roof truss	Quintal	2,468.00	
3.	Labour for hoisting and placing in proper position departmental R.S. joists, channels, angles, etc.	Quintal	13.00	
4.	M.S. or Ornamental grill of approved design, joints continuously welded with M.S., W.I. flats.			
	(*i*) Grill weighing above 10 kg/sqm and up to 12 kg.	sqm	360.00	
	(*ii*) Grill weighing above 12 kg/sqm and up to 14 kg/sqm.	sqm	387.00	
5.	M.S. gate of jail type.	Quintal	3,674.00	
6.	Collapsible gate with 40 mm × 40 mm × 6 mm tee as top and bottom guide rail, etc.	sqm	1,022.00	
7.	Supplying, fitting and fixing steel rolling shutter with 18 B.G. of approved type steel to section 75 mm wide, etc.	sqm	1,500.00	
8.	Supplying fitting and fixing steel rolling shutter.	sqm	2,000.00	
9.	M.S. Works in brackets.	Quintal	2,357.00	
10.	Supplying fitting and fixing windows and ventilators with or without integrated grills.			
	Without integrated grills	sqm	600.00	
11.	M.S. integrated grill	kg	28.00	
12.	Supplying, fitting and fixing steel door with or without integrated grills.			
	(*a*) Without integrated grills	sqm	1,483.00	
	(*b*) With integrated grills	sqm	1,510.00	
	G. Carpeter's Works			
1.	Wood work in door and window frame fitted and fixed complete.			
	(*a*) 1st class best Indian teak	cum	80,172.00	
	(*b*) Sishu, Hallak, Champ, Badam	cum	23,000.00	
	(*c*) Gamari	cum	31,000.00	

S. No.	Description of items	Unit	Rate Rs. P	Remarks
	(*d*) Sal: Siliguri	cum	28,980.00	
	(*e*) Local wood	cum	19,000.00	
2.	Wood work in post, post plates rafters, battens, truss members, purlins, etc.			
	Sal: Siliguri	cum	30,200.00	
3.	Wood work in beams and burgahs, fitted and fixed in position complete.	cum	29,900.00	
4.	M.S. clamp for fixing door and window frame.	Each	17.00	
5.	Iron but hinges of approved quality			
	50 mm × 30 mm × 0.90 mm	Each	6.10	
	50 mm × 37 mm × 1.50 mm	Each	6.50	
	50 mm × 40 mm × 2.5 mm	Each	14.20	
	75 mm × 40 mm × 1.12 mm	Each	7.75	
	75 mm × 47 mm × 1.70 mm	Each	8.40	
	75 mm × 60 mm × 3.15 mm	Each	23.80	
	100 mm × 50 mm × 1.25 mm	Each	16.00	
	100 mm × 58 mm × 1.90 mm	Each	18.50	
	100 mm × 75 mm × 3.50 mm	Each	39.00	
6.	Iron parliamentary hinges	Each	20.75	
7.	Iron catch hook	Each	5.00	
8.	Iron socket bolt	Each	16.15	
9.	Iron skeleton bolt	Each	55.00	
10.	Iron hasp bolt	Each	80.00	
11.	Ironpad bolt	Each	57.00	
12.	Double acting spring hinges	Each set	115.00	
13.	Iron gravity hinge	Each	48.00	
14.	Iron Tee hinges	Each	12.50	
15.	Helical door spring hinge	Each	55.00	
16.	Hydraulic door closer	Each	590.00	
17.	Anodised aluminium barrel/tower/socket bolt	Each	22.00	
18.	Anodised aluminium Aldrop/sliding bolt.	Each	134.00	
19.	Anodised aluminium butt hinges	Each	16.50	
20.	Anodised aluminium D-type handle	Each	19.50	
21.	Iron door handle	Each	8.15	
22.	Venetian shutters of door and windows.			
	50 mm thick shutters with 19 mm thick valve. 1st class Indian teak	sqm	5,019.00	
23.	Fixed louver shutters of door and windows.			
	1st class Indian teak	sqm	4,468.00	
24.	Glazed shutters of doors, windows, fan light, clerestory window.			
	40 mm thick shutters 1st class Indian teak	sqm	2,477.00	

S. No.	Description of items	Unit	Rate Rs. P	Remarks
25.	Glazed shutters of doors, with sheet glass of 5.5 mm thick. 50 mm thick shutters. 1st class Indian teak	sqm	3,532.00	
26.	Z-batten shutters of doors and windows. Shutters with 25 mm thick planks, 19 mm thick battens.			
	(*a*) Sishu, Hallak, Champ, Badam	sqm	910.00	
	(*b*) Gamari	sqm	1,196.00	
	(*c*) Local wood	sqm	722.00	
	(*d*) Sal, Siliguri	sqm	1,125.00	
27.	Supplying and fixing solid flush type doors of commercial quality.			
	(*a*) 35 mm thick shutters (single leaf)	sqm	902.00	
	(*b*) 25 mm thick shutters (single leaf)	sqm	775.00	
28.	Supplying and fixing factory made panel door.			
	(*i*) 25 mm thick shutters			
	(*a*) Single leaf	sqm	665.00	
	(*b*) Double leaf	sqm	710.00	
29.	Panel shutters of doors and windows with 12 mm thick particle board panel finished with commercial veneers. 25 mm thick shutters, styles and rails with 1st class Indian teak			
	(*a*) Single leaf	sqm	1,376.00	
	(*b*) Double leaf	sqm	1,835.00	
30.	Fly proof shutters with galvanised netting 256 mesh per sq. inch/22 gauge of approved quality.			
	(*a*) 35 mm thick shutters 1st class Indian teak	sqm	2,275.00	
	H. Band moulding, cornice, etc.			
1.	Band moulding (horizontal or vertical) rectangular section, made of cement plaster (4 : 1) complete. Projection up to 25 mm Depth or width (75 mm to 100 mm)	m	14.40	
2.	Multiple-band moulding made with 15 mm cement plaster (4:1) complete. Projection up to 25 mm			
	(*a*) Depth or width (75 mm to 100 mm)	m	22.00	
3.	Concrete chowkat with rabbet (in sill of door or window) made with cement concrete (4 : 2 : 1)	m	27.00	
	I. Plastering pointing, etc.			
1.	Plaster (to wall, floor, ceiling, etc.) with sand and cement.			
	(*i*) With 6 : 1 cement mortar			
	(*a*) 25 mm thick plaster	sqm	73.00	
	(*b*) 20 mm thick plaster	sqm	52.00	
	(*c*) 15 mm thick plaster	sqm	45.00	

S. No.	Description of items	Unit	Rate Rs. P	Remarks
2.	Plaster (to wall, floor, ceiling, etc.) with composite mortar of sand, lime, and cement.			
	(*i*) With (9 : 2 : 1) composite mortar			
	(*a*) 35 mm thick plaster	sqm	61.00	
3.	Plaster with surkhi and lime mortar 2 : 1. 20 mm thick plaster	sqm	48.70	
4.	Neat cement punning average 1.5 mm thick in wall, dado, window sills floor, drain, etc.	sqm	15.00	
5.	Lime punning average 3 mm thick with shell lime and stone lime (2 : 1).	sqm	27.00	
6.	Flush pointing to brickwork in cement mortar including raking out joints.	sqm	25.40	
7.	Rule pointing to brickwork in cement mortar (4 : 1) including raking out joints.	sqm	26.00	
8.	Tuck pointing to brickwork in cement mortar (3 : 1) including raking out joints.	sqm	55.00	
	J. White washing, Colour washing, Distemper, etc.			
1.	White washing including cleaning and smoothening surface thoroughly.			
	(*a*) One coat	% sqm	175.00	
	(*b*) Two coats	% sqm	291.00	
2.	Colour washing with "Ella" with a coat of white wash priming.			
	(*a*) One coat	% sqm	220.00	
	(*b*) Two coats	% sqm	430.00	
3.	Colour washing with pigments.			
	(*i*) Internal surface			
	(*a*) One coat of colour wash	% sqm	476.00	
	(*b*) Two coats of colour wash	% sqm	805.00	
	(*ii*) External surface			
	(*a*) One coat of colour wash	% sqm	476.00	
	(*b*) Two coats of colour wash	% sqm	805.00	
4.	Cement washing including cleaning and smoothening surface thoroughly.			
	(*a*) One coat	% sqm	282.00	
	(*b*) Two coats	% sqm	510.00	
5.	Applying decorative cement based paint			
	(*a*) One coat	sqm	11.20	
	(*b*) Two coats	sqm	19.00	
6.	Chalk washing one coat	sqm	2.10	
7.	Rendering the surface of walls and ceiling with plaster of paris.	sqm	30.00	

S. No.	Description of items	Unit	Rate Rs. P	Remarks
8.	Priming one coat on timber, plastered or on steel or other metal surface with sythetic enamel/oil bound primer.	sqm	14.00	
	K. Painting and varnishing, etc.			
1.	Painting with best quality sythetic enamel paint.			
	(*a*) On timber or plastered surface			
	One coat	sqm	22.00	
	Two coats	sqm	36.00	
2.	Copal varnish including preparing surface.			
	One coat	sqm	16.00	
	Two coats	sqm	24.00	
3.	French polishing to wood works.			
	(*a*) On new wood work	sqm	50.00	
	(*b*) On old French polished surface	sqm	60.00	
4.	Frosting glass by dabbing white paint	sqm	17.00	
	L. Glazier's Work			
1.	Supplying best Indian sheet glass panes set in putty and fitted and fixed with nails and putty.			
	2 mm thick	sqm	237.00	
	3 mm thick	sqm	324.00	
	4 mm thick	sqm	376.00	
2.	Supplying best Indian reinforced wire safety glass 6 mm thick including cutting and fixing complete.	sqm	887.00	
3.	Supplying best Indian sheet glass 5.5 mm thick including cutting fitting and fixing complete.	sqm	584.00	
4.	Supplying best Indian Calorex glass including fitting and fixing.	sqm	440.00	
	M. Drain, Down pipes, Chimneys, Pipes, etc.			
1.	Saucer drain up to 150 mm width in floor and up to 75 mm depth including cement plaster 3 : 1 and neat cement finish.	m	11.00	
2.	Supplying fitting and fixing cast iron down pipes.			
	(*i*) 75 mm diameter (external)	m	232.00	
	(*ii*) 100 mm diameter (external)	m	267.00	
	(*iii*) 150 mm diameter (external)	m	417.00	
	N. Thatch, Mud and Bamboo works			
1.	Digging hole in all sorts of soil for fixing bamboo posts.			
	(*a*) Depth 450 mm	Each	2.00	
	(*b*) Depth 600 mm	Each	2.50	
	(*c*) Depth 750 mm	Each	3.00	
2.	Strong bamboo frame work with 75 mm bamboo for thatch roofing.	sqm	68.00	

S. No.	*Description of items*	*Unit*	*Rate* Rs. P	*Remarks*
3.	Rice straw thatching in roof including ridges and hips.			
	(*a*) 150 mm (pressed) thick	sqm	36.00	
	(*b*) 225 mm (pressed) thick	sqm	56.00	
	O. Fenching			
1.	Supplying 7 ply galvanised strand wire 19 gauge fitted and fixed.	m	10.50	
2.	Supplying 6 ply galvanised strand wire 19 gauge fitted and fixed.	m	9.50	
3.	Double knotted woven wire 1.2 m height (11 bars), vertical 300 mm apart, horizontal spacing starting from 88 mm.	% m	4,536.00	
	P. Soling, Edging & Metalling			
1.	Brick soling with picked jhama bricks.			
	(*a*) Single brick flat soling	sqm	95.00	
	(*b*) Double brick flat soling	sqm	189.00	
2.	Brick edging 75 mm wide with picked jhama bricks.			
	(*a*) Brick on edge edging 125 mm depth.	% m	1,200.00	
	(*b*) Brick on end edging 250 mm depth	% m	2,470.00	
	Q. Maintenance of Statues and Monuments			
1.	Filling up the joints of marble or granite stone, etc. of statues after chiselling out joints including grouting with cement mortar 3 : 1.	m	13.00	
2.	Cleaning and removing stains as far as possible from the pedestals and bases below statues of granite and syenite stone.	sqm	8.50	
	R. Special Items			
1.	Antitermite treatment to bottom surface (in case of masonry foundation and basements) and sides of the excavation trenches with chemical emulsion by admixing chloropyrefcs emulsifiable concentrates (1% concentration) with water by weight at the rate of 5 liters per sqm area.	sqm	40.00	
	S. Miscellaneous Items			
1.	Number plaque of buildings (plaque size up to 225 mm × 225 mm).	Each	25.00	
2.	Stitching crack in brick wall by carefully cutting out face brick 125 mm deep into the wall.			
	(*i*) With plain cement concrete blocks ($3 : 1\frac{1}{2} : 1$) with stone chips			
	(*a*) Block size 250 × 125 × 75 mm thick	Each block	25.00	

The items included are not exhaustive, but are shown as examples. There may be several other items in each section.

20

PRACTICE QUESTIONS

A. Short questions.

Find out the correct answers from the options given.

1. Brickwork dimensions shall be measured to the nearest
   (*a*) 0.01 m (*b*) 0.02 m
   (*c*) 0.05 m
2. Except steelwork areas of the other works shall be worked out to the nearest
   (*a*) 0.001 sqm (*b*) 0.003 sqm
   (*c*) 0.01 sqm (*d*) 0.10 sqm
3. Concrete work cubic contents shall be worked out to the nearest
   (*a*) 0.001 cum (*b*) 0.01 cum
   (*c*) 0.02 cum
4. Areas of concrete slab shall be worked out to the nearest
   (*a*) 0.01 sqm (*b*) 0.002 sqm
   (*c*) 0.001 sqm
5. Steel reinforcement shall be measured to the nearest
   (*a*) 0.10 m (*b*) 0.01 m
   (*c*) 0.002 m (*d*) 0.005 m
6. Areas of steel or iron work (excluding cross-section) shall be worked out to the nearest of
   (*a*) 0.01 sqm (*b*) 0.05 sqm
   (*c*) 0.001 sqm
7. Weights of steel or iron work shall be worked out to the nearest
   (*a*) 0.01 kg (*b*) 0.05 kg
   (*c*) 1.0 kg
8. Length and width of woodwork shall be measured to the nearest
   (*a*) 0.001 m (*b*) 0.002 m
   (*c*) 0.05 m
9. Thickness of wood work shall be measured to the nearest
   (*a*) 1 mm (*b*) 2 mm
   (*c*) 5 mm (*d*) 0.01 m
10. Wooden scantlings, battens shall be measured to the nearest
   (*a*) 1 mm (*b*) 2 mm
   (*c*) 5 mm (*d*) 0.01 m

11. Cubic contents of woodwork shall be worked out to the nearest
(*a*) 0.10 cum (*b*) 0.05 cum
(*c*) 0.001 cum
12. Dimensions excepting cross-sections and thickness shall be measured to the nearest
(*a*) 0.05 m (*b*) 0.10 m
(*c*) 0.001 m
13. For glazing each pane of glass shall be measured to the nearest
(*a*) 0.01 cm (*b*) 0.10 cm
(*c*) 0.50 cm (*d*) 1.0 cm
14. Thickness of roadwork where the thickness is less than 20 cm, the thickness is measured to the nearest
(*a*) 0.01 m (*b*) 0.50 m
(*c*) 0.005 m
15. Lime concrete on roof terracing is measured per
(*a*) sqm (*b*) cum
16. Terrazzo flooring is measured per
(*a*) sqm (*b*) cum
17. For roof covering ridges, hips and valley is measured per
(*a*) sqm (*b*) rm
18. Corrugated galvanised steel sheets are measured by
(*a*) number (*b*) kg
(*c*) quintal (*d*) sqm
19. A.C. or G.C.I. sheet roofing is measured by
(*a*) quintal (*b*) sqm
(*c*) kg
20. Lime concrete or cement concrete flooring is measured in sqm stating the thickness which does not exceed
(*a*) 10 cm (*b*) 20 cm
(*c*) 15 cm
21. The unit of measurement for earthwork in excavation exceeding 1.5 m in width as well as 10 sqm on plan but not exceeding 30 cm in depth, is in
(*a*) cum (*b*) sqm
(*c*) 10 sqm
22. The unit of measurement of lime terracing on roof is in
(*a*) cum (*b*) sqm
(*c*) 10 sqm
23. The unit of measurement of wooden shutters is in
(*a*) sqm (*b*) cum
(*c*) 10 sqm
24. The unit of measurement of woodwork for door and window frames is in
(*a*) sqm (*b*) cum
(*c*) 10 sqm

25. The unit of measurement for 10 cm or half brick walls is in
(*a*) cum (*b*) sqm
(*c*) 10 sqm

26. The unit of measurement of Ridges, Hips and Valley is in
(*a*) rm (*b*) sqm
(*c*) cum

27. The unit of measurement of dividing strips for flooring is in
(*a*) kg (*b*) rm
(*c*) sqm

28. The unit of measurement of rainwater or vent pipe is in
(*a*) kg (*b*) quintal
(*c*) rm

29. For brickwork no deduction is made for area of openings up to
(*a*) 0.1 sqm (*b*) 0.2 sqm
(*c*) 0.3 sqm (*d*) 0.5 sqm

30. For brickwork, ends of lintel up to 0.1 sqm in section
(*a*) deduction is made
(*b*) no deduction is made

31. No deduction is made in brickwork for part bearing of slabs, chajja where the thickness does not exceed
(*a*) 10 cm (*b*) 15 cm
(*c*) 20 cm

32. For R.C.C. work no deduction is made for openings up to
(*a*) 0.1 sqm (*b*) 0.2 sqm
(*c*) 0.3 sqm

33. The volume occupied by reinforcement in R.C.C. work shall be
(*a*) deducted (*b*) not deducted

34. For formwork no deduction shall be made for openings up to
(*a*) 0.1 sqm (*b*) 0.4 sqm
(*c*) 0.5 sqm (*d*) 0.6 sqm

35. For paving or floor finishes no deduction shall be made for voids up to
(*a*) 0.1 sqm (*b*) 0.2 sqm
(*c*) 0.3 sqm (*d*) 0.5 sqm

36. For paving floor finishes, dado and skirting deductions for ends of dissimilar materials or other articles embedded shall not be made for areas not exceeding
(*a*) 0.01 sqm (*b*) 0.10 sqm
(*c*) 0.50 sqm

37. For plastering to brickwork no deduction shall be made for ends of joists, beams, steps and openings not exceeding each
(*a*) 0.10 sqm (*b*) 0.25 sqm
(*c*) 0.50 sqm (*d*) 1.0 sqm

38. When two faces of brickwall are plastered deduction shall be made for one face only and no addition shall be made for reveals, jambs, soffits, sills, etc. for openings each exceeding

(*a*) 0.1 sqm, but not exceeding 1.0 sqm
(*b*) 0.3 sqm, but not exceeding 1.0 sqm
(*c*) 0.5 sqm, but not exceeding 3.0 sqm

39. When both faces of brickwork are plastered, deductions shall be made for openings of each face but jambs, soffits and sills shall be measured for openings of each area above

(*a*) 1 sqm, (*b*) 3 sqm,
(*c*) 4 sqm (*d*) 5 sqm.

40. Woodwork for door and window shutters measurement is taken as per opening in the framework

(*a*) including rebate, (*b*) excluding rebate.

41. Woodwork for door and window shutters is measured

(*a*) including extra width of meeting styles,
(*b*) excluding extra width of meeting styles.

42. In case of welded steel structure allowance for weld metal

(*a*) shall be made, (*b*) shall not be made.

43. For rivet heads in riveted steel structures

(*a*) no allowance shall be made, (*b*) allowance shall be made.

44. The rivet or bolt hole for structural steel work, if its area does not exceed 0.02 sqm

(*a*) deduction shall be made, (*b*) no deduction shall be made.

45. The superficial area of G.C.I. or A.C. sheet roof coverings shall be measured on the flat

(*a*) with allowance for laps and corrugations,
(*b*) without allowance for laps and corrugations.

46. For painting or white washing or colour washing corrugated steel surfaces shall be measured flat and the area worked out shall be increased by

(*a*) 10% (*b*) 12%
(*c*) 14% (*d*) 25%

47. For painting, white washing or colour washing corrugated asbestos cement sheets surfaces shall be measured flat and the area so worked out shall be increased by

(*a*) 15% (*b*) 18%
(*c*) 20% (*d*) 25%

48. Painting of eaves-gutters, rainwater pipes, soil and ventilating pipes and steel poles shall be measured in

(*a*) sqm (*b*) rm

49. Painting up to 10 cm in width or in girth and not in conjunction with similar painted work shall be measured in

(*a*) sqm (*b*) rm

50. To convert equivalent plain area of uneven surfaces and also to include frame, cleats, etc. The multiplying factor for the panelled joinery for each face is

(*a*) 1.0 (*b*) 1.3

(*c*) 1.5 (*d*) 2

51. To convert equivalent plain area of uneven surfaces and also to include frame, cleats. The multiplying factor for partly glazed joinery for each face is
(*a*) 0.67 (*b*) 1.3
(*c*) 1.5

52. To convert equivalent plain area of uneven surfaces and also to include frame, cleats, etc. The multiplying factor for flush joinery is
(*a*) 1.0 (*b*) 1.0
(*c*) 1.3 (*d*) 1.5

53. The multiplying factor for painting collapsible gate measured flat (size of opening) all over is
(*a*) 1.0 (*b*) 1.5
(*c*) 2.0 (*d*) 2.5
(*e*) 3.0.

54. The multiplying factor for steel rolling shutters measured flat (size of opening) overall; including jamb guides, bottom rails, locking arrangement, etc. for each side is
(*a*) 1.0 (*b*) 1.1
(*c*) 1.25 (*d*) 1.4
(*e*) 1.5.

55. For R.C.C. work the length of a stirrup is
(*a*) (A + E) + 15 cm (*b*) (A + E) + 18 cm
(*c*) 2 (A + E) + 24d
where *A* and *E* are the inside depth and width of the stirrup respectively and *d* = dia. of the stirrup bar.

56. Brick or stone aggregate of 40 mm nominal size and above is measured after making of deduction of
(*a*) 5% (*b*) 7.5%
(*c*) 10% (*d*) 14% from measurement

57. Soling stone, boulders or rubble is measured after making deduction of
(*a*) 5%, (*b*) 10%,
(*c*) 11%, (*d*) 18% from the gross stack measurement.

58. The unit of lift of earthwork is
(*a*) 1.0 m (*b*) 1.4 m
(*c*) 1.5 m

59. One bag of cement is
(*a*) 0.0215 cum (*b*) 0.0347 cum
(*c*) 0.04347 cum

60. One cum of cement is
(*a*) 28.81 bags (*b*) 20.83 bags
(*c*) 80.28 bags

61. Stone chips (20 mm down) required for 1 cum of cement concrete of proportion 1 : 2 : 4 will be about

(*a*) 0.44 cum (*b*) 0.55 cum
(*c*) 0.88 cum (*d*) 0.90 cum

62. For 1 cum of cement concrete of proportion 1 : 2 : 4 the required number of cement bags is
(*a*) 4.5 (*b*) 5.5 (*c*) 6.0
(*d*) 6.34 (*e*) 6.5

63. For 1 cum of first class brickwork (metric bricks) the number of bricks required will be
(*a*) 430 (*b*) 450
(*c*) 500 (*d*) 550

64. For 10 sqm of half brickwork (with metric bricks) the number of bricks required will be
(*a*) 300 (*b*) 450
(*c*) 500 (*d*) 550

65. For single brick flat (with metric bricks) soling the number or bricks required will be
(*a*) 350 (*b*) 400
(*c*) 425 (*d*) 500

66. For 25 mm thick cement concrete (1 : 2 : 4) damp proof course the quantity of stone chips required will be
(*a*) 2.0 cum (*b*) 2.2 cum
(*c*) 2.4 cum per 100 sqm

67. While plastering 15 mm thick cement plaster (1 : 6) the number of cement bags taken into account per 100 sqm is
(*a*) 10 (*b*) 9
(*c*) 8.3 (*d*) 8.64
(*e*) 7.5

68. The estimated quantity of cement bags for 10 mm thick cement plaster per 100 sqm will be about
(*a*) 5.0 (*b*) 6.5
(*c*) 7.0 (*d*) 7.5

69. For two coats of white washing on a coat of primer to new plaster, the quantity of unslaked lime in kg required per 100 sqm area will be
(*a*) 20 (*b*) 25
(*c*) 30 (*d*) 35
(*e*) 45

70. For two coats snow-cem coating on plastered surface, the quantity of snow-cem in kg required per 100 sqm area will be
(*a*) 45 (*b*) 50
(*c*) 60 (*d*) 70

71. While doing analysis of rate for painting two coats (excluding primer coat) with ready mixed paint to new wood work the quantity of paint will be required per 100 sqm
(*a*) 10 liters (*b*) 12 liters
(*c*) 14 liters

72. For cement concrete (except for road or mass concrete) the size of coarse aggregate shall be

(*a*) 25 mm graded down to 10 mm (*b*) 20 mm graded down to 5 mm
(*c*) 15 mm graded down to 5 mm

73. First class bricks shall have an average compressive strength in kg per sq cm not less than

(*a*) 90 (*b*) 100
(*c*) 125 (*d*) 160

74. For first class brickwork the thickness of mortar joint shall not be less

(*a*) 3.0 (*b*) 5.0
(*c*) 10.0

75. Where ordinary portland cement is used for removal of props under slabs spanning up to 4.5 m may be done after

(*a*) 5 days (*b*) 7 days
(*c*) 12 days (*d*) 15 days

76. While ordinary portland cement is used removal of props under beams spanning upto 6 m may be made after expiry of

(*a*) 7 days (*b*) 14 days
(*c*) 21 days

77. Corrugated galvanised iron sheet roofing shall be laid providing side lap of

(*a*) one corrugation (*b*) one and half corrugation
(*c*) two corrugations

78. For artificial stone flooring or cement concrete flooring panel diemnsion shall not exceed

(*a*) 1.0 m (*b*) 2.0 m
(*c*) 2.5 m

79. For artificial stone flooring or cement concrete flooring the area of panel shall not be more than

(*a*) 1.0 sqm (*b*) 2.0 sqm
(*c*) 3.0 sqm

80. The rebate in shutter for closing in double shutter door and window shall not be less than

(*a*) 1 cm (*b*) 1.5 cm
(*c*) 2 cm (*d*) 2.5 cm

81. In laying of corrugated galvanised iron sheet roofing shall be done providing an end lap of

(*a*) 10 cm (*b*) 12 cm
(*c*) 15 cm (*d*) 20 cm

82. The quantity of brick ballast required for 10 cm thick lime terracing on R.C.C. roof per 100 sqm will be

(*a*) 8 cum (*b*) 10 cum
(*c*) 10.2 cum (*d*) 10.8 cum

83. Revised estimate is required due to
    (*a*) change of quantity of material, rates
    (*b*) addition of new work, changes of design
84. Supplementary estimate
    (*a*) requires comparative statement
    (*b*) comparative statement is not required
85. Plinth area
    (*a*) includes plinth offset (*b*) excludes plinth offset
86. For plinth area measurement balcony is
    (*a*) included (*b*) excluded
87. In calculation of carpet area, the areas of corridor and passage of a building will be
    (*a*) included (*b*) excluded
88. Along with the tender, a contractor has to deposit
    (*a*) security deposit (*b*) earnest money
89. The capacity of earthwork in excavation in foundation trenches in ordinary soil per day per mazdoor is
    (*a*) 2 cum (*b*) 2.35 cum
    (*c*) 2.5 cum (*d*) 3.50 cum
90. The quantity of cement concrete in foundation per day per mason will be
    (*a*) 3 cum (*b*) 4 cum
    (*c*) 5 cum (*d*) 6 cum
91. The quantity of brickwork in foundation and plinth per day per mason should be
    (*a*) 1.0 cum (*b*) 1.25 cum
    (*c*) 1.5 cum (*d*) 2.0 cum
92. The capacity of brickwork in superstructure, ground floor per day per mason is
    (*a*) 0.5 cum (*b*) 1.0 cum
    (*c*) 1.1 cum
93. The quantity of half brickwork in partition wall in sqm per day per mason should be
    (*a*) 10.0 (*b*) 8.0
    (*c*) 7.0 (*d*) 6.0
94. The capacity of 15 mm thick cement plaster on new brickwork up to first floor in sqm per mason per day should be
    (*a*) 8.0 (*b*) 10.0
    (*c*) 12.0 (*d*) 15.0
95. 10 mm thick cement plaster to ceiling can be done per mason per day
    (*a*) 5.0 (*b*) 8.0
    (*c*) 10.0 (*d*) 12.0
96. The quantity of single coat white washing over old white washed surface in sqm per painter per day is
    (*a*) 50.0 (*b*) 60.0
    (*c*) 66.0 (*d*) 70.0

97. The quantity of white washing two coats on a coat of primer in sqm per painter per day is

(*a*) 50.0 (*b*) 60.0
(*c*) 66.0

98. The quantity of snow-cem painting to new plastered surface in sqm per painter, per day is

(*a*) 50.0 (*b*) 40.0
(*c*) 30.0 (*d*) 20.0

99. The capacity of breaking of over burnt brick to ballast 40 mm down per mazdoor per day is

(*a*) 1.25 cum (*b*) 1.0 cum
(*c*) 0.75 cum

100. The capacity of breaking over burnt brick to chips in cum per day per mazdoor is

(*a*) 0.5 (*b*) 0.55 (*c*) 0.75

101. In king post roof truss, there will be :

(*a*) Even number of vertical post (*b*) One vertical post
(*c*) Minimum 2 number of vertical post (*d*) No vertical post

102. The apex line of sloping roof is called

(*a*) Apex (*b*) Ridge
(*c*) Rafter (*d*) Top

103. The portion of a wall which supports an arch is called

(*a*) Embankment (*b*) Base
(*c*) Abutment (*d*) Column

104. Stone masonry of finely dressed stones laid in cement or lime is known as

(*a*) Flint masonry (*b*) Random rubble masonry
(*c*) Rubble masonry (*d*) Ashlar masonry

105. In machine foundation, material used to prevent transmission of vibration is

(*a*) Cork (*b*) Rubber
(*c*) Felt (*d*) Any one of the above

106. The sides of an opening such as doors, windows, etc. are known as

(*a*) Jambs (*b*) Lintels
(*c*) Verticals (*d*) Heads

107. The process of keeping concrete moist for several days after finishing is termed as

(*a*) Setting (*b*) Hardening
(*c*) Curing (*d*) None of above

108. A material often used for damp proofing is

(*a*) Silica gel (*b*) Wax
(*c*) Glass wool (*d*) Bitumen

109. Plate load test is conducted at the site to find

(*a*) Depth of water table (*b*) Depth of underlying rock
(*c*) Ultimate bearing capacity
(*d*) All the above

110. Concrete hollow block masonry is normally constructed adopting
(*a*) Stretcher bond (*b*) English bond
(*c*) Flemish bond (*d*) Ashlar bond

111. The end support of an arch is known as
(*a*) Springer (*b*) Intrados
(*c*) Voussior (*d*) Abutment

112. Damp-proof course consists of a layer of
(*a*) Burt clay brick (*b*) Sand
(*c*) Timber (*d*) Cement concrete

113. Fire-resistant characteristic is improved by impregnation of the following-fire-retarding chemical
(*a*) Hydrochloric acid (*b*) Hydrogen peroxide
(*c*) Zinc chlorides (*d*) Sulphuric acid

114. Terrazzo flooring utilises which of the following as aggregate
(*a*) Granite (*b*) Marble
(*c*) Terracota (*d*) Linoleum

115. Casement window is a
(*a*) Awning window (*b*) Horizontal sliding window
(*c*) Folding window
(*d*) Hinged window which may swing in and out

116. Soil kneading operation which forms part of compaction process. The equipment used for this purpose is
(*a*) Sheep foot roller (*b*) Skimmer
(*c*) Dragline (*d*) Smooth wheel roller

117. The arrangement of supports provided underneath the existing structure without disturbing its stability is known as
(*a*) Underpinning (*b*) Scaffolding
(*c*) Shoring (*d*) Jacking

118. Under-reamed piles are predominantly used in
(*a*) Expansive soil (*b*) Sandy soils
(*c*) Permeable soil (*d*) Silty soil

119. The minimum thickness of a wall in stone mesonry cannot be less than
(*a*) 10 cm (*b*) 20 cm
(*c*) 35 cm (*d*) 50 cm

120. When a brick is cut off lengthwise, the cut out bricks are called
(*a*) king closer (*b*) queen closer
(*c*) Corbel (*d*) bat

121. A part of wall at the side of an opening in the masonry is called
(*a*) Jamb (*b*) Parapet
(*c*) Quoin (*d*) Squint

122. In horizontal D.P.C. the thickness of cement concrete (1 : 2 : 4) is kept
(*a*) 2.5 cm (*b*) 4.0 cm
(*c*) 6 cm (*d*) 8 cm

123. In R.C.C. lintels, the position of main reinforcement in concrete should be at

(*a*) the top (*b*) the bottom

(*c*) the center (*d*) any position

124. The inclined braces used in a truss to prevent the sagging of the principal ratter are called

(*a*) king post (*b*) queen poat

(*c*) tie beam (*d*) struts

125. The property of fresh concrete, in which the water in the mix tends to rise to the surface while placing and compaction is known as

(*a*) bleeding (*b*) creep

(*c*) segregation (*d*) shrinkage

126. If the slump of a concrete mix is 6 cm, its workability is considered to be

(*a*) very high (*b*) high

(*c*) medium (*d*) low

B. Broad Questions

1. (*a*) What are the different methods for estimating building works ? Explain by setting example in each.

   (*b*) State the importance of approximate estimate and its purposes.

2. Define the following terms

   (*i*) Plinth area

   (*ii*) Floor area

   (*iii*) Carpet area

   (*iv*) Covered area, Rental area

3. (*a*) State the basic qualifications of contractors.

   (*b*) Write notes on the advantages and disadvantages of the following types of contracts.

   (*i*) Item rate contract (*ii*) Lump-sum contract

   (*iii*) Turn-key job contract

4. (*a*) What do you mean by controlled concrete ? Discuss degree of control.

   (*b*) Describe briefly the procedure for statistical quality of concrete in construction works.

   (*c*) Write short notes on

   (*i*) High strength concrete,

   (*ii*) Air entrained concrete,

   (*iii*) Light weight concrete.

5. (*a*) Prepare a detailed estimate for earthwork for a stretch of a road from the data given below :

Distance in meters	0	100	200	300	400	500	600	700	800	900	1000
R.L. of ground	114.5	114.75	115.25	115.2	116.1	116.85	118.00	118.25	118.10	117.80	117.75
R.L. of formation	115 upward gradient 1 in 200 →						← Downward gradient 1 in 400 upto 600				

Formation width of road is 10 m and side slope 2 : 1 and 1 : 15 in cutting. Adopt suitable rates.

(*b*) Work out the preliminary estimate for a concrete pavement 200 mm thick in nominal mix 1 : 2 : 4 using 20 mm size maximum aggregate for a 3.75 m width for 1 km length. Assume rates and necessary data required if any.

6. Write the deatailed specifications for the following items of work
   (*i*) Lime concrete in foundation
   (*ii*) Damp-proof course
   (*iii*) Reinforced cement concrete
   (*iv*) 20 mm premixed carpet
7. (*a*) Describe briefly the item rate contract, general conditions of the contract and contract agreement.
   (*b*) Write short notes on
   (*i*) Labour contract
   (*ii*) Lump-sum contract
8. Estimate the quantities of the following items in a building from plan and section as given in the figure on a separate sheet attached.
   (*i*) Earthwork in excavation
   (*ii*) Earthwork in filling in foundation and floor
   (*iii*) CC in foundation
   (*iv*) Brickwork in foundation up to plinth level
   (*v*) DPC
   (*vi*) First class brickwork for walls
   (*vii*) 100 mm thick PCC floor
   (*viii*) RCC roof and lintel
   (*ix*) 25 mm thick floor finish (ASF)
   (*x*) Woodwork in door and window frames
9. (*a*) State the necessity of specification in construction works.
   (*b*) What factors are considered in drafting the specification for construction work.
   (*c*) Write detailed specifications for any two of the following
   (*i*) Terrazo flooring
   (*ii*) Centering and shuttering for an RCC beam and slab
   (*iii*) Earthwork in excavation and filling
   (*iv*) PCC (1 : 3 : 6) in foundation and floor
   (*d*) Assuming reasonable current rates for material and labour analyse rates for the following items of works (any two):
   (*i*) Two coats of distemper or new surface
   (*ii*) First class brickwork in cement mortar
   (*iii*) 12 mm thick cement plastering (1 : 6) on new brickwork
   (*iv*) 10 cm average lime terracing on RCC roof with 25 mm gauge overburnt brick ballast (proportion 2 : 2 : 7).
10. Write notes on the following :

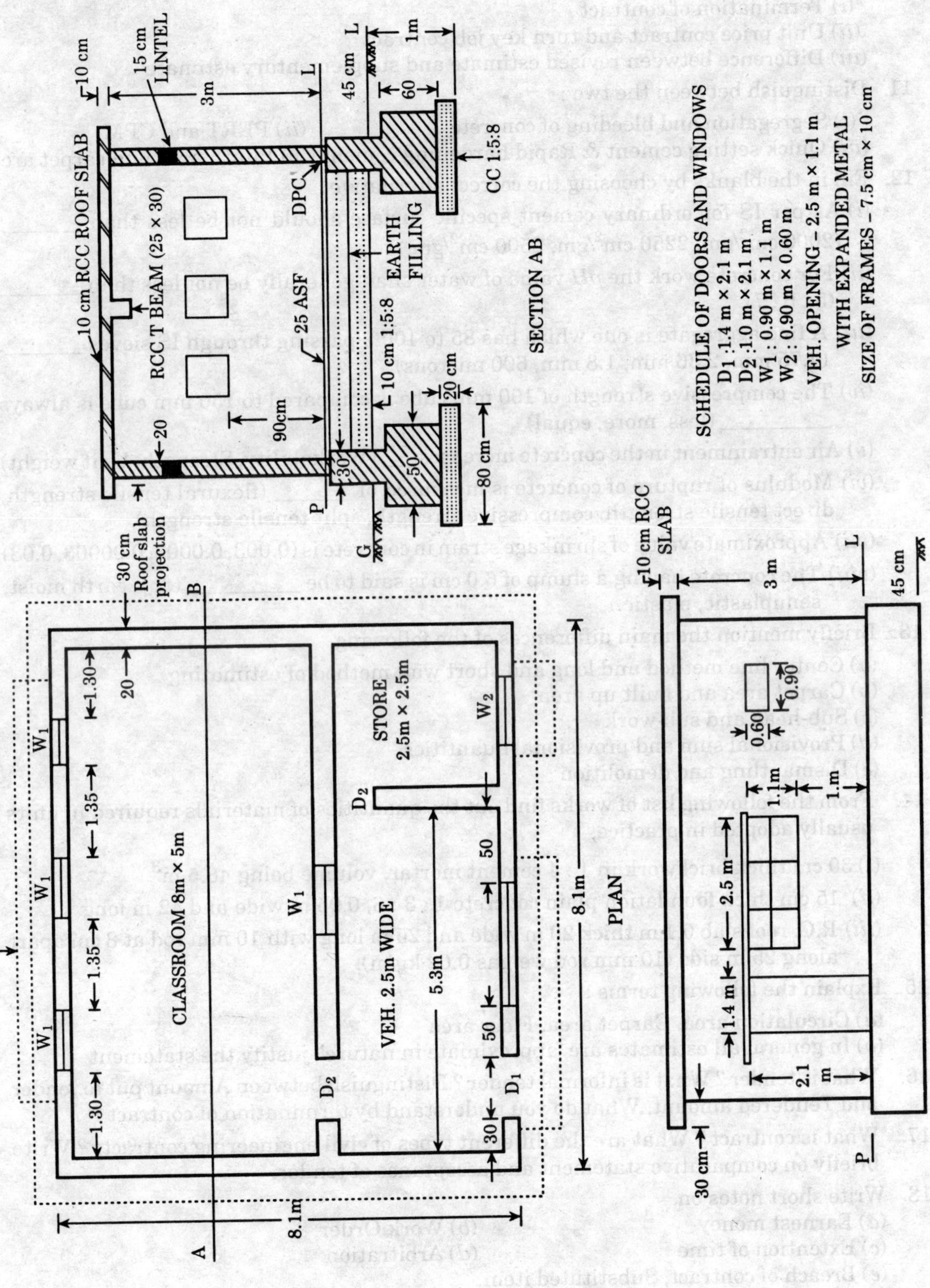
10 cm
15 cm
LINTEL
3m
L
45 cm
1m
60
RCC ROOF SLAB
10 cm RCC ROOF SLAB
RCC T BEAM (25 × 30)
DPC
CC 1:5:8
25 ASF
EARTH
FILLING
G
10 cm 1:5:8
SECTION AB
20 cm
90cm
20
30
50
80 cm
P
SCHEDULE OF DOORS AND WINDOWS
D1 : 1.4 m × 2.1 m
D2 : 1.0 m × 2.1 m
W1 : 0.90 m × 1.1 m
W2 : 0.90 m × 0.60 m
VEH. OPENING – 2.5 m × 11 m
WITH EXPANDED METAL
SIZE OF FRAMES – 7.5 cm × 10 cm
45cm PROJECTED CHAJJA
30 cm
Roof slab
projection
B
A
W1
1.30
1.35
20
CLASSROOM 8m × 5m
W1
STORE
2.5m × 2.5m
W2
D2
VEH. 2.5m WIDE
5.3m
50
D1
30
8.1m
PLAN
10 cm RCC
SLAB
0.90
0.60
1.1 m
1 m
2.5 m
1.4 m
2.1
m
30 cm

(i) Termination of contract
(ii) Unit price contract and turn key job contract
(iii) Difference between revised estimate and supplementary estimate

11. Distinguish between the two :
(i) Segregation and bleeding of concrete (ii) PERT and CPM
(iii) Quick setting cement & Rapid hardening cement (iv) Plinth area and carpet area

12. Fill in the blanks by choosing the correct alternative :
(i) As per IS for ordinary cement specific surface should not be less than _______. (2000 cm^2/gm, 2250 cm^2/gm, 2500 cm^2/gm.)
(ii) For concrete work the pH value of water shall generally be not less than_______ (5 , 6 , 7).
(iii) A fine aggregate is one which has 85 to 100% passing through IS sieves _______. (4.75 mm, 2.36 mm, 1.8 mm, 600 microns)
(iv) The compressive strength of 100 mm cube is compared to 150 mm cube is always _________ (less, more, equal)
(v) Air entrainment in the concrete increases___(Workability, Strength, Unit weight)
(vi) Modulus of rupture of concrete is measured of _______ (flexural tensile strength, direct tensile strength, compressive strength, split tensile strength).
(vii) Approximate value of shrinkage strain in concrete is (0.003, 0.0003, 0.00003, 0.03)
(viii) The concrete having a slump of 6.0 cm is said to be _________ (dry, earth moist, semiplastic, plastic.)

13. Briefly mention the main differences of the following
(a) Center line method and long and short wall method of estimating
(b) Carpet area and built up area
(c) Sub-head and sub-work
(d) Provisional sum and provisional quantities
(e) Dismantling and demolition

14. From the following list of works find out the quantities of materials required in units usually adopted in practice,
(i) 30 cm thick brickwork in 1 : 4 cement mortar, volume being 48.5 m^3
(ii) 15 cm thick foundation plain concrete 1 : 3 : 6, 0.95 m wide and 42 m long
(iii) R.C. roof slab 0.1 m thick 20 m wide and 25 m long with 10 mm rod at 8 cm apart along 25 m side (10 mm rod weighs 0.62 kg/m).

15. Explain the following terms :
(a) Circulation area, Carpet area, Floor area
(b) In general all estimates are 'approximate in nature', justify the statement

16. What is tender ? What is informal tender ? Distinguish between Amount put to tender and Tendered amount. What do you understand by termination of contract ?

17. What is contract ? What are the different types of civil engineering contracts ? Write briefly on comparative statement and acceptance of tender.

18. Write short notes on
(a) Earnest money (b) Work Order
(c) Extention of time (d) Arbitration
(e) Breach of contract, Substituted item

19. Write brief clauses of general condition of contract any four of the following :

(*a*) Rectification of defective work and removal of materials not conforming to specifications,

(*b*) Extention of the completion time of work.

20. (*a*) Discuss the provisions in Civil Engineering contract to settle dispute with the contractor,

(*b*) What is plinth area and cubic rate estimate ? Why a revised estimate is necessary? What is a detailed estimate and how is it prepared ?

21. Write short notes on any four :

(*a*) Earnest money (*b*) Refund of security deposit

(*c*) Work order (*d*) Lump-sum contract, Substituted item

22. Briefly mention the difference of the following :

(*i*) Tender notice and Tender papers (*ii*) Rate Analysis and Specification

(*iii*) Renewal and Extention of time (*iv*) Salvage value and Scrap value

(*v*) Units of measurement and units of payment.

23. What do you mean by target contract ?

A - a owner agrees to pay the actual cost plus 10% of the actual cost as the basic fees. In addition A agrees to pay 25% of the saving effected against the target cost that will be arrived at by the previous agreed rates. In case the actual cost is more than the target value,

B - a contractor will permit deduction at 25% of the excess from the basic fee payable to him. B carries out the work, whose target value works out to Rs. 2,00,000.00. What will be total fee, if the actual cost is

(*i*) Rs. 1,70,000.00 (*ii*) Rs. 2,00,000.00 (*iii*) Rs. 2,30,000.00

24. What is earthwork table ? What is price-escalation as additional terms of condition in a contract ? When whole security deposit of a contractor can be forfieted ?

25. What is site value ? How will you fix up proportionate rent of a building used for office-cum residence purpose ? What is valuation report and are different parts of the report ?

26. Write short notes on (*a*) Return frontage with some example ; (*b*) Belting method of valuation :

27. (*a*) Work out the percentage rate of annual depreciation by constant percentage method of a property assuming :

p = percentage rate of annual depreciation,

c = original cost, Sc = Scrap value, n = life of the property in years.

(*b*) Explain the rental method of valuation of a building.

28. (*a*) Define, cost, price, and value. (*b*) Enlist different types of value.

(*c*) Explain accomodation and Book value.

(*d*) Define the term Y.P. Explain both types of Y.P. fully

29. (*a*) An investor has a right to receive Rs. 50,000.00 after 6 years. Let the rate of interest be 12%. Find what amount investor should get so that he will be ready to relieve his future right.

(*b*) A loan of Rs. 50,000.00 is to be returned in 20 equal yearly installments with 6% interest. Work out the amount of interest.

30. A person purchased a plot measuring 450 sqm at the rate of Rs. 60 per sqm. Then he constructed a bungalow (on that plot) of built up area 150 sqm, the cost of construction being Rs. 900 per sqm. Now the owner wishes to let this property (plot and the bungalow together) on monthly rental basis. He expects a net return of 6% on the land cost and 12% on the bungalow cost. Considering the out goings as 30% of the income, suggest suitable monthly rent for the property to the owner.

31. A leasehold property is to produce a net annual income of Rs. 1,00,000 for the next 25 years. The owner expects a return of 10% on his capital and also sets apart a sinking fund instalment to accumulate at 5% annually to replace the capital. Determine the value of the property.

32. Write notes on the following :
 (*i*) Difference between value and cost of a property.
 (*ii*) Purpose of valuation, state any ten points.
 (*iii*) Difference between scrap value and salvage value.
 (*iv*) Security deposit and earnest money deposit.
 (*v*) The factors that affect the value of a property.

SCHEDULE OF DOORS AND WINDOWS

D_1 – 1.4 m × 2.1 m

D_2 – 1.0 m × 2.1 m

W_1 – 0.90 m × 1.1 m

W_2 – 0.90 m × 0.60 m

VEH. OPENING - 2.5 m – 1.1 m WITH EXPANDED METAL

SIZE OF FRAMES - 7.5 cm × 10 cm

33. Define valuation. What are the purposes of valuation ? Discuss the various methods of valuation of building.

34. A leasehold property is to produce a net income of Rs. 15,000/- per annum for the next 60 years. What is the value of the property ? Assume that the landlord desires a return of 6% on his capital and the sinking fund to replace the capital is also to accumulae at 6%.

35. Write notes on the following
 (*i*) Difference between depreciation and obsolescence
 (*ii*) Leasehold property and freehold property
 (*iii*) Difference between revised estimate and supplementary estimate
 (*iv*) Termination of contract
 (*v*) Unit price contract and turn key contract
 (*vi*) Scrap value and Salvage value
 (*vii*) plinth area and carpet area

ANSWERS to the A. short questions.

1. (*a*) 0.01 m	2. (*c*) sqm	3. (*b*) 0.01 cum	4. (*a*) 0.01 sqm
5. (*d*) 0.05 m	6. (*c*) 0.001 sqm	7. (*c*) 1.0 kg	8. (*b*) 0.002 m
9. (*b*) 2 mm	10. (*b*) 2 mm	11. (*c*) 0.001 cum	12. (*c*) 0.001 m
13. (*c*) 0.50 cm	14. (*c*) 0.005 m	15. (*a*) sqm	16. (*a*) sqm
17. (*b*) rm	18. (*b*) kg	19. (*c*) kg	20. (*b*) 20 cm

21. (*b*) sqm 22. (*b*) sqm 23. (*a*) sqm 24. (*b*) cum
25. (*b*) sqm 26. (*a*) rm 27. (*b*) rm 28. (*c*) rm
29. (*a*) 0.1 sqm 30. (*b*) no deduction is made 31. (*a*) 10 cm
32. (*a*) 0.1 sqm. 33. (*b*) not deducted 34. (*b*) 0.4 sqm
35. (*b*) 0.2 sqm 36. (*b*) 0.10 sqm, 37. (*a*) 0.50 sqm
38. (*a*) 0.5 sqm but not exceeding 3.0 sqm. 39. (*b*) 3 sqm
40. (*a*) including rebate 41. (*b*) excluding extra width of meeting styles
42. (*b*) shall not be made 43. (*b*) allowance shall be made
44. (*b*) no deduction shall be made
45. (*b*) without allowance for lapses and corrugations.
46. (*c*) 14% 47. (*c*) 20% 48. (*b*) rm 49. (*b*) rm
50. (*a*) 1.0 51. (*a*) 0.67 52. (*b*) 1.0 53. (*b*) 1.5
54. (*c*) 1.25 55. (*c*) (A + E) +24*d* 56. (*d*) 14%
57. (*c*) 11% 58. (*c*) 1.5 m 59. (*a*) 0.04347 cum 60. (*a*) 28.81 bags
61. (*c*) 0.88 cum 62. (*d*) 6.34 63. (*c*) 500, 64 64. (*c*) 500
65. (*c*) 425, 66 66. (*b*) 2.2 cum 67. (*d*) 8.64 68. (*d*) 7.5
69. (*c*) 30 70. (*b*) 50 71. (*b*) 12 liters
72. (*b*) 20mm graded down to 5mm
73. (*b*) to (*c*) 74. (*c*) 10 75. (*b*) 7 days 76. (*b*) 14 days
77. (*c*) two corrugations 78. (*b*) 2m 79. (*b*) 2 sqm 80. (*c*) 2 cm
81. (*c*) 15 cm 82. (*b*) 10 cum
83. (*a*) change of quantity of materials and rates
84. (*b*) comparative statement is not required 85. (*b*) excludes plinth offset
86. (*b*) excluded 87. (*b*) excluded 88. (*b*) earnest money
89. (*b*) 2.35 cum 90. (*c*) 5 cum 91. (*b*) 1.25 cum 92. (*c*) 1.1 cum
93. (*c*) 7 94. (*b*) 10 95. (*c*) 10 96. (*d*) 70
97. (*c*) 66 98. (*d*) 20 99. (*c*) 0.75 cum 100. (*b*) 0.55
101. (*b*) one vertical post 102. (*b*) Ridge 103. (*c*) abutment 104. (*d*) ashlar masonry
105. (*d*) any one of baove 106. (*a*) Jambs 107. (*c*) curing 108. (*d*) bitumen
109. (*c*) ultimate bearing capacity 110. (*a*) stretcher bond
111. (*d*) abutment 112. (*d*) cement concrete 113.(*c*) Zinc chlorides
114. (*b*) marble 115. (*d*) hinged window which may swing in and out
116. (*a*) sheepfoot roller 117. (*a*) underpinning 118. (*a*) expansive soil
119. (*b*) 20 cm 120. (*b*) queen closer 121. (*a*) jamb
122. (*a*) 2.5 cm 123. (*b*) bottom 124. (*d*) struts 125. (*a*) bleeding
126. (*d*) low

B. Broad questions

12. (*i*) 2250 cm^2, (*ii*) 7, (*iii*) 4.75, (*iv*) equal, (*v*) workability, (*vi*) flexural tensile strength, (*vii*) 0.0003, (*viii*) semiplastic.

QUESTION BANK

1. The plan & section of a building are given in Fig. Q.1A&B below. Assuming any other data if required, find out quantities for the following items of work, using standard measurement sheet. Write full description of each & every item.

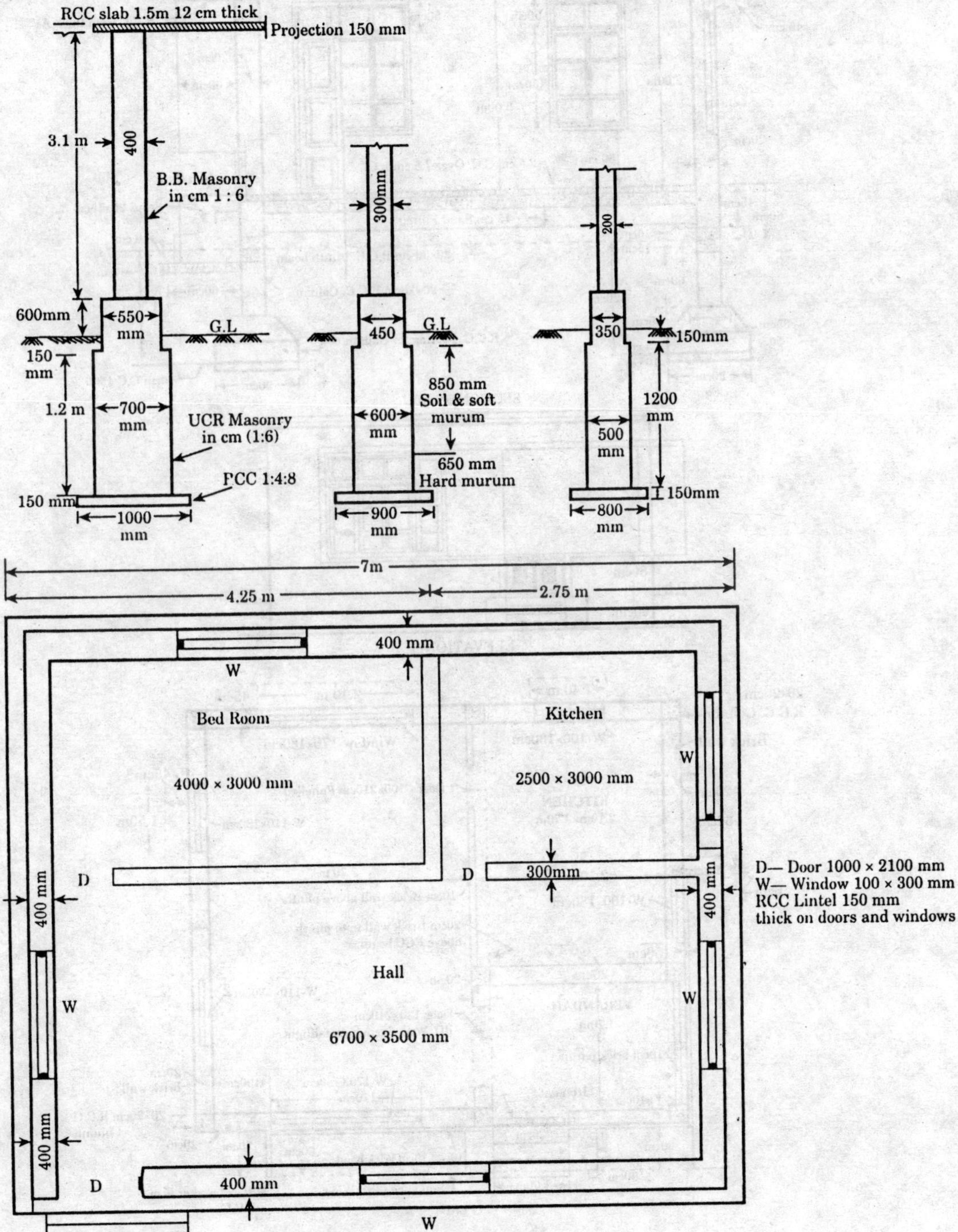

PLAN — I : SECTION OF BUILDING

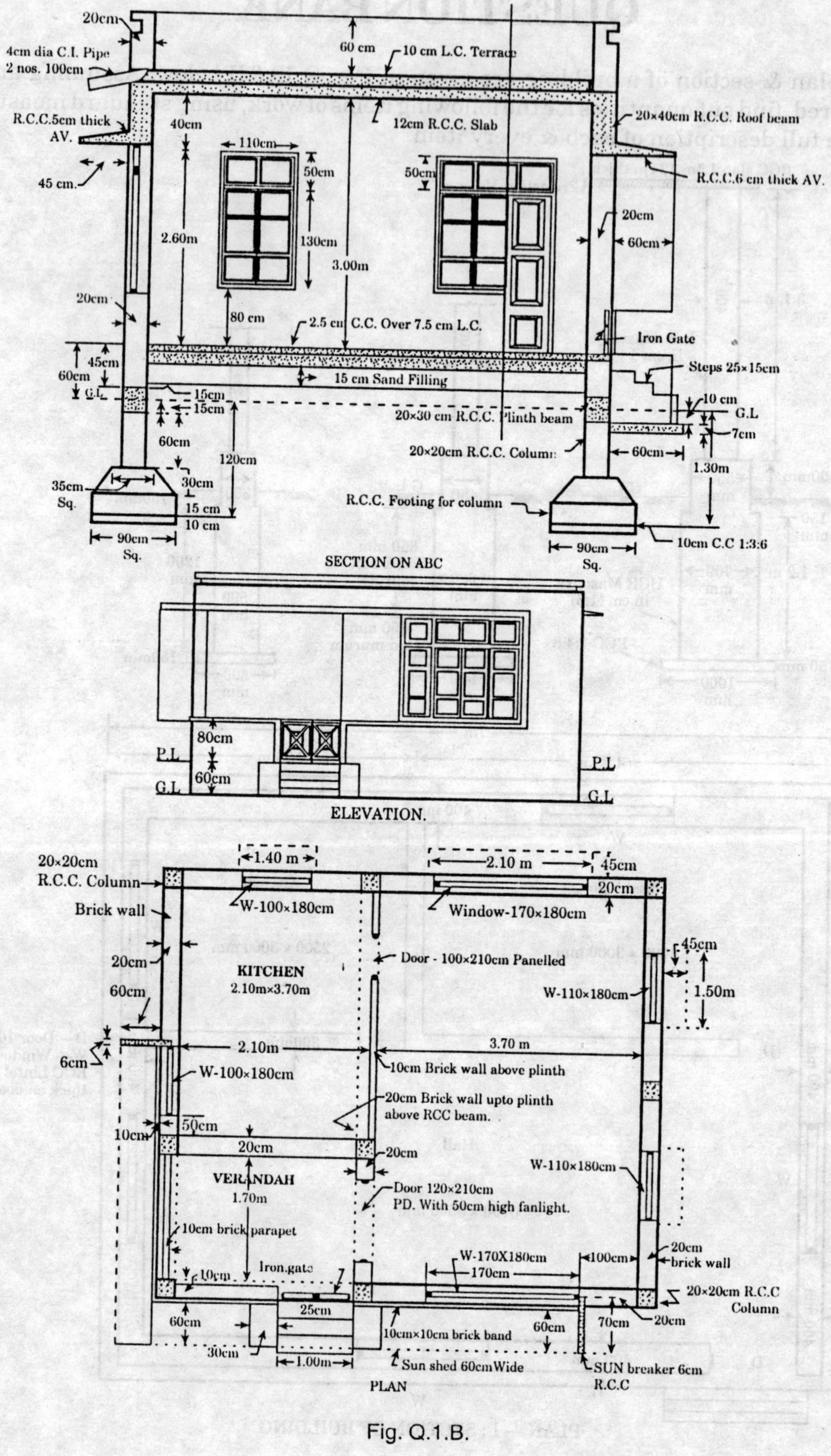
20cm
4cm dia C.I. Pipe
2 nos. 100cm
60 cm
10 cm L.C. Terrace
R.C.C.5cm thick
AV.
40cm
12cm R.C.C. Slab
20×40cm R.C.C. Roof beam
45 cm.
110cm
50cm
50cm
R.C.C.6 cm thick AV.
2.60m
130cm
3.00m
20cm
60cm
20cm
80 cm
2.5 cm C.C. Over 7.5 cm L.C.
Iron Gate
45cm
60cm
G.L
15 cm Sand Filling
Steps 25×15cm
15cm
15cm
10 cm
G.L
20×30 cm R.C.C. Plinth beam
7cm
60cm
120cm
20×20cm R.C.C. Column
60cm
1.30m
35cm
Sq.
30cm
R.C.C. Footing for column
15 cm
10 cm
90cm
Sq.
10cm C.C 1:3:6
90cm
Sq.
SECTION ON ABC
80cm
P.L
60cm
G.L
P.L
G.L
ELEVATION.
20×20cm
R.C.C. Column
1.40 m
2.10 m
45cm
20cm
W-100×180cm
Window-170×180cm
Brick wall
Door - 100×210cm Panelled
45cm
20cm
KITCHEN
2.10m×3.70m
1.50m
W-110×180cm
60cm
2.10m
3.70 m
6cm
W-100×180cm
10cm Brick wall above plinth
20cm Brick wall upto plinth
above RCC beam.
10cm
50cm
20cm
20cm
W-110×180cm
VERANDAH
1.70m
Door 120×210cm
PD. With 50cm high fanlight.
10cm brick parapet
W-170X180cm
100cm
20cm
brick wall
10cm
Iron.gate
170cm
20×20cm R.C.C
Column
25cm
60cm
70cm
20cm
60cm
10cm×10cm brick band
30cm
1.00m
Sun shed 60cmWide
SUN breaker 6cm
R.C.C
PLAN

Fig. Q.1.B.

(*a*) Excavation for foundation. (*b*) P.C.C. for foundation.

(*c*) B.B. Masonary for superstructure. (*d*) Doors & windows.

(*e*) Lintels over doors & windows.

2. (*a*) What are the different methods of preparing approximate estimate? Write the suitability of each method.

(*b*) State the rules for deduction to be made for openings for plaster work & also for deductions for openings to be made from brick masonry work.

3. (*a*) Which points are taken into cosideration while preparing rate analysis?

(*b*) Work out the rate analysis for 12 mm. thick cement plaster with neons finish to internal surface of brick masonry in superstructure.

4. (*a*) Discuss briefly the factors which affect the unit price of an item of work.

(*b*) What is meant by an item of work? What exact information is required while describing a particular item of work?

5. Prepare a preliminary estimate of a school building for 200 students with following data.

(*a*) Land is donated for the school building.

(*b*) Single storeyed load bearing structure having five class rooms, each accommodating 40 students.

(*c*) Carpet area per student $= 1.2 \text{ m}^2$.

(*d*) Carpet area of Head master's room, office & staff room is 45 m^2.

(*e*) Area of corridor, verandah, lavatories is about 20% of class room area.

(*f*) Wall area is 15% of plinth area.

(*g*) Present rate of construction is Rs.3250 per m^2.

(*h*) Cost of approach road & compound wall is 5% of building cost. Assume any other data if required.

6. (*a*) Why specifications are necessary? How the specifications are useful to contractor, supervisor & estimator?

(*b*) Write detailed specifications for:

(*i*) Excavation for foundation (*ii*) P.C.C. for foundation.

7. (*a*) Explain the situation where the following methods of valuation will be used.

(*i*) Rental method (*ii*) Cost based method

(*iii*) Profit based method (*iv*) Development method.

(*b*) Find out the present value of property from the following data.

(*i*) Built up area of the building $= 450 \text{ m}^2$.

(*ii*) Gross rent received per month is Rs.4,500/-.

(*iii*) Municipal taxes per year are 25% of gross rent per year.

(*iv*) Annual maintenance & other outgoings except sinking fund = 12% of gross rent per year.

(*v*) Expected future life = 70 years.

(*vi*) Area of plot $= 1200 \text{ m}^2$.

(*vii*) Present sale rate of land = Rs.500 per m^2.

(*viii*) Net return expected from building investment = 10% per year.

(*ix*) Net return expected from land investment = 6% per year.

(*x*) Rate of interest on redemption = 4 % per year.

8. (*a*) Distinguish between sinking fund & depreciation.

(*b*) Define:

(*i*) Annuity (*ii*) Year's purchase.

(*c*) A concrete mixer was purchased for Rs. 70,000/-. Assume salvage value of Rs. 6,000/- after six years. Calculate book value each year by calculating depreciation by constant percentage method.

9. Write short notes on **any four**:

(*a*) Importance of Bombay rent control act (*b*) Necessity of "Minimum Wages Act"

(*c*) Contract Labour Act of 1970

(*d*) Free hold property & lease hold property

(*e*) General specifications.

10. Calculate the cost of providing a two way RCC slab 15 cm thick. The slab panel effective dimensions being 4 × 4 m. It is reinforced with 12 mm. Bars at 15 cm. c/c both ways. Bars are bent up alternately at span/7 near the edges. Calculate the costs on the basis of rates prevailing at Indore City steel reinforcement are to be taken as separate item. Estimate also the quantities of material required. Assume any other data if required, suitably.

11. Derive unit rate for the following item of work —

(*a*) Ist class Brickwork in superstructure with standard modular brick 1:6 cement sand mortar.

(*b*) 6 mm. thick mosiac flooring over 2.5 cm. cement concrete floor.

12. Write detailed specifications for —

(*a*) Damp proof course.

(*b*) 1:6 cement-mortar plastering in wall.

(*c*) 1:2:4 cement concrete in RCC slab.

13. Write short notes on —

1. Prime cost.
2. General specifications and detailed specifications.
3. Building Cost Index.

14. (*a*) What is the need of valuation of a building ?

(*b*) A premise (Godown) is let on Rs.1,500/- p.m. including all taxes. However the fair rent is Rs. 2,000=00 p.m. in the locality. How much government should pay to the owner for acquiring the premise ?

15.(*a*) Accompanying figure Q. 15.A shows the plan and section of a R.C.C. column and its footing. Ten such columns are required in a building. Work-out quantities for 10 columns for following items.

(*i*) Cement concrete M_{15} for R.C.C column footings;

(*ii*) Cement concrete M_{15} for R.C.C columns;

(*iii*) Formwork for R.C.C columns;

(*iv*) m.s. reinforcement in columns and footings.

Marks will be awarded for using correct method of measurements, description of items and accuracy.

(*b*) Figure Q.15.B shows the outline of a building, work out the following.

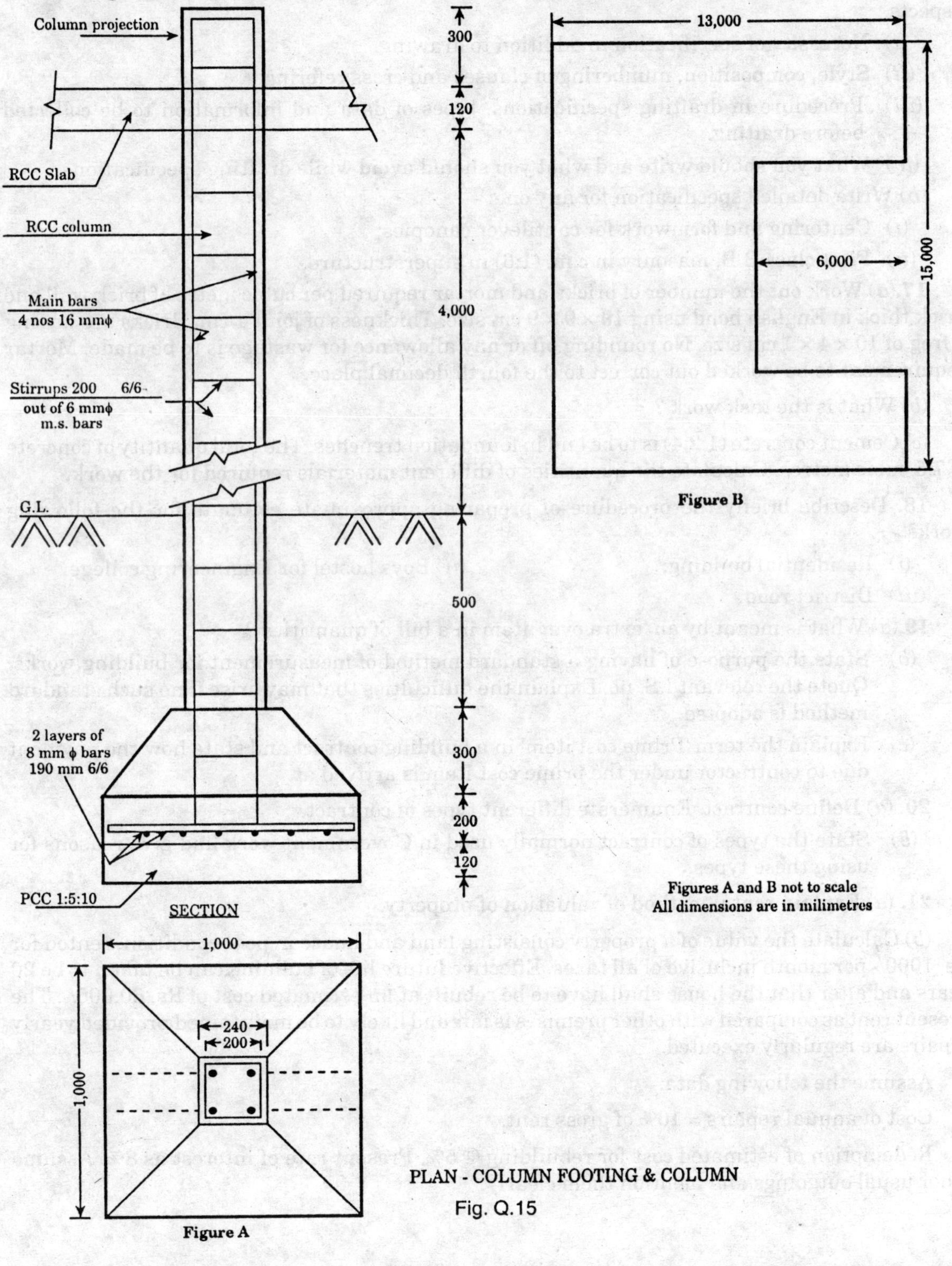

Figure A

Figure B

Figures A and B not to scale
All dimensions are in milimetres

PLAN - COLUMN FOOTING & COLUMN

Fig. Q.15

(*i*) Area of 1 m. wide plinth protection to be provided around the building.

(*ii*) Length of the edge of roof slab having 300 mm roof projection all around the building.

16.(*a*) Write a note on the art and science of writing specifications covering the following aspects.

(*i*) Necessity of specification in addition to drawing.

(*ii*) Style, composition, numbering of clauses and cross refering.

(*iii*) Procedure in drafting specifications, types of data and information to be collected before drafting.

(*iv*) What you should write and what you should avoid while drafting specifications.

(*b*) Write detailed specification for any one: -

(*i*) Centering and formwork for cantilever canopies;

(*ii*) First class B.B. masonry in c.m. (1:6) in superstructure.

17.(*a*) Work out the number of bricks and mortar required per cubic metre of brick wall one brick thick in English bond using 19 × 9 × 9 cm size. Thickness of joint 1 cm. Bricks are having a frog of 10 × 4 × 1 cm size. No rounding off or any allowance for wastage is to be made. Mortar requirement to be worked out correct to the fourth decimal place.

(*b*) What is the task work ?

(*c*) Cement concrete (1:2:4) is to be laid in foundation trenches. The total quantity of concrete is 7.5 cubic metres. Calculate the quantities of different materials required for the work.

18. Describe briefly the procedure of preparing approximate estimate for the following works.

(*i*) Residential building; (*ii*) Boys hostel for Engineering college;

(*iii*) District road.

19.(*a*) What is meant by an 'extra over' item in a bill of quantities ?

(*b*) State the purpose of having a standard method of measurement for building works. Quote the relevant I.S. no. Explain the difficulties that may arise if no such standard method is adopted.

(*c*) Explain the term 'Prime cost item' in a building contract and state how the payment due to contractor under the prime cost item is arrived at.

20. (*a*) Define contract. Enumerate different types of contract.

(*b*) State the types of contract normally used in Government work and give reasons for using these types.

21. (*a*) Explain rental method of valuation of property.

(*b*) Calculate the value of a property consisting land and house in poor condition, rented for Rs. 1000/- per month inclusive of all taxes. Effective future life of building can be taken to be 20 years and after that the house shall have to be rebuilt at an estimated cost of Rs. 60,000/-. The present rent as compared with other premises is fair and likely to be maintained provided yearly repairs are regularly executed.

Assume the following data:

Cost of annual repairs = 10% of gross rent.

Redemption of estimated cost for rebuilding @ 5%. Present rate of interest as 8%. Assume other usual outgoings and mention them clearly.

OR

21.(*a*) What is depreciation ?

(*b*) What are the different types of depreciation ?

(*c*) Explain the constant percentage method of calculating depreciation.

(*d*) Write a note on book value.

22. (*a*) Explain the procedure for submission of tender and opening of tender in case of Government work.

(*b*) State the conditions when:-

(*i*) All tenders are rejected;

(*ii*) Tenders become unqualified;

(*iii*) Time for submission of tender is extended.

23.(*a*) What are the contract documents ?

(*b*) List all documents in case of Lumpsum contract.

(*c*) Explain any three conditions of contract of the following.

(*i*) Works to be open to insepection;

(*ii*) Subletting of work;

(*iii*) Extension of time limit.

(*iv*) Compensation for delay.

24. Write short notes on **any three** of the following.

(*a*) Piece work method of executing the work;

(*b*) Building lease and Occupational lease;

(*c*) Secured Advance;

(*d*) Materials at site account;

(*e*) Arbitration.

25. Fig. Q. 25. shows the plan and section of a residential building. Workout the quantities of following items describing the item fully and recording the measurements in proper form.

(*a*) UCR masonry in c.m. (1:6) in plinth and foundation.

(*b*) Rubble filling 200 mm thick in plinth.

(*c*) Marble mosaic flooring in rooms & passage.

(*d*) 15 mm thick sand faced cement plaster (1:4) to all external surface of BK. masonry.

26. (*a*) What is bill of quantity ? State its importance.

(*b*) Write a note on D.S.R.

(*c*) Explain the terms Lead & Lift used in the description of excavation item.

(*d*) Why are the contingencies & work charged establishment amounts added to estimated cost ?

27.(*a*) Distinguish between builtup area and carpet area.

(*b*) How will you calculate cubic content of building.

(*c*) Compare Plinth area method with Cubic content method of approximate estimate.

28. (*a*) Define Task Work. State the task work for the following items.

(*i*) II class B.B. masonry in superstructure.

(*ii*) 15 mm thick cement plaster to B.K. masonry in superstructure.

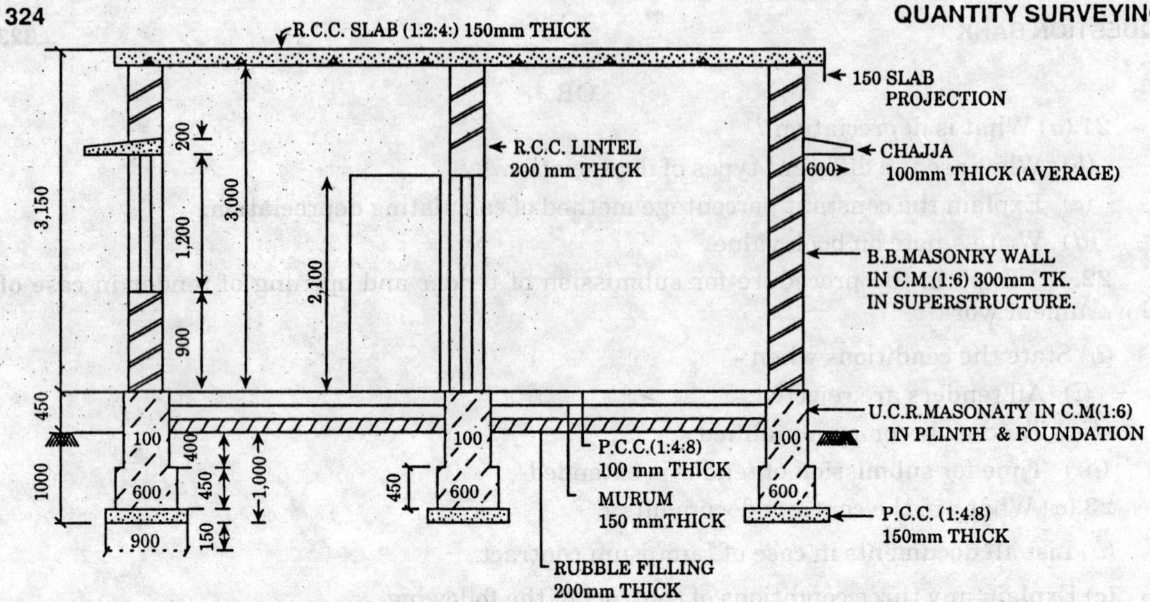

SECTIONAL ELECATION AB

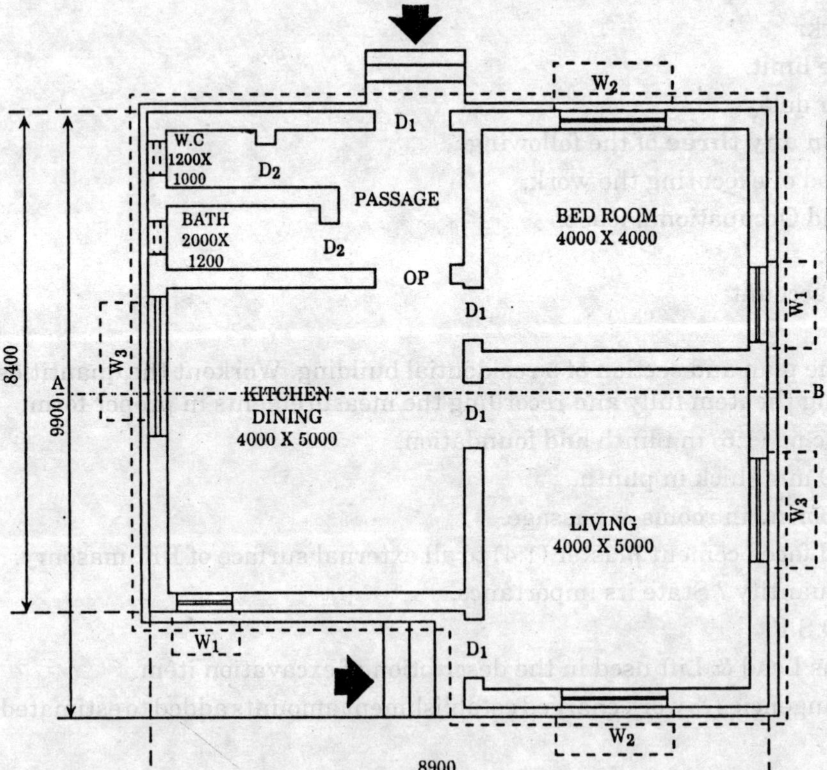

PLAN

Schedule of Openings

Sy.	*Size*	*Description*
W_1	1000×1200	Steel windows
W_2	1500×1200	Steel windows
W_3	2000×1200	Steel windows
V	600×600	Louvered
D_1	1000×2100	CCTW fully
D_2	800×2100	Panelled
OP	1000×2100	Opening

1. Hard Murum is available at 0.8 m depth from G.L.
2. Marble mosaic flooring in all rooms and passage.
3. White glazed tiles for flooring and dado in W.C. & Bath.
4. B.B. Masonary for steps Tead = 300 mm, Rise = 150 mm
5. 15 mm thick sand faced cement plaster in C.M. (1:4) provided to all external surfaces of brick masonry.
6. 100 mm thick R.C.C. Slab (1:2:4) is provided over W.C. & Bath at 2.1 m height from floor level

Scale 1 cm - 1.0 m

All dimentions in mm

Fig. Q.25.

(*b*) Prepare rate analysis for the item. 'PCC (1:4:8) in foundation'.

OR

28. (*a*) 36 m^3 of UCR masonry in cm (1:6) is to be constructed for the foundation of a school building. Calculate:-

(*i*) Requirement of different materials.

(*ii*) Numbers of masons and mazdoors required, if the work is to be completed in 10 days.

(*b*) State the rules for deductions for openings to be made from BK. masonry work in superstructure.

29. (*a*) Enumerate the types of specifications. Write the purpose of each type.

(*b*) Write the detailed specification for any one item of the following:-

(*i*) II class B.B. masonry in cm (1:6) in superstructure.

(*ii*) C.C. (1:2:4) for RCC roof slab.

30.(*a*) Distinguish between Depletion and Depreciation.

(*b*) Explain any two methods of calculating depreciation.

(*c*) A centrifugal pump was purchased in 1988 for Rs. 40,000/-. The life of pump as stated by manufacturer is 10 years. Assume any other data if required. Calculate the book value of pump in 1993.

31.(*a*) What is tender ? Explain B_1 and B_2 types of tender.

(*b*) Suggest suitable form of tender for following:-

(*i*) Transporting cement from PWD store to site of construction which is 40 km away.

(*ii*) Supply of Rubble at work site by the contractor.

(*iii*) Constructing a small sanitary unit at a Railway station.

(*c*) What are the essential characteristics of tender notice.

32.(*a*) What is a Contract ?

State essential requirements of contract.

(*b*) Describe 'Item rate contract and state its merits and demerits.

OR

(*b*) Explain Rate List and Piece Work System of carryingout the work.

33.(*a*) Write suitable clauses of conditions of contract for **any two** of following:-

(*i*) Bad quality of Work.

(*ii*) Defect liability period.

(*iii*) Stores supplied by Government to the contractor.

(*b*) Explain **any two** of the following:-

(*i*) Scrap value & Salvage value.

(*ii*) Out goings.

(*iii*) Years-Purchase.

34.(*a*) How will you prepare a Valuation report of a property consisting of a two storeyed residential building and a plot.

(*b*) A property consist of a plot of 600 m^2 area and a bunglow of 150 m^2 in area; constructed in 1960. On inspecting the present condition of bunglow, future life of bunglow is predicted as

50 years. Find out the present value of property from the following data:-

(*i*) Present sale rate of land - Rs. 400/- m^2.

(*ii*) Present Construction rate for similar building - Rs.2500/- m^2.

(*iii*) Rate of interest for redumption of Capital - 5% per year.

Assume any other data if necessary.

35.(*a*) The figure Q.35. shows a residential building for the middle class family. The details of construction are:

Foundations : 1.2 m below ground level

C.C. (1:3:6) bed 0.2 m thick, 0.9m. wide for all walls.

Uncoursed rubble masonry in cm (1:6) in two offsets below ground level, each layer 0.50 m thick and width 0.8 m and 0.70 m respectively. Above ground level 0.55 m height and 0.50 wide.

Plinth C.C.(1:3:6) 0.15 m all around.

Superstructure : Burnt brick masonary in cm (1:6) 0.30 for all walls.

Parapet wall : Burnt brick masonry in cm (1:6) 0.20 m thick and 0.80 m high all around.

R.C.C. lintels: 0.15 m thick on all openings.

R.C.C. roof slab: 0.15 m thick with C.C. (1:2:4)

Plastering: with CM (1:4) for all walls both inside and outside 12 mm thick.

Work out the quantities of **any three** of the following items:

(*i*) Uncoursed rubble masonry in cm (1:6) for foundation and plinth.

(*ii*) Burnt brick masonry in cm (1:6) for superstructure and parapet.

(*iii*) Plastering of walls in cm (1:4) 12 mm thick.

(*iv*) R.C.C. roof in C.C. (1:2:4)

(*b*) Give quantities of cement bags required to execute each of the above items - No. (*ii*) and (*iv*).

36.(*a*) An existing road is 12 cm thick and its surface has become patchy and rough. It is required to modernise the road by providing one layer of 12 cm stone macadam and two coats of surface dressing with bitumen. Calculate the quantities of various items of modernising one km length of the road which is 4 m wide.

(*b*) State the uses of preparing the approximate estimate.

(*c*) State the rules for deduction to be made from plaster work.

37.(*a*) Why are the contigency charges and work-charged establishment charges added to the estimated cost ?

(*b*) Work out the rates for **any one** of the following items:

(*i*) U.C.R. in cm (1:6) for foundation and plinth.

(*ii*) Burnt brick masonary in cm (1:6) for superstructure and parapet.

(*c*) What is task work? What are the different factors affecting the task work ?

38.(*a*) What are different types of specifications ? State the purpose of each type.

(*b*) Write detailed specification for **any one** of the following:

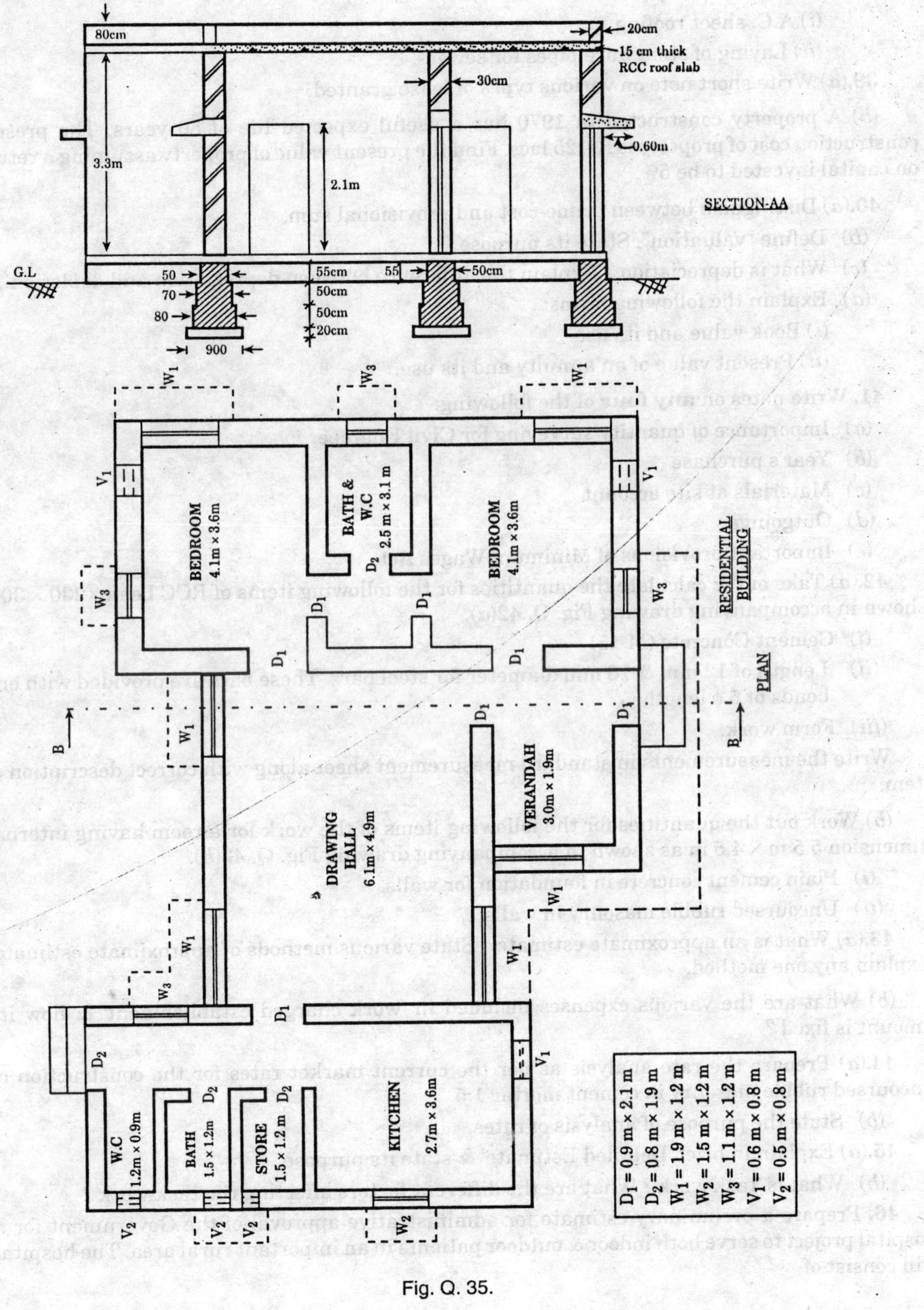

80cm
20cm
15 cm thick
RCC roof slab
30cm
0.60m
3.3m
2.1m
SECTION-AA
G.L
50
70
80
900
55cm
50cm
50cm
20cm
55
50cm
BEDROOM
4.1m × 3.6m
BATH &
W.C
2.5 m × 3.1 m
BEDROOM
4.1m × 3.6m
RESIDENTIAL
BUILDING
PLAN
VERANDAH
3.0m × 1.9m
DRAWING
HALL
6.1m × 4.9m
W.C
1.2m × 0.9m
BATH
1.5 × 1.2m
STORE
1.5 × 1.2 m
KITCHEN
2.7m × 3.6m
D1 = 0.9 m × 2.1 m
D2 = 0.8 m × 1.9 m
W1 = 1.9 m × 1.2 m
W2 = 1.5 m × 1.2 m
W3 = 1.1 m × 1.2 m
V1 = 0.6 m × 0.8 m
V2 = 0.5 m × 0.8 m

Fig. Q. 35.

(i) A.C. sheet roofing

(ii) Laying of stoneware pipes for sewers.

39.(a) Write short note on various types of lease granted.

(b) A property constructed in 1970 has a useful expected life of 80 years. The present construction cost of property is Rs. 25 lacs. Find the present value of property assuming a return on capital invested to be 5%.

40.(a) Distinguish between prime-cost and provisional sum.

(b) Define "valuation". State its purpose.

(c) What is depreciation ? Explain the difference between depreciation and depletion.

(d) Explain the following terms:

(i) Book value and its use

(ii) Present value of an annuity and its use.

41. Write notes on **any four** of the following:

(a) Importance of quantity surveying for Civil Engineer

(b) Year's purchase

(c) Materials at site account

(d) Outgoings

(e) Important provisions of Minimum Wages Act.

42.(a) Take out & calculate the quantities for the following items of RCC beam (230 × 300) shown in accompanying drawing Fig. Q. 42(a).

(i) Cement Concrete (M 15)

(ii) Length of 12 mm & 16 mm diameter for steel bars. These bars are provided with end bends of 6 ϕ length.

(iii) Form work.

Write the measurements in standard measurement sheet along with correct description of item.

(b) Work out the quantities for the following items of the work for a room having internal dimension 5.5 m × 4.5 m as shown in accompanying drawing Fig. Q. 42(b).

(i) Plain cement concrete in foundation for walls.

(ii) Uncoursed rubble masonry in walls.

43.(a) What is an approximate estimate ? State various methods of approximate estimate. Explain any one method.

(b) What are the various expenses included in 'work charged establishment' & how its amount is fixed ?

44.(a) Prepare the rate analysis as per the current market rates for the construction of uncoursed rubble masonry in cement mortar 1:5.

(b) State the purpose of analysis of rates.

45.(a) Explain in brief 'Detailed Estimate' & state its purpose.

(b) What is 'task work'? What are the different factors affecting the task work ?

46. Prepare a preliminary estimate for administrative approval of the Government for a hospital project to serve both indoor & outdoor patients in an important rural area. The hospital will consist of

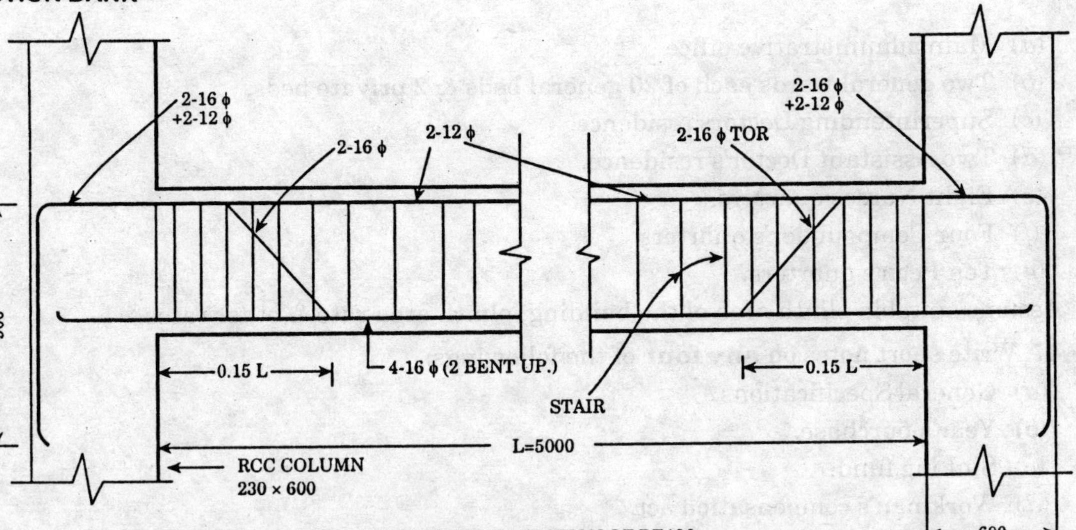

LONGITUDINAL SECTION OF BEAM

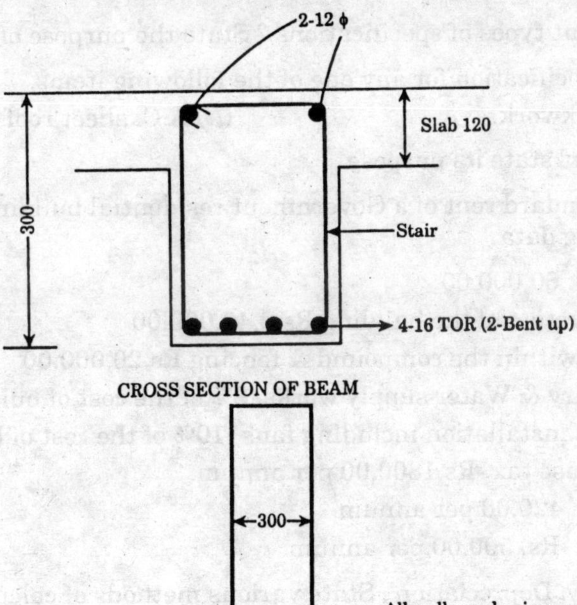

CROSS SECTION OF BEAM

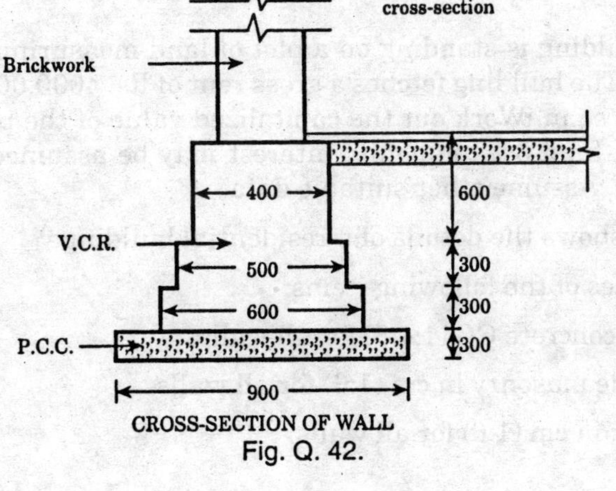

CROSS-SECTION OF WALL

Fig. Q. 42.

(*a*) Main administrative office

(*b*) Two general wards each of 20 general beds & 2 private beds.

(*c*) Superintending Doctors residence.

(*d*) Two Assistant Doctor's residence.

(*e*) Eight Nurses quarters.

(*f*) Four Compounder's quarters

(*g*) Ten Peon's quarters.

Assume suitable plinth area of the building, plinth area rate & other rates.

47. Write short notes on **any four** of the followings:

(*a*) General Specifications.

(*b*) Year's purchase.

(*c*) Sinking fund.

(*d*) Workman's compensation act.

(*e*) Rent act.

48.(*a*) What are different types of specifications ? State the purpose of each type.

(*b*) Write detailed specification for any one of the following items.

(*i*) First class brickwork. (*ii*) A.C. sheet roof convering.

49. (*a*) Define 'valuation' state its purpose.

(*b*) Calculate the standard rent of a Government residential building newly constructed from the following data

(*i*) Cost of land Rs. 60,000.00

(*ii*) Cost of construction of the building Rs.2,40,000.00

(*iii*) Cost of roads within the compound & fencing Rs.20,000.00

(*iv*) Cost of Sanitary & Water supply works, 8% of the cost of building.

(*v*) Cost of electric installation including fans -10% of the cost of building.

(*vi*) Municipal House tax -Rs.1800.00 per annum.

(*vii*) Water tax Rs. 420.00 per annum.

(*viii*) Property tax -Rs. 500.00 per annum.

50.(*a*) What is meant by 'Depreciation'. State various methods of calculating depreciation. Explain any one method.

(*b*) A three storied building is standing on a plot of land measuring 8000 sq.m. The life of the structure is 80 years. The building fetches a gross rent of Rs. 4000.00 per month. The plinth area of each storey is 400 sq.m. Work out the capitalized value of the property on the basis of 6% net yield. For sinking fund 3% compound interest may be assumed. Cost of land may be taken as Rs. 300 per sq.m. Assume other suitable data.

51.(*a*) The Fig. Q. 51 shows the details of a residential building.

Work out the quantities of the following items:

(*a*) Foundation bed concrete CC (1:4:8) for all walls.

(*b*) Uncoursed rubble masonry in cm (1:6) for all walls.

(*c*) Burnt brickwork in cm (1:6) for all walls.

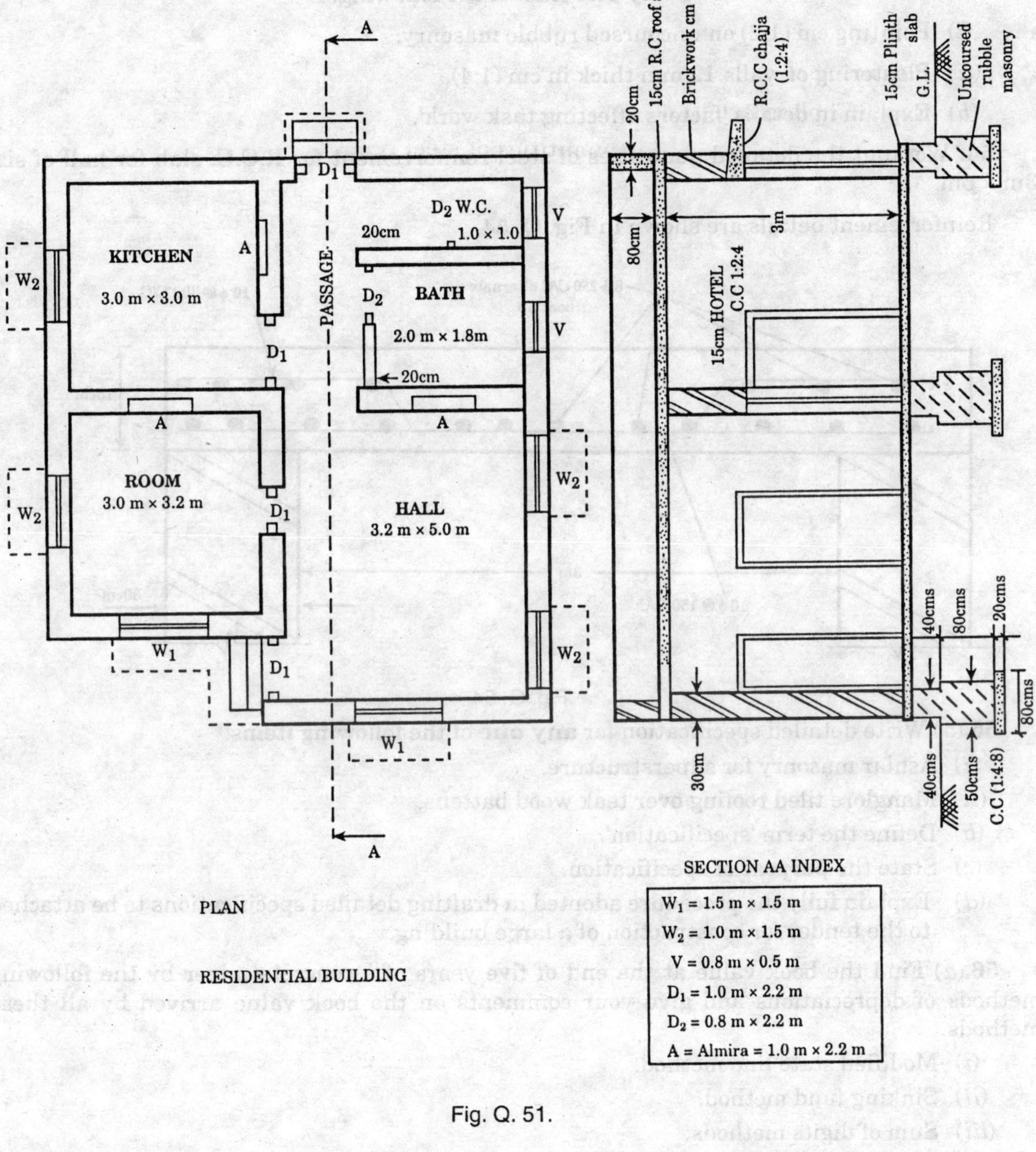

Fig. Q. 51.

52.(*a*) What is approximate estimate? State the importance of approximate estimate.

(*b*) Distinguish between **any two** of the following:

(*i*) Administrative approval and technical sanction.

(*ii*) Revised estimate and supplimentary estimate.

(*iii*) Reproduction cost and replacement cost.

53.(*a*) Workout the rates for **any one** item of the following:

(*i*) Pointing cm (1:2) on uncoursed rubble masonry.

(*ii*) Plastering of walls 12 mm thick in cm (1:4).

(*b*) Explain in details 'factors affecting task work'.

54. Workout the detailed quantities of steel reinforcement for R.C.C. slab for hall of size 3m × 6m.

Reinforcement details are shown in Fig. Q. 54.

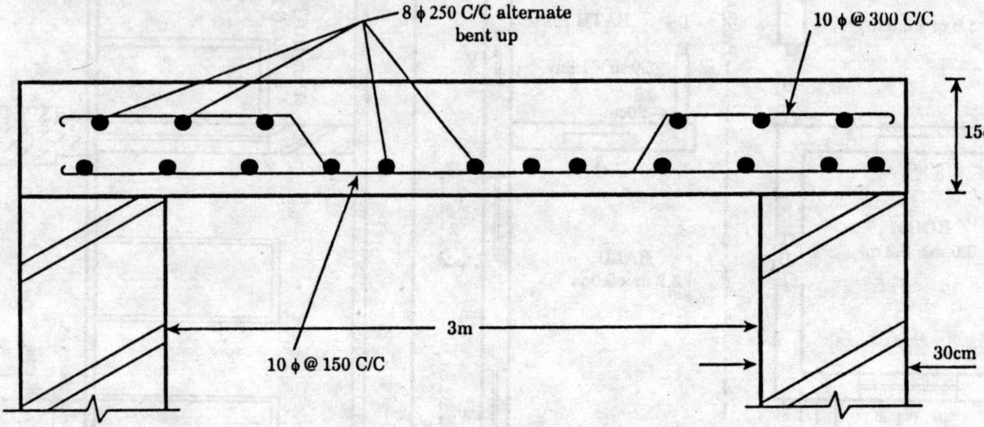

Fig. Q. 54.

55.(*a*) Write detailed specification for **any one** of the following items:

(*i*) Ashlar masonry for superstructure.

(*ii*) Manglore tiled roofing over teak wood battens.

(*b*) Define the term 'specification'.

(*c*) State the purpose of specification.

(*d*) Explain fully the procedure adopted in drafting detailed specifications to be attached to the tender for construction of a large building.

56.(*a*) Find the book value at the end of five years of a concrete mixer by the following methods of depreciations and give your comments on the book value arrived by all these methods.

(*i*) Modified state line method.

(*ii*) Sinking fund method.

(*iii*) Sum of digits methods.

Other data as given below:

(*i*) Useful life of concrete mixer - 8 years.

(*ii*) Cost of concrete mixer - Rs. 60,000/-.

(*iii*) Scrap value - 10%.

(*b*) State the procedure of preparing valuation report of a residential building for a purchaser.

57. Distinguish between **any four** of the following:

(*a*) Depletion and Description.
(*b*) Scrap value and salvage value.
(*c*) Building lease and occupational lease.
(*d*) Market value and Book value.
(*e*) Reproduction cost and Replacement cost.

58. Write short notes on **any four** of the following:
(*a*) Building cost index
(*b*) Capitalised value
(*c*) Cubic content method of approximate estimate
(*d*) Rate list method of executing the work
(*e*) Sinking fund.

59. A room measures an area of 4 m × 5 m walls are 20 cm. thick. There are two doors of size 11m × 2.4m each and two windows of size 1m × 1.5m each. If height of building from floor to ceiling is 4 m and plinth height is 0.6 m. Find the cost of plastering work of room (both sides) if cement mortar 1:4 is used for it.

Also find quantities of materials required.

60. Give analysis of rates for:
(*i*) Cement pointing in 1:4 cm.
(*ii*) First class brick masonry for superstructure.

61.(*a*) What are the different methods of preparing approximate estimates ? Explain them briefly.
(*b*) Write detailed specifications for DPC.

62. What is necessity of valuating any building ? Explain various factors on which the valuation of a building depends? What are the duties and responsibilities of a Valuer?

63. (*a*) Prepare a list of different items of works necessary for the construction of a middle class residential building in urban areas, which is required for the preparation of bill of quantities. Indicate units of payment of each item.
(*b*) What is the importance of C.S.R.?

64. A room measures an area of 4m × 5m. walls are 20 cm. thick. There are two doors of size 1.1m × 2.4m. each and two windows of size 1.1m × 1.5m. each. If height of the building from floor to ceiling is 4 m and plinth height is 0.6 m. find the quantities of materials required for brickwork in superstructure (walls only) in 1:6 cement mortar. Metric bricks are used.

65. Give the analysis of rates for —
(*i*) Cement pointing in 1:4 cm.
(*ii*) 13mm. thick plaster in 1:4 cm.

66. Write down detailed specifications for —
(*i*) Tar felting.
(*ii*) Village housing.

67. (*a*) What are the duties and responsibilities of a valuer?
(*b*) Write short notes on —
(*i*) Prime cost.
(*ii*) Building cost Index.

68. (*a*) Write down the units of measurement for the following items of works:

1. Skirting.
2. 25 cm.C.C. over 7.5 cm. L.C. floor.
3. Renewal of glass panels.
4. Coping.

(*b*) Discuss all the salient points which must be mentioned in the report of an estimate of a project.

69. Estimate the quantites of materials for a Reinforced bricks slab (roof) over a verandah 2.5.m. wide and 6 m. long. Bearing over walls to be 15 cm. and thickness of slab is one brick thick (bricks on edge). Metric bricks are used. The main reinforcement consist of 10 mm. ϕ bars @ 12 cm.c/c and distribution steel 8 mm. ϕ bars @ 22 cm. c/c.

70. Give the analysis of rate for the following items:

1. 6 mm. mosaic floor over 2.5 cm. C.C. 1:2:4.
2. Second class brick works in superstructure in 1:6 cm.

71.(*a*) What are the different methods of preparing approximate estimates ? Why it is necessary to find the approximate cost of any structure ?

(*b*) Write down detailed specifications for D.P.C.

72. Write short notes on:

1. Years purchase.
2. Rent fixation.
3. Technical sanction.
4. Supplementary and Revised estimate.

73. (*a*) What is the significant of soil exploration in selection of suitable type of foundation for any building?

(*b*) State the bearing capacity of the following soils:

(*i*) Black cotton soil (*ii*) Sandy soil.

(*iii*) Hard murram (*iv*) Soft rocks.

(*c*) How do piles bear the loads? Illustrate your answer with neat sketches.

74. (*a*) What is a damp-proof-course? What precautions are to be taken in a building to avoid possibility of dampness?

(*b*) Explain the difference between the bricks masonry and stone masonry with reference to their suitability, cost and method of construction.

75. (*a*) What are the requirements of a well designed staircase? Name the type of stair you would recommend for the following building giving suitable reasons -

(*i*) A residential building. (*ii*) A cinema theatre.

(*b*) Write a short note on "Prestressed concrete".

76. (*a*) Describe briefly the types of floors used for different types of buildings and state the reason for their choice. What factors affect the design and specifications of a floor finish?

(*b*) Write a short note on "Timber-floor".

77. (*a*) Show different parts of a parallel door with neat sketch.

(*b*) Write explanatary notes on —

(*i*) Grillage foundation (*ii*) Form works.

(*iii*) Partition walls.

78. Give analysis of rates for following items —

1. 25 mm. thick panelled window.
2. Excavation in hard rock.

79. Write down detailed specifications for following items —

1. D.P.C.
2. Mosaic flooring over cement concrete.

80. How will you find approximate quantities of materials required for the construction of a building of average type without going into detailed estimate? Find the quantities of bricks, cement and steel bars required for the construction of an office building having a plinth area of 300 sq.m.

81. (*a*) What is necessity of valuating any building?

(*b*) Workout the rent statement of a building newly constructed at a cost of Rs.1,50,000/-. The cost for sanitary, water supply and electric installations should be included. Assume any other data if required suitably.

82.(*a*) A Chowkidar's post is to be constructed with 150 mm. thick R.C.C. slab in roof, with 20 × 30 cm. R.C.C. beams and 20 × 20cm. R.C.C. columns resting on solid slab footing of 1.00m. × 1.00m. × 0.30m. thick. The foundation depths is 2.50 m. and a mass concrete of 120 mm. thickness in provided below footing. If centre line dimensions of post are 2.00m. × 3.00m. in plan and clear height above ground is 2.80 m., calculate the quantities of Excavation, R.C.C. work and centering or falsework.

(*b*) What is the total quantity of cement required for only R.C.C. work.

(*c*) Give approximate quantity of steel required for reinforcement.

83.(*a*) Write down detailed specifications for following items of work —

(*i*) Second class brick masonry in cement mortar.

(*ii*) Mosaic tiled flooring with cement base coarse.

(*iii*) White washing to buildings.

(*b*) What is importance of such specifications?

84.(*a*) Derive the unit rate for following items of work-

(*i*) R.C.C. work 1:2:4. (*ii*) Excavation in hard soil.

(*iii*) 12 mm. thick 1:4 cement plaster.

(*b*) What is a "Nominal Mustor Roll" and how is it used on construction site?

85. Calculate the cost of providing reinforced concrete slab 13 cm. thick. The outside dimensions of slab are 4m. × 3.5m. Main reinforcement bars are 12 mm. dia. spaced at 12 cm. c/c. and distribution steel is 6 mm. dia. spaced 15 cm. c/c. Assume current rates prevailing at Indore City. Steel reinforcements are to be taken under a separate item. Alternate bars are bent up at 1/7th of span from support. Estimate also the quantities of material required.

86. Derive the unit rate for the following items of work:-

(*a*) 2 cm. thick Damp Proof Course (DPC) with cement mortar 1:2.

(*b*) Ist class Brickwork in superstructure with standard modular bricks with 1:6 cement sand mortar.

87. Write short notes on:-

(*a*) Bill of quantities. (*b*) Overhead costs.

(*c*) General specifications and detailed specifications.

88. Write down detailed specifications for the following items:-

(*a*) Damp proof course. (*b*) 1:2:4 Cement Concrete in RCC Slab.

(*c*) Distempering.

89. Explain in brief the various factors on which the valuation of a building depends. What are the methods to determine present day cost? What are the duties and responsibilities of a valuer?

90. Estimate the cost of a reinforced concrete slab 12.5 cm. thick for the roof of a room 6m. × 4m. having 15 cm. bearings over the walls. The main reinforced bars are 12 mm. dia spaced at 10 cm. c/c. and the distribution bars are 8 mm. dia. spaced 20 cm.c/c. Alternate main bars are bent up at 1/5th of span from support. Steel reinforcement is to be taken under a separate item. Assume rates prevailing in Indore. Estimate also the quantities of materials required.

91. Derive the unit rate for following items of work:-

(*a*) First class brick masonry in 1:6 cement mortar.
(*b*) 13 mm. thick plaster in 1:4 cement mortar.

92. What are the different methods of preparing approximate estimates. Explain each briefly.

93. Write down the detailed specifications for the following items:-

(*a*) Painting of doors and windows.
(*b*) Lime concrete in foundations. Write short note on "Importance of C.S.R."

94. (*a*) What do you understand by valuation of real properties.

(*b*) Make computations for the value of a premises of an office block let for Rs.400/- per month including all taxes. Office block was constructed only a few months back and is in very good condition. The rent is fair as compared to the other buildings in the locality.

95. Calculate the cost of providing reinforced concrete slab 12 cm. thick. The outside dimensions of slab are 4.2m × 3m. Main reinforcement bars are 12 mm. dia. spaced 12.5 cm. c/c. and distribution bars are 6 mm. dia spaced 15 cm. c/c. Assume rates prevailing at Indore City. Steel reinforcements are to be taken under a separate item. Alternate bars are bent up at 1/5th of span from the support. Estimate also the quantities of material required.

96. Derive the unit rate for the following items of work:-

(*a*) Fully glazed window 1.0m × 1.5m. of Indian teak wood.
(*b*) 6 mm. thick mosaic flooring over 2.5 cm. cement concrete floor.

97. Write short notes on:-

(*a*) Contingencies and supervision charges. (*b*) Building cost Index.
(*c*) Prime cost.

98. Write down the detailed specification for the following items:-

(*a*) Damp-proof-course.
(*b*) 2nd class bricks masonry in 1.8 cement mortar. Write a short note on "technical-sanction"?

99. (*a*) What is the necessity of valuating any building?

(*b*) A premise (Ware house) is let on Rs.1,200/- per month including of all taxes. However the fair rent is Rs.1600/- per month in locality. How much government should pay to the owner for acquiring the premise?

100. Write down detailed specifications for —

1. Village housing. 2. Tar felting.

101. Give analysis of rates for —

1. Cement plaster in 1:4 cm.
2. 6 mm. thick mosaic floor over 2.5 cm. cement concrete.

102. Write short notes on:

1. Supervision & Contingencies charges.
2. Revised Estimate.
3. Prime Cost.
4. Importence of C.S.R.

103. Write short notes on:

1. Years Purchase.
2. Technical Sanction
3. Rent Fixation
4. Centre-line Method.

104. Estimate the quantites of materials required for a R.B. slab over a verandah 2.5 m. wide and 6m. long. Bearing over walls to be 15 cm. and thickness of slab 10 cm. *i.e.* one brick (brick on edge) thick slab. The main reinforcement consists of 10 mm. dia. bars at 16 cm.c/c. and distribution bars 6 mm. and at 23 cm.c/c. Conventional bricks of size 22 × 10 × 7cm. are used. Assume all other datas if required giving suitable reason.

105. Give analysis of rates for following items:

(*i*) 25 mm. thick fully glazed window. (*ii*) Excavation in hard soils.

106. Write down detailed specifications for following items:

(*i*) A village house. (*ii*) Damp proof course.

107. How will you find approximate quantities of materials required for the construction of a building of average type without going into detailed estimate? Find the quantities of bricks, cement and steel bars required for the construction of a residential building having a plinth area of 160 sq. m.

108. (*a*) What is necessity of valuating any building?

(*b*) A premise is let on Rs. 1500/- per month including of all taxes. However the fair rent in Rs. 1800/- per month in that locality. How much government should pay to the owner for acquiring the premise?

109. Estimate the quantities of materials required for plastering in 1:4 cm. for a room (both side) measuring 4m × 5m. The walls are one bricks thick wall using conventional bricks of size 22.5cm. × 10cm. × 7cm. There is one door measuring 1m. × 2.1m. and two windows measuring 1m. × 1.2m. Assume roof thickness 15 cm. and ceiling height 3 m. above floor. Plinth height is 60 cm. Assume other datas it require, giving suitable reasons.

110. Give analysis of rates for following items —

(*a*) Cement pointing in 1:4 cm. (*b*) 10 cm. thick partition walls in 1:4 cm.

111. (*a*) Prepare a list of different items of work necessary for the construction of a middle class residential building in urban area which are required for the preparation of bill of quantities. Indicate units of payment against each.

(*b*) Write a note on "Building Cost Index".

112. (*a*) Discuss all the salient points which must be maintained in the report of an estimate of a project.

(*b*) How the approximate cost of a bridge is determined.

113. Calculate the standard rent of a government building (residential) newly constructed, from the following datas:

(*i*)	Cost of land	Rs. 25,000/-
(*ii*)	Cost of Construction of building	Rs. 85,000/-
(*iii*)	Cost of water supply and sanitary fittings	Rs. 6,500/-
(*iv*)	Cost of electrical Installation including fans	Rs. 6,000/-
(*v*)	Municipal House Tax	Rs. 400/- per annum.
(*vi*)	Property Tax	Rs. 1,200/- per annum.

114. Calculate the cost of providing a square RCC column and its footing. The column section is 45cm. × 45cm. and footing being 350 × 350 cm. The length of the column from the bottom level of footing is 605 cm. Column consists of 8 No-20 mm. dia reinforcing steel bars as main steel and 5 mm. dia. lateral ties are spaced at 24 cm. centre to centre. The square footing has a total depth of 105 cm. at the face of the column and 30 cm. at the outer edge. It has 28 No. 12 mm. dia. bars bothways as reinforced provided in the form of a mesh. Assume suitable rates as prevailing in Indore City currently.

115. Derive the unit rate for the following items of work —

(*a*) 6 mm. thick mosaic flooring over 2.5 cm. cement concrete floor.

(*b*) 13 mm. cement plastering 1:6 cm.

116. Write short notes on:

(*i*) Building cost index. (*ii*) Various types of Estimates.

(*iii*) Technical Sanction.

117. Write down detailed specifications for the following items of work:-

(*a*) 2.5 cm. cement concrete floor. (*b*) Centering and shuttering.

(*c*) Earthwork in excavation in foundation.

118.(*a*) What is the necessity of Valuating any building.

(*b*) Workout the rent statement of a building newly constructed at a cost of Rs. 120,000/-. The cost for sanitary, water supply and electric installations should be included. Assume any other data, if required, suitably.

119. What will be the cost of construction of a beam shown in Fig. Q. 119? Steel should be taken as separate item. Also find the quantities of different materials required.

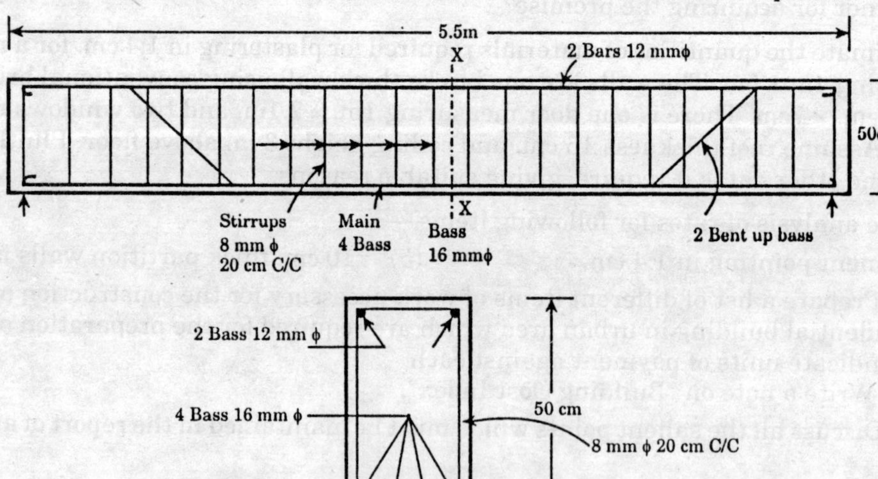

Fig. Q.119.

120. (*a*) Write down the units of measurement for the following items of work:-

(*i*) Skirting. (*ii*) Renewing of glass panels.

(*iii*) 2.5 C.C. over 7.5 cm. L.C. floor. (*iv*) Coping.

(*b*) Write short notes on —

(*i*) Contingencies and supervision charges. (*ii*) Building cost Index.

121. Give analysis of rates for the following items:-

(*i*) 25 mm. thick panelled window. (*ii*) Bricks masonry in 1:6 cement mortar.

122. (*a*) What are the different methods of preparing approximate estimates? Explain them briefly.

(*b*) Write detailed specifications for Damp-proof-Course.

123. What is necessity of valuating any building? Explain various factors on which the valuation of a building depends? What are the duties and responsibilities of a valuer?

124. Prepare a detailed estimate of a shop shown in Fig. Q. 124 and estimate the amount of cement required for its construction.

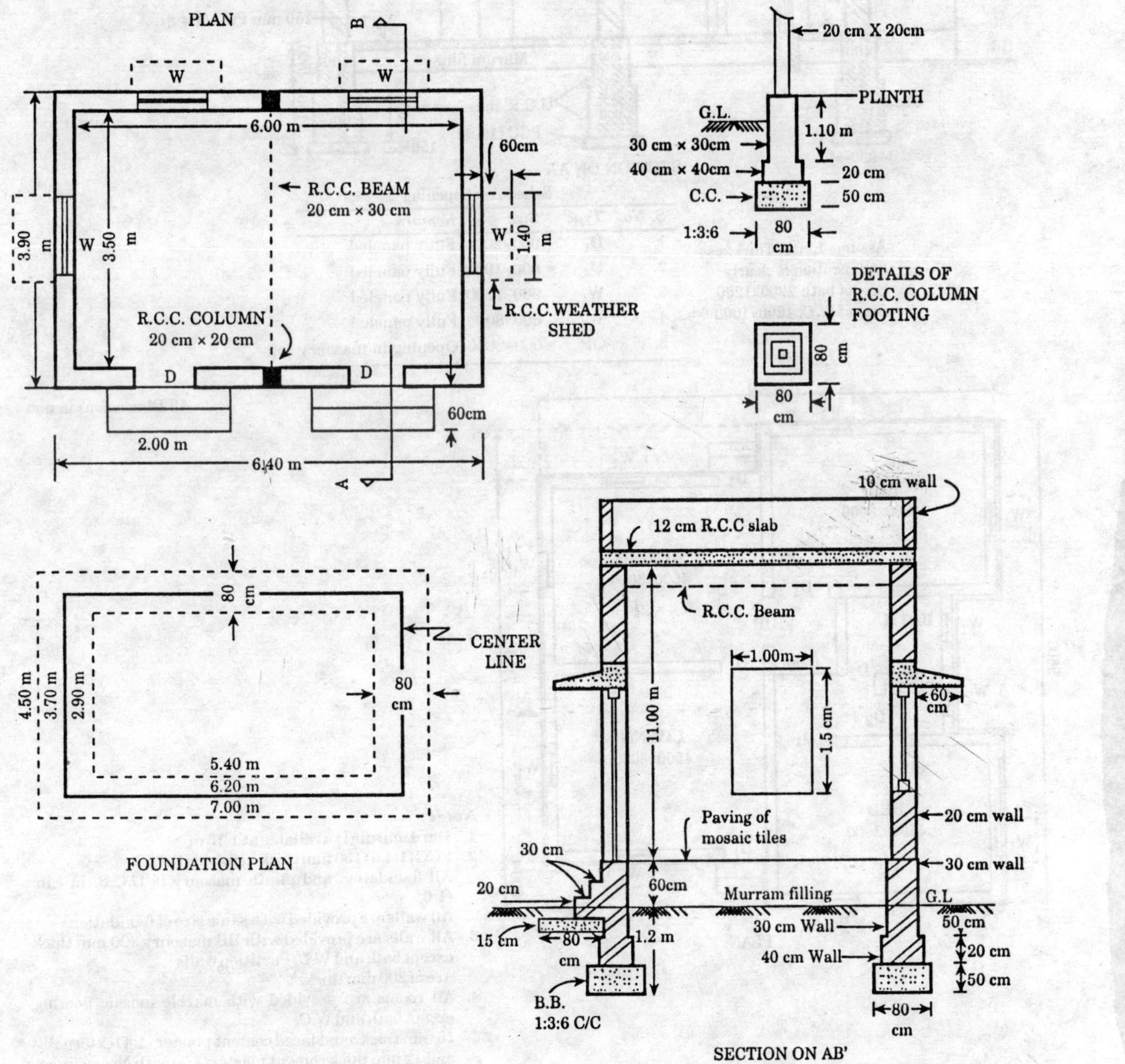

Fig. Q. 124

125. Fig. Q. 125 shows the plan and section of a residential building. Work-out the quantities of the following items.

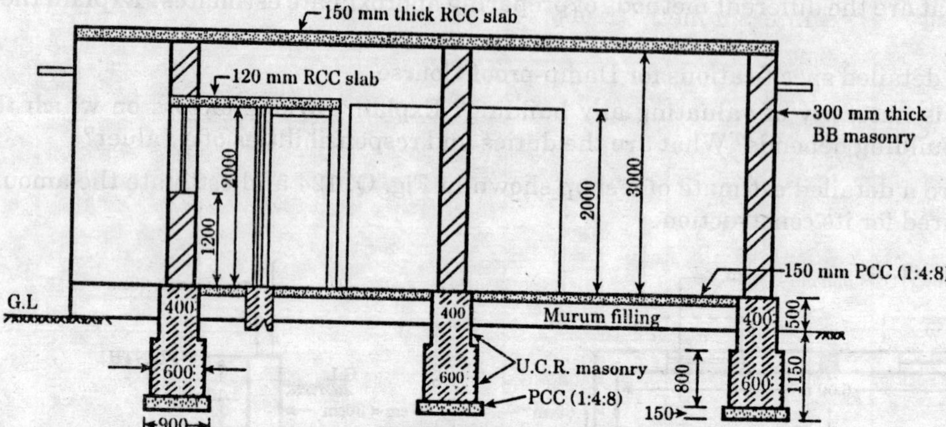

SECTION ON AA

Assume Lintel Thickness and mention it clearly
Size of bath 2200×1200
Size of W.C. 1200×1000

Schedule of opening

S. No.	Type	Size	Remark
1.	D_1	900×2000	Fully paneled
2.	D_2	800×1900	Fully paneled
3.	W_1	900×1200	Fully paneled
4.	W_2	600×800	Fully paneled
5.	OP	900×2000	Opening in masonry

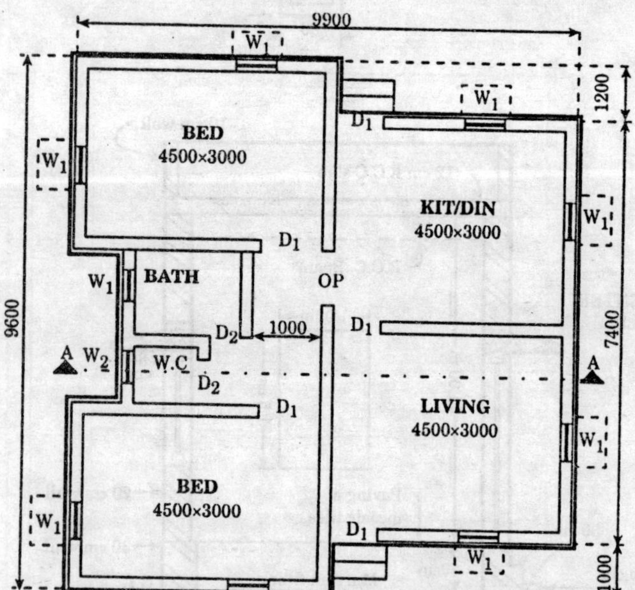

PLAN

All Dimensions in mm

Notes :

1. Hard murum is available at 1.15 m
2. PCC (1:4:8) 150 mm thick in foundation.
   All foundation and plinth masonry is U.C.R. in c.m. (1:6).
   All walls are provided with same size of foundation.
3. All walls are provided with BB masonry 300 mm thick except bath and W.C. Partition walls Are of 200 mm thick.
4. All rooms are provided with marble mosaic flooring except bath and W.C.
5. 15 mm thick sand faced cement plaster (1:4) externally and 12 mm thick cement plaster (1:4) with Neeru finish internally.

Fig. Q.125

(*a*) P.C.C. (1:4:8) in foundation.

(*b*) II class B.B. masonry in cm. (1:8) in superstructure.

(*c*) 15 mm thick sand faced cement plaster (1:4) to external surfaces of B.B. masonry walls.

(*d*) Marble mosaic flooring in all rooms and passage except W.C. & bath.

126. (*a*) Distinguish between **any two** of the following.

1. Administrative approval & Technical Sanction.
2. Revised estimate and supplimentry estimate.
3. Detailed specifications and general specification.

(*b*) A proposal of cosntructing a primary school at a village is to be prepared. Write in brief the procedure of preparing approximate estimate for this proposal.

127. (*a*) Explain the terms Work-charged establishment and contingencies.

(*b*) Work out the rate for **any one** item of the following.

1. P.C.C. (1:4:8) foundation.
2. 12 mm thick cement plaster (1:4) with neeru finish, to internal surfaces of brick masonry in superstructure.

128. (*a*) State the mode the measurement (I.S.) for the following.

1. M.S. Reinforcement for R.C.C. Work:
2. Teak Wood for door frames
3. G.I. pipe line for carrying water
4. Manglore tile ridge
5. Damp proof course
6. Cement pointing (1:3) to B.K. masonry
7. A.C. sheet roof covering.

(8) M.S. Grill for window.

(*b*) Work-out the quantity of earth for 90 m road length. Formation width 7 m. Side slope in embarkment 2:1 and that in cutting 1½:1

Chainage m	*G.L. m*	*Formation Level m*
0	125.00	123.60
30	124.60	124.00
60	122.90	123.60
90	121.60	123.20

129. (*a*) State the reasons for popularity of plinth area method of approximate estimate.

(*b*) Write detailed specifications for **any one** of the following.

1. 15 mm thick sand face cement plaster (1:4) to Brick masonry.
2. Excavation for foundation in ordinary soil.

130. (*a*) State the various methods adopted for executing minor works in department and explain any one method in details.

(*b*) State the purpose of inviting tenders for the construction of public works. What are the different tender forms? Write the procedure for scrutiny of item rate-tender.

131.(*a*) What is an engineering contract? State the requirements of Valid Contract.

(*b*) What are the types of contract? Explain the lump-sum contract and state its advantages and disadvantages?

(*c*) State the significance of Earnest money and Security deposit.

132.(*a*) State the circumstances in which the extension of time limit may be granted to contractor.

(*b*) Explain with justification what action will you suggest in following cases. (**any three**)

1. The lowest tender received is unbalanced.
2. Quality of construction work is found to be sub-standard at the time of inspection.
3. The contractor sub-lets the work without proper permission.
4. The contractor abandons the work.
5. The progress of construction work is found to be unsatisfactory.

133.(*a*) State the different methods of valuation and explain any one of them.

(*b*) Find out the present value of property from the data given below.

1. Built up area of the building - 300 m^2
2. Gross rent received per month - Rs. 3000/-
3. Municipal taxes per year - 24% of gross rent/year
4. Annual maintenance and other outgoings except sinking fund - 12% of Gross rent/year
5. Expected future life - 60 years
6. Area of plot - 800 m^2
7. Present sale rate of land - Rs. 400/- per m^2
8. Net return expected from building investment - 10% per year
9. Net return expected from land investment - 6% per year
10. Rate of interest on redumption = 4% per year

134. Write short notes on **any three** of the following.

(*a*) Arbitration

(*b*) Salvage Value and Scrap Value

(*c*) Building lease.

(*d*) Extra items.

(*e*) Book Value.

135. (*a*) Workout the rates for **any one** item of the following:

(*i*) Providing mild steel reinforcement for R.C.C. work.

(*ii*) R.C.C. work 1 : 1½ : 3 for beam with 2.0% of steel.

(*b*) Workout the materials required for one cubic metre brick wall, one brick thick in English bond using 19 × 19 × 9 cm size. Thickness of joint 1 cm. Bricks are having a frog of 10 × 4 × 1 cm size. No rounding off or any allowance for wastage is to be made. Mortar requirement to be workout correct to the fourth decimal place.

136.(*a*) Explain fully the procedure adopted in drafting detailed specifications to be attached to the tender for the construction of a large building.

(*b*) Write detailed specifications for any one item of the following:

(*i*) A.C. sheet roof covering.

(*ii*) Excavation for foundation.

137.(*a*) State the standard mode of measurement (I.S.) for concrete in R.C.C. footings, columns, beams and slabs for two storeyed R.C.C. frame structure. In your answer, clearly state the unit of measurement as well as how measured.

(*b*) Compare plinth area method with cubic content method for working out-approximate estimate of building and explain why plinth area method is more popular and widely in use.

138. Prepare a detail estimate of a Man-hole from the given drawing as shown in Fig. Q. 138 foundation and floor shall be of cc 1:3:6. Brick work shall be of wire cut brick in cm 1:6. The inner faces of the wall shall be plastered with cm 1:6 of 12 mm thick.

Workout the quantities of the following items:

(*a*) Earthwork in excavation in ordinary soil

(*b*) C.C. bed in foundation 1:3:6

(*c*) Wire-cut brickwork in cm 1:5

(*d*) Plastering in cm 1:6 of 12 mm thick.

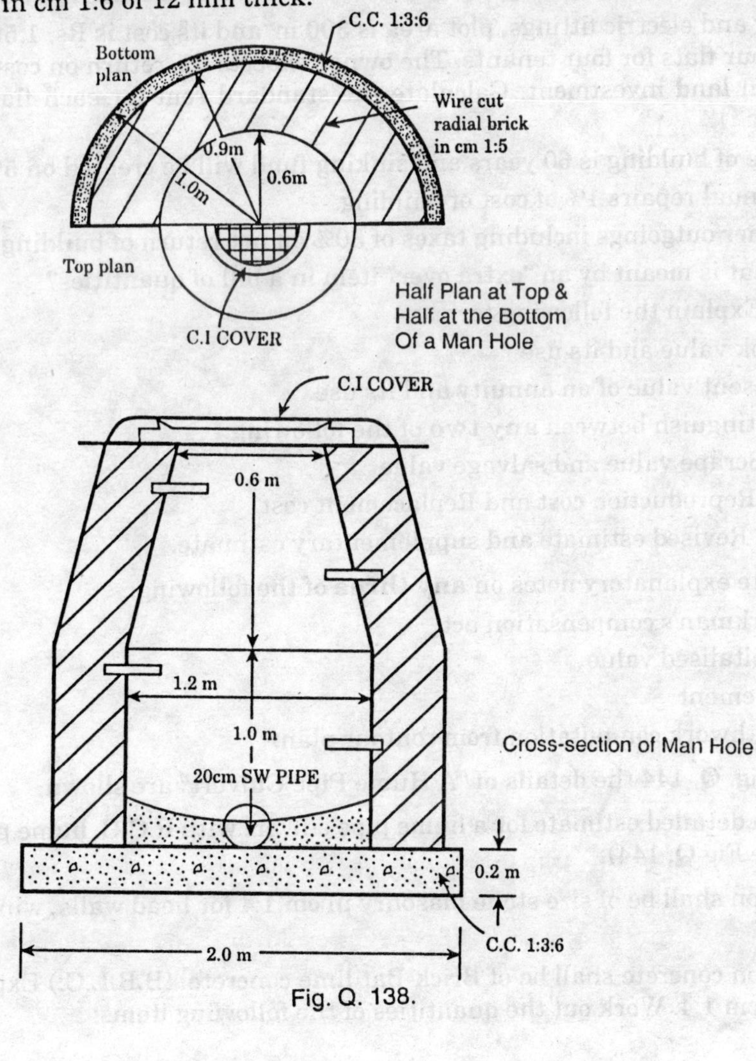

Fig. Q. 138.

139. (*a*) Explain the term depletion.

(*b*) State the different methods of calculating depreciation and explain any one method.

(*c*) The cost of construction of a new building according to present market value is Rs. 80,000/- having life of 70 years. But if the building is 15 years old, determine the depreciation amount which should be deducted from the cost of the new building at 6% compound interest.

140. (*a*) State the procedure of preparing valuation report of a residential building for a purchaser.

(*b*) A coloniser intends to purchase a land of 1,00,000 sqm. area located in the suburb of a big city to develop it into plots of 700 sqm. each after providing necessary roads and parks and other amenities. The current sale price of small plots in the neighbourhood is Rs.30/- per sqm. The coloniser wants a net profit of 20%. Workout the maximum price of the land at which the coloniser may purchase the land.

141. (*a*) Explain the term building lease and occupation lease.

(*b*) A building has been newly constructed at a total cost of Rs. 2,40,000/- including sanitary, watersupply and electric fittings, plot area is 300 m^2 and its cost is Rs. 1,50,000/-. The building consists of four flats for four tenants. The owner expects 8% return on cost of construction and 5% return on land investment. Calculate the standard rent for each flat with the following assumptions:

(*i*) Life of building is 60 years and sinking fund will be created on 5% interest basis.

(*ii*) Annual repairs 1% of cost of building.

(*iii*) Other outgoings including taxes of 30% on net return of building.

(*c*) What is meant by an "extra over" item in a bill of quantities?

142. (*a*) Explain the following terms:

(*i*) Book value and its use

(*ii*) Present value of an annuity and its use.

(*b*) Distinguish between **any two** of the following:

(*i*) Scrape value and salvage value

(*ii*) Reproduction cost and Replacement cost

(*iii*) Revised estimate and supplementary estimate.

143. Write explanatory notes on **any three** of the following:

(*a*) Workman's compensation act

(*b*) Capitalised value

(*c*) Easement

(*d*) Earthwork computation from contour plan.

144. In Fig. Q. 144 the details of "A Hume Pipe Culvert" are shown.

Prepare a detailed estimate for a hume pipe culvert with R.C.C. hume pipes from the given drawing. (See Fig Q. 144).

Foundation shall be of size stone masonry in cm.1:4 for head walls, wing walls, turn walls, and toe walls.

Foundation concrete shall be of Brick-Bat lime concrete. (B.B.L.C.) Exposed faces shall be pointed with cm 1:4. Work out the quantities of the following items:

(*a*) Earthwork in excavation in foundation in ordinary soil.

(*b*) Brick-bat lime concrete for Abutments, wing walls, turn walls, Toe walls, Brick flooring.

(*c*) S.S.M. in CM (1:4) for Abutments, wing walls, Turn walls, Toe walls.

(*d*) Pointing in CM (1:4)12 mm thick.

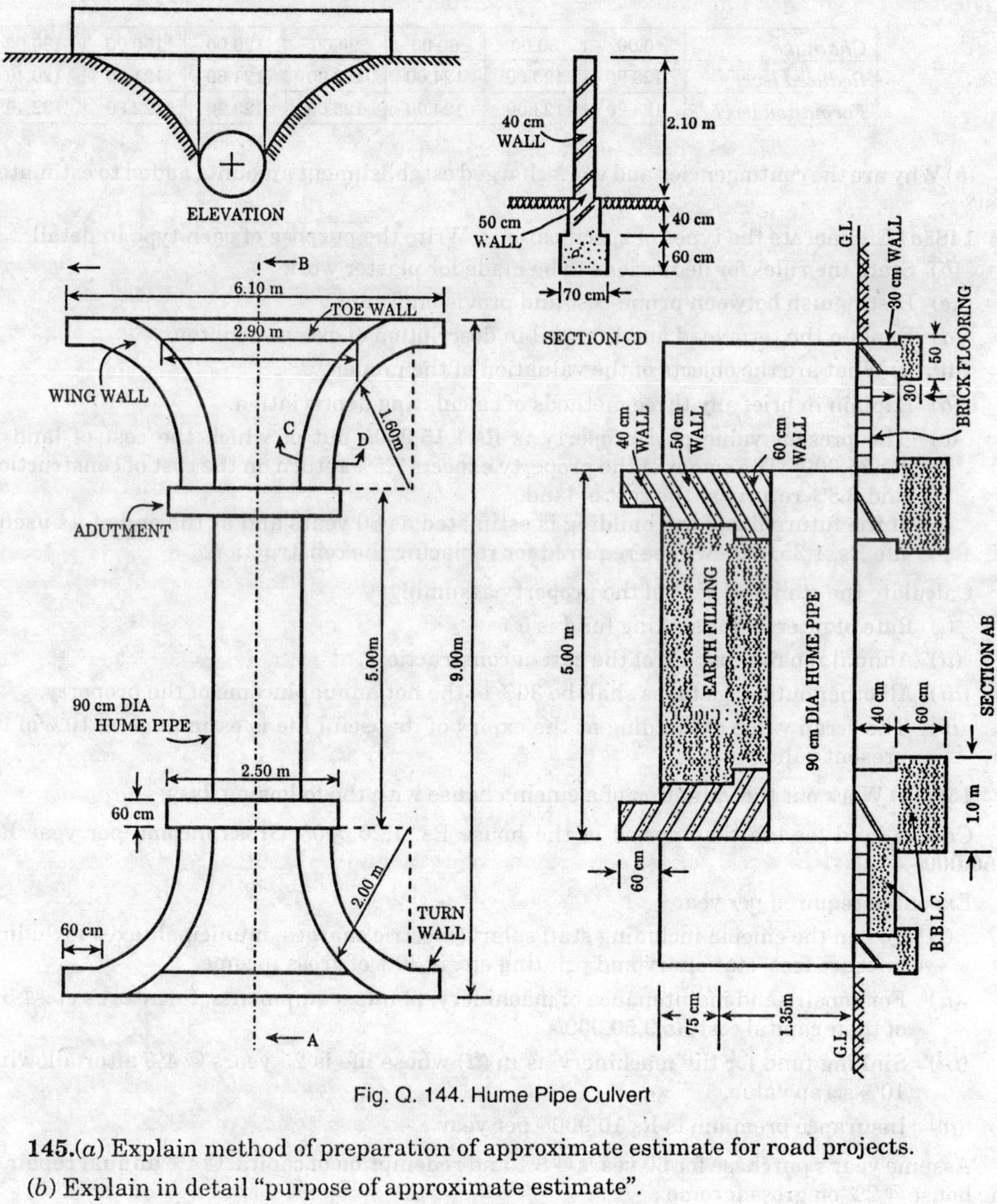

Fig. Q. 144. Hume Pipe Culvert

145.(*a*) Explain method of preparation of approximate estimate for road projects.

(*b*) Explain in detail "purpose of approximate estimate".

146.(*a*) State the purpose of analysis of rates.

(*b*) Prepare the rate analysis as per the current market rates for 20 mm thick damp proof course with cement mortar (1:2).

147.(*a*) Calculate the quantity of earthwork for 180 m of road length, formation width 10 m, slide slopes are 2:1 for banking and cutting.

Chainage	0.00	30.00	60.00	90.00	120.00	150.00	180.00
Reduced level	123.90	125.00	124.60	122.90	121.60	121.00	120.40
Formation level	123.20	123.00	124.00	123.60	123.20	122.80	122.40

(*b*) Why are the contingencies and work charged establishment amounts added to estimated cost?

148.(*a*) Enumerate the types of specifications. Write the purpose of each type in detail.

(*b*) State the rules for deductions to be made for plaster work.

(*c*) Distinguish between prime-cost and provisional sum.

(*d*) Explain the term lead and lift used in description of excavation item.

149. (*a*) What are the objects of the valuation of the property?

(*b*) Explain in brief any three methods of calculating depreciation.

(*c*) The present value of a property is Rs.1,15,000/- out of which the cost of land is Rs.25,000/- The owner of the property expects 7.5% return on the cost of construction and 6.5% return on the cost of land.
If the future life of the building is estimated as 80 years and at the end of its useful life Rs. 1,35,000/- will be required for replacing the construction.

Calculate the standard rent of the property assuming:

(*i*) Rate of interest for sinking fund is 5%

(*ii*) Annual repairs cost 1% of the cost of construction

(*iii*) All other outgoings taxes shall be 30% of the net annual income of the property.

(*iv*) The scrap value of building at the expiry of its useful life is estimated as 10% of its present value.

150. (*a*) Work out the valuation of a cinema house with the following data:

Cost of land for life time period of the house Rs. 1,20,000/- Gross income per year Rs. 7,50,000/-.

Expenses required per year:

(*i*) To run the cinema including staff salary, electric charges, municipal taxes including lincence fees, stationary and printing etc. is 30% of gross income.

(*ii*) For repairs and maintenance of machinery, plants, equipments, furnitures etc.@ 5% of their capital cost Rs.9,50,000/-

(*iii*) Sinking fund for the machinery as in (*ii*) whose life is 25 years @ 4% after allowing 10% scrap value.

(*iv*) Insurance premium is Rs.10,000/- per year.

Assume year's purchase for 60 years @ 8% and redemption of capital @ 4% annual repair of the house @ 2% on gross income.

(*b*) Define.

(*i*) Annuity (*ii*) Year's purchase

(*iii*) Specification.

151. Write short notes on **any four** of the following:

(*a*) Schedules of rates (*b*) Minimum wages act

(*c*) Factors affecting value of property (*d*) Establishment charges

(*e*) Free hold and lease hold property.

152. The accompanying sketch shows details of a building. Prepare in standard forms the detailed estimate of the quantities of the following items of work.

(*a*) Excavation (*b*) UCR masonary

(*c*) Brick work in superstructure (*d*) Internal Plastering

(*e*) PCC in foundation.

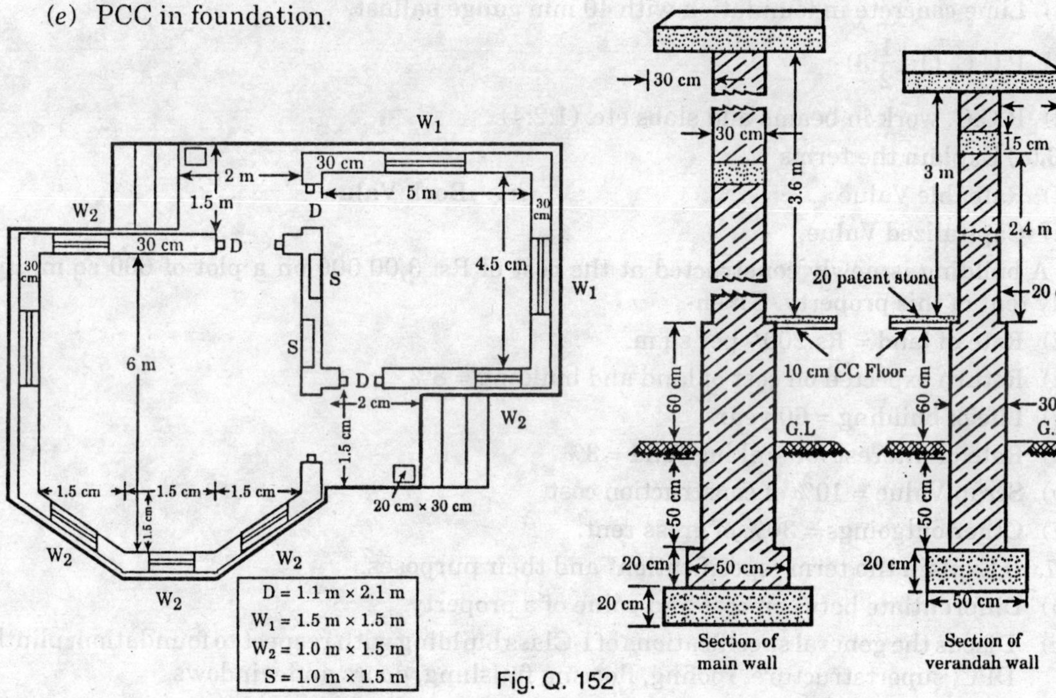

Fig. Q. 152

153. (*a*) Discuss the different types of estimates.

(*b*) It is required to draw up a preliminary estimate of a school building for 500 students in order to assess the amount of fund. The following particulars are collected :

Carpet area required per students = 1.25 sqm.

Area of corridor, verandah, lavatories etc = 20%,

Area for wall = 15% (% of plinth area in both cases)

Plinth area rate = Rs.3100/- per sq.m.

The extra cost in % of building cost for different items are as under :

Cost of water supply = 5%

Cost of sanitation = 6%

Cost of electrification = 10%

Cost of approach road and boundary wall = 3%

Contengency and w.c. establishment shall be 5% and 2.5% of total cost respectively.

154. (*a*) Explain in brief-

(*i*) Site Plan (*ii*) Layout Plan

(*iii*) Index Plan

(*b*) What are the factors on which the rates of particular item of work depends.

(*c*) Write a note on standard mode of "measurement of earth work".

155.(*a*) Define the term "task-work" and mention the factors affecting it.

(*b*) Work out the rates per cubic metre of the following items.(any two)

(*i*) Lime concrete in foundation with 40 mm gauge ballast.

(*ii*) P.C.C. $(1:1\frac{1}{2}:3)$

(*iii*) R.C.C. work in beams and slabs etc. (1:2:4)

156.(*a*) Explain the terms

(*i*) Rateable Value (*ii*) Book Value

(*iii*) Capitalized Value

(*b*) A building is newly constructed at the cost of Rs. 3,00,000 on a plot of 600 sq.m. Fix monthly rent of this property. Given-

(*i*) Rate of land = Rs.200/- per sq.m.

(*ii*) Return expected on cost of land and building = 8%

(*iii*) Life of building = 60 years.

(*iv*) Rate of interest for sinking fund = 3%

(*v*) Scrap Value = 10% of construction cost

(*vi*) Other outgoings = 30% of gross rent.

157.(*a*) Explain the term "specification" and their purposes.

(*b*) Differentiate between cost and value of a property.

(*c*) Discus the general specifications of I-Class building with respect to foundation, plinth, DPC, supertstructure, roofing, flooring finishing, doors and windows.

158.(*a*) Define the term "depreciation". What are the different methods for calculating depreciation. Discuss the declining balance method.

(*b*) A building has total cost of construction as Rs.20 lakh. Find out the depreciated value of building after 25 years. Assume total life of building to be 90 years. Scrap value may be taken as 10% of the capital cost.

159.(*a*) Mention the different methods of valuation.

(*b*) Discuss the following.

(*i*) Rent Act (*ii*) Labour Laws

(*c*) Explain the following terms.

(*i*) Dismantling and Demolition. (*ii*) Joinery

APPENDIX - I VALUATION TABLES

Table A.1

Annuity of Re. 1/- at the end of a given term

Years	Rate per cent											
	3	3.5	4	4.5	5	5.5	6	6.5	7	7.5	8	8.5
1	1.03	1.04	1.04	1.04	1.05	1.05	1.06	1.07	1.07	1.08	1.08	1.09
2	1.06	1.07	1.08	1.09	1.10	1.11	1.12	1.13	1.14	1.16	1.17	1.18
3	1.09	1.11	1.12	1.14	1.16	1.17	1.19	1.21	1.23	1.24	1.26	1.28
4	1.13	1.15	1.17	1.19	1.22	1.24	1.26	1.29	1.31	1.34	1.36	1.39
5	1.16	1.19	1.22	1.25	1.28	1.31	1.34	1.37	1.40	1.44	1.47	1.50
6	1.19	1.23	1.27	1.30	1.34	1.38	1.42	1.46	1.50	1.54	1.59	1.63
7	1.23	1.27	1.32	1.36	1.41	1.45	1.50	1.55	1.61	1.66	1.71	1.77
8	1.27	1.32	1.37	1.42	1.48	1.53	1.59	1.65	1.72	1.78	1.85	1.92
9	1.30	1.36	1.42	1.49	1.55	1.62	1.69	1.76	1.84	1.92	2.00	2.08
10	1.34	1.41	1.48	1.55	1.63	1.71	1.79	1.88	1.97	2.06	2.16	2.26
11	1.38	1.46	1.54	1.62	1.71	1.80	1.90	2.00	2.10	2.22	2.33	2.45
12	1.43	1.51	1.60	1.70	1.80	1.90	2.01	2.13	2.25	2.38	2.52	2.66
13	1.47	1.56	1.67	1.77	1.89	2.01	2.13	2.27	2.41	2.56	2.72	2.89
14	1.51	1.62	1.73	1.85	1.98	2.12	2.26	2.41	2.58	2.75	2.94	3.13
15	1.56	1.68	1.80	1.94	2.08	2.23	2.40	2.57	2.76	2.96	3.17	3.40
16	1.60	1.73	1.87	2.02	2.18	2.36	2.54	2.74	2.95	3.18	3.43	3.69
17	1.65	1.79	1.95	2.11	2.29	2.48	2.69	2.92	3.16	3.42	3.70	4.00
18	1.70	1.86	2.03	2.21	2.41	2.62	2.85	3.11	3.38	3.68	4.00	4.34
19	1.75	1.92	2.11	2.31	2.53	2.77	3.03	3.31	3.62	3.95	4.32	4.71
20	1.81	1.99	2.19	2.41	2.65	2.92	3.21	3.52	3.87	4.25	4.66	5.11
21	1.86	2.06	2.28	2.52	2.79	3.08	3.40	3.75	4.14	4.57	5.03	5.55
22	1.92	2.13	2.37	2.63	2.93	3.25	3.60	4.00	4.43	4.91	5.44	6.02
23	1.97	2.21	2.46	2.75	3.07	3.43	3.82	4.26	4.74	5.28	5.87	6.53
24	2.03	2.28	2.56	2.88	3.23	3.61	4.05	4.53	5.07	5.67	6.34	7.08
25	2.09	2.36	2.67	3.01	3.39	3.81	4.29	4.83	5.43	6.10	6.85	7.69
26	2.16	2.45	2.77	3.14	3.56	4.02	4.55	5.14	5.81	6.56	7.40	8.34
27	2.22	2.53	2.88	3.28	3.73	4.24	4.82	5.48	6.21	7.05	7.99	9.05
28	2.29	2.62	3.00	3.43	3.92	4.48	5.11	5.83	6.65	7.58	8.63	9.82
29	2.36	2.71	3.12	3.58	4.12	4.72	5.42	6.21	7.11	8.14	9.32	10.65
30	2.43	2.81	3.24	3.75	4.32	4.98	5.74	6.61	7.61	8.75	10.06	11.56
31	2.50	2.91	3.37	3.91	4.54	5.26	6.09	7.04	8.15	9.41	10.87	12.54
32	2.58	3.01	3.51	4.09	4.76	5.55	6.45	7.50	8.72	10.12	11.74	13.61
33	2.65	3.11	3.65	4.27	5.00	5.85	6.84	7.99	9.33	10.88	12.68	14.76
34	2.73	3.22	3.79	4.47	5.25	6.17	7.25	8.51	9.98	11.69	13.69	16.02
35	2.81	3.33	3.95	4.67	5.52	6.51	7.69	9.01	10.68	12.57	14.79	17.38
36	2.90	3.45	4.10	4.88	5.79	6.87	8.15	9.65	11.42	13.51	15.97	18.86
37	2.99	3.57	4.27	5.10	6.08	7.25	8.64	10.28	12.22	14.52	17.25	20.46
38	3.07	3.70	4.44	5.33	6.39	7.65	9.15	10.95	13.08	15.61	18.63	22.20

Years	*Rate per cent*											
	3	3.5	4	4.5	5	5.5	6	6.5	7	7.5	8	8.5
39	3.17	3.83	4.62	5.57	6.70	8.07	9.70	11.66	13.99	16.79	20.12	24.09
40	3.26	3.96	4.80	5.82	7.04	8.51	10.29	12.42	14.97	18.04	21.72	26.13
41	3.36	4.10	4.99	6.08	7.39	8.98	10.90	13.22	16.02	19.40	23.46	28.35
42	3.46	4.24	5.19	6.35	7.76	9.48	11.56	14.08	17.14	20.85	25.34	30.76
43	3.56	4.39	5.40	6.64	8.15	10.00	12.25	15.00	18.34	22.42	27.37	33.38
44	3.67	4.54	5.62	6.94	8.56	10.55	12.99	15.97	19.63	24.10	29.56	36.22
45	3.78	4.70	5.84	7.25	8.98	11.13	13.76	17.01	21.00	25.90	31.92	39.30
46	3.90	4.87	6.07	7.57	9.43	11.74	14.59	18.12	22.47	27.85	34.47	42.64
47	4.01	5.04	6.32	7.92	9.91	12.38	15.47	19.29	24.05	29.94	37.23	46.26
48	4.13	5.21	6.57	8.27	10.40	13.07	16.39	20.55	25.73	32.18	40.21	50.19
49	4.26	5.40	6.83	8.64	10.92	13.78	17.38	21.88	27.53	34.60	43.43	54.46
50	4.38	5.58	7.11	9.03	11.47	14.54	18.42	23.31	29.46	37.19	46.90	59.09

Annuity of Re. 1/- at the end of a given term

Years	*Rate per cent*						*Years*	*Rate per cent*					
	9	9.5	10	10.5	11	11.5		9	9.5	10	10.5	11	11.5
1	1.09	1.10	1.10	1.11	1.11	1.12	26	9.40	10.59	11.92	13.41	15.08	16.95
2	1.19	1.20	1.21	1.22	1.23	1.24	27	10.25	11.59	13.11	14.82	16.74	18.90
3	1.30	1.31	1.33	1.35	1.37	1.39	28	11.17	12.69	14.42	16.37	18.58	21.07
4	1.41	1.44	1.46	1.49	1.52	1.55	29	12.17	13.90	15.86	18.09	20.62	23.49
5	1.54	1.57	1.61	1.65	1.69	1.72	30	13.27	15.22	17.45	19.99	22.89	26.20
6	1.68	1.72	1.77	1.82	1.87	1.92	31	14.46	16.67	19.19	22.09	25.41	29.21
7	1.83	1.89	1.95	2.01	2.08	2.14	32	15.76	18.25	21.11	24.41	28.21	32.57
8	1.99	2.07	2.14	2.22	2.30	2.39	33	17.18	19.98	23.23	26.97	31.31	36.31
9	2.17	2.26	2.36	2.46	2.56	2.66	34	18.73	21.88	25.55	29.81	34.75	40.49
10	2.37	2.48	2.59	2.71	2.84	2.97	35	20.41	23.96	28.10	32.94	38.57	45.15
11	2.58	2.71	2.85	3.00	3.15	3.31	36	22.25	26.24	30.91	36.40	42.82	50.34
12	2.81	2.97	3.14	3.31	3.50	3.69	37	24.25	28.73	34.00	40.22	47.53	56.13
13	3.07	3.25	3.45	3.66	3.88	4.12	38	26.44	31.46	37.40	44.44	52.76	62.58
14	3.34	3.56	3.80	4.05	4.31	4.59	39	28.82	34.45	41.14	49.11	58.56	69.78
15	3.64	3.90	4.18	4.47	4.78	5.12	40	31.41	37.72	45.26	54.26	65.00	77.80
16	3.97	4.27	4.59	4.94	5.31	5.71	41	34.24	41.30	49.79	59.96	72.15	86.75
17	4.33	4.68	5.05	5.46	5.90	6.36	42	37.32	45.23	54.76	66.25	80.09	96.73
18	4.72	5.12	5.56	6.03	6.54	7.09	43	40.68	49.52	60.24	73.21	88.90	107.85
19	5.14	5.61	6.12	6.67	7.26	7.91	44	44.34	54.23	66.26	80.90	98.68	120.25
20	5.60	6.14	6.73	7.37	8.06	8.82	45	48.33	59.38	72.89	89.39	109.53	134.08
21	6.11	6.73	7.40	8.14	8.95	9.83	46	52.68	65.02	80.18	98.78	121.58	149.50
22	6.66	7.36	8.14	8.99	9.93	10.97	47	57.42	71.20	88.20	109.15	134.95	166.69
23	7.26	8.06	8.95	9.94	11.03	12.23	48	62.59	77.96	97.02	120.61	149.80	185.86
24	7.91	8.83	9.85	10.98	12.24	13.63	49	68.22	85.37	106.72	133.28	166.27	207.24
25	8.62	9.67	10.83	12.14	13.59	15.20	50	74.36	93.48	117.39	147.27	184.56	231.07

Table A 1.2
Present value of Re. 1/- receiveable at the end of a given term

Years	*Rate per cent*											
	3	3.5	4	4.5	5	5.5	6	6.5	7	7.5	8	8.5
1	0.971	0.966	0.962	0.957	0.957	0.948	0.943	0.939	0.935	0.930	0.926	0.922
2	0.943	0.934	0.925	0.916	0.907	0.898	0.890	0.882	0.873	0.865	0.857	0.849
3	0.915	0.902	0.889	0.876	0.864	0.852	0.840	0.828	0.816	0.805	0.794	0.783
4	0.888	0.871	0.855	0.839	0.823	0.807	0.792	0.777	0.763	0.749	0.735	0.722
5	0.863	0.842	0.822	0.802	0.784	0.765	0.747	0.730	0.713	0.697	0.681	0.665
6	0.837	0.814	0.790	0.768	0.746	0.725	0.705	0.685	0.666	0.648	0.630	0.613
7	0.813	0.786	0.760	0.735	0.711	0.687	0.665	0.644	0.623	0.603	0.583	0.565
8	0.789	0.759	0.731	0.703	0.677	0.652	0.627	0.604	0.582	0.561	0.540	0.521
9	0.766	0.734	0.703	0.673	0.645	0.618	0.592	0.567	0.544	0.522	0.500	0.480
10	0.744	0.709	0.676	0.644	0.614	0.585	0.558	0.533	0.508	0.485	0.463	0.442
11	0.722	0.685	0.650	0.616	0.585	0.555	0.527	0.500	0.475	0.451	0.429	0.408
12	0.701	0.662	0.625	0.590	0.557	0.526	0.497	0.470	0.444	0.420	0.397	0.376
13	0.681	0.639	0.601	0.564	0.530	0.499	0.469	0.441	0.415	0.391	0.368	0.346
14	0.661	0.618	0.577	0.540	0.505	0.473	0.442	0.414	0.388	0.363	0.340	0.319
15	0.642	0.597	0.555	0.517	0.481	0.448	0.417	0.389	0.362	0.338	0.315	0.294
16	0.623	0.577	0.534	0.494	0.458	0.425	0.394	0.365	0.339	0.314	0.292	0.271
17	0.605	0.557	0.513	0.473	0.436	0.402	0.371	0.343	0.317	0.292	0.270	0.250
18	0.587	0.538	0.494	0.453	0.416	0.381	0.350	0.322	0.296	0.272	0.250	0.230
19	0.570	0.520	0.475	0.433	0.396	0.362	0.331	0.302	0.277	0.253	0.232	0.212
20	0.554	0.503	0.456	0.415	0.377	0.343	0.312	0.284	0.258	0.235	0.215	0.196
21	0.538	0.486	0.439	0.397	0.359	0.325	0.294	0.266	0.242	0.219	0.199	0.180
22	0.522	0.469	0.422	0.380	0.342	0.308	0.278	0.250	0.226	0.204	0.184	0.166
23	0.507	0.453	0.406	0.363	0.326	0.292	0.262	0.235	0.211	0.189	0.170	0.153
24	0.492	0.438	0.390	0.348	0.310	0.277	0.247	0.221	0.197	0.176	0.158	0.141
25	0.478	0.423	0.375	0.333	0.295	0.262	0.233	0.207	0.184	0.164	0.146	0.130
26	0.464	0.409	0.361	0.318	0.281	0.249	0.220	0.194	0.172	0.153	0.135	0.120
27	0.450	0.395	0.347	0.305	0.268	0.236	0.207	0.183	0.161	0.142	0.125	0.111
28	0.437	0.382	0.333	0.292	0.255	0.223	0.196	0.171	0.150	0.132	0.116	0.102
29	0.424	0.369	0.321	0.279	0.243	0.212	0.185	0.161	0.141	0.123	0.107	0.094
30	0.412	0.356	0.308	0.267	0.231	0.201	0.174	0.151	0.131	0.114	0.099	0.087
31	0.400	0.344	0.296	0.256	0.220	0.190	0.164	0.142	0.123	0.106	0.092	0.080
32	0.388	0.333	0.285	0.245	0.210	0.180	0.155	0.133	0.115	0.099	0.085	0.073
33	0.377	0.321	0.274	0.234	0.200	0.171	0.146	0.125	0.107	0.092	0.079	0.068
34	0.366	0.310	0.264	0.224	0.190	0.162	0.138	0.118	0.100	0.086	0.073	0.062
35	0.355	0.300	0.253	0.214	0.181	0.154	0.130	0.110	0.094	0.080	0.068	0.058
36	0.345	0.290	0.244	0.205	0.173	0.146	0.123	0.104	0.088	0.074	0.063	0.053
37	0.335	0.280	0.234	0.196	0.164	0.138	0.116	0.097	0.082	0.069	0.058	0.049
38	0.325	0.271	0.225	0.188	0.157	0.131	0.109	0.091	0.076	0.064	0.054	0.045
39	0.316	0.261	0.217	0.180	0.149	0.124	0.103	0.086	0.071	0.060	0.050	0.042
40	0.307	0.253	0.208	0.172	0.142	0.117	0.097	0.081	0.067	0.055	0.046	0.038
41	0.298	0.244	0.200	0.165	0.135	0.111	0.092	0.076	0.062	0.052	0.043	0.035
42	0.289	0.236	0.193	0.157	0.129	0.106	0.087	0.071	0.058	0.048	0.039	0.033
43	0.281	0.228	0.185	0.151	0.123	0.100	0.082	0.067	0.055	0.045	0.037	0.030
44	0.272	0.220	0.178	0.144	0.117	0.095	0.077	0.063	0.051	0.041	0.034	0.028
45	0.264	0.213	0.171	0.138	0.111	0.090	0.073	0.059	0.048	0.039	0.031	0.025
46	0.257	0.205	0.165	0.132	0.106	0.085	0.069	0.055	0.044	0.036	0.029	0.023
47	0.249	0.199	0.158	0.126	0.101	0.081	0.065	0.052	0.042	0.033	0.027	0.022
48	0.242	0.192	0.152	0.121	0.096	0.077	0.061	0.049	0.039	0.031	0.025	0.020
49	0.235	0.185	0.146	0.116	0.092	0.073	0.058	0.046	0.036	0.029	0.023	0.018
50	0.228	0.179	0.141	0.111	0.087	0.069	0.054	0.043	0.034	0.027	0.021	0.017

Present value of Re. 1/- receiveable at the end of a given term

Years	*Rate per cent*						*Years*	*Rate per cent*					
	9	9.5	10	10.5	11	11.5		9	9.5	10	10.5	11	11.5
1	0.917	0.913	0.909	0.905	0.901	0.897	26	0.106	0.094	0.084	0.075	0.066	0.059
2	0.842	0.834	0.826	0.819	0.812	0.804	27	0.098	0.086	0.076	0.067	0.060	0.053
3	0.772	0.762	0.751	0.741	0.731	0.721	28	0.090	0.079	0.069	0.061	0.054	0.047
4	0.708	0.696	0.683	0.671	0.659	0.647	29	0.082	0.072	0.063	0.055	0.048	0.043
5	0.650	0.635	0.621	0.607	0.593	0.580	30	0.075	0.066	0.057	0.050	0.044	0.038
6	0.596	0.580	0.564	0.549	0.535	0.520	31	0.069	0.060	0.052	0.045	0.039	0.034
7	0.547	0.530	0.513	0.497	0.482	0.467	32	0.063	0.055	0.047	0.041	0.035	0.031
8	0.502	0.484	0.467	0.450	0.434	0.419	33	0.058	0.050	0.043	0.037	0.032	0.028
9	0.460	0.442	0.424	0.407	0.391	0.375	34	0.053	0.046	0.039	0.034	0.029	0.025
10	0.422	0.404	0.386	0.368	0.352	0.337	35	0.049	0.042	0.036	0.030	0.026	0.022
11	0.388	0.369	0.350	0.333	0.317	0.302	36	0.045	0.038	0.032	0.027	0.023	0.020
12	0.356	0.337	0.319	0.302	0.286	0.271	37	0.041	0.035	0.029	0.025	0.021	0.018
13	0.326	0.307	0.290	0.273	0.258	0.243	38	0.038	0.032	0.027	0.023	0.019	0.016
14	0.299	0.281	0.263	0.247	0.232	0.218	39	0.035	0.029	0.024	0.020	0.017	0.014
15	0.275	0.256	0.239	0.224	0.209	0.195	40	0.032	0.027	0.022	0.018	0.015	0.013
16	0.252	0.234	0.218	0.202	0.188	0.175	41	0.029	0.024	0.020	0.017	0.014	0.012
17	0.231	0.214	0.198	0.183	0.170	0.157	42	0.027	0.022	0.018	0.015	0.012	0.010
18	0.212	0.195	0.180	0.166	0.153	0.141	43	0.025	0.020	0.017	0.014	0.011	0.009
19	0.194	0.178	0.164	0.150	0.138	0.126	44	0.023	0.018	0.015	0.012	0.010	0.008
20	0.178	0.163	0.149	0.136	0.124	0.113	45	0.021	0.017	0.014	0.011	0.009	0.007
21	0.164	0.149	0.135	0.123	0.112	0.102	46	0.019	0.015	0.012	0.010	0.008	0.007
22	0.150	0.136	0.123	0.111	0.101	0.091	47	0.017	0.014	0.011	0.009	0.007	0.006
23	0.138	0.124	0.112	0.101	0.091	0.082	48	0.016	0.013	0.010	0.008	0.007	0.005
24	0.126	0.113	0.102	0.091	0.082	0.073	49	0.015	0.012	0.009	0.008	0.006	0.005
25	0.116	0.103	0.092	0.082	0.074	0.066	50	0.013	0.011	0.009	0.007	0.005	0.004

Table A1.3. Amount of Re. 1/- per annum at the end of a given term

Years	Rate per cent									
	2	3	4	5	5.5	6	6.5	7	7.5	8
1	1.00	1.00	1.00	1.00	1.00	1.00	1.00	1.00	1.00	1.00
2	2.02	2.03	2.04	2.05	2.05	2.06	2.07	2.07	2.08	2.08
3	3.06	3.09	3.12	3.15	3.17	3.18	3.20	3.21	3.23	3.25
4	4.12	4.18	4.25	4.31	4.34	4.37	4.41	4.44	4.47	4.51
5	5.20	5.31	5.42	5.53	5.58	5.64	5.69	5.75	5.81	5.87
6	6.31	6.47	6.63	6.80	6.89	6.98	7.06	7.15	7.24	7.34
7	7.43	7.66	7.90	8.14	8.27	8.39	8.52	8.65	8.79	8.92
8	8.58	8.89	9.21	9.55	9.72	9.90	10.08	10.26	10.45	10.64
9	9.75	10.16	10.58	11.03	11.26	11.49	11.73	11.98	12.23	12.49
10	10.95	11.46	12.01	12.58	12.88	13.18	13.49	13.82	14.15	14.49
11	12.17	12.81	13.49	14.21	14.58	14.97	15.37	15.78	16.21	16.65
12	13.41	14.19	15.03	15.92	16.39	16.87	17.37	17.89	18.42	18.98
13	14.68	15.62	16.63	17.71	18.29	18.88	19.50	20.14	20.81	21.50
14	15.97	17.09	18.29	19.60	20.29	21.02	21.77	22.55	23.37	24.21
15	17.29	18.60	20.02	21.58	22.41	23.28	24.18	25.13	26.12	27.15
16	18.64	20.16	21.82	23.66	24.64	25.67	26.75	27.89	29.08	30.32
17	20.01	21.76	23.70	25.84	27.00	28.21	29.49	30.84	32.26	33.75
18	21.41	23.41	25.65	28.13	29.48	30.91	32.41	34.00	35.68	37.45
19	22.84	25.12	27.67	30.54	32.10	33.76	35.52	37.38	39.35	41.45
20	24.30	26.87	29.78	33.07	34.87	36.79	38.83	41.00	43.30	45.76
21	25.78	28.68	31.97	35.72	37.79	39.99	42.35	44.87	47.55	50.42
22	27.30	30.54	34.25	38.51	40.86	43.39	46.10	49.01	52.12	55.46
23	28.84	32.45	36.62	41.43	44.11	47.00	50.10	53.44	57.03	60.89
24	30.42	34.43	39.08	44.50	47.54	50.82	54.35	58.18	62.31	66.76
25	32.03	36.46	41.65	47.73	51.15	54.86	58.89	63.25	67.98	73.11
26	33.67	38.55	44.31	51.11	54.97	59.16	63.72	68.68	74.08	79.95
27	35.34	40.71	47.08	54.67	58.99	63.71	68.86	74.48	80.63	87.35
28	37.05	42.93	49.97	58.40	63.23	68.53	74.	80.70	87.68	95.34
29	38.79	45.22	52.97	62.32	67.71	73.64	80.16	87.35	95.26	103.97
30	40.57	47.58	56.08	66.44	72.44	79.06	86.38	94.46	103.40	113.28
31	42.38	50.00	59.33	70.76	77.42	84.80	92.99	102.07	112.15	123.35
32	44.23	52.50	62.70	75.30	82.68	90.89	100.03	110.22	121.57	134.21
33	46.11	55.08	66.21	80.06	88.22	97.34	107.54	118.93	131.68	145.95
34	48.03	57.73	69.86	85.07	94.08	104.18	115.53	128.26	142.56	158.63
35	49.99	60.46	73.65	90.32	100.25	111.43	124.03	138.24	154.25	172.32
36	51.99	63.28	77.60	95.84	106.76	119.12	133.10	148.91	166.82	187.10
37	54.03	66.17	81.70	101.63	113.64	127.27	142.75	160.34	180.33	203.07
38	56.11	69.16	85.97	107.71	120.89	135.90	153.03	172.56	194.86	220.32
39	58.24	72.23	90.41	114.09	128.54	145.06	163.97	185.64	210.47	238.94
40	60.40	75.40	95.03	120.80	136.61	154.76	175.63	199.64	227.26	259.06
41	62.61	78.66	99.83	127.84	145.12	165.05	188.05	214.61	245.30	280.78
42	64.86	82.02	104.82	135.23	154.10	175.95	201.27	230.63	264.70	304.24
43	67.16	85.48	110.01	142.99	163.58	187.51	215.35	247.78	285.55	329.58
44	69.50	89.05	115.41	151.14	173.57	199.76	230.35	266.12	307.97	356.95
45	71.89	92.72	121.03	159.70	184.12	212.74	246.33	285.75	332.07	386.51
46	74.33	96.50	126.87	168.68	195.24	226.51	263.34	306.75	357.97	418.43
47	76.82	100.40	132.95	178.12	206.98	241.10	281.45	329.23	385.82	452.90
48	79.35	104.41	139.26	188.02	219.37	256.56	300.75	353.27	415.75	490.13
49	81.94	108.54	145.83	198.43	232.43	272.96	321.30	379.00	447.94	530.34
50	84.58	112.80	152.67	209.35	246.22	290.34	343.18	406.53	482.53	573.77

Amount of Re. 1/- per annum at the end of a given term

Years	*Rate per cent*					*Years*	*Rate per cent*				
	8.5	9	9.52	10	10.5		8.5	9	9.5	10	10.5
1	1.00	1.00	1.00	1.00	1.00	26	86.35	93.32	100.91	109.18	118.19
2	2.09	2.09	2.10	2.10	2.11	27	94.69	102.72	111.50	121.10	131.60
3	3.26	3.28	3.29	3.31	3.33	28	103.74	112.97	123.09	134.21	146.42
4	4.54	4.57	4.61	4.64	4.68	29	113.56	124.14	135.79	148.63	162.79
5	5.93	5.98	6.04	6.11	6.17	30	124.21	136.31	149.69	164.49	180.88
6	7.43	7.52	7.62	7.72	7.81	31	135.77	149.58	164.91	181.94	200.87
7	9.06	9.20	9.34	9.49	9.63	32	148.31	164.04	181.57	201.14	222.97
8	10.83	11.03	11.23	11.44	11.65	33	161.92	179.80	199.82	222.25	247.38
9	12.75	13.02	13.30	13.58	13.87	34	176.68	196.98	219.81	245.48	274.35
10	14.84	15.19	15.56	15.94	16.32	35	192.70	215.71	241.69	271.02	304.16
11	17.10	17.56	18.04	18.53	19.04	36	210.08	236.13	265.65	299.13	337.10
12	19.55	20.14	20.75	21.38	22.04	37	228.94	258.38	291.89	330.04	373.49
13	22.21	22.95	23.72	24.52	25.35	38	249.40	282.63	320.61	364.04	413.71
14	25.10	26.02	26.98	27.97	29.01	39	271.60	309.07	352.07	401.45	458.15
15	28.23	29.36	30.54	31.77	33.06	40	295.68	337.88	386.52	442.59	507.25
16	31.63	33.00	34.44	35.95	37.53	41	321.82	369.29	424.24	487.85	561.51
17	35.32	36.97	38.71	40.54	42.47	42	350.17	403.53	465.54	537.64	621.47
18	39.32	41.30	43.39	45.60	47.93	43	380.94	440.85	510.77	592.40	687.73
19	43.67	46.02	48.51	51.16	53.96	44	414.31	481.52	560.29	652.64	760.94
20	48.38	51.16	54.12	57.28	60.63	45	450.53	525.86	614.52	718.91	841.84
21	53.49	56.76	60.26	64.00	68.00	46	489.83	574.19	673.90	791.80	931.23
22	59.04	62.87	66.99	71.40	76.14	47	532.46	626.86	738.92	871.98	1030.01
23	65.05	69.53	74.35	79.54	85.13	48	578.72	684.28	810.12	960.17	1139.16
24	71.58	76.79	82.42	88.50	95.07	49	628.91	746.87	888.08	1057.19	1259.77
25	78.67	84.70	91.25	98.35	106.05	50	683.37	815.09	973.45	1163.91	1393.05

Table A1.4. Annual sinking fund for the redemption of Re. 1/- capital

Years	*Rate per cent*											
	2.5	3	3.5	4	4.5	5	6	6.5	7	7.5	8	8.5
1	1.000	1.000	1.000	1.000	1.000	1.000	1.000	1.000	1.000	1.000	1.000	1.000
2	0.494	0.493	0.491	0.490	0.489	0.488	0.485	0.484	0.483	0.482	0.481	0.480
3	0.325	0.324	0.322	0.320	0.319	0.317	0.314	0.313	0.311	0.310	0.308	0.307
4	0.241	0.239	0.237	0.235	0.234	0.232	0.229	0.227	0.225	0.224	0.222	0.220
5	0.190	0.188	0.186	0.185	0.183	0.181	0.177	0.176	0.174	0.172	0.170	0.169
6	0.157	0.155	0.153	0.151	0.149	0.147	0.143	0.142	0.140	0.138	0.136	0.135
7	0.132	0.131	0.129	0.127	0.125	0.123	0.119	0.117	0.116	0.114	0.112	0.110
8	0.114	0.112	0.110	0.109	0.107	0.105	0.101	0.099	0.097	0.096	0.094	0.092
9	0.100	0.098	0.096	0.094	0.093	0.091	0.087	0.085	0.083	0.082	0.080	0.078
10	0.089	0.087	0.085	0.083	0.081	0.080	0.076	0.074	0.072	0.071	0.069	0.067
11	0.080	0.078	0.076	0.074	0.072	0.070	0.067	0.065	0.063	0.062	0.060	0.058
12	0.072	0.070	0.068	0.067	0.065	0.063	0.059	0.058	0.056	0.054	0.053	0.051
13	0.066	0.064	0.062	0.060	0.058	0.056	0.053	0.051	0.050	0.048	0.047	0.045
14	0.061	0.059	0.057	0.055	0.053	0.051	0.048	0.046	0.044	0.043	0.041	0.040
15	0.056	0.054	0.052	0.050	0.048	0.046	0.043	0.041	0.040	0.038	0.037	0.035
16	0.052	0.050	0.048	0.046	0.044	0.042	0.039	0.037	0.036	0.034	0.033	0.032
17	0.048	0.046	0.044	0.042	0.040	0.039	0.035	0.034	0.032	0.031	0.030	0.028
18	0.045	0.043	0.041	0.039	0.037	0.036	0.032	0.031	0.029	0.028	0.027	0.025
19	0.042	0.040	0.038	0.036	0.034	0.033	0.030	0.028	0.027	0.025	0.024	0.023
20	0.039	0.037	0.035	0.034	0.032	0.030	0.027	0.026	0.024	0.023	0.022	0.021
21	0.037	0.035	0.033	0.031	0.030	0.028	0.025	0.024	0.022	0.021	0.020	0.019
22	0.035	0.033	0.031	0.029	0.028	0.026	0.023	0.022	0.020	0.019	0.018	0.017
23	0.033	0.031	0.029	0.027	0.026	0.024	0.021	0.020	0.019	0.018	0.016	0.015
24	0.031	0.029	0.027	0.026	0.024	0.022	0.020	0.018	0.017	0.016	0.015	0.014
25	0.029	0.027	0.026	0.024	0.022	0.021	0.018	0.017	0.016	0.015	0.014	0.013
26	0.028	0.026	0.024	0.023	0.021	0.020	0.017	0.016	0.015	0.013	0.013	0.012
27	0.026	0.025	0.023	0.021	0.020	0.018	0.016	0.015	0.013	0.012	0.011	0.011
28	0.025	0.023	0.022	0.020	0.019	0.017	0.015	0.013	0.012	0.011	0.010	0.010
29	0.024	0.022	0.020	0.019	0.017	0.016	0.014	0.012	0.011	0.010	0.010	0.009
30	0.023	0.021	0.019	0.018	0.016	0.015	0.013	0.012	0.011	0.010	0.009	0.008
31	0.022	0.020	0.018	0.017	0.015	0.014	0.012	0.011	0.010	0.009	0.008	0.007
32	0.021	0.019	0.017	0.016	0.015	0.013	0.011	0.010	0.009	0.008	0.007	0.007
33	0.020	0.018	0.017	0.015	0.014	0.012	0.010	0.009	0.008	0.008	0.007	0.006
34	0.019	0.017	0.016	0.014	0.013	0.012	0.010	0.009	0.008	0.007	0.006	0.006
35	0.018	0.017	0.015	0.014	0.012	0.011	0.009	0.008	0.007	0.006	0.006	0.005
36	0.017	0.016	0.014	0.013	0.012	0.010	0.008	0.008	0.007	0.006	0.005	0.005
37	0.017	0.015	0.014	0.012	0.011	0.010	0.008	0.007	0.006	0.006	0.005	0.004
38	0.016	0.014	0.013	0.012	0.010	0.009	0.007	0.007	0.006	0.005	0.005	0.004
39	0.015	0.014	0.012	0.011	0.010	0.009	0.007	0.006	0.005	0.005	0.004	0.004
40	0.015	0.013	0.012	0.011	0.009	0.008	0.006	0.006	0.005	0.004	0.004	0.003
41	0.014	0.013	0.011	0.010	0.009	0.008	0.006	0.005	0.005	0.004	0.004	0.003
42	0.014	0.012	0.011	0.010	0.008	0.007	0.006	0.005	0.004	0.004	0.003	0.003
43	0.013	0.012	0.010	0.009	0.008	0.007	0.005	0.005	0.004	0.004	0.003	0.003
44	0.013	0.011	0.010	0.009	0.008	0.007	0.005	0.004	0.004	0.003	0.003	0.002
45	0.012	0.011	0.009	0.008	0.007	0.006	0.005	0.004	0.003	0.003	0.003	0.002
46	0.012	0.010	0.009	0.008	0.007	0.006	0.004	0.004	0.003	0.003	0.002	0.002
47	0.011	0.010	0.009	0.008	0.007	0.006	0.004	0.004	0.003	0.003	0.002	0.002
48	0.011	0.010	0.008	0.007	0.006	0.005	0.004	0.003	0.003	0.002	0.002	0.002
49	0.011	0.009	0.008	0.007	0.006	0.005	0.004	0.003	0.003	0.002	0.002	0.002
50	0.010	0.009	0.008	0.007	0.006	0.005	0.003	0.003	0.002	0.002	0.002	0.001

Annual sinking fund for the redemption of Re. 1/- capital

Years	*Rate per cent*						*Years*	*Rate per cent*					
	9	9.5	10	10.5	11	11.5		9	9.5	10	10.5	11	11.5
1	1.000	1.000	1.000	1.000	1.000	1.000	26	0.011	0.010	0.009	0.008	0.008	0.007
2	0.478	0.477	0.476	0.475	0.474	0.473	27	0.010	0.009	0.008	0.008	0.007	0.006
3	0.305	0.304	0.302	0.301	0.299	0.298	28	0.009	0.008	0.007	0.007	0.006	0.006
4	0.219	0.217	0.215	0.214	0.212	0.211	29	0.008	0.007	0.007	0.006	0.006	0.005
5	0.167	0.165	0.164	0.162	0.161	0.159	30	0.007	0.007	0.006	0.006	0.005	0.005
6	0.133	0.131	0.130	0.128	0.126	0.125	31	0.007	0.006	0.005	0.005	0.005	0.004
7	0.109	0.107	0.105	0.104	0.102	0.101	32	0.006	0.006	0.005	0.004	0.004	0.004
8	0.091	0.089	0.087	0.086	0.084	0.083	33	0.006	0.005	0.004	0.004	0.004	0.003
9	0.077	0.075	0.074	0.072	0.071	0.069	34	0.005	0.005	0.004	0.004	0.003	0.003
10	0.066	0.064	0.063	0.061	0.060	0.058	35	0.005	0.004	0.004	0.003	0.003	0.003
11	0.057	0.055	0.054	0.053	0.051	0.050	36	0.004	0.004	0.003	0.003	0.003	0.002
12	0.050	0.048	0.047	0.045	0.044	0.043	37	0.004	0.003	0.003	0.003	0.002	0.002
13	0.044	0.042	0.041	0.039	0.038	0.037	38	0.004	0.003	0.003	0.002	0.002	0.002
14	0.038	0.037	0.036	0.034	0.033	0.032	39	0.003	0.003	0.002	0.002	0.002	0.002
15	0.034	0.033	0.031	0.030	0.029	0.028	40	0.003	0.003	0.002	0.002	0.002	0.001
16	0.030	0.029	0.028	0.027	0.026	0.024	41	0.003	0.002	0.002	0.002	0.002	0.001
17	0.027	0.026	0.025	0.024	0.022	0.021	42	0.002	0.002	0.002	0.002	0.001	0.001
18	0.024	0.023	0.022	0.021	0.020	0.019	43	0.002	0.002	0.002	0.001	0.001	0.001
19	0.022	0.021	0.020	0.019	0.018	0.017	44	0.002	0.002	0.002	0.001	0.001	0.001
20	0.020	0.018	0.017	0.016	0.016	0.015	45	0.002	0.002	0.001	0.001	0.001	0.001
21	0.018	0.017	0.016	0.015	0.014	0.013	46	0.002	0.001	0.001	0.001	0.001	0.001
22	0.016	0.015	0.014	0.013	0.012	0.012	47	0.002	0.001	0.001	0.001	0.001	0.001
23	0.014	0.013	0.013	0.012	0.011	0.010	48	0.001	0.001	0.001	0.001	0.001	0.001
24	0.013	0.012	0.011	0.011	0.010	0.009	49	0.001	0.001	0.001	0.001	0.001	0.001
25	0.012	0.011	0.010	0.009	0.009	0.008	50	0.001	0.001	0.001	0.001	0.001	0.000

VALUATION TABLE
Table A1.5

Present value of Re. 1/- per annum allowing interest of 4% on capital								*Present value of Re. 1/- per annum allowing interest of 4.5% on capital*						
Years	*And For Redemption of Capital at*			*Years*	*And For Redemption of Capital at*			*Years*	*And For Redemption of Capital at*			*Years*	*And For Redemption of Capital at*	
	3%	3.5%	4%		3%	3.5%	4%		3.5%	4%	4.5%		3.5%	4%
1	0.96	0.96	0.96	26	15.17	15.58	15.98	1	0.96	0.96	0.96	26	14.45	14.80
2	1.88	1.88	1.89	27	15.49	15.91	16.33	2	1.86	1.87	1.87	27	14.74	15.10
3	2.75	2.76	2.78	28	15.80	16.23	16.66	3	2.73	2.74	2.75	28	15.01	15.38
4	3.58	3.61	3.63	29	16.10	16.54	16.98	4	3.54	3.57	3.59	29	15.28	15.65
5	4.38	4.42	4.45	30	16.39	16.84	17.29	5	4.32	4.35	4.39	30	15.53	15.92
6	5.14	5.19	5.24	31	16.67	17.13	17.59	6	5.06	5.11	5.16	31	15.78	16.17
7	5.86	5.93	6.00	32	16.94	17.41	17.87	7	5.76	5.83	5.89	32	16.01	16.41
8	6.56	6.65	6.73	33	17.20	17.68	18.15	8	6.43	6.51	6.60	33	16.24	16.64
9	7.22	7.33	7.44	34	17.45	17.93	18.41	9	7.07	7.17	7.27	34	16.46	16.86
10	7.86	7.98	8.11	35	17.69	18.18	18.66	10	7.68	7.79	7.91	35	16.67	17.07
11	8.47	8.61	8.76	36	17.92	18.42	18.91	11	8.26	8.39	8.53	36	16.87	17.28
12	9.05	9.22	9.39	37	18.14	18.65	19.14	12	8.81	8.96	9.12	37	17.06	17.47
13	9.61	9.80	9.99	38	18.36	18.87	19.37	13	9.34	9.51	9.68	38	17.25	17.66
14	10.15	10.36	10.56	39	18.57	19.09	19.58	14	9.85	10.03	10.22	39	17.43	17.84
15	10.66	10.89	11.12	40	18.77	19.29	19.79	15	10.33	10.53	10.74	40	17.60	18.01
16	11.16	11.40	11.65	41	18.97	19.49	19.99	16	10.79	11.01	11.23	41	17.76	18.18
17	11.63	11.90	12.17	42	19.16	19.69	20.19	17	11.23	11.47	11.71	42	17.92	18.34
18	12.09	12.37	12.66	43	19.34	19.87	20.37	18	11.65	11.91	12.16	43	18.07	18.49
19	12.53	12.83	13.13	44	19.52	20.05	20.55	19	12.06	12.32	12.59	44	18.22	18.63
20	12.95	13.27	13.59	45	19.69	20.22	20.72	20	12.44	12.73	13.01	45	18.36	18.77
21	13.36	13.69	14.03	46	19.86	20.39	20.88	21	12.81	13.11	13.40	46	18.50	18.91
22	13.75	14.10	14.45	47	20.02	20.55	21.04	22	13.17	13.48	13.78	47	18.63	19.04
23	14.12	14.49	14.86	48	20.17	20.70	21.20	23	13.51	13.83	14.15	48	18.76	19.16
24	14.48	14.86	15.25	49	20.32	20.85	21.34	24	13.84	14.17	14.50	49	18.88	19.28
25	14.83	15.23	15.62	50	20.46	20.99	21.48	25	14.15	14.49	14.83	50	19.00	19.40

Tabel 16.5.

Years	*Present value of Re. 1/- per annum allowing interest of 5% on capital* — *And For Redemption of Capital at* 2.5%	3%	3.5%	4%	4.5%	5%	*Present value of Re. 1/- per annum allowing interest of 5.5% on capital* — And For Redemption of Capital at 3%	3.5%	4%	4.5%	5%	6.5%
1	0.95	0.95	0.95	0.95	0.95	0.95	0.95	0.95	0.95	0.95	0.95	0.95
2	1.84	1.84	1.85	1.85	1.86	1.86	1.83	1.83	1.83	1.84	1.84	1.85
3	2.67	2.68	2.69	2.70	2.71	2.72	2.64	2.65	2.66	2.68	2.69	2.70
4	3.44	3.46	3.48	3.50	3.52	3.55	3.40	3.42	3.44	3.46	3.48	3.51
5	4.16	4.20	4.23	4.26	4.30	4.33	4.11	4.14	4.17	4.21	4.24	4.27
6	4.84	4.89	4.93	4.98	5.03	5.08	4.77	4.82	4.86	4.90	4.95	5.00
7	5.48	5.54	5.60	5.66	5.72	5.79	5.39	5.45	5.51	5.56	5.62	5.68
8	6.08	6.16	6.23	6.31	6.39	6.46	5.97	6.04	6.12	6.19	6.26	6.33
9	6.65	6.74	6.83	6.92	7.01	7.11	6.52	6.60	6.69	6.78	6.86	6.95
10	7.18	7.29	7.39	7.50	7.61	7.72	7.03	7.13	7.23	7.33	7.43	7.54
11	7.69	7.81	7.93	8.05	8.18	8.31	7.51	7.63	7.74	7.86	7.98	8.09
12	8.16	8.30	8.44	8.58	8.72	8.86	7.97	8.10	8.23	8.36	8.49	8.62
13	8.62	8.77	8.92	9.08	9.24	9.39	8.40	8.54	8.68	8.83	8.97	9.12
14	9.05	9.21	9.38	9.55	9.73	9.90	8.81	8.96	9.12	9.27	9.43	9.59
15	9.45	9.64	9.82	10.01	10.19	10.38	9.19	9.36	9.53	9.70	9.87	10.04
16	9.84	10.04	10.24	10.44	10.64	10.84	9.56	9.74	9.92	10.10	10.28	10.46
17	10.21	10.42	10.63	10.85	11.06	11.27	9.91	10.10	10.29	10.48	10.67	10.86
18	10.56	10.79	11.01	11.24	11.46	11.69	10.23	10.44	10.64	10.84	11.04	11.25
19	10.90	11.13	11.37	11.61	11.85	12.09	10.55	10.76	10.97	11.18	11.40	11.61
20	11.22	11.47	11.71	11.96	12.21	12.46	10.84	11.07	11.29	11.51	11.73	11.95
21	11.52	11.78	12.04	12.30	12.56	12.82	11.13	11.36	11.59	11.82	12.05	12.28
22	11.81	12.08	12.36	12.63	12.90	13.16	11.40	11.64	11.88	12.11	12.35	12.58
23	12.09	12.37	12.66	12.94	13.21	13.49	11.65	11.90	12.15	12.39	12.64	12.88
24	12.36	12.65	12.94	13.23	13.52	13.80	11.90	12.15	12.41	12.66	12.91	13.15
25	12.61	12.92	13.21	13.51	13.80	14.09	12.13	12.40	12.66	12.91	13.17	13.41
26	12.86	13.17	13.48	13.78	14.08	14.38	12.36	12.63	12.89	13.15	13.41	13.66
27	13.09	13.41	13.73	14.04	14.34	14.64	12.57	12.84	13.12	13.38	13.64	13.90
28	13.32	13.64	13.97	14.28	14.59	14.90	12.77	13.05	13.33	13.60	13.87	14.12
29	13.53	13.87	14.20	14.52	14.83	15.14	12.97	13.25	13.54	13.81	14.08	14.33
30	13.74	14.08	14.42	14.74	15.06	15.37	13.15	13.45	13.73	14.01	14.28	14.53
31	13.94	14.29	14.63	14.96	15.28	15.59	13.33	13.63	13.92	14.20	14.47	14.72
32	14.13	14.48	14.83	15.16	15.49	15.80	13.51	13.80	14.09	14.38	14.65	14.90
33	14.31	14.67	15.02	15.36	15.69	16.00	13.67	13.97	14.26	14.55	14.82	15.08
34	14.49	14.85	15.21	15.55	15.88	16.19	13.83	14.13	14.43	14.71	14.98	15.24
35	14.66	15.03	15.38	15.73	16.06	16.37	13.98	14.29	14.58	14.87	15.14	15.39
36	14.83	15.20	15.56	15.90	16.23	16.55	14.12	14.43	14.73	15.01	15.28	15.54
37	14.98	15.36	15.72	16.07	16.40	16.71	14.26	14.57	14.87	15.16	15.42	15.67
38	15.14	15.51	15.88	16.23	16.56	16.87	14.40	14.71	15.01	15.29	15.56	15.80
39	15.28	15.66	16.03	16.38	16.71	17.02	14.53	14.84	15.14	15.42	15.68	15.93
40	15.42	15.81	16.17	16.52	16.85	17.16	14.65	14.96	15.26	15.54	15.80	16.05
41	15.56	15.95	16.31	16.66	16.99	17.29	14.77	15.08	15.38	15.66	15.92	16.16
42	15.69	16.08	16.45	16.80	17.12	17.42	14.88	15.20	15.49	15.77	16.03	16.26
43	15.82	16.21	16.58	16.92	17.25	17.55	14.99	15.31	15.60	15.88	16.13	16.36
44	15.94	16.33	16.70	17.05	17.37	17.66	15.10	15.41	15.71	15.98	16.23	16.46
45	16.06	16.45	16.82	17.16	17.48	17.77	15.20	15.52	15.81	16.08	16.32	16.55
46	16.17	16.57	16.93	17.28	17.59	17.88	15.30	15.61	15.90	16.17	16.41	16.63
47	16.28	16.68	17.04	17.38	17.70	17.98	15.39	15.71	15.99	16.26	16.50	16.71
48	16.39	16.78	17.15	17.49	17.80	18.08	15.49	15.80	16.08	16.34	16.58	16.79
49	16.50	16.89	17.25	17.59	17.89	18.17	15.57	15.88	16.17	16.42	16.66	16.86
50	16.60	16.99	17.35	17.68	17.98	18.26	15.66	15.97	16.25	16.50	16.73	16.93

Years	*Present value of Re. 1/- per annum allowing interest of 6% on capital*						*Present value of Re. 1/- per annum allowing interest of 6.5% on capital*					
	And For Redemption of Capital at						And For Redemption of Capital at					
	3.5%	4%	4.5%	5%	5.5%	6%	3.5%	4%	4.5%	5%	5.5%	6.5%
1	0.94	0.94	0.94	0.94	0.94	0.94	0.94	0.94	0.94	0.94	0.94	0.94
2	1.81	1.82	1.82	1.83	1.83	1.83	1.80	1.80	1.81	1.81	1.81	1.82
3	2.62	2.63	2.64	2.65	2.66	2.67	2.58	2.60	2.61	2.62	2.63	2.65
4	3.36	3.38	3.40	3.42	3.44	3.47	3.31	3.33	3.35	3.37	3.39	3.43
5	4.06	4.09	4.12	4.15	4.18	4.21	3.98	4.01	4.04	4.07	4.10	4.16
6	4.70	4.74	4.79	4.83	4.87	4.92	4.59	4.63	4.68	4.72	4.76	4.84
7	5.30	5.36	5.41	5.47	5.53	5.58	5.17	5.22	5.27	5.32	5.38	5.48
8	5.87	5.93	6.00	6.07	6.14	6.21	5.70	5.76	5.83	5.89	5.96	6.09
9	6.39	6.47	6.55	6.64	6.72	6.80	6.19	6.27	6.35	6.42	6.50	6.66
10	6.89	6.98	7.07	7.17	7.26	7.36	6.66	6.74	6.83	6.92	7.01	7.19
11	7.35	7.45	7.56	7.67	7.78	7.89	7.09	7.19	7.29	7.39	7.49	7.69
12	7.78	7.90	8.02	8.14	8.26	8.38	7.49	7.60	7.71	7.82	7.93	8.16
13	8.19	8.32	8.45	8.59	8.72	8.85	7.87	7.99	8.11	8.23	8.36	8.60
14	8.58	8.72	8.86	9.01	9.15	9.29	8.23	8.36	8.49	8.62	8.75	9.01
15	8.94	9.10	9.25	9.40	9.56	9.71	8.56	8.70	8.84	8.98	9.12	9.40
16	9.29	9.45	9.61	9.78	9.94	10.11	8.87	9.02	9.17	9.32	9.47	9.77
17	9.61	9.78	9.96	10.13	10.30	10.48	9.17	9.33	9.49	9.64	9.80	10.11
18	9.92	10.10	10.28	10.47	10.65	10.83	9.45	9.62	9.78	9.95	10.11	10.43
19	10.21	10.40	10.59	10.78	10.97	11.16	9.71	9.89	10.06	10.23	10.40	10.73
20	10.49	10.69	10.88	11.08	11.28	11.47	9.96	10.14	10.32	10.50	10.67	11.02
21	10.75	10.96	11.16	11.36	11.57	11.76	10.20	10.39	10.57	10.75	10.93	11.28
22	11.00	11.21	11.42	11.63	11.84	12.04	10.42	10.62	10.81	10.99	11.18	11.54
23	11.23	11.45	11.67	11.89	12.10	12.30	10.64	10.83	11.03	11.22	11.41	11.77
24	11.46	11.68	11.91	12.13	12.34	12.55	10.84	11.04	11.24	11.43	11.62	11.99
25	11.67	11.90	12.13	12.35	12.57	12.78	11.03	11.23	11.44	11.63	11.83	12.20
26	11.88	12.11	12.34	12.57	12.79	13.00	11.21	11.42	11.63	11.83	12.02	12.39
27	12.07	12.31	12.54	12.77	13.00	13.21	11.38	11.60	11.80	12.01	12.20	12.58
28	12.25	12.50	12.74	12.97	13.19	13.41	11.55	11.76	11.97	12.18	12.37	12.75
29	12.43	12.68	12.92	13.15	13.37	13.59	11.70	11.92	12.13	12.34	12.54	12.91
30	12.60	12.85	13.09	13.32	13.55	13.76	11.85	12.07	12.29	12.49	12.69	13.06
31	12.76	13.01	13.25	13.49	13.71	13.93	11.99	12.22	12.43	12.64	12.83	13.20
32	12.91	13.17	13.41	13.65	13.87	14.08	12.13	12.35	12.57	12.77	12.97	13.33
33	13.06	13.31	13.56	13.79	14.02	14.23	12.26	12.48	12.70	12.90	13.10	13.46
34	13.20	13.46	13.70	13.94	14.16	14.37	12.38	12.61	12.82	13.03	13.22	13.58
35	13.33	13.59	13.84	14.07	14.29	14.50	12.50	12.73	12.94	13.15	13.34	13.69
36	13.46	13.72	13.97	14.20	14.42	14.62	12.61	12.84	13.05	13.26	13.45	13.79
37	13.58	13.84	14.09	14.32	14.53	14.74	12.72	12.95	13.16	13.36	13.55	13.89
38	13.70	13.96	14.20	14.43	14.65	14.85	12.82	13.05	13.26	13.46	13.65	13.98
39	13.81	14.07	14.32	14.54	14.75	14.95	12.92	13.15	13.36	13.56	13.74	14.06
40	13.92	14.18	14.42	14.65	14.85	15.05	13.02	13.24	13.45	13.65	13.83	14.15
41	14.03	14.28	14.52	14.74	14.95	15.14	13.11	13.33	13.54	13.73	13.91	14.22
42	14.12	14.38	14.62	14.84	15.04	15.22	13.19	13.42	13.62	13.81	13.99	14.29
43	14.22	14.47	14.71	14.93	15.13	15.31	13.28	13.50	13.70	13.89	14.06	14.36
44	14.31	14.56	14.80	15.01	15.21	15.38	13.36	13.58	13.78	13.96	14.13	14.42
45	14.40	14.65	14.88	15.09	15.28	15.46	13.43	13.65	13.85	14.03	14.20	14.48
46	14.48	14.73	14.96	15.17	15.36	15.52	13.50	13.72	13.92	14.10	14.26	14.54
47	14.56	14.81	15.04	15.24	15.42	15.59	13.57	13.79	13.98	14.16	14.32	14.59
48	14.64	14.89	15.11	15.31	15.49	15.65	13.64	13.85	14.05	14.22	14.38	14.64
49	14.71	14.96	15.18	15.38	15.55	15.71	13.71	13.92	14.11	14.28	14.43	14.68
50	14.79	15.03	15.24	15.44	15.61	15.76	13.77	13.98	14.16	14.33	14.48	14.72

Present value of Re. 1/- per annum allowing interest of 7% on capital

Years	*And For Redemption of Capital at*							
	3.5%	4%	4.5%	5%	5.5%	6%	6.5%	7%
1	0.93	0.93	0.93	0.93	0.93	0.93	0.93	0.93
2	1.78	1.79	1.79	1.79	1.80	1.80	1.80	1.81
3	2.55	2.56	2.57	2.58	2.59	2.60	2.61	2.62
4	3.25	3.27	3.29	3.31	3.33	3.35	3.37	3.39
5	3.90	3.93	3.96	3.98	4.01	4.04	4.07	4.10
6	4.49	4.53	4.57	4.61	4.65	4.69	4.73	4.77
7	5.04	5.09	5.14	5.19	5.24	5.29	5.34	5.39
8	5.54	5.60	5.66	5.72	5.78	5.85	5.91	5.97
9	6.01	6.08	6.15	6.22	6.30	6.37	6.44	6.52
10	6.44	6.52	6.61	6.69	6.77	6.86	6.94	7.02
11	6.84	6.94	7.03	7.12	7.22	7.31	7.40	7.50
12	7.22	7.32	7.43	7.53	7.63	7.74	7.84	7.94
13	7.57	7.68	7.80	7.91	8.02	8.13	8.25	8.36
14	7.90	8.02	8.14	8.26	8.38	8.50	8.63	8.75
15	8.21	8.34	8.47	8.60	8.72	8.85	8.98	9.11
16	8.50	8.63	8.77	8.91	9.04	9.18	9.31	9.45
17	8.77	8.91	9.06	9.20	9.34	9.48	9.62	9.76
18	9.02	9.17	9.33	9.47	9.62	9.77	9.92	10.06
19	9.26	9.42	9.58	9.73	9.89	10.04	10.19	10.34
20	9.49	9.65	9.82	9.98	10.13	10.29	10.44	10.59
21	9.71	9.87	10.04	10.20	10.37	10.53	10.68	10.84
22	9.91	10.08	10.25	10.42	10.59	10.75	10.91	11.06
23	10.10	10.28	10.45	10.62	10.79	10.96	11.12	11.27
24	10.28	10.46	10.64	10.81	10.98	11.15	11.31	11.47
25	10.45	10.64	10.82	10.99	11.17	11.33	11.50	11.65
26	10.62	10.80	10.99	11.17	11.34	11.51	11.67	11.83
27	10.77	10.96	11.15	11.33	11.50	11.67	11.83	11.99
28	10.92	11.11	11.30	11.48	11.65	11.82	11.98	12.14
29	11.06	11.25	11.44	11.62	11.80	11.96	12.12	12.28
30	11.19	11.39	11.58	11.76	11.93	12.10	12.26	12.41
31	11.32	11.51	11.70	11.89	12.06	12.23	12.38	12.53
32	11.44	11.63	11.83	12.01	12.18	12.35	12.50	12.65
33	11.55	11.75	11.94	12.12	12.29	12.46	12.61	12.75
34	11.66	11.86	12.05	12.23	12.40	12.56	12.71	12.85
35	11.76	11.96	12.16	12.33	12.50	12.66	12.81	12.95
36	11.86	12.06	12.25	12.43	12.60	12.76	12.90	13.04
37	11.96	12.16	12.35	12.53	12.69	12.84	12.99	13.12
38	12.05	12.25	12.44	12.61	12.78	12.93	13.07	13.19
39	12.14	12.34	12.52	12.70	12.86	13.00	13.14	13.26
40	12.22	12.42	12.60	12.77	12.93	13.08	13.21	13.33
41	12.30	12.50	12.68	12.85	13.01	13.15	13.28	13.39
42	12.38	12.57	12.75	12.92	13.07	13.21	13.34	13.45
43	12.45	12.64	12.82	12.99	13.14	13.27	13.40	13.51
44	12.52	12.71	12.89	13.05	13.20	13.33	13.45	13.56
45	12.59	12.78	12.95	13.11	13.26	13.39	13.50	13.61
46	12.65	12.84	13.01	13.17	13.31	13.44	13.55	13.65
47	12.71	12.90	13.07	13.23	13.36	13.49	13.60	13.69
48	12.77	12.96	13.13	13.28	13.41	13.53	13.64	13.73
49	12.83	13.01	13.18	13.33	13.46	13.58	13.68	13.77
50	12.88	13.06	13.23	13.37	13.50	13.62	13.71	13.80

Present value of Re. 1/- per annum allowing interest of 7.5% on capital

Years	And For Redemption of Capital at								
	3.5%	4%	4.5%	5%	5.5%	6%	6.5%	7%	7.5%
1	0.93	0.93	0.93	0.93	0.93	0.93	0.93	0.93	0.93
2	1.77	1.77	1.77	1.78	1.78	1.78	1.79	1.79	1.80
3	2.52	2.53	2.54	2.55	2.56	2.57	2.58	2.59	2.60
4	3.20	3.22	3.24	3.26	3.28	3.29	3.31	3.33	3.35
5	3.82	3.85	3.88	3.91	3.93	3.96	3.99	4.02	4.05
6	4.39	4.43	4.47	4.50	4.54	4.58	4.62	4.66	4.69
7	4.91	4.96	5.01	5.06	5.10	5.15	5.20	5.25	5.30
8	5.39	5.45	5.51	5.56	5.62	5.68	5.74	5.80	5.86
9	5.83	5.90	5.97	6.04	6.10	6.17	6.24	6.31	6.38
10	6.24	6.32	6.39	6.47	6.55	6.63	6.71	6.79	6.86
11	6.62	6.70	6.79	6.88	6.97	7.05	7.14	7.23	7.32
12	6.97	7.06	7.16	7.26	7.35	7.45	7.54	7.64	7.74
13	7.30	7.40	7.50	7.61	7.71	7.81	7.92	8.02	8.13
14	7.60	7.71	7.82	7.93	8.05	8.16	8.27	8.38	8.49
15	7.88	8.00	8.12	8.24	8.36	8.48	8.59	8.71	8.83
16	8.15	8.28	8.40	8.53	8.65	8.78	8.90	9.02	9.14
17	8.40	8.53	8.66	8.80	8.93	9.05	9.18	9.31	9.43
18	8.63	8.77	8.91	9.05	9.18	9.31	9.45	9.58	9.71
19	8.85	9.00	9.14	9.28	9.42	9.56	9.69	9.83	9.96
20	9.06	9.21	9.36	9.50	9.65	9.79	9.92	10.06	10.19
21	9.26	9.41	9.56	9.71	9.86	10.00	10.14	10.28	10.41
22	9.44	9.60	9.75	9.90	10.05	10.20	10.34	10.48	10.62
23	9.61	9.77	9.93	10.09	10.24	10.39	10.53	10.67	10.81
24	9.78	9.94	10.10	10.26	10.41	10.56	10.71	10.85	10.98
25	9.93	10.10	10.26	10.42	10.58	10.73	10.87	11.01	11.15
26	10.08	10.25	10.41	10.57	10.73	10.88	11.03	11.17	11.30
27	10.22	10.39	10.56	10.72	10.88	11.03	11.17	11.31	11.44
28	10.35	10.52	10.69	10.86	11.01	11.16	11.31	11.44	11.57
29	10.48	10.65	10.82	10.98	11.14	11.29	11.43	11.57	11.70
30	10.60	10.77	10.94	11.10	11.26	11.41	11.55	11.68	11.81
31	10.71	10.89	11.06	11.22	11.37	11.52	11.66	11.79	11.92
32	10.82	11.00	11.17	11.33	11.48	11.63	11.77	11.89	12.02
33	10.92	11.10	11.27	11.43	11.58	11.73	11.86	11.99	12.11
34	11.02	11.20	11.37	11.53	11.68	11.82	11.95	12.08	12.19
35	11.11	11.29	11.46	11.62	11.77	11.91	12.04	12.16	12.27
36	11.20	11.38	11.55	11.70	11.85	11.99	12.12	12.24	12.35
37	11.28	11.46	11.63	11.79	11.93	12.07	12.19	12.31	12.42
38	11.37	11.54	11.71	11.86	12.01	12.14	12.26	12.38	12.48
39	11.44	11.62	11.78	11.94	12.08	12.21	12.33	12.44	12.54
40	11.52	11.69	11.86	12.01	12.15	12.28	12.39	12.50	12.59
41	11.59	11.76	11.92	12.07	12.21	12.34	12.45	12.55	12.65
42	11.66	11.83	11.99	12.14	12.27	12.39	12.50	12.60	12.69
43	11.72	11.89	12.05	12.20	12.33	12.45	12.56	12.65	12.74
44	11.78	11.95	12.11	12.25	12.38	12.50	12.60	12.70	12.78
45	11.84	12.01	12.17	12.31	12.43	12.55	12.65	12.74	12.82
46	11.90	12.07	12.22	12.36	12.48	12.59	12.69	12.78	12.85
47	11.95	12.12	12.27	12.40	12.53	12.63	12.73	12.81	12.89
48	12.00	12.17	12.32	12.45	12.57	12.67	12.77	12.85	12.92
49	12.05	12.22	12.36	12.49	12.61	12.71	12.80	12.88	12.95
50	12.10	12.26	12.41	12.53	12.65	12.75	12.83	12.91	12.97

Present value of Re. 1/- per annum allowing interest of 8% on capital

Years	And For Redemption of Capital at								
	3.5%	4.5%	5%	5.5%	6%	6.5%	7%	7.5%	8%
1	0.93	0.93	0.93	0.93	0.93	0.93	0.93	0.93	0.93
2	1.75	1.76	1.76	1.76	1.77	1.77	1.78	1.78	1.78
3	2.49	2.51	2.52	2.53	2.54	2.55	2.56	2.57	2.58
4	3.15	3.19	3.21	3.22	3.24	3.26	3.28	3.29	3.31
5	3.75	3.81	3.83	3.86	3.89	3.91	3.94	3.97	3.99
6	4.30	4.37	4.40	4.44	4.48	4.51	4.55	4.59	4.62
7	4.80	4.89	4.93	4.98	5.02	5.07	5.11	5.16	5.21
8	5.25	5.36	5.41	5.47	5.52	5.58	5.63	5.69	5.75
9	5.67	5.79	5.86	5.92	5.99	6.05	6.12	6.18	6.25
10	6.05	6.20	6.27	6.34	6.42	6.49	6.56	6.64	6.71
11	6.41	6.57	6.65	6.73	6.81	6.89	6.98	7.06	7.14
12	6.73	6.91	7.00	7.09	7.18	7.27	7.36	7.45	7.54
13	7.04	7.23	7.33	7.42	7.52	7.62	7.71	7.81	7.90
14	7.32	7.53	7.63	7.74	7.84	7.94	8.04	8.14	8.24
15	7.59	7.81	7.91	8.02	8.13	8.24	8.35	8.45	8.56
16	7.83	8.06	8.18	8.29	8.41	8.52	8.63	8.74	8.85
17	8.06	8.30	8.42	8.54	8.66	8.78	8.89	9.01	9.12
18	8.28	8.53	8.65	8.78	8.90	9.02	9.14	9.26	9.37
19	8.48	8.74	8.87	9.00	9.12	9.25	9.37	9.49	9.60
20	8.67	8.94	9.07	9.20	9.33	9.46	9.58	9.70	9.82
21	8.85	9.12	9.26	9.39	9.52	9.65	9.78	9.90	10.02
22	9.01	9.30	9.44	9.57	9.70	9.83	9.96	10.08	10.20
23	9.17	9.46	9.60	9.74	9.87	10.00	10.13	10.25	10.37
24	9.32	9.62	9.76	9.90	10.03	10.16	10.29	10.41	10.53
25	9.46	9.76	9.91	10.05	10.18	10.31	10.44	10.56	10.67
26	9.60	9.90	10.04	10.18	10.32	10.45	10.58	10.70	10.81
27	9.72	10.03	10.17	10.31	10.45	10.58	10.70	10.82	10.94
28	9.84	10.15	10.30	10.44	10.57	10.70	10.82	10.94	11.05
29	9.96	10.27	10.41	10.55	10.69	10.81	10.94	11.05	11.16
30	10.06	10.37	10.52	10.66	10.79	10.92	11.04	11.15	11.26
31	10.17	10.48	10.62	10.76	10.89	11.02	11.14	11.25	11.35
32	10.26	10.57	10.72	10.86	10.99	11.11	11.23	11.33	11.44
33	10.35	10.67	10.81	10.95	11.08	11.20	11.31	11.42	11.51
34	10.44	10.75	10.90	11.03	11.16	11.28	11.39	11.49	11.59
35	10.53	10.84	10.98	11.11	11.24	11.36	11.46	11.56	11.65
36	10.61	10.92	11.06	11.19	11.31	11.43	11.53	11.63	11.72
37	10.68	10.99	11.13	11.26	11.38	11.49	11.60	11.69	11.78
38	10.75	11.06	11.20	11.33	11.45	11.56	11.66	11.75	11.83
39	10.82	11.13	11.27	11.39	11.51	11.61	11.71	11.80	11.88
40	10.89	11.19	11.33	11.45	11.57	11.67	11.76	11.85	11.92
41	10.95	11.25	11.39	11.51	11.62	11.72	11.81	11.89	11.97
42	11.01	11.31	11.44	11.56	11.67	11.77	11.86	11.94	12.01
43	11.07	11.37	11.50	11.61	11.72	11.81	11.90	11.98	12.04
44	11.13	11.42	11.55	11.66	11.76	11.86	11.94	12.01	12.08
45	11.18	11.47	11.59	11.71	11.81	11.90	11.98	12.05	12.11
46	11.23	11.51	11.64	11.75	11.85	11.93	12.01	12.08	12.14
47	11.28	11.56	11.68	11.79	11.88	11.97	12.04	12.11	12.16
48	11.32	11.60	11.72	11.83	11.92	12.00	12.07	12.14	12.19
49	11.37	11.64	11.76	11.86	11.95	12.03	12.10	12.16	12.21
50	11.41	11.68	11.80	11.90	11.98	12.06	12.13	12.18	12.23

Present value of Re. 1/- per annum allowing interest of 9% on capital

Years	And For Redemption of Capital at											
	3.5%	4%	4.5%	5%	5.5%	6%	6.5%	7%	7.5%	8%	8.5%	9%
1	0.92	0.92	0.92	0.92	0.92	0.92	0.92	0.92	0.92	0.92	0.92	0.92
2	1.72	1.72	1.73	1.73	1.73	1.74	1.74	1.74	1.75	1.75	1.76	1.76
3	2.43	2.44	2.45	2.46	2.47	2.47	2.48	2.49	2.50	2.51	2.52	2.53
4	3.06	3.07	3.09	3.11	3.12	3.14	3.16	3.17	3.19	3.21	3.22	3.24
5	3.62	3.64	3.67	3.69	3.72	3.74	3.76	3.79	3.81	3.84	3.86	3.89
6	4.12	4.15	4.19	4.22	4.25	4.29	4.32	4.35	4.39	4.42	4.45	4.49
7	4.58	4.62	4.66	4.70	4.74	4.78	4.82	4.86	4.91	4.95	4.99	5.03
8	4.99	5.04	5.09	5.14	5.18	5.23	5.28	5.33	5.38	5.43	5.48	5.53
9	5.36	5.42	5.48	5.53	5.59	5.65	5.71	5.76	5.82	5.88	5.94	6.00
10	5.71	5.77	5.84	5.90	5.96	6.03	6.09	6.16	6.22	6.29	6.35	6.42
11	6.02	6.09	6.16	6.23	6.31	6.38	6.45	6.52	6.59	6.66	6.73	6.81
12	6.31	6.39	6.47	6.54	6.62	6.70	6.78	6.85	6.93	7.01	7.08	7.16
13	6.58	6.66	6.74	6.83	6.91	6.99	7.08	7.16	7.24	7.32	7.41	7.49
14	6.82	6.91	7.00	7.09	7.18	7.27	7.36	7.44	7.53	7.62	7.70	7.79
15	7.05	7.15	7.24	7.33	7.43	7.52	7.61	7.70	7.80	7.88	7.97	8.06
16	7.26	7.36	7.46	7.56	7.66	7.75	7.85	7.95	8.04	8.13	8.22	8.31
17	7.46	7.56	7.67	7.77	7.87	7.97	8.07	8.17	8.26	8.36	8.45	8.54
18	7.64	7.75	7.86	7.97	8.07	8.17	8.27	8.37	8.47	8.57	8.66	8.76
19	7.82	7.93	8.04	8.15	8.25	8.36	8.46	8.57	8.66	8.76	8.86	8.95
20	7.98	8.09	8.21	8.32	8.43	8.53	8.64	8.74	8.84	8.94	9.04	9.13
21	8.13	8.25	8.36	8.47	8.59	8.70	8.80	8.91	9.01	9.10	9.20	9.29
22	8.27	8.39	8.51	8.62	8.74	8.85	8.95	9.06	9.16	9.26	9.35	9.44
23	8.40	8.52	8.64	8.76	8.88	8.99	9.09	9.20	9.30	9.40	9.49	9.58
24	8.53	8.65	8.77	8.89	9.01	9.12	9.23	9.33	9.43	9.53	9.62	9.71
25	8.64	8.77	8.89	9.01	9.13	9.24	9.35	9.45	9.55	9.65	9.74	9.82
26	8.76	8.88	9.01	9.13	9.24	9.35	9.46	9.56	9.66	9.76	9.84	9.93
27	8.86	8.99	9.11	9.23	9.35	9.46	9.57	9.67	9.77	9.86	9.94	10.03
28	8.96	9.09	9.21	9.34	9.45	9.56	9.67	9.77	9.86	9.95	10.04	10.12
29	9.05	9.18	9.31	9.43	9.54	9.65	9.76	9.86	9.95	10.04	10.12	10.20
30	9.14	9.27	9.40	9.52	9.63	9.74	9.84	9.94	10.03	10.12	10.20	10.27
31	9.23	9.36	9.48	9.60	9.72	9.82	9.93	10.02	10.11	10.19	10.27	10.34
32	9.31	9.44	9.56	9.68	9.79	9.90	10.00	10.09	10.18	10.26	10.34	10.41
33	9.38	9.51	9.64	9.76	9.87	9.97	10.07	10.16	10.25	10.33	10.40	10.46
34	9.46	9.59	9.71	9.83	9.94	10.04	10.14	10.23	10.31	10.38	10.45	10.52
35	9.52	9.65	9.78	9.89	10.00	10.10	10.20	10.28	10.36	10.44	10.51	10.57
36	9.59	9.72	9.84	9.96	10.06	10.16	10.26	10.34	10.42	10.49	10.55	10.61
37	9.65	9.78	9.90	10.02	10.12	10.22	10.31	10.39	10.47	10.53	10.60	10.65
38	9.71	9.84	9.96	10.07	10.18	10.27	10.36	10.44	10.51	10.58	10.64	10.69
39	9.77	9.90	10.01	10.13	10.23	10.32	10.41	10.48	10.55	10.62	10.67	10.73
40	9.82	9.95	10.07	10.18	10.28	10.37	10.45	10.53	10.59	10.65	10.71	10.76
41	9.87	10.00	10.12	10.22	10.32	10.41	10.49	10.56	10.63	10.69	10.74	10.79
42	9.92	10.05	10.16	10.27	10.36	10.45	10.53	10.60	10.66	10.72	10.77	10.81
43	9.97	10.09	10.21	10.31	10.40	10.49	10.57	10.63	10.69	10.75	10.80	10.84
44	10.01	10.14	10.25	10.35	10.44	10.53	10.60	10.67	10.72	10.78	10.82	10.86
45	10.05	10.18	10.29	10.39	10.48	10.56	10.63	10.70	10.75	10.80	10.84	10.88
46	10.10	10.22	10.33	10.42	10.51	10.59	10.66	10.72	10.78	10.82	10.86	10.90
47	10.13	10.25	10.36	10.46	10.55	10.62	10.69	10.75	10.80	10.85	10.88	10.92
48	10.17	10.29	10.40	10.49	10.58	10.65	10.72	10.77	10.82	10.86	10.90	10.93
49	10.21	10.32	10.43	10.52	10.60	10.68	10.74	10.79	10.84	10.88	10.92	10.95
50	10.24	10.36	10.46	10.55	10.63	10.70	10.76	10.82	10.86	10.90	10.93	10.96

Present value of Re. 1/- per annum allowing interest of 10% on capital

Years	*And For Redemption of Capital at*											
	3.5%	4.5%	5%	5.5%	6%	6.5%	7%	8%	8.5%	9%	9.5%	10%
1	0.91	0.91	0.91	0.91	0.91	0.91	0.91	0.91	0.91	0.91	0.91	0.91
2	1.69	1.70	1.70	1.70	1.71	1.71	1.71	1.72	1.73	1.73	1.73	1.74
3	2.37	2.39	2.40	2.41	2.41	2.42	2.43	2.45	2.46	2.47	2.48	2.49
4	2.97	3.00	3.01	3.03	3.04	3.06	3.07	3.11	3.12	3.14	3.15	3.17
5	3.49	3.54	3.56	3.58	3.60	3.63	3.65	3.70	3.72	3.74	3.77	3.79
6	3.96	4.02	4.05	4.08	4.11	4.14	4.17	4.23	4.26	4.29	4.32	4.36
7	4.38	4.45	4.49	4.53	4.56	4.60	4.64	4.72	4.75	4.79	4.83	4.87
8	4.75	4.84	4.88	4.93	4.97	5.02	5.06	5.15	5.20	5.24	5.29	5.33
9	5.09	5.19	5.24	5.30	5.35	5.40	5.45	5.55	5.60	5.66	5.71	5.76
10	5.40	5.51	5.57	5.63	5.69	5.74	5.80	5.92	5.97	6.03	6.09	6.14
11	5.68	5.81	5.87	5.93	6.00	6.06	6.12	6.25	6.31	6.37	6.43	6.50
12	5.94	6.07	6.14	6.21	6.28	6.35	6.41	6.55	6.62	6.68	6.75	6.81
13	6.17	6.32	6.39	6.46	6.54	6.61	6.68	6.82	6.90	6.97	7.03	7.10
14	6.39	6.54	6.62	6.70	6.78	6.85	6.93	7.08	7.15	7.22	7.30	7.37
15	6.59	6.75	6.83	6.91	6.99	7.07	7.15	7.31	7.38	7.46	7.53	7.61
16	6.77	6.94	7.03	7.11	7.20	7.28	7.36	7.52	7.60	7.67	7.75	7.82
17	6.94	7.12	7.21	7.30	7.38	7.47	7.55	7.71	7.79	7.87	7.95	8.02
18	7.10	7.29	7.38	7.47	7.56	7.64	7.73	7.89	7.97	8.05	8.13	8.20
19	7.25	7.44	7.53	7.62	7.71	7.80	7.89	8.06	8.14	8.21	8.29	8.36
20	7.39	7.58	7.68	7.77	7.86	7.95	8.04	8.21	8.29	8.36	8.44	8.51
21	7.52	7.72	7.81	7.91	8.00	8.09	8.18	8.35	8.42	8.50	8.58	8.65
22	7.64	7.84	7.94	8.03	8.13	8.22	8.31	8.47	8.55	8.63	8.70	8.77
23	7.75	7.96	8.06	8.15	8.25	8.34	8.42	8.59	8.67	8.74	8.81	8.88
24	7.86	8.07	8.17	8.26	8.36	8.45	8.53	8.70	8.77	8.85	8.92	8.98
25	7.96	8.17	8.27	8.36	8.46	8.55	8.63	8.80	8.87	8.94	9.01	9.08
26	8.05	8.26	8.36	8.46	8.55	8.64	8.73	8.89	8.96	9.03	9.10	9.16
27	8.14	8.35	8.45	8.55	8.64	8.73	8.82	8.97	9.04	9.11	9.18	9.24
28	8.22	8.44	8.54	8.63	8.73	8.81	8.90	9.05	9.12	9.19	9.25	9.31
29	8.30	8.52	8.62	8.71	8.80	8.89	8.97	9.12	9.19	9.25	9.31	9.37
30	8.38	8.59	8.69	8.79	8.88	8.96	9.04	9.19	9.25	9.32	9.37	9.43
31	8.45	8.66	8.76	8.86	8.95	9.03	9.11	9.25	9.31	9.37	9.43	9.48
32	8.51	8.73	8.83	8.92	9.01	9.09	9.17	9.31	9.37	9.43	9.48	9.53
33	8.58	8.79	8.89	8.98	9.07	9.15	9.22	9.36	9.42	9.47	9.52	9.57
34	8.64	8.85	8.95	9.04	9.12	9.20	9.28	9.41	9.46	9.52	9.56	9.61
35	8.70	8.91	9.00	9.09	9.18	9.25	9.33	9.45	9.51	9.56	9.60	9.64
36	8.75	8.96	9.06	9.14	9.23	9.30	9.37	9.49	9.55	9.59	9.64	9.68
37	8.80	9.01	9.10	9.19	9.27	9.35	9.41	9.53	9.58	9.63	9.67	9.71
38	8.85	9.06	9.15	9.24	9.31	9.39	9.45	9.57	9.61	9.66	9.70	9.73
39	8.90	9.10	9.19	9.28	9.36	9.43	9.49	9.60	9.64	9.69	9.72	9.76
40	8.94	9.15	9.24	9.32	9.39	9.46	9.52	9.63	9.67	9.71	9.75	9.78
41	8.98	9.19	9.27	9.36	9.43	9.50	9.55	9.66	9.70	9.74	9.77	9.80
42	9.03	9.22	9.31	9.39	9.46	9.53	9.58	9.68	9.72	9.76	9.79	9.82
43	9.06	9.26	9.35	9.42	9.49	9.56	9.61	9.71	9.74	9.78	9.81	9.83
44	9.10	9.30	9.38	9.46	9.52	9.58	9.64	9.73	9.76	9.80	9.82	9.85
45	9.14	9.33	9.41	9.48	9.55	9.61	9.66	9.75	9.78	9.81	9.84	9.86
46	9.17	9.36	9.44	9.51	9.58	9.63	9.68	9.77	9.80	9.83	9.85	9.88
47	9.20	9.39	9.47	9.54	9.60	9.66	9.71	9.78	9.82	9.84	9.87	9.89
48	9.23	9.42	9.50	9.56	9.62	9.68	9.72	9.80	9.83	9.86	9.88	9.90
49	9.26	9.44	9.52	9.59	9.65	9.70	9.74	9.81	9.84	9.87	9.89	9.91
50	9.29	9.47	9.54	9.61	9.67	9.72	9.76	9.83	9.86	9.88	9.90	9.91

Y.P. of a reversion to a perpetuity after a given number of years

Years	*Rate per cent*											
	3	3.5	4	4.5	5	5.5	6	6.5	7	7.5	8	9
1	32.36	27.61	24.04	21.27	19.05	17.23	15.72	14.45	13.35	12.40	11.57	10.19
2	31.42	26.67	23.11	20.35	18.14	16.34	14.83	13.56	12.48	11.54	10.72	9.35
3	30.50	25.77	22.22	19.47	17.28	15.48	13.99	12.74	11.66	10.73	9.92	8.58
4	29.62	24.90	21.37	18.63	16.45	14.68	13.20	11.96	10.90	9.98	9.19	7.87
5	28.75	24.06	20.55	17.83	15.67	13.91	12.45	11.23	10.19	9.29	8.51	7.22
6	27.92	23.24	19.76	17.06	14.92	13.19	11.75	10.54	9.52	8.64	7.88	6.63
7	27.10	22.46	19.00	16.33	14.21	12.50	11.08	9.90	8.90	8.04	7.29	6.08
8	26.31	21.70	18.27	15.63	13.54	11.85	10.46	9.30	8.31	7.48	6.75	5.58
9	25.55	20.96	17.56	14.95	12.89	11.23	9.86	8.73	7.77	6.95	6.25	5.12
10	24.80	20.25	16.89	14.31	12.28	10.64	9.31	8.20	7.26	6.47	5.79	4.69
11	24.08	19.57	16.24	13.69	11.69	10.09	8.78	7.70	6.79	6.02	5.36	4.31
12	23.38	18.91	15.61	13.10	11.14	9.56	8.28	7.23	6.34	5.60	4.96	3.95
13	22.70	18.27	15.01	12.54	10.61	9.06	7.81	6.78	5.93	5.21	4.60	3.62
14	22.04	17.65	14.44	12.00	10.10	8.59	7.37	3.37	5.54	4.84	4.26	3.32
15	21.40	17.05	13.88	11.48	9.62	8.14	6.95	5.98	5.18	4.51	3.94	3.05
16	20.77	16.48	13.35	10.99	9.16	7.72	6.56	5.62	4.84	4.19	3.65	2.80
17	20.17	15.92	12.83	10.52	8.73	7.32	6.19	5.27	4.52	3.90	3.38	2.57
18	19.58	15.38	12.34	10.06	8.31	6.94	5.84	4.95	4.23	3.63	3.13	2.36
19	19.01	14.86	11.87	9.63	7.91	6.57	5.51	4.65	3.95	3.37	2.90	2.16
20	18.46	14.36	11.41	9.21	7.54	6.23	5.20	4.37	3.69	3.14	2.68	1.98
21	17.92	13.87	10.97	8.82	7.18	5.91	4.90	4.10	3.45	2.92	2.48	1.82
22	17.40	13.40	10.55	8.44	6.84	5.60	4.63	3.85	3.22	2.72	2.30	1.67
23	16.89	12.95	10.14	8.07	6.51	5.31	4.36	3.61	3.01	2.53	2.13	1.53
24	16.40	12.51	9.75	7.73	6.20	5.03	4.12	3.39	2.82	2.35	1.97	1.40
25	15.92	12.09	9.38	7.39	5.91	4.77	3.88	3.19	2.63	2.19	1.83	1.29
26	15.46	11.68	9.02	7.08	5.62	4.52	3.66	2.99	2.46	2.03	1.69	1.18
27	15.01	11.29	8.67	6.77	5.36	4.28	3.46	2.81	2.30	1.89	1.56	1.08
28	14.57	10.90	8.34	6.48	5.10	4.06	3.26	2.64	2.15	1.76	1.45	0.99
29	14.14	10.54	8.02	6.20	4.86	3.85	3.08	2.48	2.01	1.64	1.34	0.91
30	13.73	10.18	7.71	5.93	4.63	3.65	2.90	2.33	1.88	1.52	1.24	0.84
31	13.33	9.84	7.41	5.68	4.41	3.46	2.74	2.18	1.75	1.42	1.15	0.77
32	12.94	9.50	7.13	5.43	4.20	3.28	2.58	2.05	1.64	1.32	1.06	0.70
33	12.57	9.18	6.85	5.20	4.00	3.11	2.44	1.93	1.53	1.23	0.99	0.65
34	12.20	8.87	6.59	4.98	3.81	2.94	2.30	1.81	1.43	1.14	0.91	0.59
35	11.85	8.57	6.34	4.76	3.63	2.79	2.17	1.70	1.34	1.06	0.85	0.54
36	11.50	8.28	6.09	4.56	3.45	2.65	2.05	1.59	1.25	0.99	0.78	0.50
37	11.17	8.00	5.86	4.36	3.29	2.51	1.93	1.50	1.17	0.92	0.72	0.46
38	10.84	7.73	5.63	4.17	3.13	2.38	1.82	1.41	1.09	0.85	0.67	0.42
39	10.53	7.47	5.42	3.99	2.98	2.25	1.72	1.32	1.02	0.79	0.62	0.39
40	10.22	7.22	5.21	3.82	2.84	2.14	1.62	1.24	0.95	0.74	0.58	0.35
41	9.92	6.97	5.01	3.66	2.71	2.02	1.53	1.16	0.89	0.69	0.53	0.32
42	9.63	6.74	4.81	3.50	2.58	1.92	1.44	1.09	0.83	0.64	0.49	0.30
43	9.35	6.51	4.63	3.35	2.45	1.82	1.36	1.03	0.78	0.59	0.46	0.27
44	9.08	6.29	4.45	3.20	2.34	1.72	1.28	0.96	0.73	0.55	0.42	0.25
45	8.81	6.08	4.28	3.07	2.23	1.63	1.21	0.90	0.68	0.51	0.39	0.23
46	8.56	5.87	4.12	2.93	2.12	1.55	1.14	0.85	0.64	0.48	0.36	0.21
47	8.31	5.67	3.96	2.81	2.02	1.47	1.08	0.80	0.59	0.45	0.34	0.19
48	8.07	5.48	3.80	2.69	1.92	1.39	1.02	0.75	0.56	0.41	0.31	0.18
49	7.83	5.29	3.66	2.57	1.83	1.32	0.96	0.70	0.52	0.39	0.29	0.16
50	7.60	5.12	3.52	2.46	1.74	1.25	0.90	0.66	0.48	0.36	0.27	0.15

Table 16.6.
Y.P. of reversion to a perpetuity after a given number of years

Years	Rate per cent								
	10	10.5	11	11.5	12	12.5	13	14	15
1	9.09	8.62	8.19	7.80	7.44	7.11	6.81	6.27	5.80
2	8.26	7.80	7.38	6.99	6.64	6.32	6.02	5.50	5.04
3	7.51	7.06	6.65	6.27	5.93	5.62	5.33	4.82	4.38
4	6.83	6.39	5.99	5.63	5.30	4.99	4.72	4.23	3.81
5	6.21	5.78	5.40	5.05	4.73	4.44	4.18	3.71	3.31
6	5.64	5.23	4.86	4.53	4.22	3.95	3.69	3.25	2.88
7	5.13	4.73	4.38	4.06	3.77	3.51	3.27	2.85	2.51
8	4.67	4.28	3.94	3.64	3.37	3.12	2.89	2.50	2.18
9	4.24	3.88	3.55	3.26	3.01	2.77	2.56	2.20	1.90
10	3.86	3.51	3.20	2.93	2.68	2.46	2.27	1.93	1.65
11	3.50	3.18	2.88	2.63	2.40	2.19	2.01	1.69	1.43
12	3.19	2.87	2.60	2.36	2.14	1.95	1.77	1.48	1.25
13	2.90	2.60	2.34	1.11	2.91	1.73	1.57	1.30	1.08
14	2.63	2.35	2.11	1.89	1.71	1.54	1.39	1.14	0.94
15	2.39	2.13	1.90	1.70	1.52	1.37	1.23	1.00	0.82
16	2.18	1.93	1.71	1.52	1.36	1.22	1.09	0.88	0.71
17	1.98	1.74	1.54	1.37	1.21	1.08	0.96	0.77	0.62
18	1.80	1.58	1.39	1.23	1.08	0.96	0.85	0.68	0.54
19	1.64	1.43	1.25	1.10	0.97	0.85	0.75	0.59	0.47
20	1.49	1.29	1.13	0.99	0.86	0.76	0.67	0.52	0.41
21	1.35	1.17	1.02	0.88	0.77	0.67	0.59	0.46	0.35
22	1.23	1.06	0.92	0.79	0.69	0.60	0.52	0.40	0.31
23	1.12	0.96	0.82	0.71	0.61	0.53	0.46	0.35	0.27
24	1.02	0.87	0.74	0.64	0.55	0.47	0.41	0.31	0.23
25	0.92	0.78	0.67	0.57	0.49	0.42	0.36	0.27	0.20
26	0.84	0.71	0.60	0.51	0.44	0.37	0.32	0.24	0.18
27	0.76	0.64	0.54	0.46	0.39	0.33	0.28	0.21	0.15
28	0.69	0.58	0.49	0.41	0.35	0.30	0.25	0.18	0.13
29	0.63	0.53	0.44	0.37	0.31	0.26	0.22	0.16	0.12
30	0.57	0.48	0.40	0.33	0.28	0.23	0.20	0.14	0.10
31	0.52	0.43	0.36	0.30	0.25	0.21	0.17	0.12	0.09
32	0.47	0.39	0.32	0.27	0.22	0.18	0.15	0.11	0.08
33	0.43	0.35	0.29	0.24	0.20	0.16	0.14	0.09	0.07
34	0.39	0.32	0.26	0.21	0.18	0.15	0.12	0.08	0.06
35	0.36	0.29	0.24	0.19	0.16	0.13	0.11	0.07	0.05
36	0.32	0.26	0.21	0.17	0.14	0.12	0.09	0.06	0.04
37	0.29	0.24	0.19	0.15	0.13	0.10	0.08	0.06	0.04
38	0.27	0.21	0.17	0.14	0.11	0.09	0.07	0.05	0.03
39	0.24	0.19	0.16	0.12	0.10	0.08	0.07	0.04	0.03
40	0.22	0.18	0.14	0.11	0.09	0.07	0.06	0.04	0.02
41	0.20	0.16	0.13	0.10	0.08	0.06	0.05	0.03	0.02
42	0.18	0.14	0.11	0.09	0.07	0.06	0.05	0.03	0.02
43	0.17	0.13	0.10	0.08	0.06	0.05	0.04	0.03	0.02
44	0.15	0.12	0.09	0.07	0.06	0.04	0.04	0.02	0.01
45	0.14	0.11	0.08	0.06	0.05	0.04	0.03	0.02	0.01
46	0.12	0.10	0.07	0.06	0.05	0.04	0.03	0.02	0.01
47	0.11	0.09	0.07	0.05	0.04	0.03	0.02	0.02	0.01
48	0.10	0.08	0.06	0.05	0.04	0.03	0.02	0.01	0.01
49	0.09	0.07	0.05	0.04	0.03	0.02	0.02	0.01	0.01
50	0.09	0.06	0.05	0.04	0.03	0.02	0.02	0.01	0.01

Valuation Table 16.7
Mortgage instalment table showing monthly sum to redeem Rs. 100/- borrowed

Years	*Rate per cent*											
	4	4.5	5	5.5	6	6.5	7	7.5	8	8.5	9	9.5
1	8.667	8.708	8.750	8.792	8.833	8.875	8.917	8.958	9.000	9.042	9.083	9.125
2	4.418	4.450	4.482	4.513	4.545	4.577	4.609	4.641	4.673	4.705	4.737	4.769
3	3.003	3.031	3.060	3.089	3.118	3.146	3.175	3.204	3.234	3.263	3.292	3.321
4	2.296	2.323	2.350	2.377	2.405	2.433	2.460	2.488	2.516	2.544	2.572	2.601
5	1.872	1.898	1.925	1.951	1.978	2.005	2.032	2.060	2.087	2.115	2.142	2.170
6	1.590	1.616	1.642	1.668	1.695	1.721	1.748	1.775	1.803	1.830	1.858	1.885
7	1.388	1.414	1.440	1.466	1.493	1.519	1.546	1.573	1.601	1.628	1.656	1.684
8	1.238	1.263	1.289	1.316	1.342	1.369	1.396	1.423	1.450	1.478	1.506	1.534
9	1.121	1.146	1.172	1.199	1.225	1.252	1.279	1.306	1.334	1.362	1.390	1.418
10	1.027	1.053	1.079	1.106	1.132	1.159	1.186	1.214	1.242	1.270	1.299	1.327
11	0.951	0.977	1.003	1.030	1.057	1.084	1.111	1.139	1.167	1.196	1.225	1.254
12	0.888	0.914	0.940	0.967	0.994	1.021	1.049	1.077	1.106	1.135	1.164	1.193
13	0.835	0.861	0.887	0.914	0.941	0.969	0.997	1.026	1.054	1.084	1.113	1.143
14	0.789	0.815	0.842	0.869	0.897	0.925	0.953	0.982	1.011	1.040	1.070	1.101
15	0.750	0.776	0.803	0.830	0.858	0.886	0.915	0.944	0.974	1.004	1.034	1.065
16	0.715	0.742	0.769	0.797	0.825	0.853	0.882	0.912	0.941	0.972	1.002	1.034
17	0.685	0.712	0.739	0.767	0.795	0.824	0.854	0.883	0.914	0.944	0.975	1.007
18	0.658	0.685	0.713	0.741	0.770	0.799	0.828	0.859	0.889	0.920	0.952	0.984
19	0.634	0.662	0.690	0.718	0.747	0.776	0.806	0.837	0.868	0.899	0.931	0.963
20	0.613	0.641	0.669	0.697	0.727	0.756	0.787	0.817	0.849	0.881	0.913	0.946
21	0.594	0.622	0.650	0.679	0.708	0.738	0.769	0.800	0.832	0.864	0.897	0.930
22	0.577	0.605	0.633	0.662	0.692	0.722	0.753	0.785	0.817	0.849	0.883	0.916
23	0.561	0.589	0.618	0.647	0.677	0.708	0.739	0.771	0.804	0.836	0.870	0.904
24	0.547	0.575	0.604	0.634	0.664	0.695	0.727	0.759	0.791	0.825	0.859	0.893
25	0.533	0.562	0.591	0.621	0.652	0.683	0.715	0.748	0.781	0.814	0.848	0.883
26	0.521	0.550	0.580	0.610	0.641	0.672	0.705	0.737	0.771	0.805	0.839	0.874
27	0.510	0.539	0.569	0.600	0.631	0.663	0.695	0.728	0.762	0.796	0.831	0.866
28	0.500	0.529	0.559	0.590	0.622	0.654	0.687	0.720	0.754	0.789	0.824	0.859
29	0.491	0.520	0.550	0.581	0.613	0.646	0.679	0.712	0.747	0.782	0.817	0.853
30	0.482	0.512	0.542	0.573	0.605	0.638	0.672	0.706	0.740	0.775	0.811	0.847
31	0.474	0.504	0.534	0.566	0.598	0.631	0.665	0.699	0.734	0.770	0.806	0.842
32	0.466	0.496	0.527	0.559	0.592	0.625	0.659	0.694	0.729	0.765	0.801	0.838
33	0.459	0.490	0.521	0.553	0.586	0.619	0.653	0.688	0.724	0.760	0.796	0.833
34	0.453	0.483	0.515	0.547	0.580	0.614	0.648	0.683	0.719	0.755	0.792	0.830
35	0.446	0.477	0.509	0.541	0.575	0.609	0.644	0.679	0.715	0.752	0.789	0.826
36	0.441	0.472	0.504	0.536	0.570	0.604	0.639	0.675	0.711	0.748	0.785	0.823
37	0.435	0.467	0.499	0.532	0.565	0.600	0.635	0.671	0.708	0.745	0.782	0.820
38	0.430	0.462	0.494	0.527	0.561	0.596	0.632	0.668	0.704	0.742	0.779	0.818
39	0.426	0.457	0.490	0.523	0.557	0.592	0.628	0.665	0.702	0.739	0.777	0.815
40	0.421	0.453	0.486	0.519	0.554	0.589	0.625	0.662	0.699	0.737	0.775	0.813
41	0.417	0.449	0.482	0.516	0.550	0.586	0.622	0.659	0.696	0.734	0.773	0.811
42	0.413	0.445	0.478	0.512	0.547	0.583	0.619	0.656	0.694	0.732	0.771	0.810
43	0.409	0.442	0.475	0.509	0.544	0.580	0.617	0.654	0.692	0.730	0.769	0.808
44	0.406	0.438	0.472	0.506	0.542	0.578	0.615	0.652	0.690	0.728	0.767	0.807
45	0.402	0.435	0.469	0.504	0.539	0.575	0.612	0.650	0.688	0.727	0.766	0.805
46	0.399	0.432	0.466	0.501	0.537	0.573	0.610	0.648	0.687	0.725	0.765	0.804
47	0.396	0.429	0.463	0.499	0.535	0.571	0.609	0.647	0.685	0.724	0.763	0.803
48	0.393	0.427	0.461	0.496	0.532	0.569	0.607	0.645	0.684	0.723	0.762	0.802
49	0.390	0.424	0.459	0.494	0.531	0.568	0.605	0.644	0.682	0.722	0.761	0.801
50	0.388	0.422	0.456	0.492	0.529	0.566	0.604	0.642	0.681	0.721	0.760	0.800

Mortgage instalment table showing monthly sum to redeem Rs. 100/- borrowed

Years	*Rate per cent*						*Years*	*Rate per cent*					
	10	10.5	11	11.5	12	12.5		10	10.5	11	11.5	12	12.5
1	9.167	9.208	9.250	9.292	9.333	9.375	26	0.910	0.946	0.982	1.018	1.055	1.093
2	4.802	4.834	4.866	4.898	4.931	4.963	27	0.902	0.938	0.975	1.012	1.049	1.087
3	3.351	3.380	3.410	3.440	3.470	3.499	28	0.895	0.932	0.969	1.006	1.044	1.082
4	2.629	2.657	2.686	2.715	2.744	2.773	29	0.889	0.926	0.963	1.001	1.039	1.077
5	2.198	2.226	2.255	2.283	2.312	2.340	30	0.884	0.921	0.959	0.996	1.035	1.073
6	1.913	1.942	1.970	1.998	2.027	2.056	31	0.879	0.916	0.954	0.992	1.031	1.069
7	1.712	1.740	1.768	1.797	1.826	1.855	32	0.875	0.912	0.950	0.989	1.027	1.066
8	1.562	1.591	1.619	1.648	1.678	1.707	33	0.871	0.909	0.947	0.985	1.024	1.063
9	1.447	1.476	1.505	1.534	1.564	1.594	34	0.867	0.905	0.944	0.983	1.022	1.061
10	1.356	1.385	1.415	1.445	1.475	1.505	35	0.864	0,902	0.941	0.980	1.019	1.059
11	1.283	1.313	1.343	1.373	1.403	1.434	36	0.861	0.900	0.939	0.978	1.017	1.057
12	1.223	1.253	1.284	1.314	1.345	1.377	37	0.859	0.897	0.936	0.976	1.015	1.055
13	1.173	1.204	1.235	1.266	1.297	1.329	38	0.856	0.895	0.934	0.974	1.014	1.054
14	1.131	1.162	1.194	1.225	1.257	1.290	39	0.854	0.893	0.933	0.972	1.012	1.052
15	1.096	1.127	1.159	1.191	1.224	1.256	40	0.852	0.891	0.931	0.971	1.011	1.051
16	1.065	1.097	1.129	1.162	1.195	1.228	41	0.850	0.890	0.930	0.970	1.010	1.050
17	1.039	1.071	1.104	1.137	1.170	1.204	42	0.849	0.888	0.928	0.968	1.009	1.049
18	1.016	1.049	1.082	1.116	1.149	1.184	43	0.847	0.887	0.927	0.967	1.008	1.048
19	0.996	1.029	1.063	1.097	1.131	1.166	44	0.846	0.886	0.926	0.966	1.007	1.048
20	0.979	1.012	1.046	1.081	1.116	1.151	45	0.845	0.885	0.925	0.966	1.006	1.047
21	0.964	0.998	1.032	1.067	1.102	1.138	46	0.844	0.884	0.924	0.965	1.005	1.046
22	0.950	0.984	1.019	1.054	1.090	1.126	47	0.843	0.883	0.924	0.964	1.005	1.046
23	0.938	0.973	1.008	1.044	1.080	1.116	48	0.842	0.882	0.923	0.964	1.004	1.045
24	0.927	0.963	0.998	1.034	1.071	1.107	49	0.841	0.882	0.922	0.963	1.004	1.045
25	0.918	0.954	0.990	1.026	1.062	1.100	50	0.840	0.881	0.922	0.962	1.003	1.045

Table 16.8. Depreciation percentage at 3.5%

Age in Years	*Life of building in years*									
	30	35	40	45	50	55	60	65	70	75
1	1.940	1.500	1.180	0.950	0.760	0.620	0.510	0.420	0.350	0.290
2	3.948	3.053	2.401	1.933	1.547	1.262	1.038	0.855	0.712	0.590
3	6.026	4.659	3.665	2.951	2.361	1.926	1.584	1.305	1.087	0.901
4	8.177	6.322	4.974	4.004	3.203	2.613	2.150	1.770	1.475	1.222
5	10.403	8.044	6.328	5.094	4.076	3.325	2.735	2.252	1.877	1.555
6	12.707	9.825	7.729	6.223	4.978	4.061	3.341	2.751	2.293	1.900
7	15.092	11.669	9.180	7.390	5.912	4.823	3.967	3.267	2.723	2.256
8	17.560	13.578	10.681	8.599	6.879	5.612	4.616	3.802	3.168	2.625
9	20.115	15.553	12.235	9.850	7.880	6.428	5.288	4.355	3.629	3.007
10	22.759	17.597	13.843	11.145	8.916	7.273	5.983	4.927	4.106	3.402
11	25.495	19.713	15.508	12.485	9.988	8.148	6.702	5.520	4.600	3.811
12	28.328	21.903	17.230	13.872	11.097	9.053	7.447	6.133	5.111	4.235
13	31.259	24.170	19.013	15.307	12.246	9.990	8.218	6.767	5.640	4.673
14	34.293	26.516	20.859	16.793	13.435	10.960	9.015	7.424	6.187	5.126
15	37.434	28.944	22.769	18.331	14.665	11.963	9.841	8.104	6.753	5.596
16	40.684	31.457	24.746	19.922	15.938	13.002	10.695	8.808	7.340	6.082
17	44.048	34.058	26.792	21.570	17.256	14.077	11.580	9.536	7.947	6.584
18	47.529	36.750	28.910	23.275	18.620	15.190	12.495	10.290	8.575	7.105
19	51.133	39.536	31.101	25.039	20.031	16.341	13.442	11.070	9.225	7.644
20	54.862	42.419	33.370	26.866	21.492	17.533	14.423	11.877	9.898	8.201
21	58.723	45.404	35.718	28.756	23.005	18.767	15.437	12.713	10.594	8.778
22	62.718	48.493	38.148	30.712	24 570	20.044	16.488	13.578	11.315	9.375
23	66.853	51.691	40.663	32.737	26.190	21.365	17.575	14.473	12.061	9.994
24	71.133	55.000	43.266	34.833	27.867	22.733	18.700	15.400	12.833	10.633
25	75.563	58.425	45.961	37.002	29.602	24.149	19.864	16.359	13.632	11.295
26	80.147	61.969	48.749	39.247	31.398	25.614	21.070	17.351	14.460	11.981
27	84.892	65.639	51.636	41.571	33.257	27.131	22.317	18.379	15.316	12.690
28	89.804	69.436	54.623	43.976	35.181	28.700	23.608	19.442	16.202	13.424
29	94.887	73.366	57.715	46.465	37.172	30.325	24.944	20.542	17.119	14.184
30	–	77.434	60.915	49.041	39.233	32.006	26.328	21.681	18.068	14.971
31	–	81.644	64.227	51.708	41.366	33.746	27.759	22.860	19.050	15.785
32	–	86.002	67.655	54.468	43.574	35.547	29.241	24.080	20.067	16.627
33	–	90.512	71.203	57.324	45.859	37.411	30.774	25.343	21.119	17.499
34	–	95.180	74.875	60.280	48.224	39.341	32.361	26.650	22.209	18.401
35	–	–	78.675	63.340	50.672	41.338	34.004	28.003	23.336	19.335
36	–	–	82.609	66.507	53.206	43.405	35.704	29.403	24.503	20.302
37	–	–	86.680	69.785	55.828	45.544	37.463	30.852	25.710	21.303
38	–	–	90.894	73.177	58.542	47.758	39.285	32.352	26.960	22.338
39	–	–	95.255	76.688	61.351	50.049	41.170	33.904	28.254	23.410
40	–	–	–	80.323	64.258	52.421	43.121	35.511	29.593	24.520
41	–	–	–	84.084	67.267	54.876	45.140	37.174	30.978	25.668
42	–	–	–	87.977	70.381	57.416	47.230	38.895	32.413	26.856
43	–	–	–	92.006	73.605	60.046	49.393	40.676	33.897	28.086
44	–	–	–	96.176	76.941	62.768	51.631	42.520	35.433	29.359
45	–	–	–	–	80.394	65.584	53.949	44.428	37.023	30.677
46	–	–	–	–	83.968	68.500	56.347	46.403	38.669	32.040
47	–	–	–	–	87.667	71.517	58.829	48.447	40.373	33.452
48	–	–	–	–	91.495	74.641	61.398	50.563	42.136	34.913
49	–	–	–	–	95.457	77.873	64.057	52.753	43.961	36.424
50	–	–	–	–	–	81.219	66.809	55.019	45.849	37.989

Table II : Requirement of materials for different items of work

Requirement of different materials of construction items of work shall be computed on the basis of the quantities shown in the chart subject to a variation of plus/minus five per cent.

Sl. No.	*Description of items* (1)	(2)	Unit (3)	Name of materials required (4)	*Quantity of materials required* (5)
1.	10 mm. cement plaster	2:1	% sq.m.	1. Cement	0.54 cu.m.
				2. Sand	1.08 cu.m.
2.	- do -	3:1	"	1. Cement	0.40 cu.m.
				2. Sand	1.20 cu.m.
3.	- do -	4:1	"	1. Cement	0.30 cu.m.
				2. Sand	1.00 cu.m.
4.	- do -	6:1	"	1. Cement	0.20 cum
				2. Sand	1.20 cum
5.	15 mm cement plaster	2:1	"	1. Cement	0.80 cum
				2. Sand	1.20 cum
6.	- do -	3:1	"	1. Cement	0.60 cum
				2. Sand	1.80 cum
7.	- do -	4:1	"	1. Cement	0.46 cum
				2. Sand	1.84 cum
8.	- do -	6:1	"	1. Cement	0.30 cum
				2. Sand	1.80 cum
9.	20 mm cement plaster	3:1	"	1. Cement	0.80 cum
				2. Sand	2.40 cum
10.	- do -	4:1	"	1. Cement	0.60 cum
				2. Sand	2.40 cum
11.	- do -	6:1	"	1. Cement	0.40 cum
				2. Sand	2.40 cum
12.	25 mm. cement plaster	3:1	"	1. Cement	0.884 cum
				2. Sand	2.65 cum
13.	- do -	4:1	"	1. Cement	0.71 cum
				2. Sand	2.84 cum
14.	- do -	6:1	"	1. Cement	0.472 cum
				2. Sand	2.84 cum
15.	Cement flush pointing	3:1	"	1. Cement	0.122 cu.m.
				2. Sand	1.366 cu.m.
16.	Cement flush pointing	4:1	"	1. Cement	0.092 cu.m.
				2. Sand	0.366 cu.m.
17.	Ruled pointing	3:1	"	1. Cement	0.122 cu.m.
				2. Sand	0.365 cu.m.
18.	Brick work in cement	2:1	cu.m.	1. Brick	389 Nos.
				2. Cement	0.15 cu.m.
				3. Sand	0.30 cu.m.
19.	- do -	3:1	"	1. Brick	389 Nos.
				2. Cement	0.107 cu.m.
				3. Sand	0.33 cu.m.
20.	- do -	4:1	"	1. Brick	389 Nos.
				2. Cement	0.083 cu.m.
				3. Sand	0.33 cu.m.

(*Contd...*)

(1)		(2)	(3)	(4)	(5)
21.	- do -	5:1	"	1. Brick	389 Nos.
				2. Cement	0.06 cu.m.
				3. Sand	0.33 cu.m.
22.	- do -	6:1	"	1. Brick	389 Nos.
				2. Cement	0.05 cu.m.
				3. Sand	0.33 cu.m.
23.	Brick work in cement mortar with modular bricks	1:4	Cu.m.	1. Bricks	500 Nos.
				2. Cement	0.0805 cu.m.
				3. Sand	0.322 cu.m.
24.	- do -	(6:1)	"	1. Bricks	500 Nos.
				2. Cement	0.0537 cu.m.
				3. Sand	0.322 cu.m.
25.	125 mm. thick brick wall	3:1	% sq.m.	1. Brick	4951 Nos.
				2. Cement	1.22 cu.m.
				3. Sand	3.66 cu.m.
26.	- do -	4:1	"	1. Brick	4951 Nos.
				2. Cement	0.914 cu.m.
				3. Sand	3.66 cu.m.
27.	100 mm thick brick wall with modular bricks	1:4	"	1. Brick	5065 Nos.
				2. Cement	0.73 cu.m.
				3. Sand	2.90 cu.m.
28.	7.5 mm thick brick wall	3:1	"	1. Brick	3014 Nos.
				2. Cement	0.762 cu.m.
				3. Sand	2.286 cu.m.
28 (A).	- do -	4:1	"	1. Brick	3014 Nos.
				2. Cement	0.57 cu.m.
				3. Sand	2.28 cu.m.
29.	Cement concrete with jhama chips	4:2:1	cu.m.	1. Jhama chips (6.0 to 19 mm.)	0.9 cu.m.
				2. Sand	0.45 cu.m.
				3. Cement	0.225 cu.m.
30.	- do -	5:2 1/2:1	"	1. Jhama chips (-do-)	0.93 cu.m.
				2. Sand	0.465 cu.m.
				3. Cement	0.186 cu.m.
31.	- do -	6:3:1	"	1. Jhama chips (-do-)	0.96 cu.m.
				2. Sand	0.48 cu.m.
				3. Cement	0.16 cu.m.
32.	- do -	8:4:1	"	1. Jhama chips	0.98 cu.m.
				2. Sand	0.49 cu.m.
				3. Cement	0.122 cu.m.
33.	Cement concrete with stone chips	4:2:1	"	1. Stone chips (6.0 to 19 mm.)	0.88 cu.m.
				2. Sand	0.44 cu.m.

(Contd...)

(1)		(2)	(3)	(4)	(5)
				3. Cement	0.22 cu.m.
34.	- do -	3:1 1/2:1	"	1. Stone chips (-do-)	0.86 cu.m.
				2. Sand	0.43 cu.m.
				3. Cement	0.286 cu.m.
35.	- do -	5:2 1/2:1	"	1. Stone chips (-do-)	0.92 cu.m.
				2. Sand	0.46 cu.m.
				3. Cement	0.18 cu.m.
36.	Cement concrete with stone chips.	6:3:1	cu.m.	1. Stone chips (6.0 to 19 mm.)	0.924 cu.m.
				2. Sand	0.462 cu.m.
				3. Cement	0.155 cu.m.
37.	- do -	8:4:1	"	1. Stone chips	0.96 cu.m.
				2. Sand	0.48 cu.m.
				3. Cement	0.12 cu.m.
38.	25 mm. artificial stone floor with jhama chips (which includes 3 mm. thick neat cement finish)	4:2:1	%sq.m.	1. Jhama chips (5 to 12 mm.)	2.268 cu.m.
				2. Sand	1.14 cu.m.
				3. Cement	0.872 cu.m.
39.	20 mm. -do-	4:2:1	"	1. Jhama chips (-do-)	1.716 cu.m.
				2. Sand	0.858 cu.m.
				3. Cement	0.732 cu.m.
40.	25 mm. - do - with stone chips	4:2:1	"	1. Stone chip (-do-)	2.23 cu.m.
				2. Sand	1.12 cu.m.
				3. Cement	0.857 cu.m.
41.	20 mm. - do -	4:2:1	"	1. Stone chips (-do-)	1.676 cu.m.
				2. Sand	0.838 cu.m.
				3. Cement	0.702 cu.m.
42.	37 mm. - do -	4:2:1	"	1. Stone chips (-do-)	3.35 cu.m.
				2. Sand	1.675 cu.m.
				3. Cement	1.142 cu.m.
43.	37 mm. - do - with jhama chips - do -	4:2:1	"	1. Jhama chips (-do-)	3.43 cu.m.
				2. Sand	1.72 cu.m.
				3. Cement	1.172 cu.m.
44.	7.5 cm. lime terracing in roof with brick khoa, surki, lime (7:2:2) including finishing.		sq.m.	1. Jhama khoa	0.075 cu.m
				2. Surki	0.021 cu.m.
				3. Lime	0.021 cu.m.
45.	10 cm. lime terracing in roof with brick khoa, surki lime (7:2:2) including finishing.		sq.m.	1. Jhama khoa	0.10 cu.m.
				2. Surki	0.028 cu.m.
				3. Lime	0.028 cu.m.

(*Contd...*)

(1)		(2)	(3)	(4)	(5)
46.	12.5 cm. (-do-)	(-do-)	"	1. Jhama khoa 2. Surki 3. Lime	0.125 cu.m. 0.036 cu.m. 0.036 cu.m.
47.	15 cm. -do-	-do-		1. Jhama khoa 2. Surki 3. Lime	0.15 cu.m. 0.043 cu.m. 0.043 cu.m.
48.	50 mm thick R.C. slab with stone chips (4:2:1) and with 0.8% reinforcement.		% sq.m.	1. Stone chips (6.0 to 19 mm.) 2. Sand 3. Cement 4. Steel 5. Shuttering	4.47 cu.m. 2.23 cu.m. 1.12 cu.m. 322.60 kg. 100 sq.m
49.	75 mm thick R.C. slab with stone chips (4:2:1) and with 0.8% reinforcement.		% sq.m.	1. Stone chips (-do-) 2. Sand 3. Cement 4. Steel 5. Shuttering	6.7 cu.m. 3.35 cu.m. 1.675 cu.m. 482.62 kg. 100 sq.m
50.	100 mm R.C. slab with stone chips (4:2:1) and with 0.8% reinforcement.		% sq.m.	1. Stone chips (-do-) 2. Sand 3. Cement 4. Steel 5. Shuttering	8.93 cu.m. 4.47 cu.m. 2.23 cu.m. 683.54 kg. 100 sq.m
51.	125 mm R.C. slab with stone chips (4:2:1) and with 0.8% reinforcement.		% sq.m.	1. Stone chips (6.0 to 19 mm.) 2. Sand 3. Cement 4. Steel 5. Shuttering	11.18 cu.m. 5.59 cu.m. 2.80 cu.m. 787.44 kg. 100 sq.m
52.	150 mm -d0-	-do- (4:2:1)	% sq.m.	1. Stone chips (-do-) 2. Sand 3. Cement 4. Steel 5. Shuttering	13.4 cu.m. 6.7 cu.m. 3.35 cu.m. 955.08 kg. 100 sq.m
53.	Single brick flat soling (conventional size)		sq.m.	Brick	32 Nos.
54.	Brick on edge soling (conventional size)		sq.m.	Brick	54 Nos.
55.	7.5 mm wide brick-on-edge edging.		%m.	Brick	820 Nos.
56.	7.5 mm. brick-on-edge edging.		sq.m.	Brick	410 Nos.
57.	25 mm thick (finished) terrazo work, cast in situ floor 9 mm thick terrazo topping, laying and finished to 6 mm thick after final grinding in ordinary grey colour.		% sqm	1. Grey cement	0.83 cum

(*Cont*i

(1)	(2)	(3)	(4)	(5)
			2. Coarse sand	0.85 cum
			3. Stone chips	1.72 cum
			4. Marble chips	1420 kg
			5. Marble powder	0.126 cum
58.	-do- in black or red colour	% sqm	1. Grey cement	0.83 cum
			2. Coarse sand	0.86 cum
			3. Stone chips	1.72 cum
			4. Marble chips	1420 kg
			5. Marble powder	0.126 cum
			6. Pigment	40 kg
59.	-do- In silver grey	% sqm	1. Grey cement	0.63 cum
			2. Coarse sand	0.86 cum
			3. Stone chips	1.72 cum
			4. White cement	0.20 cum
			5. Marble chips	1420 kg
			6. Marble powder	0.126 cum
60.	-do- in pink, green, yellow, light green colour	% sqm	1. Grey cement	0.43 cum
			2. Coarse sand	0.86 cum
			3. Stone chips	1.72 cum
			4. White cement	0.40 cum
			5. Marble chips	1420 kg
			6. Marble powder	0.126 cum
			7. Pigment	0.40 kg
61.	25 mm thick (finished) terrsazo work, cast in situ in floor. 12 mm thick terrazo topping, laying and finished to 9 mm thick after final grinding. In ordinary grey colour.	% sqm	1. Grey cement	0.926 cum
			2. Coarse sand	0.72 cum
			3. Stone chips	1.44 cum
			4. Marble chips	1734 kg
			5. Marble powder	0.170 cum
62.	-do- In black and red colour	% sqm	1. Grey cement	0.926 cum
			2. Coarse sand	0.72 cum
			3. Stone chips	1.44 cum
			4. Marble chips	1734 kg
			5. Marble powder	0.170 cum
			6. Pigment	57 kg
63.	-do- In silver grey	% sqm	1. Grey cement	0.634 cum
			2. Coarse sand	0.72 cum
			3. Stone chips	1.44 cum
			4. White cement	0.283 cum
			5. Marble chips	1734 kg
			6. Marble powder	0.170 cum
64.	-do- In cream, green, yellow, light green colour	% sqm	1. Grey cement	0.36 cum

(Contd...)

(1)		(2)	(3)	(4)	(5)
				2. Coarse sand	0.72 cum
				3. Stone chips	1.44 cum
				4. White cement	0.566 cum
				5. Marble chips	1734 kg
				6. Marble powder	0.170 cum
				7. Pigment	57 kg
65.	20 mm thick (finished) terrazo work in floor with precast tiles set in lime/cement mortar (3:1) and sides with admixture of pigment as and when necessary and white cement/grey. In ordinary grey colour				
	(*a*) When sand and cement mortar is used in bed	% sqm		1. Grey cement	1.507 cum
				2. Coarse sand	2.67 cum
	(*b*) When lime mortar is used in bed	% sqm		1. Unslaked lime	5.65 quintal
				2. Surkhi	2.67 cum
				3. Grey cement	0.616 cum
66.	-do- In black and red colour	% sqm			
	(*a*) When sand and cement mortar is used in bed			1. Grey cement	1.506 cum
				2. Coarse sand	2.67 cum
				3. Pigment	31 kg
	(*b*) When lime mortar is used in bed	% sqm		1. Unslaked lime	5.65 cum
				2. Surkhi	2.67 cum
				3. Grey cement	0.616 cum
				4. Pigment	31 kg
67.	-do- In Silver grey				
	(*a*) When sand cement mortar is used in bed			1. Grey cement	1.352 cum
				2. White cement	0.154 cum
				3. Coarse sand	2.67 cum
	(*b*) When lime mortar is used in bed			1. Unslaked lime	3.65 quintal
				2. Surkhi	2.67 cum
				3. Grey cement	0.462 cum
				4. White cement	0.154 cum
68.	-do- In pink, cream, yellow light green colour				
	(a) When sand cement mortar is used in bed	% sqm		1. Grey cement	1.198 cum
				2. White cement	0.308 cum
				3. Coarse sand	2.67 cum
				4. Pigment	31 kg
	(b) When lime mortar is used in bed	% sqm		1. Unslaked lime	3.65 quintal
				2. Surkhi	2.67 cum
				3. Grey cement	0.308 cum
				4. White cement	0.308 cum
				5. Pigment	31 kg

N.B. Ordinary (grey) cement required for slurry @1.75 kg/sqm is not included in the above consumption chart from serial 57.

Apppendix III

CONVERSION TABLE

(A) Linear:

1 inch = 25.400 milimetres
1 millimetre = 0.0394 inches
1 metre = 3.281 ft.= 1.094 yards
1 foot = 0.3050 metre
1 mile = 1.6090 kilometres
1 centimetre = 0.3940 inch
1 metre = 39.3701 inches
1 kilometre = 1093.61 yards = 0.621 mile

(B) Area:

1 sq. inch = 6.451 sq.cm.
1 sq. cm. = 0.155 sq. inch
1 sq. metre = 10.764 sq. ft.
1 sq.ft. = 0.0929 sq. metre
1 acre = 0.405 hectare
1 sq. mile = 2.590 sq. kilometre

(C) Capacity and Volume:

1 imp. gallon = 4.546 litres
1 litre = 0.22 gallons
1 cu. inch = 16.387 $cm.^2$
$1cm.^3$ = 0.61 cu. inch
1 cu.ft.= 0.0283 $m.^3$
1 m^3 = 35.315 cu. ft.

(D) Weight:

1 ton = 1.016 tonnes
1 tonne = 0.9840 tons
1 ton = 2240 lbs. = 1016 kgs.
1 tonne = 1000 kg. = 2204.622 lbs.
1 lb. 0.454 kilograms
1 hundred weight = 50.8 kilogram = 0.508 quintal
1 kilogram = 2.2050 lbs.
1 quintal = 1.968 cwt.

(E) Linear Density:

1 lb./ft. = 1.488 kg.m.
1 kg./ m. = 0.672 lb./ft.

(F) Density:

$1lb./ft.^3$ = 16.019 $kg./m^3$
$1kg./m^3$ = 0.624 $lb./ft.^3$
$1lbs./in^3$ = 27.680 $gm./cm^3$
1 $gm./cm^3$ = 0.0361 $lb./inch^3$

(G) Temperature:

(Relation between Fahrenheit Centrigrade Scale)

$$°F = (°F - 32) \times \frac{5°}{9}\ C$$

$$°C = \left(°C \times \frac{9}{5} + 32\right)°F$$

Appendix IV

Areas, Weights and Perimeters of M.S. and Tor Steel round bars

Diameter in mm	*Sectional area in sq.mm*	*Weights per metre in kg*	*Perimeter in mm*
5	20.0	0.16	15.7
6	28.3	0.22	18.8
8	50.3	0.39	25.1
10	78.6	0.62	31.4
12	113.0	0.89	37.7
16	201.0	1.58	50.3
20	314.0	2.47	62.8
22	380.0	2.98	69.1
25	491.0	3.85	78.5
28	616.0	4.83	88.0
32	804.0	6.31	100.5
36	1018.0	7.99	113.1
40	1257.0	9.86	125.7
45	1590.0	12.40	157.1

(*i*) Standard weight per metre in kg = $0.00618 \times d^2$;
where d = diameter of the bar in mm.

(*ii*) Weight of M.S. plate per sq. metre = $7.85 \times t$;
where t = thickness of the plate in mm.

(*iii*) Weight of 1 cum of M.S. or Tor Steel = 7,850 kg

(*iv*) Weight of 1 bag of cement = 50 kg

(*v*) Volume of 1 bag of cement = 0.347 cum

(*vi*) 1 cum of cement = 28.82 bags

Appendix - V

PROPERTIES OF SECTIONS

Section	*Area*	*Moment of inertia*	*Section Modulus*	*Radius of Gyration*
Triangle 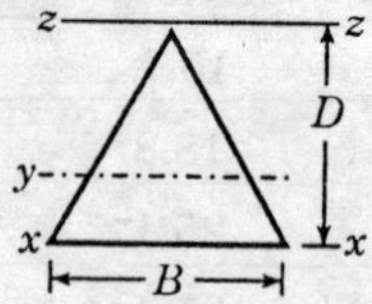	BD/2	X-X, $\frac{BD^3}{36}$ Y-Y, $\frac{BD^3}{12}$ Z-Z, $\frac{BD^3}{4}$	X-X Base $\frac{BD^2}{12}$ Apex $\frac{BD^2}{24}$	About X-X 0.236D
Trapezium 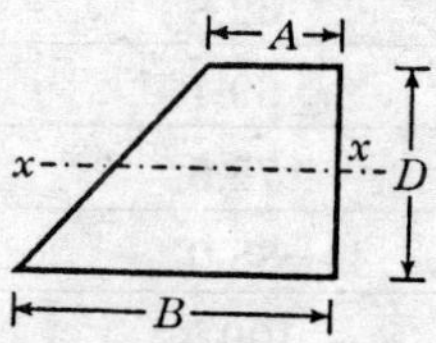	$(A+B)\,\frac{D}{2}$	X-X, 2 $\frac{(B+4\,BA+A^2)}{36\,(A+B)}D^2$	X-X, $\frac{(B^2+4BA+A^2)}{36\,(A+B)\,(D-Y)}D^2$	About X-X $\sqrt{\frac{2\,(B^2+4BA+A^2}{36\,(A+B)^2}}$
Rectangle 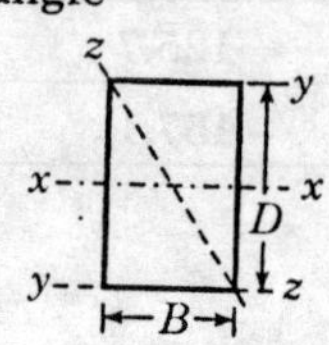	*BD*	X-X, $\frac{BD^3}{12}$ Y-Y,= $\frac{BD^3}{6}$ Z-Z, $\frac{B^3\,D^3}{6\,(B^3+D^3)}$	X-X, $\frac{BD^2}{6}$ Top or Base Z-Z, $\frac{B^2\,D^2}{6\sqrt{B^2+D^2}}$	About X-X, 0.289
Hollow rectangle 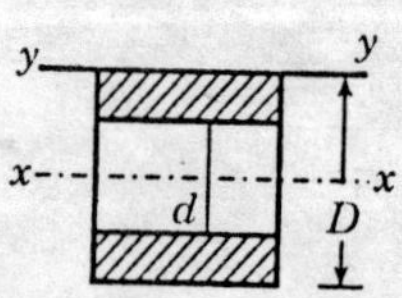	*B(D–d)*	X-X, $\frac{B\,(D^3-d^3)}{12}$ Y-Y, $Ixx+\frac{BD^2\,(D-d)}{4}$	X-X, Top or Base $\frac{B\,(D^2-d^2)}{6D}$	About X-X, $\sqrt{\frac{D^2+dD+d^2}{12}}$
Flanged beam 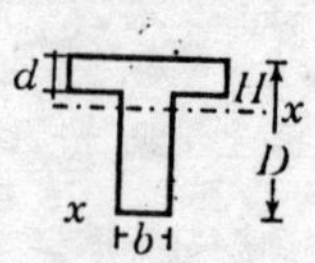	$Bd+b$ $(D-d)$	X-X, $=\frac{1}{3}\,[BN^3+b\,(D-N)^3$ $-(N-D)^3\,(B-b)]$	X-X, $\frac{I\,x\,x}{D-N}$	About X-X $\frac{\sqrt{I_x-x}}{A}$
Square 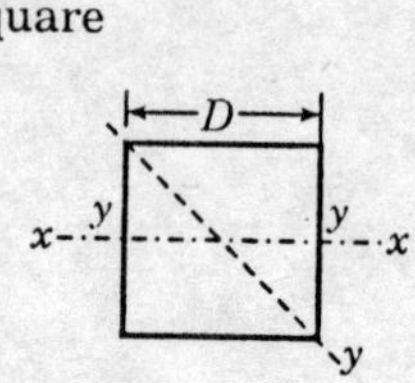	D^2	X-X $\frac{D^4}{12}$ Y-Y $\frac{D^4}{12}$	X-X $\frac{D^2}{6}$ Y-Y 0.118D^2	About X-X or Y-Y 0.2689D.

Section	*Area*	*Moment of inertia*	*Section Modulus*	*Radius of Gyration*
Regular hexagon on face 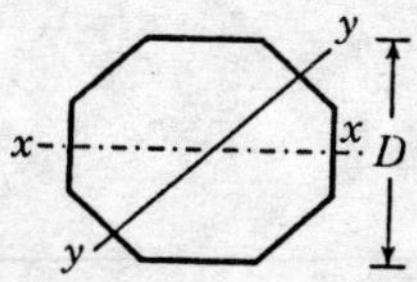	$0.866D^2$	X-X, $0.06\ D^4$ Y-Y, $0.06\ D^4$	X-X, $0.12\ D^2$ Y–Y, $0.104\ D^2$	About X-X or Y-Y 0.263 D
Regular hexagon on edge 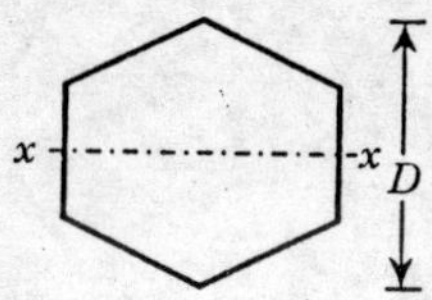	$0.65\ D^2$	X-X, $0.0338\ D^4$	X-X, $0.0676\ D^3$	About X-X, 0.228D
Regular octagon 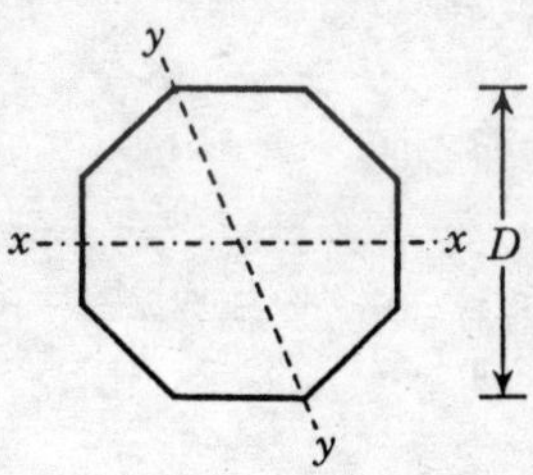	$0.828\ D^2$	X-X, $0.055\ D^4$ Y-Y, $0.055\ D^4$	X-X, $0.109\ D^3$ Y-Y, $0.1016\ D^3$	About X-X or Y-Y 0.257 D
Circle 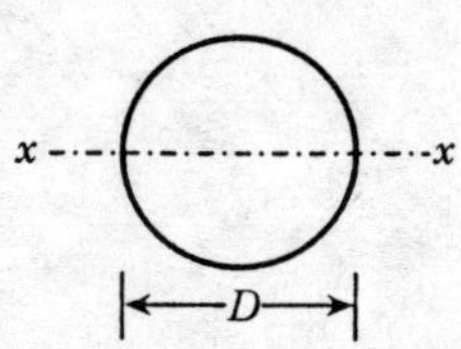	$0.7854\ D^2$	X-X, $\frac{\pi}{64} D^2$	X-X, $\frac{\pi}{32} D^2$	About X-X, $\frac{D}{4}$
Hollow circle 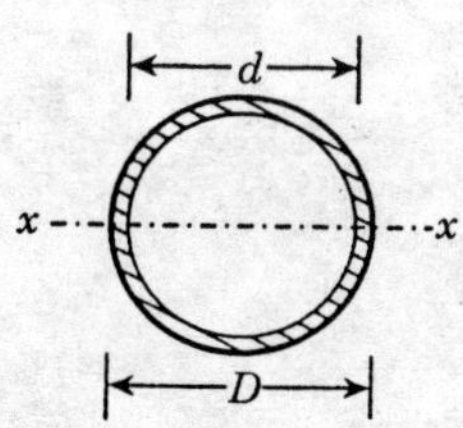	0.7754 $(D^2 - d^2)$	X-X, $\frac{\pi}{64}(D^4 - d^4)$	X-X, $\frac{\pi}{32}\frac{(D^4 - d^4)}{D}$	$\frac{1}{4}\sqrt{D^2 + d^2}$

Section	*Area*	*Moment of inertia*	*Section Modulus*	*Radius of Gyration*
Quarter circle (inner) 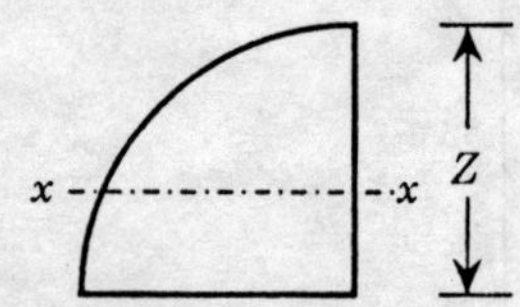	$0.7854\ R^2$	$X\text{-}X$, $0.0518\ R^4$	$X\text{-}X$, $0.129\ R^3$	$0.264\ R$
Quarter circle (outer) 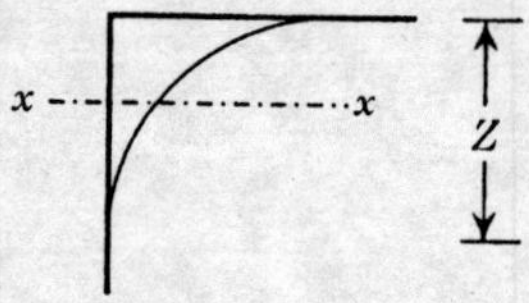	$0.2146\ R^2$	$X\text{-}X$ $0.0075\ R^4$	$X\text{-}X$, $0.0095\ R^3$	$0.187\ R$

Appendix VI
Mensuration Formulae

Sl. No.	*Item with figure*	*Formulae*
1.	Retangle 	Perimeter $= 2\ (AB + BC)$ Area $=$ Length $\times$ Breadth $= AB \times BC$
2.	Square 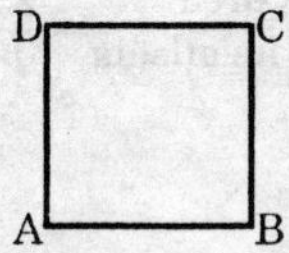	Perimeter $= 4 \times AB$ Area $= A\,B^2$ sq. units Side of the square $= \sqrt{\text{Area}} = \sqrt{A\,B^2}$
3.	Right-angled Triangle 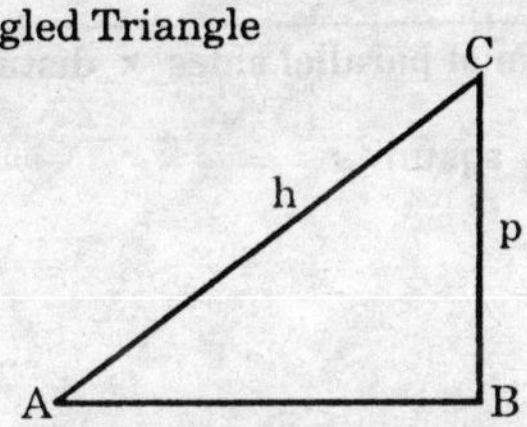	Hypotenuse $= \sqrt{\text{base}^2 + \text{perpendicular}^2}$ $h = \sqrt{b^2 + p^2}$
4.	Isoscelels rightangled triangle 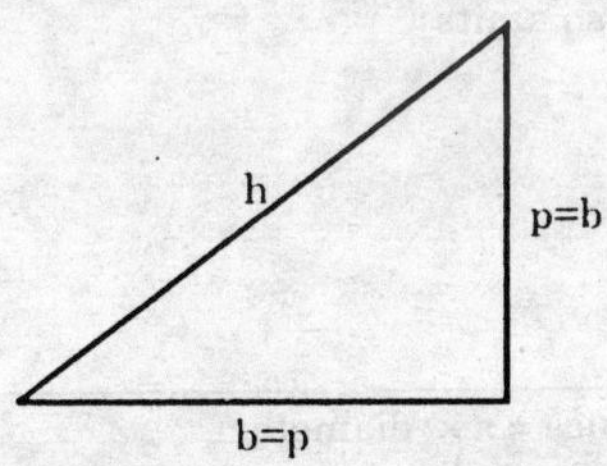	Hypoteneuse $= h = \sqrt{2} \times (\text{base}^2)$ $= b\,\sqrt{2} = p\sqrt{2}$
5.	Equilateral triangle 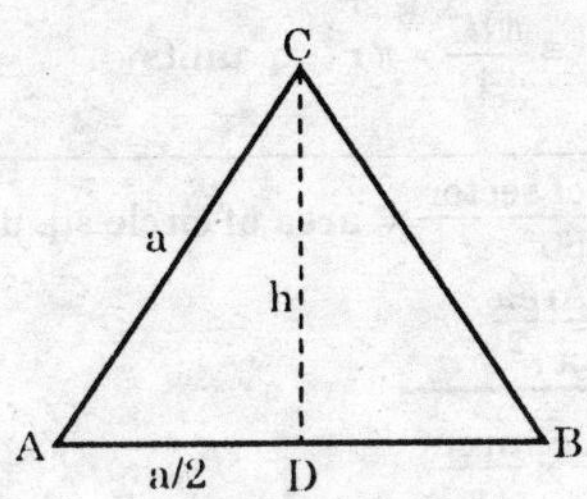	Height = Side $\times \dfrac{\sqrt{3}}{2}$
6.	Triangle 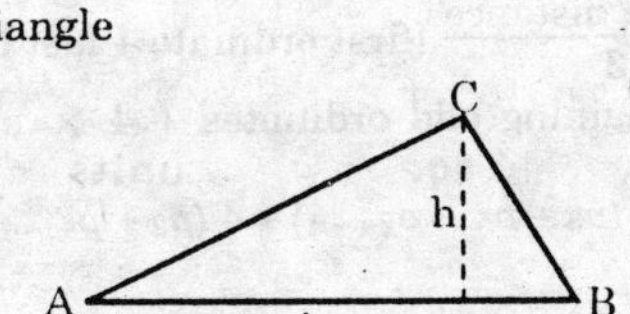	Area = 1/2 base $\times$ height = 1/2 $b\ h$ sq. units Height $= \dfrac{2 \times \text{area}}{\text{base}}$ Base $= \dfrac{2 \times \text{area}}{\text{height}}$

Sl. No.	*Item with figure*	*Formulae*
7.	Parallelogram 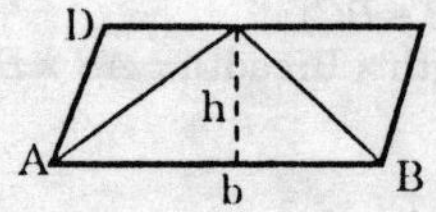	Area = base × height = $b \times h$ sq. units Base $b = \frac{\text{area}}{\text{height}}$ Height, $h = \frac{\text{area}}{\text{base}}$
8.	Quadrilateral 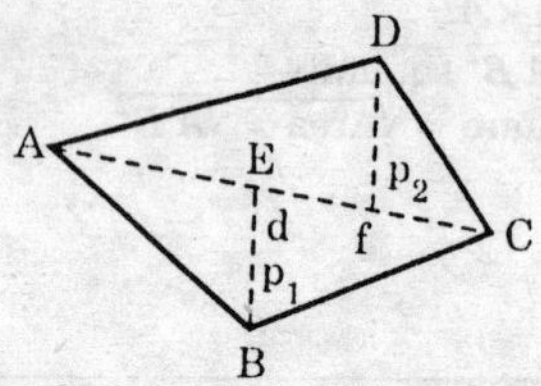	Area = 1/2 diagonal × (sum of its offsets) = $1/2 \times d\ (p_1 + p_2)$ sq. units Diagonal = $\frac{2 \times \text{area}}{\text{sum of its offsets}} = \frac{2 \times \text{area}}{p_1 + p_2}$
9.	Trapezoid 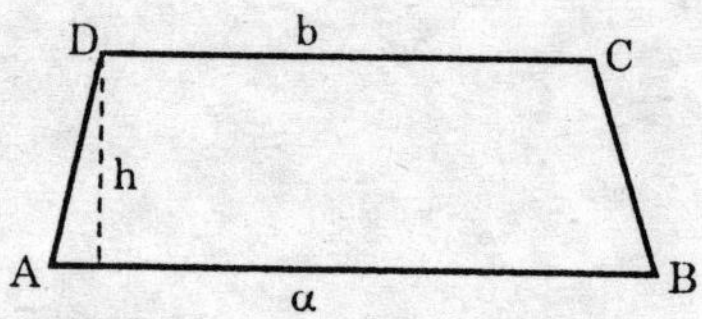	Area = 1/2 sum of parallel sides × distance between them = $1/2\ (a + b)\ h$ sq. units
10.	Polygon 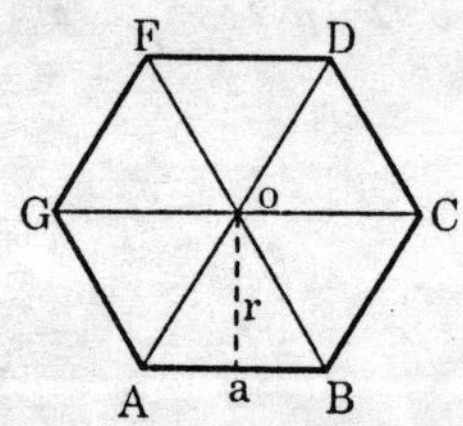	Area = $\frac{\text{Number of sides}}{2}$ × side × radius of inscribed circle. = $n/2 \times a\ r$ sq. units
11.	Circle 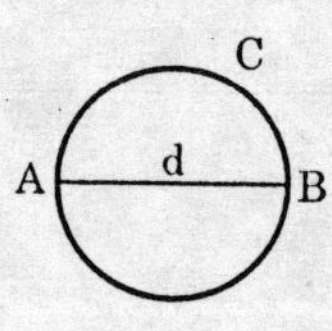	Circumference = $\pi \times$ diameter = πd. Diameter, $d = \frac{\text{circumference}}{\pi}$ Area $= \frac{\pi d^2}{4} = \pi r^2$ sq. units
12.	Sector 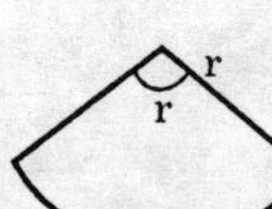	Area = $\frac{\text{angle of sector}}{360°}$ × area of circle sq. units $= 360 \times \frac{\text{Area}}{\pi r^2}$ $r = \sqrt{\frac{360}{\alpha} \times \frac{\text{area}}{\pi}}$
13.	Simpson's Rule 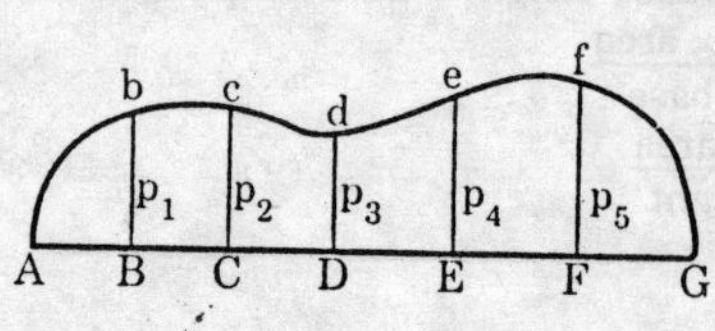	Area = $\frac{\text{common distance}}{3}$ {first ordinate + last ordinate + 2 × sum of remaining odd ordinates + 4 × sum of even ordinates} sq. units $d/3$ $\{P_1 + P_{2n+1} + 2\ (p_3 + p_5 \ldots p_{2n-1}) + 4\ (p_2 + p_4 \ldots p_{2n})$ sq. units

Sl. No.	*Item with figure*	*Formulae*
14.	Elipse 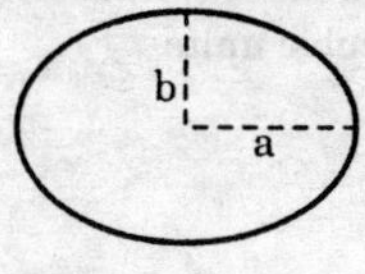	Area = semi-major axis × semi-minor axis sq. units = $\pi.a.b$ sq. units
15.	Rectangular solid 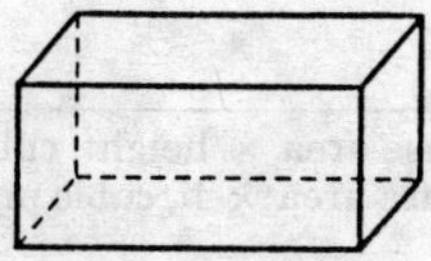	Volume = length × breadth × depth or = length × area of end or = breadth × area of side or = depth × area of base = $a \times b \times c$ cubic units
16.	Cube 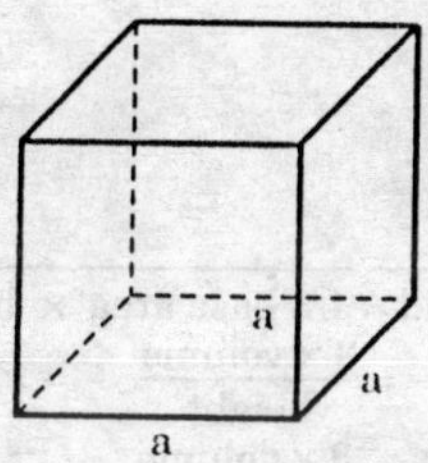	Volume = a^3 cubic units side = √volume
17.	Parallelopiped 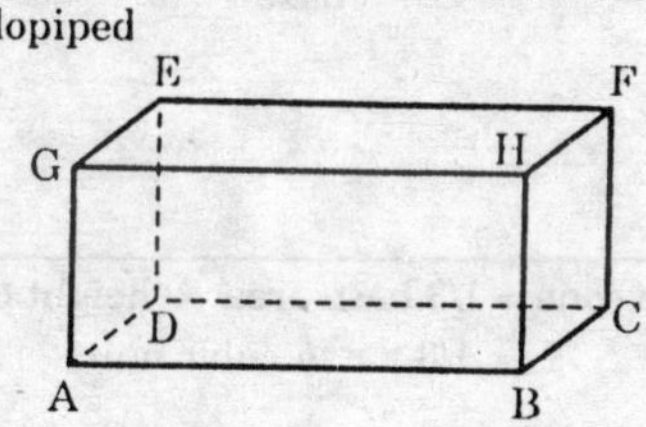	Volume = area of base × height cubic units
18.	Triangular prism 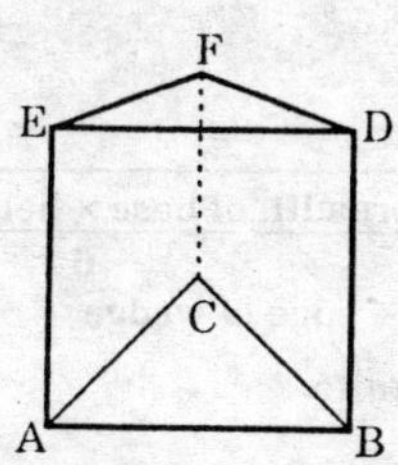	Volume = area of base × height cubic units =Area of the tringle ABC × height DB, cubic units Base of any prism = Volume/height Height of any prism = Volume/base
19.	Prism 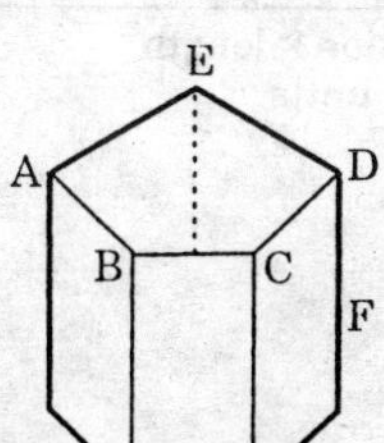	Volume = cross section × length, cubic units Cross section of prism = Volume/length Length of prism = Volume/cross section

Sl. No.	*Item with figure*	*Formulae*
20.	Cylinder 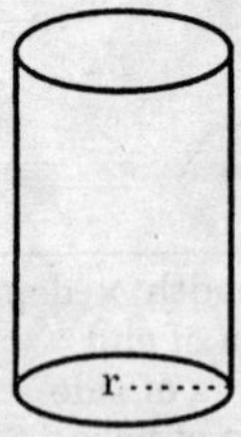	Volume = base area × height, cubic units $= \pi r^2 \times h$, cubic units
21.	Tetrahedron Triangular pyramid 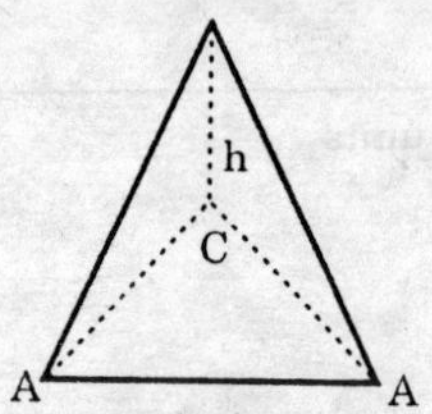	Volume = 1/3 base area × height, cubic units = 1/3 base area × h, cubic units
22.	Pyramid 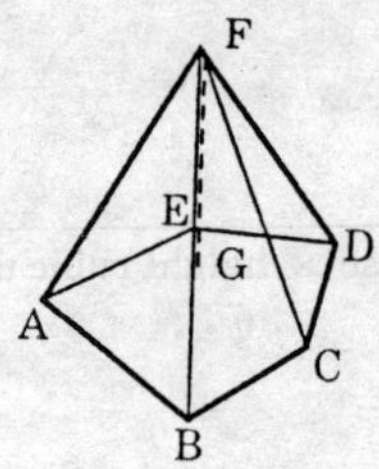	Volume of pyramid = 1/3 base area × height cubic units Base of pyramid $= \dfrac{3 \times \text{volume}}{\text{height}}$ Height of pyramid $= \dfrac{3 \times \text{volume}}{\text{base}}$
23.	Cone 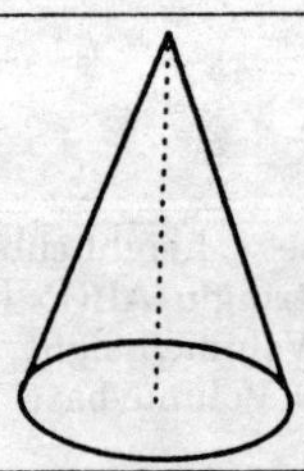	Volume of cone = 1/3 base area × height cubic units $= 1/3\ \pi\ r^2\ h$ cubic units
24.	Wedge 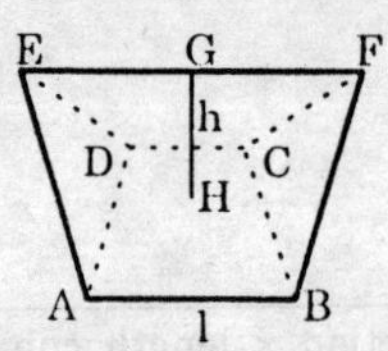	Volume of wedge $= \dfrac{\text{breadth of base} \times \text{height of wedge}}{6}$ × 2 × length of base + edge of wedge $= \dfrac{\partial h}{6}(2\,l + e)$ cubic units
25.	Oblique Frustum of Right Regular Prism 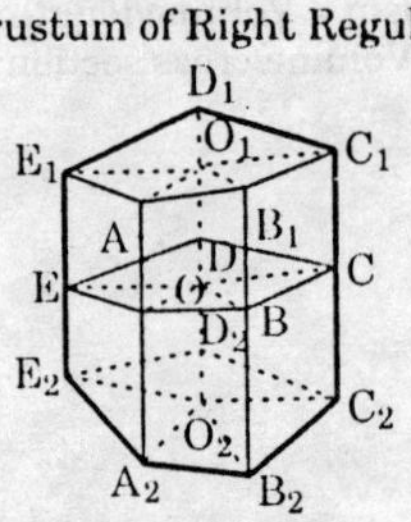	Volume = Cross section × length $= A_1\, l$ cubic units

Sl. No.	*Item with figure*	*Formulae*
26.	Frustum of pyramid 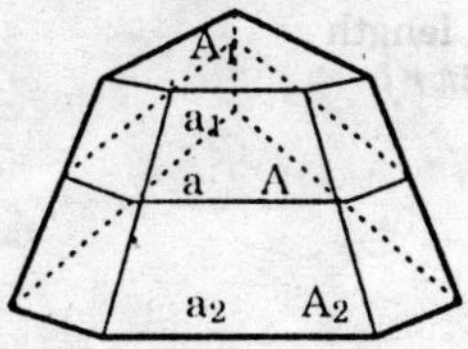	Volume $= \frac{h}{3}(A_1 + A_2 + 4A)$ cubic units $= \frac{h}{3}(A_1 + A_2 + \sqrt{A_1 A_2})$ cubic units
27.	Frustum of cone 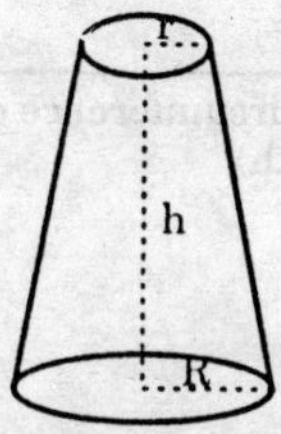	Volume $= \frac{h}{3}(\pi R^3 + \pi r^2 + \sqrt{\pi R^2 r^2})$ $= \frac{\pi h}{3}(R^2 + r^2 + Rr)$ cubic units
28.	Zone of sphere 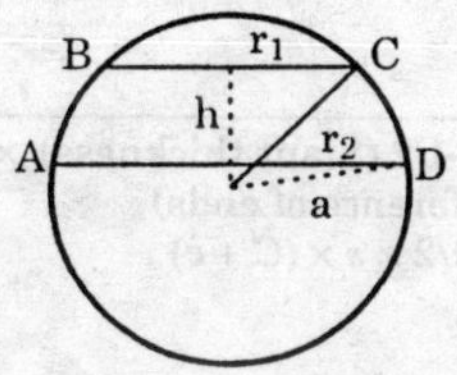	Volume $= \frac{\pi}{6} \times$ height $\times$ (3 $\times$ sum of squares of radii of ends + height^2) $= \frac{\pi h}{6}\{3(r_1^2 + r_2^2 + h^2)\}$ cubic units
29.	Sphere 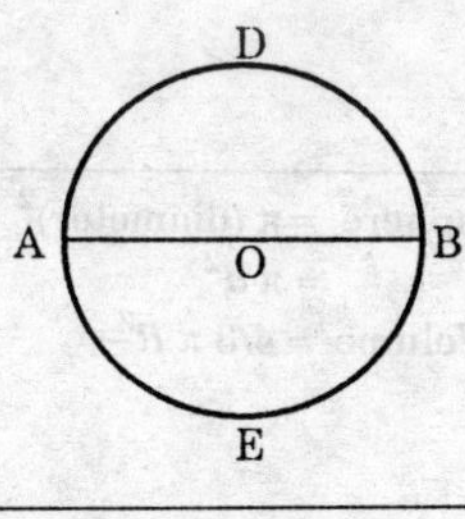	Volume $= \frac{\pi}{6} \times (\text{diameter})^3$ $= \frac{\pi d^3}{6}$ Diameter $= \sqrt[3]{\frac{6 \text{ volume}}{\pi}}$
30.	Sector of sphere 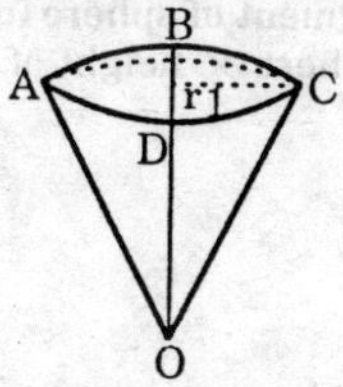	Volume = 2/3 (radius of sphere)^2 × (height of segment) $2/3\, \pi r^2 h$ cubic units
31.	Cylinder 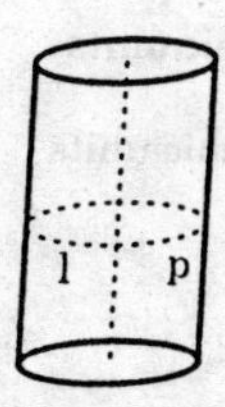	Curved surface = perimeter of cross section × length = *p.l.* sq. units

Sl. No.	*Item with figure*	*Formulae*
32.	**Oblique frusta of right circular cylinder** 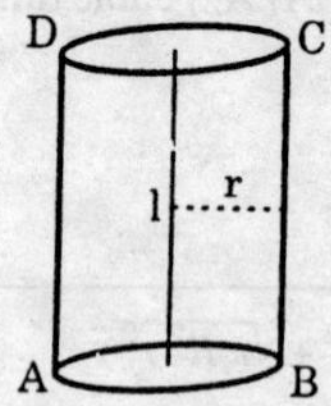	**Curved surface = Circumference of the cross section × length** $= 2\pi r l$
33.	**Right circular cone** 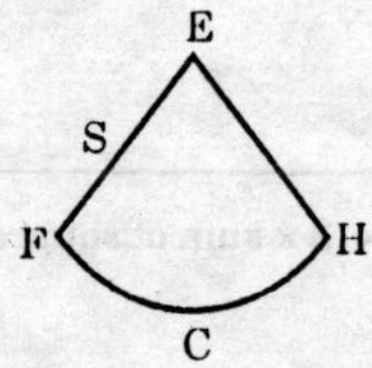	**Curved surface = 1/2 (circumference of base) × (slant length)** $= \frac{1}{2} CS$
34.	**Frusta of right circular cone** 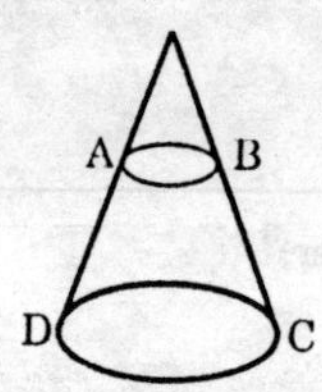	**Curved surface = (1/2 (Slant thickness) × (sum of circumference of ends)** $= 1/2 \times s \times (C + c)$
35.	**Sphere** 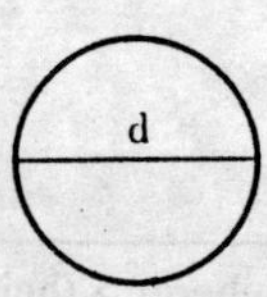	**Curved surface of sphere** $= \pi$ **(diameter)**^{2} $= \pi d^2$ **Volume** $= 4/3\ \pi R^3$
36.	**Segment or zone of sphere** 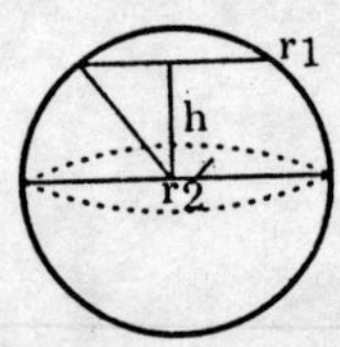	**Curved surface of segment of sphere (or of zone of sphere)** $= \pi \times$ **Diameter of sphere × height of segment (or of zone)** $S = \pi dh$.
37.	**Spherical shell** 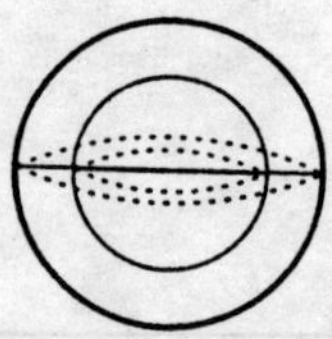	**Volume** $= \frac{\pi}{6} (D^3 - d^3)$ **cubic units** $= \frac{4\pi}{3} (R^3 - r^3)$ **cubic units**

Sl. No.	Item with figure	Formulae
38.	Oblate spheroids 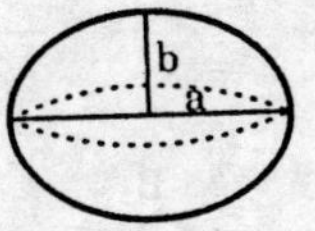	Volume $= 4/3\ \pi a^2 b$ cubic units
39.	Prolate spheroids 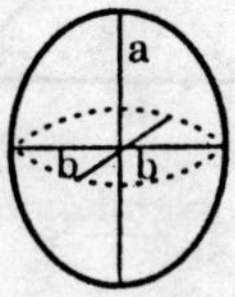	Volume $= 4/3\ \pi a b^2$ cubic units

Notations:

A = Area of base ; A_1 = Area at top section ; A_2 = Area at bottom section ; A_3 = Area at mid-section ; a = Semi-major axis ; b = semi-minor axis ;

B = Base length ; D = Diameter ; H = height ; L = Slant height 1

P = Perimeter of base ; P_1 = Perimeter at top section ; P = Perimeter at bottom section ; R = Radius ; R_1 = Radius at base ;

π = Ratio of circumference to diameter of circle = 22/7 = 3.141

$\pi^2 = 9.87$; $\pi^3 = 31.00$; $1/\pi = 0.32$; $\sqrt{\pi} = 1.77$.

Appendix VII

TRIGONOMETRICAL FORMULAE

Oblique angle triangles

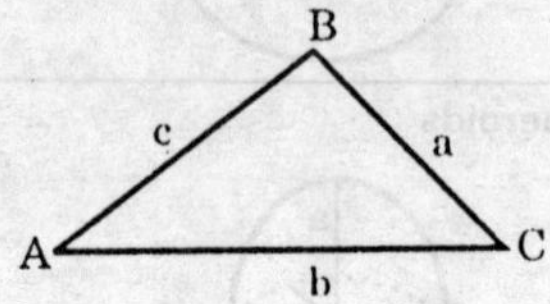

Given	*Required*	*Formulae*
A, c, a	*C*	$C = \dfrac{a \sin C}{\sin A}$
A, a, b	*B*	$\sin B = \dfrac{b \sin A}{a}$
a, b, c	*A*	$\tan A = \dfrac{a \sin C}{b - a \cos C}$
a, b, c	*A, B, C*	$\sin A = \dfrac{2 \text{ area}}{bc}$
		$\sin B = \dfrac{2 \text{ area}}{ac}$
		$\sin C = \dfrac{2 \text{ area}}{ab}$
A, B, c, a	Area	$= \dfrac{a^2 \sin B \sin C}{2 \sin A}$
A, b, c	Area	$= 1/2\ (bc \text{ Sin } A)$
a, b, c	Area	$= \sqrt{s\,(s-a)\,(s-b)\,(s-c)}$
		where, $s = \dfrac{a+b+c}{2}$

Right Angle Triangle

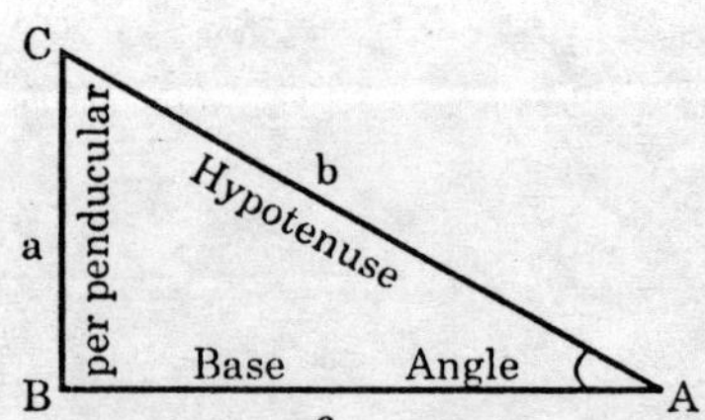

$$\text{sine} = \frac{\text{Perpendicular}}{\text{Hypotenuse}} \quad \text{cosine} = \frac{\text{Base}}{\text{Hypoteneuse}} \quad \text{tangent} = \frac{\text{Perpendicular}}{\text{Base}}$$

$$\text{cotan} = \frac{\text{Base}}{\text{Perpendicular}} \quad \text{sec tan} = \frac{\text{Hypoteneuse}}{\text{Base}} \quad \text{cosec} = \frac{\text{Hypoteneuse}}{\text{Perpendicular}}$$

$$\text{Hypoteneuse} = \sqrt{\text{Base}^2 + \text{Perpendicular}^2} \quad \text{Base} = \sqrt{\text{Hypoteneuse}^2 - \text{Base}^2}$$

Appendix - VIII
WEIGHT OF ENGINEERING MATERIALS

Alum	1,696 gm/cum
Aluminium sheets per mm thickness	2.8 kg/cum
Asbestos flat sheets 6 mm thickness	12.21 kg/sqm
Asbestos corrugatedor traford sheets 6 mm thickness	17.09 kg/sqm
Ashes, cinder	740 kg/cum
Asphalt	2,200 kg/cum
Bitumen	1,040 kg/cum
Brass	8,550 kg/cum
Bel metal	8,720 kg/cum
Bricks clay kiln burnt 1st. class	1,760 kg/cum
Ballast (brick)	1,200 kg/cum
Masonry (brick)	1,920 kg/cum
Cement ordinary aluminous	1,440 kg/cum
Chalk	1,938 kg/cum
Stone chips	2,420 kg/cum
Hollow blocks (25 mm thick)	2,563 kg/cum
Clay dry lump	1,040 kg/cum
Copper sheet per mm thickness	8.97 kg/sqm
Fire brick	2,083 kg/cum
Fire clay	2,243 kg/cum
Glass common	2,530 kg/cum
Lead	11,374 kg/cum
Lead sheet per mm thickness	11 kg/cum
Leather	897 kg/cum
Lime stone	1,360 kg/cum
Unslaked lime	960 kg/cum
Slaked lime	640 kg/cum
Concrete with brick ballast	1,920 kg/cum
Mortar cement	2,080 kg/cum
Mortar lime	1,760 kg/cum
Mortar gypsum	1,200 kg/cum
Sand dry coarse	1,600 kg/cum
Sand wet coarse	1,900 kg/cum
Sand wet River	2,000 kg/cum
Sand wet River	1,840 kg/cum
Stone	2,515 kg/cum
Shale	2,595 kg/cum
Shellac gum	509 kg/cum
Steel cast	7,850 kg/cum

Steel mild	7,850 kg/cum
Steel hard	7,810 kg/cum
Corrugated steel sheets, galvanised	
16 gauge	16,405 kg/cum
18 gauge	13,085 kg/cum
20 gauge	10,204 kg/cum
22 gauge	8,398 kg/cum
24 gauge	6,933 kg/cum
Stone, Basalt	2,850 – 2,960 kg/cum
Stone Granite	2,640 – 2,800 kg/cum
Stone Laterite	2,080 – 2,400 kg/cum
Lime stone	2,400 – 2,640 kg/cum
Marble	2,620 kg/cum
Marble chips	1,802 kg/cum
Quartz rock	2,640 kg/cum
Sand stone	2,240 – 2,400 kg/cum
Slate	2,800 kg/cum
Stone metal or chips	1,600 – 1,920 kg/cum
Snow	0,096 kg/cum
Soap stone	2,643 kg/cum
Rubble stone masonry	2,080 kg/cum
Ashlar stone masonry	2,640 kg/cum
Marble dressed	2,700 kg/cum
Coal Tar	1,121 kg/cum
Pitch	1,281 kg/cum
Terra cota (solid)	2,080 kg/cum
Country tile	63,354 kg/sqm
Timber Hard wood	640 – 960 kg/cum
Timber Light wood	400 – 480 kg/cum
Timber Medium wood	480 – 640 kg/cum
Fresh water	1,000 kg/cum
Sea water	1,025 kg/cum

Appendix IX

METRIC STANDARD TABLES
ROLLED STEEL I BEAMS DIMENSIONS AND PROPERTIES

Size Depth X Width h × b	Wt. per metre	Section Area	Thickness		Moment of Intertia		Ratio of Gyration		Modulii of section		Maximum size of flange Rivet
			Flange	Web	I_{xx}	I_{yy}	R_{xx}	R_{yy}	Z_{xx}	Z_{yy}	
mm	kg	cm^2	mm	mm	cm^4	cm^4	cm	cm	cm^3	cm^3	mm
150 × 50	7.1	9.01	4.6	3.0	322.1	9.2	5.98	1.01	42.9	3.7	6
175 × 50	8.1	10.28	4.8	3.2	479.3	9.7	6.83	0.97	54.8	3.9	6
200 × 60	9.9	12.64	5.0	3.4	780.7	17.3	7.86	1.17	78.1	5.8	6
255 × 80	12.8	16.28	5.0	3.7	1308.5	40.5	8.97	1.58	116.3	10.1	12
75 × 50	6.1	7.71	5.0	3.7	72.7	10.0	3.07	1.14	19.4	4.0	6
100 × 50	8.0	10.21	6.4	4.0	168.0	12.7	4.06	1.12	33.6	5.1	6
125 × 75	11.9	15.12	6.5	4.4	406.8	43.4	5.19	1.69	65.1	11.6	12
150 × 80	14.2	18.08	6.8	4.8	688.2	55.2	6.17	1.75	91.8	13.8	12
175 × 90	16.7	21.30	6.9	5.1	1096.2	79.6	7.17	1.93	125.3	17.7	12
200 × 100	19.8	25.27	7.3	5.4	1696.6	115.4	8.19	2.13	169.7	23.1	16
225 × 100	23.5	29.92	8.6	5.8	2501.9	112.7	9.15	1.94	222.4	22.5	16
250 × 125	27.9	35.53	8.2	6.1	3717.8	193.4	10.23	2.33	297.4	30.9	22
275 × 140	33.0	42.02	8.8	6.4	5375.3	287.0	11.31	2.61	302.4	41.0	22
300 × 150	37.7	48.08	9.4	6.7	7332.9	376.2	12.35	2.80	488.9	50.2	22
325 × 165	43.1	54.90	9.8	7.0	9874.6	510.8	13.41	3.05	607.7	61.9	25
350 × 165	49.5	63.01	11.4	7.4	13158.3	631.9	14.45	3.17	751.9	76.6	25
400 × 165	56.9	72.43	12.5	8.0	19306.3	716.4	16.33	3.15	965.3	86.8	25
450 × 170	65.3	83.14	13.4	8.6	27536.1	853.0	18.20	3.20	1223.8	100.4	25
500 × 180	75.0	95.50	14.1	9.2	38579.0	1063.9	20.10	3.34	1543.2	118.2	28
550 × 190	86.3	109.97	15.0	9.9	53161.6	1335.1	21.99	3.48	1933.2	140.5	32
600 × 210	99.5	126.69	15.5	10.5	72867.6	1821.9	23.98	3.79	2428.9	173.5	25.32
100 × 75	11.5	14.60	7.2	4.0	257.5	40.8	4.20	1.67	51.5	10.9	12
125 × 75	13.0	16.60	7.6	4.4	449.0	43.7	5.20	1.62	71.8	11.7	12
150 × 80	14.9	19.00	7.6	4.8	726.4	52.6	6.18	1.66	96.9	13.1	12
175 × 90	19.3	24.62	8.6	5.5	1272.0	85.0	7.19	1.86	145.4	18.9	12
200 × 100	25.4	32.33	10.8	5.7	2235.4	150.0	8.32	2.15	223.5	30.0	16
225 × 110	31.2	39.72	11.8	6.5	3441.8	218.3	9.31	2.34	305.9	39.7	20
250 × 125	37.3	47.53	12.5	6.9	5131.6	334.5	10.39	2.65	410.5	53.5	22
300 × 140	44.2	56.26	12.4	7.5	8603.6	453.9	12.37	2.84	573.6	64.8	22
350 × 140	52.4	66.71	14.2	8.1	13630.3	537.7	14.29	2.84	778.9	76.8	22

Appendix IX
METRIC STANDARD TABLES I-BEAMS (Continued)

Size Depth × Width h × b	*Wt. per metre*	*Section Area*	*Thickness*		*Moment of Inertia*		*Ratio of Gyration*		*Modulii of section*		*Maximum size of flange Rivet*
			Flange	*Web*	I_{xx}	I_{yy}	R_{xx}	R_{yy}	Z_{xx}	Z_{yy}	
mm	kg	cm^2	mm	mm	cm^4	cm^4	cm	cm	cm^3	cm^3	mm
400 × 140	61.6	78.46	16.0	8.9	20458.4	622.1	16.15	2.82	1022.9	88.9	22
450 × 150	72.4	92.27	17.4	9.4	30390.8	834.0	18.15	3.01	1350.7	111.2	22
500 × 180	86.9	110.74	17.2	10.2	45218.3	1369.8	20.21	3.52	1808.7	152.2	28
550 × 190	103.7	132.11	19.3	11.2	64893.6	1833.8	22.16	3.73	2359.8	193.0	32
600 × 210	122.6	156.21	20.8	12.0	91813.0	2651.0	24.24	4.12	3060.4	252.5	25.32
150 × 100	17.0	21.67	7.0	5.4	8.9.1	94.8	6.22	2.09	111.9	19.0	16
175 × 125	22.1	28.11	7.4	5.8	1509.4	188.6	7.33	2.99	172.5	30.2	22
200 × 140	28.8	36.71	9.0	6.1	2624.5	328.8	8.46	2.59	262.5	47.0	22
225 × 150	33.9	43.24	9.9	6.4	3920.5	448.6	9.52	3.22	348.5	59.8	22
250 × 200	40.9	52.05	9.0	6.7	5943.1	857.5	10.69	4.06	475.4	85.7	22.32
300 × 200	48.1	61.33	10.0	7.4	9821.6	990.1	12.66	4.02	654.8	99.0	22.32
350 × 200	56.9	72.50	11.4	8.0	15521.7	1175.9	14.63	4.03	887.0	117.6	22.32
400 × 200	66.7	85.01	13.0	8.6	23426.7	1388.0	16.60	4.04	1171.3	138.8	22.32
450 × 200	79.4	101.15	15.4	9.2	35057.6	1706.7	18.63	4.11	1558.1	170.7	22.32
500 × 250	95.2	121.22	14.7	9.9	52290.9	2987.8	20.77	4.96	2091.6	239.0	32
550 × 250	112.5	143.34	17.6	10.5	74906.1	3740.6	22.86	5.11	2723.9	299.2	32
600 × 250	133.7	170.38	21.3	11.2	106198.5	4702.5	24.97	5.25	3540.0	376.2	32
600 × 250	145.1	184.86	23.6	11.8	115626.6	5298.3	25.01	5.35	3854.2	423.9	32
150 × 150	27.1	34.48	9.0	5.4	1455.6	431.7	6.50	3.54	194.1	57.6	22
150 × 150	30.6	38.98	9.0	8.4	1540.0	460.3	6.29	3.44	205.3	60.2	22
150 × 150	34.6	44.08	9.0	11.8	1635.6	494.9	6.09	3.35	21.1	63.2	22
200 × 200	37.3	47.54	9.0	6.1	3608.4	967.1	8.71	4.51	360.8	96.7	22.32
200 × 200	40.0	50.94	9.0	7.8	3721.8	994.6	8.55	4.42	372.2	98.6	22.32
225 × 225	43.1	54.94	9.1	6.5	5279.5	1353.8	9.80	4.96	469.3	120.3	28
225 × 225	46.8	59.66	9.1	8.6	5478.8	1396.6	9.58	4.84	487.0	123.0	28
250 × 250	51.0	64.96	9.7	6.9	7736.5	1961.3	10.91	5.49	618.9	156.9	32
250 × 250	54.7	69.71	9.7	8.8	7983.9	2011.7	10.70	5.37	638.7	159.7	32
300 × 250	58.8	74.85	10.6	7.6	12545.2	2193.6	12.95	5.41	836.3	175.5	32
300 × 250	63.0	80.25	10.6	9.4	12950.2	2246.7	12.70	5.29	863.3	178.4	32
350 × 250	67.4	85.91	11.6	8.3	19159.7	2451.4	14.93	5.34	1094.8	196.1	32
350 × 250	72.4	92.21	11.6	10.1	19802.8	2510.5	14.65	5.22	1131.6	199.4	32
400 × 250	77.4	98.66	12.7	9.1	28083.5	2728.3	16.87	5.26	1404.2	218.3	32
400 × 250	82.2	104.66	12.7	10.6	28823.5	2783.0	16.61	5.16	1444.2	221.3	32
450 × 250	87.2	111.14	13.7	9.8	39210.8	2985.2	18.78	5.18	1742.7	238.8	32
450 × 250	92.5	117.89	13.7	11.3	40349.9	3045.0	18.50	5.08	1793.3	242.1	32

Appendix IX

METRIC STANDARD TABLES ROLLED STEEL CHANNELS DIMENSIONS AND PROPERTIES

Size Depth × Width h × b	Wt. per metre	Section Area	Thickness		Moment of Inertia		Radii of Gyration		Modulii of section		Maximum size of flange Rivet
			Flange	Web	I_{xx}	I_{yy}	R_{xx}	R_{yy}	Z_{xx}	Z_{yy}	
mm	kg	cm^2	mm	mm	cm^4	cm^4	cm	cm	cm^3	cm^3	mm
100 × 45	5.8	7.41	5.1	3.0	123.8	14.9	4.09	1.42	24.8	4.8	1.40
125 × 50	7.9	10.07	6.6	3.0	270.0	25.7	5.18	1.60	43.2	7.6	1.64
150 × 55	9.9	12.65	6.9	3.6	471.1	37.9	6.10	1.73	62.8	9.9	1.66
175 × 60	11.2	14.24	6.9	3.6	719.9	50.5	7.11	1.88	82.3	11.9	1.75
200 × 70	13.9	17.77	7.1	4.1	1161.2	84.2	8.08	2.18	116.1	16.7	1.97
75 × 40	5.7	7.26	6.0	3.7	66.1	11.5	3.02	1.26	17.6	4.3	1.35
100 × 50	7.9	10.02	6.4	4.0	164.7	24.8	4.06	1.57	32.9	7.3	1.62
125 × 65	10.7	13.67	6.6	4.4	356.8	57.2	5.11	2.05	57.1	12.8	2.04
150 × 75	14.4	18.36	7.8	4.8	697.2	103.2	6.16	2.37	93.0	20.2	2.38
175 × 75	17.6	22.40	9.5	5.1	1148.4	126.5	7.16	2.38	131.3	24.8	2.40
200 × 75	20.6	26.22	10.8	5.5	1725.5	146.9	8.11	2.37	172.6	28.5	2.35
225 × 90	24.0	30.53	10.2	5.8	2547.9	209.5	9.14	2.62	226.5	32.0	2.46
250 × 100	28.0	35.65	10.7	6.1	3687.9	298.4	10.17	2.89	295.0	40.9	2.70
300 × 100	33.1	42.11	11.6	6.7	6047.9	346.0	11.98	2.87	403.2	46.4	2.55
350 × 100	38.8	49.47	12.5	7.4	9312.6	394.6	13.72	2.82	532.1	52.0	2.41
400 × 100	45.7	58.25	14.0	8.0	13989.5	460.4	15.50	2.81	699.5	60.2	2.36
75 × 40	6.8	8.67	7.3	4.4	76.0	12.6	2.96	1.21	20.3	4.7	1.13
100 × 50	9.2	11.70	7.5	4.7	186.7	25.9	4.00	1.49	37.3	7.5	1.53
125 × 65	12.7	16.19	8.1	5.0	416.4	59.9	5.07	1.92	66.6	13.1	1.94
150 × 75	16.4	20.88	9.0	5.4	779.4	102.3	6.11	2.21	103.9	19.4	2.22
175 × 75	19.1	24.38	10.2	5.7	1223.3	121.0	7.08	2.23	139.8	22.8	2.20
200 × 75	22.1	28.21	11.4	6.1	1819.3	140.4	8.03	2.23	181.9	26.3	2.17
225 × 80	25.9	33.01	12.4	6.4	2694.6	187.2	9.03	2.38	239.5	32.8	2.30
250 × 80	30.4	38.67	14.1	7.1	3816.8	219.1	9.94	2.38	305.3	38.4	2.30
300 × 90	35.8	45.64	13.6	7.6	6362.6	310.8	11.81	2.61	424.2	46.8	2.36
350 × 100	42.1	53.66	13.5	8.1	10008.0	430.6	13.66	2.83	571.9	57.0	2.44
400 × 100	49.4	62.93	15.3	8.6	15082.8	504.8	15.48	2.83	754.1	66.6	2.42

Appendix IX METRIC STANDARD TABLES
ROLLED STEEL EQUAL ANGLES DIMENSIONS AND PROPERTIES

Size A × B × t mm	Wt per metre kg.	Section Area cm^2	Centre of Gravity C_{xx} = C_{yy} cm	Moment of Inertia I_{xx} = I_{yy} cm^4	Radius of Gyration r_{xx} = r_{yy} cm	Section Moduli Z_{xx} = Z_{yy} cm^3	Size A × B mm	Wt per metre kg.	Section Area cm^2	Centre of Gravity C_{xx} = C_{yy} cm	Moment of Inertia I_{xx} = I_{yy} cm^4	Radius of Gyration r_{xx} = r_{yy} cm	Section Moduli Z_{xx} = Z_{yy} cm^3
20 × 20 × 3	0.9	1.12	0.59	0.4	0.58	0.3	70 × 70 × 5	5.3	6.77	1.89	31.1	2.15	6.1
20 × 20 × 4	1.1	1.45	0.63	0.5	0.58	0.4	70 × 70 × 6	6.4	8.06	1.94	36.8	2.14	7.3
25 × 25 × 3	1.1	1.41	0.71	0.8	0.73	0.4	70 × 70 × 8	8.3	10.58	2.02	47.4	2.12	9.5
25 × 25 × 4	1.4	1.84	0.75	1.0	0.73	0.6	70 × 70 × 10	10.2	13.02	2.10	57.2	2.10	11.7
25 × 25 × 5	1.8	2.25	0.79	1.2	0.72	0.7	75 × 75 × 5	5.7	7.27	2.02	38.7	2.31	7.1
30 × 30 × 3	1.4	1.73	0.83	1.4	0.89	0.6	75 × 75 × 6	6.8	8.66	2.06	45.7	2.30	8.4
30 × 30 × 4	1.8	2.26	0.87	1.8	0.89	0.8	75 × 75 × 8	8.9	11.38	2.14	59.0	2.28	11.0
30 × 30 × 5	2.2	2.77	0.92	2.1	0.88	1.0	75 × 75 × 10	11.0	14.02	22.20	71.4	2.26	13.5
35 × 35 × 3	1.6	2.03	0.95	2.3	1.05	0.9	80 × 80 × 6	7.3	9.29	2.18	56.0	2.46	9.6
35 × 35 × 4	2.1	2.66	1.00	2.9	1.05	1.2	80 × 80 × 8	9.6	12.21	2.27	72.5	2.44	12.6
35 × 35 × 5	2.6	3.27	1.04	3.5	1.04	1.4	80 × 80 × 10	11.8	15.05	2.34	87.7	2.41	15.5
35 × 35 × 6	3.0	3.86	1.08	4.1	1.03	1.7	80 × 80 × 12	14.0	17.81	2.42	101.9	2.39	18.3
40 × 40 × 3	1.8	2.34	1.08	3.4	1.21	1.2	90 × 90 × 6	8.2	10.47	2.42	80.1	2.77	12.2
40 × 40 × 4	2.4	3.07	1.12	4.5	1.21	1.6	90 × 90 × 8	10.8	13.79	2.51	104.2	2.75	16.0
40 × 40 × 5	3.0	3.78	1.16	5.4	1.20	1.9	90 × 90 × 10	13.4	17.03	2.59	126.7	2.73	19.8
40 × 40 × 6	3.5	4.47	1.20	6.3	1.19	2.3	90 × 90 × 12	15.8	20.19	2.66	147.9	2.71	23.3
45 × 45 × 3	2.1	2.64	1.20	5.0	1.38	1.5	100 × 100 × 6	9.2	11.67	2.67	111.3	3.09	15.2
45 × 45 × 4	2.7	3.47	1.25	6.5	1.37	2.0	100 × 100 × 8	12.1	15.39	2.76	145.1	3.07	20.0
45 × 45 × 5	3.4	4.28	1.29	7.9	1.36	2.5	100 × 100 × 10	14.9	19.03	2.84	177.0	3.05	24.7
45 × 45 × 6	4.0	5.07	1.33	9.2	1.35	2.9	100 × 100 × 12	17.7	22.59	2.92	207.0	3.03	29.2
50 × 50 × 3	2.3	2.95	1.32	6.9	1.53	1.9	110 × 110 × 8	13.4	17.02	3.00	195.0	2.38	24.4
50 × 50 × 4	3.0	3.88	1.37	9.1	1.53	2.5	110 × 110 × 10	16.5	21.06	3.08	238.4	2.36	30.1
50 × 50 × 5	3.8	4.79	1.41	11.0	1.52	3.1	110 × 110 × 12	19.6	25.02	3.16	279.6	3.34	35.7
50 × 50 × 6	4.5	5.68	1.45	12.9	1.31	3.6	110 × 110 × 15	24.2	30.81	3.27	337.4	3.31	43.7
55 × 55 × 5	4.1	5.27	1.53	14.7	1.67	3.7	130 × 130 × 8	15.9	20.22	3.50	328.3	4.03	34.5
55 × 55 × 6	4.9	6.26	1.57	17.3	1.66	4.4	130 × 130 × 10	19.7	25.06	3.58	402.7	4.01	42.7
55 × 55 × 8	6.4	8.18	1.65	22.0	1.64	5.7	130 × 130 × 12	23.4	29.82	3.66	473.8	3.99	50.7
55 × 55 × 10	7.9	10.2	1.72	26.3	1.62	7.0	130 × 130 × 15	28.9	36.81	3.78	574.6	3.95	62.3
60 × 60 × 5	4.5	5.75	1.65	19.2	1.82	4.4	150 × 150 × 10	22.8	29.03	4.06	622.4	4.63	56.9
60 × 60 × 6	5.4	6.84	1.69	22.6	1.82	5.2	150 × 150 × 12	27.2	34.59	4.14	735.4	4.61	67.7
60 × 60 × 8	7.0	8.96	1.77	29.0	1.80	6.8	150 × 150 × 15	33.6	42.78	4.26	896.8	4.58	83.5
60 × 60 × 10	8.6	11.00	1.85	34.8	1.78	8.4	150 × 150 × 18	39.9	50.79	4.38	1048.9	4.54	98.7
65 × 65 × 5	4.9	6.25	1.77	24.7	1.99	5.2	200 × 200 × 12	36.6	46.61	5.36	1788.9	6.20	122.2
65 × 65 × 6	5.8	7.44	1.86	29.1	1.98	6.2	200 × 200 × 15	45.4	57.80	5.49	2197.7	6.17	151.4
65 × 65 × 8	7.7	9.76	1.89	37.4	1.96	8.1	200 × 200 × 18	54.0	68.81	5.61	2588.7	6.13	179.9
65 × 65 × 10	9.4	12.00	1.97	45.0	1.94	9.9	200 × 200 × 25	73.6	93.80	5.88	3436.3	6.05	243.3

Appendix IX
METRIC STANDARD TABLES
ROLLED STEEL UNEQUAL ANGLES DIMENSIONS AND PROPERTIES

Size A × B × t	Wt. per metre	Section Area	Centre of Gravity		Moment of Intertia		Radit of Gyration		Modulii of Section	
			C_{xx}	C_{yy}	I_{xx}	I_{yy}	r_{xx}	r_{yy}	Z_{xx}	Z_{yy}
mm	kg	cm^2	cm	cm	cm^4	cm^4	cm	cm	cm^3	cm^3
30 × 20 × 3	1.1	1.41	0.98	0.49	1.2	0.4	0.92	0.54	0.6	0.3
30 × 20 × 4	1.4	1.84	1.02	0.53	1.5	0.5	0.92	0.54	0.8	0.4
30 × 20 × 5	1.8	2.25	1.06	0.57	1.9	0.6	0.91	0.53	1.0	0.4
40 × 25 × 3	1.5	1.88	1.30	0.57	3.0	0.9	1.25	0.68	1.1	0.5
40 × 25 × 4	1.9	2.46	1.35	0.62	3.8	1.1	1.25	0.68	1.4	0.6
40 × 25 × 5	2.4	3.02	1.39	0.66	4.6	1.4	1.24	0.67	1.8	0.7
40 × 25 × 6	2.8	3.56	1.43	0.69	5.4	1.6	1.23	0.66	2.1	0.9
45 × 30 × 3	1.7	2.18	1.42	0.69	4.4	1.5	1.42	0.84	1.4	0.7
45 × 30 × 4	2.2	2.86	1.47	0.73	5.7	2.0	1.41	0.84	1.9	0.9
45 × 30 × 5	2.8	3.52	1.51	0.77	6.9	2.4	1.40	0.83	2.3	1.1
45 × 30 × 6	3.3	4.16	1.55	0.81	8.0	2.8	1.39	0.82	2.7	1.3
50 × 30 × 3	1.8	2.34	1.63	0.65	5.9	1.6	1.59	0.82	1.7	2.0
50 × 30 × 4	2.4	3.07	1.68	0.70	7.7	2.1	1.58	0.82	2.3	2.3
50 × 30 × 5	3.0	3.78	1.72	0.74	9.3	2.5	1.57	0.81	2.8	3.0
50 × 30 × 6	3.5	4.47	1.76	0.78	10.9	2.9	1.56	0.80	3.4	2.5
60 × 40 × 5	3.7	4.76	1.95	0.96	16.9	6.0	1.89	1.12	4.2	3.0
60 × 40 × 6	4.4	5.65	1.99	1.00	19.9	7.0	1.88	1.11	5.0	2.5
60 × 40 × 8	5.8	7.37	2.07	1.08	25.4	8.0	1.86	1.10	6.5	3.0
65 × 45 × 3	4.1	5.26	2.07	1.08	22.1	8.6	2.05	1.28	5.0	3.9
65 × 45 × 6	4.9	6.25	2.11	1.12	26.0	10.1	2.04	1.27	5.9	2.5
65 × 45 × 8	6.4	8.17	2.19	1.20	33.2	12.8	2.02	1.25	7.7	3.9
70 × 45 × 5	4.3	5.52	2.27	1.04	27.2	8.8	2.22	1.26	5.7	2.5
70 × 45 × 6	5.2	6.65	2.32	1.09	32.0	10.3	2.21	1.25	6.8	3.0
70 × 45 × 8	6.7	8.58	2.40	1.16	41.0	13.1	2.19	1.24	8.9	3.9
70 × 45 × 10	8.3	10.52	2.48	1.24	49.3	15.6	2.16	1.22	10.9	4.8
75 × 50 × 5	4.7	6.02	2.39	1.16	34.1	12.2	2.38	1.42	6.7	3.2
75 × 50 × 6	5.6	7.16	2.44	1.20	40.3	14.3	2.37	1.41	8.0	3.8
75 × 50 × 8	7.4	9.38	2.52	1.28	51.8	18.3	2.35	1.40	10.4	4.9
75 × 50 × 10	9.0	11.58	2.60	1.36	62.3	21.8	2.33	1.38	12.7	6.0
80 × 50 × 5	4.9	6.27	2.60	1.12	40.6	12.3	2.55	1.40	7.5	3.2
80 × 50 × 6	5.9	7.46	2.64	1.16	48.0	14.4	2.54	1.39	9.0	3.8
80 × 50 × 8	7.7	9.78	2.73	1.24	61.9	18.5	2.52	1.37	11.7	4.9
80 × 50 × 10	9.4	12.02	2.81	1.32	74.7	22.1	2.49	1.36	14.4	6.0

Appendix X

STRUCTURAL STEEL BARS
Square and Round Bars

Diameter of Width Across	*Weight per Metre W*		*Sectional A*		*Perimeter*		*Length in per Ton*	
mm	*kg*	*kg*	cm^2	cm^2	cm^2	cm^2		
5.0	0.20	0.15	0.25	0.20	2.0	1.57	5000	6667
5.5	0.24	0.19	0.30	0.24	2.2	1.73	4167	5263
6.0	0.28	0.22	0.36	0.28	2.4	1.88	3571	4545
7.0	0.38	0.30	0.49	0.38	2.8	2.20	2632	3333
8.0	0.50	0.39	0.64	0.50	3.2	2.51	2000	2564
9.0	0.64	0.50	0.81	0.64	3.6	2.83	1563	2000
10.0	0.78	0.62	1.00	0.79	4.0	3.14	1282	1613
11	0.95	0.75	1.21	0.95	4.4	3.46	1053	1333
12	1.13	0.89	1.44	1.13	4.8	3.77	885	1124
14	1.54	12.1	1.96	1.54	5.6	4.40	449	826
16	2.01	1.58	2.59	2.01	6.4	5.03	498	633
18	2.54	2.00	3.24	2.54	7.2	5.65	394	500
20	3.14	2.47	4.00	3.14	8.0	6.28	3.19	405
22	3.80	2.98	4.84	3.80	8.8	6.91	263	336
25	4.91	3.85	6.25	4.91	10.0	7.85	204	260
28	6.15	4.83	7.84	6.16	11.2	8.80	163	207
32	8.04	6.31	10.24	8.04	12.8	10.05	124	159
36	10.17	7.99	12.96	10.18	14.4	11.31	98	125
40	12.56	9.86	16.00	12.57	16.0	12.57	80	101
45	15.90	12.49	20.25	15.90	18.0	14.14	63	80
50	19.62	15.41	25.00	19.64	20.0	15.71	51	65
56	24.62	19.34	31.36	24.63	22.4	17.69	41	52
63	31.16	24.47	39.69	31.17	25.2	19.79	32	41
71	39.57	31.08	50.41	39.59	28.4	22.30	25	32
80	50.24	39.46	64.00	50.26	32.0	25.13	20	25
90	63.58	49.94	81.00	63.62	36.0	28.27	16	20
100	78.50	61.66	100.00	78.54	40.0	31.42	13	16
110	94.98	74.60	121.00	95.03	44.0	34.56	11	13
125	122.66	96.34	156.25	122.72	50.0	39.27	8	10
140	153.86	120.84	190.00	152.94	56.0	43.98	6	8
160	200.96	157.84	256.00	201.06	64.0	50.27	5	6
180	254.34	199.76	324.00	254.47	72.0	56.55	4	5
200	314.00	246.62	400.00	314.16	80.0	62.83	3	4

Note: 1. Refer to Round Bar column for ribbed-torsteel calculations

Appendix - XI
Conversion Table

Multiply by	*To convert*	*To*	
2.54	Inches	Centimeters	0.39371
30.48	Feet	Centimeters	0.03281
0.3937	Millimeters	Inches	
0.9144	Yards	Meters	1.094
1,609.31	Miles	Meters	0.000621
3.281	Meters	Feet	0.3048
39.37	Meters	Inches	
1,853.27	Nautical miles	meters	0.00054
6.45137	Square inches	Sq. Cms.	0.15501
0.093	Square feet	Sq. mts	10.7643
0.83610	Square yards	Sq.mts	1.19603
2.58989	Square miles	Sq. kilometers	0.38616
16.38618	Cubic inches	Cub. Cms.	0.06103
28.33	Cubic feet	Liters	0.353
0.02832	Cubic feet	Cub. meters	35.31658
6.24	Cubic feet	Imp. gallons	0.1602
0.76451	Cubic yards	Imp. gallons	1.30802
0.3732	Pounds	Kilogrammes	2.68
50.80238	Cwt	Kilogrammes	0.01968
1,016.04754	Tons	Kilogrammes	0.00098
4.54346	Imp. gallons	Liters	0.22010
3.785	U.S. gallons	Liters	0.264
0.56793	Pints	Liters	1.76077
219.97	Cubic meters	Imp. gallons,	
264.2	Cubic meters	U.S. gallons	
61.022	Liters	Cubic inches	
3.531	Hectoliters	Cubic feet	
2.84	Hectoliters	Bushels	
36.34766	Bushels	Liters	
10.000	Imp. gallons of water	Pounds	
	To obtain	*From*	*Multiply by above*
0.454	Pounds of water	Liters	0.2202
70.31	lbs per sq.in. (psi)	Gms per sq. cm^2	0.01422
0.07031	lbs per sq.in. (psi)	kg/cm^2	14.22272
4.88241	lbs per sq. foot	kg/sqm kg/m^2	0.20482
0.00049	lbs per sq.foot	kg/sq.cm. kg/cm^2	2,049.1807
0.24803	lbs per fathom	kg/mtr.	4.0318
1.48816	lbs per foot	kg/mtr	0.6719
0.49606	lbs per yard	kg/mtr.	2.0159
3,333.4784	Tons/foot	kg/mtr.	0.0003
2.3	lbs per sq. in (psi)	Head of water (ft.)	0.434
0.7	lbs per sq.in. (psi)	Head of water (m)	1.4283

Multiply by	To convert	To	
0.068	lbs per sq.in. (psi)	Atmosphere	14.7
1.136	Quarts	Liters	
157.4944	Tons per sq.in	Kg/cm^2	0.0063
1.574944	Tons per sq.in	Kg/mm^2	0.635
10,936.59840	Tons per sq.foot.	Kg/mtr.^{2}	0.0001
0.0361	Gm./cm^3	lb. per cubic inch	
62.40	Gm./cm^3	lb. per cubic foot	0.016
0.593	lb per cub. yard	Kg/mtr.^{3}	1.686
16.02	lb per cub. foot	Kg/mtr.^{3} (m^3/kg)	0.624
0.4047	Acres	Hecter	2.471
11,960.00	Hecter	Yards^2	
0.00155	Sq. mm	Sq. inch	
0.0998	lb per Imp. gallon	Kgm/liter, Kg.liter	10.02
0.13825	Foot pound	Kilogram meters	7.2333
0.33	Foot tons	Ton meter	3.00
309.680	Foot tons	Kilogram meters	0.0032
25.80667	Inch tons	Kilogram meters	0.0388
41.62314	Inch^4	cm^4	0.0240
0.62138	Kilometers	Miles	1.6093
3,280.8693	Kilometers	Foot	
0.00453	Imp. gallons	Cubic meters, m^3	219.98
1.60931	Miles per hour	Kilometer per hour	0.6214
1.467	Miles per hour	Foot per second	
746.00	Horse power	Watts	0.00134
3.415	Watt hour	B.T.U.	0.293
737.30	Kilo watt	Footpound/S	
0.293	Kilo watt	K cal/second	
0.707	H.P.	B.T.U./sec.	
0.178	H.P.	Kcal/sec.	
33,000.00	H.P.	Foot pounds/min	
76.00	H.P	Kg-m/sec.	0.01216

Multiply by	To convert	To	
44.00	Watts	Foot pounds/min.	0.0227
0.10	Watts	Kg-m/sec	10.00
0.948	Kilowatt	B.T.U./sec.	
860.00	Kilowatt hour (kWh)	k cal	
426.9	K. cal	Kg/m	
3.968	Kcal : Kg calories	B.T.U.	0.252
4,184.00	Kcal : Kg calories	Joules	0.00024

	To obtain	From	Multiply by above.
0.738	Joules	Foot pounds	1.356
0.1124	k cal/ m^3	B.T.U./ foot^3	8.9

1.8	K cal/kilogram (kg)	B.T.U./pound	0.5556
14.7	Atmospheres	lb/Sq. inch	0.068
2.713	B.T.U./Sq. foot	Kg. Calories/m^3	0.369
1.033	Atmosphere	Kg/ cm^2	
0.293	B.T.U.	Watt hour	3.415
0.9	German candles	English candles	1.111
88.00	Miles per hour	Foot/min.	0.01134
197.00	Meters per sec.	Foot/min	0.00508
25,200.00	Therm (=100,000 B.T.U.)	k cal	
1.093659	Tons per sq. foot	Kg/ cm^2	
5.43	Imp. Gallon/Sq. Yard	Liter/m^2	1.845
	To obtain	*From*	*Multiply by above.*

Temperature

Celsius

$$(0°C) = \frac{5}{9}(°F - 32)$$

Fahrenheit

$$(°F) = \frac{9}{5}°C + 32$$